Contents

KU-052-423

BIRMINGHAM CITY UNIVERSITY
Book no. 35710551
Subject no. 363.348 Dav
LIBRARY

Contents in detail

Acknowledgements

This book has been prepared by the authors for RedR – *Engineers for Disaster Relief*, a registered charity which recruits and trains specialists worldwide for rapid deployment with relief agencies in emergencies.

For the first edition, Andrew Chalinder prepared initial drafts of the chapters on management and logistics and Shona McKenzie prepared the initial draft of the chapter on personal effectiveness. Bob Reed, of WEDC, provided substantial information for the chapter on environmental sanitation. For the second edition, the chapter on telecommunications draws substantially on a training document prepared for RedR by Rob Lowe, of the former Cable & Wireless Emergency Response Unit and now an independent consultant. The illustrations for the book were prepared by Ethan Danielson who also revised figures and prepared new illustrations for the second edition.

Those who reviewed sections of the book and/or contributed resource material, advice and information include: John Adams, Kojo Afful, John Alexander, David Ball, Steve Barker, Edmund Booth, Tom Bowyer, Fergus Boyle, Neil Brown, Gordon Browne, Richard Cansdale, Jim Clarke, Carolyn Crook, Pat Diskett, David Ede, Richard Fletcher, Tim Foster, Martin Gans, Brian Garstang, Samuel Ghebremariam, Mike Goodhand, Arnie Goren, Toby Gould, Peter Guthrie, Hans Hartung, Ian Henderson, Robert Hodgson, Jim Howard, Bill Ixer, Peter Kolsky, Jon Lane, Barbara Luckhurst, Richard Luff, Andrew MacAndrew, David MacMullan, Moira McLure, Woldu Mahary, Stuart Manser, Duncan Miller, Paul Naylor, Jerry Ockelford, Ron Ockwell, Nigel Osmaston, Chris Palmer, Derek Pennington, Bob Reed, Richard Seremak, Peter Smith, Paul Smith-Lomas, Madeleine Thomson, Kim Waterhouse, Derek Webb, Martin Wegelin, Lucy Wickham, David Williamson, Martin Wilson and Gunter Wittenberg. CIRIA (the Construction Industry Research and Information Association in the UK) assisted in the early stages of preparation of the first edition.

Members of the advisory group for the publication of the first edition of the book were: Charles Ainger, Neal Burton, Peter Guthrie, Jim Howard, Moira McLure, Joy Morgan, Bob Reed, Paul Sherlock and Derek Webb.

The second edition has benefited from additional contributions of advice, resource material and information from: Joseph Ashmore, Mark Buttle, Tom Corsellis, Tom De Veer, Sue Ellis, Tim Foster, Toby Gould, Tim Hayward, Tom Hutton-Stott, Rob Lowe, Richard Luff, Pete Manfield, Richard Seremak and Hans Wentink.

We are grateful to Debby Potts and Diane Davis for their advice, encouragement and support.

Financial support for the first edition was provided by the Nuffield Foundation, the former UK Overseas Development Administration (now the

Department for International Development), the Appeal Fund for the Lord Mayor of London and Shepherd Building Group.

Every effort has been made to trace the owners of copyright and to give due acknowledgement to the sources used.

The publishers would like to thank Howard Davies/www.exileimages.co.uk for permission to use the cover photograph showing distribution of Oxfam household water containers in Macedonia.

Introduction

Purpose of the book

The purpose of this book is to increase the effectiveness of relief workers in providing humanitarian assistance during an emergency. To achieve this purpose, the book provides practical information relevant to the field worker, with a minimum of supporting theoretical background.

The book does not aim to set out specific policy guidelines relating to humanitarian assistance – each agency will have its own policy framework, principles and mode of operating.

A note on terminology

The term 'emergency' is used in this book to describe the situation arising in the aftermath of a disaster, such as a drought or a famine and as a result of conflict. The first edition of the book frequently used the term 'refugees' to refer to a broad group of people who have been directly affected by disaster and need assistance in the subsequent emergency. This second edition has avoided the blanket term 'refugees' to recognize the considerable numbers of people who are variously affected by disaster. They include people who are displaced internally within their own country as well as refugees who, in the stricter legal sense, have crossed an international border.

Who should read this book?

The first edition of *Engineering in Emergencies* was primarily written with the relief engineer in mind. However, much of the content proved of interest and practical value to a range of relief workers and those considering humanitarian relief work for the first time. This revised and updated edition builds on this wide appeal to provide an introduction to humanitarian relief, not just for engineers but for anyone working in the field or considering doing so.

It is assumed that readers have a professional or practical competence and work experience in their speciality. It is not assumed that they have had prior experience in the provision of humanitarian assistance. The book aims to give practical information on areas outside someone's particular speciality. For instance, it will give a field programme manager information on the basic monitoring and implementation of a sanitation programme. It does not aim to provide detailed, highly specialized information to those who are already experienced in the provision of humanitarian assistance but it may be useful to them as an *aide-mémoire*. Where readers have any doubt about their professional competence to deal with some of the technical topics dealt with in the book, they should consult a suitably qualified person.

Scope

The book is based on the experience of many people working in a variety of different relief settings. The first edition was primarily based on experience in predominantly tropical zones. This second edition has drawn upon recent experience in cooler climates and European emergencies. The response to disasters in urban areas may require highly specialized inputs which are not specifically addressed in this book.

In addition to detailed technical information, the wider nature of emergencies and humanitarian practice is dealt with and a brief overview of the humanitarian relief system is given. Practical guidelines are given on assessment, planning, management and personal effectiveness. An important chapter on personal security is included which recognizes the hazardous, insecure environments in which many relief workers find themselves operating as a result of civil unrest, high crime rates, collapsed states and conflict. The role of telecommunications in facilitating efficient and secure operations is addressed by the addition of a chapter on the topic. To complement these chapters, practical training in both personal security and the use of radios and satellite phones is highly recommended.

Reflecting the experiences of relief workers, the book sometimes takes a panoramic view, for example, of planning for a settlement for displaced people, and sometimes gives highly detailed information – for example, of the installation of an electric submersible borehole pump.

How to use this book

Experience from the first edition has shown that readers are likely to dip into chapters or sections of interest rather than to read the book from beginning to end. To facilitate this, a detailed contents list and an index have been provided. The Bibliography includes documents that have been specifically referred to in the text and material that, while not directly referred to, may be of value to the reader who wishes to go into more depth on a particular topic. The text is copiously cross-referenced.

Feedback

The world of humanitarian relief continues to change and evolve. This edition has benefited from the feedback given by many people with field experience. We are keen to continue to receive feedback and suggestions for future publications. Please send them to the authors at RedR, 1 Great George Street, London SW1P 3AA, London, UK or by e-mail to: info@redr.demon.co.uk

Disclaimer

This book is intended for those working in humanitarian assistance where resources, including time, may be limited due to the urgency of their work. Readers must use their skill and judgement to apply the principles and information included in this book to the circumstances in which they find themselves. RedR, the authors and the publisher assume no responsibility for and make no warranty with respect to the results of using the techniques and procedures described in this book. RedR, the authors and the publisher accept no liability for any damage or loss whatsoever resulting from the use of or reliance upon any information contained in this book. Any standards referred to in the text should be checked to ensure compliance with the existing laws and regulations of the country concerned.

1 Emergencies

Most emergencies have complex causes and require complex responses if a durable solution is to be found. The initial response in an emergency may seem simple – provide protection, shelter, clean water and food. However, the manner in which this humanitarian relief is provided can have profound consequences for the affected society. Relief workers need to be aware of the complexities of the emergency and the consequences that may result from their actions.

The aim of this chapter, therefore, is to give a brief introduction to emergencies and their effects on people. To gain a deeper understanding of the nature and causes of disasters and the impact of humanitarian aid consult the Bibliography which lists key references and periodicals in the sector.

1.1 An overview of disasters and emergencies

1.1.1 Disasters and emergencies

A disaster results in a serious disruption of society, involving widespread human suffering and physical loss or damage, and stretches the community's normal coping mechanisms to breaking point.

The term 'natural disaster' is commonly used when referring to the impact of a natural hazard on a community – such as an earthquake, flood, hurricane, volcanic eruption, etc. The degree to which an individual or community is vulnerable to the hazard will significantly determine the impact of the hazard on their lives. The event becomes a disaster when the community's capacity to cope is overwhelmed, causing death or injury, loss of property, and economic damage. The situation is then declared an emergency and external assistance is requested.

The use of the term 'natural disaster' might suggest that a disaster is simply due to natural forces. But the human race has had a significant impact on the environment which influences the frequency and intensity of major hazards such as hurricanes, floods and droughts. In addition, our ability to predict, prepare for and mitigate the impact of natural hazards influences our vulnerability. Vulnerability varies tremendously and those who are poor and live in precarious circumstances are generally the most vulnerable. Therefore, the degree to which a hazard creates a disaster is not simply due to 'natural forces'.

Complex humanitarian emergencies have a number of causes, arising, for example, from political or military actions which may exacerbate drought, famine and poor living conditions, or which result in conflict and disruption to normal life. A complex emergency often involves a large and, sometimes, rapid displacement of people. This may be as a consequence or as an objective of the violence, due to 'ethnic cleansing' and genocide. A feature of a complex emergency is that relief assistance can itself become entangled in the politics of the situation.

This book focuses on responses to complex political emergencies. Nevertheless, much of the guidance may also be useful in responding to the impact of natural hazards provided, as with any emergency, due consideration is given to the context in which the relief assistance is provided.

Table 1.1 gives a generally accepted guide to the severity of an emergency using the crude mortality rate, which is expressed as the number of deaths per 10 000 people per day.

Table 1.1 Crude mortality rates in emergencies

Crude mortality rate deaths/10 000/day	*Severity of emergency*
Up to 0.5	'Normal' – non-emergency rate
< 1.0	Under control
> 1.0	Very serious
> 2.0	Out of control
> 5.0	Catastrophic

1.1.2 Relief and development

Disasters and the responses to them are shaped by and in turn strongly influence the state of development of a country or society:

- Inappropriate development increases vulnerability to disasters
- Disasters seriously retard development
- Inappropriate and insensitive relief programmes can exacerbate attempts to recover from crisis
- Disasters may provide opportunities for change.

An indicator of the level of development of a society is its ability to deal with disaster, whether by prevention (preferable) or by effective response. The impact of a drought on food availability, for example, is far greater in a developing country which has an unstable or unresponsive political system, limited food stocks, poor food distribution systems and little foreign exchange for food imports.

Chronic emergencies due to protracted conflict (e.g. Angola, Afghanistan, Sudan, Sri Lanka, Somalia, Liberia and Sierra Leone) can lurch from one crisis to another. People may be displaced several times from one place to another and may eventually return home only to be displaced again as conflict continues in a cyclical pattern. In such situations 'humanitarian action' is not simply the provision of aid and the personnel to save and preserve lives. It involves programmes that work towards promoting peace, preserving livelihoods and limiting the long-term psychological and physical impact on those affected. Without such an approach lives may be saved in the short term without coming any nearer to longer-term sustainable solutions.

Humanitarian relief programmes, therefore, need to plan for both immediate relief and the promotion of peaceful, sustainable development. Such programmes have included reconciliation, peace-building, conflict prevention and capacity building to complement more material-focused relief. They are not distinct activities as one clearly has an influence on another. For example, what might appear to be the relatively straightforward provision of food, water and shelter could, if not carried out sensitively, contribute to friction and discord among rival communities.

While the immediate impact of a disaster is by definition, negative, there may be opportunities for positive change. At the very least, a disaster can provide the opportunity to learn how to prevent, or lessen the impact, of a disaster happening again, for instance, by re-assessing and improving traditional building techniques or putting in place early warning systems. Corrupt or ineffective political or social systems may be replaced. There may even be localized economic benefits through the influx of aid and exposure to new technologies.

In responding to a disaster it is important to recognise these potentially positive aspects as one of the key elements in recovering from a disaster is the hope that there may be a better future, if not for this generation, then for the children. Effective disaster relief should lay the foundations for long-term development.

Implications for the relief worker

The implications of the relationship between disasters and development at the field level can easily be lost in the early, hectic stage of an emergency. It may be necessary to revise approaches taken in the immediate phase to better reflect long-term needs. The style of working and management should adapt to the changing circumstances as the response moves from one of 'relief' to 'development'. Sensitivity to the impact of technology and solutions implemented in an emergency can make a significant difference to long-term recovery and development prospects. Existing local technology, skills, community structures, development initiatives, supply networks, materials, government policy and many other factors all have an important bearing on the long-term success of technology and techniques introduced in an emergency.

In an insecure environment, perhaps due to open or low-intensity conflict, it is clearly necessary for the individual relief worker to be aware of the context in which they are working. This is vital for effective programmes so that they are appropriate and sensitive to long-term needs and positively support efforts for peace and reconciliation. It is also vital for the security of staff and the partners with whom they work (see Chapter 4).

1.2 The people in emergencies

1.2.1 Directly and indirectly affected people

An appreciation of who is affected and how they might feel can assist the relief worker to understand people's reactions in an emergency. Affected people include:

- The direct victims – people affected directly, such as the sick and injured, and those who suffer the loss of relatives, friends, homes and possessions.
- People living within the disaster-affected area will probably experience severe disruption themselves, and may suffer from the loss of skills where there has been an exodus of people. On the other hand they may perceive a benefit with, for example, increased access to land or business.
- Communities who become hosts to large numbers of displaced people may experience local disruption causing, for example, a rise in prices, shortages of materials, food and water, and loss of agricultural land.
- People who are indirectly affected due to the impact of a relief programme. This can extend to an entire country or region following a large-scale relief effort. Examples of this include the redirection of funding and resources from development work to emergency relief, the impact on employment (both negative and positive), and abrupt changes to the national economy.
- The helpers, both local and international relief workers, will undergo changes in their lives. They will each have their reasons for being involved in relief work which may not always be clear or easily understood by fellow helpers and those receiving assistance.
- Host governments and their employees may already have enough to do coping with their own problems. An influx of large numbers of people may put unbearable strain on already creaky systems.
- Donor communities – there may be effective mobilization of people and resources for humanitarian relief and an increased knowledge and awareness of global problems. However, funds used for emergency relief will have been drawn from other budgets such as those used for long-term development. Compassion fatigue may set in, which may limit the response to later emergencies.

1.2.2 Refugees and displaced people

The formal definition of a 'refugee' is very important because it determines refugee status and the legal protection and assistance a refugee is entitled to receive from international bodies, such as the UN.

The 1951 'UN Convention Relating to the Status of Refugees', drafted by the office of the United Nations High Commissioner for Refugees (UNHCR), defined a refugee as:

> Any person who owing to well founded fear of being persecuted for reasons of race, religion, nationality, membership of a particular social group or political opinion, is outside the country of his nationality and is unable, or owing to fear is unwilling to avail himself of the protection of that country; or who, not having a nationality and being outside the country of his former habitual residence, is unable, or having such fear is unwilling to return to it.

The 1951 definition was found to be too restrictive and many amendments have subsequently been made. The 1967 'Protocol Relating to the Status of Refugees' amended the definition to apply to 'all persons crossing an international border in genuine fear of persecution'.

In 1969 the 'Organization of African Unity Convention Governing the Specific Aspects of Refugee Problems in Africa' was adopted regionally to widen the definition of persecution to include 'those fleeing war, civil disturbance or violence generally'.

Over the years, UNHCR has made many adjustments to the original understanding of the term 'refugee' in order to afford protection and assistance to a wider group of people.

In circumstances where the numbers of people involved, their rapid rate of arrival and the urgency of their needs make it impractical to be able to determine the refugee status of each individual, UNHCR has provided protection and assistance to groups of persons, as distinct from individuals. Figure 1.1 shows the global trend in the estimated number of refugees.

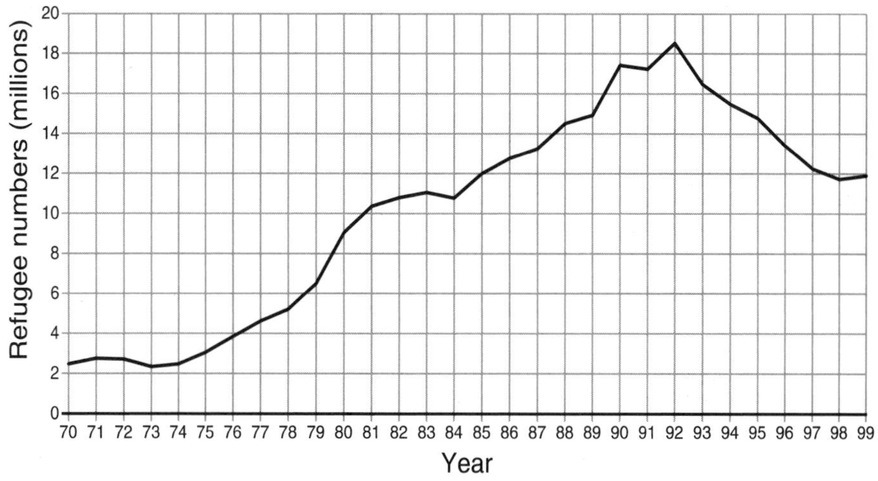

Figure 1.1 Global numbers of refugees, 1970–99
Source UNHCR, 2000

It is illegal for a country party to the 1951 Convention to return a refugee to the country from which they have fled. Furthermore, host governments are responsible for the safety of, assistance to, and law and order among refugees in their country.

Internally displaced persons (IDPs)

Many people are internally displaced as a result of armed conflict, human rights abuses or natural hazards. They are particularly vulnerable, because they do not have the opportunity or economic power to seek asylum across a border and become formal refugees and therefore entitled to international protection. Their own government may even view them as 'enemies of the state'. There are no specific international instruments covering the internally displaced. The UN has produced a booklet, *Guiding Principles on Internal Displacement* (OCHA, 2000) which is based on existing international law covering a person's basic rights.

Figures for IDPs are difficult to calculate. In the year 2000, the Special Representative of the UN Secretary-General for Internally Displaced Persons estimated there were between 20 and 25 million IDPs worldwide, though other estimates were higher.

There are many examples of where the plight of refugees and internally displaced persons have become inextricably linked. In these situations UNHCR has been mandated to provide protection and assistance to all who have fled their homes.

1.2.3 Power relations and vulnerability

A disaster will clearly have a major impact on how people live. A community can be disrupted, affecting family and community structures, and local and state politics. These changes can significantly impact on the vulnerability of people in different ways. The following is a brief overview of some key issues to consider – there will be others depending on the situation. See Chapter 5 for approaches to carrying out an assessment.

General

- How do people normally live and what have been the major changes in their lives?
- How are people coping: are they collecting water, gathering fuelwood, cooking, building shelters, looking after livestock, or trading?
- Are people looking after the injured and vulnerable?
- Do people have the tools and materials to look after themselves? If not, what do they need?
- What skills, expertise, qualifications and experience do people have that could be effectively utilized in the recovery?
- Who are the community leaders? Are traditional power structures intact or has there been a rearrangement of power and influence? Who really represents the majority of the affected population?

State of physical and mental health

- Does everyone, including the ill, the old, and people with disabilities, have access to adequate quantities of drinking water and food?
- What food did people eat before the emergency? Do they have access to acceptable food? Do they have the means to prepare food?
- Does their understanding of diseases and hygiene pose a serious risk to health?
- Are people living in overcrowded, insanitary conditions?
- Are people 'trapped' in a temporary settlement, unable to go beyond the confines of the camp?
- Do people appear confused? Depressed?

Income

- How did people earn their livelihood previously and can they still find employment?
- Is there a loss or reduction in household income and purchasing power?

Ethnicity

- Are there any ethnic dimensions to the disaster?
- Is it an ethnically homogeneous group of people?
- Are people from minority ethnic groups able to access water, food, shelter and health services?
- If there are ethnic differences are they likely to be a source of friction, or even conflict?

Gender – women

- What is the proportion of women in the population? (Women and children often constitute up to 80% of the people in a refugee camp.)
- Are women having to take on extra responsibilities and become non-traditional heads of households (because the men are elsewhere)?
- How can women be involved in the management of the relief effort without adding to their already considerable activities?
- Are there places or times of the day when women are more vulnerable to sexual violence (e.g. toilets at night-time)?
- Are women stressed as a result of fear and actual harm due to sexual assault?
- Are women under considerable extra stress due to the additional responsibilities of providing for family members?

Gender – men

- Are young men away fighting? Are they being forcibly recruited into armies or militias?
- Can men, who normally spend their lives working to provide for the family, share in caring for the family?
- Have their traditional roles changed or vanished altogether? Have the traditional male leaders been usurped by younger militants?

Age – children

- Are children especially at risk due to a lack of physical shelter and protection?
- Are there unaccompanied children separated from parental and family care?
- Are children traumatized by the suffering of their parents and other family members?
- Are older children involved in fighting as 'child-soldiers'?

Age – the elderly

- Do traditional support networks for older people still function?
- Have housebound older people become 'invisible' to support organizations?
- Do older people need additional support for looking after young dependants whose parents are missing?

- Are the chronic health, mobility and mental problems of older people addressed through adapting facilities and procedures to provide equal access?

Class/caste

- Have traditional class roles been reinforced or changed and how does this impact on access to traditional support and external humanitarian relief? Do the higher classes benefit disproportionately?

Education

- Does education play a part in access to support and opportunities for coping?

Religion

- What part does religion play in people's lives?
- Do people interpret their plight in religious terms and what is the implication for the relief effort if they do?
- Is everyone of the same religious persuasion or are there several different religious groups within the affected population? Can the different religious groups live and work together?

People with disabilities

- Are people with disabilities 'invisible' to support organizations?
- Should all facilities be adapted for people with disabilities or only in areas where they have been identified?

Problems relating particularly to refugees and displaced people

- Why are people here?
- How have they travelled here?
- How could life have been so intolerable as to make people flee their own homes?
- What have people endured to get here?
- How are they reacting to their flight now, and how will they react tomorrow and in the next few weeks?
- Is the migrating population of a different ethnic and cultural background to the host population, and if so, what are the implications?
- Does their new environment pose a potential risk to their health – are they exposed to unfamiliar diseases to which they lack immunity?

Coping mechanisms

In dealing with such problems, people – either as individuals or as a community – depend on a range of coping mechanisms, including personal qualities and community or social structures:

- Family, including the extended family, distant relatives, the clan.
- Religion, support groups associated with churches, mosques, temples, and traditional spiritual societies.

- Institutions; traditional structures (chieftaincy, elders), local government bodies, political parties.
- Economic groups; informal arrangements, co-operatives, trade unions, trade and professional societies (farmers, teachers).
- Determination; when faced with adversity many people, either as groups or individuals, discover hidden strengths.
- Social groups; friends, neighbours, women's and men's societies.

People affected by disaster are likely to draw strength from traditional social groups. There may be political factions overlaying more traditional associations and an emergency may provide the opportunity for a realignment of internal power structures. Emergency planning and management should be influenced by an understanding of social grouping and community leadership. Relief workers need to understand these structures and mechanisms and consider the effect of their activities on them. In seeking to work with community leaders it is clearly important to distinguish between true community representatives and those seeking to take advantage of the situation.

1.3 Humanitarian principles and standards

With a steady increase in disasters in the 1990s and a growth in the number of non-governmental organizations (NGOs) there was a concerted effort to define and codify principles and standards of humanitarian policy and action. Underpinning the effort was a concern for the welfare of humankind, an emphasis on fundamental human rights and the need to address the underlying causes of conflict. Complementary issues addressed were those of impartiality, neutrality, transparency, better co-ordination among agencies and the competence of relief workers.

The principles by which different agencies operate can vary significantly. On the issue of neutrality, for example, many have felt that neutrality was not possible in practice, especially when advocating for the rights of the oppressed. Others have felt that only by being perceived as neutral could those affected by conflict be assisted. It is important, therefore, for the relief worker to know and understand the principles of the agency for whom they work as they directly impact on the role and actions of the individual.

Various initiatives have attempted to agree a body of principles and professional standards in disaster relief for improving agency performance and accountability. The main initiatives are briefly listed below.

1.3.1 The Red Cross and Red Crescent Movement – fundamental principles

Seven Fundamental Principles guide the International Red Cross and Red Crescent Movement:

Humanity – The International Red Cross and Red Crescent Movement, born of a desire to bring assistance without discrimination to the wounded on the battlefield, endeavours, in its international and national capacity, to prevent and alleviate human suffering wherever it may be found. Its purpose is to protect human life and health and to ensure respect for the human being. It promotes mutual understanding, friendship, co-operation and lasting peace amongst all people.

Impartiality – It makes no discrimination as to nationality, race, religious beliefs, class or political opinions. It endeavours to relieve the suffering of individuals, being guided solely by their needs, and to give priority to the most urgent cases of distress.

Neutrality – In order to continue to enjoy the confidence of all, the Movement may not take sides in hostilities or engage at any time in controversies of a political, racial, religious or ideological nature.

Independence – The Movement is independent. The National Societies, while auxiliaries in the humanitarian services of their governments and subject to the laws of their respective countries, must always maintain their autonomy so that they may be able at all times to act in accordance with the principles of the Movement.

Voluntary service – It is a voluntary relief movement not prompted in any manner by desire for gain.

Unity – There can be only one Red Cross or one Red Crescent Society in any one country. It must be open to all. It must carry its humanitarian work throughout its territory.

Universality – The International Red Cross and Red Crescent Movement, in which all Societies have equal status and share equal responsibilities and duties in helping each other, is worldwide.

1.3.2 Red Cross and Red Crescent/NGO Code of Conduct

The label 'charitable' does not ensure relief work is always in the best interests of those assisted. Disaster relief is a complex activity and in addition to the experienced larger agencies there are many small groups, often coming into existence to assist in one specific disaster or working in a specialized field. All agencies, large and small, need guiding principles against which to check their activities. The NGO Code of Conduct was the product of a collaborative inter-agency effort which set standards for the provision of humanitarian aid (see Box 1.1). Agencies who support the Code and are endeavouring to incorporate its principles into their work can be found in the annual 'World Disasters Report' or on the International Federation of Red Cross and Red Crescent Societies web site: www.ifrc.org.

1.3.3 InterAction's PVO Standards

InterAction, a membership association of US private voluntary organizations (PVOs), exists to enhance the effectiveness and professional capacities of its members engaged in international humanitarian efforts. All InterAction members have to certify compliance with PVO Standards established and periodically amended by the InterAction association of members. The standards define a financial, operational and ethical code of conduct which is intended to ensure

Box 1.1 Code of Conduct for The International Red Cross and Red Crescent Movement and NGOs in Disaster Relief

Principal commitments:

1. The humanitarian imperative comes first.
2. Aid is given regardless of the race, creed or nationality of the recipients and without adverse distinction of any kind. Aid priorities are calculated on the basis of need alone.
3. Aid will not be used to further a particular political or religious standpoint.
4. We shall endeavour not to act as instruments of government foreign policy.
5. We shall respect culture and custom.
6. We shall attempt to build disaster response on local capacities.
7. Ways shall be found to involve programme beneficiaries in the management of relief aid.
8. Relief aid must strive to reduce future vulnerabilities to disaster as well as meeting basic needs.
9. We hold ourselves accountable to both those we seek to assist and those from whom we accept resources.
10. In our information, publicity and advertising activities, we shall recognize disaster victims as dignified human beings, not hopeless objects.

and strengthen public confidence in the integrity, quality and effectiveness of member organizations and their programmes. For the complete standards see the InterAction web site: www.interaction.org.

1.3.4 Humanitarian Accountability Project

The objective of the Humanitarian Accountability Project (otherwise known as the 'Ombudsman Project') is to provide a means whereby those affected by disaster and conflict can critically comment on the performance of both international and local systems of humanitarian assistance. It is intended to form part of a wider effort to improve accountability and quality within both the international humanitarian system and local disaster response. For more information and progress on the project see the web site: www.oneworld.org/ombudsman.

1.3.5 The Sphere Project

The Sphere Project arose due to a concern that an increase in worldwide demand for humanitarian relief could lead to inconsistent quality in relief assistance. In mid-1997 two major agency networks, the Steering Committee for Humanitarian Response (SCHR) and InterAction, launched the initiative based on the core principles of meeting essential human needs and restoring life with dignity. SCHR is an alliance of organizations for voluntary action created to improve co-ordination and co-operation among humanitarian agencies. The members are: CARE International, Caritas Internationalis, International Federation of Red Cross and Red Crescent Societies, International Save the Children Alliance,

Lutheran World Federation, Médecins Sans Frontières, Oxfam International and the World Council of Churches.

The aim of the Project is to improve the quality of assistance provided to people affected by disasters, and to enhance the accountability of the humanitarian system in disaster response. The Humanitarian Charter and Minimum Standards are key features of the project.

The Humanitarian Charter affirms the following fundamental principles:

- The right to life with dignity as reflected in a variety of legal measures. International humanitarian law (IHL) makes specific provision for assistance to civilians during conflict.
- The distinction between combatants and non-combatants underpinned by the 1949 Geneva Conventions and their Additional Protocols of 1977. There is great concern at the very high number of civilian casualties due to war.
- The principle of 'non-refoulement' that no refugee shall be sent back to a country in which his or her life or freedom would be threatened.

The Minimum Standards are based on the experience of agencies providing humanitarian assistance. Various factors will determine whether these standards can be met in a specific context. Agencies undertake to make every effort to achieve them to ensure people have access to at least minimum levels of service in water supply, sanitation, nutrition, food aid, shelter, site planning and health to achieve everyone's basic right to life with dignity. The standards can be used as guides for assessments, decision-making tools for programme planning, monitoring tools in implementation and evaluation, and to provide common ground for interagency co-ordination.

Sphere has focused attention on the need for a professional approach to meeting the needs of those affected by disasters. It has also emphasized the accountability of donors (institutional and private) and individuals to the recipients of humanitarian aid. It also means that individual relief workers are more accountable, not only to recipients, but also to their organization and the donors who fund humanitarian relief.

A summary of the Sphere Minimum Standards can be found in Appendix 3. The standards are also referred to in the main body of the text. The complete Sphere handbook and updates on how Sphere is used in practice can be accessed at the web site: www.sphereproject.org.

1.3.6 The Geneva Conventions and Protocols

Relief workers are often involved in assisting civilians caught up in armed conflict. It is, therefore, important to be familiar with relevant human rights standards and international legal provisions that apply in times of armed conflict. International humanitarian law (IHL) comprise the rules that seek to protect people who are not or are no longer taking part in hostilities. The Geneva Conventions of 1949 and their Additional Protocols of 1977 are the main instruments of IHL. The Fourth Geneva Convention of 1949 specifically concerns the protection of civilians. The two additional Protocols of 1977 strengthen the protection of victims of international (Protocol I) and non-international (Protocol II) armed conflicts. For further information see Darcy (1977) and the ICRC web site: www.icrc.org.

2 The humanitarian relief system

Relief workers operate as part of a diverse system which functions to provide humanitarian assistance to people affected by disasters. This chapter gives an overview of the relief system and brief details on some of the major agencies involved.

2.1 Sources of relief

When a major disaster occurs, the immediate victims of the disaster respond and cope as best they can. A community's own ability to cope with disaster is considered in Chapter 1. For a major disaster outside assistance can be provided through a number of channels including:

- Neighbouring communities. Such communities may extend across national boundaries as with the Malawian communities who gave refuge to Mozambican refugees in the late 1980s.
- National or local governments, either of the country directly affected by the disaster, or of the country or region to which affected people have fled.
- Outside governments, either directly or channelled through other agencies.
- Multilateral agencies such as the United Nations system.
- The Red Cross and Red Crescent Movement.
- Local and international non-governmental organizations (NGOs), including religious organizations.
- The private sector and specialized institutions.
- Military organizations.

2.2 Government agencies and co-ordination mechanisms

2.2.1 Co-ordination mechanisms

In most cases, the responsibility for disaster management ultimately rests with the government of the affected country, whether it is the country that has been directly affected or a nearby country which is host to refugees. Whether or not the government is willing or capable to assume this responsibility has a big impact on the success of the response to the disaster.

In some countries, the co-ordination of the response to a disaster may be carried out through a special forum comprising representatives of government departments and possibly of other bodies. These include major donors, UN agencies, NGOs and the Red Cross/Red Crescent Movement. The forum may deal not only with immediate disaster relief, but also with the formulation of long-term planning and preparedness measures, including risk reduction and contingency planning.

Governments may establish a specialist agency or office to co-ordinate and oversee relief operations. Examples include the Ethiopian Disaster Prevention and Preparedness Commission, the Indian Government Natural Disaster Management Control Room and the El Salvador National Emergency Committee.

A 'lead agency' often acts as a co-ordinator for the international agencies and NGOs. The UN office for the Co-ordination of Humanitarian Affairs (OCHA) has the mandate within the UN to co-ordinate the collective efforts of the international community, in particular those of the UN system (see Section 2.3). Where refugees are concerned UNHCR is often the lead agency. In other circumstances the agency acting as 'lead agency' may be agreed between the government and agencies involved.

The co-ordination of humanitarian aid is greatly complicated where, due to the breakdown of political or civil structures, there is no functioning government. In such complex emergencies, the United Nations is generally seen as the global organization through which negotiations between parties can be conducted and humanitarian relief co-ordinated. This is considered further in Section 2.3.

Co-ordination at the operational field level

Large bodies, such as a national forum, are inappropriate for dealing with operational detail. The co-ordination of specific sectors such as food, water and sanitation is carried out by specific sub-groups. Box 2.1 shows the functions of a co-ordinating sub-group.

A water sub-group, for example, might involve the field engineers of the government water authority, UNICEF (as a UN agency with expertise in water), UNHCR (if the water supply is for refugees), NGOs such as Oxfam, involved in the water sector and, possibly, private sector members involved in water provision (such as water tankering and well drilling contractors). Membership of the sub-group should also include representatives of the affected community.

The process of co-ordination will require regular meetings and a reporting mechanism (see Chapter 6). In the initial stages of a response, co-ordination meetings are likely to be every few days. As implementation gets underway, meetings at the local level may become weekly. At a broader inter-agency level, meetings to co-ordinate and assess implementation are likely to be once a month.

Integration of all relevant specialist areas and affected groups into the planning process is desirable and can help focus relief effort on priority areas. The people affected by the disaster should be involved as much as is practically possible, although sometimes this may not be acceptable to the host government, especially if these people are refugees. Involvement can be achieved

Box 2.1 Functions of a co-ordinating sub-group

To share information:

- To make known each agency's capabilities and resources.
- To maintain lists of personnel.
- To report activities regularly.
- To disseminate information and know-how.

To divide tasks and responsibilities:

- To agree needs and priorities.
- To allocate and agree responsibilities for each task.

To establish working guidelines:

- To agree on standards to ensure an appropriate level of service.
- To avoid confusion that may arise from different agency approaches.

To convene working sessions:

- To standardize equipment.
- To focus on specific issues, plans and problems; for example, to decide on wage rates for local labour.
- To share access to workshops and spare parts.
- To establish and maintain inter-agency co-operation in such areas as the briefing and training of staff and the recruitment and representation of the affected population.

To interact with other bodies:

- To represent the views of the sector at the disaster response co-ordination forum.
- To co-ordinate with other agencies not directly involved in the sector.

through their representatives – but be aware that special efforts may be needed to ensure that the needs of certain groups are represented (children, ethnic minorities etc.). Chapter 5 describes a range of methods for assessing the needs, preferences and resources of refugees.

2.2.2 Donors

The type and scale of response to an emergency is dependent on how donors, either local or external, react to appeals for humanitarian relief. External governments normally donate funds and materials for distribution and use by the governments of affected countries, by the United Nations agencies and by NGOs. However, in some cases, external governments may take a more direct role. The UK's Department for International Development (DFID), for example, has its own emergency response team to carry out initial assessments, take an active role in field co-ordination and deploy skilled personnel in relief teams. The US Office of Foreign Disaster Assistance (OFDA) provides technical assistance in the form of an Assessment Team or, for a more rapid or

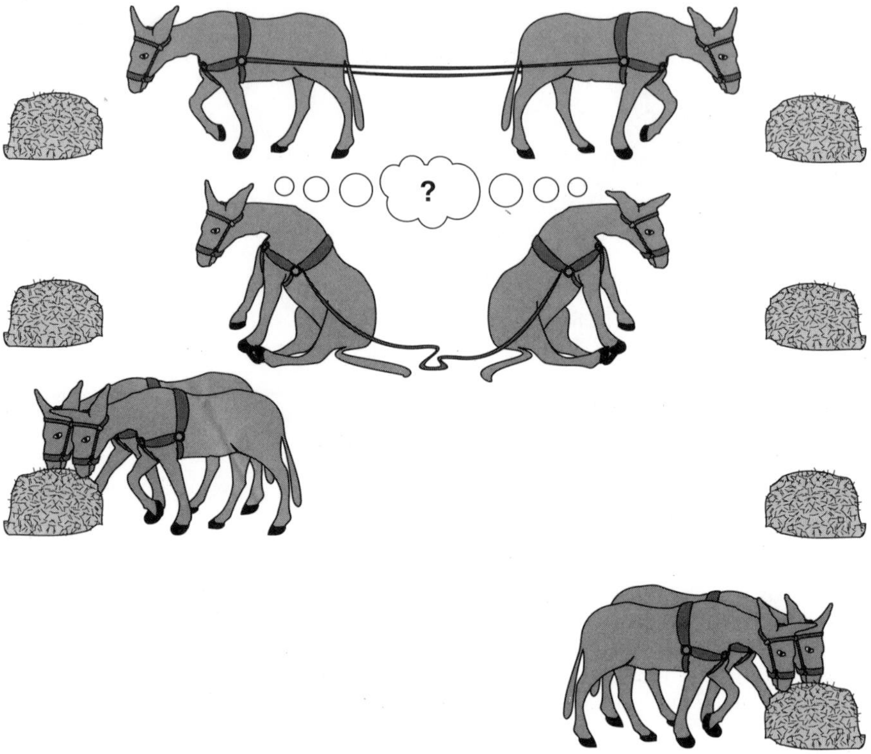

Figure 2.1 A co-ordinated response

continuous response, through the deployment of a Disaster Assistance Response Team (DART).

Donor governments are heavily influenced by public opinion and political and strategic considerations. Factors which influence public opinion include: the short-term reaction of the media in that country; the public's own experience of disaster; links to the affected country (cultural, colonial, religious, linguistic etc.); and that society's attitude to the effectiveness and morality of aid.

2.3 The United Nations system

The role of the United Nations and its agencies in disaster and emergency relief is:

- To provide aid for humanitarian relief and for rehabilitation.
- To protect and support those affected by disaster, such as refugees.
- To prevent and resolve conflict.

While some UN agencies have reserve funds that can be used in an emergency, the material assistance that UN agencies provide is heavily dependent on the outcome of appeals for voluntary contributions from governments and private sources. When a disaster occurs, this system means that for many UN agencies, funding is unpredictable and cannot be guaranteed. At a time when great demands are being made on the agencies, they have to devote significant amounts of time and effort to fundraising. This situation is not unique to the UN.

Where peace-keeping operations are involved, the UN must act within the directives of the Security Council. Obtaining a rapid consensus in times of crisis can be difficult, often resulting in delayed and inadequate humanitarian relief.

The work of different UN organizations overlaps in some areas and this has the potential, especially in an emergency, to duplicate efforts or even to create confusion. Partly in an effort to overcome these problems, the UN Office for the Co-ordination of Humanitarian Affairs (OCHA) was created.

OCHA – UN Office for the Co-ordination of Humanitarian Affairs

OCHA has the mandate to mobilize and co-ordinate the collective efforts of the international community, in particular those of the UN system, to meet the needs of those affected by natural and environmental disasters, and complex emergencies.

OCHA co-ordinates primarily through the Inter-Agency Standing Committee (IASC), which is chaired by the head of OCHA, as Emergency Relief Co-ordinator (ERC), with the participation of humanitarian partners, including the Red Cross Movement and NGOs. IASC works for inter-agency decision making in response to complex emergencies, including needs assessments, consolidated inter-agency appeals (CAPS), field co-ordination arrangements and the development of humanitarian policies. The ERC may appoint a Humanitarian Co-ordinator to co-ordinate the overall humanitarian effort at the field level.

OCHA can field a UN Disaster Assessment and Co-ordination (UNDAC) team to assist in needs assessment and the co-ordination of relief activities. It can also help establish an On-site Operations Co-ordination Centre to support the local emergency management authority.

OCHA provides information on humanitarian issues and crises through:

- A Humanitarian Early Warning System (HEWS).
- Integrated Regional Information Networks (IRINs) who issue daily and weekly reports, as well as thematic studies.
- ReliefWeb (www.reliefweb.int) a web site that provides up-to-date information on complex emergencies and natural disasters, including a map centre.

UNHCR (Office of the United Nations High Commissioner for Refugees)

The two main functions of UNHCR are to:

- Provide protection to refugees while seeking durable solutions to their problems.
- Assure the provision of material humanitarian assistance as required.

The term 'protection' includes the principle of 'non-refoulement' which means that people should not be forcibly returned to a country where they fear persecution. Material humanitarian assistance may include shelter, food, water and sanitation, health, and social services. For the purposes of UNHCR, a refugee is defined by the 1951 'UN Convention Relating to the Status of Refugees' and its subsequent amendments (see 1.2.2). UNHCR lists the following durable solutions to the problems of refugees, in order of preference:

- Voluntary repatriation of refugees and reintegration into their country of origin.
- Integration into a country of asylum.
- Resettlement in a third country.

Normally, UNHCR does not implement its own programmes but channels assistance through implementing partners such as NGOs, national and local authorities in the country concerned, specialist agencies of the United Nations and private agencies. Relief work is administered and co-ordinated in the field by UNHCR programme officers. The structure of offices in the field varies, but typically includes:

- A field office or unit in the refugee-affected area.
- A sub-office in a strategic provincial location.
- A branch office/UNHCR country office.
- A regional office, encompassing several countries.

OHCHR – UN Office of the High Commissioner for Human Rights

OHCHR promotes universal respect for and observance of human rights through providing technical support, information and education to strengthen national human rights capacities. The Office also undertakes monitoring of UN human rights operations.

UNICEF (United Nations Children's Fund)

UNICEF co-operates with developing countries to improve and extend services to benefit children, including services to women and girls. Although the emphasis of UNICEF's assistance is on long-term development programmes for children, it will respond to disasters if there are important needs of children and mothers to be met. Compared with most UN agencies, UNICEF has a broad and flexible mandate which allows it to provide assistance in circumstances where other agencies could not act. Examples include Cambodia in 1979–81, where UNICEF shared the lead agency role with ICRC, and Sudan since 1989 where UNICEF, through Operation Lifeline Sudan, has been involved in negotiating safe passage for aid. Emergency work is administered in the field through specialist programme officers responsible to the UNICEF Country Representative.

WFP – World Food Programme

WFP is the world's largest multilateral food aid organization. It initiates and co-ordinates food aid for humanitarian relief, rehabilitation and reconstruction in addition to supporting longer-term development projects.

WHO – World Health Organization

WHO acts in a co-ordinating role at an international level and supports national health authorities to maintain and improve levels of health. WHO's

Division of Emergency and Humanitarian Action (EHA) co-ordinates health-related responses to emergencies and natural disasters in partnership with other humanitarian agencies.

UNDP (Development Programme)

The United Nations Development Programme is the world's largest channel for multilateral development assistance. Its programmes cover a very broad range of development activities in support of national and regional plans. In an emergency, UNDP is primarily concerned with development issues related to both the emergency and the provision of technical assistance in disaster management. It is a core member of the United Nations Disaster Management Team (UN-DMT) but it does not become operationally involved in emergency relief.

UN-DMT (Disaster Management Team)

Within each disaster-prone country there is a permanent UN Disaster Management Team (UN-DMT), chaired by the UN resident co-ordinator (usually the UNDP resident representative). Membership of the UN-DMT will be determined by the type of disasters expected to occur and the UN agencies present in each country.

The aim of the UN-DMT is to provide an effective, co-ordinated UN response to support a government when a disaster strikes. It also aims to co-ordinate UN assistance in post-disaster rehabilitation and disaster mitigation measures as part of long-term development programmes. The UN-DMT has only a co-ordinating role and cannot override the roles and functions of the individual UN organizations represented in the DMT. In countries where there is a national forum for disaster response co-ordination, the United Nations will be represented by the UN-DMT.

2.4 The International Red Cross and Red Crescent Movement

The component bodies of the International Red Cross and Red Crescent Movement are the International Committee of the Red Cross (ICRC), the International Federation of Red Cross and Red Crescent Societies, and the National Red Cross and Red Crescent Societies. They are related to each other as shown in Figure 2.2. The International Conference of the Red Cross and Red Crescent is the supreme body of the Movement and determines major policy. It meets every four years, bringing together delegates of ICRC, the Federation and the National Societies and representatives of those states which are party to the Geneva Conventions.

The Council of Delegates is the assembly of the Movement and comprises representatives of ICRC, the Federation and delegates of all the National Societies. It meets every two years and gives opinions on policy and subjects of common interest to the Movement.

The International Committee of the Red Cross (ICRC), based in Geneva, works to protect and assist victims of armed conflict and civil strife, including prisoners of war and political detainees. Consequently the ICRC works in conflict zones.

The International Federation of Red Cross and Red Crescent Societies, IFRC, based in Geneva, supports the work of the National Societies and provides and co-ordinates assistance at an international level to victims of natural disasters or epidemics. A particular responsibility of the Federation is to assist refugees outside conflict areas, in close co-operation with UNHCR.

Individual National Societies carry out a range of activities in health care and social services. Programmes in developing countries include health education, vaccination campaigns and training for medical and social workers. National Societies also provide relief to displaced persons and victims of natural disasters, supported by other National Societies in donor nations through the Federation.

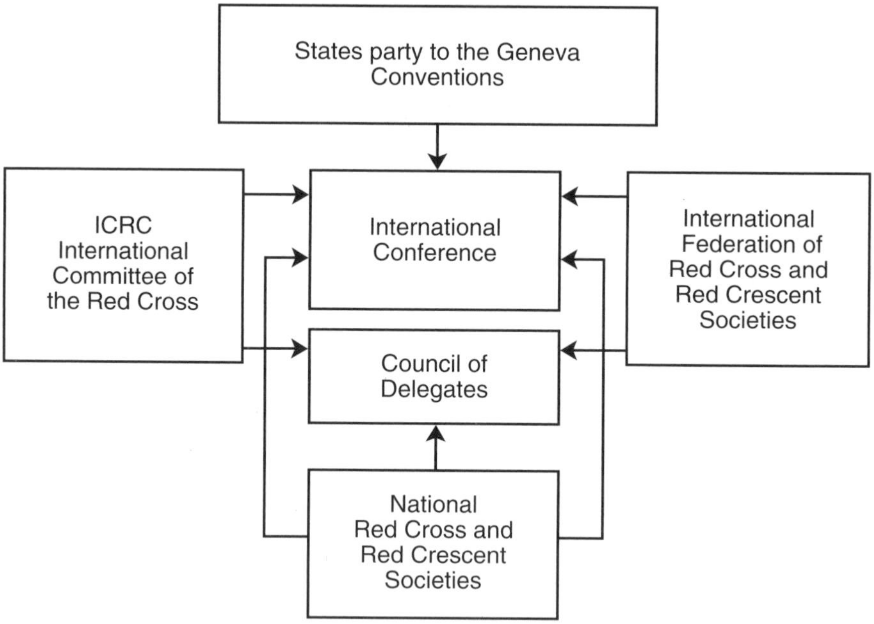

Figure 2.2 The International Red Cross and Red Crescent Movement

2.5 NGOs (non-governmental organizations)

The term NGO is commonly used to describe a range of organizations who work independently of individual governments. NGOs vary in size, expertise and funding, ranging from large international organizations such as CARE and Save the Children through to small, indigenous community-based groups. NGOs may also be termed private voluntary organizations (PVOs) or voluntary agencies (volags). NGOs have become increasingly important in emergency relief, because they are seen as a quick and effective way of channelling emergency relief funds.

NGO funding comes from voluntary donations, grants from donor governments and from multilateral agencies (the European Union and United Nations agencies). The source of NGO funding will have a heavy influence on NGO policies and how they operate in the field. Some NGOs try to ensure that they receive funds from a number of sources to retain independence. NGOs are usually accountable to their donors through some form of committee of trustees.

NGOs frequently collaborate in a variety of networks to present a united front to lobby for action and raise funds.

In the field, an effective NGO co-ordination mechanism is necessary to avoid duplication of activities and to provide mutual support. Such a structure may be established by the host government, by a leading UN agency, or by the NGOs themselves. In large programmes, sub-groups may be established for the different sectors of health, nutrition, water, etc. (see Box 2.1).

The competence and effectiveness of NGOs vary considerably. Large and well-established NGOs may be staffed by experienced adminstrators and specialists and be well equipped to respond to disasters. Smaller new NGOs, particularly those formed in response to particular disasters, may be run by highly motivated staff but they may require significant inputs from more experienced staff and technical specialists.

International NGOs and NGO co-ordinating bodies

International NGOs channel emergency relief either directly through their own operational emergency programmes or through partner organizations working in the affected area. Religious organizations often work through local representatives of their faith.

A trend in the structural development of larger NGOs has been the establishment of member organizations in other countries. Associations are often informal and are guided by a generally agreed aim and purpose. It is common for members to adopt the original name and identify the specific agency by country; for instance, Oxfam (America), MSF (Holland), SCF (Denmark). There may be significant policy and operational differences between agencies of the same name but different country.

National and local NGOs

Indigenous NGOs may operate at a regional or national level, or be much smaller and work with a particular community. A local NGO is often the first organization to respond to an emergency and it may be drawn into immediate relief work despite being a 'development agency'. Because of its local knowledge and understanding of community structures and culture, such an NGO can provide an excellent link between external agencies and a community. However, it is very easy for such small NGOs to be swamped by the short-term activities of large external agencies. When compared with well-funded external agencies, there is a danger that local NGOs may appear inadequate and lose credibility with their target community as a result.

External agencies who fund local NGOs should assess their capacity to cope with the extent of relief aid and the accompanying administration, and, where needed, provide appropriate training and support.

2.6 The private sector and research institutions

2.6.1 Private sector

The private sector can be involved in the relief system at different levels: manufacturing and supplying equipment; providing consultancy and training services; and as contractors in the field.

The manufacture and supply of equipment for emergencies is an expanding industry. Some companies have developed equipment for specific emergency use which they may be able to supply at short notice, such as water tanks and shelter facilities.

Although it is rare for major consulting firms to be involved in the early stages of an emergency, private individual consultants are often hired by UN agencies and NGOs for initial 'needs assessment' assignments, and in the later stages of emergencies consultants may be employed where specialist skills are required. Consultants may also provide specialist training to relief agencies.

At the field level, employing local contractors may be the most effective way of meeting urgent needs such as transporting relief goods and food, rehabilitating and constructing roads, constructing water systems, and drilling boreholes. Contractors are often immediately available and are familiar with local conditions. Managing a series of private contracts can be more efficient than building up an agency's own workforce and equipment for short-term actions.

2.6.2 Specialist institutions

An increasing number of specialist institutions carry out research, run training courses and provide technical assistance in emergency and disaster management. They can offer expertise in the fields of vulnerability analysis, risk reduction, disaster preparedness, disaster management, emergency relief, and programme evaluation. These institutions may be a useful source of information and support for relief workers preparing for deployment. They may also be a valuable source of information and advice when in the field. See Appendix 2 for useful web sites.

2.7 Military organizations

Logistical and material support

Military forces usually have a wide range of equipment and expertise which can be used to support humanitarian relief efforts. National military forces can play a vital role in relief work following the impact of a natural hazard, such as an earthquake. However, whilst the military may have expertise in a broad range of activities they must be used with care. Lessons learned from past relief efforts highlight a number of concerns:

- Military forces need to be prepared for humanitarian relief work if they are to adapt appropriately to their changed roles.
- Ordered planning along military lines may be inappropriate for civilian populations. Refugee camps, for example, cannot be designed and run as military bases but need to take into account specific social needs.

- The military option can be expensive. The average cost of one flight of a Hercules transport aircraft, for example, can be equivalent to the purchase of a grain truck and fuel for several months.

Conflict, peacekeeping and peace enforcement

Relief workers may have to deal with various forms of military organization, including:

- Regular military forces party to a conflict.
- National military forces enforcing security in and around refugee camps, particularly in border areas.
- International forces, sometimes under UN control, protecting humanitarian relief or acting as peace-keepers or peace-enforcers.
- Local militias acting in support of national military forces.
- Irregular or guerilla forces with links to distinct communities.

In conflict situations, lead humanitarian agencies try to agree operational procedures between the agencies and the parties to a conflict. All agencies then work within these procedures. Underpinning these agreements must be an understanding by the combatants of the agencies' objectives. For example, the Red Cross or Red Crescent is a widely known and understood symbol of non-partisan humanitarian assistance. However, even where such an understanding exists it is becoming increasingly common for combatants to target humanitarian efforts.

In some cases, the international community has deemed it necessary to intervene militarily to facilitate the delivery of humanitarian aid. In the majority of cases international intervention has been through the UN. The intervention of UN forces in support of humanitarian relief is governed by resolutions passed by the Security Council, which can often be diplomatically vague. Such intervention is usually highly controversial, debated at length and influenced not only by the views of individual member states but also by other key international organizations, such as NATO. There have been an increasing number of scenarios where the humanitarian aid community and the military of various countries have found themselves working alongside each other and personnel from both cultures need to be prepared for this eventuality.

CIMIC – Civil-Military Co-operation

CIMIC is the term used for civil-military co-operation. From the military point of view, the role of CIMIC is to maintain the support and co-operation of the civilian population and civil authorities towards achieving political and military objectives. A Civil-Military Co-ordination Centre (CMCC) may be established as an interface between the military and civil authorities and agencies.

Before approaching the military, check:

- Your agency policy – some NGOs refuse to work with military organizations.
- The current and possible future relationship between the military and the local population and different factions – could your links with the military jeopardize the present or future work of your organization?

If working with the military is acceptable, then it has the potential to provide significant support, expertise and equipment.

In dealing with the military it is important to understand the hierarchy and deal with people at the appropriate level. Table 2.1 gives an indication of the ranks and responsibilities within military forces.

Table 2.1 Ranks and responsibilities within military forces (based on the British Army)

Rank	*Typical command unit*	*Administrative role*	*Technical role*
NCOs			
Corporal (Cpl)	Section of 8–10 soldiers	Corporals and Sergeants may be: clerks, drivers and storekeepers	NCOs may be technicians and/ or supervisors of artisans and non-technical soldiers.
Sergeant (Sgt)	Platoon or Troop of 30–40 soldiers		
Warrant Officer	Group of soldiers or technicians	Chief clerks	
Officers			
Lieutenant (Lt) Captain (Capt)	Platoon or Troop of 35–45 soldiers	Officers have various admin. roles according to rank and size of command unit	Officers may be engineers and consultants, may command technical units and are often university graduates or chartered engineers.
Major (Maj)	Company or Squadron of 120–200 officers and soldiers		
Lt Colonel (Lt Col) Colonel (Col)	Battalions or Regiment of 600–700 all ranks		
Brigadier (Brig)	Brigade = 2+ Battalions		
Major General	Divisional Commander		

3 Personal effectiveness

Working in emergency relief requires both professional competence and personal resilience. For many people the professional challenges are fairly straightforward, if tough. It is the personal difficulties one encounters that cause the biggest problems. Dealing with different cultures, poor food, crowded living conditions and cultural clashes are all part of the challenge. It is important to be prepared for these challenges and to take action to deal with them. This chapter outlines some of the measures you can take to enhance your personal effectiveness.

3.1 Who will be effective?

Before working in emergency relief, both you and the aid agency employing you should assess:

- Your professional competence to do the job.
- Your likely personal effectiveness.

Professional competence is relatively easy to check through interview and curriculum vitae. Personal effectiveness is more difficult to assess but is affected by motivation, personality, and how you manage your behaviour.

Motivation Strong personal motivation is likely to play a major part in the decision to work in emergency relief and can be very helpful in maintaining commitment. It is important to understand your own motivation and the motivations of others, and that they will not necessarily be the same. Figure 3.1 illustrates common motivating factors. While there is no single correct set of motivating factors, some factors are more helpful than others. A strong motivation for high pay and a place in the sun is fairly obviously not the best motivation for relief work. Less obviously, perhaps, an overwhelming desire to help the poor and innocent victims of disaster, in order to feel wanted and receive gratitude, may cause problems when you are confronted with ungrateful refugees who appear far from poor and innocent.

Personality Relief workers have a wide range of personalities. While there is no single personality type that is ideal for an emergency, some useful traits include:

- An ability to listen.
- A sense of responsibility.

Figure 3.1 Possible motivating factors

- An ability to take decisions.
- A sense of humour.
- Tolerance of others' habits, culture, religion.
- A sense of adventure.
- Perseverance.
- An ability to work with a diverse team of people.
- An ability to relax.

Given a suitable blend of motivation and personality, personal effectiveness depends on the management of your own behaviour. While it is difficult to change one's personality it is possible to change or modify behaviour. Training courses dealing with personal effectiveness exist – use them. If you have some doubts about your personal aptitudes, it may be useful to identify any traits you have which are likely to be either helpful or a hindrance in terms of personal effectiveness. Ask a friend to help you in this process, but beware – it can be a very painful if illuminating process.

3.2 Personal planning

To function effectively in emergency relief work and to return to normal life successfully, it is helpful to make plans for what to do before, during and after an assignment. Do this whether you are an expatriate working on an overseas posting or whether you are a member of the local staff. Table 3.1 summarizes the issues concerned, which are detailed more fully in the following pages.

3.2.1 Before your assignment

Before applying for an assignment, consider the following:

- The effects on yourself: are you willing to work in conditions of poor security, discomfort, grief? How do you cope in a different culture, with a new language?
- The effects on your home life: how does your family feel, will they cope while you are away?
- The effects on your career: if you are looking for leave from regular employment, consider the effect on colleagues.
- The agency with whom you propose to work, its aims, objectives, working methods and support systems. Has it got the funds, staffing and experience to do the job required? What are its expectations of staff behaviour (such as its views on religious affiliation and practice) and work-loads (for example, provision for rest and recuperation)?
- Issues of conscience: are there any issues of conscience which might make it difficult for you to work in emergency relief? (political situation, corruption, sexism, racism – see Section 3.5.3).
- Your colleagues in the field: try to get some information about the type of people with whom you are likely to work.
- Returning home: for many people it is easier to take part in relief work than it is to return to normality.

If you are satisfied on these counts then you are more likely to be able to work effectively. If you are not, then perhaps you should not go on an assignment now. There will be other opportunities to go on assignments or other ways to give humanitarian assistance. If you decide that you are ready for an assignment, and one is offered, it is important to make preparations. Some can be

Table 3.1 Factors to consider before, during and after an assignment

Before	*During*	*After*
deciding to go	job specification	debrief
preparation and training	security	health
work/travel documents	communications	maintaining contacts
briefing and induction	team considerations	publicity
domestic arrangements	domestic considerations	employment
health	health	training/educating others
work aids	cultural sensitivity	
personal effects	media	
insurance	going home	

made in advance of any offer being made, some need to be made at the last minute.

Initial preparation

You can begin preparing for work in humanitarian relief long before you are offered a post. This section is written from the perspective of a RedR member going on assignment but it can be adapted to preparing for work in humanitarian relief generally. It would be particularly useful to consult the RedR web site (www.redr.org) for further information or updates.

Training – would you benefit from additional training? – RedR runs a wide range of courses and so do other organizations – see www.redr.org for the latest training programme and links to other relevant sites.

Reference library – consider building up your own reference library of useful manuals, etc. – refer to the Bibliography and www.redr.org.

Information – try to follow the news about humanitarian disasters. An understanding of the history and context of a disaster is invaluable. Beware, humanitarian disasters are not always well reported nationally. Consider, for instance, regularly tuning in to an international radio or TV station (BBC World Service, Voice of America, Radio France International etc.) or visiting appropriate web sites (see Appendix 2 and www.redr.org for links).

Family, friends, colleagues and the boss – discuss arrangements that need to be made for you to leave at short notice.

Will – write one and then keep it up-to-date.

Pension – will you be able to maintain contributions while on assignment?

Power of attorney – discuss with your solicitor/bank. Sign an indefinite/ long-term agreement now or ensure that one can be drawn up very quickly later.

Passport – it should be valid for at least another one to two years and have sufficient pages for visas. Some countries insist on having a full clear page for their visa and insist that the passport is valid well beyond the period of the intended visit.

Driving Licence – it should be valid for one to two years. If you travel often consider obtaining an International Driving Licence.

Photographs – maintain a stock of at least 10 passport size photographs – you can never have too many for visas, ID cards, contracts etc.

Insurance – check that any insurance policies you have (mortgage, life, personal accident, personal effects, cash etc.) will not be invalidated by accepting an assignment, especially if working in a conflict zone.

Health — discuss with your doctor whether you are fit to go on an assignment. Keep a record of your blood group. Keep your vaccinations up-to-date for as wide a range of countries as possible. Some courses of injections have to be taken over a period of months (e.g. Hepatitis B) while others cannot be given at the same time as each other. So you cannot have them all at once at the last moment! Table 3.2 is only a guide to vaccinations. Contact your medical advisor for the latest information on what is required for specific locations.

Table 3.2 Lead times and duration of common vaccinations
(As of March 2001. This is a guide only. Always obtain current medical advice in your country)

	Approx. time to allow for vaccination (from 1st dose to being effective)	*Booster interval*
Diphtheria	4 weeks	10 years
Hepatitis A	6–12 months	10 years
Hepatitis B[1]	5 months	3–5 years
Yellow fever	0	10 years
Rabies[2]	5 weeks	2–3 years
Tetanus	18 weeks	10 years
Typhoid	0	3 years
Polio	12 weeks	10 years
Measles, mumps, rubella	0	life
Meningitis	0	3 years
Japanese Encephalitis[3]	3 weeks	3 years

It is advised that:
(1) Health workers for any destination should have Hepatitis B immunization.
(2) All veterinarians/livestock specialists should have rabies immunization.
(3) Courses should be completed at least two weeks before departure because of the risks of a serious reaction to the vaccine.
BCG only for children < 5 years and those staying in area of high tuberculosis prevalence. Booster interval 20 years +.

Make sure you always have a spare set of glasses/contact lenses. Keep your dental checks and work up-to-date. Consider a personal stress management plan before you leave, including preparations for returning home (see 3.4). See Appendix 2 for useful travel health web sites.

Preparation immediately prior to an assignment

Ask for as much detail regarding:

- Terms and conditions.
- Insurance cover.
- The project you will be working on and your job description.
- Your team colleagues.
- Country of assignment – especially security, living and health conditions.
- The employing agency.

Better to pull out earlier rather than later if you are unhappy about any of the above.

Family Discuss the assignment and make a joint decision whether to accept it – remember the assignment is often more stressful for the family than the member.

Personal security

Relief work can involve a degree of insecurity. The risks you run will depend on a number of factors. When considering whether or not to accept an assignment, you have a very important question to ask:

Are the inevitable personal risks faced during the assignment justified by the possible benefits to the people assisted?

To help answer this question, you should:

- Find out about the current situation in the country from press reports, returning relief workers, the deploying agency, the web, etc.
- Ask the deploying agency in detail about their security arrangements in the country.
- Discuss the risks and benefits with friends, colleagues and family.

See Chapter 4 for further guidance on personal security.

Employer How will leaving on assignment affect your current project, colleagues and career? Is your employer prepared to release you?

Initial preparations Check all those things that you should have done before you reached this stage! (see 'Initial preparation'). Start making your own preparations as soon as possible. Even with the best intentions the agency may not be able to provide all the information, maps, manuals, medicines, equipment etc. which you may require or find useful.

What to do once the assignment is confirmed

Do not hesitate to contact the agency to fill in any information gaps. Ask them to send you any relevant available information.

Health

- Vaccinations – double check you have everything for the country of assignment. Will the agency be able to help with any vaccinations you still need?
- Malaria prophylaxis and other special medical requirements – check what is required and obtain sufficient supplies of the appropriate drugs yourself unless you are sure the agency will provide them. The regime and type of malaria prophylaxis depends on where you are going. Obtain medical advice and start taking the prophylaxis in good time. Remember to continue taking it for the recommended period after leaving the malarial region.

Insurance

- Check the agency is providing adequate health and accident cover, including cover for medical evacuation. Read the People in Aid report: 'Under-Cover? Insurance for Aid Workers' (www.peopleinaid.org) which is the result of research into levels of insurance cover available to aid workers.

Personal

- Leave your contact details (the agency, the duty station etc.) with family and friends.
- Arrange for forwarding/holding of mail.
- Decide how to deal with your e-mail.
- Revise the message on your answer phone/voice mail.
- Pay outstanding bills and make arrangements for paying bills while you are away.
- Pay off any credit card balance. Consider leaving your account in credit if you will be using the card whilst away.
- Cancel newspapers and the milk, and work out what to do with the cat . . .

Work

- Clear your desk.
- Leave your contact details (the agency, the duty station etc.) with key people.

Pack

Use the sample checklist that follows for guidance.

Packing suggestions

General

- Photocopy original critical documents (e.g. passport) and place in a safe place. Note telephone numbers for reporting lost credit cards, etc.
- Pack a change of clothes, your wash bag and essential medicines in your carry-on flight luggage in case your main luggage goes astray.
- A locked rigid suitcase protects your possessions from damage and pilfering better than a soft kit bag. Include stuff sacks and a number of plastic bags.
- Take a small bag/back pack for field trips and short journeys.
- Take clothing and footwear appropriate to the climate, culture and nature of the work – remember even 'hot' climates can be cold at night. A number of thin layers of clothing is more flexible than a smaller number of thicker layers. Natural fibres are more comfortable in warm climates than man-made fibres.
- Electrical equipment – check voltage, plugs and adapters.
- Computer equipment – do you need to take your own? Will your software be compatible with that of the agency? Remember anti-virus software is essential.
- Include a set of 'smart' clothes.
- Do not take anything remotely military in style or appearance.
- Check which items the agency will provide before buying your own.
- Take a note of the contact details for RedR's Technical Support Service: techsupport@redr.demon.co.uk.

Box 3.1 Packing checklist to be adapted as required

Documents
- Contract
- Insurance documents
- Travel ticket(s)
- Passport with exit and entry visas as appropriate
- Work permits
- Ordres de Mission/Letter of introduction
- Health certificates
- Record of blood group
- National and international driving licence
- Plenty of passport photographs
- Address book
- Health insurance card
- Business cards
- Identity card(s)
- Contact details for home, work, agency etc.

Electrical/electronic equipment
- Laptop computer, mains and surge adapter, mouse etc.
- Emergency boot/ recovery disks
- Range of printer drivers
- Portable printer, mains adapter, spare ink cartridge and cable
- Modem, mains adapter, cable and line test meter
- SW radio, mains adapter, aerial and spare batteries
- Walkman with cassettes/ CDs/MP3
- International mains adapter

Finances
- Cash – hard and local currencies as appropriate
- Travellers' cheques – check best currency and denominations
- Credit and direct debit cards, latter for cash withdrawals

Clothing
- Jeans, trousers, skirts
- Jacket and tie, smart dress/ kilt/suit
- Night-shirt/dress, pyjamas
- Shorts
- A couple of sets of long loose cotton clothing
- Sun hat and glasses
- Underwear
- Long and short sleeved shirts
- Jumper
- Socks
- Flip-flops/sandals
- Stout shoes/work boots
- Hangers
- Towel
- Waterproof jacket with hood
- Swimming costume

Stationery
- Hard backed note book
- Ring binder with dividers
- Airmail writing paper and envelopes
- Small paper hole punch
- Small stapler + staples
- Calculator – solar and battery
- Glue
- Ball point pens
- Pencils
- Pencil sharpener
- Eraser
- Highlighter
- Large permanent marker
- Clothes marker
- Scissors
- String

Toiletries
- Shampoo and soap
- Hairbrush and comb (a fine tooth comb will keep lice at bay)
- Razor, shaving soap, brush etc.
- Tooth brush/Toothpaste
- Dental floss (useful also as an impromptu washing line!)
- Nail clippers/scissors
- Liquid clothes detergent
- Foot powder and cream
- Tampons, contraceptives
- Spare glasses/contact lenses and copy of optical prescription
- Contact lens solution

Equipment – mini tool kit
- Camera, films and spare batteries
- Torch and spare batteries
- Swiss army knife or 'Leatherman' with cork screw and bottle opener
- Steel tape measure
- Electrician's screwdriver
- Electrical test meter with battery test feature
- Compass
- Stopwatch
- Altimeter
- Clinometer/Abney level
- GPS

References
- Technical reference books/ manuals
- *Engineering in Emergencies*
- Sphere Handbook
- Maps – country and major city maps
- Language guide/dictionary

Miscellaneous
- Mosquito net and Permethrin bednet treatment kit (*recent research has shown that bednets alone are not sufficient to reduce malaria transmission but treatment with insecticide renders even nets with holes protective*)
- Sleeping bag, cotton liner and foam bedroll
- Umbrella
- Reading material
- Airline blindfold
- Cigarette lighter
- Length of washing line and clothes pegs
- Unbreakable one litre water bottle
- 'Goodies' – for you and your colleagues

If on a RedR assignment consider borrowing a RedR tool kit – see www.redr.org

Medical kits

Before going on assignment, check with your agency whether you have to prepare your own medical and first aid kits – the agency should cover the cost. See Box 3.2 for guidance. Take a personal medical kit to keep in your room and a smaller personal first aid kit to carry with you in the field.

Box 3.2 A guide to medical kits

Personal medical kit

Sun block
Disinfectant
Painkillers (aspirin or paracetamol)
Bandages and sticking plasters
Scissors
Antiseptic cream or powder
Antihistamine
Malaria prophylaxis and treatment
Condoms and other contraceptives
Water purification tablets or drops
Sterile needle kit
Oral rehydration salts (ORS)
Insect repellent (DEET-based)
Strip thermometer
Mosquito net
Needles and syringes (*where local supplies cannot be relied upon – especially in areas where Hepatitis B and HIV are prevalent. Ensure you obtain a medical prescription for countries which would suspect anyone carrying them of being a drug addict, e.g. Malaysia.*)
Personal medicines (*and a list of their generic names*)

Vehicle first aid kit

Sterile gauzes
Many non-sterile gauzes
A few large, thin green gauzes
Stretch bandages
Adhesive plasters, large and small
Triangular bandages
Cotton wool
Soap
Antiseptic or Gentian Violet
Re-usable or disposable gloves
Scissors
Matches and a candle
Torch and batteries
A small container
Pen and notebook
Oral rehydration salts (ORS)

Personal first aid kit

Sticking plasters and antiseptic cream
Painkillers
Water bottle and water purification tablets (*iodine preferable*)
Anti-diarrhoea medicine

During your agency briefing

From Human Resources

Contract including:

- Job description – as detailed as possible under the circumstances.
- Salary – how much, how will it be paid and where?
- Expenses – what expenses are reimbursable; how will they be reimbursed; will you be given an advance in headquarters and/or in the field; is a daily allowance (per diem) paid in the field, etc.?
- Insurance cover provided by the agency – is it adequate?
- Other terms and conditions – accommodation, food, field transport, time off in the field, rest and recuperation (R&R), etc.

Other points:

- Living conditions, health considerations, local health care, personal mail.
- Leave contact details of your next-of-kin with the agency.

From the Desk Officer/Technical Section

- Security situation – ask about the security situation. You can refuse the assignment if you feel the risk is too great.
- Security plan – obtain details of any security plan, including evacuation arrangements. Find out who is responsible for the management of security in the team.
- Country – geography, climate, politics, economics, social situation, location of work, road conditions, language (basic greetings), introduction to key cultural issues, type of clothes to wear, photography, maps etc.
- Assignment – description, background, responsibilities, reporting lines, technical information, logistical and financial systems and constraints.
- Ask for copies of latest situation reports.
- Is there a hand-over report from your predecessor?
- Are all the manuals, spare parts lists, tools and equipment necessary to do your job available on the ground? If not, make clear to the agency the tools and equipment you will require to do the job and that they should provide them.
- Agency – mandate, policies, local team structure and members, methods of reporting, communications, policies relating to the media, issues of conscience, rules of conduct.

From the Accounts Department

- Advance for expenses or advance against per diem.
- Expense forms and procedures.
- Provide bank details for salary and expense payments.

From the Administration/Travel section

- Entry visas and travel tickets – check baggage restrictions and overweight allowances (there and back).
- Driving licence – is your national licence valid in the assignment country or do you need an International Driving Licence?
- Letters of introduction, Ordres de Mission, etc.
- Identity card(s).
- Medical insurance/evacuation cards.
- Information required by immigration on arrival: contact name and address in country, job details, introductory letter, money, etc.
- Clarify what arrangements have been made to meet you on arrival.
- Offer to carry the agency mailbag.

From the Health section

- Health considerations for the region. Have there been any health concerns within the team?
- Pre-departure medical examination (including a chest X-ray).
- Malaria prophylaxis and treatment, impregnated mosquito net, other special medicines, etc. as appropriate.
- Ask for their basic medical or field first aid kit.
- Consult medical web site links (www.redr.org).
- Some agencies ask for or recommend an HIV test – check their policy.

Consult the People in Aid project web site for their health and safety guidelines on preventing HIV/AIDS (www.peopleinaid.org).

The People in Aid project

People in Aid is an international network of development and disaster response agencies which promotes best staff management practice in aid agencies. It has established a 'Code of Best Practice in the Management and Support of Aid Personnel'. The project also produces 'Health & Safety Guidelines for Aid Workers' which provides practical advice on safety in the field. See their web site for further information (www.peopleinaid.org).

3.2.2 During an assignment

On arrival, introduce yourself to all the staff and find out about your role. Get some sort of induction and briefing at the local office, including a security briefing. Find out how the office operates and how it perceives the emergency situation. Find out what documentation you need, particularly any ID cards that are required. Find out where the best place is to keep your passport.

Job specification

Ask specifically about their interpretation of your job specification as this may vary from the one you were given at head office. If there are differences, let them know, but be prepared to be flexible and adapt to their requirements. If the tasks are significantly different from those you were expecting, you should not panic. If you feel you would like to tackle the work suggested, ask for support – for example, ask your agency to get the extra tools or reference materials you need. RedR may be able to help in this respect. Take time to assess for yourself what needs to be done and how much you can realistically achieve. Do not bite off more than you can chew.

Security

Familiarize yourself with the agency's security policies and procedures, particularly their evacuation procedures. Are they satisfactory? If not, notify the responsible staff and ask for and expect action. What security restrictions apply: travel, photography, curfews? (see Chapter 4)

Communication

Check that you understand to whom you must report and how often this is expected of you. If this contact is by radio, do you know how to use it and what type of messages you can send? Do you have a direct line of communication to your main office? Make sure you know how to contact home (mail, telephone), when to forward your personal mail and how letters from home reach you. Keeping your family in touch with what you are doing helps them to relate more easily with what you have been through when you get home, and reminds them of their importance to you.

Team considerations

Teams are generally put together on the basis of professional roles. In emergency relief work, you are likely to be both living and working with your team-mates (see also Section 6.2.6). Therefore it is important to recognize the interpersonal aspects of teamwork, which may be less well defined than the professional ones but are no less important. Be particularly aware of cultural differences and of your own and others' vulnerabilities and needs. Do not forget your extended team members; it is not just your local colleagues who make your work possible, but also those working in head office, packing crates, collecting clothes and the like. In emergency situations this work may include several volunteers who would love to hear from you that their efforts were appreciated in the field.

Domestic considerations

It is important that you and your colleagues have adequate food, accommodation and domestic facilities. You are there to help relieve misery, not to share it unnecessarily.

Ensure that you and your team members have decent accommodation as soon as is practicable. If necessary, delegate responsibility for this to one member of the team. Adopt a staged approach and improve living quarters and facilities as soon as is practicable. If possible, rent a house or hotel. Try to ensure that each member has his/her own personal space – at the minimum a tent, preferably a room. Try to ensure that the living accommodation is clean, secure and has proper washing and sanitation facilities. Ensure that domestic chores are carried out regularly – this is as important for morale as it is for hygiene. If possible, hire someone to do this. Ensure that adequate amounts of nutritious food are served regularly and hygienically. If possible, hire a cook to prepare all meals.

If you have to share accommodation with colleagues, recognize that this may cause problems. Let your fellow residents know if you have any special needs, such as a room close to the toilet if you have to get up a lot during the night. Be flexible and adaptable, but if things become unbearable, sit down and talk it through – you may not be the only one who is suffering.

Health

Remember that you are no use to anyone when you are ill, so be prepared and avoid burning up all your energy in the first week. Take precautions and if you do contract an illness treat it effectively (see also Section 3.3). Find out where your local medical and dental facilities are and what they offer. Ensure that your colleagues know your blood group and any particular worries you may have, such as ensuring that only your own sterile needles are used on you. Stress is likely to be your major occupational hazard, so set up your own support system for coping before it sets in. Decide where to take a five-minute break from work and allocate and plan time for relaxation.

Departure

Start planning your departure as early as possible. In addition to handover reports and activities in your work, plan your journey home. Consider a stepping stones approach (see Section 3.4). If possible, take photographs to share with friends, colleagues and other relief workers when you get home. You may be asked to share your experiences at public meetings or at training courses.

3.2.3 After your assignment

Debriefing

Debriefing is beneficial both to you and to the agency. The agency receives useful feedback on the project; you have an opportunity to talk to someone who is interested and you can suggest improvements. If debriefing is offered, take it; if not, ask for it. You should be offered at least one debriefing on work-related matters and one debriefing concerning personal matters. These may either be in-country or on return home. Your debriefing should allow you to comment on:

- The work you did and areas which still require attention.
- The successes and frustrations of your work.
- How well the agency treated you personally.
- The support you received both locally and from your home or head office.
- How you feel the local office is responding to the situation.
- How you feel the organization could be more effective in the future.

If at all possible, write a brief assignment report – it is valuable from a professional point of view and it is one method of self-debriefing.

Be constructive in any criticisms you make as this way people are more likely to want to listen to you.

You may be offered counselling or stress debriefing with a qualified counsellor. This is not to be taken as any indication that you were unable to cope – it is simply an acknowledgement that you have faced some pretty tough challenges. If you are not offered the counselling but feel that you would like it, find a counsellor. If you need help finding a counsellor, RedR may be able to help.

It can be very helpful to talk to people who have had similar experiences to your own. Ask your agency or RedR to put you in touch with people who may be living in your area and were working in the same country. Offer to help agencies in preparing or training prospective relief workers – you will have an eager audience who will greatly appreciate hearing about your work.

While family and friends are important in the debriefing process, it is important to recognize that they may have had a lot to cope with themselves and may not be able to relate to your experiences. Do not expect too much of them in this respect.

Health
Have a thorough medical checkup on your return. Let your own doctor know where you have been, what you have been doing and any problem you had while on assignment. If you think you have malaria, insist on being tested and treated immediately – it is sometimes misdiagnosed as flu. If you become ill within six months of your assignment, visit your doctor and remind her/him of your assignment.

Maintaining contacts
Keeping in touch with the friends you made on assignment will help you feel that you have not simply abandoned them to their problems and forgotten them completely. However, it is inevitable that you will lose touch with many of them. For some people this process of 'letting go' is very painful and takes a surprisingly long time, frequently months, sometimes years. If you find it difficult, contact other people who have had similar experiences and discuss it – you will find you are not alone.

Publicity
Talking about your work to the public, either at meetings or through the press, is an effective way of continuing to support the work that you have been doing. It is also a useful way of debriefing yourself. See Section 3.6 for tips on using the media. Take a public speaking course if you are not used to speaking in public.

Employment
Returning to your old job may be a relief after your assignment – it may also be a major anti-climax. Your colleagues may resent the fact that you have been allowed leave or that they have had to cover for you while you were away. Take time to find out what they think about your absence.

If you are interested in continuing in the same line of work, let organizations know by sending a letter and copy of your CV. If you have not contacted RedR, do so now. If you would like to be more prepared for a future assignment, find out what training courses are available.

3.3 Personal health care

Some reasons to take good care of your health on assignment:

- Healthy people work more effectively and efficiently.
- You may not have access to the standard of medical aid you would like.
- When ill you become a burden to others.

Working in emergency relief, you are likely to be exposed to many causes of illness – see Figure 3.2. In addition to increased exposure to illness, a high workload with heavy responsibilities can increase stress and lower your resistance to disease. In such circumstances it is important to take precautions to minimize the risk of becoming ill (see Box 3.3). For relief workers, road accidents and malaria are the most likely causes of death or serious illness.

Make contingency plans for illness – for example, find out where appropriately qualified medical staff and health facilities are situated.

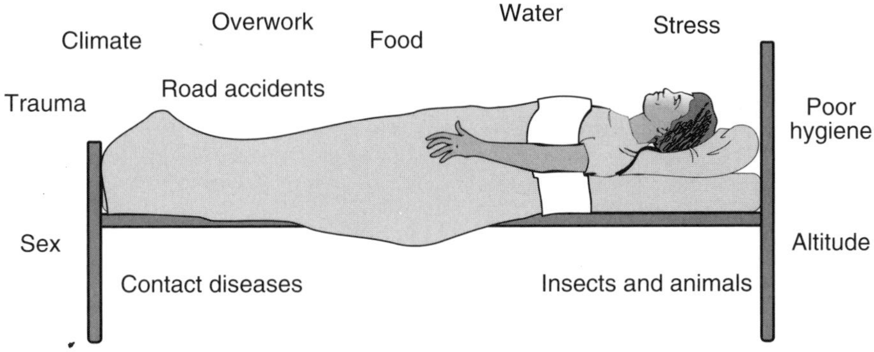

Figure 3.2 Possible causes of illness in relief workers

What to do if you become ill

Watch out for signs of illness such as: diarrhoea, vomiting, skin changes, fever, pain, ear and eye infections, excessive tiredness or drowsiness. On discovering symptoms act immediately. Do not try to 'soldier on' – it usually ends up with someone else carrying your burdens.

- Find out what is causing the symptoms as soon as they appear.
- Treat the illness as soon as possible.
- Rest when you are advised to do so. Do not resume heavy work until you have recovered or you may well relapse.
- Try to discover and remove the cause of the illness (for instance, by getting a better mosquito net, or not drinking dirty water again).

If you feel very tired and lacking in energy, check that you are eating enough of the right food and drinking sufficient liquid. In dry climates, even when you do not appear to be sweating, you can dehydrate rapidly. If you are physically active in the heat you may need to drink several litres of water per day. Ensure that you drink enough so that you need to urinate at least twice per day.

Accidents

Accidents happen more frequently when you are tired or under pressure. Anything from a cut or graze to a blood transfusion can be potentially dangerous due to the risk of infection. Along with malaria, road accidents are the most likely cause of illness or death among relief workers. Motorcycles are particularly hazardous, especially when an 'emergency mentality' develops and normal standards of safety slip – avoid using motorcycles if possible. See Section 17.2 for more details on vehicle management.

If an accident occurs:

- Clean and protect all cuts and grazes however minor.
- Avoid contaminating yourself if treating wounds of colleagues or friends.
- Ensure your colleagues know what to do if you have an accident and that they know where to find sterile needles and so on, should these be required.
- Be aware that the risk of infection from blood transfusion is high (malaria, typhoid, HIV). Choose your own donor if possible.

Box 3.3 Precautions against illness on assignment

Nutrition
Take care that you eat regularly and sufficiently, especially if physically active.

Drink enough water – you should pee twice a day.

If your urine is strong and discomfort is felt when peeing, drink more fluids.

Eating out
If eating out, eat only hot cooked food.

Drink hot tea or coffee or sealed bottles of beer. Only drink soft drinks if you are sure the bottles cannot be opened and resealed.

If in any doubt about hygiene, do not consume salads, peeled fruit, water, ice or ice-cream.

Never drink local beer or share drinking vessels – say it is against your culture.

Try to eat when the restaurant is busy – the food is more likely to be freshly made.

Wash your hands and clean any suspicious looking cutlery and crockery, especially glasses or beakers.

Eating in
If cooking for yourself take extra care over hygiene. Wash all fruit and raw vegetables in clean water (add a tiny drop of bleach or washing up liquid).

If employing a cook, check and inspect hygiene practices regularly.

Ensure all drinking water is safe: boiled or otherwise sterilized.

Clothing
In hot climates, protect yourself from the sun – use a hat, sunscreen and sunglasses.

Wear stout protective footwear – strong shoes or boots. Avoid open sandals. If working in the bush, wear long trousers.

In cold climates, remember that several layers of clothing insulate better than sheer bulk – a good combination is thermal underwear, T-shirt, shirt, light sweater, heavy sweater. Ensure you have adequate waterproof clothing, footwear and gloves.

Personal hygiene
Personal hygiene is very important for good morale.

Make sure that you wash daily and change your clothes regularly, especially underclothes. Have your clothes washed, rinsed and, in hot climates, ironed properly and regularly to kill bugs.

Ensure that your bed linen is changed regularly. If you are using a sleeping bag, use a sheet liner and wash it regularly.

Accidents
Ensure there is an agreed and widely understood procedure to deal with accidents.

Ensure there is a proper first aid kit in all project vehicles.

Know your own blood group and ensure others know it.

Always carry a small personal first aid kit for your personal use.

Treat cuts, grazes and bites immediately, to prevent infection.

Drive carefully and ensure that project drivers do likewise. Refuse to travel with dangerous drivers. If doing a lot of driving, hire a good local driver.

Avoid night driving if possible.

Insects and animals
Avoid them – they carry disease and parasites. Ask around for what to beware of. Do not keep pets.

Mosquitoes: use insect repellents to minimize biting in the evenings. Use a treated mosquito net at night.

Ticks and leeches: if working in the bush, check yourself regularly.

Snakes and scorpions: use a torch if walking at night. Check your shoes in the morning before putting them on.

Alcohol
Never drink and drive. Avoid drinking local brews. Never share drinking vessels. Be sensible and use alcohol wisely.

Sex
If you develop a sexual relationship, ensure that you take sensible health precautions. Always use a condom, even if using other contraceptives. If using the pill, ensure that you have an adequate supply and be aware that it may be less effective in certain circumstances.

Diseases
Ensure that you have taken the correct vaccinations and that they are kept up to date. If located in a malarial region, take your anti-malarials and use a mosquito net.

Stress
High levels of stress can increase the risk of illness. Have a sensible stress management plan, including enough rest and relaxation (see Section 3.4)

- Get statements from accident witnesses if appropriate.
- Write a clear record afterwards. Include: events leading up to the accident, what actually occurred, the date, time and precise location, who was present, who was injured and the nature of the injuries, what action was taken and what follow up is required.

3.4 Stress

Disaster situations are abnormal, sometimes severely so. Stress reactions are normal in an abnormal situation. Stress may be cumulative due to the build up of every day concerns over time. Traumatic stress is caused by a sudden, unexpected and violent event which severely impacts upon and harms or threatens an individual. Trauma is a very severe state of stress. In the short term, cumulative stress may increase your output and make you more efficient. In the longer term, exposure to unacceptable levels of cumulative stress may lead to poor work performance, illness, mental breakdown or burn-out. Recognize the factors which cause cumulative stress, its symptoms and how to deal with it.

Factors which cause stress

Factors which cause stress include:

- Exposure to other people's suffering and grief; an inevitable part of working in an emergency.
- Poor personal security.
- High self-expectations. Are you determined to 'prove yourself'?
- Feeling indispensable – nobody is.
- Living accommodation, health and nutrition.
- Organizational culture. Is there a workaholic mentality?
- Interpersonal relationships.
- Work environment – have you the right tools, facilities, finance, etc. for your job?
- Climate.

Symptoms of stress

The first step in dealing with stress is to recognize it. It is difficult to diagnose stress in a colleague and particularly difficult to diagnose it in yourself, partly because stress affects your ability to think clearly. Common symptoms include:

- Problems sleeping.
- Headaches or muscular twitches.
- Unusual difficulty with normal mental activities such as analysing simple problems, formulating plans, writing reports.
- Mind racing, jumping from subject to subject.
- Indecisiveness, inconsistency.
- Poor concentration, disorientation, confusion.

- Increase or decrease in activity.
- Inability to rest or let go.
- Social withdrawal.
- Periods of crying.
- Increased alcohol or drug intake.
- Increased dependency on 'pick-me-ups'.
- Self-neglect.
- Hypervigilance.
- Increase in racist or sexist statements.
- Increased complaints about minor health problems.

Emotional effects include:

- Mood swings.
- Anxiety, depression, guilt.
- Wanting to do more to help.
- Irritability, restlessness, anger, need to attribute blame.
- Feeling heroic, exhilarated, invulnerable.
- Feelings of isolation, abandonment.
- Strong identification with emergency victims.

Exposure to a severe traumatic situation may result in physical symptoms including:

- Insomnia, nightmares, flashbacks.
- Undue fatigue.
- Excessive startle, muscle tremor.
- Vomiting and diarrhoea.
- Recurrent headaches, body pain, dizziness.
- Sweating and shivering.
- Increased heartbeat, breathing and blood pressure.

Dealing with stress

The effects of stress can manifest themselves before you go on assignment and can continue long after you return. Prepare a plan for stress management before you go on assignment, while your head is still clear.

Before you go

- Make sure your family understands what you are doing and why.
- Be prepared – get as much information as possible before leaving about the job, country, situation, and where possible share it with family and friends.

While on assignment

- Try to stay healthy and physically fit.
- Know what to do when a crisis occurs, for instance, a security or medical problem.
- Watch out for signs of stress in yourself and colleagues, possibly by using the buddy system (see below).

- Identify ways of defusing stress by taking a break or talking to a friend.
- Prepare for leaving and returning home. Consider returning by 'stepping stones' (see below).

After your assignment

- Remember, for most people, returning home is more difficult than leaving.
- Make sure you are debriefed properly by your agency on both technical and personal matters.
- If you have any difficulties coming to terms with anything that happened during your assignment, go to a qualified counsellor.
- Contact people who have been working under similar conditions for an understanding chat.
- Giving talks and presentations about your assignment, particularly to other relief workers, is an excellent way of coming to terms with your work and passing on your experience to others.

Treatment of acute traumatic stress

Where acute stress or trauma has occurred, treatment must be properly structured and controlled, where possible in accordance with appropriate medical advice. All cases of acute stress should be referred to your agency who should have a policy for treating such cases. The following guidelines are suggested:

- Initial defusion; it is essential to 'let it all out' on or near the scene within 48 hours.
- Rest and take a break from work, preferably away from the area of the incident.
- Allow the sufferers to ventilate feelings with someone who is a qualified counsellor or informally with people who have been through the same ordeal and with whom the sufferer can identify. It is important that this is done in a confidential and supportive atmosphere. Criticism of the professional performance of colleagues should be dealt with in a separate forum.
- Make every effort to enable the sufferer to return to work. Complete withdrawal from the scene may make it more difficult to come to terms with the situation. However, complete withdrawal may be the only option and the sufferer must be supported in this. On no account should suggestions be made that this was a failure to cope.

Coping mechanisms

Here are some suggestions on coping with stress. Choose some and add some of your own.

- Eat well, exercise properly and take proper rest.
- Schedule a time for relaxation at the end of each day.
- Set yourself realistic goals and make sure your colleagues understand what these are. Do not be afraid to say NO.

- Make sure you get reasonable, regular breaks away from work. As a minimum, this should be at least one day off per week and a few days away from site every four to six weeks. In difficult circumstances more breaks may be needed.
- Try to ensure that you have some private space into which you can retreat from time to time, whether to read, to listen to music or simply to stare into space.
- A little alcohol may help in socializing, but be sensible and control your intake.
- Talk to friends with similar experiences.
- Try not to get too emotionally involved with the cause or effects of the crisis.
- Encourage yourself by thinking positively about what you can do, even if this is only a very small part of what needs to be done.
- Everyone likes to feel someone cares. Keep an eye on your colleagues' stress and fatigue levels.
- In emergency work, strong personal relationships frequently develop. Be aware that this may happen and consider the consequences on other relationships you may have (see below).
- Keep in touch with family and friends while you are away, even if only by brief postcard.
- Remember you are not indispensable, nor need you feel isolated.
- Keep a personal diary. It is useful in work as a record for reports. It is useful personally as a way of letting off steam at the time and may be useful afterwards in helping you come to terms with returning home.

Buddy system

Recognizing and acknowledging stress at an early stage and taking appropriate action may save the need for drastic action at a later stage. However, recognizing and acknowledging stress is not easy because:

- It is difficult to recognize stress in yourself, as by its nature, stress may impair your ability to analyse.
- There may well be strong subconscious cultural taboos which result in a reluctance to acknowledge that one is suffering from stress. These taboos may make it difficult to point out to colleagues that you believe they are suffering from stress.

The 'buddy system' is one method of dealing with the reluctance to acknowledge stress at an early stage and allows one to take appropriate action. It is a form of informal contract with a friend or colleague which works as follows:

- Before any signs of stress are manifested, make an agreement with one friend or colleague (the buddy) to:
  - Watch each other for signs of stress.
  - Point this out tactfully and in private at an early stage.
  - Suggest some course of action, such as a few days leave, or a chance to go and talk.

Relationships

Working as part of a team in difficult and dangerous conditions can result in the formation of strong personal relationships, some of which may be mutually supportive and positive, some of which may turn out to be acrimonious and negative. If you are working on a short assignment, the best way of dealing with a negative relationship may well be to 'live and let live' so long as it is not affecting your work. If it does begin to affect work, then it becomes a management issue and appropriate managerial action may be required (see Chapter 6).

Supportive, positive relationships can be very important in coping with the difficulties of a situation. However there are a number of issues to be confronted:

- Time spent working in an emergency is time away from your normal life. How would you relate to this person or these people in your normal life?
- How will this relationship affect other relationships 'back home'?
- If a relationship develops into a sexual relationship:
  - Consider the effects on partners (if any) back home.
  - Consider the effects on your friends and colleagues with whom you are living and working.
  - Consider the effects on any local customs or taboos.
  - Protect yourself against pregnancy and disease.

Emergency relief work is frequently carried out in situations where there has been a massive breakdown in civil society and where great evil has been perpetrated. Against this background, the immediate benefits to be gained from a comforting, supportive sexual relationship may seem to outweigh the long-term costs of dealing with the consequences of such a relationship when returning to normality. How you deal with these issues is a personal matter but it is important to be prepared.

Returning home – stepping stones

Returning home to normality may mean leaving the intense relationships that have developed in difficult circumstances. Your perspective may have been changed dramatically by your experiences on assignment. By contrast, the generality of life back home is likely to have changed little. You will need some time to re-adjust. It is not sensible to go straight from an assignment back into normal life and work. Plan your return home as early as possible, before you go on assignment if possible.

Take some time out between leaving your place of work on assignment and returning to normal life and work back home. If possible, take a few days to wind down away from your assignment, for example in the capital city of the country of work or a nearby country. Plan a few days' holiday close to home before attempting to get back into the full swing of normal life. If you have a partner, take a few days' break together. Return by stepping stones.

3.5 Working with different cultures

When working in humanitarian relief you will meet people from many different cultures. Cultural differences may be refreshing – they may also lead to many problems, threatening your patience and security, and increasing anxiety and stress. It is important to recognize when you are faced with a cultural issue and to accept that you may have to live with it.

3.5.1 Cultural awareness

Being culturally aware does not mean knowing everything about a different society but it does mean knowing to expect differences. If possible, speak to someone from your own culture who has experience of living in the area and ask them about their observations. Keep an open mind, do not make instant conclusions about what you see but take time to find out what it really means.

To work effectively with other cultures, it is important to understand your own culture. For example, why do you make certain gestures, keep strict time, show respect to animals or not eat meat? Keep an eye open for some of the factors and practices mentioned in Table 3.3.

Sensitivity

Begin by learning to show respect. Learn a few words of greeting in the local language and use them. Throughout your stay, show a willingness to learn by befriending locals, trying the local food or joining in local activities. Aim to be courteous, tolerant, flexible, friendly, patient, non-judgemental, prepared to learn and prepared to adapt.

Do not assume your ways are better – they are only different.

3.5.2 Culture shock

While adapting to the surrounding cultures, it is a good idea to let people know about your own culture to help explain your actions. People are generally very tolerant of newcomers and do not expect them to learn everything. Have your own realistic expectations; do not expect ever to be fully accepted by the different societies. The degree to which you need to adapt and the extent to which it is possible will vary with the nature of the culture you are working in (that of the host community and of the refugees) and the type of emergency work in which you are engaged. An inability to accept and be considerate of the differences between your own and other cultures is referred to as culture shock. This can manifest itself as:

- Withdrawal: showing no interest at all in the other culture and cutting yourself off by setting up your own small community.
- Aggression: responding to the culture with hostility, proclaiming your own ways superior.
- Over-identification: excessive readiness to abandon your own culture for a new one.

Culture shock may be a problem on arriving in a new country. For many people, the most difficult form of culture shock is that experienced on returning home.

Table 3.3 Observing cultural factors and practices

Politeness	What are the basic rules of politeness and decency?
Greetings	How and when should you say hello?
Respect	Who should be shown respect and how? (for instance, the use of 'tu' and 'vous' in French).
Body language	What gestures are rude? How should one sit? Is eye/body contact acceptable?
Physical contact	What is expected – shaking and holding hands, kissing, embracing?
Space	What is personal or public space?
Appearance	What is the appropriate dress code?
Gender	What are the attitudes to women? Sharing of household tasks? Ways of showing respect to either sex?
Age	Are elders respected? Are there different ways of greeting young and old?
Time	How punctual are you expected to be? What does 'now' mean?
Loyalty	Is this respected? Is nepotism common? Is non-conformity allowed?
Decision making	Are decisions made by individuals? by group? apparently by nobody?
Hierarchy	Is the hierarchical structure authoritarian and well defined? Participative and loose? Democratic? Anarchic?
Risk taking	Is it frowned on?
Emotions	What can be shown?
Relationships	What are the rules for socializing outside work?
Social practices	Is waiting in line the norm? How should you call for attention?
Disagreement	Should one express disagreement openly? Is saving face more important than frankness?
Attitude to work	Is work seen as good in itself? Or merely a means to an end?
Fatalism	Can people really take effective action or is everything 'God willing?'
Attitude to nature	What respect is due to animals, trees, watering places?
Law	Does it exist in a formal sense? Is it respected?

3.5.3 Issues of conscience

Working in emergency relief brings you into contact with people of very different cultures, motivations and outlooks. Sometimes these differences and the nature of the work you are doing may raise serious issues of conscience.

Your right to raise and pursue your own issues of conscience should be tempered by consideration of the implications on your own work and security and that of your colleagues and the people involved in the disaster. If you are an expatriate worker, you are a guest in the country and as such should recognize that you may have to consider different courses of action than if you were in your own country. While you may be free to leave and pursue your issues of conscience from a position of relative security, others may not have this freedom.

Some typical issues of conscience which you are likely to face include corruption, politics, religion, violence, apathy, a different attitude to the value of human life and sexism. If these issues of conscience are likely to impair your work, then it may be that emergency relief work is not for you. Most relief agencies will have policies relating to some of these issues. Find out what the policies are before you leave and check that you can live with them.

Corruption is one of the most common issues of conscience faced by relief workers. Corrupt practices range from the trivial, like asking your secretary's sister who works at the airport to get you on Friday's plane home, to the serious, such as selling off emergency food supplies destined for starving refugees. Different societies tolerate different levels or forms of corruption. Accepting bribes, backhanders or gratuities may be the only way for a poorly paid government clerk to support his family.

Very often it is possible to avoid paying bribes if you make it clear that it is strictly against your policy. It is much easier to start such corrupt practices than it is to stop them. Before becoming involved, consult with experienced colleagues, check that there is absolutely no other way and ensure that you have the support of your agency.

3.6 Publicity and the media

The media is a powerful tool which can be used to bring the plight of victims of disaster to world attention and to mobilize support and assistance. As with any powerful tool, treat it with respect. The media is interested in you as an emergency relief worker and as a representative of a relief agency. As a representative, you should have a clear understanding of your agency's media policy.

When on assignment, as a general guide, only speak to reporters once you have permission from your organization. Stay within the guidelines given to you. If you feel that you have something to promote, ask your manager to set up an interview. After you return from an assignment, remember that the work of the agency continues. If you have serious criticisms of an agency, it is only fair to bring them to the attention of that agency first before raising them elsewhere. To voice criticisms of an agency in the media is a very serious matter. It should not be done lightly.

The following are some suggestions on how to handle an interview (adapted from UNHCR, 1993):

- **Be prepared:** Ask for a list of questions beforehand, know exactly why and when they are visiting/phoning and what they want to know.
- **Be concise:** Know what you want to say and say it – remember two or three key points (no more) and make sure they come through.
- **Be factual but conversational:** Have some facts and figures at your fingertips that everyone (your granny and great uncle) can understand. For example, rather than 'we're pumping into the reticulation system 100 m^3 of water per day to the camp' say 'we're managing to supply the bare minimum of water for the camp's 10 000 people'.
- **Be yourself:** Journalists are there for a good story. They do not want to make your life miserable. Relax, get to know them and keep in touch with them.
- **Be truthful and protection minded:** If you do not know the answer to a question or do not want to give an answer on a particular point say so – 'I need to check my facts before I answer that'. Consider the effects of what you say on the security of aid workers, colleagues and people affected by the emergency.
- **Know the groundrules:** It may be possible to be quoted only as 'a relief worker' to avoid you or your colleagues being placed in jeopardy; for instance, if you point out human rights violations. Some information can be given 'off the record' to point journalists in the direction of a story. Do not abuse the groundrules – journalists are not fools.
- **Be interesting:** Have some human interest stories to tell – the children who are no longer dying from diarrhoea, examples of the efforts the people are making for themselves and how you are helping.
- **Be positive:** Avoid criticizing other agencies – all agencies are in the same boat.
- **Be thoughtful:** Never be afraid to pause and think about your reply.
- **Be photogenic:** You are a hardworking field representative of your agency; look the part.
- **Be quiet:** When you have finished. Try not to interfere with the story subsequently. If there is a serious problem, call in the agency press officer – do not harass journalists yourself.

4 Personal security

Humanitarian relief is often necessary in locations subject to conflict or significant levels of insecurity. This will expose relief workers to higher levels of risk than they would normally face. You must therefore be prepared for such situations. The personal security of you and your colleagues should be your highest priority. This is not simply a selfish viewpoint. Major security incidents can severely disrupt and possibly close a humanitarian assistance programme. It is normal, and sensible, to feel worried or afraid when working in an insecure and possibly violent environment. To ignore this feeling or push it to one side is dangerous – discuss your concerns with friends, colleagues and your manager. It is important to take a considered, rational approach to your security and the security of others.

Most agencies will state that every staff member can decide to pull out of a project if they feel the risks they are running are too high. When taking up a new post you should be given information on the security situation before being asked to sign a contract and then a security briefing as part of the induction process.

This chapter provides guidelines on how to minimise personal risk. For more detailed guidance on security management for agencies see Van Brabant (2000).

'Security' refers to risks to staff and assets due to intentional violence. 'Safety' refers to hazards such as vehicle accidents, natural and work-related hazards and medical risks. Safety is not specifically covered in this chapter although managing the hazards is covered elsewhere in relevant sections of the book. Accidents and medical conditions are a significant cause of death and injury to relief workers. It is stressed here, therefore, that managers and individuals need to be as much 'safety aware' as 'security aware'.

The term 'protection' refers to the legal protection of a civilian population (e.g. the protection of refugees). See Paul (1999) for specific guidance on protection.

4.1 Situation awareness

Threshold of acceptable risk

Is it worth the risk? A starting point for anyone working in a complex, insecure environment is to clearly understand your job and the aims of the organization for which you work. This will help to determine an acceptable threshold of risk beyond which you should not be prepared to go. If your specific mission is of a life-saving nature – people are in desperate need of food and they need it today – then you are likely to have a higher threshold of risk than someone, for example, who is working on a micro-credit savings scheme where a visit delayed for a few days to let a violent situation cool down will not have such an adverse impact. Each individual and agency will have their own threshold of acceptable risk – be sure you have thought through the level of risk you are willing to accept.

Agency mandate

What is the agency mandate? Each organization has its core focus or mandate which shapes its operational programmes. It may be emergency relief, long-term development, skills exchange, human rights and so on. It is important for the individual, and agency managers, to understand the agency mandate as this helps to establish operational boundaries beyond which the agency, and individual staff, should not go without clearly thinking through the consequences.

> **Box 4.1**
>
> **Confused mandates?**
>
> In the course of helping to develop water supplies for displaced people you witness human rights abuses. You report what you see to your manager. The agency publicizes the abuses without informing you and thinking through the consequences for field staff. You are put in a very vulnerable position.
>
> In this example, the agency mandate of emergency relief has expanded to include reporting on human rights abuses. This may seem very commendable but the security implications for you and the people you are working with must be considered very carefully before action is taken.

Values and principles

What are your values and principles and those of the agency for which you are working? The Red Cross/NGO Code of Conduct (see Box 1.1) expresses commonly held principles which many agencies have accepted. Of importance to you and your security are some of the practical dilemmas of putting principles into practice. What does it mean to be *neutral* if you are working with and advocating for the rights of an oppressed community? Are you really *impartial* when you clearly do not have the resources or means of access to work with civilians on the other side of the conflict lines? Does what your agency say match with what others perceive?

You may be challenged on your stated principles by a range of people from local staff to militias at checkpoints. Be prepared to put your position as an individual, as a team and as an agency. Inconsistency and confused arguments can lead to suspicion and misunderstandings. National and international staff need to understand the agency position and as a team you need to come to an understanding.

Historical, political, social and economic context

What is the historical, political, social and economic context in which you are working? The context in which you work is crucial to how you behave, what you say and do, and the day-to-day decisions you make concerning your project and your security. A knowledge of the history and politics of a region will help you to understand relationships and grievances between people. It will also help you to look at yourself from someone else's viewpoint to try to appreciate how others might view you. Might you be viewed with suspicion, especially if your own society has historical and political links?

The national and local economy will influence employment opportunities and the level of poverty and crime. You might, for example, be seen as a threat, real or imagined, to someone's business.

An understanding of society and cultural norms can help you to behave appropriately and avoid upsetting people. A knowledge of traditional 'codes' can help in understanding incidents and patterns of crimes. Avoid jumping to conclusions and interpreting according to your own code and beliefs without checking against local norms.

Being context aware will not only aid your security but also your project planning and practice.

4.2 Security strategies

There are three generally recognized strategies for trying to manage risk: acceptance, protection and deterrence. The acceptance strategy seeks to reduce risk by increasing acceptance of your presence and work. Protection is the more traditional approach to security of 'hardening the target' to reduce vulnerability by the use of protective measures. Deterrence aims to deter the threat with a counter-threat.

4.2.1 Acceptance

There is a danger in assuming that because you are a humanitarian relief worker you will be automatically accepted and understood by everyone – and that your agency will be accepted as well. But acceptance cannot be assumed. It may not be clear to anyone outside the aid world who you are, who you work for, and why. It is often difficult for those outside the aid community to distinguish between NGOs, UN agencies, private companies, the government of the country of origin of your agency, and so on. Your humanitarian role and what you are trying to achieve may simply not be understood.

With a greater understanding of who you are and what you are trying to achieve may come an enhanced respect and acceptance of you and your work, at the local level, and for your agency programme, on a broader level. This can result in:

- A recognition that you are no longer a threat and, therefore, not a target.
- General support for your work which may result in helpful advice and information.
- Advanced warning of potential security threats.
- Efforts made by combatants to avoid harm to agency staff and assets.

Gaining acceptance can be achieved in several ways but it may require a conscious public relations effort on the part of agency staff and managers. Key to this approach on a personal level are your behaviour and the relationships you develop.

Relationships

Your style and approach to relationships will have a bearing on how you are perceived by others. For example, approaching work relationships purely from the point of view of getting the job done in the quickest possible time without regard for the individuals involved can upset people. In an emergency you may feel that you do not have the time to spend on what might appear to be social niceties. But an investment in relationships can have significant work, social and security benefits. It is not time wasted.

However, there is a need for a balance in relationships. You may wish to maintain some distance in a relationship for political or work reasons and to avoid misunderstandings. It is useful if you can collectively review your relationships, from the point of view of security, with your team members and be open to each other's views.

Behaviour

Individual behaviour conveys many messages and what may appear acceptable to one person may create anger, resentment and envy in others. Such misunderstandings can lead to threats against the individual. Factors that can be significant include:

- The clothing you wear ('military-style', agency T-shirts, culturally insensitive).
- Cultural acceptance of hair style and body decoration.
- Posture and bearing (aggressive and threatening versus confident but not arrogant).
- Insensitive comments made in public places.
- The consumption of alcohol and its acceptance in society, or different levels of society, in particular the quantity consumed, in certain places at certain times of the day.
- The vehicle you drive (during and outside work), the wealth or benefits the vehicle portrays and the way the vehicle is driven.

4.2.2 Protection

Hardening yourself as a potential target, with protective procedures and devices, has been a common response to reduce vulnerability to threats. Key elements of a protection strategy are:

Reduce exposure
Respect curfews and 'no go' areas (sometimes self-imposed).
Withdraw from an insecure location.
Limit the amount of cash and valuables that you carry (but carry enough cash to satisfy robbers).
Use older, possibly rented, cars rather than attractive, new vehicles.

Reduce or increase visibility
Some situations require a low profile – blend into the background by removing agency logos and house signs, not wearing agency T-shirts, etc.

In other situations in which your agency has a high level of acceptance maintain a high profile – display agency logo, signs and flag, wear agency T-shirts, etc.

Strength in numbers
Don't go out alone or live alone.
Travel in convoy or in tandem with another vehicle.
Live near to the office and colleague's houses.
Watch out for each other, whether travelling/walking together or living together. Establish or join a 'neighbourhood watch' scheme.

Protective devices
Helmet or flak jacket – if you have to wear them ask yourself if you have reached a threshold of acceptable risk: should you be there at all?
Use blast and sniper walls, and bomb shelters in conflict zones.
For house protection you might consider high walls with barbed wire, strengthened locked doors, barred windows, guard dog or geese (to warn of intruders), burglar alarms, and exterior lighting.
Use a radio to maintain communications. Have a procedure for 'calling-in'. Look after hand-held radios as they are often a target for thieves.

Protective procedures
Control or monitor visitors to an office or house.
Wear your ID card and encourage others to do the same especially where people frequently come and go. An ID card is often useful to establish who you are if stopped by 'the authorities'. It may be commonplace to be asked for your card to obtain entry to agency and government offices.
In certain circumstances it may be advantageous to announce your movements in advance to warring parties and seek their consent for travel.

Hardening the target may be a necessary, but not sufficient, security strategy. High walls, barbed wire and strong locks may provide greater physical protection but what impact might this have on your image? Protection may need to be adjusted and combined with other strategies. There may also become a point where protection measures hinder your work to such an extent that you can no longer be effective. That is when you need to review the approach and your programme.

4.2.3 Deterrence

Relief workers and agencies have limited means to deter a threat with a counter-threat. Deterrence measures can be categorized into:

- Legal, political and economic sanctions.
- Threatened suspension of a project or withdrawal.
- Armed protection.

Relief workers may look for legal protection under existing national and international law but this is unlikely to be effective in most situations.

At an international level attempts have been made to influence governments and non-state actors through political pressure and the imposition of economic sanctions. The individual relief worker needs to assess the effect such pressures may have on their own security if working in the country or region concerned.

Adopting armed protection is clearly an extreme strategy that can have a profound impact on the image and perception of your agency and colleague agencies. In itself it is a high-risk strategy. If you have to consider armed protection then you may have reached the threshold of acceptable risk. If your agency adopts armed protection then it signals a moment of decision for all staff as it is a recognition of a clear change in level of risk and strategy. You have to decide if it might be wiser to personally withdraw.

The form of armed protection can range from lightly armed warehouse guards, to deter a criminal threat, to fully armed convoy escorts to deal with a military threat. Whatever the form of armed protection there are three key issues to consider: is armed protection acceptable in principle, appropriate in the context and capable of being managed by the agency? Thinking through these questions with your colleagues will aid a rational response to the issue.

For a more complete discussion on armed protection see Chapter 6 of Van Brabant (2000).

4.3 Security procedures

Security procedures are established by security managers to ensure everyone conducts themselves appropriately as a team. Procedures should be based on:

- The agency mission in the country.
- An understanding of the context in which the agency operates.
- An assessment of current and possible future threats.
- An assessment of the vulnerability of the agency and individual staff.
- A conscious mix of security strategies based on the above considerations.
- Any practical constraints.

You should receive documentation and a briefing from your agency on procedures to be followed. If you do not, ask for them.

Procedures can be divided into preventive and reactive measures. Preventive measures are standard operating procedures which are followed in the normal course of work. Reactive measures are sometimes called contingencies which are guidelines to respond to an incident.

4.3.1 Standard Operating Procedures (SOPs)

Standard Operating Procedures (SOPs) guide our daily actions and they generally comprise the following elements:

- Statement of purpose – what the SOP is trying to achieve.
- The tasks – what needs to be done and how.
- Responsibilities – who does what.
- Timing – when actions are taken or their sequence.
- Supporting documents for the procedure (e.g. radio call signs).

SOPs typically cover activities related to: personnel management, financial management, vehicle movement, checkpoints, beneficiary registration and verification, site assessment and management, relief commodities distribution, radio communications, incident reporting and so on. Many of these SOPs will cover procedures which will have already been established as part of good management practice. Good security practice should be incorporated into good management practice.

Specific recommendations for SOPs are not given here because each procedure must be based on a clear understanding of the situation and to whom the procedure applies. What might be acceptable in one location may be unacceptable elsewhere. For example, is it customary to switch the vehicle engine off at a checkpoint or is it recommended to leave it running? A change in practice from the norm can draw unwanted attention and may increase your vulnerability. When you are new to a country it is important to ensure you know the correct procedures, even for an experienced relief worker. If you find they are not appropriate then perhaps the situation has changed and it is time for a review. Each individual has the responsibility to alert the security manager to inappropriate or outdated procedures.

4.3.2 Contingencies

Even if we follow all the correct procedures there is no guarantee that we will avoid a security incident. Therefore, we need to be prepared to react when necessary. Contingencies are guidelines for responding to an incident and they typically cover medical evacuations (Medevac), staff death, staff disappearance, abduction/kidnapping/hostage situations, assault, ambush, bomb threat, withdrawal (evacuation/relocation/hibernation).

There are two key components to a contingency plan:

- Reaction in the field to the incident.
- How the incident is managed by the agency.

The anticipation of likely scenarios, agreeing responses as a team, and incident response drills can help to clarify and consolidate how you would collectively react when faced with danger. Working through responses may also be reassuring but beware of overconfidence that might lead to recklessness.

If you know that the agency has a plan of action when you are involved in an incident then this can also give reassurance. If you are taken hostage, for example, it can be reassuring and practically useful if you know what efforts will be made to secure your release and the best way for you to react and complement such efforts.

Box 4.2

Evacuation

A key contingency is withdrawal from a programme. For many relief workers this can mean evacuation. An agency should have an up-to-date evacuation plan, or plans, if the situation demands. For the individual this means at least knowing the following:

- The latest version of the plan as it affects you.
- How a movement to assembly (concentration) points prior to evacuation is authorized and arranged.
- Where your concentration point, and alternatives, are located.
- Communication procedures during a crisis.
- What up-to-date visas you should have.
- How to hand over your work responsibilities to local staff or partners. If this is not possible then how to close down your project.
  Hand over can involve the disposal or safeguarding of sensitive files (personnel, project, financial), the delegation of authority, payment of remaining staff and any debts.
- What to do with agency assets: vehicles, radios, project equipment.
- Personal baggage allowance.

In unpredictable situations it is advisable to prepare a 'grab bag' for a rapid departure. The bag should contain essentials for survival during evacuation and on arrival, including an agreed cash minimum, passport (with visas kept up-to-date), relevant papers, toiletries, change of clothing, etc.

4.4 Self-management, teamwork and preparedness

4.4.1 Self-management

Being security aware means consciously managing how you live and work:

- Be conscious of the image you project. Are you quietly confident and respectful?
- Avoid drawing attention to yourself through behaviour, manner or dress.
- Try to avoid routines to make it difficult for someone to predict your movements, especially where the movement of money is concerned (e.g. regular staff pay days).
- Be suspicious of what is unusual, risky or threatening. Be aware of your environment and notice when things are not normal (empty markets, quiet streets that are usually busy).
- Tact and diplomacy can be refined through conscious effort.
- The management of anger (in yourself and in others) can also be consciously developed.

- Your decision-making capacity is impaired if you are stressed. How do you monitor your stress levels? What are the implications for others and how might they help? (see Section 3.4).
- Keep healthy by eating, resting and sleeping well.

4.4.2 Teamwork

If one person takes a risk they can put at risk the whole team and mission. There is no such thing as a personal risk. Teamwork is critical to working in an insecure environment. If your team is not working effectively this can adversely impact on your collective security. Action must be taken to resolve problems. Everyone has a part to play in ensuring:

- Mutual understanding and support.
- A recognition of hierarchy, the need for discipline at critical times, and a sharing of responsibilities.
- Roles recognize and draw upon strengths and weaknesses.
- Effective communication and the sharing of security-related information.

A specific area which can greatly benefit from mutual support is in the management of stress (refer to Section 3.4).

4.4.3 Preparation

Being prepared means:

- Taking advantage of training in personal security and radio communications before going on an assignment.
- Obtaining a security briefing *before* signing a contract so that you can make an informed decision on committing yourself or not.
- Briefing yourself on the situation by talking to people who have recent experience of the area, by reading reports in newspapers and on the web, by reading agency reports.
- Obtaining a security briefing before you arrive at your location and getting an update soon after arrival.
- Identifying the specific threats in your location and obtaining specialist briefing, if necessary e.g. landmines awareness.
- Keeping yourself updated.
- Avoiding complacency.

Complacency can set in when, after a time, you become used to living in an insecure environment but nothing serious happens to you or your colleagues. A false sense of confidence and invulnerability may result in lax procedures, e.g. staying in a location for too long or delaying a return to base to finish a job. You and your team must guard against such complacency by regularly reviewing how you operate and the habits to which you become accustomed. It is not uncommon for a new arrival to be surprised at the risks people take and the absence of security measures. See such criticism as a prompt for a security review. Complacency can be fatal.

5 Assessment and planning

In the immediate aftermath of a disaster, there will always be a tension between starting implementation quickly with inadequate information and taking valuable time to formulate a more effective response. A common message from experienced relief workers is that it is very important to take time to assess carefully what needs to be done and to resist the temptation of rushing headlong into poorly thought-out actions.

This chapter deals with the process of collecting and analysing information and of formulating plans. Specific assessment techniques are described. Detailed information which is required on specific topics is dealt with in other chapters.

In carrying out assessments and making plans, adopt a staged approach: identify priority actions quickly and get started; monitor and evaluate the effects of these actions; decide what needs to be changed and develop more comprehensive plans.

Assessment and planning are essential and ongoing processes, and should not be confined to the initial stages of an emergency.

5.1 Assessment

5.1.1 Needs and resources

In international law people affected by disasters are entitled to protection and assistance. Governments and parties to a conflict are required to provide assistance or to allow it to be provided. They are also obliged to prevent and refrain from violating basic human rights. It is recognised that those with primary responsibility for providing humanitarian assistance may be unwilling or unable to do so. Humanitarian agencies fulfil this role but require acceptance by governments and, in a conflict, by warring parties to be able to satisfy the basic right of people to life with dignity.

Assessments, therefore, clearly take account of the rights of individuals to a minimum standard of assistance. But in complex emergencies assessments also need to ensure that assistance does not inadvertently increase the vulnerability of those being assisted or favour parties to a conflict through politically insensitive and inappropriate relief. An assessment should also consider the risks to staff and fellow agencies and partners of working in a particular environment. See chapter 4 for guidance on personal security.

To prepare and implement an effective response after a disaster:

- Determine and prioritize the needs of the affected people.
- Assess the resources that may be mobilized to meet these needs.

- Formulate plans and implement a response.
- Monitor progress, evaluate results and adjust programme.

In carrying out an assessment, the principle should be to collect *enough* information to implement an *effective* response. Time spent collecting unnecessary information is time wasted. On the other hand, not doing an adequate assessment may lead to much more effort, time and money wasted on an ineffective response. Focus on the most relevant factors (the question 'so what?' is a useful test of relevance – ask it frequently). Try to keep an open mind – list all possible options; brainstorming may be useful here (see 5.3.2).

While each disaster will have a unique set of needs and resources, it is useful to anticipate what some of the needs and resources may be.

Needs

After a disaster, the immediate needs of the affected population are likely to include, to varying degrees, the following examples:

- Protection from violence or harassment:
  Consider the effects of temporary settlement location and layout, access roads, provision of services, access to water and fuel.
- Shelter from the elements:
  Consider the provision of blankets, plastic sheeting for shelters, tents, building materials, tools.
- Food and fuel:
  How is the food going to reach the settlement? Vehicles required? Access by road – river crossings? Food distribution, feeding centres? Is there adequate fuel? How can it be transported to the people in need? Have they got matches?
- Water and sanitation:
  Have people enough safe water to drink, cook, wash? What sort of latrine facilities are needed? What about soap? Vector control? Hygiene promotion?
- Medical care:
  Clinical care for injuries, acute illnesses. Community care for diarrhoeas – education, oral rehydration therapy? Vaccinations?
- Social services:
  Tracing of relatives, support for rape victims, care of unaccompanied children.

This is not a comprehensive checklist and there will be many other needs which will vary with the circumstances. Although some needs will be stark and clear, it is important to avoid making assumptions about other people's real needs. Let them tell you. The approach and techniques in this chapter are given to help you establish what they are.

Secondary needs which should be addressed include training and institution building.

The relief worker should be aware of all these needs and also aware of how any particular type of response may affect them. For example, the design and location of water points and latrines may have a significant effect on the security of women and children using these facilities.

Resources

To meet these needs, resources have to be mobilized. Such resources include:

- Human resources, such as those affected, your team, yourself.
- Natural resources such as: trees, topography, water, soil, stone.
- Infrastructural resources, such as transport (roads, rail, rivers, airports) and communication systems (phone, fax, mail).
- Institutional resources, such as local government, outside agencies, local commercial sector, local markets, the military.
- Financial resources.
- Information resources, such as the media.

A key element in mobilizing these resources is the need to get the relief team into position and operational. This includes arranging team accommodation, sufficient vehicles for personal transport, and communication equipment.

5.1.2 The assessment process

Assessments may be carried out at different stages of an emergency and at different levels. They may include:

- Rapid reconnaissance: formulation of general plans in the immediate aftermath of crisis. This may involve multi-disciplinary teams from emergency response units of major relief agencies. Their task is to identify the overall situation, the scale of response needed and specific sectors which require priority action. For example, is there a problem with access to the site by road? If a road is required, get a road engineer to do a more detailed assessment.
- Outline design: assessment of the needs of specific sectors. For example, an experienced needs assessment engineer may draw up a detailed proposal and an outline design for a water project, including the specification and ordering of key equipment.
- Detailed design: the engineer responsible for implementing a specific sanitation project may have to assess which type of latrine is acceptable and how large-scale construction can be managed.
- Monitoring: this should be done both during construction and during any subsequent operation. Monitoring may reveal further needs to be addressed – requiring further assessment and planning.
- Evaluation: checking the effectiveness of a response is essential if lessons are to be learned and future responses improved.

Assessment can begin long before the relief worker arrives on site. The following is a brief guide to the process of carrying out an assessment:

- Collect as much secondary information as possible before departure, using press reports; situation reports from aid agencies or government departments; conversations with relief workers who have returned from the area; maps of the area from specialist shops or major bookstores; aerial photography or satellite imagery; reports or books from university libraries such as the School of Oriental and African Studies in London; reports from major consulting firms who have operated in the area.

- Make a list of people you intend to consult on arrival (government officials, aid agency staff, local people, refugees – see 5.3.1 on interviewing). This information should be provided by the agency – if they do not have the information, impress on them the importance of such support.
- On arrival in the country, find out what secondary information is available in the country office of the aid agency. Have any assessments already been carried out by this agency or by any other aid agency? Ask about assessments that cover other sectors – an assessment by a health team may contain information that is valuable to an engineer.
- If flying to the site, ask the pilot to do a few circuits over the affected area before landing. If this is not feasible, arrange to fly over the site as soon as is possible. Take as many photographs as you can at this point and make notes.
- On arrival at the site, find out who are the key people to meet and what information has already been collected. Get to the site quickly and drive or walk around as much as you can. Stop and talk to people – explain what you are doing and what information you need. Do not just talk to the leaders (usually men) – speak to the women and to the children. Observe – and ask your colleagues to be aware – what did the driver see? Climb on to vantage points and observe. Do not assume that information written in a report is necessarily more accurate than information given by people you meet on the side of the road. Make notes and sketches, on the spot if you can, or as soon afterwards as is practicable. Take photographs where possible. A polaroid camera that will print photographs instantaneously is an invaluable piece of equipment on assessment and so is a digital camera for including pictures in reports.
- Where it is feasible, collect information as part of a multi-disciplinary team and share impressions to put together a more comprehensive assessment of needs and resources.

Stages in an assessment

A schematic schedule of activities and stages in carrying out an assessment is given in Figure 5.1. The actual amount of time allocated to each stage will depend on the nature of the assessment and the emergency or crisis for which the response is intended. Even where recommendations for action are required 'yesterday', there is a need to think through the whole process.

Preparation for the assessment

In preparing for an assessment, ask the following questions:

- Where and when will the assessment be carried out and how long will it take? How much time is available?
- Who will use the information? What type of information is required? Which assessment methods are appropriate?
- What are the planning constraints? Are funds available? Are there budget deadlines?

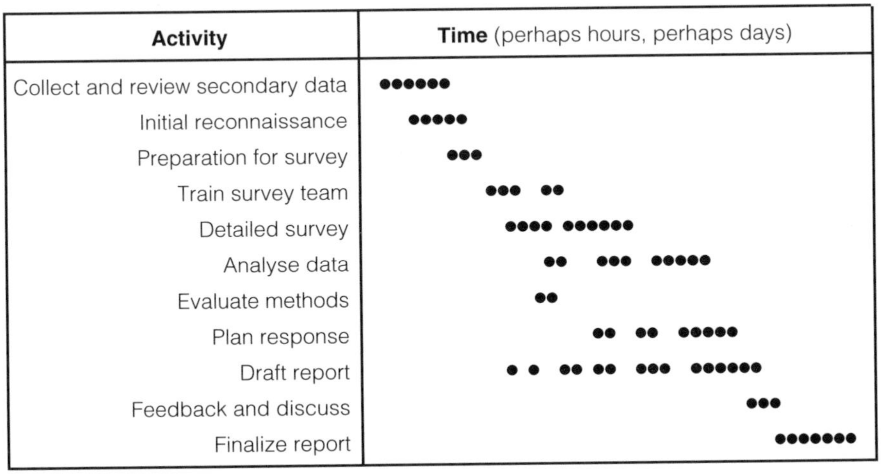
Activity
Time (perhaps hours, perhaps days)
Collect and review secondary data
Initial reconnaissance
Preparation for survey
Train survey team
Detailed survey
Analyse data
Evaluate methods
Plan response
Draft report
Feedback and discuss
Finalize report

Figure 5.1 Activities in an assessment

- Who will be in the assessment team? What training do they need?
- What equipment is required to collect and analyse information?
- What analysis and reporting procedures will be used?
- Are all relevant sources of information being considered? Do not forget, for example:
  - The press.
  - Published reports, maps, books, air photos, satellite imagery, etc.
  - Local government officials.
  - Relief agency offices and other aid workers.
  - The people affected.
  - Local people (host community).
  - Observation (walk, drive, fly).
  - Physical measurement (engineering surveying).
  - Consultants, contractors (may have drawings, reports or plans).

5.1.3 Writing an assessment report

Whenever an assessment is carried out and information collected, a report should be prepared, even if it is only one page (see Section 6.4.1). The results of even the briefest assessment may be very useful to other relief workers. Before writing a report, ask yourself: who will read the report and what will it be used for? How does this affect what should be in the report and how should it be presented? Consider all the steps involved in reporting: preparation of a draft, discussion, review and revision, finalization and distribution. The report should be finalized as soon as possible after the assessment is completed. Key findings should, where possible, be discussed with those who have participated in the assessment, whether as informants or as assessment team members. This can be done by preparing a draft report and circulating it for comment. Comments should be noted in the report.

The report should be kept as brief as possible. Use a logical structure and write in short clear sentences. For reports on major assessments, a suggested outline is given in Box 5.1.

Box 5.1 Outline of an assessment report

- Title, authors, agency, location, date.
- Executive summary, 1 page: key recommendations, proposals, main budget and staffing requirements, responsibilities for implementation.
- Action plan, 1–2 pages.
- Introduction, 1–2 pages: objectives of assessment, background to work, methodology used.
- Presentation of key results, 1–2 pages.
- Detailed recommendations, 1–2 pages.
- Resource implications (human, financial, institutional etc.), 1–2 pages.
- Terms of reference (if they have been specified).
- Appendices: relevant analyses of data collected, maps, design drawings etc.

5.2 Planning in emergencies

Planning involves a number of key activities:

- Anticipating future conditions and events.
- Setting objectives and priorities.
- Programming the sequence of actions to meet the objectives.
- Allocating realistic times for each activity.
- Financial budgeting.
- Identifying staffing and resource requirements.
- Developing methods and procedures of working.

In the initial phase of an emergency, there may be little time for these activities, but they each need consideration. Planning is closely linked to management – see Chapter 6.

5.2.1 Planning framework

The planning cycle

When planning a response, keep in mind the various phases of the cycle of a project, from initial assessment, through implementation with monitoring to evaluation, as illustrated in Figure 5.2. A common, almost defining, feature of an emergency is the speed with which the situation changes. Therefore planning must be flexible and must be tied in closely with implementation.

- Collect enough information to make initial implementation effective and to avoid obvious mistakes. Include in a plan the time and resources to monitor, evaluate and modify the plan.

- Get going! Even if obvious mistakes have been avoided, less obvious ones will become apparent with implementation.

In this book the collection and analysis of information before implementation is termed *assessment*, during implementation, it is termed *monitoring*, and after implementation it is called *evaluation*. Many of the techniques appropriate for assessment may also be used in monitoring and evaluation.

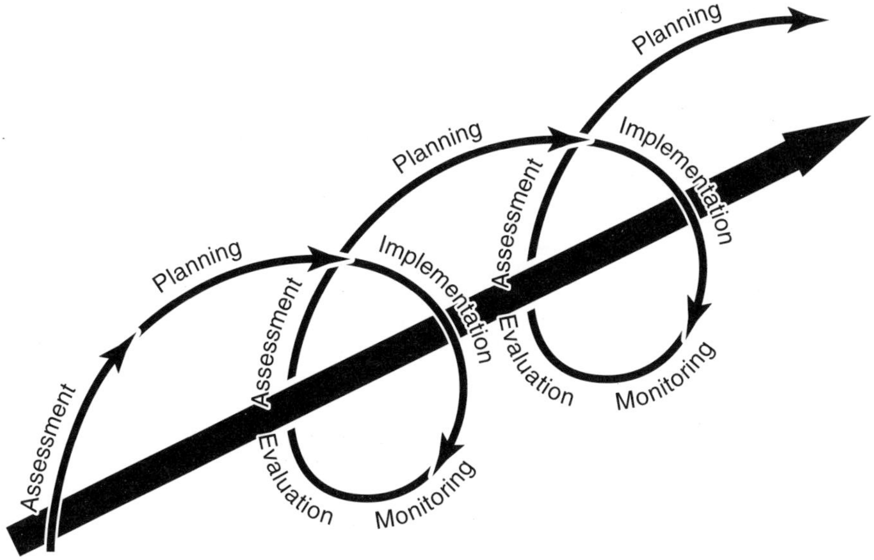

Figure 5.2 The planning cycle

Logical framework planning tool

When developing a plan, use a logical planning framework. This requires:

- An understanding of the aims, objectives and priorities of the response.
- A knowledge of the cycle of assessment, planning, implementation, monitoring and evaluation.
- A focus on the people for whom the response is intended.
- A co-ordinated multi-sectoral approach.

The overall goal of a humanitarian response to a crisis might typically be 'to relieve the suffering of the affected population'. To achieve this goal a number of aims may be defined which could include 'ensure minimum standards of health for displaced communities'. This may be further broken down into a hierarchy of objectives, one of which might be 'provide an adequate safe water supply'. This objective may itself have a number of lower order objectives, such as locating a suitable source or contracting a tankering service. Priority objectives may be agreed through a ranking exercise such as direct matrix ranking (see Section 5.3.5).

The logical framework is a tool to assist project management throughout the project cycle. It is now commonplace for donors to require agencies to complete a 'logframe' in applications for funding. The following is a brief description of a logframe. Refer to Figure 5.3 and Table 5.1.

The Narrative Summary is the general description of the project comprising:

- The **Aim** (or Goal) to which the project contributes.
- The **Purpose** of the project.
- The **Outputs** required to achieve the Purpose.
- The **Activities** required to achieve the Outputs.

This should form a logical sequence such that activities lead to outputs which lead to achieving the purpose and contribute to the overall aim.

However, there are external factors which can influence the outcome of a project and **assumptions** have to be made. The assumptions may relate to natural phenomena (e.g. the start of the rains), political considerations (e.g. access to the affected community), social and cultural issues, the dependence on other projects, and so on. The assumptions are the conditions for the project to be successful. This can be tested by the IF and THEN logic. IF the necessary conditions (the objectives in the narrative summary) AND the sufficient conditions (the assumptions) are met THEN the next level of objectives will be achieved (see Figure 5.3).

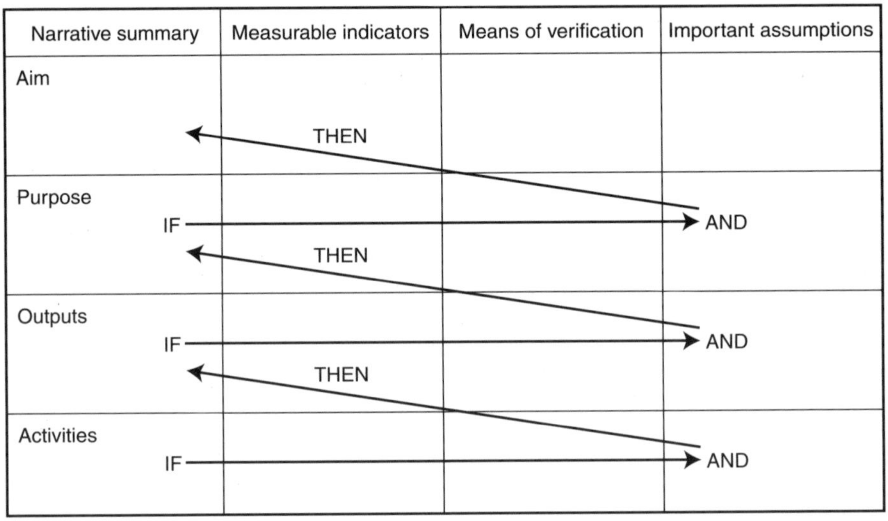

Figure 5.3 The logical framework planning tool

Indicators measure the result of the project. They should be measurable and often stated in terms of quantity and time. It is useful to differentiate between output indicators (e.g. the number of latrines installed) and impact indicators (e.g. the incidence of diarrhoea in the target group). Impact indicators often depend on other factors such as the success of complementary projects.

The **means of verification** identify the sources of information that will show what has been achieved. In some cases the means of verification will involve an activity in itself, such as a survey.

The activities can be used to draw up a project budget and a bar chart. The logframe is a useful document throughout the project and is referred to in monitoring and evaluation. Note that the sample logframe in Table 5.1 has been abbreviated and can be expanded to involve more activities to complete the project.

People-oriented planning

Experience shows that responses are more effective when the roles of different groups within an affected population are recognized and incorporated into plans. Relief workers should be aware of which groups are vulnerable and why, and the effect of relief interventions on this vulnerability. Consider a typical example: engineers may be responsible for installing a water supply and the location of tapstands. In this instance, supplying water may mean that people need no longer travel over a minefield to the nearest river and this clearly reduces the vulnerability of the water-carriers. If, however, the tapstands are located in secluded areas, where young women are in danger of attack, this may increase their vulnerability to a different form of danger.

The concept of people-oriented planning has been developed to help relief workers identify such vulnerable groups and to target responses appropriately. Techniques which have been developed to apply the concept in practice include:

- Refugee population profile and context analysis.
- Activities analysis.
- Analysis of use and control of resources.

Details of these tools are given in Section 5.3.7.

Multi-sectoral approach

Experience shows that a co-ordinated multi-sectoral approach is necessary in emergencies. This means that engineers, health workers, social services staff, logisticians, administrators, and protection officers must recognize the importance of each other's work and the contribution it makes towards meeting vital needs. See Chapter 2 for more details.

Where there are gaps in staffing, specialists such as engineers may have to undertake tasks which are outside their specialist area but are necessary to the success of the overall project. An example might be the carrying out of a survey on the customs relating to defecation and hygiene practices, in order to design an effective sanitation project.

5.2.2 Principles and guidelines

Some general principles which may help in formulating a plan in an emergency are given below, followed by guidelines that apply to engineering schemes.

Table 5.1 An abbreviated sample logframe for a sanitation programme

Narrative summary	*Measurable indicators*	*Means of verification*	*Important assumptions*
Aim To ensure minimum standards of health for displaced communities	Mortality and morbidity rates reduced to 1 per 10 000 people/day within 4 months	Health records Grave counts Community consultation	
Purpose To reduce the incidence and severity of sanitation related disease	Mortality and morbidity rates of sanitation related disease reduced to 'normal' levels within 4 months	Health records	Access to the community Community participation
Outputs **1** The safe containment of excreta	No more than 20 people per latrine within 3 months	Latrine monitoring forms Community maps	The population does not significantly increase
2 Improvement in hygiene practices	Within 3 months: 90% of latrines kept clean and hygienic 80% of people washing hands with soap 90% of children's faeces safely disposed 80% of settlement clear of solid waste	Focus group discussions Structured observation	Soap and water containers available Sufficient tools available
Activities **1** Sites identified for latrines	Sites demarcated within 2 weeks to cater for 125% of the population	Observation Site map	Sufficient space available
2 Rapid survey of defecation and hygiene practices	25% sample of recognised male and female community leaders interviewed within 1 month	Semi-structured interviews Exploratory observation	Willingness to take part in survey
3 Facilitate community involvement in future sanitation provision	Recruit and train one community facilitator per 1000 population within 1 month	Names of facilitators	Suitable people available for recruitment and training
4 Construct latrines to agreed community design	Designs agreed with community within 1 month Artisans recruited and trained within 1 month Sufficient latrines constructed within 3 months to serve the whole community	Demonstration latrines to agreed design Names of artisans and training records Project records	Agreement on designs Sufficient artisans available
5 Identify and train latrine attendants	Community to select latrine attendant for each latrine within 1 month	Notes from community meetings	Cultural acceptability of posts
6 Provide handwashing facilities at sanitation sites	Handwashing facilities in place at 90% of sites within 3 months	Observation Monitoring forms	Soap and washing containers available

Principles for planning in emergencies

A staged approach Plan on the basis of a staged approach. Identify priority actions and get going. Plan to upgrade later. Develop plans as the situation becomes clearer and time allows.

Participation and self-reliance Mobilizing the community's own resources – skills, knowhow, adaptability, fortitude – can be invaluable to the relief effort and can restore some measure of hope, confidence and dignity to people. Although, in certain circumstances, the need for a rapid response may be a constraint, the general principle should be to encourage participation and self-reliance where possible. Simply treating affected people as helpless victims and recipients of aid can result in a dependency syndrome. (See Section 1.2.3.) Participation by host and neighbouring communities is particularly important.

A long-term view 'Temporary settlements' often become permanent. Therefore, plan the response for the long term even though an open political commitment by governments and agencies to a long-term response may not be readily forthcoming. Planning for the long term raises the issue of sustainability – who is going to run the settlement after the initial emergency period is over? What funds will be available? What impact will it have on the environment? What about children's education? Keep long-term development needs in mind.

Flexibility It is important to plan for expansion – in the short term, more people may arrive; in the long term normal population growth may result in increases of 3–4 per cent per annum. Similarly, it is important to recognize that displaced people may return home in months if the political situation changes either in the host community or back home.

Appropriate technical support The technical support provided in humanitarian relief should, if possible, be compatible with local skills and capabilities (see below for guidelines relating to engineering schemes). An extreme example of inappropriate technical support might be the provision of free, imported, pre-fabricated housing when all that is required are supplies of timber poles and galvanized roofing sheet at subsidized, affordable prices.

Guidelines relating to engineering schemes

A reliable energy source What fuel will the displaced people use for cooking? Is heating required? Are there constraints on the availability of petrol or diesel? Is there a reliable electrical power supply and is equipment compatible with it? Is solar power an option for pumping, lighting, cold chain refrigerators, etc.?

Consumables, spares, tools and materials Are consumables such as lubricating oil and brake fluid readily available? What will the impact be if the consumables can no longer be obtained? Can spare parts be obtained? Equipment may require special tools to dismantle and assemble critical parts. Are these tools available or can they be made locally (such items as special pullers, bearing replacement tools etc.).

Skills availability and training Are the skills available locally to install, operate and maintain equipment and/or will training be required? Is there enough time and support to train personnel for essential tasks? Where possible, match equipment to the training and experience of existing local operation and maintenance personnel.

Standardization Try to ensure that the equipment used in the emergency is matched to the equipment already used locally. Check what standard equipment is specified by government departments. It may be tempting to import a sophisticated piece of equipment that can do everything and more, but it may quickly become useless if it cannot be maintained beyond its first service. There may be occasions when the only feasible emergency solution is to introduce an unfamiliar technology. It is then important to ensure that, after the immediate emergency phase is over, steps are taken to replace the technology with a more locally acceptable solution. It is unlikely that the necessary skills, training and spare parts supply system can be established within the time frame of a relief programme to ensure its long-term sustainability.

Local purchase The purchase of locally available equipment can have the following advantages:

- Quick purchase and installation.
- Local operator and mechanic familiarity.
- Ancillary fittings, spare parts and replacement units available at relatively short notice.
- Minimization of problems associated with keeping the equipment running when the emergency is over.
- Benefits to the local economy.

Check local experience with local engineers. Check that equipment complies with standardization policies. As far as possible, assess supplier efficiency, stocks and support services before making a commitment to specific equipment.

5.2.3 Planning bar charts

For an assessment to lead to implementation, an action plan is required. This could be presented as a bar chart – see Box 5.2. For an example of a bar chart for use in camp planning, see Chapter 20, Figure 20.2. An action plan should cover the following:

- Key activities; list all relevant activities. The level of detail depends on the scope of the plan. For a high level co-ordination plan, one item might be to install a water supply system. The engineer charged with installing the system may break this down into 20 sub-activities.

- Target dates or milestones: What are the critical dates? What is critical about them? Which is most important at the water points: having the taps installed or having water available?
- Responsibilities: Who is responsible for activities that may affect the programme? Have these responsibilites, activities and scheduling plans been agreed? What happens if targets are not met?
- Critical path activities: If speed is required, focus on critical path activities. Column 2 in Box 5.2 helps identify critical path activities. Can activities be moved from the critical path, or can they be shortened?

When listing activities and allocating times to them, remember to include the 'soft' activities as well as the 'hard'. Liaising with local government officials may

Box 5.2 Sample bar chart for planning a water supply system*

Activity	Task that must be completed before this begins	Respons-ibility	Week number and date 1 10/9	2 17/9	3 24/9	4 1/10	5 8/10
1 Protect existing water sources		MSF	●●●				
2 Procure plastic containers		Concern	●●●				
3 Organize tankering		CARE	●●●●	●●●●●	●●●●●●	●●●	
4 Survey water sources			●●				
5 Design water supply system	4			●●			
6 Order equipment	5			●			
7 Ship equipment	6			●●●●●			
8 Recruit and train water team				●●●●●	●●	●●●	●●
9 Prepare sites for tanks and pipes	4,8,10			●●●●			
10 Liaise with local authorities			●●	●●●	●●●●	●●	●●●●

* This chart is used to illustrate the planning process – refer to Chapters 11, 12, 13 and 14 for details of the key activities required for planning a water supply system.

consume much of your time and be an essential feature of your work, but it is easily overlooked when drawing up time allocations. Other 'soft' activities that may consume significant quantities of time include: travel, recruitment, induction, training, conflict resolution, monitoring of contractors, labour supervision and meetings.

5.3 Techniques for the collection and analysis of information

This section gives brief guidance on a number of techniques that may be used for the collection and analysis of information. The techniques, which have been widely used in rapid rural appraisal, are adaptable and most of them can be used both for very rapid assessment, taking a few minutes in the field, and for more in-depth analysis when more time is available. Where possible, analyse information as it is collected. This helps to ensure that important data are collected and it avoids the collection of that which is unnecessary. Remember to evaluate the methods you are using. Try and run a pilot study first, even if it is only one morning's work. Always try and cross-check key information. Box 5.3 gives some guidelines for organizing the fieldwork in an assessment.

Box 5.3 Guidelines for fieldwork

- If working in a team, agree responsibilities within the team and agree a team leader.
- Plan and agree, with the whole team, each day's activities, including writing field notes.
- Explain objectives of assessment to key informants (the people affected, government officials).
- Cross-check – compare information from different sources and evaluate methods of collection.
- Use and update checklists to remind team members of key questions.
- Stop collecting information when sufficient has been obtained for planning purposes.
- Share key findings with members of the target group and invite and note their response.

Information may be obtained in several ways:

- Reading published literature such as books, journal articles, agency reports, press reports, maps, air photos, satellite imagery.
- Rapid appraisal: interviews, ranking, participatory mapping, direct observation.
- Physical survey: levelling, geophysical, topographical, sanitary.
- Questionnaire survey: interviews according to a standard form.

- Epidemiological survey: monitoring of health data collected at clinics, hospitals and so on can help to identify which parts of the camp have the highest incidence of sanitation-related diseases which might, for example, suggest the starting point for a defecation control programme.

5.3.1 Interviewing

Whether it is talking to government officials in the capital city or to displaced people encountered by the roadside, asking questions in a 'semi-structured interview' is one of the major methods by which information can be obtained.

One of the first steps in interviewing is to identify key informants who have specialized, detailed or overview knowledge on a particular topic. This includes government officials and aid agency staff in the capital and at the site, other aid workers, displaced and host community representatives. Where possible, select informants from different parts of the affected society. Include women, men, children, the elderly, artisans, labourers, professionals and religious and political leaders. In established communities, outsiders (such as school-teachers) who have had time to observe local people from the inside can often give very valuable information. In displaced populations, remember that traditional information systems may have been severely disrupted and new systems may be emerging.

Interviews may be held with individuals or with groups. Where possible, interviews should be carried out by a team which includes members from the displaced and host population. Sometimes the team may consist of only yourself, or yourself and an interpreter. See Box 5.4.

5.3.2 Brainstorming

Brainstorming is a technique for generating ideas. It is carried out in small groups and its aim is to elicit all ideas, no matter how bizarre, that occur to people in the group, relating to a specific theme. Avoid assessing the validity of suggested ideas because once this happens, group members may become inhibited and start searching for the 'correct' ideas.

The ideas can be called out by members of the group and written down quickly by one or two facilitators. Alternatively, blank cards can be handed out and members of the group asked to write down quickly what comes into their minds. Once the group has exhausted its supply of ideas, the ideas generated may be grouped, ranked or prioritized.

5.3.3 Direct observation

Direct observation is useful for cross-checking other assessment methods and can often be undertaken concurrently with other methods, such as interviewing. In some cases it may be the only method that is feasible. Ask your colleagues what they see – a local driver may see and interpret visual evidence in a very different way to an outsider. Differentiate between observations (they had a fridge-freezer in their pick-up) and interpretations (they were clearly wealthy).

It is useful to make notes of what has been observed. Where possible, take photographs; they are worth many pages of notes. A polaroid camera allows

Box 5.4 Guidelines for interviewing

Before

- Select an appropriate team. Consider, age, gender, ethnicity, social status, of both the team and the informants. For example, if interviewing women, it is generally better to use women interviewers.
- Identify key issues on the topic you wish to discuss. Be clear about what your objectives are for the interview.
- Select appropriate informants, according to the profile of the population and the information required. Beware of the temptation to focus exclusively on the well-dressed, better educated, English-speaking males. This is particularly important in water and sanitation for example.
- Keep a low profile and fit in with informants' schedules.
- Dress appropriately.
- If time permits, run some pilot interviews first. Start within the team – interview each other about some controversial topic. It is useful to have an interviewer, a respondent and an observer. This will improve interviewing techniques and is a useful team-building exercise.
- Try to keep interviews short: the maximum duration of interviews for individuals should be 45 minutes and for groups it should not exceed two hours.

During

- Be sensitive. Start with appropriate greetings. Explain the purpose of the interview.
- Be aware of correct behaviour. Avoid knowing looks or smiles between team members.
- Be observant. Observe non-verbal messages and be clear about what they mean (avoiding one's eyes may be a sign of respect in one culture and a sign of insincerity in another).
- Start with broad questions. Find out what is important to the informant and deal with that first.
- Use open questions liberally ('who? why? what? where? when? how?'). Be careful when asking 'why' questions. Use closed questions (Yes or No answers) for clarification.
- Avoid leading questions. Instead of: 'Is your water supply adequate?' say: 'Tell me about your water supply'.
- Avoid giving advice – you are there to learn, not to teach.
- One member of the team should take notes. Other members should concentrate on asking questions. Make notes in a duplicate book (or use carbon paper) as copies may be needed and photocopying facilities are not always available. If detailed notetaking is not possible in the interview, make notes as soon as possible afterwards.
- Distinguish clearly in the notes between verbal responses, observations and interpretations. Use literal quotations in the notes – they are illuminating.

Continued opposite.

Continued from previous page.

- Clarify and feed back important points: for example, 'So what you've said is: "the main problem with the water supply is that we have to queue for two hours at the tapstand".'

After

- Check the notes of the interview with each member of the team.
- Check if colleagues had any other observations you may have missed.
- Briefly discuss how the interview went – for example, 'that was a good way of asking that question' or 'we hit a problem with that question, how can we improve our approach next time?'

you to produce an instantaneous image which can be attached to your field notes.

5.3.4 Participatory mapping

Participatory mapping can be carried out very rapidly with one or two local people or can take much longer and involve large groups of people. It can:

- Provide an insight into the knowledge of the people concerned, be they host or displaced communities.
- Help to understand patterns of behaviour, where people go and why they go there – this may be important in planning sanitation. Different groups of people are likely to produce different maps of the same area, reflecting their activities and priorities.
- Establish where people would like facilities such as water points or latrines.
- Design camp layouts that are acceptable to camp inhabitants.

Participatory mapping can be done quickly, either individually or in groups. It can take as little as five minutes, for example, using a stick to draw in the sand on the ground and using stones, leaves and the like to locate specific items of interest. Existing maps or aerial photos should be used where possible. Even apparently uneducated people can rapidly grasp the idea behind mapping – drawing with a stick on the sand may save hours of walking or driving. Get different groups to draw maps of the same area (old women, young children, elders) to see what is important to each group.

5.3.5 Ranking

Ranking can be used to identify people's priorities or preferences. There are many ways in which ranking can be carried out. Two methods likely to be of interest to engineers are preference ranking and direct matrix ranking. The methods can be used in very different settings, from a discussion at a feeding centre to analysis of options for major programme interventions, such as the selection of a new site for a temporary settlement. As with the other techniques described in this section, depending on the time available and level of detail required, ranking can take a few minutes with a small group of people or can occupy many more people for longer periods. When involving other people in ranking exercises it is important to ask the right questions in the right way (see 5.3.1 on interviewing).

Preference ranking

Preference ranking can give an idea of the relative importance of different issues or problems to individuals or groups. It does not explicitly provide information on why people have these preferences.

Table 5.2 Example of preference ranking of problems in water collection

		*Respondents' scores**				
Problem	*A*	*B*	*C*	*D*	*E*	*Score*
Distance to source	4	3	2	5	2	16
Queueing time	3	4	3	2	3	15
Small containers	5	6	5	6	4	26
Lack of storage	2	5	6	4	6	23
Steep hill	1	2	4	1	1	9
Security at taps	6	1	1	3	5	16

* 6 = most important, 1 = least important

For example, in a situation where people are known to have problems in collecting enough water, interviewees might be asked to identify 5–6 of the main problems they encounter. Either as a group or individually, interviewees should then rank these problems – see Table 5.2. In the example shown, the absence of small containers and lack of storage get the highest total score and are clearly the most important problems for the group as a whole. Security is an important issue for respondents A and E – why? Follow up with detailed questions if appropriate.

Matrix ranking

Matrix ranking can be used to analyse a range of options according to objective criteria, for example, choosing the sites for a temporary settlement or the selection of the best candidate for store manager. It can be used by one person to make the selection as objective as possible; it can be used by a group of planners to give a balanced assessment of the group's views or it can be used directly with the target group, to stimulate discussion in a structured way. Where the target group takes part, the technique can often shed light on the reasons behind the choice of option – understanding these reasons may be as important as selecting the right option.

Matrix ranking involves drawing up a list of options and a list of criteria by which the options will be ranked. These criteria may be given different weightings according to their importance. The technique is outlined below with a hypothetical example on toilet choice among a group of knowledgeable users. (see also 20.2.3).

- Ask the group to describe the types of toilet facility that they know. When they have finished, introduce any types that you may wish them to consider.
- Draw up a matrix of criteria, weightings and options for toilets as in Table 5.3.
- Ask for criteria by which one would judge a toilet. If someone mentions something bad about one type, such as the lack of privacy, then use the positive criteria, such as 'plenty of privacy', in the analysis.
- Give each criterion a weighting factor. One method of doing this is to ask the respondents to award a number of points to each criterion, depending on its importance. For example the criterion could be weighted from 10 to 100, with 100 being very important. If lack of smells is deemed comparatively unimportant, this might attract a total of only 20 per cent.
- Ask the group to allocate scores (perhaps marks out of 100) to each type of toilet according to each criterion. Some toilets may get no points. This process may take some time and involve quite a lot of discussion. Note the key points emerging through the discussion.
- Multiply the score under each criterion by the weighting accorded to that criterion to get the weighted score. The option with the highest weighted score is the preferred option.

Table 5.3 Example of how to use matrix ranking in the selection of toilet types

		*Toilet type**							
Criterion	*Weighting factor, %*	*Bush*		*Communal latrine*		*Ordinary family pit*		*VIP family*	
Privacy	90	*80*	72	*20*	18	*70*	63	*70*	63
Distance	80	*30*	24	*20*	16	*70*	56	*70*	56
Bright inside	20	*80*	16	*60*	12	*80*	16	*20*	4
Access at night	60	*40*	24	*50*	30	*80*	48	*80*	48
Lack of smells	20	*90*	18	*10*	2	*40*	8	*80*	16
Easy to clean	40	*70*	28	*0*	0	*70*	28	*70*	28
Prevents disease	50	*30*	15	*30*	15	*60*	30	*70*	35
Total score			197		93		249		250
Ranking			3		4		2		1

* The first number is 'marks out of 100' for that toilet type; the second is the score adjusted by the weighting factor. For example, 'Communal latrine' scores *50* under the 'access at night' criterion, which is weighted at 60%. Thus, the overall weighting for access at night is 60% of 50 = 30.

In this hypothetical example the VIP latrine was ranked number one, closely followed by the ordinary pit and going into the bush. The communal latrine was last. This exercise could be repeated with other groups, involving different criteria. For example, the sanitation team itself could use the method with criteria such as cost and speed of construction included. The technique should be used as a guide. There is likely to be little point in spending too much time refining the weighting system or method of analysis. See Chapter 20 for the use of matrix ranking in selecting a site for a temporary settlement.

5.3.6 Questionnaire surveys

Questionnaire surveys allow you to collect quantifiable data which can be analysed statistically. One of their principal strengths is that if they have been properly prepared, they can generate large amounts of data in a short space of time. An engineer could use questionnaire surveys to collect information on, for example, water usage at waterpoints or on household sanitation practices. Before carrying out a questionnaire survey, be very clear about how you are going to analyse and use the information collected. Allow enough time for analysis – at least as much as for collection.

To carry out a questionnaire survey:

- Design the questionnaire form carefully. This takes time and skill.
- Select competent enumerators. See 6.2.2.
- Always carry out a pilot study before embarking on large-scale data collection. Use the pilot study to check the wording and usefulness of questions, to identify any gaps and to assess the competence of the enumerators.

The questionnaire form should have the minimum number of questions required, should be easy to use and to analyse. Questions should be ordered logically, moving from the general to the particular. The form should be laid out clearly and with sufficient space to write the answers in the boxes. With cluttered questionnaires it is easy for enumerators to miss some of the questions. Box 5.5 illustrates what might be the first page of a survey form for collecting information on household water usage.

Use simple, direct, 'closed' questions, which have a limited range of possible answers. 'Have you collected any water today?', is a closed question (answer Yes or No), as is 'What container did you use?'. 'What do you feel about the water facilities?' is an open question. Open questions are more difficult to analyse and may produce both illuminating and mystifying responses. They are more appropriate in other contexts, such as semi-structured interviewing, but may be used at the end of the questionnaire.

5.3.7 Refugee profiles, context, activities and resources

The material in this section has been adapted from Anderson (1994). In order to work effectively with refugees, it is useful to have a good understanding of the potentials of and constraints upon the refugees:

- What is the make-up of the group of refugees and what skills and resources have they got?

Box 5.5 Example of a questionnaire survey form

Title: Household water survey, Incuda Refugee Camp, 1994

Date:____________ Interviewer:________________________

Location:______________ Household number:____________

1 *Introduce yourself and explain purpose of survey*

2 Respondent's characteristics:

Male [] Female [] Age: 10–15 [] 16–30 [] 31–50 [] 51+ []

3 Where do you collect your water from?

1 Standpipe [] 2 Water tanker [] 3 Streams [] 4 Pond [] 5 Other:__________

4 What do you use water from different sources for?

	Source of water				
Use	Standpipe	Tanker	Streams	Pond	Other
Drinking					
Cooking					
Bathing					
Laundry					
Dishes					

6 What containers do you use to collect water?

Jerrycans [] Buckets [] Pots [] Other [] describe________________

Page 1

- What alleviation measures are they already taking themselves?
- Which groups need priority support?
- How much time do they have available for emergency relief work?
- Who is available for work?

To answer such practical questions, some techniques have been developed which are described below (see also Section 1.2).

Refugee profile and context

A group of refugees is never one homogeneous mass of people. It may include children without parents, angry young men, despairing elders, highly motivated professionals and cynical politicans. A common characteristic of refugee populations is that social structures have been disrupted and traditional roles may no longer apply. The relief worker should have a good understanding of who the refugees are, their background and the context in which they now operate. To gain such an understanding the following questions should be posed:

Refugee profiles:

- Do they consist of families or separate individuals?
- What is the balance of males and females?
- Are there many single heads of households?
- Are there many unaccompanied children?
- Are there many professionals or educated people in the group?
- Are there important ethnic differences in the group?

Refugee context:

- What are the social hierarchies and power structures, including protection mechanisms for women and children?
- What are the common religious beliefs and practices?
- What formal institutional structures exist, such as government bureaucracies?
- What are the economic, legal and political conditions?
- What attitudes prevail towards refugees, in both the originating and the host country?
- What are the attitudes to aid workers, and of aid workers?

More detailed knowledge of the context in which the refugees find themselves may be obtained through an analysis of their activities and on who uses and controls resources.

Analysis of activities and resource use

A refugee society is likely to be in a state of considerable flux, so some knowledge of what people did before they became refugees and what they do now is useful to the planner. Use Table 5.4 to analyse the activities of different groups. The nature of a disaster and subsequent emergency and any humanitarian relief interventions can have great impact on people's access to, and control of, resources. Use Table 5.5 to understand how these resources are accessed or controlled.

Table 5.4 Example of an activities analysis

Current activities of refugees	*Who? Gender/age*	*Where?*	*When? How long?*
Protection			
Production of goods			
Pottery	Older women	At home	Dry season
Metalwork etc	Men	Village workshop	Every day
... and services			
Teaching, etc	Women and men	School and home	Weekdays
Agriculture			
Ploughing	Mainly men	Field	Seasonal
Weeding	Mainly women	Field	As required
Care of livestock			
Harvesting			
Household			
Water collection	Women	From source	Every day
Childcare	Children		Irregular
Social/political/ religious			
Community meetings			
Ceremonies, etc			

Table 5.5 Resource use and control

Lost resource	**Who used?**	**Who controlled?**
Land		
Shelter		
Income		
Tools, etc		
Brought along	**Who uses?**	**Who has?**
Skills:		
Technical		
Managerial		
Political		
Agricultural etc		
Knowledge		
Literacy		
Medicine etc.		
Provided	**To whom?**	**How?** (Where? By whom? When?)
Protection		
Food		
Shelter		
Clothing		
Education		

6 Management

Working as a relief worker involves some form of management, from self-management to the organization of a labour force of hundreds. An ability to work with a wide range of people is essential. You may have to manage many more people and act at a more senior level than you would have done in your normal work or you may be a senior person working in a junior position to which you are not accustomed. If you are working in the initial phase of an emergency, you may have to set up basic management procedures that can be developed at a later stage. You may be part of a large organization with clearly defined management systems and hierarchies or you may be working with a small flexible organization where you have considerable freedom to develop your own management system.

The purpose of this chapter is to describe the principal areas of management encountered on assignment, and to suggest some practical methods that have been found useful in the field. Adapt them to your own requirements.

Related chapters include 5, 7 and 20.

6.1 Management functions, styles and structures

6.1.1 Functions of management

The job of the manager is to organize resources such as people, money and time to turn plans or concepts into reality. This involves four key activities:

- Planning (see Section 5.2).
- Leading – causing people to take effective action. This means taking decisions; communicating clearly; and selecting, training and motivating people.
- Organizing – includes developing a structure within which the objectives can be met; delegation of authority (responsibility cannot be delegated); and establishing supportive relationships.
- Controlling – involves establishing performance standards; monitoring and evaluation of performance; and correction of performance as required.

Chapter 5 deals with the process of assessment and planning at the conceptual stage. As a manager your job is to put the plan into action. This requires an ongoing process of assessment and planning (see 5.2.1 Figure 5.2).

Clarity and *understanding* are two important characteristics of good management. Everyone, including the manager, should be clear about the objectives of the team, their role in achieving those objectives, and their position within the team (see 6.4.2).

A key principle of management in emergency relief is that involvement of the affected community, although not always easy, is desirable.

6.1.2 Management styles

Management styles tend to reflect the personality of the individual manager, the organization, and those being managed. Recognize and adopt whichever style is appropriate to a particular situation. The most effective style will depend on the speed with which decisions need to be taken and the type of person being managed. Styles which are relevant to emergency leadership include:

- Directive – the leader directs with minimal subordinate participation in decision-making.
- Participative – the leader uses suggestions from team members in decision-making; emphasis is placed on staff functioning as a team.
- Achievement-oriented – the leader sets challenges and goals for staff and delegates responsibility to them, showing confidence that they can achieve these goals with little supervision.
- Supportive – the leader shows a friendly interest in people; builds strong interpersonal relationships; creates a supportive work environment.

For example, in the immediate aftermath of a disaster, when immediate action is called for, the manager may need to adopt a directive style. As the immediate emergency passes, a more participative and achievement-oriented style may be more effective. In some cultures, a very directive form of management is the norm, while in others, a consultative approach is expected. Find out what traditional management styles are used and adapt them to the circumstances.

6.1.3 Management structures

On arrival, or before if possible, get to know the management structure, systems and procedures of the agency. As far as possible, clarify your role and responsibilities, who reports to you and to whom you report. Be aware that in a fast-changing situation other staff may not have a clear idea of your (or their) role. Get as full a briefing as possible. As an employee of an organization, you can expect a certain amount of support and guidance. Likewise, as a manager, recognize that the people below you in the structure should get the same from you.

Bureaucratic management systems requiring prolonged procedures, several signatures and rubber stamps can be very frustrating, but they often have to be followed if any progress is to be made.

During an emergency programme, a manager must recognize and deal with key players such as the agency itself, the co-ordinating or lead agency, such as UNHCR, the host government and the people directly affected. The manager should have an understanding of the traditional social structures of the people concerned and their significance for the design and implemention of a relief programme (see Chapters 1, 2 and 5). The trauma of a disaster may well provoke changes in traditional social orders and it is important to understand such changes.

6.1.4 Professionalism

Attitude

Attitudes of relief workers may range from enthusiastic amateurism to professional cynicism, from inexperienced clumsiness, to considered and experienced efficiency, and from altruism to avarice. Whilst you may feel that you are a responsible person doing a professional job, many of your colleagues may appear otherwise. Recognize that you may have to work with people whose motivation is very different from your own (see Chapter 3). There will be a range of attitudes displayed by representatives of the host government, the host community and the people affected, from support to antagonism, from gratitude to resentment.

Always keep clear sight of your own objectives and the overall objectives of the programme. Try not to let personalities get in the way of sound professional judgement. Remember why you are there. Work with people on a friendly professional basis. Be patient and tolerant. Retain a sense of perspective and a sense of humour.

Technical competence

Although recruited for your specialist skills, do not be surprised if you are asked to do something which is completely outside your specialization. For example, even if recruited to install a water system in a camp, you may well be asked to design and organize a latrine construction programme or build an access road. Although many emergency engineering tasks are well within the scope of the experienced engineer, there is a need to balance the enthusiasm to help out with a realistic assessment of your own and your agency's technical competence. This will always be a personal judgement. Bear in mind the following:

- Be willing to undertake unexpected tasks but recognize the boundaries of your expertise and do not be afraid to make these clear to others.
- Ask for professional assistance. Your employing organization should be able to provide technical support. If not, RedR may be able to provide advice and information through its Technical Support Service. See www.redr.org for details.
- You can always ask for additional staff to be recruited.
- Be prepared to say 'no', but have valid reasons for doing this.
- Be aware of hazards, for example those posed by dangerous chemicals such as chlorine or those caused by dangerous work practices such as excavations in unsupported soil.
- Avoid promising anything you cannot deliver. It is better to be cautious from the outset than to get swept along with the high expectations that are common in emergencies.

Accountability

As a professional, you must be accountable for your work, just as you would be in your regular job. However, the emergency will demand both quick decisions and action which you may feel might result in unprofessional work.

Standards during an emergency are not as high as you may be used to; corners may have to be cut and compromises made. This is acceptable if it is meeting the overall aim, which is to respond rapidly to the immediate needs of large numbers of people. In most cases, the aim is not to construct engineering masterpieces. Try to plan work using a phased response, so that it can be improved at a later date.

If you are responsible for administering large amounts of cash, ensure that you keep clear accounts (see Section 6.7.4).

Keep your agency informed of your key decisions. If in doubt about a certain course of action, discuss it with your manager. Do not be hurried into a difficult decision. In the long term, objectives are usually better served if the correct decision is taken over a couple of days than if a wrong and irreversible decision is taken instantaneously.

Safety and hazards

There may be a certain amount of resistance to a 'safety mentality', especially in the aftermath of a disaster. However, there is no point in compounding one disaster with another. Whilst safety standards in an emergency may well be different from those you are used to, the approach to safety should be the same:

- Safe working practice is of the highest priority.
- Awareness: be aware of the safety implications of all work and ensure that all staff are also aware. Be aware of any local safety regulations.
- Individual and collective responsibility: ensure that all staff know that they should speak up if they feel they are being asked to do something which is unsafe or if they see someone else doing something unsafe.
- Treat all accidents as soon as is possible. Prepare contingency plans for accidents, such as having medical evacuation plans and a designated health centre for referral. Ensure that a first aid kit is on site and that someone knows how to use it.
- Record all serious accidents. An employee affected by an accident should sign any report about the accident. This will help to protect both the employee and the employer against any future legal action, should this occur. Ensure that all supervisory level staff know and understand the importance of this requirement and that the procedure is enforced. Comply, and be seen to comply, with any investigation that may result from an accident. This will become very important if for any reason the agency is viewed as being responsible for an accident.

Be particularly careful of the following hazards:

- Fire: especially when handling fuel, fuel tanks (especially when empty), gas and cooking stoves.
- Working above or below ground: check scaffolding and trench or well-digging practice and take appropriate precautions.
- Road accidents: poor driving practice is common in emergencies (see Section 17.2.3).
- Working in or near water: drowning or infection.
- Food and water: ensure that these are prepared hygienically.

- Hostility: people affected by a disaster may react abnormally in a work situation. Try to choose work teams who know and trust each other. Be wary of dangerous ethnic mixes.

(See also Section 6.3 and Chapters 3, 12 and 17.)

6.2 Managing people

6.2.1 Self-management

An essential part of effective management is self-management. While this is true in normal life, it is essential when working in an emergency. This includes being realistic about your abilities and your needs. Give yourself time to plan and reflect. Prioritize your own work, the tasks to be done, people to be seen and rest to be taken. At the beginning of every week, draw up a list of tasks to be completed in the coming week, allocate a time to each task and write them in your diary. Before accepting new tasks, consider which tasks will have to be deferred or delegated. Likewise, each night go through the same process for the next day and plan your work in accordance with the weekly objectives. The process of planning work in this manner helps to organize tasks, places things in perspective and gives a sense of order to a seemingly chaotic situation.

Build into your work programme half an hour every day to reflect upon events. This is best done at the end of the day. Look back upon the day and ask yourself what went well and not so well. Why did it go well? What have you learnt from the day about your staff, other agencies, the work programme, local work practices? How can you use these experiences in future? Why did problems occur? What could you do in future to avoid the same mistakes? Was it your fault or somebody else's? If it was yours, how can you avoid the same response in future? If another person's, what can you do to influence their actions the next time a similar circumstance arises? For some people, such reflection is helped by keeping a diary.

6.2.2 Recruitment

A key element in working with a successful team is the recruitment of the right people, and particularly of good supervisory staff. If possible, use existing social systems to find staff. In some instances, good supervisory staff may be suggested by the workforce.

Your agency should be, and be seen to be, a fair and non-partisan employer. Check its recruitment policies and any requirements of the host government. It may be very important to have a good ethnic spread of employees and a balance between refugees and the host community. Be wary of 'my brother', or cousin, uncle, or grandmother, who are suddenly experts in the very discipline you need. Familiarize yourself with any local employment laws that exist. There may be strictly enforceable regulations referring to health benefits, insurance, termination of employment and associated payments.

For much of the time you may be turning away people eager for a job. Treat all enquiries courteously and fairly. If there are no vacancies, tell people that there are no vacancies at present, but ask for written details and keep them on file – you never know when you might need someone. A 'NO VACANCIES' sign outside the office will sometimes deter people.

In selecting a candidate for a job, decide what criteria are to be used in assessment. Criteria can include professional skills, personal attributes, literacy, numeracy, eyesight (drivers), the respect accorded by the community (extension agents). Think about how flexible you may want the employee to be. At a later date you may want the employee to work at another location or to do a different job. Ensure that the job title and description cover this.

Decide on an interview procedure and consider setting a small task that reflects the nature of the work they will have to do. For example, if interviewing supervisory staff, ask the candidate to measure the height and width of the room and write it down for you. Consider a probationary period. (See 5.3.5 for a ranking method and use it to rank candidates against a list of criteria.) Local circumstances sometimes interfere with the equal opportunities policy of an agency. For example, if the job is based in an insecure area and the candidate is from a rival ethnic group, you could be placing the person at undue risk. Be aware of this, take advice and use your best judgement.

Once recruited, professional and supervisory staff should be issued with a clear employment contract (see Box 6.1). Individual contracts are not necessary for every employee, but standard terms and conditions should apply.

Ensure that staff are given adequate induction. It is particularly important that supervisory staff understand their task. Employees responsible for keeping records are very important to the programme. Ensure that they are well briefed.

Box 6.1 Items to include in an employment contract

Name of employer and employee.
Date of commencement (and completion if fixed term employment).
Rate of remuneration.
Frequency of payment: for example, weekly, monthly.
Hours of work.
Terms related to holidays, public holiday pay, religious days etc.
Terms related to sickness and injury benefits.
Length of notice required for contract termination by both parties.
Any disciplinary rules applicable to employee.
Grievance procedure.
An attached job description.

If you have to recruit people, at the very minimum, prepare a job description for each post and decide on a recruitment procedure. The job description should contain an outline of specific responsibilities, tasks and reporting lines. A sample employment contract and job description are attached in Appendix 7.

6.2.3 Motivation

Motivation involves encouraging people to perform a task well. To motivate staff and workers, consider the following.

Casual labourers

- Show interest in people by visiting them at their workplace and talking to them. Find out what they need to do their job well.
- Give recognition to work well done.
- Provide breaks where, for example, bread and tea are served, not only to give workers a sense that the agency values them, but also to ensure physical fitness to perform the task.
- Discuss the length and timing of the work day with them. They will have other commitments. Try to accommodate these.
- Take account of the climate. In hot climates, people may wish to work in cooler periods of the day, such as early in the morning and late in the evening, or even at night. Provide shaded rest areas and plenty of potable water. In cold climates, it may be necessary to provide clothing, hot food and a warm rest area.
- For dirty jobs, provide washing facilities.
- Where the work may damage clothing, provide overalls – people may have only the clothes they stand in.

Long-term workers

All of the above apply and in addition:

- Agency T-shirts are always popular as a sign of team membership and belonging. In addition to a safety function, protective clothing such as raincoats, hard hats or boots can be a significant status symbol for employees.
- Access to healthcare is very important to people. Encourage the agency to pay for this.
- Show that the agency values them as people and not just for their work. For example, provide mosquito nets in a malarial area.
- Make the work as interesting and varied as you can.

Professional counterpart engineers

- Establish mutual respect and acknowledge that there is a two way sharing of knowledge.
- Delegate authority.
- Recognize accomplishments and provide opportunities to tackle problems and overcome obstacles.

6.2.4 Working with a large labour force

Whether building latrines, laying a pipeline or constructing a road, it may be necessary to mobilize a large labour force. Such a labour force requires proper management.

Consider using a contractor to hire and manage labour. This may save you a great deal of time in labour management, but it does require effective contract management (see Section 6.3).

Paid or voluntary labour

There may be strong views about whether labour should be provided voluntarily or paid. (Table 6.1 lists some of the issues to consider.) In some cases, local labour laws may preclude refugees from paid work.

Table 6.1 Paid or voluntary labour

Voluntary labour	*Paid labour*
May be difficult to motivate and manage	Should be readily available
May cause bottlenecks and time delays	May get the job done quickly
May keep costs down	May push costs up
May demand a lot of management time	Needs a lot of supervision
May promote a sense of ownership and participation	Implies a legal employer/employee relationship
	Will not work voluntarily again
	Assigns high value to paid tasks and low value to unpaid

Once paid labour has started, it is extremely difficult to return to a voluntary basis. Therefore, decide as early as possible whether labour will be paid or voluntary, and if payment is to be made, to whom. This should be a common policy decision, co-ordinated amongst all agencies that employ labour.

As a guide, an approach frequently adopted is to pay for communal work, such as the construction of an access road, but not for private work such as the excavation of family latrines. It is important to have an agreed salary structure across all organizations employing paid labour.

Paying for labour assigns a value to a certain task. The work of the paid labourer digging trenches may be perceived as having a higher value than that of an unpaid community health educator.

A willingness to undertake certain tasks voluntarily may be an indicator of the community's perception of the importance of those tasks. If people lack the motivation to dig their own pits for latrines, then they are unlikely to have the motivation to use and maintain them properly.

Managing a large labour force

Get a good assistant. Look for someone who can act as a translator and understands both basic engineering principles and the local culture. It is important that the assistant is respected by the community.

Set up an effective supervisory structure. Plan a hierarchy on the basis of one manager or supervisor responsible directly for no more than eight to twelve people. See Figure 6.1.

Pay people on time. People get angry if not paid on time. Have a regular pay day and ensure that wages are paid on this day. This is important for morale and the safety of you and your staff.

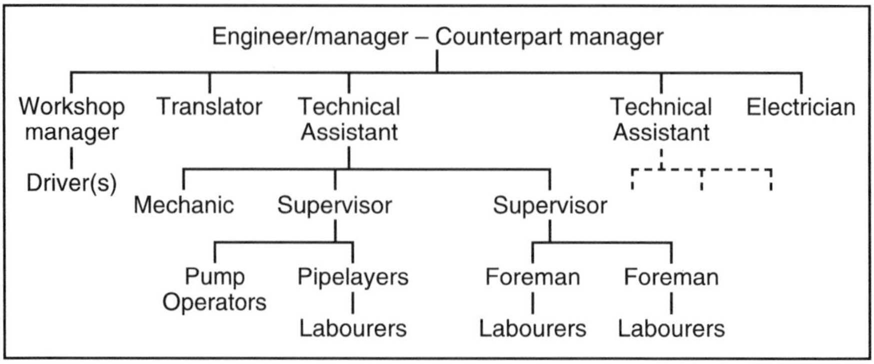

Figure 6.1 A typical field management structure

Minimize the number of work sites to no more than three or four. Employ new labour at each site, but consider moving supervisory staff from site to site as work is completed. This helps with quality control and saves time.

Explain how long the job is expected to last. Always let people know how long they can expect to be employed. If you intend to change from employing displaced people to local labour, or vice versa, everyone must know and agree this at the outset. Misunderstandings can be very dangerous.

Keep clear records. Record major events and keep a daily log. Get supervisors to keep their own log and to record daily attendance, including any overtime or extra work. This can go a long way in avoiding misunderstandings and resolving disputes. Major events which should be recorded include:

- Employment contracts.
- Disciplinary notices and details of the background.
- Pay increases with dates.
- If relevant, records of leave days taken.
- Details of any disputes or accidents.

Remember the people coming after you. Someone is going to have to take over where you left off. Remember how you felt when you started.

6.2.5 Working with host and displaced communities

Host and displaced communities can offer the engineer/manager:

- Technical expertise and knowledge of local materials, skills and methods.
- An understanding of and advice on cultural sensitivities.
- The opportunity for the manager to learn new ideas.
- Assistance with negotiation and advice on organization of work.

It is worth spending some time identifying skilled and trained engineers, technicians, supervisors and overseers within the displaced or host community. Working with local knowledge and methods, problems can be approached from appropriate and novel angles. In emergencies, managers will be faced with many situations that they do not quite understand or lack the cultural knowledge to resolve. Labour negotiations are a glaring example of this.

Do listen, question, consult, show respect, discuss.

Do not jump to conclusions, be dismissive or act without considering the consequences.

In stressful circumstances it may be difficult to retain sensitivity, and the needs of other cultures may be the last thing on your mind. Strive to retain this sensitivity.

6.2.6 Working with colleagues

In a relief situation it is common to be working as part of a management hierarchy. You will be managing people and you will be managed by others. In some circumstances you may be very much on your own, but in most cases you are likely to be working with colleagues who are your professional peers. They may be professionals of other disciplines working in your own location or other professionals of your own discipline working in other locations.

Working with colleagues requires teamwork. This is as much of a skill as is management or leadership and is particularly important in difficult circumstances where, in addition to working together, you may have to share accommodation and meals. Although it is not necessary to like your colleagues, you do have to work with them. Resist the temptation to 'do your own thing' – you are part of a team. Do not challenge or undermine the leadership, unless there is a very strong reason – the team leader needs and deserves support from the team.

Remember your colleagues in remote locations. They may need the support of the team and it should not be a case of 'out of sight, out of mind'. It may be useful to have a bar chart in the main office for recording arrivals and departures of team members, dates for rest and relaxation, handover periods, and so on.

Teams are generally put together on the basis of professional skills. However, for a team to work, the interpersonal dynamics must also work. This depends to a large extent on the personalities and attitudes of the team members. An understanding of how teams function can help.

Team roles

While the professional and hierarchical roles within a team are often fairly well defined, there are a number of other roles which, if understood, can help the team to function more effectively. Such roles might be, for example, that of 'ideas generator', 'finisher', 'motivator' or 'mediator'. An effective team will ensure that a broad spectrum of roles is covered. If a team consists entirely of 'idea generators' then, while it may generate many innovative ideas, it is likely to be weak on planning, implementing and following through. Each team member should be aware of the strengths and weaknesses of the team as a whole and be prepared to work on the weaknesses.

Team dynamics

In emergencies, teams will be continually changing. It is important that team members are open to newcomers and make them feel part of the team. When a new member joins the team, the team itself becomes a new team. There are several stages in team formation, often termed 'forming, storming, norming and performing'. The sequence and emphasis of these stages may vary somewhat and several stages may be taking place at the same time if new members are joining the team.

In the forming stage, team members get to know each other and to understand their formal roles. In the storming stage, conflicts may arise that need to be resolved. Such conflict resolution, if managed well, can be a positive achievement for the team (see Section 6.5.2). In the norming stage, team members begin to understand how they will work together and will focus on the task to be carried out. In the performing stage, the team is functioning well, with mutual trust and an ability to deal with conflict.

6.3 Working with contractors

In an emergency, commercial contractors can be invaluable for tasks such as road construction, water tankering, borehole drilling or pipeline laying. Local contractors understand the local culture and environment. However, in an emergency there may be:

- Little choice of contractor and hence little competition.
- Lower quality of work from contractors.
- Insecurity and a reluctance by contractors to work in a particular area.
- An opportunity for the contractor to inflate the price or to take shortcuts.
- A distorted labour and materials market.
- Poor legal enforcement procedures.

However, the basic principles of good contract management apply equally to emergencies as to any other form of engineering works.

Safety

Throughout the management of a contract, it is your responsibility to ensure that all reasonable steps are taken to maintain safe working conditions. It is not acceptable to expose to further hazards people who have probably only recently been in very risky situations. Take a systematic approach to managing risk by consciously examining what could potentially cause harm to people so that you can assess whether enough precautions have been taken to minimize risk. It is good practice to go through simple steps with your counterpart, supervisors or contractor to assess risk:

1. Look for hazards – what might cause harm?
2. Decide who might be harmed and how. This includes members of the community as well as the workers.
3. Evaluate the risks
   - can the hazard be removed or avoided?
   - if not, how can the risks be controlled?
4. Review your risk assessment as the situation changes with, for example, new equipment, people, and methods.

It may be possible to control risk by:

- Looking for an alternative way of doing the job.
- Preventing access to the hazard, for example, fencing, guards.
- Reducing exposure to the hazard by organising the work effectively.
- Providing protective clothing: boots, gloves, hard hats, etc.
- Providing welfare facilities: washing area, hygienic site sanitation, first aid.

Failure to take simple precautions can cost a great deal in the longer term – and it may cost a life.

Enforcement

As the agency's representative, it is up to you to see that the contractor delivers what is agreed and that this is what you require.

Payment. Ultimately the best method of enforcing a contract is through payment. For this reason, the method and timing of contractual payments must be very carefully considered and agreed before signing a contract. Think about incentives for good performance and retentions or penalties for poor performance. Although penalties may not be enforceable in practice, including them in the contract may in itself convince the contractor of your professionalism. Make it clear that you expect the contractor to make a fair profit – but that it must be fair.

Capability. Check that the contractor is capable of meeting the terms of the contract. Where are their water tankers? What have they built before? Get independent confirmation before going ahead. If this is not possible, and if there is time, set a small contract first to verify capabilities.

Monitoring. Monitoring performance can promote compliance with a contract. Regularly observe the work in progress. If necessary, hire specific monitors for this purpose. An example would be a supervisor employed to check the trench length dug per day on a pipe trenching contract. Balance the need for monitoring against the appearance of policing. Let other people know what the contractor is supposed to be doing. If the people know that the tanker contractor is supposed to supply them with ten tanker loads per day, they will try to ensure that they receive that amount and will let you know if this does not happen.

Financial information. The need to negotiate a new contract or an addition to an existing one can arise at any time. At the earliest opportunity, familiarize yourself with local labour rates and prices of materials and transport. This will help if contracts need to be agreed on the spot or if detailed negotiation is required.

Fairness and flexibility. Fairness and consideration towards the contractor helps to build a good working relationship and should ensure a reliable service. Be prepared to be flexible. Remember, the important thing is to get the job done and unusual circumstances may call for an unusual response.

Legality. In an emergency situation, the agency as the client may be in a poor legal position with regard to enforcing the terms and conditions of a contract. However, if a large contract is to be signed, consider using a local lawyer to draw up and witness the contract.

Professional relationship. Try to maintain a friendly professional relationship with the contractor. As far as is possible, avoid accepting gifts or lifts from the contractor. Ensure that your supervisory staff are also aware of the need for a professionally distant relationship.

Record keeping. It is important that the agency is kept informed of progress. From your own point of view, it is wise to record important events and details and keep them on file. Regular reports to your manager should include information about any contracts that you have running.

Procedures

During the early phase of an emergency there will almost certainly be insufficient time to enter into a formal tendering process. Make as much effort as time allows to secure the best contract. Give the contractor as much information as possible about the job and ask for enough details to check that the price is reasonable. Contractors should submit estimates broken down in terms of time, labour and materials. Think through the consequences and clearly define the responsibilities for all parties to the contract. If the contract is to be large and there is sufficient time for formal contractual procedures, asking for tenders from several contractors may help to limit the possibility of overcharging. Be aware of the possibility of cartels. Be prepared to negotiate parts of contracts separately, especially if it is cheaper to source materials separately.

A contract requires formal agreement, implementation, supervision, enforcement and payment according to terms. Before any contractual terms and conditions are agreed, think through all possible problems and make suitable provisions in the contract. The written document should be clear and concise so that the contractor knows precisely what is expected, what standard is required and at what time the contract should be completed. Clarity leads to understanding and agreement, makes disputes less likely and is your best ally if disputes arise.

Normally there are three phases to the contract process:

- Invitation to tender – usually sent by the customer to selected bidders.
- Tender – an offer to do a job for a certain price using specified materials, techniques and methods.
- Acceptance – the client agrees to a tendered offer for a specific price. In the UK, when a formal letter of offer has been formally accepted by the client, the contract is legally binding. In the absence of more detailed country specific procedures, this is probably a good principle to follow, but do check local custom/law. Make it clear from the outset what principles you are following.

Agency policy with regard to setting contracts will dictate much of the process needed to finalize a contract. For example, UN agencies normally require three bids before granting a contract, and this is almost always granted on price. NGOs tend to be less formal.

Types of contract

Select the type of contract according to the circumstances. Types of contract include:

- Lump sum/Fixed price – agreed rate for the job. This is the simplest to administer.

- Cost-plus or Time and Lime – contractor gets materials and labour costs plus an agreed percentage. This type of contract should be avoided as it encourages high spending and lengthy work.
- Labour only – a fixed sum for labour, where the agency supplies materials. This is not generally recommended as the contract is breached if the agency fails to supply materials. It may be necessary if materials are not easily available to the contractor. Useful to consider as an alternative to direct labour.
- Incentive or Target Cost – incentives are given for achievement and penalties for underachievement. It can be combined with other types of contract.

It is very likely that some form of inflation proofing will be required. Local currencies are often very weak. One way of resolving this is to agree a price in hard currency (usually US$) and to pay in that currency if it is available and acceptable, or to use the exchange rate current at the time of payment.

Contents of a contract

A contract is usually made up of three documents: the Conditions of Contract; the Specifications; and the Bill of Quantities. Contracts during an emergency can be condensed to one document, but have in mind the three categories. In drawing up a contract, consider the following:

- Responsibilities: Who delivers materials to site? Who is responsible for security of materials? Who pays for breakages? Who pays for downtime? What legal safety requirements apply? What happens if the site becomes inaccessible? Who provides fuel and who pays if it is unavailable?
- Specification of work; for instance, the concrete mix, the pressure rating of pipes, the thickness of concrete – how will these be monitored?
- Timescale – set realistic targets.
- Include sketches or drawings.
- Separate contracts – it may be cheaper to source materials elsewhere.
- Terms of payment – when, how much; incentives, penalties; retention of payment until, for example, pipes are tested and are not leaking; hard or local currency; inflation.
- Payment according to what rate? Per load or total volume? Per cubic metre of excavation? Person days? Weight or item? (particularly important for unloading).
- Retainers – it may be better to pay a retainer than to lose a good contractor whilst waiting for a decision.
- Keep the contract as clear, simple and brief as possible.

See Appendix 5 for a sample contract.

6.4 Information and communication

6.4.1 Information and record keeping

During an emergency there is an enormous amount of information passing between colleagues and agencies. As a manager and an employee, you are part

Box 6.2 Case history of simple contract for construction of 16 ferrocement tanks in Kenya

1 First tank constructed under supervision by agency engineer, with some on the job training. The total number of man hours was determined.

2 Agreement with 'labour only' contract based on time taken for first tank (less 10 per cent to account for learning), plus agreed percentage for contractor's profit.

3 Thereafter any saving in time or labour is to contractor's benefit.

Agency knows in advance the price for the next 15 tanks.

of that process and will have to decide what information has to be passed on, to whom it should go, in which form and at what time. Staff members who are responsible to you must be kept informed, not just about the details necessary for them to do their work but also about general situational and policy information. Particularly important is reporting back to your team members about meetings you have attended on their behalf and what has been decided at these meetings.

Information needs processing: it has to be collected, recorded, analysed and passed on (see Chapter 5). As a manager, consider the following methods:

- Field book: carry it at all times and record information as it occurs.
- Personal diary: note down key events of the day, such as meetings, decisions, achievements; also record feelings and odd occurrences (such as the hail-storm, the big dust-devil).
- Office diaries and logs (see Section 6.6.1).

Keep records of decisions and the circumstances that prevailed when they were made. Circumstances are fast-changing during an emergency, and a decision made by you today can appear to be curious and inappropriate next week when you have gone.

6.4.2 Communication

Achieving the clarity and understanding essential to effective management requires good communication. Likewise, the point of communication is the achievement of clarity and understanding – it is not simply the transmission of masses of information. Before initiating a formal communication ask 'why am I communicating?' A good communication should:

- Explain why the communication is being made.
- Clarify what is expected of people as a result of the communication.
- State who should receive the communication – distribution and level of confidentiality.
- Provide any information needed to enable the required action to be taken.

While it is wise to minimize report writing and paperwork, it is important that your agency is kept informed about work progress and the general situation as you see it. As you are their representative, the agency will be relying on your field level information to help them to make decisions about future policy. Many agencies will have regular reporting procedures which might include a weekly 'sitrep' (SITuation REPort) or a daily debrief – see Appendix 4 for an example. While regular sitreps may not be your responsibility, detailed reports of work progress and all matters pertaining to the areas of your direct responsibility will be. Ideally, reports should be sent every two weeks or, as an absolute minimum, every month. The frequency of reporting should be checked with the agency. Even if not required by the agency, regular reporting is a good professional habit.

Prepare good handover notes for your successor. They help the newcomer to understand the context and thinking behind decisions; the detail of design and the stage of progress. Handover notes are best written as a continuous process. This avoids a last-minute dash to complete some notes and it makes the exercise more satisfactory for all concerned.

6.4.3 Meetings

Meetings will be an inevitable and necessary part of your work. They can be viewed as tiresome chores or useful venues for gathering information and making collective decisions (see Chapter 2 for co-ordination meetings). At a meeting, you are a representative of your agency and will be viewed as such by others. Expect to be asked to give an opinion on an issue which is outside your area of expertise. If you are not briefed on this issue, say so, and defer comment until you have discussed the issue with your manager.

To increase the efficiency of meetings, prepare for a meeting, consider what you want out of it and ensure the meeting is conducted properly (including any follow-up). As a manager you will need to call regular meetings for your team and it is at these meetings that you will have most opportunity to manage the proceedings. Demonstrating a planned and organized approach to meetings will help you to influence meetings called by others.

Meetings may be held for the following reasons:

- Sharing of information – this can consist of straightforward reports about circumstances related to your area of work.
- Discussion and consultation – to air certain ideas or to get advice.
- Decision-making, including ratification of something which may have been agreed informally in the field or at the last meeting.
- Review of previous decisions and action taken. Were they the correct decisions? Has the agreed action been taken? Are modifications needed?

Procedures for effective meetings

Hold meetings regularly and select a suitable location. Actions agreed at previous meetings can be followed up and progress can be monitored. The location should facilitate discussion – avoid noisy or dusty areas, or places where one or more attendee can keep dodging back to the office or site.

Have an agenda. Draw this up with input from the participants, and circulate it in advance so that they can be prepared. If it is not possible to circulate an agenda beforehand, at the beginning of the meeting list the items to be discussed and prioritize them. At the end of the meeting, ask for items for the next meeting. It can be useful to set time limits for each item. At the outset of the meeting, clarify the estimated finishing time of the meeting and see if everyone is happy with it.

Introduce everyone. In a rapidly changing situation, you may know all present but they may not know each other. Ensure that everyone knows everyone else's name and role.

Have a chair and a minute taker. These people should be told in advance of their position for the meeting and what is required of them. Even with informal meetings, someone should take a chairing role. Good chairing involves:

- Preparation: of the agenda, attendance, timing, duration and location.
- Control: state purpose of meeting; introduce each member and the agenda items; ensure that agenda is dealt with on time; use questions, statements and summaries to progress the meeting and to arrive at a result; ensure outcomes and decisions are recorded in the minutes; minimize one's own participation whilst encouraging and controlling participation by all present; draw attention to points of agreement rather than disagreement; encourage the meeting to build on points of agreement. The person chairing should, if holding strong personal views on a particular subject, relinquish the chair while that subject is being discussed.
- Follow up: Ensure agreements and action are recorded, with names and dates; check minutes; check up on actions at the following meeting.

Minute takers should record briefly but accurately the outcomes and agreed action points. If unclear on what exactly has been decided, ask for clarification – this can do wonders to focus the minds of those present. Table 6.2 below is an example of how minutes and action points from meetings can be combined.

Table 6.2 Format for taking minutes

Meeting: .... Location: .... Date: ....

Present: .... Apologies: ....

Item number	Details	Key outcomes/Action agreed	By whom	When

Adapted from Gawlinski & Graessle, 1988

6.5 Negotiation and conflict resolution

6.5.1 Negotiation

Working with other people always involves negotiation. An obvious example is the negotiation of a contract for the construction of a road. A less obvious example is the negotiation of your sleeping accommodation with your colleagues.

A good negotiation process should result in both parties discussing and arranging the terms of an agreement, and improving a relationship as trust, understanding and respect are built up. Each party to the negotiation will have a clearer understanding of the constraints and priorities under which the other side has to work. This is very important during an emergency, where good relationships help to achieve speedy results. A good negotiation takes place when:

- Parties believe that they will benefit from the process.
- There is sufficient trust, so that each side believes that the other will honour their part of the bargain.
- Parties enter the negotiation realizing that the solution may give them less than they want, but will not cost them more than they can afford to lose.

Although the aim of a good negotiation is a WIN–WIN outcome, you may have to negotiate with parties who will attempt to attain an unfair advantage (a WIN–LOSE outcome). Where one party behaves thus, future outcomes may become LOSE–LOSE as trust is lost and the relationship deteriorates. In the circumstances of an emergency, however, they may not be interested in building a long-term relationship. Take account of the following:

- People: Focus on the problem rather than on personalities.
- Interests: Focus on common interests not individual positions.
- Options: Generate a variety of options before deciding what to do.
- Criteria: Insist that the result be based on some objective standards.

(Adapted from Fisher & Ury, 1992)

Prepare thoroughly for important negotiations. Be clear in your own mind what you want to get out of the negotiation. A useful exercise is to sit down and draw up a 'shopping list' for yourself, including 'ideal' and 'worst possible' position. When you have done this for yourself, think yourself into the position of the other party and ask yourself what they want out of the negotiation. The areas of overlap between the two shopping lists will be the area where the negotiation can take place and agreement be reached.

Some points to bear in mind when negotiating:

- Consider where the negotiation is to take place, who will conduct it, who will be present, and the timescale.
- Ask lots of questions. This will help you to discover more about the other party's needs, it slows things down (which provides thinking time) and shows that you are interested in their point of view.
- Let people know your motives. This helps the other party to understand why you are making a certain suggestion and avoids guessing and suspicion. Try to understand their motives.
- Repeat your key offers or demands regularly – repetition will encourage the other party to believe you are serious.

- Avoid using irritating expressions such as 'reasonable', 'fair' or 'generous offer' – the implication is that the other party is being unfair, which does not make for a co-operative atmosphere.
- Avoid verbal defend/attack spirals.
- Avoid diluting good arguments with weaker ones. Quality of argument is better than quantity of reasons.
- Be prepared to walk away if you are not satisfied. Avoid making large concessions simply to obtain a settlement. People may return with new demands if they feel you are an easy touch.
- Flag behaviour changes. Use phrases such as 'I'd like to suggest . . .' or 'Could I ask if . . .'. They are clear, and request the listening and perception of the other party.
- Saying 'I don't understand' or 'I don't know' gives you time, and the other party may think they have an advantage.
- If someone tells you that you will have to do better, ask 'how much better?' Encourage them to be specific.
- Broaden options. Be innovative and be prepared to consider the unusual.

In certain circumstances, such as where there is only one contractor available, you may have to look at negotiating on more than just price. This could be the length of contract, guarantee of payment, hard currency and such like. Recognize and make the most of your assets.

6.5.2 Conflict resolution

Working in emergencies is very stressful, demands and expectations are high, and people place themselves and others under inordinate pressure. Conflict is inevitable and can arise from:

- Personality clashes.
- Conflicting objectives – an agency often does not recognize that people working for it have different objectives within the overall agency aim. The accountant may want to keep costs down and the engineer may want to spend more to provide an improved service. Both will be working within the broader aims, but each has somewhat differing objectives.
- Competition for scarce resources.
- Cultural differences (see Section 3.5).
- Communication problems/distortion – a particular problem when people within an agency are geographically remote from each other. Misunderstandings lead to confusion and conflict.

Although conflict can be destructive, conflict resolution, if well managed, can be positive and constructive. The process of conflict resolution has much in common with that of good negotiation. Some additional tactics that may help to resolve a conflict include the following:

- Focus on the issues rather than the personalities. It is generally easier to resolve conflict over issues than it is over personalities.

- Encourage differences to emerge and confront them.
- Recognize and accept feelings.
- Concentrate on finding solutions rather than apportioning blame.
- Use a step-by-step procedure for resolving differences – do not expect to solve all the problems at once.

The objective of conflict resolution is to achieve a lasting solution to personal or group differences. Managers should try to serve as facilitators rather than judges. This means helping the parties to resolve their own conflict and requires communication rather than direct resolution of the conflict. It is unlikely that solutions that are imposed on the parties will be long lasting. If, through facilitation, the conflict still cannot be resolved, it may help to call on the assistance of a third party or mediator.

6.6 Office practice

6.6.1 Filing system

Accurate records are necessary for efficient adminstration and management. They are essential for future reference. As a temporary staff member on a project, you owe it to your successors to maintain a good filing system. If you have not inherited a well kept system, you should make it a priority to ensure that one is installed. Initially, set up a very basic system that can be expanded as time permits. The most important point about a filing system is that it is easy to use – a filing system that is difficult will not be used. In setting up a new system, consider:

- A newcomer who does not know the system.
- Information you regularly use.
- Information which provides background.
- Miscellaneous files – avoid them.
- A uniform approach so that everyone can use the files. Think in terms of large groupings of information and then sub-divide these. Thus, a filing section on *REPORTS* might have files on 'settlements', 'health status', 'tour visits', 'contractors' performance' and 'engineering works'.
- Understandable instructions on the filing procedure. A diagram may be helpful.
- Duration of current files – this will not be a problem in the initial phase of an emergency, but needs to be considered if the emergency continues for some time. Current files should contain no more than the last 12 months' entries. They should then be archived or dumped.

It is better to spend some time setting up a comprehensive filing system with an assistant once time allows.

Files which are regularly used will include those holding communications (faxes, notes on telephone or radio conversations, letters, etc.), design data, minutes from meetings, accounts, addresses and contact names of agencies or government departments and the like. Less frequently used files might hold background information such as personnel data, equipment specifications, orders and delivery of equipment, reports and vehicle maintenance.

It is useful to keep a day file of everything that comes in and out of the office on a particular date. This information is then copied to the relevant main files once office and staff are properly established. If the office receives a great deal of written or verbal communication, it may prove advantageous to keep a separate communications day file. Ensure all incoming official telephone and radio messages are recorded and passed on. A messages logsheet may help – include a 'message received' column for initialing by the receiver of the message. Maintain an office diary and record where everyone is or should be. It can be helpful to use a wall board showing the whereabouts of each vehicle, its date of departure, date of return, driver and the name of the staff member with the vehicle.

Security of records

If you are working in an insecure environment consider the implications for staff if personnel records were to get into the hands of parties wishing to persecute particular groups of people. This may be for a variety of reasons: political, religious, ethnic, geographical affiliations or working for 'Western' agencies. Carefully manage such sensitive information and have a contingency plan to take or destroy all records when the programme is closed down or if you have to leave in a hurry during an evacuation. Consider both paper and computer records and the range of records that may be sensitive: personnel, finance, communications (e-mail, letters, day file, etc.). See Van Brabant (2000) for futher guidance on managing security.

6.6.2 Office procedures

On arrival, ensure that you are fully briefed about office procedures and systems. As a manager, you should know how staff are supposed to carry out their tasks and it is important that you lead by example. For example, as an engineer, you may be placing orders for materials and equipment. How should this be done? Check if there is a set procedure for this. Is it the same for local and international purchases? If not, who controls the cash to make local purchases? Do you need quotes?

Try to ensure that all those who need to know about office procedures at least know that the procedures exist. If you need to introduce an office procedure ensure that:

- It does not contradict an existing procedure.
- Your manager agrees with the need and chosen method.
- All those it applies to are aware of its existence – put it in writing, copy it to the office procedures file, and circulate it to the relevant people.

Ensure that good supplies of the following stationery are maintained: paper, envelopes, pens, pencils, paperclips, staplers, erasers, erasing fluid, typewriter ribbons, printer ink cartridges, notebooks, files, labels, duplicating pads, carbon paper. Order office equipment as soon as possible: photocopiers; computers;

calculators; typewriters; waste paper bins; chairs; desks; lockable filing cabinets; safe for documents and money; lights; candles (for when the power goes down); a stand-by generator; heaters (if in a cold country); fans (nice in a hot country); shelving; facilities for making hot drinks and preparing food. Many of the items above are not essential in the initial stages of an emergency but should be procured as soon as possible.

Where an emergency programme is being run from an existing office with many other functions, it may be necessary to agree such things as: times when the emergency staff can use existing radio links or fax machines; access to vehicles; attendance at regular office/team meetings; use of a photocopier; charges for tea/coffee.

Where crime or general insecurity is an issue, ensure security procedures are in place and adhered to. See Van Brabant (2000) for further guidance.

6.7 Financial management

6.7.1 Budgeting

A budget is an estimate, or forecast, of income and expenditure. As a field manager, you are likely to be asked by your agency to estimate your required expenditure budget, which is the amount of money a certain project or programme is expected to cost. The agency will use this to look for the necessary moneys from donors. In emergencies, agencies may have to prepare budgets at very short notice. Anticipate this by:

- Familiarizing yourself with the budgeting procedures of the agency.
- Getting price lists of standard agency stock items.
- Ascertaining local costs and keeping them up to date.

In drawing up a budget:

- State clearly what your budget covers (for instance, the water supply for 40 000 refugees). If the numbers suddenly increase, then you have more chance of getting additional funds.
- Expect inflation of costs in the emergency area.
- Allow generous margins for local costs.
- Make generous estimates of operation and maintenance costs.
- Incorporate flexibility for increasing numbers of beneficiaries.
- Budget for the long-term – it is far easier for agencies to secure funding for projects during the initial stages of an emergency.

Avoid miscellaneous items, but it is legitimate to put in a contingency item of 5–10 per cent of the total.

6.7.2 Budget codes

It is normal practice for a project budget to be split down into a number of allocation headings. Most agencies will have budget coding systems – find out what they are and use them. If a budget has been approved, a grant (approved budget) will be made for that programme. For this purpose, the grant will have a title or code, and this will then be sub-coded under budget items. Table 6.3 gives an example of an emergency water programme in Afghanistan. Separate coded items may be termed a budget line. In this instance, £1000 expenditure on local purchases would be entered in the accounts as: AFG 12 A – 1000.

Table 6.3 An example of a budget for an emergency water programme

Grant No. AFG 12 *Code*	*Item*	*£83 000* *Cost, £*
A	local materials purchase	9 000
B	local salaries	8 000
C	pumps, generators	17 000
E	vehicle running costs	2 500
F	office costs	1 500
G	travel subsistence	1 000
H	operation and maintenance	15 000
I	accommodation	2 000
J	air fares	3 000
K	pipes, fittings	4 000
L	water equipment	20 000

Some items can be difficult to code, or can be entered under a number of different codes. This can be useful if one or more budget lines are spent and others underspent. For example, if a new set of tyres were needed for a vehicle, they could be entered under A, E, or H. Having said this, it is far better to use regular budget monitoring to anticipate shortfalls and find additional funding or to re-allocate within the grant.

6.7.3 Monitoring

Once a budget has been agreed, as the manager in the field you should regularly monitor cash flow. This may seem tedious, but it is necessary if the agency is to supply the funds required. Compare actual expenditure with the amount budgeted and if there are significant differences, find out why. If necessary, warn the head office of the need for additional funding. Draw up budgets as shown in Table 6.4 (cost budget) and Table 6.5 (cash flow budget).

Table 6.5 shows that, in this example, the peak demand for cash will be during Weeks 1 and 2. If work is to start immediately, it is necessary to ensure that there is sufficient cash available on-site to pay for the work. Monitoring during the first week showed that the trench digging cost 160 per cent of the budgeted estimate. After the first week had been monitored, the engineer would have been able to revise the budget in anticipation of increased costs in Week 2. This would have meant that additional cash could have been requested for labour payments in subsequent weeks.

Table 6.4 Example of cost budget for water installation

Task	*Materials*	*Labour*	*Cost £* *Transport*	*Totals*
Site preparations	150	200	50	400
Dig trench	300	700	0	1000
Construct tanks	0	300	150	450
Pump house	350	70	20	440
Construct store	350	70	20	440
Install tapstands	250	300	20	570
Lay pipe and make connections	200	200	0	400
Total	1600	1840	260	3700

Table 6.5 Example of cash flow budget for water installation

Task	*Cash needed £*							
	Week 1		*Week 2*		*Week 3*		*Week 4*	
	budget	*actual*	*budget*	*actual*	*budget*	*actual*	*budget*	*actual*
Site preparations	300	400	100	200	0	0	0	0
Dig trench	500	800	300	500	150	200	50	100
Construct tanks	0	0	300	300	150	150	0	0
Pump houses	0	0	350	450	0	0	90	90
Construct store	350	0	90	400	0	0	0	0
Install tapstands	0	0	270	270	150	300	150	150
Lay pipe and make connections	0	0	150	250	150	150	100	100
Totals	1150	1200	1560	2370	600	800	390	440

6.7.4 Regular accounting

An agency has a responsibility to its donors to ensure that money is spent for the purpose for which it was donated. Increasingly, donors are demanding more detailed accounting for funds they have made available for emergencies. In addition to discharging this responsibility, accounts provide valuable information for project planning and management. As a field manager you should be able to account for all moneys issued to you. You will be expected to provide invoices and receipts (or if these are not available, personal notes) in support of your accounts.

To keep track of funds, make a note of every transaction and where possible obtain receipts – even in remote markets, these may be available. Keep a receipt book or supply of credit card-sized pieces of paper in your wallet. If no receipt is obtained, write your own – note the date, time, item purchased, amount and currency, and sign the note. The simple rule is 'something out – something in': if you pay out some money that has to be accounted for – put a note back in. Similarly, note any income that you receive.

Periodically check that your own personal accounts are in order. Leaving this to the end of your assignment can cause much frustration.

Free accounting tools for NGOs can be downloaded from the Mango website – see Appendix 2.

6.7.5 Security of cash

If the theft of cash is a concern then consider the measures listed below:

- Check on agency insurance for loss and theft of cash.
- Minimize the use of cash through using traveller's cheques, payment by cheque and/or bank transfer, or credit card.
- Investigate informal transaction systems, especially in collapsed states where formal banking does not exist. This may mean depositing cash in a foreign account to cover costs incurred locally.
- Be discreet! Work on a 'need to know' basis to minimize the number of people who know when a cash transfer will take place. Use agreed code words to disguise conversations about cash over the radio or telephone.
- Anticipate the bulk of cash handed over in a bank when exchanging international for local currency. Ask for large denomination notes or arrange collection in smaller instalments.
- Where is the greater risk – during cash transfer or where it is kept? Decide whether to limit the amount kept in a safe (more transfers) or reduce the number of transfers (more kept in the safe).
- Arrange for cash transfers to be made just before they are paid out to minimize time kept in the office.
- Arrange for contractors, suppliers, field staff and service providers to come to you for payment rather than you go to them.
- Do not keep all your cash in one place – spread the risk.
- Avoid routine and predictability such as the monthly payroll, the arrival of international staff with cash, visits to the bank, etc.

Whatever happens, remember your life and the life of your colleagues are worth more than any cash you might be tempted to protect during a robbery.

6.8 Training

6.8.1 Organizing training

While working on an emergency programme, you may be introducing new ideas, technology and methodologies to an area. You will also be leaving in a short space of time. After the immediate life-saving phase of the emergency response, training is probably one of the most useful things that you can do while working on your programme. Good training makes people more competent and confident in their work. Training can:

- Pass on skills and knowledge.
- Help to ensure the long-term success of the programme.
- Build local self-reliance.
- Strengthen and reinforce local institutions.

Everyone on your team will require some form of training. The pump operator will have to know about the specific engine and the regular daily checks that need to be made. Likewise, staff employed to manage a construction programme will need training on, for example, procedures for ordering materials and monitoring progress. Good supervision should result in the identification of training needs. Once these needs are identified, design a training programme to fit both the needs and the work conditions. This should be a continuous and ongoing process. The types of training that are likely to be applicable in an emergency are:

- *Induction:* a short time at the start of the job to clarify the nature of the work, how the organization functions and the role of the inductee in the organization.
- *On the job training:* where instructions or explanations are given from time to time. This should be done in a planned and systematic manner. The worker should not just be told to get on with the job, but be introduced to the task and gradually given increasing responsibility for it.
- *Shadowing or counterpart training.* You will almost inevitably be 'shadowed', either formally or informally. Take the opportunity to pass on any skills you can – and learn new ones.
- *Formal training sessions, seminars, workshops.* Seminars and workshops can be used for reviewing progress and for sharing each other's experience and knowledge.
- *Practical demonstrations.*

Running training courses requires considerable expertise. If you have not got the necessary experience, there is a good chance that there is a significant training capacity among the population with whom you are working. For example, community health educators are often familiar with training techniques, and they may have just the skill you need to help with training staff members. If you have to organize a training session or workshop, consider:

- The training needs to be met.
- The specific objectives of the training session. What do you want the trainees to be able to do at the end of the session that they could not do at the beginning?
- The methods to be used and the trainer's and trainees' capacities in such fields as language, reading and writing skills.
- The location and facilities required – for example, on site, in a classroom.
- The time available – try not to pack in too much.

It may be appropriate to train the people who are going to train others, so benefiting from a multiplier effect. For example, if a large number of maintenance staff are employed, consider training their supervisor. She/he will then be well placed to pass on this knowledge to the staff.

There may occasionally be a need to look for training opportunities outside the organization. This is only likely if an emergency is long term. It may happen that a large engineering programme is to be handed over to local staff management. It is unrealistic and unfair to do this without equipping the staff members with the necessary skills.

6.8.2 Training yourself

In between relief assignments you can share your knowledge and experience with others through contributing to training. You can take advantage of training to enhance your own knowledge and skills. Short and long courses are available. Consult the RedR Training Programme on the RedR web site and the Humanitarian Assistance Training Inventory (HATI) on the OCHA web site (Appendix 2).

7 Logistics

Humanitarian assistance in emergencies frequently involves supplying food, water, shelter and medical aid to people who have fled to relatively inaccessible areas. Good logistics planning is critical to the success of an emergency programme, and engineers or relief workers should have an understanding of how a logistics system should operate.

This chapter gives a brief overview of the type of logistics systems typical of international relief operations, and highlights some of the elements that have particular relevance to the engineer.

An invaluable reference for this chapter is UNHCR's *Supplies and Food Aid Handbook* (1989).

7.1 Overview of a logistics system

Logistics is about getting the right thing to the right place at the right time at the right cost. The processes involved in a logistics operation include:

- Assessment of requirements and budget (see Chapter 5).
- Detailed specification of goods and equipment needed.
- Communication of these requirements to suppliers, usually via an intermediary (such as a head office).
- Procurement (either locally or internationally) and consignment (includes packaging).
- Transport and supply.
- Delivery and storage, including reordering.
- Distribution.

A logistics system (see Figure 7.1) will be composed of:

- A communications network.
- A transport system for people and goods by land, air and water.
- Storage facilities – located throughout the system as transit stores between modes of transport or final pre-distribution stores.
- Control systems – this will include records and reports to control the flow of goods through the system.
- Personnel – to monitor the system by conducting checks and inspections; to provide management and supervision at key control points; to drive and unload vehicles.

Before specifying goods or equipment, consider all aspects of the logistics process and system and how it might affect timing in your plans.

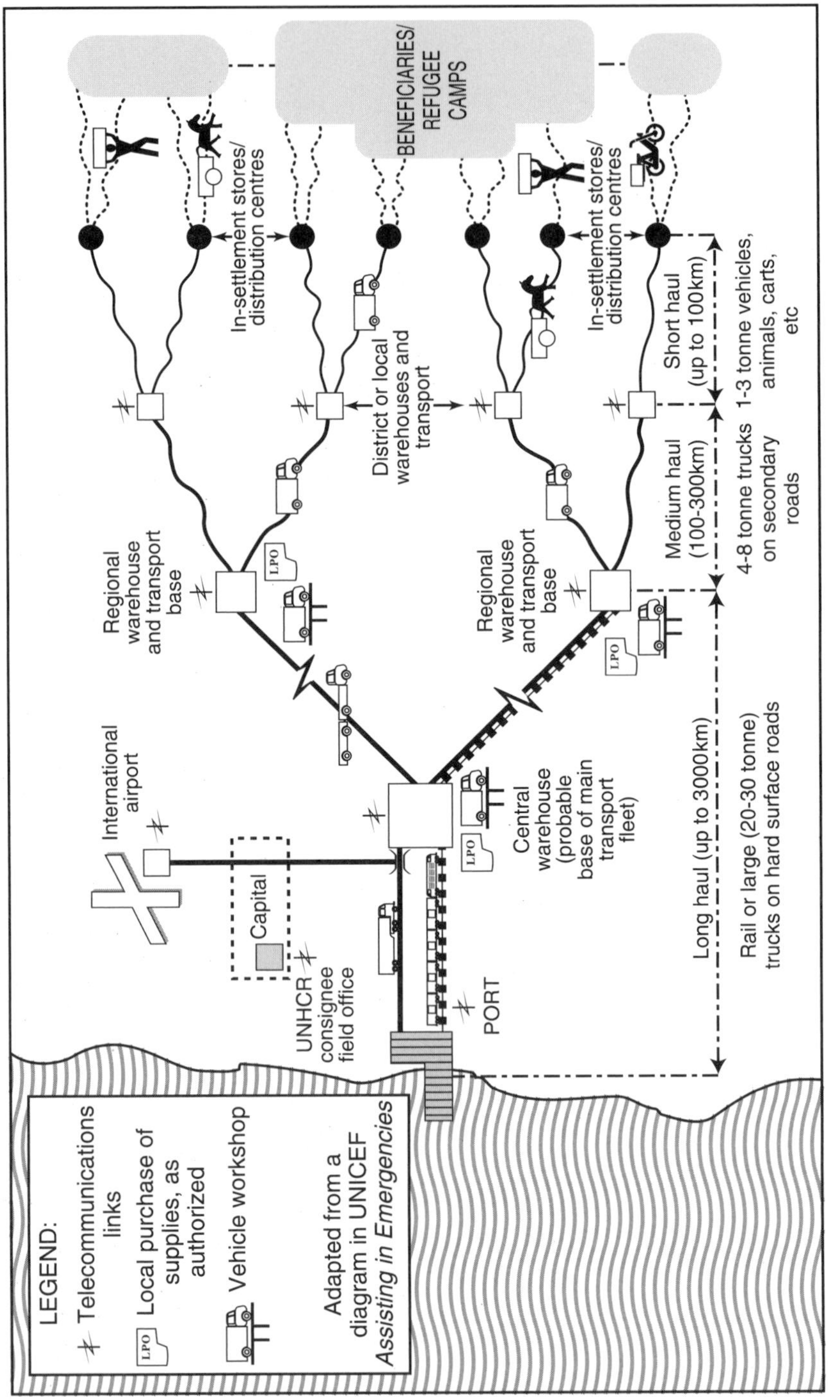

Figure 7.1 Components of a logistics system

In the early stages of an emergency, speed of response is required. Equipment that is ordered from outside the country can take a long time to arrive at the final destination. Make full use of local resources, even though they may appear to be an expensive option.

7.2 Procurement

Procurement involves specification, ordering, purchase, packaging and dispatch. Field workers are involved mainly in specification and ordering, although they may have to do some local purchasing themselves.

7.2.1 Specifying

Unless items are specified and ordered accurately, there is a real danger that incorrect or inappropriate goods will travel through the logistics system. This is expensive and wasteful, but more importantly, will hinder the provision of services to the beneficiary population.

Specifying technical items accurately is particularly important. People reading and dealing with the order may not have an understanding of technical terms. Misunderstandings can easily happen, resulting in your order being returned for clarification, or the wrong items being purchased and sent to you in the field.

To be understood, a good purchase specification should:

- Be clear and unambiguous.
- Include details of intended use, and a sketch where possible.
- Use standard agency stock item reference codes where applicable, such as spare parts numbers.
- Provide the person reading it with the information they need to purchase the item.
- Be in the language of the person responsible for the purchase.

The details that need to be specified depend on the item being ordered. Specification guides for particular items can be found in the relevant chapters of the book. See, for example, specifications for a generator in Table 16.1. Do not specify a particular make or model unless you have good reasons, such as: existing local usage; maintenance and spare parts available locally; government regulations or controls on the use of certain makes of equipment.

The purchasing officer will have more scope to supply equipment quickly if not restricted to one supplier. Take care to specify a particular standard if you require it, to avoid purchase of inferior-quality items on a lowest cost basis. Strength, durability and reliability may be cheaper in the long run than initial capital savings.

7.2.2 Ordering

A simple system for ordering should include:

- A procedure for securing quotes – this stage will most probably be bypassed in the initial stages of an emergency.

- A procedure for placing a firm order.
- A procedure for notifying delivery time to the field.

Quotes should be obtained from a number of suppliers on the basis of a specification supplied by the field. Suppliers should be asked to quote against a detailed specification on:

- Price.
- Delivery time – may take precedence over exact specification.
- Terms, such as FOB, CIF (these abbreviations are explained in Section 7.3).

If you are ordering vehicles or other mechanical equipment, be sure to take local advice before specifying the order (see Chapters 15, 16 and 17).

If the agency does not have a standard order form and reference system, establish one. This is particularly important where there is a high staff turnover. Orders should be placed on a standard duplicate order form with:

- Exact details of the consignee (the person to whom the goods are to be delivered) including the address.
- The project number.
- A purchase order number.

The specification should be attached to the order form (see Figure 7.2).

If large quantities or expensive goods are being supplied from a previously unknown regional source, it is worth considering a visit to the supplier. This will help to confirm that the items are being supplied to the correct specification and that the supplier can supply in accordance with the quote they have tendered. Ask for the consignment to be inspected prior to shipment. Know the lead time for delivery of the item and order well in advance of this (see Section 7.5). Short lead times are usually more important than exact specifications. For this reason, ensure that suppliers are bound by performance and delivery clauses, and follow up all orders.

Any special packaging should be detailed when the order is placed. Normally goods supplied for export have to be export packaged to prevent damage in transit and for insurance purposes. If purchased locally, specify that goods should be packaged to minimize the risk of transit damage, and that they may be rejected if they are damaged as a result of poor packaging.

It is essential that you know the lead time between identifying a need, placing an order and actually receiving the goods into the store. Local and international purchases can take a considerable time to arrive.

7.2.3 Purchasing

While major purchases should, if possible, be left to logistics staff, you may have to purchase some goods or equipment locally. If you are involved with a lot of local purchases, employ an assistant specifically for this task, familiarize yourself with local purchasing procedures, and regularly check the availability and price of items you may require. Ideally, your purchasing assistant should have a technical background and an understanding of the local market. If it is necessary to employ a non-technical person for the task, take some time to explain exactly what you mean when you specify an item. For example, if

AGENCY NAME ADDRESS	PURCHASE ORDER NO. DATE
TO (supplier's details)	SHIP TO (consignee)
SUPPLIER'S REFERENCE *This will be the reference number of the original quote*	PROJECT REFERENCE NUMBER
Please supply the following goods and/or services, subject to the specification set out in your quote of../../.. and ref. no.	SHIPPING MARKS *This will include any special ID marks, e.g. project number, agency logo.*

ITEM	GOODS	QUANTITY	UNIT PRICE	AMOUNT
REMARKS				

GENERAL INSTRUCTIONS Please retain this original and return the copy duly signed and dated as evidence of your acceptance of this order.	
	SIGNATURE *Person placing order*

Figure 7.2 A sample order form

ordering a lot of pipe fittings for a water system, go with the person to the suppliers in the first instance, and explain the options. Provide samples and diagrams or sketches to the assistant and the supplier.

7.3 Supply and transport

7.3.1 Freight

INCOTERMS (International Commercial Terms) provides a set of international rules for the interpretation of the terms used in international trade contracts. The following are some of the more commonly used terms:

EXW Ex-Works. This means that the supplier's responsibility is to make goods available at his premises. The buyer bears the full cost and risk involved in bringing the goods from these premises to the desired destination.

FOB Free On Board – (named port of shipment). The seller must place the goods on board a ship or other carrier at the port of shipment named in the sales contract. The risk of loss or damage remains with the supplier until the goods pass the ship's rail. Similar abbreviations apply for Airport, Rail or Truck transport (FOA, FOR, FOT).

C&F Cost and Freight – (named port of destination). The supplier must pay the costs and freight charges necessary to bring the goods to the named destination. The risk of loss or damage to the goods is transferred to the buyer once the goods pass the ship's rail in the port of shipment.

CIF Cost, Insurance and Freight – (named port of destination). Basically the same as C&F but the supplier has to provide shipping insurance against loss and damage during carriage.

The consignee is the person or agency that has responsibility for clearing goods through customs once they have arrived in the country. Normally this will be your agency. In some circumstances, your agency may have an agreement with another agency that has existing customs duty exemption. For example, in refugee emergencies, UNHCR frequently agrees to clear relief goods for partner agencies. In this case, the consignee would be your agency, care of (c/o) whichever UNHCR sub-office had responsibility for clearing the goods.

Transhipment is the term used when goods have to be transferred from one method of transport to another, for instance, from ship to rail to truck. It entails additional handling and increases the risk of goods being lost or damaged.

For local or regional purchases, try to have the goods delivered to the site of final use or as close to it as the supplier can manage. This may be termed 'Free delivered warehouse . . . (final destination)'. If this can be agreed, the cost of the goods includes delivery. The supplier has responsibility for the goods until they are delivered to the consignee at the final destination. Only goods delivered in an acceptable condition have to be paid for.

7.3.2 Transport

Agency involvement in organizing the method of carriage for freight goods will largely depend upon the nature of the supply contract. In general, the agency or relief worker should spend as little time as possible in handling and carriage of goods – leave it to the shippers. However, during the early stages of an emergency, the agency may have no choice but to organize transportation. This will depend on:

- Urgency of shipment.
- Size of shipment: weight and volume.
- Origin of goods: supplier's location.
- Normal transportation routes and scheduled services between the point of origin and the destination.
- Ports of entry, receiving facilities and transportation infrastructure at the destination.
- Relative costs and budgetary limitations.

Sea freight

Sea freight is normally used when shipment of goods is non-urgent and large volumes and weights are involved, such as food supplies. It is the least expensive form of transport, but has major limitations, including:

- Lead time for delivery to port of destination can be very long and unreliable, even for scheduled liner services.
- Goods can only be moved to a sea or river port; after this they need to be transhipped for onward delivery to the final destination.
- Goods delivered to sea ports can frequently be tied up for long periods awaiting berthing, unloading and customs clearance.

Air freight

Air freight is the fastest and most reliable shipping option. It is also by far the most expensive. It is used when:

- Goods are needed urgently, as occurs in the early stages of an emergency.
- Goods have a high value.
- Goods are low volume and low weight.
- Transport by other means is not possible.

Air freight can be sent by scheduled or charter flights or by military transport. With scheduled flights, freight is carried by airlines that have established handling and clearance procedures at the airport of arrival. Charter flights are often used to deliver goods directly to the disaster area or when it is economic to charter a whole aircraft. With military transport it is important to check the level of military assistance available to assist with tasks such as unloading.

When expecting urgent goods via scheduled air freight, contact the airline for advice on clearance procedures. Airlines vary in efficiency and, during an emergency, airport procedures can be completely disrupted. If the goods you require are particularly urgent, check to see if it is necessary to meet the aircraft to ensure speedy and safe clearance of freight.

Dealing with charter flights

Charter flights will demand a great deal more time and attention from field staff. Unlike scheduled airlines, charter flights have as their priority speedy turn-around time. They are best handled by experienced logisticians. However, if you have to deal with a charter flight:

- Prepare for the arrival. Local authorities may be unused to dealing with such flights, so make sure that all formalities required before the plane arrives have been resolved, such as flight clearance, advance paper work, notification of cargo contents.
- Ensure that the runway is in good repair and long enough for the plane coming in (see Section 18.6). Check with airlines and local civil aviation authorities, or measure the runway, and send details back to the office arranging the charter for them to check.
- Notify your head office of any flying restrictions which apply, for instance, no night flying. Likewise, arrange for the flight to arrive at such a time that you will not break any curfews on the way back from the airstrip after unloading.
- Check what staff and labour are needed for unloading and have them organized and ready. Arrange for a forklift to be ready (see 7.5.3). Check with the charter company that the type of aircraft is suitable for local unloading facilities.
- Check for ground support, particularly electrical power for jet aircraft. If this is not available the captain of the aircraft will need to keep one engine running and will be even more anxious to unload, putting more pressure on you – so be prepared. Check the availability of the correct fuel.
- Keep the runway clear – make sure people and animals are kept away and move any other obstructions. (See also Section 18.6).

Charter flights are rarely on time, but do make sure that you have plenty of advance warning of the ETA (Estimated Time of Arrival). The head office should provide you with this. However, be prepared for a long wait and do not let the unloading crew disappear from the airstrip. You must be ready for the plane when it arrives.

Road transport

Road transport offers the greatest flexibility for inland transport with regard to capacities, scheduling and routing (see also Chapters 17 and 18). Consider the following when planning road transport:

- The route: can the destinations be reached by road or track? Are there alternative routes – roads can close because of poor weather, security problems, blockages, bridges collapsing and such like. See Chapter 18.
- Vehicles: What is the nature and quantity of goods to be transported, and the time and frequency of each trip? What is the maximum vehicle size that the roads and bridges can take? One heavy truck can be thousands of times more damaging to a road than a light truck. It is generally easier to choose vehicles to suit the road than to build a new road to accommodate heavy vehicles. The most useful and flexible vehicle is a 10 tonne capacity, rigid, multi-axle driven, high-sided dropside truck. Heavy articulated trucks are to be avoided

if possible. Identify additional trucks, or sources for borrowing or renting trucks, if volumes to be moved increase or existing vehicles go out of service due to mechanical failure. See Chapter 17.

- The availability of fuel, spare parts and maintenance facilities: Do workshop and fuel facilities have to be set up? – adequate servicing facilities are rarely available in emergency areas. Downtime may be anything up to 25 per cent for vehicle breakdown, lack of fuel and general maintenance. Establish maintenance facilities at transit stores and warehouses. Stockpile against future shortages.
- Consider the use of contractors to move goods rather than importing and managing a dedicated fleet of vehicles.

Drive the route to inspect its condition and suitability for various types of vehicle.

Terms for commercial trucking contracts
If you plan to use a trucking contractor, you will have to negotiate a contract. In addition to the general points discussed in Sections 6.3 and 6.5, consider the following:

- Trucking contracts are quoted per tonne of cargo, either per trip per truck to/from a specified destination, or per truck for a given time period, preferably with unlimited mileage. Vehicle capacity should be stipulated. Costs can include or exclude loading and unloading.
- Costs of maintenance and vehicle insurance are borne by the contractor. Agree on who has responsibility in case of accidents, loss or theft of the vehicle or its load, inaccessibility of destination due to road condition or security problems, if vehicles are idle due to fuel shortages etc.
- If the contractor provides the driver, retain the right to review selection and request driver replacement if she/he proves unsatisfactory.
- Contractors should provide replacement vehicles in the event of a time consuming breakdown.
- Make provision to terminate or extend a contract at short notice.

(From UNHCR, 1989)

Transport by people and animals
Some remote or mountainous areas may not be accessible to motor vehicles. Use Table 7.1 as a guide when planning to use transport by people or animals. Speed will depend on many factors, but as a guide allow 3–5 km/h.

Rail and water
If navigable waterways exist, they may offer a viable alternative to road or rail transport, particularly to remote locations.

Rail transport should be considered when the goods to be moved are bulky and have to be transported over long distances. Typically, rail transport over more than 400 km can cost 80 per cent less than comparable road transport.

Table 7.1 Load carrying capacities of people and animals

Method of transport	*Approx load carrying capacity, kg*
People	
Head or shoulder load	20–35
Backload	35–70
Pack animals	
Donkey	50–120
Horse	100–150
Camel	200–300
Animal carts (single animal)	
Donkey	200–400
Ox	500–1000
Horse	up to 1200

7.3.3 Specialist items

Specialist items such as vaccines and chemicals will require special handling and transport arrangements.

Cold chain

Some items such as vaccines need to be kept within a certain temperature range to ensure their viability. For this reason, they are transported and stored in chilled containers right up to the point of use. The chilled storage from supplier to final destination is called the 'cold chain'. To avoid possible breakdown in the cold chain, the transport method chosen should use the quickest and safest route. Considerations about the cold chain will be of particular relevance if you are involved in the logistics operation of a medical agency.

Items requiring cold chain transport will usually be sent by air freight, in which case they will be in insulated cool boxes, possibly containing ice. Packed this way, the vaccines will normally be good for up to 72 hours. You should ensure that the sending office notifies the field well in advance of dispatch of the vaccines and when they are expected to arrive.

If you are expecting to receive cold chain items, always check with the medical staff for handling and storage requirements. Vaccines are frequently packed with a 'tell-tale'. This is an indicator which will detect when a vaccine has gone outside its temperature range. In their simplest form, tell-tales are colour indicators which change when the vial has been at a higher than acceptable temperature for an unacceptable period. If you think that the cold chain has been broken at any time, do not throw the vaccines away but refer your concern to the senior medical officer. Make sure that chilled or refrigerated containers are not opened until there is another suitable container chilled to the right temperature to accept the contents. Keep all polystyrene boxes for future use. If you need to make an insulated container, use materials such as polystyrene, newspaper, straw and clothing to provide the insulation.

If road transport is being used, refrigerated containers or trailers will be used. Leave the vaccines on the truck until the reception area is prepared. It is better to pay the truck to wait than to have a vital consignment of vaccines wasted. If you are dealing with a large quantity of vaccines, consider renting a refrigerated trailer to stand at the store for the duration of the programme. Simply mount a diesel generator on to the trailer to provide the power.

Airports sometimes have cold storage facilities; check this with the authorities.

Solar powered refrigerators are available. UNHCR and WHO have standard specifications for these and if you are involved with a cold chain, this type of refrigerator may be worth considering. See Chapter 16 for information on solar panels.

Chemicals

Transport and handling of chemicals such as chlorine, insecticides and pesticides must be carefully monitored and controlled. Ensure that all hazardous chemicals are clearly labelled, properly packaged, and that the necessary permits for transport are obtained. Chlorine needs specialized IATA packing and has to be packed in 5 kg lots for passenger cargo and 25 kg drums for commercial flights. Guidelines provided by the supplier must be followed. Where possible, any recommended safety equipment and clothing should be used.

Be aware of the risks associated with handling these goods and brief others about them. Chemicals should be stored under lock and key so that unauthorized personnel cannot get access to them.

7.4 Documentation

7.4.1 Waybills and bills of lading

Whichever form of transport is being used to carry freight, a document which forms the contract for carriage, handling, dispatch and delivery of the shipment to the consignee should be provided. This document itemizes the contents of each shipment, it allows the captain or driver to acknowledge delivery of the freight on board, and it allows the consignee to confirm receipt of the consignment at the destination. For air, road and rail, the document is called a 'waybill'. For carriage by ship, the document is called a 'bill of lading'. Packing and contents lists will normally be attached to the waybill or bill of lading. More details on air and truck waybills are given below.

Air waybill

The carrier, or his agent, contacts the consignee on arrival and hands over a copy of the air waybill (see Figure 7.3), the packing list and any other documents attached to package number one of the consignment. The original air waybill is important as it is the official record of the consignment details. It will be handed directly to the relevant officials at the destination by the captain. Field staff will only usually see a copy of this.

Truck waybills

When valuable cargo is being transported by truck, waybills should be used for every truck load. They must show information about the shipper, the

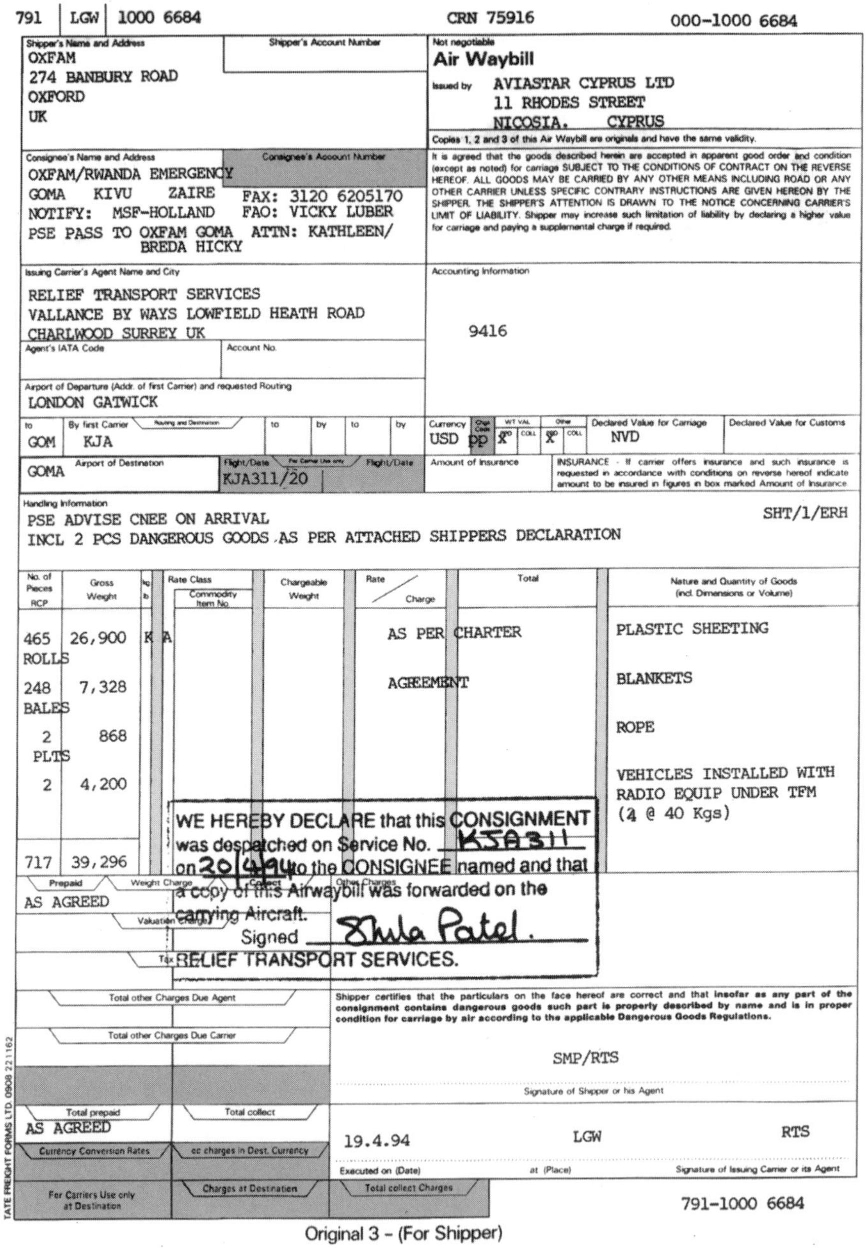

791 | LGW | 1000 6684 CRN 75916 000-1000 6684

Shipper's Name and Address: OXFAM, 274 BANBURY ROAD, OXFORD, UK

Shipper's Account Number

Not negotiable

Air Waybill

Issued by AVIASTAR CYPRUS LTD, 11 RHODES STREET, NICOSIA. CYPRUS

Copies 1, 2 and 3 of this Air Waybill are originals and have the same validity.

Consignee's Name and Address: OXFAM/RWANDA EMERGENCY, GOMA KIVU ZAIRE FAX: 3120 6205170, NOTIFY: MSF-HOLLAND FAO: VICKY LUBER, PSE PASS TO OXFAM GOMA ATTN: KATHLEEN/ BREDA HICKY

Consignee's Account Number

It is agreed that the goods described herein are accepted in apparent good order and condition (except as noted) for carriage SUBJECT TO THE CONDITIONS OF CONTRACT ON THE REVERSE HEREOF. ALL GOODS MAY BE CARRIED BY ANY OTHER MEANS INCLUDING ROAD OR ANY OTHER CARRIER UNLESS SPECIFIC CONTRARY INSTRUCTIONS ARE GIVEN HEREON BY THE SHIPPER. THE SHIPPER'S ATTENTION IS DRAWN TO THE NOTICE CONCERNING CARRIER'S LIMIT OF LIABILITY. Shipper may increase such limitation of liability by declaring a higher value for carriage and paying a supplemental charge if required.

Issuing Carrier's Agent Name and City: RELIEF TRANSPORT SERVICES, VALLANCE BY WAYS LOWFIELD HEATH ROAD, CHARLWOOD SURREY UK

Accounting Information: 9416

Agent's IATA Code | Account No.

Airport of Departure (Addr. of first Carrier) and requested Routing: LONDON GATWICK

to	By first Carrier (Routing and Destination)	to	by	to	by	Currency	Chgs Code	WT VAL PPD / COLL	Other PPD / COLL	Declared Value for Carriage	Declared Value for Customs
GOM	KJA					USD	PP	X	X	NVD	

Airport of Destination: GOMA | Flight/Date: KJA311/20 | For Carrier Use only | Flight/Date | Amount of Insurance | INSURANCE - If carrier offers insurance and such insurance is requested in accordance with conditions on reverse hereof indicate amount to be insured in figures in box marked Amount of Insurance.

Handling Information: PSE ADVISE CNEE ON ARRIVAL, INCL 2 PCS DANGEROUS GOODS AS PER ATTACHED SHIPPERS DECLARATION SHT/1/ERH

No. of Pieces RCP	Gross Weight	kg/lb	Rate Class / Commodity Item No.	Chargeable Weight	Rate / Charge	Total	Nature and Quantity of Goods (incl. Dimensions or Volume)
465 ROLLS	26,900	K	A		AS PER CHARTER AGREEMENT		PLASTIC SHEETING
248 BALES	7,328						BLANKETS
2 PLTS	868						ROPE
2	4,200						VEHICLES INSTALLED WITH RADIO EQUIP UNDER TFM (4 @ 40 Kgs)
717	39,296						

WE HEREBY DECLARE that this CONSIGNMENT was despatched on Service No. KJA311 on 20/4/94 to the CONSIGNEE named and that a copy of this Airwaybill was forwarded on the carrying Aircraft. Signed Shila Patel. RELIEF TRANSPORT SERVICES.

Prepaid | Weight Charge | Collect | Other Charges

AS AGREED

Valuation Charge

Tax

Total other Charges Due Agent

Total other Charges Due Carrier

Shipper certifies that the particulars on the face hereof are correct and that insofar as any part of the consignment contains dangerous goods such part is properly described by name and is in proper condition for carriage by air according to the applicable Dangerous Goods Regulations.

SMP/RTS

Signature of Shipper or his Agent

Total prepaid: AS AGREED | Total collect

Currency Conversion Rates | cc charges in Dest. Currency

19.4.94 | LGW | RTS

Executed on (Date) | at (Place) | Signature of Issuing Carrier or its Agent

For Carriers Use only at Destination | Charges at Destination | Total collect Charges

791-1000 6684

TATE FREIGHT FORMS LTD. 0908 221162

Original 3 - (For Shipper)

Figure 7.3 An example of an air waybill

consignee, the exact number of packages, the gross weight of the consignment (important for bulk items such as food and grain) and the shipping marks. A packing list or issue voucher providing a detailed description of the consignment should be attached to the waybill. The carrier should prepare a waybill in triplicate:

- Copies 1 and 2 go to the consignee with the goods.
- Copy 1 is kept by the consignee; copy 2 must be signed by the consignee and returned to the consignor.
- Copy 3, signed by the driver, stays with the shipper, to be matched against the returned Copy 2 to confirm delivery.

If trucks have to cross international borders, additional customs documentation and driver and vehicle identification will be necessary. Find out the exact local requirements.

7.4.2 Customs: import and export documentation

All international shipments must have the following documents:

- Original bill of lading or waybill.
- Commercial invoice.
- Packing list.

These will be needed for customs officials at the port of departure and arrival. If the goods are being gifted to the country of final destination a 'Certificate of Gift' will be required. Other documents or notification might include:

- Certificate of Origin – states country where goods originated.
- Dangerous Goods Certificate (DGR) – for items such as chemicals; vehicles also need a DGR when leaving certain countries of origin.
- Phytosanitary Certificate – very important to have certification that food is 'fit for human consumption'.
- Insurance Certificate – if CIF (see Section 7.3.1).

Documents should be sent to the field as early as possible and copies must always be sent prior to the arrival of goods. This will allow field staff to discuss the consignment with local customs officials and identify any shortfalls or missing documents necessary to comply with local customs regulations. Whenever possible, have as much of the local clearance procedure resolved before the goods arrive.

Customs clearance is at best a difficult task. It is time consuming, pedantic and can be extremely frustrating if you want something urgently and it has to stand at the airport for days or weeks because a formality has not been complied with. Whenever possible, contract a reputable local forwarding agent to handle the delivery and clearance of your goods.

It may be worthwhile employing a member of staff specifically to deal with customs clearance, especially if no suitable agent is available. This staff member must have sufficient authority and ability to deal directly with customs and to take the necessary decisions. A petty cash float is essential.

Always check and abide by the agency policy on inducements.

Items for importation which commonly cause problems

- Vehicles. It is always difficult to obtain customs clearance for these. Make sure that all vehicle identification numbers are correct (chassis and engine numbers). It often helps to have a registration plate on the vehicle when it arrives. If the vehicles are to be fitted with radio communication equipment, import these separately.
- Radio communication equipment. Apply for a licence as soon as possible – it may take weeks or months to arrive. Consider importing on someone else's licence – check the agency policy on this first.
- Drugs and chemicals can be difficult if they are not approved for use by the Ministry of Health or, in the case of insecticides or pesticides, by the Ministry of Agriculture. Check acceptability prior to ordering.
- Foodstuffs can be difficult. Be aware of cultural sensitivities such as Halal meat – make sure it has any relevant certification. Ensure that it is fit for human consumption.
- Clothing. Some countries, such as Iran, will not permit the import of clothing. Some may need a certificate of fumigation.

7.5 Receiving, storing and issuing goods

A good storage system, once installed, should:

- Ensure that the programme has what it needs, when it needs it. The stores system should adapt to the needs of the emergency: minimum bureaucracy, open at weekends etc.
- Provide a degree of security and protection against theft.
- Provide protection against the elements.
- Ensure that sufficient stock items are carried at all times.

See also 19.2.1.

7.5.1 Stores management

Establish a stores management system using a staged approach. In the initial phases of the emergency, a simple 'in/out' record in a notebook may be all that is feasible. This system can be upgraded as soon as the opportunity arises. Good control over all goods moving in and out of the store makes it possible to detect any shortfalls or damage. Theft should always be dealt with vigorously as the alternative is a continuation and possible escalation of the problem.

Stores management starts with the preparation of the store for the incoming goods. You will need to know the volume and nature of the goods before you can identify suitable facilities. Ideally, stores should be cool and dry, with the facility to lock doors and entrances against intruders. For further details on store preparation see Section 19.2. For food or cement, raise the goods above floor level by using wooden pallets. Make sure that protruding nails will not damage the goods.

Personnel

If possible, recruit people with previous experience in storekeeping. It is important that both you and the community being served can trust the stores personnel. Both men and women can run a store and there are often advantages in employing women in such tasks. Make sure that stores personnel are given clear job descriptions, responsibilities and instructions. If possible, choose a stores system with which the storekeepers are already familiar – the simpler the better. Spend some time making sure everyone is clear about the system. It is vital that the storekeepers understand their responsibility for the goods once the goods have been received by them.

Employ enough guards for round-the-clock security. Provide night guards with torches and blankets and consider giving them whistles to raise the alarm. In many situations, a guard will expect to be provided with a weapon such as a machete; you should consider the implications of this very carefully before issuing one. Where possible, make random checks on the stores and the guards.

Record keeping

It is necessary to maintain records of all incoming and outgoing stock. These records can be used to check against a physical stock check and inspection. Stock checks should be made frequently. Establish this procedure from the outset. Any discrepancies in recorded and actual stock levels should be fully investigated and necessary action should be taken to prevent a recurrence. Staff will recognize that their work and the stock is regularly monitored. For the first month, do a regular weekly check and an occasional random or unannounced check.

The complexity of the stores record system will depend upon the type of store (large stores for bulky items, such as food or blankets, or small stores for engineering spares). Adapt the following to suit the type of store:

- Stock control ledger – shows receipts and issues, sources or destinations, quantities and item descriptions. Each entry should be cross referenced to the corresponding official receipt/issue voucher or waybill.
- Store card – should be established for every item held in stock. Receipts and issues should be recorded and a current balance shown (see Figure 7.4).

<table>
<tr><td colspan="4">STORE CARD
Minimum quantity:</td><td colspan="3">Card no:_______
Units/Package/Item Code:</td></tr>
<tr><td>Init. by</td><td>Date</td><td>Received from/ Issued to</td><td>Location stack or bin no.</td><td>Amount received</td><td>Amount issued</td><td>Balance</td></tr>
<tr><td></td><td></td><td></td><td></td><td></td><td></td><td></td></tr>
<tr><td></td><td></td><td></td><td></td><td></td><td></td><td></td></tr>
</table>

Figure 7.4 An example of a store card
Adapted from UNHCR (1989)

- Stack record card (or bin record card for spare parts) – should be affixed to each stack or bin in the store, giving a description of the item and location, receipts, issues, the current balance and initials. If the stack is made up of food items, the reverse of the card can be used to record any treatments (fumigations etc.).
- Stores inspection record – should be completed every time the senior storekeeper completes an inspection.
- Monthly summary report – should be provided by the senior storekeeper. It should include details on current stock levels, total receipts and issues for each line item, and any significant actions taken during the period. It should also include information on necessary repairs and supply re-orders.

Receiving and issuing goods

- All arriving consignments must be counted and inspected during unloading. Check for damage.
- Quantities received should tally with the waybill or packing list. If there is evidence of tampering, carefully inspect for missing contents.
- Record quantities received and any damaged or missing items.
- Ensure that porters handle and stack goods (especially food and cement bags) such that damage is minimized.
- On issuing consignments, drivers are responsible for counting packages onto their vehicles. The storekeeper should observe the vehicles being loaded and ensure that drivers sign to acknowledge receipt of goods.
- Issue vouchers should be in triplicate:
  - One for you as manager.
  - One for the storekeeper.
  - One for the receiver, to be signed and sent back with the driver.
- Rubber stamps are useful as they are difficult to forge and officials like to see lots of stamps and signatures.

Stock control

Build in plenty of contingency for delays and problems. Two important stock-keeping rules are given in Box 7.1.

Box 7.1 Stock-keeping rules

80/20 rule	20 per cent of stock items will be used 80 per cent of the time and 80 per cent used only 20 per cent of the time.
A.B.C. rule	Place stock items into three categories: A = Items critical to the functioning of the project (e.g. spare generator) B = 20 per cent of items (80/20 rule) C = Remainder

Examples of 'A' category items include diesel injectors for an engine or impellers for a water pump, as they are critical items. Although not often replaced, it is essential that these items are carried in stock, as without them the machines will not function.

In the 'B' category, if you are running diesel engines on your programme, oil filters will certainly fall into the 20 per cent of items in your store which will be used 80 per cent of the time. Split the stock of filters in two separate parts of the store and only allow issues from one 'bin' at a time. At the bottom of the bin should be a card saying 'Place order and start using other bin'. When the first bin is empty, start using the other bin and place an order for more oil filters. This should be timed so that the new order arrives before the second bin is empty. In this way, the system is simple and self-triggering. The manager should ensure that there is adequate liaison between all staff; for example, the vehicle workshop and stores.

Manual or computerized system

Locally employed staff are more likely to be familiar with paper record systems and will adapt easily to a new manual paper system. However, keep manual systems as simple as possible. Documents must be easily understood by all who use them. Ideally everyone involved in the system should understand why it is necessary, how it works and why they are keeping the records they are being asked to keep. Overprint records with the local language.

Use of computers for stock control and stores management should be avoided. They are liable to damage or breakage due to dust, poor handling, and so on and there is a significant risk of theft.

7.5.2 Storage of specialist items

Dangerous items include fuels, explosives, compressed gases, insecticides, pesticides and other flammable, chlorine-based, toxic or corrosive substances. They should be be supplied with markings denoting the nature of the hazard and warning instructions regarding their handling and storage. Ensure that these warnings are heeded.

- Warn staff of the dangers associated with the goods.
- Stack with due care.
- Store flammable substances away from the main building, and prohibit smoking or open flames within 10 metres of the storage area. Have fire extinguishers available nearby. Sand and blankets can be used to help extinguish fires.
- Volatile substances which vaporize easily must be kept cool.
- Never store chemicals or cement in the same store as food.

High value and non-flammable hazardous goods should be stored in a separate lockable area within the main store. A simple structure can be constructed for this purpose.

Medical supplies should be carefully managed. This must be done in close consultation with the medical team working on the programme. Antibiotics and vaccines require temperature-controlled storage (see Section 7.3.3). Other drugs and supplies can be of a very high value and have a short shelf life. Lock drugs away in a safe room such as a cargo container.

7.5.3 Goods handling equipment

Preparations

Before arrival of heavy or bulky items, consider how they are going to be unloaded. Accidents can happen in the rush and enthusiasm to unload long-awaited and essential items. Truck drivers want to off-load as soon as possible and be away back home. Safety should be high on the agenda whether loading or unloading.

Be safety minded

Preparations and procedures for unloading include:

- Prepare a good site for the vehicle to park. Use topography to your advantage, build ramps or dips if needed. Make sure there is good grip underfoot. Prepare any lifting tackle over the parking area.
- Know the type of vehicle coming. Is it closed or open?
- Keep onlookers well away from the area.
- The driver will definitely be in a rush, but do not let haste compromise safety. Better to pay an extra day's hire than to have a serious accident.

Use the following as a guide for safe manual handling:

- 25 kg maximum safe lift per person.
- 200 kg maximum crate weight.
- 1.5 m × 1.5 m × 1.5 m maximum crate size.

Manual equipment

Frequently, heavy items, such as generators, need to be manually handled. Labour for these tasks is usually readily available, but caution must be taken when handling heavy individual items. Simple techniques and equipment can be used to reduce the burden on labourers. Equipment such as ropes, pulleys, chain blocks and tripods will be useful (see Appendix 19). If a particularly heavy item is to be unloaded, a tripod and pulley can be used to lift the item off the bed of the truck whilst the truck drives away. The item is then lowered straight on to the ground. Once on the ground, it can be manoeuvred by using rollers made of short trees or poles and hand winches ('Tirfors').

Consider the use of ramps, either by building a ramp up to the height of the vehicle or by digging out a slope and reversing the vehicle down (see 17.2.4, Figure 17.5).

As a last resort, some items can be dropped off trucks. If this really has to be done, make sure that there is something on the ground to break the fall, such as old tyres. The item can be anchored to a tree, vehicle or other fixed object while the truck drives slowly away. Try to ensure that the item falls squarely to the ground. *Never use this method for unloading any piece of equipment such as a generator, which may be damaged in the fall.*

Powered equipment

Winches Winches are useful for dragging and lowering equipment. If used in conjunction with tripods and pulleys they can also lift heavy items, in which case they should be fitted with a brake. Drum winches mounted to the front of vehicles are useful for handling heavy items in the field. Ensure that the weight of the load is less than that of the vehicle. Attend to the condition and rating of the wire rope. The rope should be rated well above the capacity of the winch. Do not let people stand in the path of the rope and prevent anyone from touching the drum itself whilst in use.

Forklift A forklift may be essential when unloading transport aircraft or when handling heavy palleted items. If large volumes of goods are being handled on a regular basis, buy a forklift. For short-term use, see if one can be hired.

The standard forklift needs a flat, even surface. For rough terrain (such as a temporary warehouse or airstrip) a construction site forklift is more appropriate. Use Box 7.2 as a guide for specifying a forklift.

Box 7.2 Items to consider when specifying forklifts

Maximum weight to be lifted.
Maximum lift height.
Minimum height clearance (e.g. in warehouse).
Type of engine – depends on warehouse ventilation and available fuel.
Wheel base: long (more stable) or short (more manoeuvrable).
Number of wheels – 4 is better than 3.
Tyres – specify pneumatic not cushion.
Attachments: fork extender is useful for aircraft; single spike; 3-hook jib; backhoe.

Hydraulic loaders These are cranes, mounted on the back of trucks, for self unloading. If available, they are very useful for unloading heavy items. A vehicle with a hydraulic loader can park next to a loaded vehicle and unload within the crane's reach. If available, hire hydraulic loaders if heavy items are being transported and handled.

Ordering powered handling equipment Before ordering any equipment, be sure that it is necessary. Know where it will work and ensure that an appropriate model is ordered. If using powered handling equipment, order surplus capacity, as the programme will become dependent upon the equipment. As with all mechanical equipment, consider maintenance requirements and order spares. Hydraulic machines need to be maintained in dust-free environments. If hydraulic machines are ordered or provided, always make sure that a good spares package is provided, including pipes, seals and fluids.

8 Telecommunications

8.1 Introduction

Emergency programmes are dependent upon good communications for security, logistics and programming. The most suitable communication system(s) for a particular programme will depend upon:

- Communication distance (the next town or thousands of kilometres).
- Communication method (voice, fax, data, etc).
- Communication within or external to the organization (e.g. partner agencies).
- Security of communications if working in an insecure environment.
- Budget: for capital and running costs.

The most common options are:

- Landline telephone.
- Mobile telephone.
- VHF radio network of base station and hand-held type for communication over short distances.
- HF (also called Short Wave) radio for longer distance communication.
- Satellite telephones for rapid set-up and more secure global communications.

A multi-layered approach to communication can provide e-mail, fax, voice and telephone capability. The capability and cost of equipment available to relief agencies are changing all the time. But whatever the technology the human factor remains vital in any communications network. The most advanced system in the world is useless if it cannot be set up and operated properly. Therefore, the training of staff in the correct use of equipment is essential.

The nature of emergencies requires communications systems to be set up quickly and to be flexible for easy expansion. Emergency satellite communications are highly mobile and quick and easy to set up. For this reason it is worthwhile considering a phased approach using satellite communications initially and phasing in radio which is cheaper to operate but not as quick and easy to install. In insecure environments, satellite communications can complement and provide a relatively secure back-up to the radio system.

8.2 Safety first

Telecommunications equipment is powered by electricity and electricity can kill! Refer to Section 16.1.2 in the chapter on 'Electrical plant' for guidelines on safety and safety rules for working with electricity. In particular, when working with telecommunications equipment, take note of the following:

Electric shock Attend an appropriate first aid course and display a poster showing what to do in the case of electric shock. Consult the guidelines for dealing with a casualty given in Section 16.1.2.

Installation Obtain and consult the installation notes that should have come with the equipment. If you do not feel competent then consult a suitably qualified electrician or colleagues in other agencies who do know.

Isolating switch All electrical circuits should have a means of isolation. In a radio room arrange for all equipment to be supplied from one isolation switch (providing the load is within the limits of the supply). The whole station can then be made safe quickly in case of malfunction or fire.

Earthing All items of equipment must be separately earthed. This can be done using their individual mains cable earth wires or by bonding the metal cases of all equipment to earth using a suitable wire. It can be highly dangerous to use equipment that has not been correctly earthed. If a reliable mains earth is unavailable then drive a metal stake, preferably copper, at least one metre into damp ground and use this as a station earth.

Wiring It is good practice to use double insulated cable no matter what voltage is carried. It is a legal requirement in many countries on any voltages above 25 V. All cables must be terminated with suitable connectors at each end. Cables should not pose a tripping or overhead hazard. Overhead cables need to be at least 3.5 metres above ground, where people are present, and at least 6 metres where vehicles may pass. For a long overhead span, a suspension wire should be used to relieve strain on the supply cable.

Antennas Antenna wires are thin and practically invisible, especially at night, and so if they are placed near the ground they can severely injure someone. The wires may also be carrying dangerous voltages. If it is impossible to elevate the wires out of the way then make them visible: attach flags of tape or string along the hazardous length. Temporary structures (masts) installed in field conditions are often not as stable as permanent masts. Avoid having people working (or camping) within the 'fall-over' area.

Radio frequency hazards The non-ionizing radiation emitted by antennas will affect the human body above certain power density levels. The eyes and the genitals are particularly sensitive. Do not use handheld radios that have damaged antennas or if the 'bobble' at the top of the antenna is missing. Satellite terminals pose a hazard. The energy density from the antenna is particularly high and it is focused in one direction. The antenna should have a radiation hazard notice on it advising a 'safe' distance – take account of this when setting up the antenna and warn others in the vicinity.

Working at heights In the rush of a relief mission it may be tempting to take unnecessary risks: to use makeshift ladders, walk on weak roofs and so on. Take extreme care. Consider the consequences of you being on the elevated structure when it fails! Trees are useful alternative masts. Standing on roofs in areas where security is an issue can make you a target.

Lightning protection Antennas erected in the open and as high as possible will generally transmit the most efficiently. However, the antenna then becomes a potential lightning conductor. Unfortunately there is no simple rule that can be applied to relieve the situation. Precautions that can be taken include: masts and the outer conductor of coaxial cable can be bonded to earth *outside* the building, This also helps in reducing the build up of static electricity. To achieve adequate protection requires large diameter cables and an extensive earth system which is not achievable in the 'field' environment. As a *minimum* the antenna should be provided with a bond wire of at least 1.5 mm^2 cross sectional area. Bond this to any buried metallic water pipes (NOT gas pipes!). Alternatively, use earth-spikes driven into the ground. Realistically however, this kind of earthing system will suffice for static discharge but will not protect against a lightning strike. To be safe, in the event of lightning, abandon the radio room. Do not be tempted to remove or handle electrical connections as lethal static voltages could be present. Equipment is replaceable, people are not.

8.3 Frequency, wavelength and physical effects

There is a fixed relationship between the frequency and the wavelength of a radio wave. Radio waves travel at the speed of light (about 300 million metres / second).

The free space relationship for radio waves becomes:

300 000 000/frequency = wavelength

Table 8.1 Frequency ranges for radio transmission

300 kHz–3 MHz	Medium frequency and medium wave broadcasting
3–30 MHz	High frequency (HF) long distance and long range mobile communications
30–300 MHz	Very High Frequency (VHF) short range and mobile communications
300 MHz–3 GHz	Ultra High Frequency (UHF) short range mobile communications, point to point links, commercial operators (e.g. taxis)
3–30 GHz	(SHF) point to point links, radar, satellite communications

Radio waves are affected by the environment and medium through which they travel:

- Waves are *absorbed* when they pass through objects like buildings, trees and the ground.
- Waves are *refracted* when they pass through materials of varying density like the atmosphere (this effect increases the radio horizon because the radio waves are refracted downwards as they pass through the atmosphere).
- *Diffraction* occurs when a wave passes over the edge of an obstacle and some of its energy is bent in the direction of the obstacle.
- *Reflection* occurs when waves encounter surfaces along their path.

The combined effect of all these mechanisms is to provide what is called *multi-path* propagation. This can be advantageous as signals may be received in places where they would not otherwise reach. Conversely, the multi-path signals may cancel each other and no signal will be detected. It is for this reason that the signal strength can sometimes be improved by moving either the transmitter or receiver. For VHF communications this may be as little as a few centimetres. For HF moving a few metres is usually adequate.

Noise from natural or manmade sources, such as static from thunderstorms, will also affect the quality of the radio signal. When using radio 'on the move' the combined effects of all the above may appear in rapid succession resulting in a fluctuation in signal level and quality.

8.4 Radio equipment selection

Radio equipment is expensive and mistakes during specification and installation should be avoided. When selecting radio equipment, it is best to decide what is required of the system and then take this information to a communications specialist for advice. Specific makes and models are not as important as compatibility with existing equipment. It is well worth getting a specialist to install the system and train people how to use and maintain it properly.

The information a specialist needs to know:

- Which frequency ranges are required? Which frequencies do other agencies use? Which frequency will you be permitted to use? Which is the best frequency for the area?
- What distances are involved? Short distances around town, long distances across a country or global communications to HQ?
- The number of people requiring hand held sets; the number of car-mounted mobile sets; the number of base stations.
- Intermittent or continuous use.
- Type of use and therefore how rugged the equipment needs to be.
- Currently available and planned power supply.
- What technical support is available? Are spare parts available locally? Is there a local agent and is the agent competent?

8.5 VHF (Very High Frequency) radio

VHF radio (30–300 MHz) is normally used for local communication (e.g. around a town or a refugee camp) although the use of repeaters can vastly increase the range (see below). Manufacturers and suppliers of commercial VHF equipment include: Motorola, Yaesu, and Icom.

Good VHF communication requires 'line of sight' between transmitter and receiver. An obstacle will inhibit the strength of the signal. Buildings in a town will greatly weaken a signal and a hill will absorb it.

Typical VHF radio range:

- Handheld to handheld – about 5 km depending on terrain.
- Vehicle to vehicle – about 20 km depending on terrain.
- Vehicle to base – about 30 km depending on terrain.
- Base to base – about 50 km depending on terrain.

To improve VHF transmission and reception:

- Transmit from a high point.
- Mount antennas as high as possible e.g. on the roof of buildings, at the top of a mast, on the roof of a car.
- If in a car, drive out of valleys or areas with significant obstacles to a direct signal path.

The effective range of VHF radios can be significantly increased by using repeaters. A repeater receives on one frequency and re-transmits on another at a higher power. This is sometimes referred to as a duplex system whereas transmission and reception on the same frequency is a simplex system. A repeater sited on top of a hill or a building can command a much greater area than a radio located in a valley or in the centre of a town among buildings. Repeaters need a power supply and many rely upon solar-charged batteries. There is a danger, therefore, that a duplex system used heavily at night could run out of power until recharged again during the day.

Squelch is a method of filtering out the 'noise' or hiss which can overlay transmissions. The squelch facility is normally automatic on modern radios although squelch can be switched on or off on some radios.

Channel scanning allows several channels to be constantly monitored. This can be useful when working on an inter-agency basis and in an insecure environment.

8.6 HF (High Frequency) radio

HF radio (3–30 MHz) provides medium to long range communications for voice, data, e-mail and fax messages.

HF radio transceivers can be base stations or vehicle-mounted mobile sets. Manufacturers and suppliers of commercial grade HF equipment include: Codan, Barrett, Icom, Yaesu.

The required signal is superimposed on a carrier wave by a process called 'modulation'. The most commonly used HF carrier wave is Single Side Band

(SSB). SSB reduces the power required to send a signal and uses only half the radio bandwidth which allows more channels for communication within the HF spectrum. Communications may be on Upper Side Band (USB) or Lower Side Band (LSB). There is sometimes a control to switch from USB to LSB.

Figure 8.1 illustrates how HF radio waves are propagated.

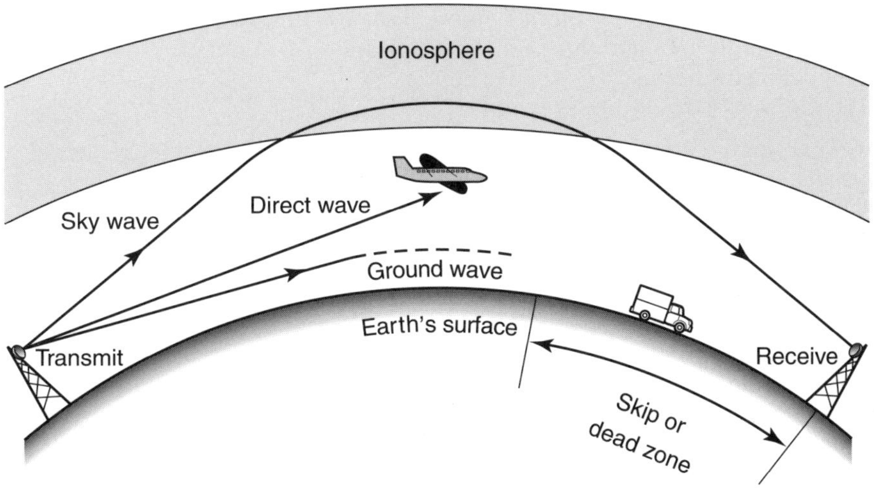

Figure 8.1 High frequency radio transmission

- The ground wave travels close to the Earth's surface and is attenuated by ground absorption and diffraction.
- The direct, or space wave, travels between transmitter and receiver directly and by ground or object reflection.
- The sky wave is reflected by the ionosphere.

The degree of reflection will depend on frequency and the density and height of the ionosphere which will vary according to the time of day, the season and the activity of the sun. Generally, low HF frequencies will tend to be absorbed by the ionosphere and high HF frequencies will tend to pass straight through.

To be able to maintain good communications throughout the day and night it may be necessary to switch between three or four frequencies to cope with the varying conditions. General rules of thumb for HF communications:

- The higher the sun, the higher the frequency.
- The greater the distance, the higher the frequency

It can often occur that mobile radio communication can be maintained for several kilometres from the base station using the ground wave but as the vehicle continues this signal fades and the sky wave has not yet been reached (see Figure 8.1). The vehicle has entered the 'skip zone' which is an area where radio communication with the current equipment set up is not possible. If it is important to be able to communicate in this zone then adjustments should be made. Changes to the orientation of the antenna can make a significant difference but it is advisable to seek specialist advice.

Typical HF radio ranges:

Vehicle to vehicle – about 50 km on groundwave then there may be a dead zone (skip zone) until the sky wave becomes useable up to hundreds of kilometres.

Base to vehicle as for vehicle to vehicle.

Base to base range on ground wave – about 100 km, then dead zone until sky wave is useable. Range can then be thousands of kilometres depending on ionospheric conditions.

HF radio features typically include:

- An automated facility to determine the most suitable available frequency at a particular time of day or night.
- Channel scanning to monitor a range of frequencies.
- Selective calling (Selcall) allows an operator to call a single transceiver by transmitting a coded signal. There are several benefits to Selcall which include individual calling; base and mobiles can be muted as the radio will only respond to a specific Selcall; confirmation of a call being received; identification of caller; unattended operation; and emergency Selcall which activates a predetermined calling sequence in an emergency.
- GPS tracking and mapping involves connecting a GPS receiver to the HF radio. It is then possible to poll (call) the radio to identify its location.

8.7 Antennas

The correct design, erection and orientation of an antenna is crucial for efficient transmission. Antennas resonate at the frequency of transmission. Except for a few special cases all antennas are limited to their design frequency plus or minus a few per cent. Using an antenna outside its design parameters may produce harmful voltages or currents at the radio equipment antenna terminals. Damage to the equipment may result.

The height of an antenna above ground directly affects how much voltage is induced from the electric field of a radio wave, particularly for HF radio. In practice, doubling the height can double the received signal strength.

For most practical purposes mobile antennas are vertical. However, it is impractical to size them at the optimum length as they would be far too long. Therefore, they tend to be about two metres in length and either pre-tuned to a particular frequency by a coil within the antenna or tuned using an electronic antenna tuning unit (ATU).

8.8 Satellite communications

There are a number of current and planned providers of satellite communications. The longest running provider is Inmarsat which was established as a joint co-operative venture of governments but is now a privatized company. About 40 land earth stations (LES) around the world link Inmarsat satellites with international telecommunications networks. LESs are owned by independent telecommunications operators. Coverage is most of the world except the poles.

Inmarsat provide a range of communication systems. Individual manufacturers supply the 'satphone' hardware for access to these systems.

- The 'A' system is the original analogue service providing phone, telex, fax and data.
- The 'B' system was the digital successor to the 'A' service, offering a similar range of services but at lower cost. Supports high speed data services up to 64 kbps and connection into international ISDN networks. Can be used for telepresence and telemedicine using video and data communications.
- The 'C' system is a store and forward messaging, data, telex and email service. Often used in road transport management, it has been used for the monitoring and management of aid vehicles and convoys.
- The 'D+' system is very compact (personal CD player size) and provides global two-way data communications. With an integrated GPS facility it can be used for vehicle and container tracking and tracing.
- The 'M' system is a digital voice, low-speed data and fax service.

The 'mini M' phone is a compact successor to the 'M' system providing the same services but in a smaller package weighing about 2 kg and the size of a laptop computer. This has been the most common 'satphone' used in emergency relief. It is quick and easy to set up and use.

Inmarsat's fourth generation satellite network, the Broadband Global Area Network (B-GAN), will enable the delivery of internet and intranet content, video, fax, e-mail, voice and LAN access at speeds up to 432 kbps. The network is planned to be operational in 2004.

Other systems are providing a variety of services including multi-mode cellular and satellite hand-held phones. Globalstar is a consortium of international telecommunications companies providing multiple services. Globalstar's 48 low-earth-orbiting (LEO) satellites link into existing fixed and cellular telephone networks.

8.9 Radio operation

Digital and HF radio systems should be separated as they and their associated cables can interfere with each other. Avoid, for example, positioning satellite terminals (digital) adjacent to HF radios. Generally, try to keep communications equipment some distance away from general office equipment.

Radio conversations are not like telephone conversations. The listening station cannot interrupt a transmission if they do not understand a point and only one user can transmit a radio message at any one time. Therefore, keep radio use to a minimum and keep transmissions short. This can take discipline and practice but writing messages down beforehand can help.

Call signs are used to identify the caller and the station or individual to be called. In situations where security is an issue they should not refer to specific people or places but be anonymous to the casual listener. Letters of the phonetic alphabet (Box 8.1) are often adopted as call signs. For example: 'Romeo, this is Juliet'.

Box 8.1 Phonetic alphabet

Alpha	**F**oxtrot	**K**ilo	**P**apa	**U**niform
Bravo	**G**olf	**L**ima	**Q**uebec	**V**ictor
Charlie	**H**otel	**M**ike	**R**omeo	**W**hiskey
Delta	**I**ndia	**N**ovember	**S**ierra	**X**-ray
Echo	**J**uliet	**O**scar	**T**ango	**Y**ankee
				Zulu

Poor reception and misunderstood messages can cause a great deal of confusion. Use standard procedural words ('pro-words') (Box 8.2) and the internationally recognized phonetic alphabet to spell long or difficult words.

Box 8.2 Procedural words

Hello – *the 'alert'*
Go ahead – *I am ready*
Roger – *I understand*
Over – *invitation for you to transmit*
Out – *I am closing down (returning to listening)*
Standby – *wait while I deal with your request*
Repeat – *I will repeat the last message (do not use in a conflict zone as this can mean 'fire again' to the military!)*

Wait – *I am busy*
Listening – *I am prepared to take calls*
Say again –
Say all after –
Say all before –
Spell (I Spell) – *words requiring phonetic spelling*
Message – *I have a message that requires writing down*

It is advisable to keep a notebook by each radio and a log of all incoming and outgoing messages. This can help to record transmission problems and monitor the best frequencies for different times of the day.

Security

Radio transmissions are not private. Anyone with a suitable receiver can listen. Therefore, exercise sensitivity when discussing programme matters. Do not transmit politically sensitive information. Take care when discussing the movement of money or supplies and when cars or personnel are travelling. Code words and phrases are used by agencies to make messages more secure. Codes are used, for example, for the names of agencies, locations, times, types of people, security incidents, etc. However, avoid a long list of codes or complex codes as they can become confusing and impractical.

Digital satellite communications are inherently secure between the satphone, via a satellite, to a land earth station (LES) or another satphone. However, once calls enter an LES and public telephone network they are open to eavesdropping. A way to maintain confidentiality is to use encryption for which similar encryption devices will be required at each end of the communication link. However, most relief agencies in most situations will want to maintain transparency of operations and the use of encryption may not be appropriate.

Power supply

In a relief or remote situation the regular provision of electric power is uncertain. Batteries (12 V) are often used as the main power source or as a back-up. There are several options for recharging: a running vehicle, solar power or a generator. Batteries need maintenance – even 'maintenance-free' batteries! Very expensive radio equipment can be made useless because someone forgot to top up the battery with distilled water. Keep terminals clean, protect them from damp by coating with Vaseline, or special grease, and check they are tight. Inverters can supply 'mains voltage' from 12 V batteries to office and radio equipment.

Inter-agency communications

There are major advantages to sharing communication facilities with other agencies. This can be from sharing frequencies, for low levels of radio traffic, to network equipment and telecommunications expertise. One VHF repeater, for example, established in a good location can provide a service for several agencies. The cost of providing a repeater, peripheral power equipment, mast and a technician can be shared by each agency.

8.10 Legal issues

Given the sensitivity of communications systems it is advisable to obtain the correct permissions before transmissions begin. The permission may be in the form of a licence to operate or permission to transmit. It can be difficult to obtain permission quickly. The Tampere Convention of 1998 on the 'Provision of Telecommunication Resources for Disaster Mitigation and Relief Operations' includes article 9 on *Regulatory Barriers* in which states are urged 'to reduce or remove regulatory barriers to the use of telecommunication resources for disaster mitigation and relief'.

The government department responsible for telecommunications generally has responsibility for issuing licences. The ministry with responsibility for the emergency may be willing to facilitate the process. Likewise, the UN lead agency may be able to assist. When applying for an operating licence be prepared to provide technical specifications for the equipment you are planning to use. Some countries will only allow single frequencies and so will not allow the use of multi-frequency, user programmable equipment. Find out this kind of information before ordering any equipment. If international communications are necessary, special permissions may be required from both countries.

9 Environmental health

Emergencies due to drought, famine, and conflict, often result in the displacement of people who may become refugees or find themselves in overcrowded refugee-like situations. Environmental health problems can quickly arise both in these situations, and in the aftermath of sudden impact disasters such as earthquakes and floods. The measures considered in this chapter are of relevance to a range of disaster situations.

This chapter provides guidelines on the establishment of an environmental health programme and on methods of hygiene promotion. Detailed guidelines on specific engineering measures will be found in the following chapters:

Chapter 10 – Environmental sanitation: excreta disposal, sullage, refuse disposal, the disposal of dead bodies, and insects and rodents.
Chapter 11 – Emergency water supply.
Chapter 12 – Water source development.
Chapter 13 – Water storage, treatment and distribution.

9.1 Priorities

9.1.1 The health of a disaster-affected population

One of the most important tasks of engineers and other relief workers is to improve the standards of environmental health. This may involve the provision of improved sanitation, adequate water supplies, and decent shelter. It may also involve the promotion of improved hygiene practices. At the very least, specialist relief workers, such as engineers, should be aware of all the elements of an environmental health programme and work closely with the affected population, administrators, and health workers.

Displacement and health

The impact of displacement on people's health will depend on a number of factors, including their condition prior to becoming displaced, the effects of migration, and the prevalence of disease at their point of arrival. People may not have been previously exposed to certain diseases and may therefore lack immunity. Rural people may find themselves living in overcrowded settlements with the unfamiliar problems of high density living. Displaced town dwellers, who may have previously enjoyed safe piped water supplies, urban sanitation and relatively comprehensive health services, may have to adjust to a lower standard of amenities.

The range of health problems found in displaced populations is often similar to that occurring in many poor communities in the world. Common problems include diarrhoea, nutritional deficiencies, pneumonia and other respiratory infections, malaria, worms, anaemia, tuberculosis, measles, eye and skin infections, and genito-urinary problems. Although epidemics occur relatively infrequently, outbreaks of diseases such as measles or cholera pose a serious threat.

The range of health problems commonly encountered in emergencies is demonstrated by the example shown in Figure 9.1. It indicates the major causes of death of children (one of the most vulnerable groups) in a refugee camp in the Horn of Africa.

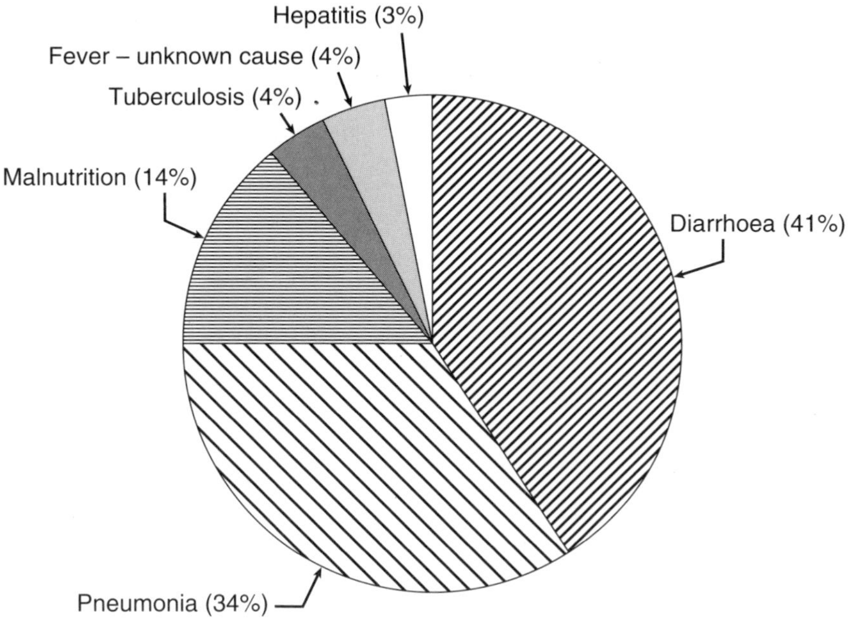

Figure 9.1 The major reported causes of death in children under 5 years Hartisheik A Camp, eastern Ethiopia, 1989

Source: SCF(UK)/UNHCR/Ethiopian MoH and ARA, 1989

The three main causes of death indicated in Figure 9.1 – diarrhoea, pneumonia and malnutrition – which accounted for 89 per cent of all deaths, are typical of many emergencies.

People's susceptibility to infection varies, but it is likely to be greater in the very young and the old, in the malnourished, and in people who are already weak. The malnutrition/infection cycle is particularly evident in malnourished children, who often suffer from diarrhoea, which in turn exacerbates malnutrition. Respiratory infections, such as pneumonia, may lead to malnutrition, especially in cold, wet conditions where shelter is poor.

Environmental diseases

Diseases caused by poor environmental conditions are frequently related to the faecal–oral route of contamination. Figure 9.2 illustrates the important routes

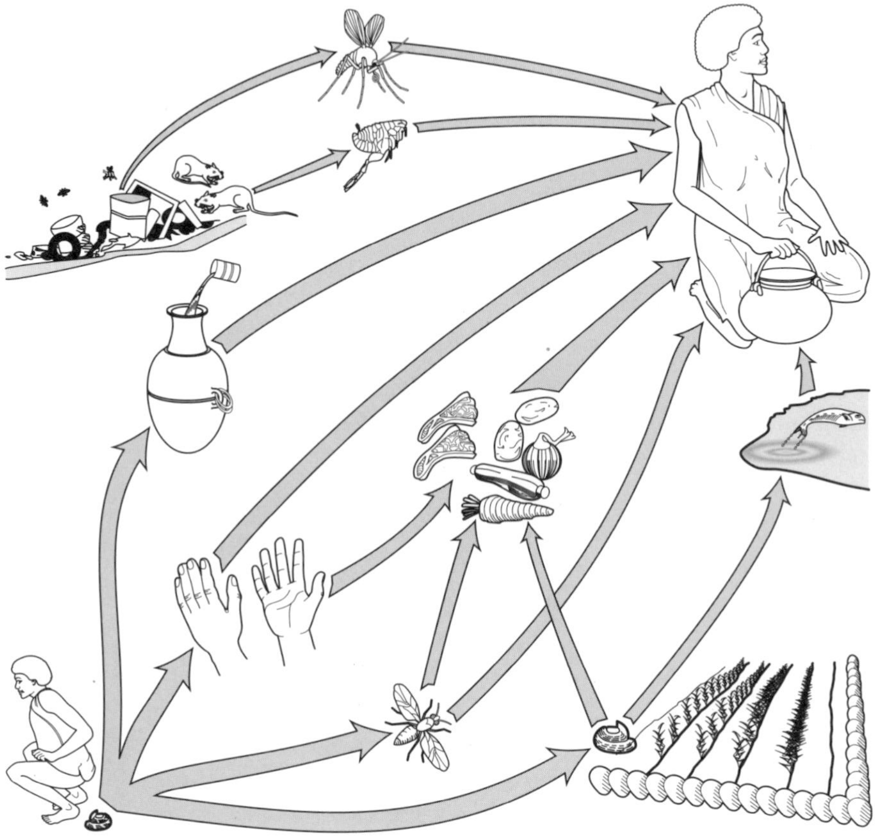

Figure 9.2 Important disease transmission routes related to poor environmental sanitation

by which faeces reach the mouth and the way in which the poor disposal of rubbish can create breeding sites for mosquitoes and attract rodents that may harbour disease transmitting fleas.

Environmental diseases of particular importance in emergencies include:

- Faecal–oral diseases, including most of the diarrhoeas. These diseases can be caused by drinking contaminated water, by poor personal hygiene (dirty hands) and by poor food hygiene (cooking, contamination by flies). These diseases can be particularly virulent in overcrowded unsanitary conditions and are frequently the major causes of illness and death in epidemics.
- Soil-transmitted diseases, such as roundworm, where the soil is contaminated by human excreta. These diseases are not usually critical in the short term.
- Water-based diseases, such as schistosomiasis, where the disease vector is present in water contaminated by human excreta. This disease is not critical in the short term.

- Shelter-related diseases, such as pneumonia, where people become more susceptible to infection due to being cold and wet. These diseases can be very important in the short term.
- Diseases caused by insect and rodent vectors, including water-related diseases, such as malaria. Malaria requires the presence of water for the disease vector, the mosquito, to breed. It can quickly cause illness and death.

Excreta is a major source of disease unless there is a barrier to the faecal–oral route. Urine is considerably less dangerous than faeces and is usually sterile, although it can contain certain pathogens. These are either uncommon or require an aquatic intermediate host before they can infect humans (as with schistosomiasis). It is usually sufficient to prevent urination into water courses.

9.1.2 Environmental health controls

Environmental controls aim to prevent infection by interrupting the routes of disease transmission (Figure 9.2). Vaccination complements environmental controls and gives additional protection by improving a person's ability to withstand disease once infected. The number of possible routes of infection mean that a range of measures is necessary to interrupt transmission. The measures require outside intervention, such as those of an engineering nature, and individual action, such as the maintenance of good personal hygiene. For example, an engineer can ensure that water emerging from the tap is safe to drink, but the user must handle the water properly after collection to prevent contamination before it is consumed. A selection of engineering and personal measures required to control the transmission of environmentally related diseases is shown in Table 9.1. Engineering interventions to provide good sanitation facilities must be complemented by health promotion and education so that people take the required measures in personal hygiene.

Environmental measures required to control infectious diseases include:

- The provision of an adequate quantity of water.
- The provision and consumption of water of an acceptable quality.
- The safe containment or disposal of excreta.
- The promotion of appropriate hygienic practices. Such practices often require an increased use of water.
- The provision of adequate shelter, including blankets.
- The maintenance of a sanitary environment.

Note that improvements in water and sanitation often reduce the severity of a disease more than its incidence.

9.1.3 Establishing an environmental health programme

An environmental health programme may be planned and implemented by a single agency working with the affected community or by a public health coordinating committee representing several agencies, government departments

Table 9.1 Control of environmental diseases

Type of disease	*Personal measures:* Drink safe water / *Engineering measures:* Provide safe water (quality)	Dispose of excreta safely / Control defecation, provide latrines	Wash and clean regularly / Provide enough water (quantity)	Store and cook food properly / Provide cooking utensils, fuel etc.	Dispose of wastewater safely / Ensure adequate drainage
Faecal–oral:					
○ Water-borne*	●●●	●●●	–	●●	–
○ Water-scarce* (e.g. diarrhoeas)	–	●●●	●●●	–	–
Skin/eye infections					
○ Water-scarce*	–	–	●●●	–	●
Excreta-related:					
○ Water-based* (e.g. schistosomiasis)	●●	●●●	–	–	–
Water-related* (e.g. malaria)	–	–	–	–	●
Soil-based	–	●●	●	●●	–
Food-based	–	●●	●●●	●●●	–

**Water-borne:* pathogens in water which is swallowed; *Water-scarce:* personal hygiene affected by lack of water; *Water-based:* pathogens infect humans through contact with water; *Water-related:* spread by vectors (e.g. mosquitoes) which live near or breed in water.
Importance of measures: ●●● High ● Low

and the affected community. The planning, personnel, and methods used will vary, but a similar approach is appropriate in each case.

- Identify the needs and establish priorities, by carrying out an assessment (see Chapter 5).
- Identify the resources needed to deal with these needs (staff, time, skills, equipment, materials, funds).
- Prepare an outline plan. Details can be filled in later.
- Begin implementation as soon as possible. Adopt a staged approach. Start with minimum levels and plan to upgrade later.
- Set up an effective reporting system and ensure it is used. Monitor progress, using appropriate indicators (see Chapter 5). Evaluate the programme and revise as necessary.

Establish a programme of action to deal with the environmental health problems that might arise. Base it on a clear identification of existing and likely future problems and the most appropriate ways of solving them.

Identify the needs and establish priorities

Establish a small team for field work: counterpart, translator, driver and assistants. The size of the team will depend on the situation and the scale of the problem but it should be small enough to establish quickly and to manage easily.

Carry out an initial rapid survey (see Box 9.1). Talk to key people about current and potential health problems. Contact government and relief agency health service staff, leaders and selected members of the community. Observe the terrain, soils, the state of the environment and people's hygiene behaviour. Do not concentrate only on the technical factors. For example, the choice and development of a poor water source may seem an engineering problem, but what are the broader factors affecting a water supply? Culturally, it may not be possible to share an alternative safer source with other people for reasons such as religion or class. Politically, the use of a source by displaced people may create friction with existing users. Environmentally, a source may be of very poor quality and economically it may cost too much to treat, or the treatment technology may not be available.

Box 9.1 Checklist for an initial rapid field survey

- Identify and contact community leaders and local authority officials.
- How many people are affected by the emergency?
- Does a health information system exist which can give disease specific morbidity and mortality data?
  - If people are ill – why are they ill?
  - If people are dying – what are they dying from?
- What are the current, or likely, diseases related to the environment?
- Are people living in overcrowded conditions?
- Do people have adequate shelter?
- Existing defecation – is it hygienic and safe?
- Existing water supply – is it enough and safe to drink?
- Personal hygiene – do people have the means to keep themselves clean?
- Drainage – is there ponding and flooding, or the potential for flooding?
- Is solid waste a problem?
- What is the current and potential risk of the spread of disease by insect and rodent vectors?
- Is there a health risk due to livestock numbers and habits?
- Is there a health risk related to the disposal of dead bodies?
- Who are the government departments and other agencies working in the environmental health sector?

Methods of gathering information: Observation and interviews with the people affected (women, men and children), community leaders, local authorities, medical personnel, and other humanitarian agencies.

It will not be possible, and probably not desirable, to give equal emphasis to solving all the identified problems simultaneously. Prioritize actions in an ordered way. Give priority to establishing a minimum level of service necessary to sustain minimum levels of health. Improve the level of service later as time and resources allow. For example, it may be necessary to restrict defecation to certain areas (defecation fields) as an interim measure before latrines can be built.

Prioritize – and revise – control measures by regularly monitoring disease incidence and severity. Liaise with health workers to monitor disease. For example, if the incidence of diarrhoea continues at a high level after the provision of an adequate, chlorinated supply of water, there is little point in spending any more effort in 'fine tuning' the water supply system as there are likely to be other reasons for a continuing high diarrhoea rate. Make sanitation the top priority, if it is not already, and further investigate excreta-disposal methods and hygiene practices (including what happens to the water after collection). Remember, the aim is to reduce ill-health, not to construct the best water supply system possible at the expense of other vital needs.

Box 9.2 gives a practical example of how priorities can be established.

Special emphasis should be given to the problems of the vulnerable: the young, old, sick and pregnant. Additional measures may be needed to ensure that they benefit from the services provided:

- Social measures – such as ensuring that water is collected for those unable to get to a tapstand.
- Careful design – for example, latrines with suitably sized squat plates for the young and hand rails for the elderly.

Identify resources

To implement the programme, resources will need to be mobilized and utilized including: staff, time, skills and knowledge, equipment, materials and funds.

Be realistic about what can be achieved using existing resources within the time available. If necessary, ask as soon as possible for further assistance. Well-argued programme proposals supported with facts and figures (and an explanation of the consequences of not acting as proposed) are more likely to be supported by an agency than straightforward demands for funds and materials.

The right environmental health team is a key ingredient for a successful programme. In putting together a team:

- Decide on the priorities.
- Draw up a list and organizational chart of staff required.
- Outline staff responsibilities.
- Agree a system of reporting within and outside the programme (for example, with medical agencies and community leaders).

Refer to Chapter 6 for details of the management aspects of running a programme: staff recruitment, payment, personnel management, training, and so on.

See Figure 9.3 for a typical organizational chart of personnel required to implement the above programme. An expatriate manager should have a local counterpart.

The number of staff required will vary depending on the type and scale of the programme and the response of the community. One male and one female supervisor will be required for each male and female communal latrine. Sanitarians monitor latrine use and condition. Hygiene promoters promote good

Box 9.2 Establishing environmental health priorities

A limited study was undertaken to investigate the reasons for rising mortality and morbidity rates as a result of diarrhoea in a Sudanese refugee camp in Uganda. People with diarrhoea (cases) and without diarrhoea (controls) were informally interviewed by survey teams. The interviews were supported by observation of people's homes and their environment. The greatest differences between the behaviour of the cases and the controls were noted, as shown in Table 9.2.

Table 9.2 The effect of various factors on diarrhoea occurrence in a Sudanese refugee camp

Factors	*Cases with diarrhoea (%)*	*Controls without diarrhoea (%)*
Drinking water:		
drank safe water	50	80
had clean water storage containers	50	75
covered water storage containers	27	45
Hygiene:		
covered cooked food during storage	23	50
washed raw food before eating	31	80
were aware of faecal–oral route	35	65
Latrine: kept compound free of excreta	46	80

The respondents were also asked their views on how the problem of ill-health could be solved. The majority replied that a greater personal effort was required to keep their environment clean. Other factors included: allocating plots to individual families, more tools, clean water, and insecticide for flies. Based on the survey, the following list of priority interventions was drawn up:

- Increase the availability of safe drinking water.
- Promote the storage of drinking water in clean, covered containers. This may mean distributing more containers.
- Promote improved food hygiene, particularly regarding the storage of cooked food and the washing of raw food.
- Increase people's awareness of the faecal–oral route of disease transmission.
- Encourage people to make a greater personal effort to keep their environment clean. This may require the allocation of specific plots for each family.

Source: Morgan, 1993

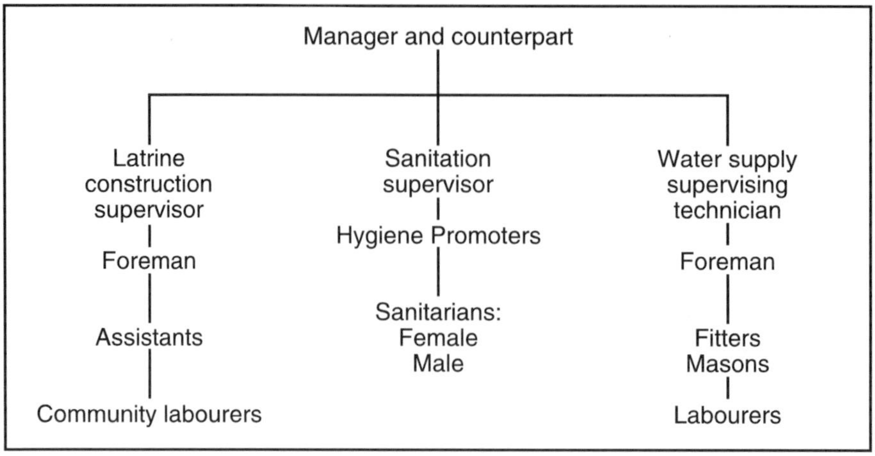

Figure 9.3 A sample organizational chart for an environmental health programme

hygiene practices by working through community facilitators. It has been suggested that one male and one female facilitator per 2000 people is required with one supervisor for eight facilitators (Ferron et al., 2000).

Where the local government services extend their support to the affected population, appropriate staff may be seconded from relevant government departments. For example, during the period of influx of Mozambican refugees into Malawi, one Malawian government environmental health officer was assigned per 1000 refugees to carry out preventive health care measures. The environmental health officer worked through a health committee of ten refugee community representatives. Each representative was given training in basic primary health care and environmental sanitation measures.

Prepare a plan

Even though there will be little time for detailed planning in the early stages of an emergency, develop a flexible outline plan of action and adapt it to the changing circumstances. It is helpful to use a bar chart to plan the timing of programme activities (see Chapter 5 for further details). Figure 9.4 gives an indication of the type of activities that are required. The priorities will be different for different situations.

Implementation

Get going as soon as possible.

Team communication and reporting

Regularly monitor the effectiveness of the measures and the health profile of the population. Adapt the programme and activities according to the feedback. Monitoring can be carried out by the environmental health team members, and regular team meetings will assist this. Seek the views of the population at risk and employ them in monitoring their own situation.

Activity	Month			
	1	2	3	4
Assess, plan and form a team	••••	••	••	••
Control indiscriminate defecation	•••••••••••••	••••• • •	• • • •	• • • •
Protect existing water sources	•••••••••••••	•••••••		
Construct latrines	•••	•••••••••••••	•••••••••••••	•••••••••••••
Run information campaign on environmental health measures	••••• •	• • • •	• • • •	• • • • •
Hygiene promotion	•••••••••••••	• •	• •	• •
Upgrade water supply system	•••	•••••••••••••	•••••••••••••	••••
Attend co-ordination meetings	• • • •	• •	• •	•
Monitor impact, change plans	••• •	• • • • • •	• • • •••••	• • • • •
Collect and dispose of rubbish	•••••••••	•••••••••••••	•••••••••••••	•••••••••••••

Figure 9.4 An example of an environmental health programme bar chart

Ensure good communication between partner agencies. Give progress reports at the appropriate subgroup co-ordination meetings. These meetings provide an opportunity for the engineer to obtain important information on health statistics, expected population changes, logistical problems, and so on.

A health information system

A health information system aims to identify and understand the health problems of the affected population so that interventions are targeted appropriately. A system should be supported and utilized by staff involved in environmental health programmes as it provides the basis for programme interventions and adjustments, particularly in the water and sanitation sectors.

The Sphere minimum standards in health services describes the requirements for an effective health information system. See Appendix 3 for a summary of the standards. In particular, Analysis standard 2 states:

> 'The health information system regularly collects relevant data on population, diseases, injuries, environmental conditions and health services in a standardised format in order to detect major health problems.'

There may be an existing local health information system or it may be necessary to initiate a new or parallel system. If the local health authority is not in a position to manage the system then responsibility is assigned to an individual agency which co-ordinates between the partners involved in the relief response. In the initial stages of an emergency, the health information system normally collects data on demography, mortality and its causes, morbidity and priority activities such as sanitation, water, food, nutrition and shelter. Five of the key indicators of effectiveness of interventions given in Sphere Health Services analysis standard 4 are:

- Decreasing death rate aiming towards less than 1/10 000/day.
- The under-5 mortality rate (U-5MR) is reduced to no more than 2/10 000/ day.
- Epidemics/diseases are controlled.
- There is access to adequate water.
- Adequate sanitation facilities are available.

Refer also to Table 1.1 'Crude mortality rates in emergencies'.

9.1.4 Cholera control

Specific action may need to be taken to control particular diseases. Cholera is an important example of a disease which, if left unchecked, can kill many people rapidly.

Facts about cholera

(From Bartram and Howard, 1994)

- The main danger from cholera is rapid dehydration (see Box 9.3). Unless patients are rehydrated quickly they can die, sometimes in a few hours.
- Most cholera cases can be treated successfully with oral rehydration therapy. The few that become severely dehydrated need intravenous fluid initially, and antibiotic treatment.
- Neither vaccination, quarantine, nor travel restrictions prevent cholera from spreading.
- In the long term, improved water supply, sanitation, hygiene and better living conditions are crucial to preventing cholera.
- 90 per cent of cholera cases are mild and therefore may be difficult to distinguish from other cases of acute diarrhoea. Many infected people have no symptoms but **they can be carriers and infect others**.
- Even in a cholera outbreak, more children may die from other types of diarrhoea than from cholera itself.

Cholera in temporary settlements

A plan to cope with a potential cholera outbreak must be considered, and preparations made, in the aftermath of a disaster in a cholera endemic area. During an outbreak of cholera in a camp for displaced people, commonly 1–4 per cent of the population are attacked, of whom about 20 per cent may be expected to be severely attacked and require hospitalization. Use these guideline figures when taking preparatory measures prior to a potential outbreak. Estimate the size of isolation areas needed and the equipment, materials, water supply and sanitation facilities likely to be required. Prepare staff through adequate training. For further guidance see, for example, Hausman (1994).

Box 9.3 Assessment and treatment of dehydration

Assess the degree of dehydration of someone with diarrhoea using the following guide (WHO, 1991):

Table 9.3 Assessing degrees of dehydration

1. Look at:			
Condition	Well, alert	*Restless, irritable	*Lethargic or unconscious
Eyes	Normal	Sunken	Very sunken and dry
Tears	Present	Absent	Absent
Mouth and tongue	Moist	Dry	Very dry
Thirst	Drinks normally, not thirsty	*Thirsty, drinks eagerly	*Drinks poorly or not able to drink
2. Lift the skin between two fingers and release	Skin falls back quickly	*Skin falls back slowly	*Skin falls back very slowly
3. Decide	No sign of dehydration	Two or more signs, including at least one marked*; there is some dehydration	Two or more signs, including at least one marked*; there is severe dehydration

The skin pinch may be less useful in people with marasmus (severe wasting) or kwashiorkor (malnutrition with swelling of the feet, hands and face), or obese people. Tears are a relevant sign only for infants and young children.

Prevention and treatment of dehydration using rehydration drink

To prevent and treat dehydration, give plenty of liquids or rehydration drink. Use small sachets of Oral Rehydration Salts (ORS), if available, for mixing with water. If not available, prepare a rehydration drink as follows:

To one litre of water add:
- two level tablespoons of sugar (or honey)
- ¼ teaspoon of salt
- ¼ teaspoon of sodium bicarbonate (baking soda).

If there is no baking soda use another ¼ teaspoon of salt. Add a small amount of fruit juice if available. The drink should be no more salty than tears. Sip regularly until urinating is normal. An adult needs at least three litres per day and a child at least one litre or a glass of liquid for each watery stool passed, whichever quantity is the greater.

Recognizing cholera

Cholera should be suspected when:

- An adult develops severe dehydration from acute watery diarrhoea, usually with vomiting (see Box 9.3).
- There is a sudden increase in patients with acute watery diarrhoea.

Practical ways to prevent the spread of cholera

Cholera is transmitted by the faecal–oral route. People can be infected but not show any signs of sickness. Their faeces will contain the *Cholera vibrio* bacterium. Without firm action up to 50 per cent of patients with cholera may die. Firm action can reduce this figure to 1–10 per cent of patients. Standard measures used in controlling cholera include:

- Monitor the supply of food, especially at markets, and its preparation.
- Provide safe excreta-disposal facilities, ensure they are used and prevent indiscriminate defecation (see Chapter 10).
- Control excessive numbers of flies, especially around latrines/defecation areas (see Section 10.8).
- Ensure a safe and adequate supply of drinking and washing water (see Chapters 11, 12 and 13).
- Prevent the use of contaminated water sources (see Chapter 11).
- Implement a public cholera information campaign, telling people the measures they can personally take to control transmission (see Section 9.2).
- Establish emergency isolation centres. Isolate and treat severe cases under conditions which treat all wastes before disposal (see below).
- Establish oral rehydration therapy (ORT) centres to rehydrate moderate cases (see Box 9.3).
- Train personnel to recognize cholera symptoms early and to give oral rehydration salt solution (ORS) (see Box 9.3).
- Use patient records to plot outbreaks on a map of the settlement.
- Follow up cases to determine where the patients came from and their living conditions. Contact people who had been in contact with patients and institute preventive measures as necessary.

Figure 9.5 shows the layout of a typical emergency cholera treatment centre. More details on construction are given in Chapter 19. Two points are of particular relevance here:

- Control: access to the centre should be restricted to patients and those giving care. Passage between sections should be through shallow footbaths containing disinfectant placed across doorways. Staff are advised to wear rubber boots or shoes.
- Site: not close to other buildings, but accessible by vehicle. There should be access to a water supply. Allow space for extension if attack rates or population increases.

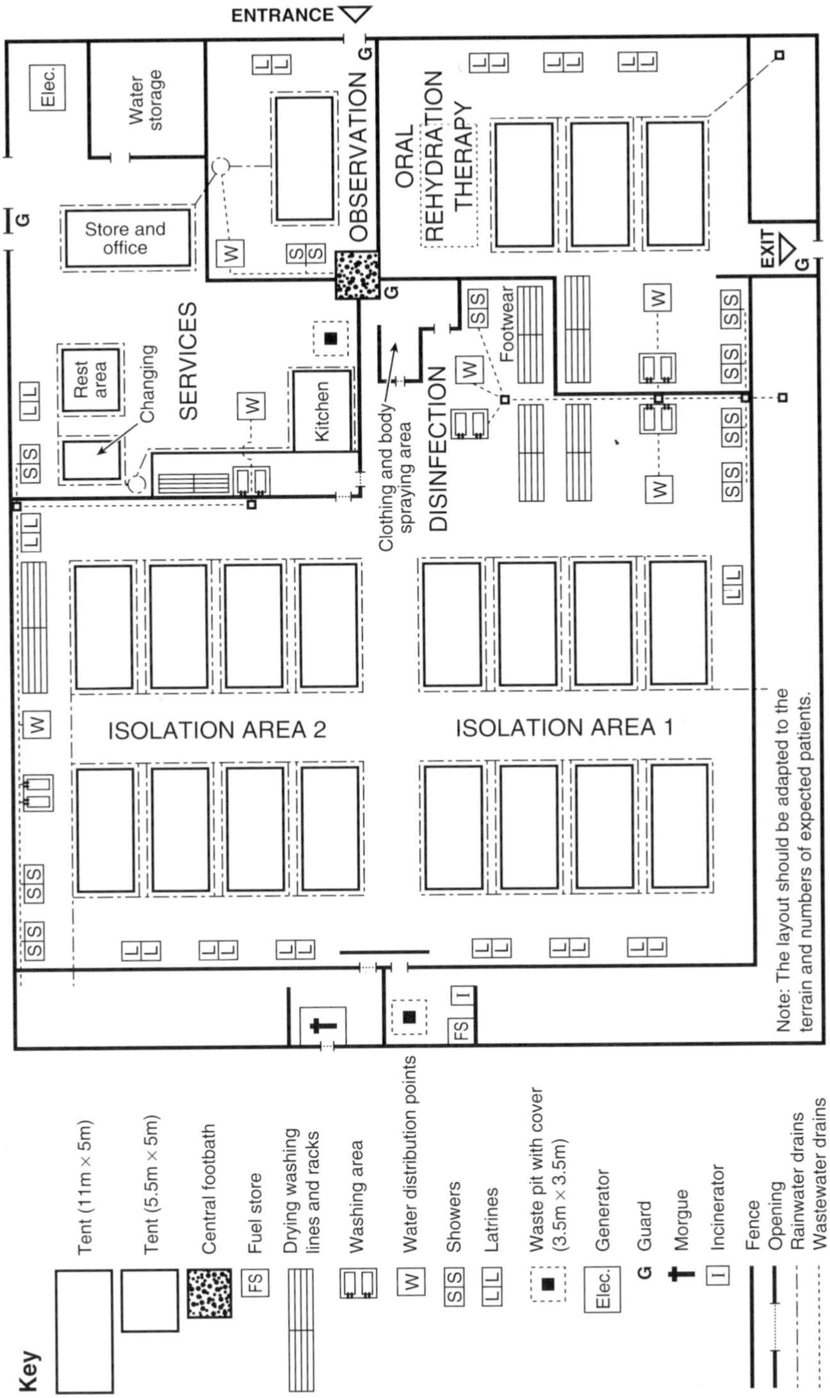

Figure 9.5 Plan of an emergency cholera treatment centre

Source: MSF, undated

Disinfection

(Note: 0.05% = 500 mg/l; 0.2% = 2000 mg/l)

- Change disinfectant in footbaths regularly.
- Wash new arrivals in 0.05% chlorine solution (see Section 13.3.3).
- Disinfect stretchers and vehicles transporting patients.
- Immerse clothes in 0.2% chlorine solution.
- Staff, patients and guardians should wash their hands with soap and 0.05% chlorine solution.
- Wash floors and beds with 0.2% chlorine solution each day.
- Place half a cup of 2% chlorine solution in each bucket and receptacle used for stools and vomit. Empty in the latrines. Rinse after emptying with 0.2% chlorine solution.
- Wash latrine slabs regularly with 0.2% chlorine solution.
- Wash eating and cooking utensils in 0.05% chlorine solution and rinse them in clean water.
- Ensure water for drinking is safe by chlorinating to give at least 0.2 mg/l residual chlorine (see Section 13.3.3).

The wastewater (sullage) load is high due to the washing facilities, footbaths and general washing down that is required. Pay particular attention to the safe disposal of the sullage (see Section 10.5).

Wash dead bodies with 2% chlorine solution, block orifices with cotton wool soaked in chlorine solution, and wrap in plastic sacks. Bury bodies as soon as possible, explaining the reason for a quick burial to relatives (see Section 10.7).

9.2 Hygiene promotion

People may know the hygienic practices they should be following but lack the means to follow them. It is clearly no use promoting the washing of hands with soap and water if there is no soap. Hygiene promotion is not just about providing information but it includes the provision of appropriate materials, facilities and support to enable people to follow good hygienic practices.

People will need to access sufficient water and facilities to wash themselves and their clothing. If nobody else has taken the responsibility, arrange the purchase and distribution of hygiene kits. Kits typically comprise: soap, washing bowls, water containers, food storage containers, sanitary towels, nappies (or nappy materials), anal cleansing materials (paper, corn cobs), and cloth material for covering and cleaning. Consult community representatives before making assumptions about what is appropriate.

The supply of clean water containers is very important as people may not have anything in which to collect or store water. They should preferably have covers for hygienic storage. Plastic or galvanized containers can often be purchased locally. Recycled plastic vegetable oil jerry cans may be suitable for water collection. Water jars for home storage may be made on site (see Section 13.2.7). Oxfam have developed a 14 litre water container with a tap for specific use in emergencies. It has a snap-on lid, a cap for a hygienic seal and can be easily cleaned. As the container stacks easily it does not take up as much space as jerry cans in freighting. Unlike many 'collapsible' plastic containers it is durable.

Communal washing facilities, for men and women, may need to be established. All communal services will need to be supervised and maintained either by employed staff or community committees. Again, consult with the users when designing and siting community facilities.

The following is a checklist of hygiene promotion measures that might be taken in an emergency.

- Carry out a rapid assessment:
  - What are the commonly accepted beliefs and practices concerning hygiene within the community?
  - What do people understand about the relationship between water, sanitation, shelter, insect and rodent vectors, and disease?
  - What are the commonly followed hygiene practices – washing hands after defecation, storage and covering of water and food, disposal of children's faeces, etc.?
  - What are the gaps in facilities, tools and equipment that do not allow people to follow hygienic practices?
  - Are there community health workers or extension agents within the community who can be recruited into a hygiene promotion programme?
  - Are there existing hygiene promotion activities?
- Develop contacts with and enlist the support of community leaders for hygiene promotion activities.
- Liaise with other agencies to co-ordinate activities and identify areas for collaboration.
- Recruit and train campaign staff to provide key hygiene-related information to the public.
- Attend agency co-ordination meetings to learn from others and to provide feedback on concerns expressed as a result of the hygiene promotion activities.
- Recruit and train public-latrine attendants to ensure cleaning and maintenance of public latrines and to encourage hand-washing following use of latrines.
- Recruit and train community facilitators to promote the benefits of family latrines and to mobilize the community to dig family latrines.
- Recruit and train mobile sanitation teams to remove and bury scattered faeces. Teams can be informal promoters of sanitation facilities (defecation fields or latrines).
- Recruit and train water source attendants to prevent defecation near water sources and to explain the dangers of such practices.
- Identify and prevent access to contaminated water sources. Recruit and train staff to monitor access and explain the dangers of using the contaminated water.
- Monitor the risk of solid waste accumulation and, if necessary, employ mobile sanitation teams in the promotion of appropriate collection and disposal.

- Monitor the availability and use of soap and containers for water and food.
- Organise the procurement, distribution and use of hygiene kits.
- Discuss with community members how animals can be effectively managed from a hygiene perspective.
- During an outbreak of diarrhoeal disease (including cholera) keep the community informed of the extent and severity of the outbreak and the benefits of reporting cases promptly.

Information campaigns

In the immediate emergency phase it may be necessary to initiate information campaigns on specific public health risks (where to defecate, measures to control prevalent diseases, etc.) and to develop these activities in the longer term interest of raising the general level of hygiene and health.

- As soon as possible, establish and train a team to mount information campaigns and to liaise with community representatives and volunteers.
- Keep messages clear and simple. Do not try to cover a broad range of topics but concentrate on the priority issues. Liaise with other agencies so that messages are consistent and complementary.
- Work through existing social structures (religious leaders, women's groups) where they still exist and are identifiable. Consider establishing representative committees where there is no existing group with whom to work.
- Plan messages and the method of promotion with community representatives so that cultural background and practices are taken into account.
- Be careful that the messages and health promotion methods do not imply that people are to blame for their own or their children's ill health.
- Based on feedback, adapt approaches to reflect the changes in conditions and health status over time.
- Ensure new arrivals in temporary settlements are made aware of the hygiene measures being promoted, why they are being promoted, and the rules regarding defecation, rubbish disposal and water collection.

In many societies women play a major role in latrine maintenance, excreta disposal, domestic and personal hygiene, and in the education of young children. Therefore, women's importance in health promotion should be recognized and utilized. Actively involving women does not mean disregarding the men, or children, but ensures women are not bypassed. Be aware of possible changes in gender roles due to the emergency and the value of working with children in establishing hygienic practices at an early age.

There are a range of methods employed in disseminating information: announcements by loud hailer, posters, drama, and songs. Meetings can be called for specific groups, such as the family, clan, or section. Captive audiences can be found at clinics, feeding centres, food distribution centres, water collection points, and so on. Longer-term hygiene promotion measures can be implemented as an emergency moves out of the immediate phase. See the Bibliography for further information, in particular: Ferron et al. 2000.

10 Environmental sanitation

The environmental sanitation measures which need urgent attention in an emergency include the safe disposal of excreta and sullage, the provision of adequate drainage, the safe disposal of refuse and insect and rodent control. These measures should not be taken in isolation but within the context of an overall environmental health programme, as described in Chapter 9. It is especially important that hygiene promotion is integrated with the sanitation programme.

10.1 Excreta disposal – assessment and planning

The emphasis of this section is on the short-term provision of excreta disposal facilities for displaced people in temporary settlements. The methods described may also be suited to other circumstances; for example, where traditional methods of excreta disposal used by non-displaced people are, or will soon become, inadequate in the circumstances of the emergency. Some guidelines on longer-term measures are also given.

10.1.1 A strategy for action

It takes time to develop an ideal system of excreta disposal and so a staged approach of incremental improvement must be adopted. The following stages are typical:

- Carry out a rapid survey to establish current excreta disposal practices and the physical parameters of the site which might affect the choice of disposal method.
- Prepare a sanitation plan and mobilize the necessary resources (people, money, materials and equipment). Use a staged approach.
- The immediate measures needed are likely to be controlling indiscriminate defecation at the earliest opportunity whilst initiating temporary measures which can be improved later. Prevent defecation in critical areas and then establish controlled defecation fields (see Section 10.2).
- Medium-term measures may include the construction of communal trench latrines or shallow family latrines (see Section 10.3).

Experience indicates that a move to family latrines for everyone as soon as possible is the most effective form of sanitation. Aim for the Sphere minimum standards for excreta disposal (see Appendix 3). Key extracts from the standard follows:

Excreta disposal standard 1: access to, and number of toilets
People have sufficient numbers of toilets, sufficiently close to their dwellings to allow them rapid, safe and acceptable access at all times of the day and night.
Key indicators:

- Maximum of 20 people per toilet.
- Use of toilets is arranged by household(s) and/or segregated by sex.
- Toilets are no more than 50 metres from dwellings, or no more than one minute's walk.
- Separate toilets for women and men are available in public places (markets, distribution centres, health centres etc.).

See Sphere (2000) for further indicators and guidance notes.

At each stage there should be regular contact with the affected community, both as individuals and through their representatives. Close co-operation is essential to promote the hygienic use and management of facilities. Adjust methods and determine hygiene promotion needs based on user feedback.

The survey

Find out about the current situation by carrying out a site survey, and include the surroundings beyond the immediately affected area. Draw a plan of the site. Use the following questions as the start of a checklist:

- What is the estimated population and how are people distributed across the site?
- How does the terrain slope and what are the drainage patterns?
- What is the depth and permeability of the soil, and can it be dug easily by hand?
- What is the level of the groundwater table?
- What natural construction materials are available (trees, bush, grass for screens, stone, etc.) and what can be purchased locally?
- Where are people presently defecating and why? Is it hygienic?
- Are there existing sanitation facilities and what condition are they in? Are they being used? Can they be extended or adapted for use?
- Are present defecation practices in danger of directly polluting water sources or the food chain?
- Are there any people familiar with the construction of latrines?
- Are women, men and children prepared to use defecation fields, communal latrines or family latrines?
- What are the current beliefs and traditions concerning excreta disposal?
- What are the attitudes towards the excreta of babies and young children?
- Is there space for the construction of sanitation facilities?
- When does the seasonal rain fall and what will be its impact on sanitation?

See Chapters 5 and 9 for further guidance on general and health-related surveys.

10.1.2 Factors to consider

Volumes of human excreta

Faeces, water, anal cleansing material and any additional waste materials are deposited in latrines. In an emergency, latrines will be intensively used and short-term accumulation rates will be high. Base short-term accumulation rates on the volume of fresh excreta: 1–2 litres per person per day (this figure includes urine but excludes cleaning materials and washing water). If the soil is permeable, liquid will quickly percolate away and the accumulation rate will be considerably lower than this. In impermeable soils, there will be little percolation and the latrine will have to store the full liquid volume in the short term. Ensure that no other liquid enters the latrine (such as surface runoff or water from washing).

Excreta is reduced in volume as it decomposes. The mechanisms involved include: evaporation, digestion and the release of gases, the leaching of soluble substances, and consolidation under the deposition of fresh wastes. The rate at which sludge is accumulated is affected by the amount of faeces and water, the type of anal cleansing material and the intensity of usage, but it will be between 40 and 90 litres/person/year.

Social and cultural considerations

Traditional practices and beliefs concerning the disposal of human faeces can crucially affect the acceptability and impact of excreta disposal methods. These beliefs are as vital to consider and understand as the management and technical aspects of the proposed solutions. The following points are particularly important.

Place of defecation Acceptable or preferred places of defecation vary widely. Defecation may take place inside or outside the house or compound, at a distance from the compound behind bushes, in open fields, in gulleys, near or over water. The place of defecation may vary from day to night-time. Children may use only the compound area and be afraid of using a latrine. The old and infirm may have physical difficulties in moving far from a shelter or compound. Women and men may not use the same place. In some societies communal defecation areas are unacceptable.

Disposal of children's faeces Children under the age of three will not use latrines. In wealthy communities, the provision of nappies, washing facilities and a refuse collection system (for disposable nappies) should be sufficient. In poorer, less developed communities, the faeces of babies and young children are sometimes erroneously considered harmless, and therefore less care may be taken over the disposal of their faeces. In fact, they are more harmful than adults' faeces. Therefore, positive action should be taken to ensure that children's faeces are disposed of carefully, and this will involve close consultation with mothers on basic hygiene. The safe disposal of children's faeces may be encouraged by the provision of a small hoe to mothers, so that they can cover the faeces.

Anal cleansing Water, paper, stones, maize cobs and other materials are used for cleaning the anus. Traditional practice may have to be adapted to the circumstances of the emergency. Materials may need to be supplied or substituted. The safe disposal of babies' anal cleansing materials may need to be promoted.

The accumulation of non-degradable anal cleansing materials can markedly affect the life of a latrine. Some materials will block water-flushed systems. Traditional anal cleansing practices must be taken into account when choosing technical options.

Handwashing Handwashing following defecation may be normal practice. Where handwashing is not customary, it will need to be promoted. It is important to ensure water for handwashing is available. Water and soap will need to be provided at communal washing points.

Menstruation Women of child-bearing age may experience problems in obtaining suitable materials for the absorption and disposal of menstrual blood, and this can soon become apparent in communal latrines. Menstruation is a sensitive issue which is often not easy to discuss in public. It is important that the supply and disposal of adequate, appropriate materials is addressed.

Maintenance of latrines

All latrines need regular cleaning, but emergency communal latrines, especially, require constant supervision and cleaning if they are to be kept in a sanitary condition. There may be cultural norms which affect the degree to which certain individuals in a society are prepared to be involved in the handling of faeces and the cleaning of latrines. This can affect the use and care of latrines and the recruitment of sanitarians, latrine supervisors and cleaners.

In general, small coherent groups, such as families, are more likely to take responsibility for care and maintenance than large disparate groups.

Community involvement

The implementation of sanitation measures requires the co-operation of users if facilities are to be used hygienically and kept in a sanitary condition. Therefore, as soon as possible, it is important to establish some form of liaison with the community so that sanitation can be discussed; by establishing a sanitation committee for example. The committee can be formed using the community contacts established during the surveys and include community representatives, agency staff, government personnel and groups involved in hygiene education. In a temporary settlement, the sanitation committee will be one of several camp committees. In a large community, or in a community comprised of different groups of people, it may be necessary to establish a number of sanitation sub-committees. Sanitation committee responsibilities are:

- To raise awareness of the importance of effective sanitation.
- To decide on the best sanitation option.
- To recruit and organize people for latrine construction, supervision, maintenance and management.
- To provide regular monitoring of the sanitation measures.

Immediate excreta disposal measures are likely to be predominantly an organizational and management task in which community co-operation is essential. Medium- to longer-term solutions must be carefully planned with the users after the immediate emergency measures have been implemented.

Displaced people may be reluctant to expend time and energy on the construction of latrines if they hope to return home in the near future. Latrine construction can also be seen as a sign of long-term displacement and the displaced community or the host government may be reluctant to accept such measures for this reason. Therefore, the level of community commitment to the development of improved sanitation will vary, and must be judged in discussions with them.

Staffing

Emergency sanitation programmes are staff-intensive involving organizational, communication and monitoring tasks in addition to construction. A family latrine programme, for example, will involve staff in the promotion of latrines, giving advice on siting and construction, the purchase and distribution of materials, the production of latrine slabs and so on.

A typical staffing structure for an excreta disposal programme in a camp of 50 000 people is shown in Table 10.1 (from Adams, 1999).

10.2 Excreta – immediate actions

Immediate actions include the control of indiscriminate defecation and the provision of designated defecation sites.

10.2.1 Control of indiscriminate defecation

Indiscriminate defecation can pose a health risk to individuals, water sources and food supplies. Therefore, a major priority at the beginning of an emergency is to control indiscriminate defecation. In particular, prevent defecation:

- By the side of, or into, rivers, streams, lakes, and within 15 m of all water sources.
- Within the vicinity of water storage and treatment facilities.
- On slopes uphill of camps and water sources.
- In fields of crops destined for human consumption.
- Along public roads.
- Within the vicinity of communal buildings such as clinics and feeding centres.
- Within the vicinity of food storage and preparation facilities.

Controlling where people defecate can be highly unpopular, especially if traditional practices are insanitary. But in an emergency, where the health of many people is at risk, firm action must be taken. Make sure people know what is happening and which areas are prohibited. It may be necessary to fence off critical areas and post guards to prevent defecation. The regular inspection of upstream water courses is advisable.

Table 10.1 Examples of staff needs for an excreta disposal project for 50 000 people

Phase	*Main activities*[1]	*Staff type*	*Nos.*
I: Days	*Setting up and running defecation fields, hygiene promotion*		
	Site management, administration, logistics etc.	Manager, storekeeper, buyer, administrator, driver	5
	Setting up 10 defecation fields	Labourers and team leaders[2]	110
	Maintaining 10 defecation fields	Labourers and team leaders[2]	60
	Hygiene promotion and information exchange	Hygiene promoters and team leaders	55
II: Weeks	*Constructing and running public pit latrines*		
	Site management, administration, logistics etc.	Manager, storekeepers, buyer, administrator, drivers	8
	Construction of public pit latrines	Skilled workers, labourers and team leaders	210
	Cleaning and maintaining public pit latrines	Cleaners and team leaders	85
	Hygiene promotion and information exchange	Hygiene promoters and team leaders	55
III: Months	*Family pit latrine programme*		
	Site management, administration, logistics etc.	Manager, storekeepers, buyer, administrator, drivers	8
	Advising population on latrine siting and construction	Latrine technicians and team leaders[3]	55
	Concrete latrine slab production	Masons, labourers and team leaders	22
	Hygiene promotion and information exchange. Programme monitoring	Hygiene promoters and team leaders	55

1. These activities overlap as the situation and programme develop. Defecation fields will be managed while the public latrines are being built. The family latrines may be started before the public latrine programme is finished etc.
2. Workers setting up and then maintaining defecation fields may be the same staff, who move straight onto maintenance as soon as the defecation fields go into use.
3. Latrine technicians may have a role which overlaps with that of the hygiene promoters and it may be possible to combine the two jobs.

Stopping defecation in certain areas might suggest, erroneously, that defecation is acceptable everywhere else. Therefore, as soon as possible, it is a good idea to designate defecation sites or facilities and prohibit defecation from all other areas. Make sure people know where it is permissible to defecate, by using public announcements passed through community representatives. Ensure that new arrivals to a camp know where they should not defecate and are told where they can defecate. Firm control must be exercised.

10.2.2 Defecation fields

In many cases, the only immediate solution to excreta containment is to designate defecation fields. These fields localize contamination and make it easier to manage the safe disposal of excreta. Defecation fields have a limited lifespan and can only be used once in the short term, so prepare new fields well in advance of existing fields filling up. Defecation fields become difficult to supervise over time, they take up a lot of space and they are not easy to keep in a hygienically acceptable state. They are only a short-term measure until alternative solutions are developed. Key points include:

- Defecation fields should be made as large as it is possible to manage safely. Allow about $0.25m^2$ per person per day.
- Space fields according to the distribution of people in the camp, to allow easy user access without too far to walk. Fields should be at least 30 m from shelters and stores.
- Locate on land sloping away from shelters, food stores and surface water sources. Avoid areas liable to flooding. The soil should be easy to dig to cover faeces. People may prefer a site with trees and bush, although open land may be easier to manage. Consult and agree the plans for the defecation fields with the users before they are implemented. This is especially important for people who are not used to defecating in public.
- Defecation fields need supervision and management – appoint sanitary assistants to do this job.
- Ensure polluted surface runoff is disposed of safely, and does not contaminate downstream water sources.
- Designate male and female defecation fields.
- Provide water and soap for handwashing at the exits to defecation fields.

There are two types of defecation field: open and trench. Both are laid out by dividing a field into strips.

Open defecation field

Defecation is allowed within each opened 1.5 m wide strip (Figure 10.1). Users should be directed to keep to one side of the strip and leave a space free of excreta for access. If strips are too long (>20 m) the furthest ends may not be used. To encourage full use of a strip, people should enter along one path and leave by another. Several strips can be opened if large numbers of people are using the field at the same time. Space the open strips to provide some privacy. New strips can be spaced away from used strips, to reduce the fly and smell nuisance. On sloping sites, strips should follow the contours of the land. Use the lower strips first, to avoid contaminating unused strips on lower ground.

In a hot, dry climate, faeces can be left uncovered to dry out under the sun. In a wet, humid climate, the sterilizing effect of the sun may not be complete and it is then better to cover with soil, to prevent fly breeding and to reduce smells. Strips which have been marked out by light ploughing or hoeing provide loose soil for cover.

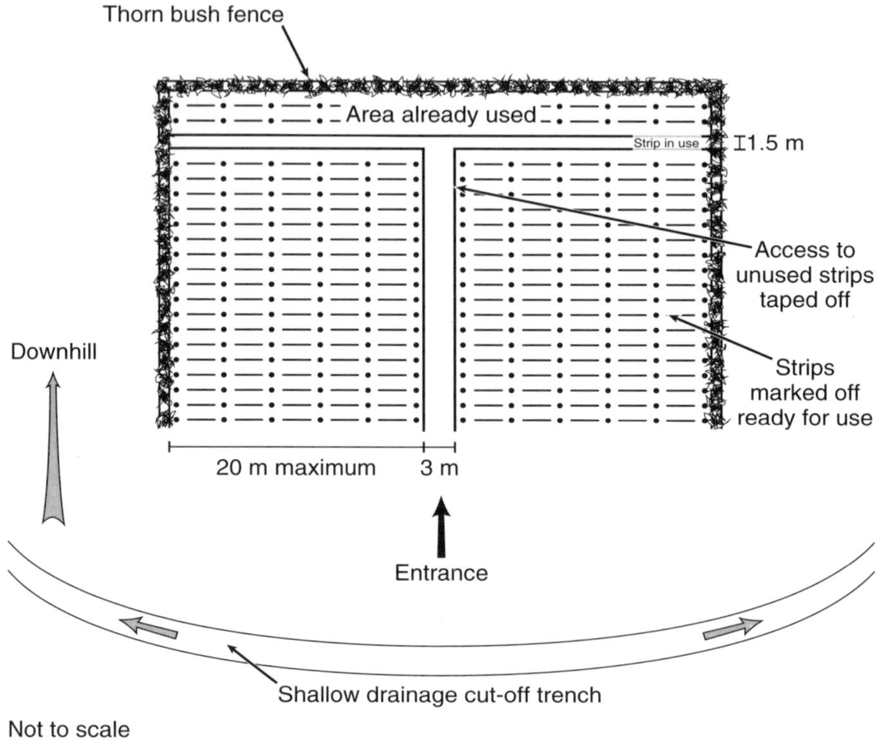

Figure 10.1 An open defecation field
Source: Reed, 1994

Trench defecation field

Open defecation fields can be improved by digging shallow trenches, about 150 mm deep, into which the users excrete (see Figure 10.2). The advantages are that excreta can be easily covered and pathways can be kept clear. Each strip can be fully utilized by only opening up a trench as required, although if there are many users, several trenches can be opened at the same time. On sloping ground, place the excavated soil on the downhill side of the trench as it is easier to squat facing uphill.

Defecation field operation and management

Defecation fields must be well managed and constantly supervised. Supervisors must be recruited, trained, and given authority to ensure the defecation fields are used properly. Employ a minimum of two people per field. Community co-operation is essential.

The furthest part of a field is used first. This avoids people walking across contaminated ground. Strips can be marked out by stones, shallow furrows, screens of plastic sheeting or marker poles and tapes. Management is made easier if poles are joined by cloth or tape. Access to strips not in use should be prevented by temporary fencing or tape.

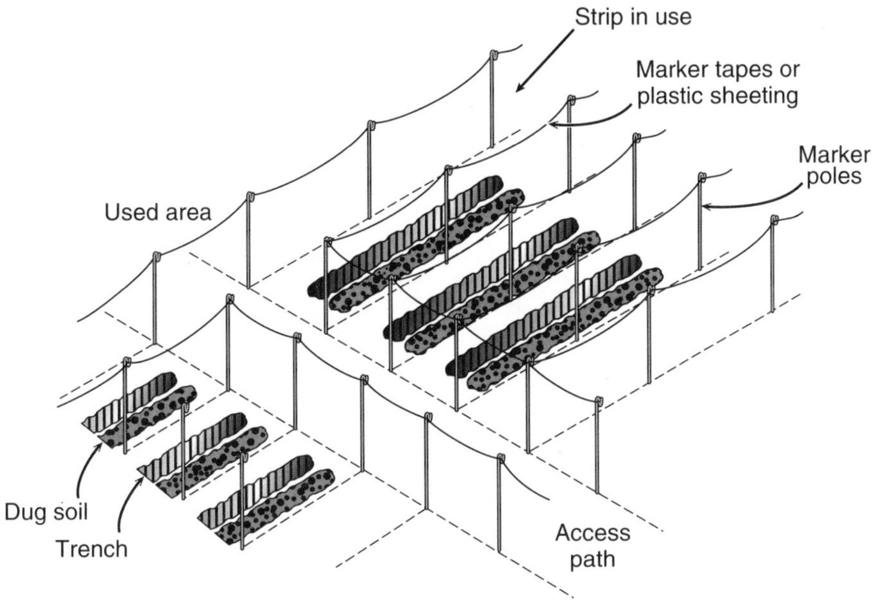

Figure 10.2 A trench defecation field
Source: Reed, 1994

Animals must be controlled and/or a thorn bush fence erected, to prevent animals entering defecation fields.

Anal cleansing material may have to be supplied if it is not otherwise available, and this must be discussed with the users. If water is used, it should be provided at the entrance to the defecation field with small pots for personal use. If solid material is used, it must be deposited in a container at the end of each strip and then buried or burnt. Material left on the ground can become a health hazard if re-used or if it blows about.

Water and soap for handwashing should be provided.

Do not remove excreta from the field. Excreta must be covered with soil to a depth of at least 100 mm to prevent fly breeding and reduce odours. Soil or sand may have to be brought to the site if there is little or no topsoil. Fouled sections of trench must be covered immediately after use.

10.3 Medium-term measures for excreta disposal

Medium-term measures for excreta disposal include the provision of communal latrines and shallow latrines for families.

10.3.1 General guidelines for latrines

Communal trench and pit latrines

Communal latrines need the close co-operation of the users and considerable external supervisory and management support if they are to remain effective.

Therefore, communal latrines will only be a short- to medium-term solution. If people are to remain in one place for any length of time, some form of excreta disposal which can be more easily managed at the family, or small group, level will need to be developed. This will often be a form of pit latrine.

If pit latrines are to last for a long period, consider the construction of twin-pit latrines. Construct each pit to provide sludge storage for at least a year (two years is preferable). The contents will digest during storage and become innocuous whilst the other pit is being used. The digested sludge can be removed after one to two years and the pit re-used.

Children may not be happy using pit latrines, even if they are shallow, because the inside of a latrine is often dark, and children may have a fear of falling down the hole. Therefore, an alternative should be made available for young children to use if they are not to defecate indiscriminately. One solution is to include a small squat hole in the latrine design. The main latrine privacy screen or wall should not surround the smaller squat hole but leave it in the open, with a cover. Children generally do not require the same privacy as adults, and they are likely to prefer to defecate outside where they can be seen if they have a problem. Parents may also be reassured as children will always be in view.

Construction cost and time Sufficient allowance must be made at the planning and budgeting stage for the significant cost of latrine building materials and the time required for their construction. Extended linings and twin-pit latrines will add substantially to costs. To service a large population, the overall costs of implementation and management can be considerable.

Siting and numbers It is preferable to construct a large number of well-spaced latrines than to build a small number of large latrines. People will probably use the latrine closest to their shelter but they may use other latrines on the way to feeding centres, food distribution points, bathing areas, and so on. Normally, position communal latrines at a reasonable distance away from dwellings (30 m) but not so far away that people will not use the latrine (a maximum of 250 m). Site latrines at least 15 m away from a water source (see 'Groundwater pollution' below). Where possible, site communal latrines on the prevailing downwind edge of camps. However, in large camps they may have to be sited centrally. Avoid depressions or dry water courses which could fill with rainfall runoff. Take into account drainage patterns, and protect latrines with a shallow cut-off drain to divert rainfall runoff. Discuss the location of latrines with all the groups of the community who will use them. Ask men and women separately and remember to ask the children. See Chapter 5 for more details.

In most cases, it should be possible to estimate the number of users based on the latrine's proximity to shelters. Refer to the sections on individual latrines for the recommended number of users per type of latrine. Communal latrines are often used at night. Therefore, some form of lighting may need to be provided. In initial planning, allow space for at least three times the initial number of latrines, to account for used and filled latrines.

Ground conditions and linings

Dig trial pits to investigate the soils. The ground must be soft enough to dig, but firm enough to be self-supporting. Constructing a lining is significant extra work. In firm soils, it may only be necessary to line the depth of the topsoil. Unstable soils must be lined. Pits dug in clay in the dry season may appear stable, but they can quickly collapse when the clay becomes wet following rain or a rise in the groundwater table.

Line short-term pits using wooden boards or bush poles and brushwood. Longer-term linings will require more durable materials which can add considerably to the cost and time required for construction. Linings include blockwork, bricks, stone masonry, coral, and rot-resistant or treated timber. Bamboo submerged in sludge will decay in less than a year. Seal the top 0.5 m of a lining. The lining below 0.5 m must allow liquid to percolate out of the pit but prevent the ingress of surrounding sand or soil.

Latrines in rocky or shallow groundwater areas In a rocky area with little soil cover or where the groundwater table is near the surface, it is only possible to dig a shallow trench or pit. If necessary, extend the lining above ground level to create a sealed chamber for increased storage capacity. Some of the refugee camps for Rwandan refugees in Goma, Zaire (1994), were sited on a former volcanic lava flow. The soil cover was very thin and non-existent in some places, so emergency latrines were constructed over rock depressions and natural rock fissures.

Latrines in low permeability soils Advise users not to put water they have used for washing into latrines dug in low-permeability soils. A small amount of water helps decomposition, but excessive amounts can make the contents offensive, provide breeding grounds for mosquitoes, and possibly result in flooding of the pit. Ensure that surface runoff is directed away from the pit. This can be done by using earth dug from the hole to raise the floor of the latrine above the surrounding land.

Groundwater pollution

The risk of contamination of wells and boreholes near trench and pit latrines will depend on the fluctuation of the groundwater table and the soils. The principal hazard is the movement of pathogens of faecal origin from latrines to the water table. The following guidelines can be applied.

Trenches or pits dug in the unsaturated zone above the water table Soils and unconsolidated strata appear to remove 90 per cent of bacteria within 2 m of the bacteria moving from a pit (Lewis et al., 1980). In fine soils, therefore, there is a low risk of groundwater pollution if the distance between an unlined trench or pit and the water table is greater than 2 m. The flushing action of intense rainfall will speed up the movement of pollutants, and the safe distance must be increased in high rainfall areas. The presence of rock fissures will allow the rapid and unpredictable passage of pollutants to the water table.

Trenches or pits dug in the saturated zone below the water table Latrine trenches and pits may penetrate the water table in areas where the groundwater level is high, allowing bacteria and viruses to move significant distances in flowing groundwater. It is recommended that pit latrines should be sited at least 15 m from a water abstraction point in most fine soils (Franceys et al., 1992).

This distance should be increased if water abstraction rates are high and in areas of coarse gravel and fissured rock. A Sphere key indicator: 'Latrines and soakaways in most soils are at least 30 m from any groundwater source and the bottom of any latrine is at least 1.5 m above the water table. Drainage or spillage from defecation systems does not run towards any surface water source or shallow groundwater source.'

Groundwater pollution will extend in the direction of the groundwater flow (which is mainly horizontal) with little vertical distribution except in fissured rock. Therefore, water can be safely abstracted from below the polluted zone (see Figure 10.3) provided that the well is adequately sealed at the level of pollution and the abstraction rate is not high enough to draw polluted water into the well (Franceys et al., 1992).

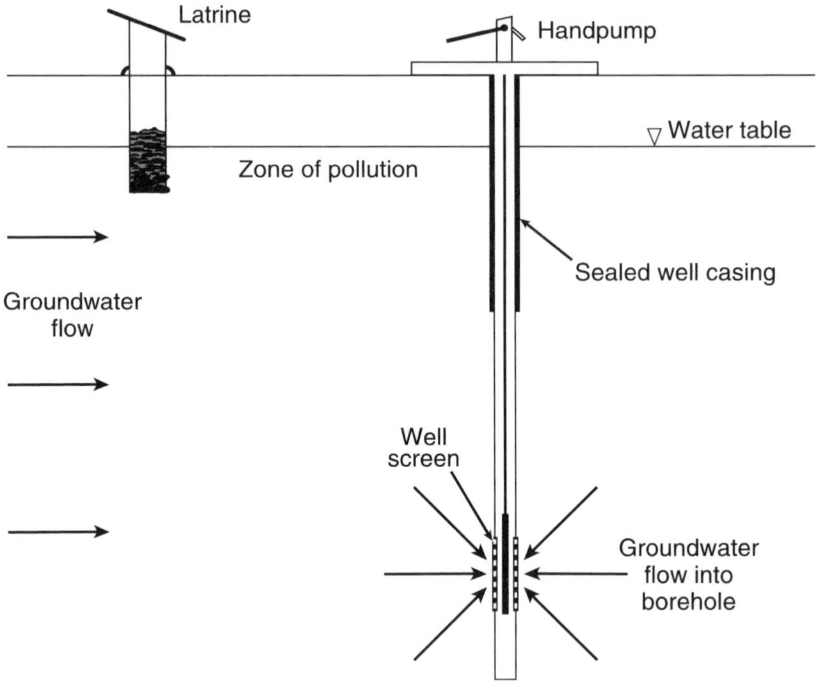

Figure 10.3 Abstracting water from below the pollution zone
Source: Franceys et al., 1992

If the pollution of a shallow water table is a cause for concern, it may be necessary to restrict the depth of latrines and raise them above ground level using an extended lining to achieve an adequate pit volume.

Latrine use and maintenance

At the entrance to communal latrines, provide anal cleansing material and soil in buckets for users to cover their excreta after defecation. Latrine supervisors should add a further 50–100 mm of soil cover periodically to reduce fly breeding. The frequency of additional covering will vary from daily to weekly, depending mainly on the weather. At the exit to communal latrines, provide water and soap for handwashing. Instruct supervisors to ensure that all latrine users wash their hands after defecation.

People will not use communal latrines that are in a poor condition, so supervisors should monitor their use and rate of filling, and ensure that they are cleaned regularly. The foot-rests, any plastic ground sheeting and the surrounding area should be scrubbed with water every few hours, and almost constantly during periods of peak use. Provide latrine supervisors with adequate protective clothing and equipment for cleaning. Ensure supervisors understand and follow appropriate personal hygiene procedures. Employ hygiene agents to monitor regularly the use and maintenance of family latrines and to promote good hygiene practices.

Where necessary, use public information campaigns to ensure people know how to use and look after communal and family latrines.

When a latrine is full

It is essential for full latrines to have some soil cover to reduce fly breeding. Aim to fill emergency shallow trench and family latrines with soil when full to within 150 mm of the surface. It is much better, however, to have a soil cover of 0.5 m. Therefore, close deeper latrines when full to within 0.5 m of the surface. See 10.8.1, for a fuller explanation of soil cover and fly breeding. See 10.1.2, which deals with volumes of human excreta, for guidance on latrine filling rates.

Prepare new latrines in advance of closing existing latrines. Remove any superstructure from the old latrine and backfill with soil. Heap and compact the soil in a mound to allow for settlement and to mark the site. Fence off the area until the contents and backfill have settled.

In certain circumstances, where it may not be possible to dig new latrines, for example if there is no space or if soil conditions do not permit, it may be necessary to organize pumping out of full latrines. This is a major task requiring careful planning and specialized equipment.

10.3.2 Communal latrines

Trench latrines

Communal trench latrines can be quickly prepared to provide a short- to medium-term solution. There are two basic types: shallow and deep trench latrines (Figures 10.4 and 10.5). Their lifespan will depend on the number of users and the latrine size. A shallow trench latrine may last 2–4 weeks while a deep trench may last 1–3 months.

Provide sufficient latrines to cope with peak use in the morning and evening. Design for a maximum of 50 people per metre length of trench (or per cubicle) per day. Adapt usage criteria based on experience, aiming for a more manageable 25 people per cubicle per day.

Communal trench latrines must be constantly supervised and maintained if they are to remain in a sanitary condition. Latrine supervisors must regularly clean the foot boards and surrounding area, and periodically cover the trench contents with 50–100 mm of soil, raked level. The success of communal latrines

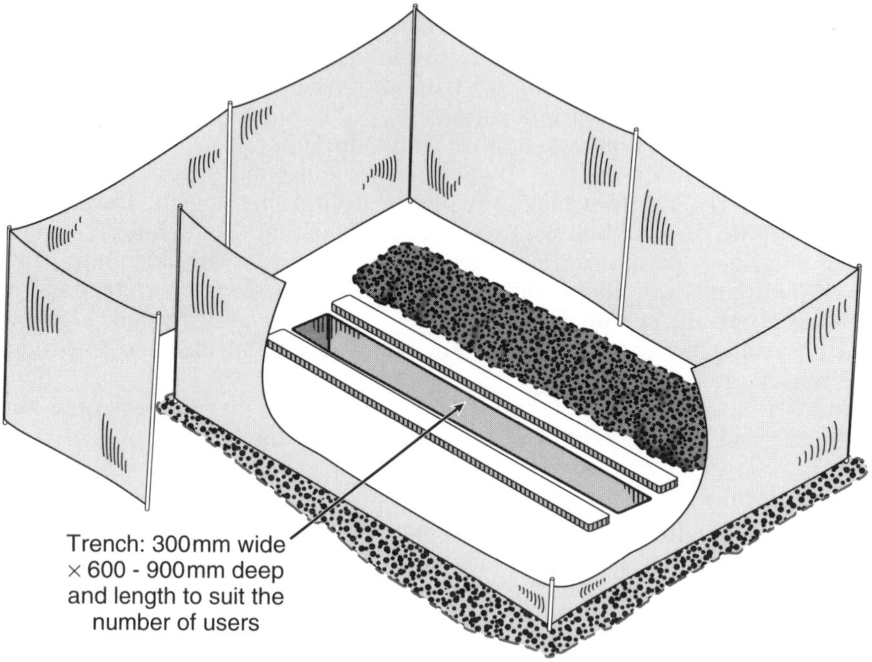

Figure 10.4 A shallow trench latrine
Source: Reed, 1994

relies heavily on the co-operation of the users. Therefore, community representatives must be involved from the beginning. Refer to the general guidelines on latrine use and maintenance given in 10.3.1.

Provide anal cleansing materials, soil for covering excreta, and water and soap for handwashing.

Shallow trench latrines Figure 10.4 shows a suggested layout for a shallow trench latrine. Place boards either side of the narrow trench or place further boards across the trench in pairs. The layout is similar to the deep trench latrine described in the next section, but quicker and easier to prepare.

Deep trench latrines A suggested layout of a deep trench latrine is shown in Figure 10.5. Adjust the final design on the basis of the materials available and consultation with the users' representatives. The latrine must be acceptable to the users or they will not use it.

In collapsing soils, line the trench with timber or poles and follow safe working practices to protect the diggers. Protect the edge of the trench from erosion and soiling by a 1.5 m wide sheet of plastic or oiled cloth attached to the underside of the timber floor plates. Arrange for about 0.5 m of the sheet to hang inside the trench. Use local materials or plastic sheeting for the optional screening (dependent on users' wishes). Excavated soil is used as soil cover for the trench and is obtained through the rear screen, so arrange both the front and rear screens for easy access.

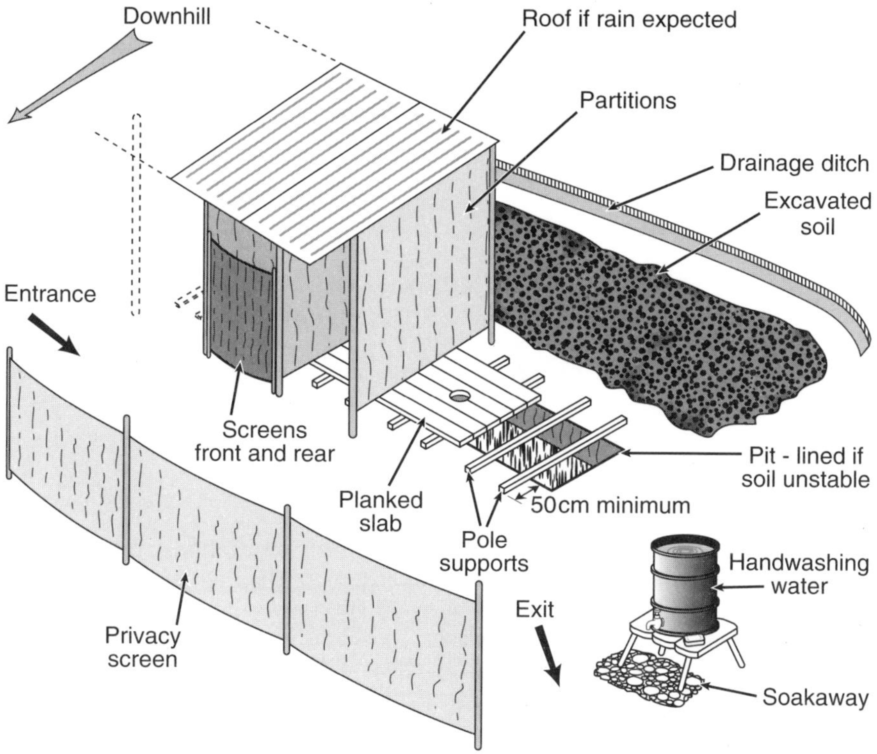

Figure 10.5 A deep trench latrine
Adapted from Reed, 1994

Table 10.2 Guideline design figures for a latrine with cubicles

Number of cubicles (maximum 300 people per day)	6 per latrine
Cubicle width	0.9 m
Length of trench	5.6 m
Width of trench	0.8 m
Depth of trench	max 2.0 m
Timber floor plate	130 mm × 40 mm × 5.6 m
Timber foot-rests	130 mm × 40 mm
Gap between foot-rests (vary and adjust with experience)	150 mm to 250 mm
Provide firm handrail supports in at least one cubicle for the infirm and elderly	

In areas subject to rain, cover the site with a shelter during excavation and place the spoil on the uphill side of the trench. Dig cut-off ditches to divert rainfall runoff. Form an overhanging roof with plastic sheeting to divert rainwater away from the trench to prevent it collapsing. Cover the excavated soil to prevent rainfall erosion. Design the superstructure for ease of dismantling and re-erection over a new trench. If required by the users, erect a privacy screen of local materials or plastic sheeting in front of the cubicle entrances.

When covering a full trench, remove the superstructure, fold the plastic ground sheet over the trench contents and backfill with the remaining soil.

10.4 Pit latrines

Early in an emergency pit latrines will need to be constructed for hospitals, feeding centres and reception centres. As soon as possible it will be necessary to promote the construction of latrines at the family level. For guidance, a pit capacity of 1.5 m^3 should serve ten people for about six months (Reed and Dean, 1994). Refer to section 10.3 for further general guidelines applicable to pit latrines.

10.4.1 Improvements to existing latrines

Where there are existing facilities, for example in clinics or schools, they may need to be improved, especially for what might be heavier than normal use. Improvements can include cleaning, strengthening of floors or slab supports, repair of superstructure, modifications for children, the elderly and infirm. The company Monarflex supply a lightweight polypropylene squatting slab (590 × 790 mm) with removable cover which can be used to quickly upgrade existing facilities. Being plastic they are easy to clean and resistant to urine and faeces. There are slots for anchoring to support timbers and tying into concrete structures.

10.4.2 Borehole latrines

Boreholes can be hand drilled using augers up to a diameter of 0.5 m in favourable soils. It takes time for two people to hand drill a large diameter hole. Manual drilling rates vary, averaging around 1.5 m per hour, depending on the diameter of the hole and the soils. It is better to machine drill borehole latrines when many have to be drilled quickly in an emergency. To obtain any useful capacity, the latrine must be drilled deeper than dug pits. However, the depth may be restricted by the groundwater table which must be at least 2 m below the bottom of the borehole if contamination is to be minimized. As with the shallow family latrine, wooden boards can be used as foot-rests and a simple screen erected. Provide a cover for the squatting hole to reduce fly nuisance.

A 300 mm diameter borehole of 5 m depth will last a family of five about two years.

Advantages of borehole latrines:

- Lining is only necessary near the top (use a pipe or woven matting).
- A slab is not absolutely necessary, although it is preferable.

Disadvantages of borehole latrines:

- The small diameter can lead to fouling near the surface and possible blockage.

- The relatively small volume may mean a limited lifespan during heavy usage in an emergency.

Because of these disadvantages, borehole latrines are not recommended for communal use.

10.4.3 Simple pit latrines

The simple pit latrine is a squatting slab placed over a hole in the ground. The hole in the slab should have a tightly fitting cover to prevent the movement of flies and to reduce odours. The superstructure need only be a simple screen and, in a dry climate, it is not essential to have a roof.

A squatting platform for short-term pits can be made from poles lashed together, and a woven grass mat or plastic sheeting can be used as a screen. Treated timber poles will last longer than untreated poles. The poles can be covered with a plastic sheet to seal the pit and give a more hygienic latrine floor for cleaning.

A simple pit latrine suitable for emergency use is shown in Figure 10.6. The spiral design provides privacy and limits light inside to discourage flies. The absence of a door reduces contact with potentially contaminated surfaces.

A concrete slab provides a durable support and seals the pit. It is also more easily cleaned than rough poles and earth floors. Concrete slabs may be reinforced or unreinforced. Steel bar for reinforced concrete slabs may be expensive and difficult to acquire. A domed slab, as shown in Figure 10.7, avoids the need for reinforcement by transmitting the load through the arch to the ground at the periphery.

There are several methods of casting a domed slab (see Brandberg 1997).

10.4.4 Ventilated improved pit (VIP) latrines

The ventilated improved pit (VIP) latrine significantly reduces odour and fly problems, but only if constructed, used and maintained correctly. There are many examples of VIP latrines which do not work as intended because of deficiencies in construction or in aftercare and use. The basic VIP latrine is shown in Figure 10.8. Construct the latrine so that the prevailing wind blows in through the entrance. This combines with the wind flow across the top of the ventilation pipe to draw air through the latrine as shown, so reducing odour.

Flies are reduced by keeping the inside of the latrine superstructure in subdued light. Flies which enter or breed in the pit are attracted by the relatively bright light at the top of the vent pipe. They pass up the pipe and, if a fly screen is positioned at the top as it should be, they cannot escape and eventually die and fall back into the pit.

Key factors for the effectiveness of fly control in a VIP latrine are:

- Subdued semi-darkness, inside the superstructure. Opaque walls and roof, and either a self-closing door or a spiral structure (see Figure 10.8) ensures sufficient darkness. The inside should not be so dark that people cannot see what they are doing, but dark in contrast to the vent pipe light.

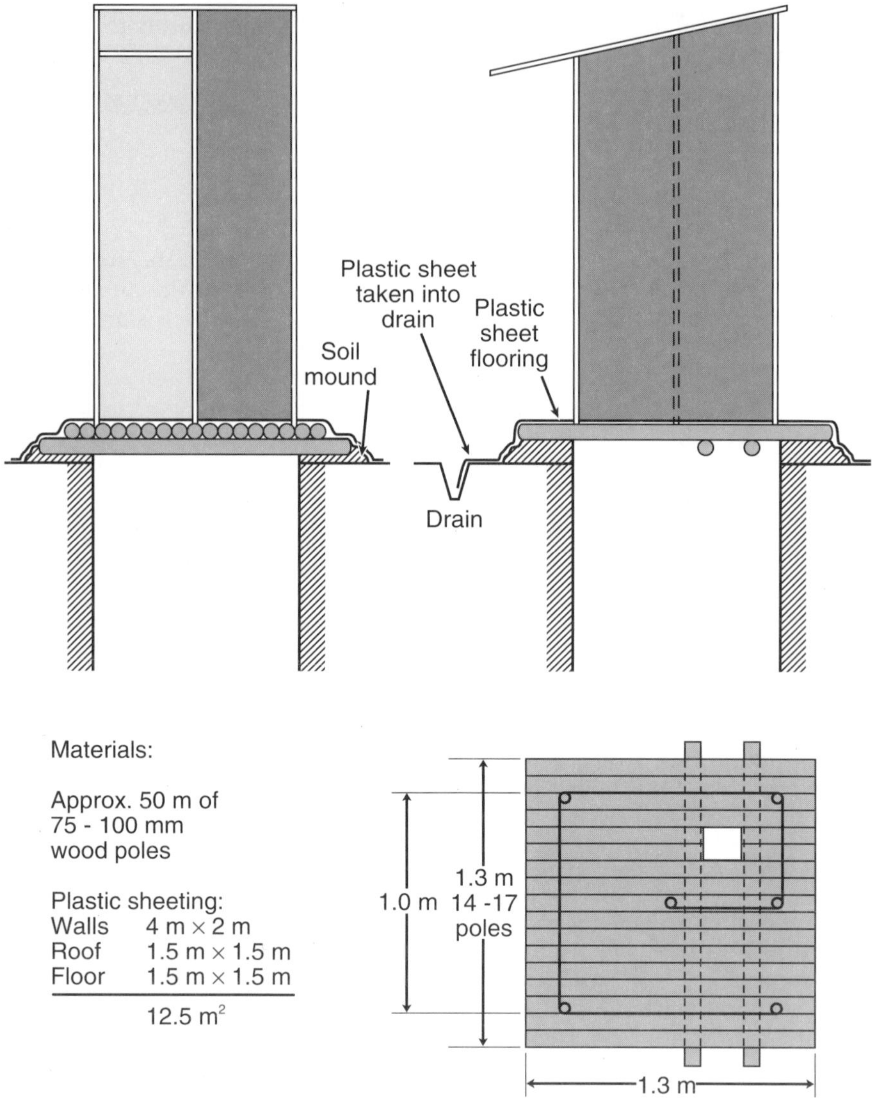

Figure 10.6 A simple pit latrine

- A well-maintained fly screen. Fly control will break down if the screen is only slightly broken. Mild steel 'fly-screen' quickly corrodes in the aggressive vent pipe gases. PVC coated fibreglass may last four or five years before weakening. Aluminium and stainless steel screens last well but they are not often available.

Note that mosquitoes are not attracted to light in the same way as flies, so a VIP latrine does not control mosquitoes. However, mosquitoes will only breed in a pit if there is standing water.

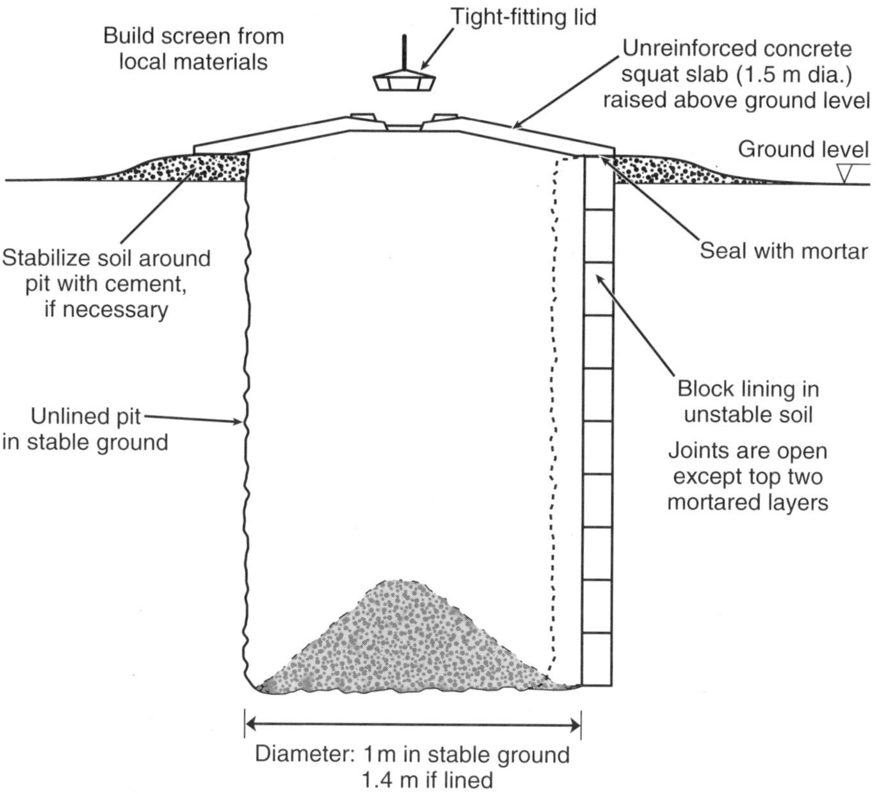

Figure 10.7 A simple pit latrine with an unreinforced concrete slab

Because ventilated improved pit (VIP) latrines need a dark interior, a vent pipe and a durable fly screen, they are more expensive and take longer to construct than simple pit latrines. This will mean they are not a viable option in many emergency scenarios.

See the Bibliography for further information on the various types of excreta disposal systems for longer-term use.

10.5 Disposal of sullage and runoff

10.5.1 Sullage

Sullage is wastewater from washing, food preparation and wasted tap water. Standing pools of polluted water can pose a health hazard through the encouragement of mosquito and fly breeding. They are also a hazard to children who play in or near them. It is therefore important to dispose of sullage safely. The main sources of sullage are water points, and service centres such as clinics and feeding centres.

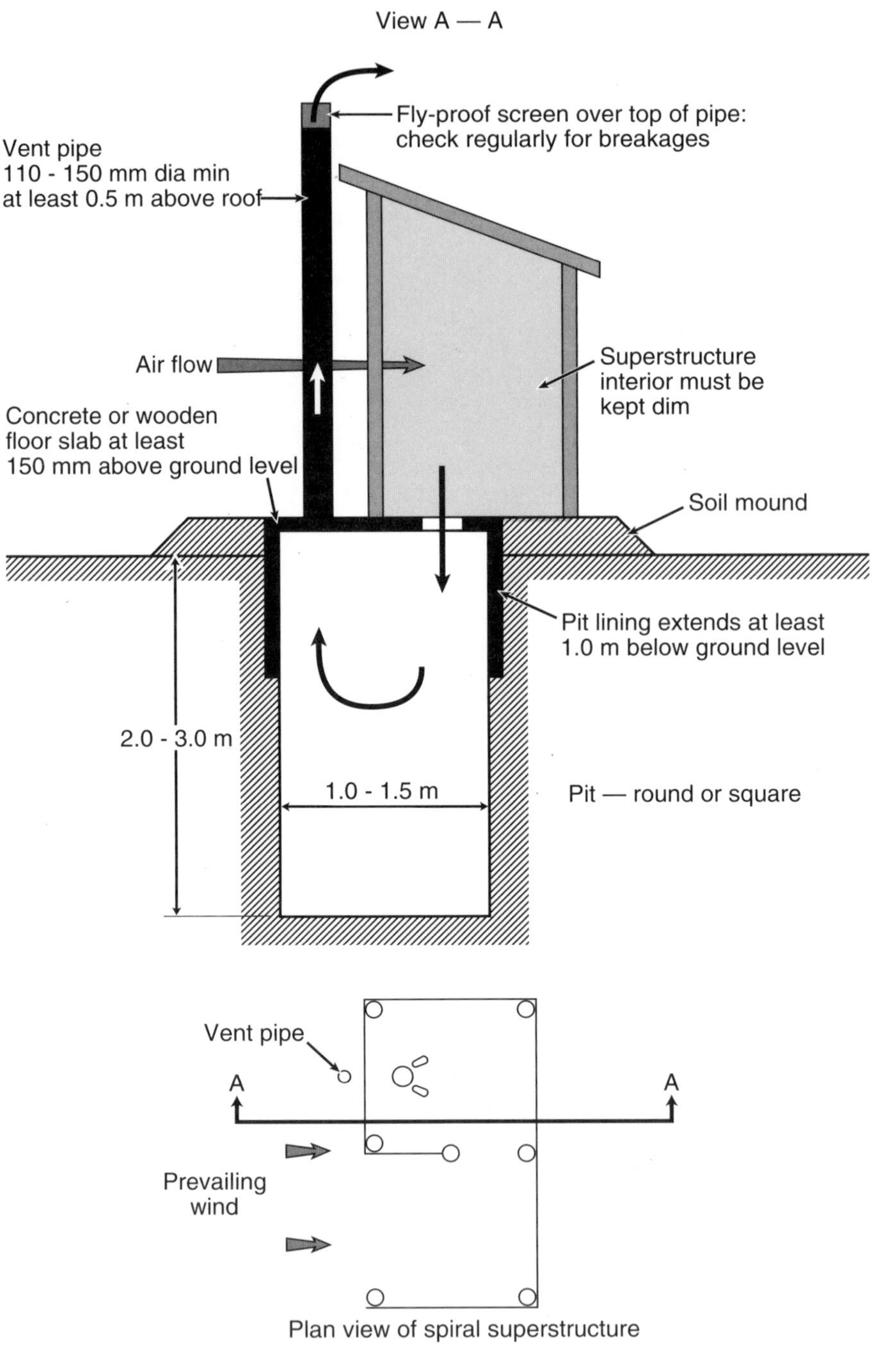

Figure 10.8 A ventilated improved pit (VIP) latrine

Where water is carried to the home by hand, volumes of domestic sullage are generally low and are well dispersed. Therefore, domestic sullage rarely poses a serious health hazard and is not considered further in this book. In certain circumstances, domestic sullage can be used productively, as in the irrigation of quick-growing fruit trees such as papaya.

The volumes of sullage generated from service centres will vary according to the type of water supply available and individual needs. As a planning guide use 55 litres per person per day for field hospitals and 25 litres per person per day for feeding centres (Reed and Dean, 1994). A cholera hospital will produce considerably higher volumes because of higher water use and this waste water must be dealt with very carefully.

Wherever possible, dispose of sullage close to the point of origin. This avoids spreading the problems created by sullage and the need for drainage channels or long pipes.

Soakaways

Do not dispose of sullage with a high organic loading into stagnant river pools and dry stream beds; it may become anaerobic and offensive. Soakaways are appropriate where the soils are sufficiently permeable. Size a soak pit or trench based on sullage volume and the infiltration capacity of the soil. Refer to Table A20.5 in Appendix 20 for guideline wastewater infiltration rates according to soil type. Carry out field tests to determine actual infiltration rates. After some time, the floor of the pit will clog and most infiltration will take place through the pit walls. Therefore, do not include the area of the floor when calculating the area required for infiltration. Only use the wall area below the level of the inlet pipe for infiltration calculations.

A covered soakaway is shown in Figure 10.9. The stones simply support the sides and roof of an unlined pit. Stones are unnecessary if the pit has a stable, porous lining.

Infiltration trenches (Figure 10.10) are an alternative to soakaways if the area required for infiltration is large or the local ground conditions prevent the digging of a pit.

Grease traps Sullage with a high solids content should be strained, otherwise the soil pores will quickly become blocked. Use a woven sacking strainer or similar. Remove grease with a grease trap (Figure 10.11). Regularly inspect and remove accumulated solids and grease in strainers and grease traps. Site a grease trap upstream of a soakaway or infiltration trench.

Rock and impermeable soils

The disposal of sullage poses special difficulties in rock or heavy clay soil conditions where soakaways are inappropriate and disposal to water courses is not feasible. The following methods can be considered, but they all have significant drawbacks.

Evaporation pans Evaporation pans are shallow ponds which hold water and allow it to evaporate. Disposal of strained sullage to evaporation pans is feasible where:

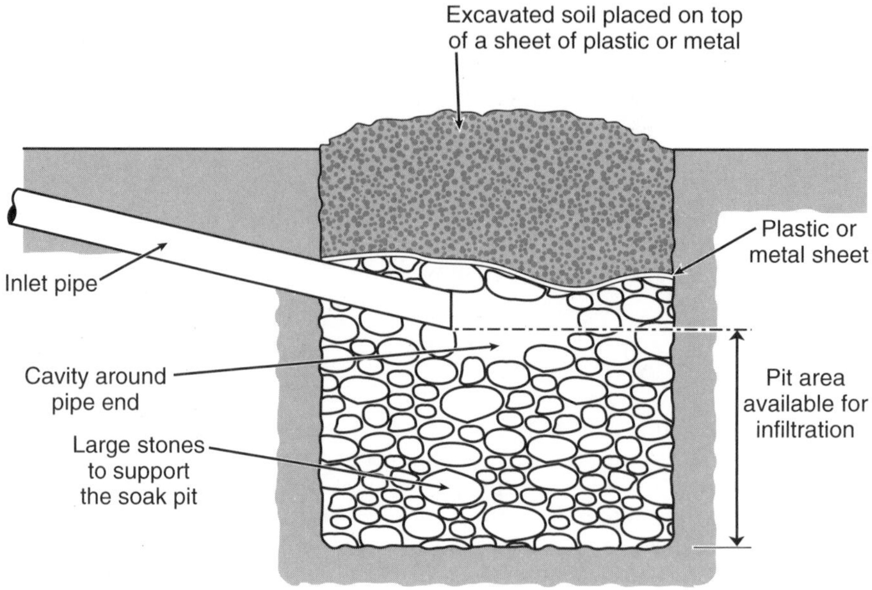

Figure 10.9 A covered soakaway

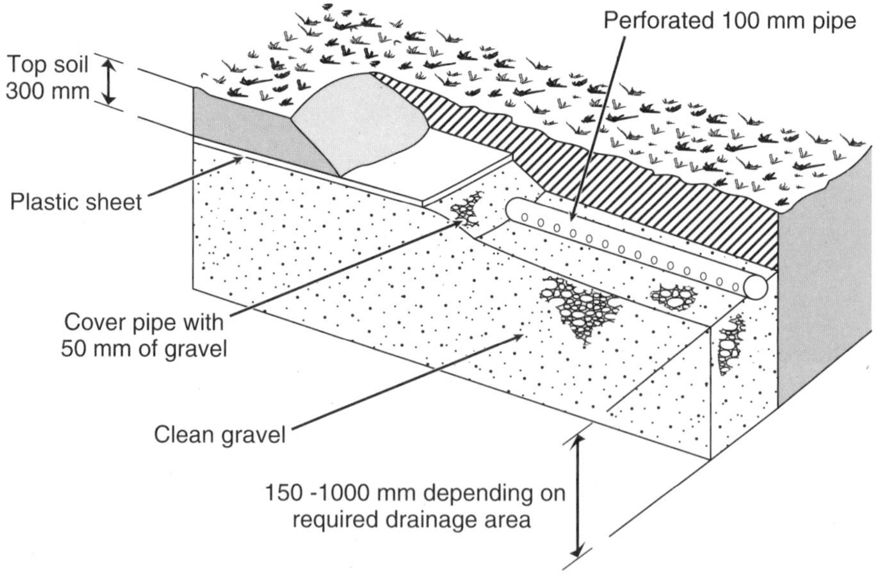

Figure 10.10 An infiltration trench
Source: Reed, 1994

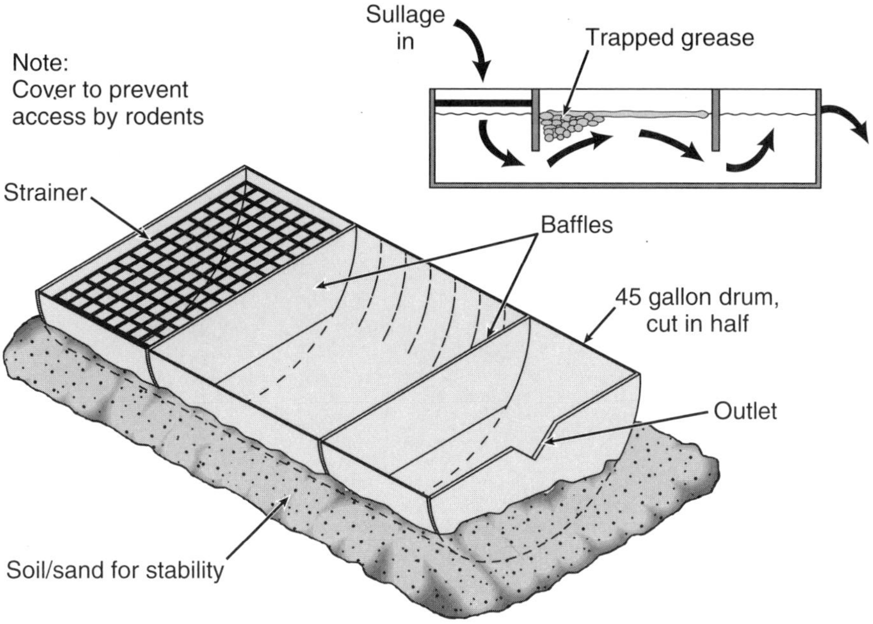

Figure 10.11 A simple grease trap

- The climate is arid and the net seasonal or annual evaporation to rainfall balance is favourable for the period in which evaporation pans are in use. Ascertain local evaporation and rainfall rates. As a rough guide, evaporation rates may vary from negligible in cold, humid conditions to as much as 5–10 mm/day in hot arid regions.
- Sufficient land is available. Even a high evaporation rate of 5 mm/day requires 200 m^2 of surface area per cubic metre of liquid per day.
- Pans can be sited away from habitation to reduce mosquito and fly hazards.

The intermittent filling and drying out of shallow pans will help to reduce mosquito breeding. Unlined pans make use of what soil absorptive capacity is available. Evaporation pans require close and careful management if they are to be effective.

Evaporation/evapotranspiration beds Evaporation beds rely on capillary action to draw water to the surface of shallow sand beds for evaporation to the atmosphere. Evapotranspiration beds are planted with grass or other vegetation which increases the movement of water from the root zone for transpiration through the leaves. There is very little storage for any rain which falls on a bed and this must also be removed by evaporation, so beds are only suited to a dry, arid climate. Figure 10.12 shows the cross-section of one type of evapotranspiration bed. The performance of evapotranspiration beds depends on a range of factors including climate, hydraulic loading, capillary rise, soil, vegetation and construction. As a guide, typical loading rates of about 2 l/m^2/day have been reported in arid areas of the western USA (EPA, 1980).

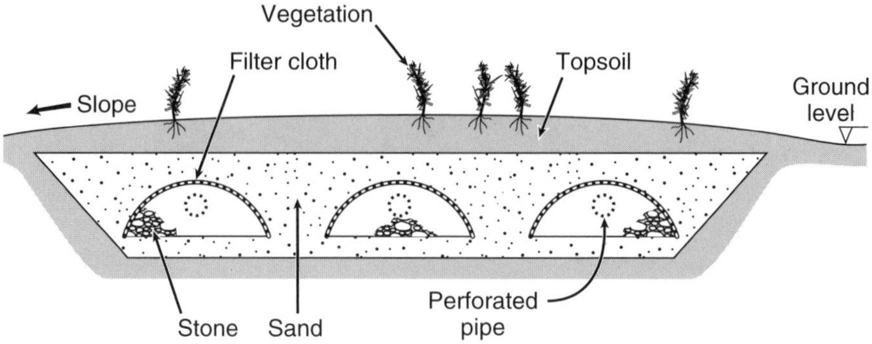

Figure 10.12 An evapotranspiration bed
Source: EPA, 1980

Irrigation Irrigation using sullage on a small scale may be appropriate. However, larger-scale irrigation takes time to establish and requires careful management. The health risks associated with irrigating vegetable plots will depend on the origin of the sullage. There may also be a danger that, at times, when there is insufficient sullage to water a productive garden regularly, excessive valuable drinking water might be diverted for use in irrigation.

10.5.2 Rainfall runoff

Rainfall runoff should be controlled because it can cause:

- Erosion: in tropical areas, intense rainfall can, in a matter of minutes, generate large quantities of surface runoff. This can cause quite dramatic and disastrous soil erosion. See Chapter 18 for a more detailed discussion of drainage and erosion control.
- Pollution: in a densely populated refugee settlement, any runoff is likely to be grossly polluted. This runoff will pollute any water source it enters.
- Disease: standing pools of surface water are ideal sites for mosquitoes. These pools are also unhygienic and can directly transmit a number of diseases (see Chapter 9).

When siting a temporary settlement, the drainage of surface water should be considered. Problems can be anticipated and mitigated by correct siting. If there is a choice, choose a site with only a slight slope to drain surface water without causing soil erosion.

The guidelines in Chapter 18 describe safe gradients, ditch side slopes and erosion control methods. Integrate drainage plans with other infrastructural development, such as road construction, to avoid one plan creating a problem for the other. Dig cut-off channels uphill of a site so that they divert runoff to natural drainage channels away from shelters and services. Plan a network of drains so that small drains from shelters channel into community, block, sector and main drains. Drain areas of standing water which could provide breeding grounds for mosquitoes. Consider filling in depressions to avoid areas of standing water.

The maintenance of drainage channels is important. Employ sanitarians and give them responsibility for drain inspection and cleaning.

10.6 Refuse disposal

10.6.1 Sources and types of refuse

Apart from being an unsightly nuisance, refuse can pose serious health problems if it is not properly controlled. Refuse encourages fly breeding and attracts rats and other animals, which can all be a nuisance and transmit disease. In an initial environmental health survey:

- Identify the sources and types of refuse.
- Prioritize the sources of refuse in terms of existing and potential health hazards.
- Arrange for the control and safe disposal of refuse according to the priorities established above.

The main sources of refuse are likely to be communal centres such as feeding centres, slaughter areas, food distribution points and clinics. In some cases, the packaging from relief items can be a major source of refuse if it cannot be recycled for other uses. Plastic bags and containers, and metal and glass objects will often be highly prized items and be automatically recycled.

10.6.2 Refuse collection

Sphere solid waste management standard 2: solid waste containers/pits, states: People have the means to dispose of their domestic waste conveniently and effectively. The key indicators for this standard are:

- No dwelling is more than 15 m from a refuse container or household refuse pit, or 100 m from a communal refuse pit.
- One 100-litre refuse container is available per 10 families, where domestic refuse is not buried on site.

Old 200-litre oil drums cut in half, with drainage holes in the bottom, are suitable for both general and service centre collection points. Larger containers are too heavy to handle. Keep containers covered to prevent scavenging by animals and children, and empty at least once a day.

People can be encouraged to make their own refuse baskets out of bamboo, cane and similar materials by agencies offering to buy some of them.

Establish a regular system of refuse collection. Recruit a refuse collection and disposal team and equip them with suitable tools and protective clothing (gloves and boots). UNRWA have reported using 2.5 workers per 1000 camp residents to keep communal areas clean and to collect and transport solid waste in wheelbarrows within a refugee camp (WHO/UNEP, 1991). A truck, tractor and trailer, or donkey cart may be necessary for regular collection and transportation from a transfer station to disposal sites some distance from dwellings.

Burning at local rubbish collection tips within a site is not recommended as combustion is often incomplete and the resulting heaps can become fly and rodent infested. They also pose a fire risk.

10.6.3 Refuse disposal methods

A combination of incineration and burial remote from dwellings is recommended for the safe disposal of solid wastes. Simple burning may not achieve sufficiently high temperatures to destroy all pathogens and it is inappropriate for high moisture content wastes such as food waste. However, burning will reduce the volume of non-hazardous dry waste prior to burial.

Bury wastes in a trench (Figure 10.13) or in a pit (Figure 10.14). Cover refuse every day. Fence the burial area to prevent both animal and human scavengers. Place wire mesh over the waste before backfilling where there is a chance that animals might dig up the trench when scavenging for food. The final soil cover should be at least 0.5 m deep to prevent fly breeding.

Consult with the affected population and local government officials concerning the location of waste disposal sites. Bury refuse downwind and away from dwellings. Ensure groundwater is not contaminated.

10.6.4 Hospital wastes

Apart from general hospital rubbish which can be handled with the general refuse, there are two types of hospital waste which must be dealt with separately: sharps and pathological wastes.

Sharps (blades, needles, syringes, etc.) should be placed in sealed containers. A container can be made from an old milk powder tin with a hole in the top or it can be a WHO/UNICEF-approved cardboard 'sharp box'. Containers should be stored securely to prevent theft. Sharps can be incinerated or, in the absence of efficient incineration, buried at the bottom of waste disposal pits or in a hand

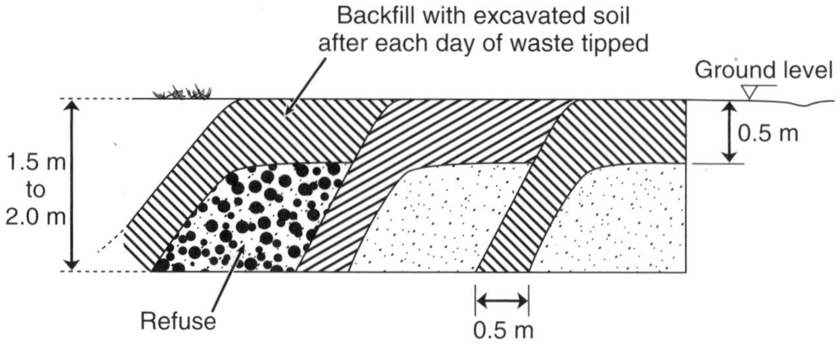

Figure 10.13 Solid waste burial trench

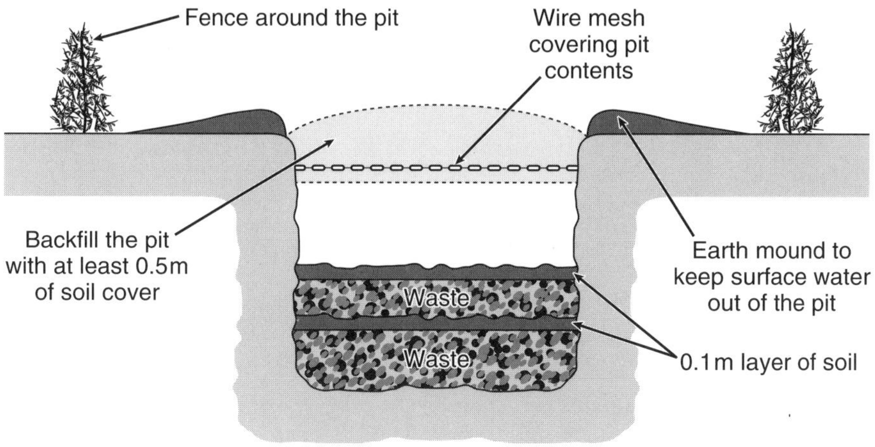

Figure 10.14 Solid waste burial pit

or machine-bored hole in the ground to avoid harm to potential scavengers (human and animal).

All non-metallic wastes, which have been in contact with body fluids, should be collected in clearly identified plastic bags tied at the top. High temperatures are required to completely destroy pathological material and burning in a simple fire will not completely destroy the pathogens. Therefore, burial as deep as possible is recommended.

Incineration

Efficient incineration is required to reduce soiled cloth, dressings, parts of human bodies and 'sharps' to a harmless ash with no possibility of the residue or the flue gases containing viruses or potentially harmful sharps or chemicals. The elimination of viruses is particularly important due to the risk of the spread of hepatitis and AIDS. High temperatures and relatively long residence times are the principal requirements for effective incineration. A temperature above 850°C is necessary for sterilization and reduction of sharps. A simple burner will not do the job and could increase risk arising from the waste.

The design shown in Figure 10.15 has been developed by De Montfort University in the UK and successfully operated in Europe, Africa and Asia. It comprises a single chamber cross-draught furnace. The outer casing is constructed of common brick while the inner core requires fire brick. Its capacity is between 7 and 13 kg of mixed waste per hour. Initial heating to bring it up to the operating temperature is achieved by burning wood, coal or dry waste assisted by small amounts of diesel oil or kerosene. Once up to temperature the waste material alone fuels incineration. The incinerator relies upon correct construction, operation and maintenance for safe and successful operation. For more information about the incinerator, various developments, drawings and instructions for construction and operation see: http://www.appsci.dmu.ac.uk/mwi/.

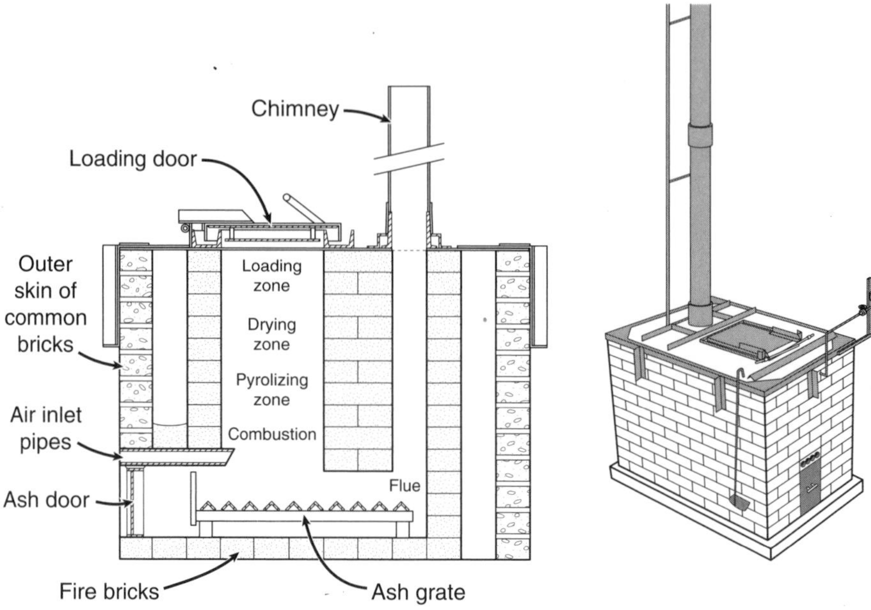

Figure 10.15 A medical waste incinerator
Source: De Montfort University, Leicester, UK, 2000

10.7 Disposal of the dead

10.7.1 Cultural practices and needs

To the family, relatives and friends of a dead person, the process of burial will be highly significant and emotional. It will be difficult for the relief worker to understand the feelings and attitudes of individuals in such circumstances fully, but it is important to try to appreciate and meet people's needs concerning funeral procedures and burial. The following should be recognized (adapted from Wilson and Harrell-Bond, 1990):

- Misunderstandings about funeral arrangements can sometimes cause friction between relief agencies and the people being assisted.
- The lack of an acceptable funeral and burial may leave social issues unresolved and contribute to grief among the bereaved resulting in additional trauma.
- People often expend scarce resources on funeral rites and graves.
- In many societies, memorials are a way of responding to the lack of proper burial or mourning for those who died in war, exile or disaster. Memorials may be a way of healing wounds.
- Burial cloth may need to be made available. Blankets or sleeping mats could be used where no cloth is available.

- Cement is often required for grave markers.
- 'Burial societies' are sometimes formed within the affected population, and agencies should work with them where they exist.
- Deaths may not be reported and bodies secretly buried if families fear a reduction in their food rations and other relief items as a result of a family death.

In certain circumstances, such as in the immediate aftermath of a disaster, relief workers may have to organize the collection and burial of large numbers of dead bodies. This is a harrowing task for all concerned and special provision should be made for the emotional support of all those involved.

10.7.2 Burial

Burial, if culturally acceptable, is the best option for disposal of the dead. Dead bodies pose a minimal health risk unless the death was associated with certain diseases, such as cholera. In the case of typhus or plague, dead bodies may harbour infected lice or fleas. There is no good health reason for cremation but some societies may prefer it.

Make arrangements for the burial of the dead as soon as possible. Locate burial areas in consultation with the people and the local authorities and consider the soil conditions and water table. Sufficient space must be made available, bearing in mind that different religious groups may want separate burial grounds and people may wish to bury relatives together.

Establish a method of recording the identity of deceased persons and causes of death. Records are used to monitor mortality rate, the incidence of disease, population, and for the tracing of individuals. However, use records with care, as burial may also take place outside recognized burial grounds.

10.8 Insects and rodents

Insects and rodents can be a nuisance, spoil or destroy food, and transmit disease; that is, they act as disease vectors.

The control of pests is a specialist subject requiring a full understanding of pest identification, life-cycles and control options. This section can only briefly mention the options available and emphasize the importance of environmental management as the priority preventive control measure. Consult local departments responsible for pest control and talk to other specialists, in particular medical entomologists, for relevant advice. See the Bibliography for further information.

10.8.1 Insect control

Insect-borne diseases can pose a hazard in normal circumstances, but for displaced populations these problems can be exacerbated (Thomson, 1990):

- People may move from a non-malarious area into an area where malaria is prevalent, or where the parasite strain differs. They may then lack the immunity of the local population.
- People may pass through areas infested with particular insect vectors (such as tsetse flies or sandflies).
- People may have to settle on land which is not normally inhabited because of insect vectors.
- People may find themselves living in overcrowded and unhygienic conditions which favour an increase in insect vectors (for instance, lice and flies).
- Problems may be compounded by the breakdown of long-term vector control programmes.

Common insect vectors and the health risks they pose are listed in Table 10.3.

Table 10.3 Insect vectors which pose significant health risks

Insect vector	*Health risks*	*Favoured environments*
Anophelene mosquitoes	Malaria; Filariasis	Surface water with little or no pollution, especially in the periphery of flooded areas and streams; puddles, wells, footprints
Culicine mosquitoes:		
– *Aedes*	Yellow fever; Dengue	Clean water containers in or around dwellings; water storage; rainwater in discarded containers
– *Culex quinquefasciatus*	Filariasis; Nuisance biter	Organically polluted water (latrines)
Flies	Diarrhoeal disease; Eye infections (particularly infants and children)	Excreta; exposed food; dead animals
Mites	Scabies; Scrub typhus	Overcrowding and poor personal hygiene
Lice	Epidemic typhus; Relapsing fever	Overcrowding and poor personal hygiene
Fleas	Plague (from infected rats); Endemic typhus	Overcrowding and poor personal hygiene
Ticks	Relapsing fever; Spotted fever	Overcrowding and poor personal hygiene

Note: The priority given to Dengue vectors depends on the incidence of the severe forms of the disease.
Adapted from UNHCR, 1999 and Lines & Kolsky, undated

Mosquitoes

Life-cycle

- Eggs laid on the water surface hatch into larvae in a few days and suspend themselves from the surface to breathe air.
- The larvae develop into pupae which remain suspended from the surface and change into adults after 1–3 days.
- The female adult needs a blood meal before laying viable eggs.
- The cycle from egg to adult can be as short as nine days in hot conditions.
- Adult mosquitoes fly up to 3 km from their breeding site. Wind may carry them further.

Environmental control methods The primary method of mosquito control is through the management of potential breeding sites. The type of breeding site preferred by each mosquito group can vary from region to region, although some generalities can be made (Table 10.3). If possible, obtain reliable information on the most appropriate control measures for specific mosquito groups in a particular area. The value of obtaining specialist advice is shown by the following important example.

The *Anopheles gambiae* species of mosquito is a major vector of malaria. The following guidelines for engineering action to control *Anopheles gambiae* mosquito in Africa have been suggested (Lines & Kolsky, undated):

- Drain standing unpolluted water within seven days of it forming, before larvae can mature.
- Maintain and keep drains clear. Larvae will tend to cling to the sides of drains or where the surface is broken by earth or emerging vegetation.
- The smallest puddles, streams and drains are the most important. Clean up after construction work and encourage the filling in of puddles.
- Eliminate puddles, ponds and borrow pits (pits used for the extraction of construction materials). In ponds greater than a metre deep, larvae are only found at the edges, so minimize the perimeter of ponds and make the edges steep and straight.
- *Anopheles gambiae* larvae are not found in ruts and potholes disturbed by passing vehicles. Deal with the water beside the road, not on it.
- Vegetation at surface water edges should either be eliminated or very thick. *Anopheles gambiae* larvae prefer the sun or partial shade. They do not like thick bush.

The last point means that it is probably better to leave a densely overgrown swamp rather than clear it of thick vegetation. However, reed swamps may be infested with *Anopheles funestus*, which can be just as undesirable as *Anopheles gambiae*. This example highlights the need to obtain specialist advice on the correct identification of species and the best action to take in each instance.

Organically polluted water is not a breeding site for malaria-transmitting *Anophelene* mosquitoes (although they may breed in muddy water) but it is favourable to the *Culex* mosquito larvae which transmit filariasis.

The use of a mosquito net (bed net) gives protection from mosquito biting. Nets impregnated with insecticide are even more effective.

Chemical control methods The chemical control of mosquitoes supplements environmental management measures. The main chemical control methods used against mosquitoes are residual spraying and larviciding. Space spraying is also sometimes used.

- Residual spraying is directed against adult female mosquitoes which feed on people in and around shelters and buildings. Spray persistent insecticide onto exposed surfaces. Depending on the insecticide, it will remain active for two or three months. Consult with the local authorities and choose an available insecticide against which local mosquitoes have not built up resistance. The most suitable machines for internal residual spraying are hand-operated, continuously pumped or pre-pressurized knapsack sprayers. They should be cleaned daily and regularly serviced, with particular attention given to preventing and repairing leaks.
- Larviciding: known breeding sites which are not sources of drinking water can be treated with insecticide or light oil.
- Space spraying is the outdoor application of insecticides as mists or fogs. This is very expensive and not normally appropriate for malaria vectors in Africa, as the mosquitoes rest indoors and can be controlled with residual spraying. Space spraying has been used in refugee camps in Thailand to control *Aedes aegypti* mosquitoes but it was not found to be very effective. The treatment of breeding sites in the water supply with a larvicide (Temephos granules) was found to be more effective.

Domestic flies

Flies closely associated with humans (*Musca domestica* and *Musca sorbens*) may transmit disease by the mechanical transfer of pathogens from wastes to human food, eyes and open wounds.

Life-cycle

- Eggs are white and about 1 mm long. They are laid in rotting organic waste including excreta, kitchen waste, surgical dressings and corpses.
- Eggs hatch into white larvae (maggots) which feed on the warm waste under the surface.
- The maggots mature rapidly and burrow (up to several metres) away from the warm, moist waste to a drier place to pupate. They may burrow as deep as 50 cm in broken soil.
- The adults finally emerge and burrow to the surface.
- The rate of development depends on temperature and takes from about a week at 35°C to more than a month at 16°C.
- The distance travelled by flies will vary according to circumstances. They will tend to remain within a few hundred metres of a breeding site, but have been known to travel up to 20 miles (Busvine, 1982).

Environmental control methods Preventive control methods are aimed at reducing breeding sites. Identify potential fly breeding sites when carrying out initial and follow-up environmental surveys. Employ the measures for the safe disposal of excreta and refuse described in this book. Note the depth of broken soil through which fly maggots are able to burrow and bury waste and excreta under a 0.5 m final layer of compacted soil to prevent fly breeding. Waste bagged in closed plastic sacks is a supplementary or alternative control measure. Excreta covered with a very thin layer of soil may not be very effective in deterring fly breeding. Fly eggs and larvae require a moist environment in which to develop. If defecation fields are the only places available for defecation then in sunny, dry climates it may be better to leave excreta exposed to dry out. Wherever possible, screen food and potential breeding sites to deny access to flies.

Chemical control methods Only use chemicals as a supplement to good hygienic practices. It may be essential to use chemicals, however, when conditions result in a rapid increase in the fly population. Do not apply chemicals directly to breeding sites (such as latrine pits) as they may be harmful to fly parasites and predators which tend to control fly breeding. The main method of chemical control used against flies is space treatment.

Suitable insecticides can be obtained for use in ultra low volume (ULV) applications, such as mists or fogs, at a concentration of less than 5 l/ha. There is a variety of equipment available for space spraying (see WHO, 1990). Some of the most appropriate equipment is the knapsack mist blower and the thermomechanical fog generator. Both these machines are portable, easy to maintain and safe to operate.

The best time to spray for flies is usually in the early morning and in the evening when atmospheric conditions tend to keep the insecticide close to the ground. Restrict treatment to the areas where flies are seen, such as defecation fields and rubbish dumps. However, if flies are present throughout a whole area, a complete settlement or camp may need to be treated.

Space spraying can be effective against flies but it is very expensive and its use must be weighed against other control methods.

Other insect pests

Improved living conditions and good hygiene will help to control other domestic insect pests such as fleas and cockroaches. Effective hygiene promotion which is integrated with the sanitation programme is important in this respect. Set an example of good housekeeping at communal centres (feeding centres) and food stores. Residual spraying, carried out for mosquito control, may also reduce other insect pests, including sandflies. (Sandflies are responsible for the transmission of leishmaniasis).

Consult with medical and specialist personnel on the preventive techniques described and further measures which could be adopted.

Insecticides

Insecticides need careful, knowledgeable use. They also need a great deal of careful organization and good logistical support. Seek specialist advice and co-ordinate actions with national programmes (see Lacarin and Reed, 1999).

WHO/FAO produce data sheets on pesticides; these data sheets can be obtained from the Division of Control of Tropical Diseases, WHO, Geneva.

WHO has categorized insecticides according to hazard (Table 10.4). Only insecticides in the 'slightly hazardous' and 'acute hazard unlikely' categories should be considered for use in temporary settlements, unless the training and supervision of personnel is of a high standard.

Table 10.4 Insecticides categorized according to hazard

Extremely hazardous	dieldrin
Highly hazardous	chlordecone, dichlorvos, dioxathion, fenthion
Moderately hazardous	bendiocarb, bioallethrin, carbaryl, chlordane, chlorphoxim, chlopyrifos, DDT, diazinon, dimethoate, dioxacarb, endosulfan, fenchlorphos, fenitrothion, HCH, naled, propoxur, pyrethrins, toxaphene
Slightly hazardous	allethrin, bromophos, malathion, pirimiphos-methyl, resmethrin, trichlorfon
Acute hazard unlikely in normal use	bioresmethrin, cypermethrin, deltamethrin, jodfenphos, permethrin, phenothrin, temephos, tetrachlorvinphos

Table 10.5 Selected insecticides for mosquito and fly control

Control method	*Insecticide*
	Mosquito control
Space treatment	Pyrethroids Organophosphates: pirimiphos-methyl Carbamates: bendiocarb
Residual spraying	Organochlorines: DDT, HCH (BHC) Organophosphates: fenitrothion, malathion, pirimiphos-methyl Carbamates: bendiocarb, propoxur
Larviciding	Organophosphates: malathion, temephos
	Fly control
Space treatment	Pyrethroids OR combined with or replaced by organophosphates: bromophos, dichlorvos, fenchlorphos, malathion, pirimiphos-methyl

For a more complete guide to insecticides refer to MSF, 1992; WHO, 1984b; and Lacarin and Reed, 1999

Spraying

Plan and organize spraying carefully. Liaise with the affected population to explain the purpose of spraying, the spraying procedure, and the importance of removing or covering items which might be harmed (food, cooking utensils, animals, and so on).

Typical personnel required for residual spraying:

- Spray teams of five people comprising a leader (preferably a health worker), two sprayers and two insecticide carriers.
- Three people to mix and issue insecticide to the teams and to keep a record of the insecticide used.

Spray training should include familiarization with spray routines, care and operation of equipment, knowledge of the hazards involved and the precautions to be taken (see Box 10.1).

10.8.2 Rodent control

Infections are transmitted by rodents to humans in several ways:

- Rat bite fever – by a bite.
- Leptospirosis (Weil's disease) – by rodent urine.
- Murine typhus and plague – by infected rat fleas.

The main rodent pests of concern are the house mouse, the brown Norway rat and the black rat (also known as the roof or ship's rat). Several other field rodents are reservoirs of infection which may be transmitted to humans, causing leishmaniasis and plague. Normally, contact with field rodents is limited, but may be increased where displaced people move into the habitat of field rodents or when field rodents move into human settlements following a disaster, such as flooding.

> *WARNING: Flea-borne diseases*
>
> *Whenever there is a possibility of a flea-borne disease (such as plague or murine typhus), action must first be taken against fleas carried by the rats before rat control measures are taken. Otherwise, fleas may transfer from the dead rats to humans, thereby encouraging disease transmission.*

Environmental control methods

Follow the guidelines for good environmental management described in the relevant sections of this book, with particular reference to sanitary refuse disposal. Reduce and inspect potential nesting sites such as discarded packaging, collections of rubbish and stocks of firewood. Protect potential rodent food supplies by the regular inspection, cleaning and sweeping of food stores, kitchens and distribution areas.

Carry out rodent proofing measures. Buildings, especially food stores, can be rodent proofed by closing all holes greater than 6 mm (the smallest hole that a young mouse can enter) with rodent proof material (metal plates, cement mortar). Check gaps under doors, where services (pipes and cables) pass through walls, and windows and other openings used for ventilation.

Lay traps to restrict the number of rodents. Offer an incentive to encourage the catching and killing of rats (for instance, payment for rat tails).

Box 10.1 Safety precautions when using insecticide

- Read insecticide labels. They should give the following information: the identity of the product; its effectiveness against pests; safe handling procedures; and treatment in case of poisoning.
- Wash and destroy all empty insecticide containers before burial.
- Insecticides in the 'Extremely Hazardous' and 'Highly Hazardous' WHO classification should not be used.
- Secure insecticide containers properly when transporting in vehicles and ensure that the vehicle is well ventilated.
- Inspect containers for damage after transport and check the vehicle is not contaminated.
- Never transport or store insecticides and food together.
- Never transfer insecticides to unmarked containers.
- Provide separate working clothes for those who handle pesticides and splashproof clothing for those handling concentrate.
- Provide soap and water for washing after concentrates are mixed and for washing before eating and at the end of work.
- Spillage: ensure protective footwear and clothing is worn; soak up liquids with absorbent material (e.g. sand); place material and swept solid formulations in plastic bags and bury.
- Keep records of: insecticides received, used, and in store; places treated; and containers buried.
- Empty and clean spraying equipment after use and ensure unused insecticide is returned to store.
- Ensure wastewater from washing associated with insecticide is not disposed of near water supplies. Use an isolated soakaway.
- Keep children away from insecticides, application equipment and stores.

Adapted from Murlis and Stephenson, 1981

Chemical control methods

Only use rodenticides in situations which are under strict control, such as in secure food stores with well trained staff. General use in a post-disaster or refugee camp situation can be very dangerous. In some cases, rats may be a source of human food and the consumption of poisoned rats could be lethal (see Box 10.2 for safety precautions).

Box 10.2 Safety precautions when using rodent poison

- Only use rat poison if rats are not a source of human food.
- Employ only well-trained staff and apply rodenticides under strictly controlled conditions.
- Handle poisons with caution. Rodent poisons are toxic to man and domestic animals.
- Whenever possible, use the less hazardous chronic anticoagulant poisons as they must be consumed for several days before they are effective.
- Wear protective plastic or rubber gloves and dust masks when preparing baits as some poisons can penetrate the skin. They should not be inhaled.
- Wear gloves and take care when handling rodent corpses, which should be incinerated or buried in a deep hole.
- At the end of a campaign, collect the remaining bait and incinerate or bury it.

Rodenticides are of two types: acute or single-dose poisons; and chronic or multiple dose poisons.

- Acute poisons are used when a rapid kill is important. Death can occur within 30 minutes of a single feed. However, there are drawbacks, as the rodent must consume sufficient poison before it takes effect. Pre-baiting with untreated food accustoms the rodent to feeding at the same sites on the same foodstuff. The bait is easier and quicker to consume if it is slightly damp. Acute poisons are more hazardous to humans and domestic animals than chronic poisons. Therefore, chronic (multiple dose) poisons are the preferred option.
- Chronic poisons are slow-acting and several feeds are necessary over a few days before they effect a kill. A widely used anticoagulant chronic poison is 'warfarin'. Typically, dose baits for rats and mice at 250 ppm (parts per million) or 0.025% of active warfarin: 250 ppm (0.025%) = 1 part of 0.5% concentrate to 19 parts of bait.

Chronic poisons are available already mixed with food materials as bait or baits can be made up – meat, fish, grains or nuts can be used. Place bait in small piles (100–200 g for rats and 25 g for mice) where rodents will easily find it and before they reach food stocks. Poisons are also available as liquids or soluble formulations. Monitor the effect of poisoning. Rodents begin to die after about a week, when there should be a reduction in feeding. Feeding on bait should stop after 3–5 weeks. Try one of the following actions if there is continued feeding:

- Extend the area being baited.
- Change the bait.
- Change the poison.
- Investigate the possible arrival of new rodents.

Mice can be more difficult to control than rats. They sample small amounts of food from different sources so a large number of bait sites are more effective. Use a mixture of 0.025% warfarin and 0.1% calciferol against mice.

11 Emergency water supply

Solving a water supply problem will need a range of skills and involve engineering in its broadest sense. Organization, management and negotiation may be just as important as technical design and construction.

This chapter provides guidelines on the rapid assessment of existing water supplies and suggests immediate actions for the development of an emergency supply. The focus is on the initial phase of an emergency. Guidelines on how much water people need and the quality of water to be supplied are given here; further details on water pumping, storage, treatment, distribution and longer-term development are given in Chapters 12, 13 and 14.

11.1 Assessment

11.1.1 Assessment approach

Use a staged approach:

- Carry out an initial rapid assessment of the health of the affected population and the condition of existing water supplies. In conjunction with health workers and the affected people, determine priority needs and the immediate actions required.
- Get started quickly.
- Monitor impact of actions, adjust as necessary and carry out further assessment to determine the next steps.
- Plan and initiate a programme of longer-term actions.

When assessing and planning water supply needs, it may be useful to bear in mind some basic groundrules:

- Assume all surface water is polluted. Groundwater from properly protected boreholes is likely to be bacteriologically safe.
- A large amount of reasonably safe water is preferable to a small amount of very pure water.
- Avoid collection from the source by individuals: distribute water to the people.

Use Table 11.1 in assessing water supplies and Chapter 5 for general guidelines on assessment. Refer to Section 11.2 for likely immediate actions. Wherever feasible, consult and work with the following people during the assessment and in subsequent implementation: representatives of local

Table 11.1 A guide to assessing water supplies

Question	*Comments*
How many people are affected and where are they?	Consult the people affected, local authorities and those involved in registration. Estimate new arrivals and departures.
Are people suffering from water related diseases and are any likely to appear?	Consult the health information system. Find out what diseases are common and what are the causes. Check the location of high disease incidence.
Do people have a water problem now? Is one likely to arise soon?	Ask them. Ask local people about seasonal effects on water supply. Anticipate the arrival or departure of people.
Has everyone enough water for drinking, washing, cooking?	Carry out a survey; Check with different groups of people (young, old, men, women). They should have access to 15 l/p/d (Sphere).
Is there enough water at the source? How long will it last?	If the source is adequate, but people are not using enough water, then distribution or collection may be a problem.
Are there intermittent shortages?	Storage in strategically located tanks may help and can also provide an element of treatment (see Chapter 13).
Is the water close enough?	Carrying water takes considerable time and effort. If the collection point is more than a few hundred metres from the home then consumption will be low.
Are there enough containers?	It is difficult to collect and store water without containers of a suitable size and opening for filling.
Is wastage significant?	Check leaking pipes, taps left open or broken.
Do people practise good hygiene? Have they the means to?	If people practise good hygiene they may be able to cope with quite a poor quality water. If they do not, supplying high quality water will not, in itself, solve a disease problem.
Is the source contaminated? Is treatment necessary?	Check using sanitary survey and/or use a microbiological test kit (see Section 11.1.2).
Is chlorination possible without pre-treatment? Can pre-treatment be set up quickly?	See Chapter 13.
Are there alternative sources nearby?	Look, ask local people and the authorities. Enquire about any potential problems in accessing and using them.
Is there time to develop this or nearby sources?	Consider logistics, staff, funding, materials, equipment.
If water sources are poor:	
• Is tankering water feasible?	Logistics, reliable access, cost (see Section 11.5).
• Are people able and willing to move?	Politics, transport, availability of suitable alternative sites?

government, the Ministry of Health, the water authority, the local community, displaced people and relevant relief agency staff (for example, health personnel).

Estimate daily water requirements using the water consumption figures given in 11.4.1 (Box 11.2). If water-related diseases are present, find out which groups of people are affected – is disease related to location, age, gender, ethnicity . . .?

11.1.2 Contamination of water sources

In the overcrowded conditions common in the initial phase of an emergency, water contaminated by pathogens can cause illness and death through disease in a very short period of time. While it is strongly recommended that, in such circumstances, water supplies be chlorinated as soon as possible (see 13.3.3) it is important to assess the level of contamination. This can be done in two complementary ways:

- Water quality tests, which indicate actual contamination at the time of the test. They do not indicate the potential for contamination or what control measures are needed. See 11.4 for more details on water quality. Various portable kits have been developed for water quality testing in the field. An example is the Oxfam/Delagua kit (Oxfam, 1988).
- Sanitary surveys, which indicate likely sources of contamination and give guidance on ways of removing such sources (see below).

Prevent contamination of the water by protecting the source. Chlorinate the water supply to ensure the water is safe to drink.

Using sanitary surveys

A sanitary survey is an on-site assessment of the condition of a water supply, and of the practices associated with it which could pose a danger to health. The survey can be carried out quickly, without the need for specialist equipment. A sanitary survey reporting system has been developed (Lloyd and Helmer, 1991) to identify possible sources of contamination and provide a 'risk score' for a source. An example of a sanitary survey form applied to a river water source is shown in Box 11.1 and Figure 11.1.

Use the form as a checklist and to produce a 'risk score' which can be used to compare alternative sources (see Section 5.3.5 for ranking techniques). Prepare a sketch of the source to accompany the form. The form and sketch can be used as a record of work which needs to be done. See Appendix 8 for further examples of sanitary survey forms.

Sanitary surveys may be particularly useful in drought emergencies where there is a need to assess quickly the condition of a large number of water supplies distributed over a wide geographical area. Where a number of people are involved in source assessment, sanitary surveys help to ensure a standard approach. The results of the surveys can be used to draw up a list of sources – or communities – needing priority attention.

Carry out sanitary surveys regularly on critical water sources to monitor any changes and indicate further actions.

Box 11.1 A sample sanitary survey form

SANITARY SURVEY FORM

Type of source: ________________ Location: ________________

Date of survey: ___________ Survey carried out by: ________________

Sanitary survey question	Yes	No
Is the refugee camp within 1 km of the river?		
Is it upstream of drinking water collection points?		
Are people defecating close to the river?		
Are there defecation areas upstream of drinking water collection points?		
Is surface runoff from the camp likely?		
Are people washing or bathing upstream of drinking water collection points?		
Are animal watering points located upstream?		
Is there any other source of pollution upstream (villages, dead animals)?		
Are people walking into the water to fill containers?		
Are the containers clean?		
Risk score: Add up the number of 'Yes' answers		

11.2 Immediate actions

There are often simple, immediate measures which can be taken to improve a poor water supply. These should not be overlooked in the rush to install a more comprehensive water supply system. Even packaged water supply systems take time to be delivered, erected, and commissioned. During this time, much can be done to improve the situation and many lives saved through quick action.

If adequate amounts of safe water cannot be supplied reliably then people may have to move. This is a major logistical and, frequently, political operation.

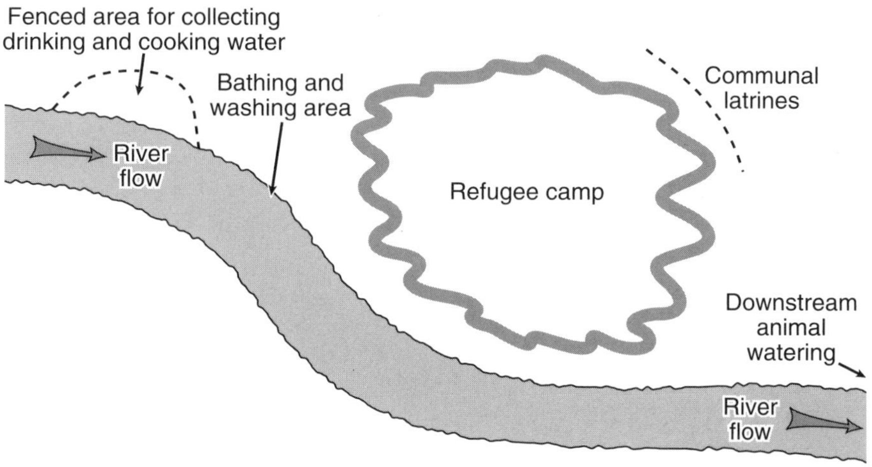

Figure 11.1 Controlled access to a river water source

Organize your team

You will not be effective acting alone. As soon as possible, recruit a team of assistants. See Chapter 6 for more details.

Protect the source

- Locate defecation areas far away and downhill from water sources.
- Control access to open water sources to give protected upstream water collection points, washing areas downstream of the water collection points, and animal watering points further downstream of any habitation (see Figure 11.1).
- Protect upstream drinking water sources by constructing fencing and walkways for water collection. Appoint supervisory guards.
- Protect wells and springs. Immediate protection can be provided by fencing, rainfall runoff trenches and embankments, and low walls around open wells.

Organize tankering

- Organize tankering, but only if really necessary. See Section 11.5.

Organize distribution

- Organize controlled distribution from heavily used point sources (such as springs, wells and standposts) to prevent wastage, damage to structures and contamination of the sources. Point source supervisors may be necessary. Ensure that the weak, sick and elderly receive adequate water.
- Minimize wastage. It is often necessary to ration water to prevent wastage. Significant amounts of water can be wasted through tank and pipe leakage, spillage, and children playing with taps, valves, etc. Control wastage through distribution at certain times of the day for different sections of a settlement, or limit the amount of water collected per person from a point source.

Provide containers for collection and storage

- Suitable containers for both the storage and collection of water may be in short supply. If so, locate, purchase and transport containers (5, 10 and 20 litres) to the point of use. Buckets have the advantage that they can be transported more easily by 'nesting'. Avoid thin plastic buckets and non-rigid collapsible plastic containers which soon crack.
- The transportation of light, empty, bulky containers can be expensive. Recycle empty cooking oil containers.
- Oxfam have developed a 14-litre water container with lid and tap for household use.

Provide community support and hygiene promotion

- Let people know what is happening and what actions are expected of them.
- Make sure that community support for the weak, sick, and elderly means that they are adequately supplied. If community support is lacking, organize support through extension workers.
- Initiate a hygiene promotion campaign (See Chapter 9). While it can take a long time to change certain culturally determined practices, other practices such as the hygienic collection of water may be improved dramatically in the short term.

Provide basic water storage and treatment

- Provide pumps, fuel and spares, and other vital equipment (this can be a major logistics operation).
- Pipe the water to storage tanks and thence to temporary tapstands. Institutions providing basic services (such as clinics and feeding centres) will need storage containers of a higher capacity than domestic containers. Emergency storage tanks such as pillow tanks can be very useful for short-term storage in the initial phase of the response. Commercially available rectangular steel tanks can be purchased in most major towns (see Section 13.2).
- Chlorinate the water supplied. In extreme circumstances, such as where water is heavily polluted and there is a serious risk of disease outbreak, chlorine may be added directly to individual water containers at the point of collection, using for example small syringes. See Section 13.3.3 on how to calculate dosage rates. Be aware that some people may refuse to drink water chlorinated in this way because of the taste of chlorine or the perception that something harmful is being added to the water.
- Set up pre-treatment of the source water (see Section 13.3.1).

Monitor and evaluate

- Initiate simple monitoring of the levels of both surface and groundwater sources. Measure the level of surface waters with rigidly fixed graduated gauge posts. Measure well levels early each morning with a dip gauge or simple string and weight.
- Monitor the demand for water.

- Liaise with health workers to identify any change in disease incidence.
- If the water supply is satisfactory, look at other priorities.

11.3 Medium- to long-term actions

11.3.1 The medium term

Once the basic measures have been taken to safeguard existing sources, assess the medium- to long-term needs. Unless people quickly move on from the site, it will be necessary to upgrade the supply. This may mean the development of additional or new sources. The prime considerations are:

- Adequate storage of water – at least 24 hours supply:
  - As a reserve of water.
  - As a buffer between the source and distribution points to allow for settlement and further treatment.
- Appropriate treatment of water. The basic treatment of surface water usually involves settlement in storage tanks and chlorination. While chlorination is recommended, uncontaminated groundwater can be supplied directly.
- Efficient distribution of water:
  - To eliminate direct user contact with water sources.
  - To avoid large concentrations of people at collection points.
  - To reduce wastage of water at crowded collection points.
  - To reduce waiting time at crowded collection points.
  - To reduce walking and carrying distances.
  - To ensure a fair distribution to all.

Treatment and distribution can be improved and developed as time allows. See Chapter 13 for more details.

11.3.2 The longer term

'Emergencies' may last a long time (see 1.1.1). In emergencies, where it is clear that many thousands of people will be resident in a settlement for at least a year or more, a reliable, well designed supply system will be needed. Make an early decision to develop an emergency supply with a properly designed distribution system. This avoids undue expenditure and worry on the maintenance of a temporary, possibly fragile, system. Funds are better spent on a well designed, more permanent system.

Refer to the relevant chapters of this manual, and the Bibliography, for specific guidance on water treatment, pumping and distribution for more permanent water supply systems.

11.3.3 Levels of service and local water supplies

The development of an emergency supply must take into account the length of time for which the supply will be required and the minimum level of service necessary to protect people's health. The level of service will be influenced by:

- What is possible. Are numbers changing rapidly? Are resources available?
- Changes in disease patterns – requiring changes in the quantity and quality of water supplied.
- Basic needs – what is the minimum level of service needed to maintain people's health?
- The levels of service that the people expect. In some temporary settlements, very basic levels of service are better than what they had previously. In others, people may have been used to much higher levels.
- The level of service available to local communities. In a temporary settlement, with large numbers of people living closely together, a high level of service is essential to guard against contamination of the source water and the widespread outbreak of disease. Thus water may be treated, chlorinated and distributed through standposts in the camp while local people continue to use unimproved traditional water sources.

At the same time as improving the water supply for a displaced population, it may be desirable to improve supplies for the host community for the following reasons:

- Local water supplies may be exposed to increased risk of contamination and depletion with the arrival of many displaced people.
- It is possible that the outbreak of disease due to poor water sources in a local community could spread to the displaced people.
- Local improvements might help to alleviate any resentment that may be caused by the higher service levels often found in a temporary settlement.

11.4 Water quantity and quality

11.4.1 How much water do people need?

People need water for drinking, washing and cooking. The minimum quantity of drinking water required for human survival will vary, depending upon the climate, the amount and type of food intake, and human activity. Minimum drinking water requirements will lie in the range 3–5 litres/person/day but more will be needed in a hot, dry and windy climate, and if people are active. Washing and cooking will add to the quantity of water an individual needs, although washing water does not have to be of drinking water quality. Box 11.2 gives estimates of water requirements.

Remember that the more water that is supplied, the more wastewater there will be. This must be disposed of safely. Estimates of the quantity of water people use must take into account all the seasonally available water sources. In the wet season, water courses are flowing, and water for washing and cooking will be more readily available. At the height of the dry season, sources of water may be scarce. Large quantities of water may have to be provided for animals.

Small-scale irrigation may be possible where there is a surplus supply of water. But approach small-scale irrigation with care. For example, 0.1 hectare (1000 m^2) of land will require something like 5000 litres of water/day

Box 11.2 Water requirements

Minimum for survival	3–5 litres/person/day
Minimum for basic domestic needs	15 litres/person/day (Sphere key indicator)
Health centres and hospitals	5 litres/outpatient 40–60 litres/inpatient/day Additional quantities may be needed for laundry, flushing toilets, etc.
Cholera centres	60 litres/patient/day 15 litres/carer/day
Therapeutic feeding centres	15–30 litres/person/day 15 litres/carer/day
Water-flushed toilets	20–40 litres/user/day for conventional flush 3–5 litres/user/day for pour-flush
Anal washing	1–2 litres/person/day
Public toilets	1–2 litres/user/day for hand washing 2–8 litres/cubicle/day for cleaning toilet
Livestock	20–40 litres/large animal/day (cattle, donkeys, mules, horses) 5 litres/small animal/day (sheep, goats)
Small scale irrigation	Wide variation but in the order of 3–6 mm/m^2/day

(5 mm/day for each 1 m^2) to irrigate. This is enough water to satisfy the minimum water requirement of 1000 thirsty people. If the guard at a tank and standpost has a small garden, check how much drinking water is being used to irrigate it!

How much water are people actually using?

Official figures for camp populations are notorious for being overestimated – sometimes over double the actual population. Estimating per capita consumption from the official population figures may imply that the per capita consumption is too low. Cross-check such estimates by carrying out spot-checks at tapstands and at individual households (see Chapter 5 for appropriate methods).

11.4.2 Drinking water quality

The quality of drinking water is determined by physical, chemical, radiological and microbiological characteristics. In most emergencies, the microbiological quality of water is by far the most important consideration. A physical characteristic that is very important is turbidity – this inhibits the effectiveness of chlorination (see 13.3.1) and hence the microbiological quality of the water. Salinity, a chemical characteristic, is important if it prevents people drinking the water. Similarly, chlorine levels, although eliminating pathogens may, because of the taste, induce people to use better tasting but contaminated sources.

Microbiological water quality

It is not practical to test water for all disease-causing organisms – pathogens – that may occur in water, but there are bacteria from the human gut which will always be present as a result of faecal contamination. These 'indicator bacteria' are a warning that there may be harmful pathogens and parasites present. *Escherichia coli (E.coli)* are the most commonly used 'indicator bacteria'. The microbiological quality of drinking water can be indicated by the number of faecal coliforms/100 ml or *E.coli*/100 ml. (Note: *Escherichia coli* may not be directly harmful in themselves, although there are some strains of *E.coli* which are a cause of diarrhoea, especially in young children).

WHO sets guidelines which are intended for use by countries as a basis for the development of water quality standards. National water quality standards may differ from the WHO guidelines. The World Health Organization (WHO) guidelines for a bacteriologically safe water supply have been set at 0 faecal coliforms/100 ml. However, although it may be a desirable target to reach eventually, this guideline is not practical in many untreated, or partially treated, supplies in developing countries. An acceptable and attainable microbiological water quality will depend on individual circumstances.

Where people are living in overcrowded, and possibly insanitary, conditions the water supply should be chlorinated if at all possible. In a properly chlorinated supply, all bacteria will be killed so there is no point in testing for *E.coli* bacteria. Instead, it will be easier and quicker to ensure water is safe to drink by simply checking there is a chlorine residual at the point of delivery. For further information on chlorination see Section 13.3.3.

In other types of emergency, such as drought, where numerous scattered sources are involved and where chlorination of water supplies may not be desirable or feasible, it may be important to assess microbiological quality. This should be done in conjunction with sanitary surveys (see Section 11.1).

Chemical and physical water quality

The chemical and physical quality of a water supply may have a direct health implication or affect a consumer's acceptance of that particular water for drinking. WHO guideline values are based on lifelong consumption. If the value of a constituent chemical is exceeded over a short time period, it does not necessarily mean the water is unfit for drinking. How much a value can be exceeded and for how long will depend on the substance concerned. Appropriate action, if any, must consider the feasibility of water treatment and balance the potentially adverse effects of the constituent chemical against alternative, possibly microbiologically contaminated, sources. Table 11.2 is a guide to selected chemical and physical characteristics of water relevant to emergency supplies.

For further information on acceptable drinking water levels for a chemical substance based on health effects see the *Drinking Water Standards and Health Advisories* tables of the US Environmental Protection Agency Office of Science and Technology home page at http://www.epa.gov/OST. A 'Health Advisory' provides technical guidance on the concentration of a chemical in drinking water that is not expected to cause any adverse noncarcinogenic effects for short-term (one day and ten days) or lifetime exposure.

Sphere water supply standard 2: water quality

'Water at the point of collection is palatable, and of sufficient quality to be drunk and used for personal and domestic hygiene without causing significant risk to health due to water-borne diseases, or to chemical or radiological contamination from short term use.'

Key indicators:

- There are no more than 10 faecal coliforms per 100 ml at the point of delivery for undisinfected supplies.
- Sanitary survey indicates low risk of faecal contamination.
- For piped water supplies to populations over 10 000 people, or for all water supplies at times of risk or presence of diarrhoea epidemic, water is treated with a residual disinfectant to an acceptable standard (e.g. residual free chlorine at the tap is 0.2–0.5 mg/litre and turbidity is below 5 NTU, see Table 11.2 for units).
- Total dissolved solids are no more than 1000 mg/litre (approximately 2000 µs/cm electrical conductivity for simple field measurement), and water is palatable to users.
- No significant negative health effect due to chemical or radiological contamination from short-term use, or from the planned duration of use of the water source, is detected (including carry-over of treatment chemicals), and assessment shows no significant probability of such an effect.

11.5 Water tankering

11.5.1 Is tankering necessary and viable?

If possible, avoid tankering water. It is expensive and difficult to organize. Tankering should be seen as no more than an interim measure to allow for the development of new water sources or the improvement of existing supplies. If there is no viable solution to the water problem then people should be relocated. However, tankering may be unavoidable in the short term if no other options are immediately available. In some circumstances, usually for political or security reasons, people may not be able to relocate, and tankering has to be continued over a prolonged period of time at great expense.

Even a small temporary settlement will require perhaps hundreds of tonnes of water every day. This is a major logistical operation, requiring a fleet of tankers and passable roads.

11.5.2 Organizing tankering

Use the following key points as a checklist when organizing tankering.

- Management: tankering must be well organized and closely managed. Identify capable and reliable supervisors. Monitor number and amount of deliveries. The camp residents may be able to help with this – if they know how

Table 11.3 Guideline values for selected chemical and physical parameters of drinking water

Chemical/ physical parameter	*Critical values and potential problems*		*Possible actions*
Iron and manganese	Guideline values: Iron < 0.3 mg/l Manganese < 0.1 mg/l	Iron and manganese are not directly harmful but in high enough concentrations they can give water an unpleasant taste. The potential danger is that an otherwise safe groundwater may be rejected by users in favour of a polluted surface source	Remove iron by aeration. Seek and treat alternative surface water sources. (See 13.3)
Fluoride	Fluoride critical values: < 1 mg/l Tooth decay 1 mg/l Protection against tooth decay > 1.5 mg/l Mottling of teeth > 4 mg/l Adverse effect on bone growth	Short-term exposure to high fluoride levels in an emergency are unlikely to be critical. However, if an emergency supply becomes permanent then long-term exposure would be important	Obtain a standard fluoride test kit and assess the fluoride concentration of alternative sources. If possible, choose a low fluoride source
Chlorides and sulphates (See note on TDS and conductivity below)	Chlorides are detected by taste above the range, 200–300 mg/l Sulphates are detected by taste above the range, 200–900 mg/l	Water with high concentrations of chlorides and sulphates may be unpleasant to drink. However, it is not likely to be harmful due solely to the high level of salts. Some communities can tolerate concentrations which may be unacceptable to others. This may be significant where people have been displaced to an area with a high concentration of salts in the water to which they are not accustomed	Seek alternative sources, if possible
Nitrates	Nitrate guideline value < 45 mg/l	In infants, nitrates can cause methaemoglobonaemia which may be fatal. This does not occur in adults. Nitrates in water may originate from fertilizer seepage and organic pollution. Groundwater movement from latrines and septic tanks may give rise to nitrates in well and spring water	Test for nitrates. Monitor feeding centre and clinic supplies. Investigate the source of high nitrates and close down offending latrines, septic tanks, etc.

Continued

Table 11.3 (cont.)

Chemical/ physical parameter	*Critical values and potential problems*		*Possible actions*
Turbidity	Preferred drinking water level: < 5 NTU For the efficient disinfection of water: < 1 NTU	Turbidity is caused by suspended solids in water and is measured optically. See note on turbidity units below. Highly turbid water can encourage bacterial growth, reduce the effect of disinfection, and increase chlorine demand	Treat water to reduce high turbidity levels (See Section 13.3)
Colour		The colour of water can be affected by substances arising from organic matter, iron and manganese or industrial wastes. The colour of a safe water becomes significant if people prefer to use an alternative unsafe supply	If there is no ready alternative supply and the water is tested and found to be safe, then explain the reason for the colour to the users
Taste/smell		Certain tastes and odours may indicate characteristics of a water that should be investigated further (e.g. organic pollution). A safe water with a distinctive taste and smell may be rejected by users in favour of an unsafe source	Investigate and identify the reason for the taste and smell. Treat, if possible, or seek an alternative source
pH	pH range of most natural waters: 4 to 9	Low pH can contribute to the corrosion of metals in contact with the water, in particular pipes and pumps. The resulting corrosion can affect taste and a water's acceptability. In the absence of a distribution system, however, pH is of minor significance	Choose pump and pipe materials carefully for the abstraction and distribution of low pH water

Chlorides and sulphates are the principal ions contributing to the Total Dissolved Solids (TDS) in water which comprise inorganic salts and small amounts of organic matter. The TDS can be estimated from electrical conductivity (EC). The relationship between TDS and EC depends on the proportions of the various ions and is specific to each water type. Research has shown that for most waters, the value of conductivity in μS/cm (microSiemens/cm) multiplied by a factor in the range 0.55–0.70 will give an approximation to TDS in mg/l.
Turbidity units. For all practical purposes the following turbidity units are interchangeable: Nepholometric Turbidity Units (NTU), Jackson Turbidity Units (JTU), Formazin Turbidity Units (FTU), and American Public Health Association Turbidity Units (APHA).
Chemical and pH levels can be tested in the field using simple colour comparator kits

much they are supposed to receive, they may be the most insistent monitors of tanker performance.

- Water source: get clearance from both the relevant authorities and the owners that a water source can be used for tanker loading. It may not be obvious who should be consulted about using a source. Get good local advice. Potential water sources include existing urban supplies and boreholes belonging to private companies or institutions such as churches and schools.
- Contracts: in contracts with private tankering contractors, stipulate delivery targets and a means of payment based on the amount of water delivered. At the outset, agree a method of measuring the quantity of water delivered and establish a monitoring and recording system (refer to Section 6.3). Private contractors may be drawn away from their regular work by the opportunity of earning an increased income through emergency tankering. Check the effect on the local population of the withdrawal of such vehicles from their usual work.
- Route: survey the route from the water source to the points of discharge – road surfaces, bridge crossings, fords, etc. (see Chapter 18). Note any potential problems that might arise due to regular tanker traffic and changes in the weather. Deal with them in advance to avoid future disruption.
- Transport: identify the most appropriate means of transport. Can the route take articulated trucks or rigid trucks only? What capacity (load) can the route sustain – are there bridge weight restrictions, etc.? If tanker trucks are not available, can flat-bed trucks fitted with secured rigid or flexible tanks be used? Are tractor-pulled trailers more appropriate to the conditions? Check what each tanker formerly carried and ensure that each tank is cleaned thoroughly with detergent and chlorinated before use. It is difficult to clean fuel and oil tankers adequately but it may be the only option. Tankers may be available from the military, fire services, drink factories, breweries, dairies, etc. Ensure adequate arrangements are made for the maintenance of tankers. If tankers are contracted, specifically cover maintenance in the contract so that responsibilities are clear. Ensure the provision of sufficient spares, tyres, tools, consumable materials (such as lubricants, welding rods, etc.), mechanics, and provide a basic on-site working area. Arrange for standby trucks to cover for breakdowns and for those trucks that have to be taken out of service for repair and maintenance.
- Fuel: who will supply the fuel and lubricants? How will they be obtained? Where will they be safely stored? Arrange for adequate stocks of fuel.
- Personnel: a good relationship with the drivers is important. There must be sufficient drivers to allow for driver rest days. Make clear the division of responsibilities for loading, off-loading and chlorination (if included) between supervisors, drivers, driver assistants and pump operators. Will emergency tankering mean operators of an existing pump installation working longer hours and, if so, what arrangements need to be made? Will guards be required for parked tankers, pumps, and stores?
- Working hours: establish and agree tankering schedules with all concerned. Is it feasible, safe, and necessary, to consider night-time operations?

See Chapters 6 and 18 for details on management of contractors and information on roads and crossings.

Chlorination of a tankered supply (see also Section 13.3.3)

Where possible, chlorinate the tankered water at the tanker filling point:

- The chlorine dose can be accurately controlled as the tanker will either be of a known volume or the volume can be calculated.
- The chlorine will be thoroughly mixed on the journey to the distribution site.
- The total time needed for filling, transporting and off-loading will, in most cases, give the minimum recommended chlorine contact time of 30 minutes.

Remember that turbid water needs more chlorine and reduces the chlorine's effectiveness. Regularly monitor the free residual chlorine at the tapstands. Provide protective clothing for workers and somewhere secure and ventilated to store the source of chlorine (in powder or liquid form).

Tankering schedules

The estimation of tankering schedules is illustrated by the worked example shown in Box 11.3.

11.5.3 Water distribution with tankers

Key points:

- Identify distribution sites on the basis of:
  - A fair and equal distribution of the water.
  - Easy access and turnaround space for tankers.
  - Good drainage from the distribution point.
  - Space for storage to give a 24 hour reserve.
  - The development of the site for ease of off-loading, increased storage and improved distribution.
- Do people have sufficient containers in which to collect water and how will they be filled? Some containers have small filler holes resulting in spillage and a lot of wasted water. Can the containers be filled from the taps?
- Can tankers off-load at high speed into storage? Tankers are expensive to run and should be used to transport water, not to distribute it. They should not off-load directly into individual family containers, which takes a long time, but into static storage tanks which can be done much more quickly. Set up static tanks as soon as possible. Consider fitting extra discharge pipes to the tanker to speed up off-loading.
- Establish a well-organized system of distribution. Use stewards and roped queues to control crowds waiting for water.

People will be anxious about getting their share of water at the first delivery. Ensure that people know there will be a regular distribution. Ease anxiety and avoid overloading one site by arranging that, with the first delivery of water on the first day, all the tankers arrive at their allotted sites and deliver at the same time. Try to build up adequate stocks of water quickly.

In some cases, where tankering is the immediate emergency water supply solution, tankers may have to discharge directly into individual containers. It is

Box 11.3 Worked example of a tankering schedule

A new camp currently serves 10 000 people. There are no sources of water in the camp. Water will have to be trucked along a rough 10 km track from a single borehole source until sources can be developed nearby.

Estimate the quantity of water to be tankered.

Population:	10 000
Minimum water requirement:	15 l/person/day
Daily water requirement	150 000 l
Allow 20% extra for wastage and for new arrivals:	30 000 l
Water to be tankered:	180 000 l/day

Survey the 10 km route and identify a suitable means of transporting the water. Rigid (5 000-litre) tankers are found suitable and can be hired. Estimate the journey time from filling point to distribution point. Do not overestimate speed. One-way journey time @ 20 km/h is 30 minutes.

The borehole pump discharges at 5 l/s. Time to fill a 5000 l tanker: 17 minutes.

Off-loading is by gravity through a 75 mm (3 in) diameter hose. Each distribution site has been chosen to give a 1.5 m head difference between tanker outlet and receiving tank. This allows a tanker to discharge by gravity in about six minutes.

Calculate the turnaround time (total delivery time plus the return journey) for each site.

Time to fill tanker:	17 minutes
Journey time from filling point to distribution point:	30
Time for off-loading tanker:	6
Return journey time to filling point:	30
Net turnaround time:	83
Add 30% for contingencies	25
Gross turnaround time	108 minutes = 1.8 hours

The number of journeys and tankers required can now be determined. Include a generous contingency time for rest breaks (for drivers, pump operators and supervisors) and for refuelling, maintenance, breakdowns and punctures. Contingency time is very variable, particularly if the refuelling point is some distance away. In this example, a contingency time of 30% is taken. The following estimate assumes all the distribution points are approximately the same distance from the borehole source. This is clearly not always going to be the case.

$$\text{Number of deliveries per tanker in a day} = \frac{\text{working hours in a day}}{\text{gross turnaround time}} = \frac{12}{1.8} = 6\ (a)$$

$$\text{Total number of deliveries in a day} = \frac{\text{daily tankered water}}{\text{volume per tanker}} = \frac{180\,000}{5000} = 36\ (b)$$

Number of tankers (b/a) = 6

Summary: A total of six tankers of 5000 l capacity will be required to make six deliveries each per day to supply enough water at 15 l/person/day for 10 000 people.

extremely important to be ready and organized for the first distributions, otherwise there will be chaos.

Figure 11.2 shows how an organized method of distribution from the rear tap bar of a tanker or tapstand can be effected by erecting simple rope fences. The arrows show the movement of the collectors (who walk round the outside of the fence) and the route of their containers (which are taken, filled and returned to them by the supervisors).

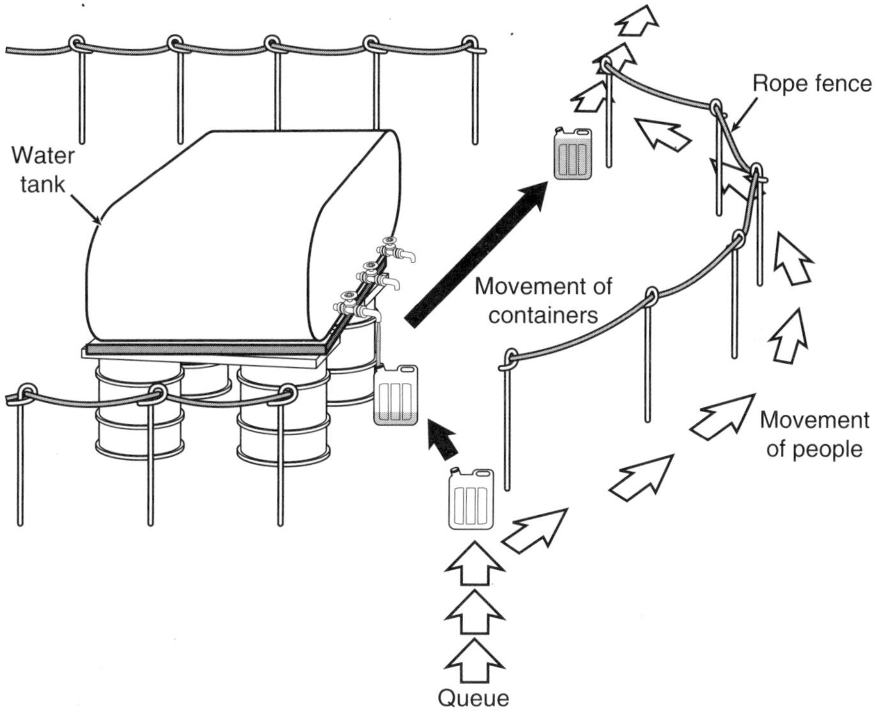

Figure 11.2 Water distribution point

Static tanks for distribution

The advantages of erecting static tanks at distribution sites are:

- The tankering operation can be separated from queues and possible unrest.
- Reduced tanker turnaround time. Tankers can discharge more quickly into tanks than into individual containers. Reduced turnaround time means that more water can be delivered. If sufficient water is already being delivered, the number of tankers can be reduced. Higher flow rates can be achieved by using large diameter hoses, several hoses for discharge or both. On flat terrain, gravity discharge restricts the height of the receiving tank. Use pumps to lift water to an elevated tank, if necessary.
- People do not need to queue for so long to collect water because they can use taps fed continuously by the tanks.

- Tanks provide a reserve of water for when there is a break in supply. The greater the storage at the distribution site the better. A tankered water supply is vulnerable to tanker and pump breakdowns, fuel supply problems, and heavy rain preventing tanker movement along the supply route.
- The storage of water can have a beneficial effect on the quality of water. Suspended solids in turbid water have time to settle in the storage tanks. Tanks, however, need regular cleaning to remove the settled solids. The number of water-borne pathogens significantly decreases during storage.

Water storage tanks for quick erection, and flexible and rigid tanks for mounting on flat-bed trucks are described in Section 13.2.

12 Water source development

12.1 Water source assessment

A staged approach to water source development is necessary in an emergency, to provide a basic water supply rapidly, with the option of further development later. Chapter 11 describes the rapid assessment methods for existing water sources and the immediate actions needed to protect them from gross pollution. This chapter describes the development of water sources to supply water in the longer term.

Table 12.1 gives some guidelines on the assessment of different water sources. Use Table 12.2 as a checklist of major factors you should consider when assessing and selecting suitable water sources. If a range of water sources is available and a choice has to be made, use matrix ranking to analyse the options (see Chapter 5). To decide which sources to exploit:

- Estimate the yield of existing springs, dug wells and boreholes (see the relevant sections of this chapter and Appendix 9). Is the yield sufficient to meet the demand for water?
- Carry out a sanitary survey of the existing sources as explained in Section 11.1.2. What measures are needed to safeguard the quality of the source water?
- Determine the time, materials and equipment needed to protect, improve and further develop the existing sources. Compare the advantages of using the existing sources against the development of new sources.
- Decide the best option:
  - Springs should always be considered first, if they exist.
  - Surface water sources can be used quickly, although quality is usually poor and treatment will be required.
  - In an emergency, time will be the most imporatant factor: dug wells may be an alternative, but consider the time required to dig and line them – in some cases, the cost of deeper concrete ring-lined dug wells can approach the cost of drilling a borehole and in some limited circumstances, hand drilled or jetted wells are feasible.
  - Consider a combination of sources.
  - Machine drilled boreholes may be necessary if they are the only feasible source.

Further details on the choice of water source are given in the relevant sections. If work is to be carried out on sources which are currently in use, an alternative supply of water must be made available to maintain continuity of supply. Whatever source is chosen, start with a simple system and improve it later to take account of variations in flow, water levels, and the medium- to long-term needs of the population served.

Table 12.1 A guide to water source selection

Source	*Surface water*		*Groundwater*		
	River, stream, lake	*Rainfall collection*	*Spring*	*Shallow well*	*Deep well*
Yield	May be seasonally variable – assess lowest yields	Unlikely to meet total demand; may be useful as supplement	Seasonally variable; wide variation between yields of springs	Seasonally variable; wide variation between yields of wells	Yield fairly constant – except in droughts; wide variation in yields between boreholes
Collection	Stream diversion or pumped abstraction Control access	Collect from roofs or divert surface runoff to ground tanks	Protect and develop gravity flow to supply	Protect and cover; hand or motor pump to storage	Motor pump to storage; handpump if yield low and depth < 45 m
Notes	Often easily accessible and developed first in emergency Treatment required	Simple to implement if materials and equipment are available	Good source Quick to develop Use if available	Needs good organization Needs diggable soil Can be dangerous (see 12.3.4)	Expensive High skill Specialized equipment Time needed to mobilize

See also Section 13.1, Table 13.2, for more information on water source quality and treatment

The water cycle

In assessing water sources, it is useful to bear in mind the water cycle (see Figure 12.1) – where does the water come from, how is it stored and where does it go to? To maintain a water balance:

$$\text{Inflow} = \text{Outflow} + \text{Change in storage volume}$$

This equation can be applied to a range of timescales and catchment sizes. Abstracting water from a source changes this balance and the implications of this change should be assessed. Monitor water sources to give an early warning of possible failure through pools drying up, wells pumping dry etc. Historical data may exist on flow rates and well levels, but can be difficult to find or not available. In long-term programmes, data collected in the first year will be valuable in subsequent years.

- Surface waters: monitor flow rates, volumes of lakes and pools, evaporation, rainfall, seepage (if feasible), and key dates of hydrological relevance (such as the onset of seasonal river flow, the start of the rains). See also 12.2.1.
- Groundwater: monitor the static and dynamic (pumping) water levels in wells. Take regular measurements of static well water levels early in the morning before water is pumped or collected.

Table 12.2 Water source assessment

Questions	*Remarks*
Quantity: is the yield sufficient to meet the demand for water, for the duration of the emergency?	See 11.4.1 and the guidance on yield measurements given in this chapter
Quality: is water treatment necessary and feasible?	See 11.4.2. Treatment requires: equipment, skills, chemicals and a logistics system. See Chapter 13
Time: how much time is needed to develop the source?	Drinking water must be made available while a source is developed
Technology: are there both skills and technology available for source development?	Use local skills and technology if possible
Energy: can gravity be used or is pumping required?	Where possible, use gravity fed supplies
Money: how much is the overall cost?	Funding will be required for both source development and subsequent operation and maintenance
What are the legal, social and political rights concerning the source?	Source development must be sensitive to the water rights and welfare of everyone

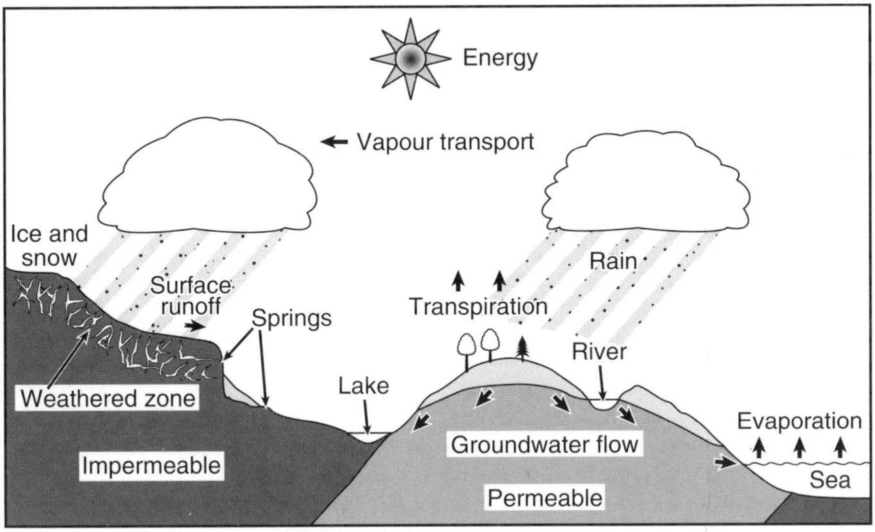

Figure 12.1 The water cycle

Use sanitary surveys (see 11.1.2) to monitor the actual or potential contamination of sources.

12.2 Surface water

12.2.1 Assessment of surface water sources

The quality of surface water from rivers, streams, lakes and reservoirs is usually poor, and, although some upland surface sources can be relatively free from pollution, surface water normally needs treatment before it can be supplied as safe drinking water. See Chapter 13 for guidelines on water treatment and Section 11.3 on protecting the source by controlling access.

In the wet season, surface waters have large sediment loads and this can make water treatment difficult and costly. In the dry season, algal growth in lakes, reservoirs, tanks and pools can inhibit treatment. Anticipate seasonal variations in flow and water levels. Find out, from local people, the months in which the water courses are dry. Look for stream flow data in water department offices.

To know the amount of water available for supply, it will be necessary to measure, or estimate, the current and future flow in a stream. Refer to Appendix 9 for several methods of determining flow rate in an open water course.

Where water is stored in lakes or dams, allow for losses through seepage and evaporation. The rate of evaporation depends upon temperature, sunshine, humidity and wind. Under dry, tropical conditions, evaporation rates of 4–7 mm/day are typical. In hot desert areas, annual evaporation may exceed 2.5 m. In cooler, more humid regions, annual evaporation may be considerably less than 1 m. Seepage rates depend on the permeability of the retaining walls and floor of the dam or lake.

12.2.2 Abstraction from surface water sources

Water can be abstracted from surface water sources by:

- Flow diversion into an off-take channel or pipe.
- Pumping from infiltration galleries or wells.
- Pumping directly from the source (see 14.3.2).

Flow diversion

Water can be pumped or diverted directly from the main stream into a side channel or pipe but the intake may dry or flood as water levels vary. To cope with fluctuating water levels, conventional intakes incorporate a diversion structure which increases and maintains the level of the water. A conventional diversion structure is a weir of masonry or reinforced concrete (Figure 12.2).

Where possible, use a natural barrier, such as a rock bar across the channel. If that is not possible, it may be necessary to construct a diversion structure. In an emergency, there is unlikely to be enough time to build conventional permanent structures. In low-flowing streams, temporary diversions can be constructed out of boulders, sandbags, gabions (see Appendix 17), brushwood,

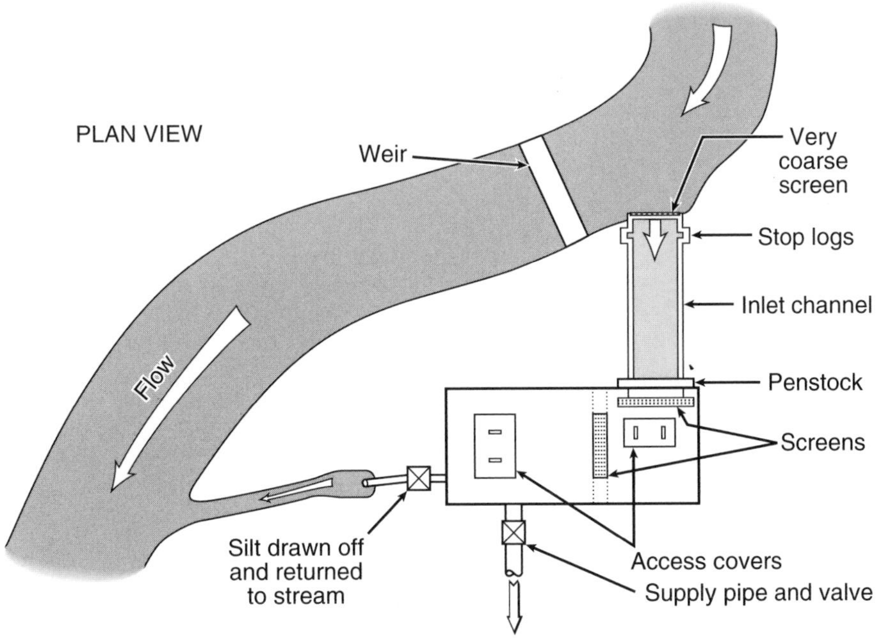

Figure 12.2 A diversion structure for a stream intake

earth, sawn timber and felled trees. First build an intake channel, or fix a pipe above the flow, and then raise the water level by creating the temporary structure.

Infiltration wells and galleries

The generally poor quality of surface waters can be improved by using the natural filtration of surrounding permeable soils. In particular, turbidity levels can be significantly reduced (see Section 13.3.1).

Riverside wells If the permeability of river bank soils is sufficient, filtered surface water can be collected from a well or wells dug adjacent to the source. (See 12.3.4 for dug well construction.) The yield of riverside wells is determined by soil permeability, the extent of the soil formations, the distance from the river, and the hydraulic gradient of the water moving to the well.

Use a hand auger to assist in determining the site of a riverside well (12.3.3). Starting near the river bank, hand drill a series of holes and move progressively further away. This will give information about the nature of the soil and the presence of any clay. If possible, before proceeding with construction, temporarily line the auger hole with plastic pipe and screen and carry out pumping tests to estimate yields (see 12.3.5 and Appendix 11). Site riverside wells above the river flood level and at least 20 m, or more, from the river bank. This gives sufficient time for the natural purification of the water through the soils to occur, and protects wells from bankside erosion. Sink wells at least 1m below the level of the river bed to take advantage of any sub-surface flow in the dry season.

The side of the river bed will clog over time but scouring during periods of high flow will remove sediment to restore the infiltration rate.

Infiltration galleries Infiltration galleries may be constructed on the bank of a stream or river or in the bed of the water course as shown in Figure 12.3. An infiltration gallery comprises a trench in which is placed a slotted, drilled or open jointed pipe, or purpose made well screen. The trench is usually backfilled with gravel media. The gravel enables pipes or screens with larger openings to be used and improves hydraulic conductivity around the infiltration pipe. If several layers of gravel are used, gravel size should increase towards the infiltration pipe.

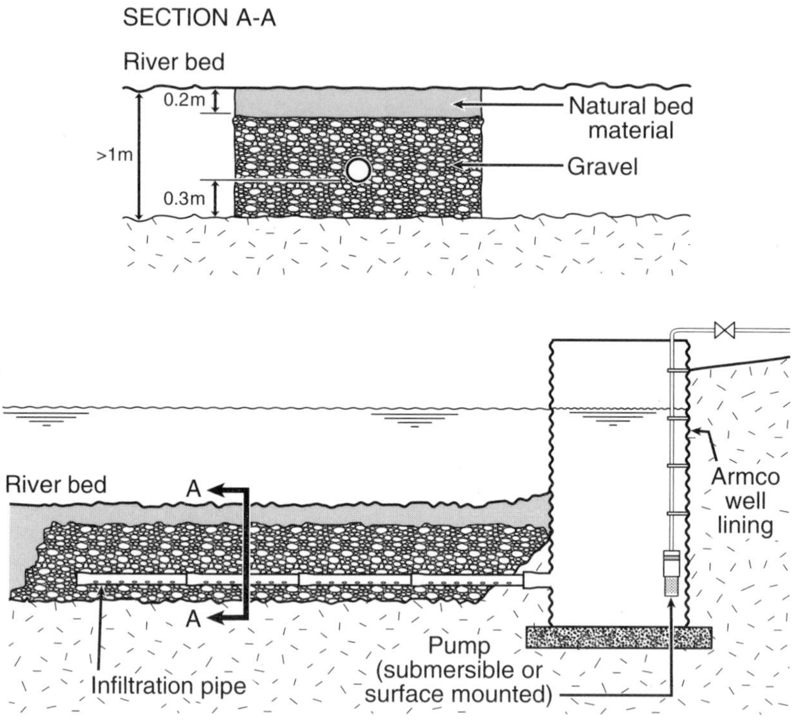

Figure 12.3 A river bed infiltration gallery

Use the guidelines for riverside wells to site bankside infiltration galleries. If the river bank soils are unsuitable for riverside wells or infiltration galleries (for example, because of low permeability) then infiltration galleries may be constructed in the bed of an existing water course or lake, as shown in Figure 12.3. It is only practical to construct an infiltration gallery in a water course during periods of minimal flow in the dry season. Due to residual sub-surface flow, dewatering pumps may be required during construction to enable the infiltration trench to be excavated. Take adequate safety precautions when digging the trench.

Regular flood flows over the surface of a river bed displace settled silt and renew the uppermost layers. Therefore, the clogging of infiltration media is more of a problem in a static source, such as a lake, than in a flowing stream or river.

Key elements in the design of an infiltration gallery are: the hydraulic gradient driving the water through the river bed material; and the hydraulic conductivity of that material. In most cases, the hydraulic gradient will be low because the infiltration pipe can only be placed at a relatively shallow depth. Therefore, it is important that the material in the river bed has a high hydraulic conductivity (frequently the case) and that the dimensions of the slotted infiltration pipe are chosen correctly. Design criteria for infiltration galleries are similar to those for boreholes (see 12.3.6) and are given in Box 12.1. If the length of gallery is restricted by the width of the stream bed, place the pipe in-line with the water course, use more than one gallery, or do both. Box 12.2 gives an example of a calculation to design an infiltration gallery.

Box 12.1 Design criteria for infiltration galleries

- Flow velocity in the infiltration pipe should be a maximum of 1.5 m/s to limit head losses.
- Entrance velocity through the pipe or screen openings should be a maximum of 0.03m/s to keep flow losses to a minimum.
- Hole or slot sizes in the pipe or screen should be based on the size of the surrounding gravel media (see Table 12.9, Section 12.3.6).
- Optimum sizing of gravel media is similar to sizing for an artificial gravel pack for a borehole (see 12.3.6). The grading curve of the gravel media should be similar to that of the river bed material, but the values for each percentage passing should be 6 to 7 times greater. See Appendix 20 for an explanation of grading curves. In the absence of equipment for a sieve analysis, an adequate rough estimate of gravel size can be made based on the above guidelines. In practice, choice of readily available material will be the greatest determinant of gravel size.
- Estimate the required surface area of the layer of gravel media from its approximate hydraulic conductivity (k). See Appendix 10 for values of k for different materials. A practical guide figure for river gravels is 4–12 m/h.
- Place the infiltration pipe at least 1 metre below the stream bed. Place at least 0.3 m of gravel media below the pipe.
- The width of a river bed infiltration trench should be approximately twice the depth at which the pipe is buried.
- If more than one infiltration pipe is placed in a river bed they should be at least 3 m apart.

Infiltration wells Where the hydraulic gradient and permeability of the river bed material are adequate, a point source infiltration well may be used. Infiltration wells (Figure 12.4) are similar to infiltration galleries. Sink a porous ring column into the permeable stream bed. Prevent the ingress of unfiltered surface water by either sealing the buried top of the ring column or extending the column above the flood level. The yield can be increased by:

Box 12.2 Calculation of slotted pipe dimensions for an infiltration gallery

Given: Supply required – 15 litres/person/day for 10 000 people = 150 000 litres/day
10 pumping hours/day, i.e. pumping rate = 4.2 l/s

At flow velocity of 1.5 m/s, diameter of the infiltration pipe = 60 mm.
At entrance velocity of 0.03 m/s, infiltration open area needed = $0.0042/0.03\ m^2$ = $0.14\ m^2$
Two infiltration holes of 5 mm diameter every 50 mm gives an open area of $7.85 \times 10^{-4}\ m^2$/metre length of pipe. Therefore the length of infiltration pipe required is $0.14/7.85 \times 10^{-4}$ = 178m (giving a flow of 1.4 l/min/metre of pipe).

This can be compared with field results from Waiya dam, Kenya (IRC, 1990): infiltration pipe of PVC, 100 mm diameter, 21 m length, holes of 5 mm diameter at 50 mm intervals gave a yield of 22 l/min (1 litre/min/m).

A manufactured well screen could be used to achieve the open area of $0.14\ m^2$ described above. A PVC well screen of diameter 60 mm and slot width 3 mm has about 25% open area. The area of screen per metre length is $\pi d = 0.2$ m and the open area of screen = $0.25 \times 0.2 = 0.05\ m^2/m$. The length of screen to give $0.14\ m^2$ open area is 0.14/0.05 m = 2.8 m.

However, with such short lengths, the permeability of the material in the river bed may be a constraining factor. If the river bed material is sufficiently permeable and the collapse resistance of the well screen is sufficient to withstand the weight of media (or the screen is suitably protected), the length of infiltration pipe required can be greatly reduced by the use of manufactured well screen.

- Adding several infiltration pipes radiating from the well.
- Combining the well with an infiltration pipe or pipes.
- Interconnecting several infiltration wells.

Water can be abstracted directly from an infiltration well by a submersible pump. This is not advisable, however, in rivers with high seasonal flows and where access for maintenance could be a problem. In these situations, connect through a pipe to a collector well or sump in the channel bank and pump water from there. Figure 12.5 shows how a well screen could be used for river bed abstraction.

12.2.3 Small dams

Conventional dams are unlikely to form part of an emergency water supply because of the time and expense involved in construction. The construction of dams requires specialized skills and has many possible hazards. In emergencies, small gravity dams with a maximum water depth of 2 m (comprising 3 m crest height, with 1 m freeboard) may be appropriate in order to:

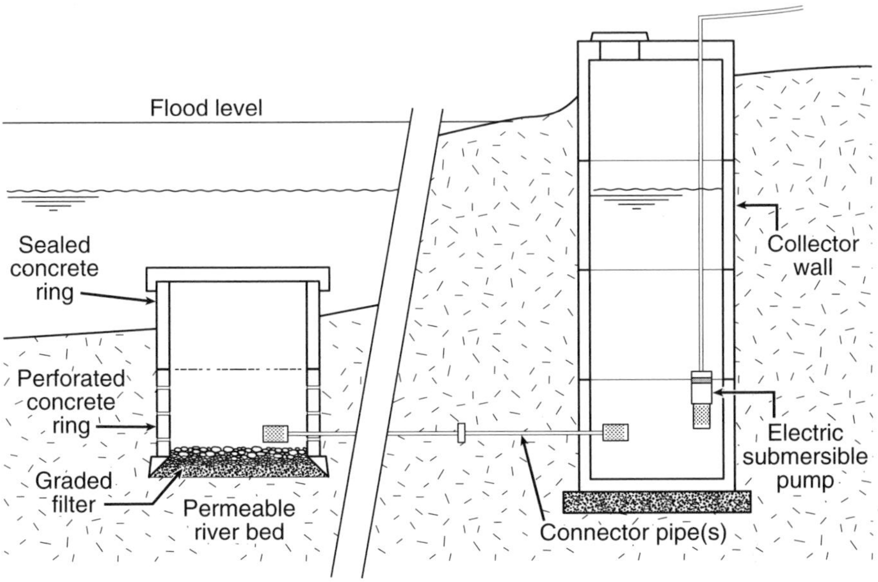

Figure 12.4 An infiltration well

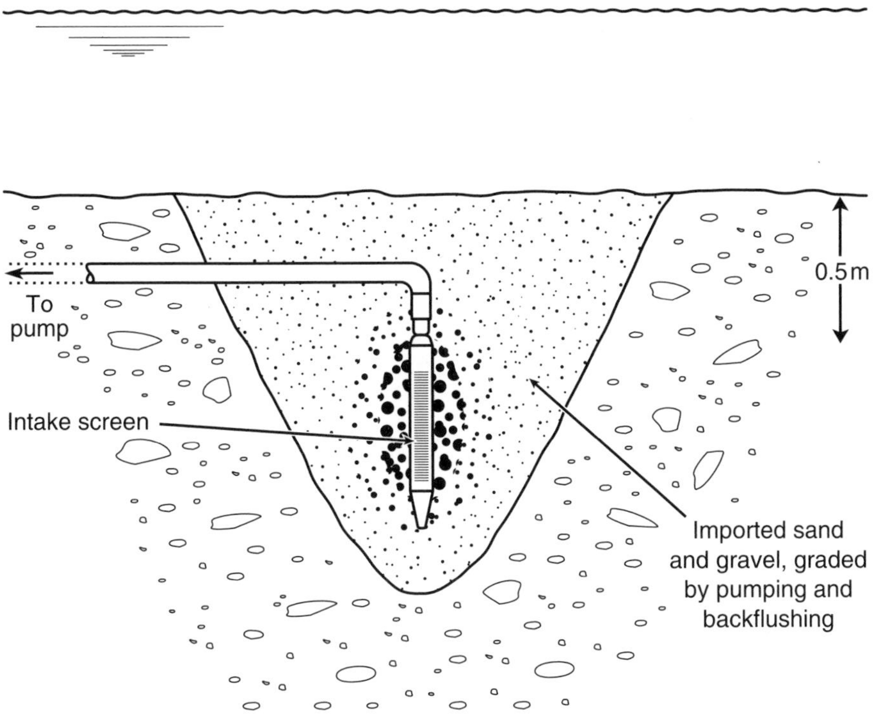

Figure 12.5 A well screen used for river bed abstraction

- Supplement an existing supply by storing rainfall runoff.
- Temporarily block a low-flowing water course in the dry season to give a reservoir of water until the river floods in the wet season.
- Form a sub-surface dam to store water in stream beds with intermittent flows.

Warning

Before contructing any dam, always consider the effect of a sudden failure of the dam on people downstream. Even a low dam may impound large quantities of water, which can cause considerable damage if released suddenly.

Legal and social considerations

The damming of a water course can be a very sensitive issue and is usually controlled by law. Authorization may be required to construct the smallest of dams and it is important to follow procedures.

Downstream populations may be reliant on trickle flows in the dry season and close liaison with community leaders is essential. Discuss the effects of construction work, and ensure there is enough water for everyone during the dam filling period.

Some principles of small dam design

A dam can be constructed of earth, masonry, rock, and gabions. Very temporary low-level dams can be formed from vegetation and earth.

Streams draining small catchments have proportionally more erratic flow rates than larger rivers. In tropical areas, where rainfall may be intense and runoff high, a trickling brook a few centimetres deep may, in a matter of hours, turn into a raging torrent a metre or more deep, sweeping away any poorly designed or constructed obstruction such as a small dam. This is likely to happen in the middle of dam construction and at the dead of night. A well designed spillway is critical, to cope with high stream flows. The spillway must be able to pass the highest flows safely; that is, without overtopping of the dam. Overtopping will lead to rapid and catastrophic failure.

In tropical areas, silt loads may be very high. All that silt will be deposited behind the dam, sometimes completely silting up a small dam in the first rainy season. Silt loads are likely to be high in steep catchments where soils have poor vegetative cover.

The three main forces acting on a gravity dam are:

- The pressure of water on the upstream face.
- The weight of the dam which prevents overturning.

- The vertical uplift force on the base of the dam due to the pressure of water which seeps into the dam or beneath it. Seepage can be reduced by using a cut-off trench beneath the dam or by laying an impermeable layer, such as clay or plastic, in the reservoir upstream of the dam.

A good site for a dam is where the valley is narrow, where there is a good impermeable foundation for the dam, where the valley upstream of the dam can store large quantities of water (where it is wide and gently sloping) and where a spillway can be easily constructed (such as where one side of the valley is rock).

A low earth dam (< 1 metre) built for the duration of the dry season and designed to be washed away at high streamflows may not require a spillway. In all other circumstances a properly designed spillway is essential if a dam is to survive high stream flows. Even low dams may store large quantities of water which, if suddenly released downstream, may cause considerable damage.

Construction of small earth dams

The construction of an earth dam is feasible where there are locally available natural materials suitable for dam construction, and where there is a means of moving earth – by conventional earth moving plant, modified agricultural equipment, or animal drawn scoops.

The simplest type of earth dam is a homogeneous (single soil) embankment dam. Refer to Appendix 20 for how to recognize and estimate soil composition. Use material containing 20–30 per cent clay with a mixture of sand and gravel, and only a small amount of silt. Avoid heavy cracking clays unless they are mixed with coarser material. Do not use anthill material, as it can either directly introduce or attract termites to the embankment and weaken the structure. Choose relatively flat slopes of at least 3:1 upstream and 2:1 downstream.

Control of seepage Problems are mainly due to excessive seepage. Slumping and failure may eventually occur if dam material is lost from the toe due to the flushing action of seepage. A filter at the toe prevents the migration of dam material. In a dam constructed on an impermeable foundation, seepage can be controlled by a filter and stone toe and a gravel drain as shown in Figure 12.6. The filter example in Figure 12.6 refers to the 15 per cent size which is defined as the mesh size through which passes 15 per cent of the material (see 'filter rule' in Appendix 20). A dam constructed on a permeable foundation will require an upstream clay blanket, as shown in Figure 12.7, or a deep clay-filled cut-off trench. A gravel toe drain is also needed. (Refer to Appendix 20 for typical soil permeabilities and how to determine permeability.)

Spillway design The spillway should be capable of carrying the maximum likely flood at flow velocities low enough to prevent erosion.

In order to determine the peak flood, an estimate of the catchment size and runoff is needed. In many areas there is little reliable hydrological information on which to base these estimates. One approach is to assume a full dam, saturated ground and 100 per cent runoff. Estimate the catchment area draining to the dam site from a topographical map or rapid ground survey. Calculate the runoff based on the highest expected daily rainfall. This will give an

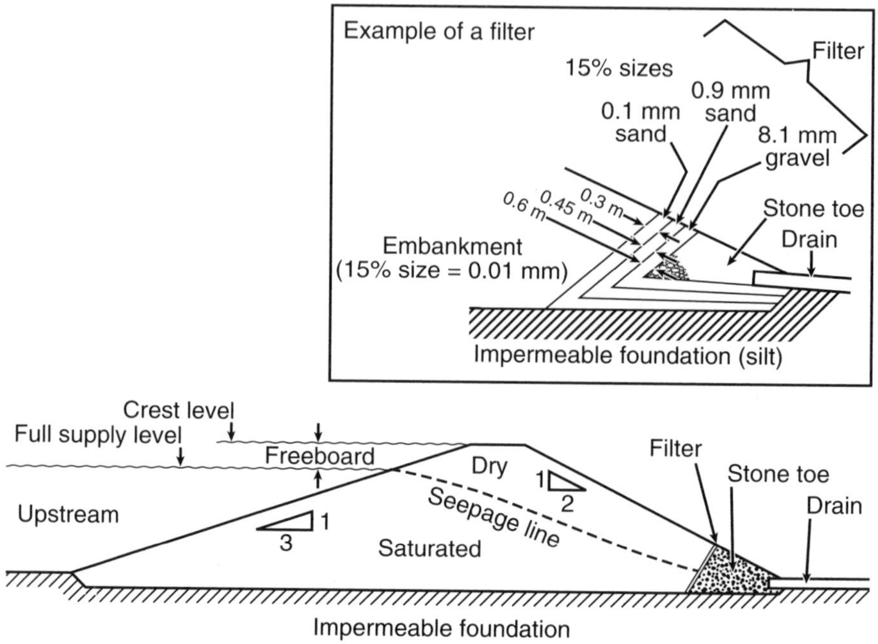

Figure 12.6 Earth embankment dam with a stone toe and drainage

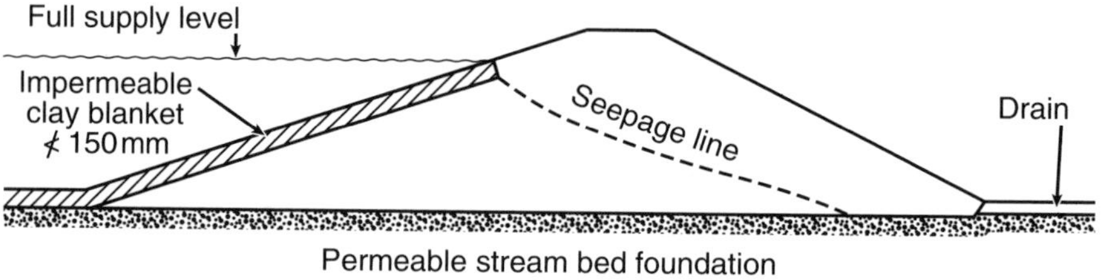

Figure 12.7 Earth embankment dam on a permeable foundation

estimate for peak flow over 24 hours. Allow a generous safety factor – it is better to have an oversized spillway than an overtopped and failed dam. For further guidance on discharge measurements refer to Appendix 9.

To determine the best size to build a small earth dam spillway, use the following guidelines (Nelson, 1985):

- Flow over a grassed spillway should not exceed 2.5 m/s. For ungrassed spillways in arid climates construct a wider spillway with lower flow velocities.
- Freeboard of at least 1 metre.
- Maximum depth of flow of 0.5 metres.
- The spillway outlet should be wider than the inlet to spread the flow evenly over the return slope. To ensure even flow, the outlet width should not be more than 1.5 times the inlet width.

- Select the flattest return slope available.
- Use stone pitching, gabions, or a concrete sill to help prevent erosion. Alternatively, site the dam to take advantage of a natural rock spillway.

A typical spillway design, including an extension to the dam wall to prevent erosion of the toe, is shown in Figure 12.8.

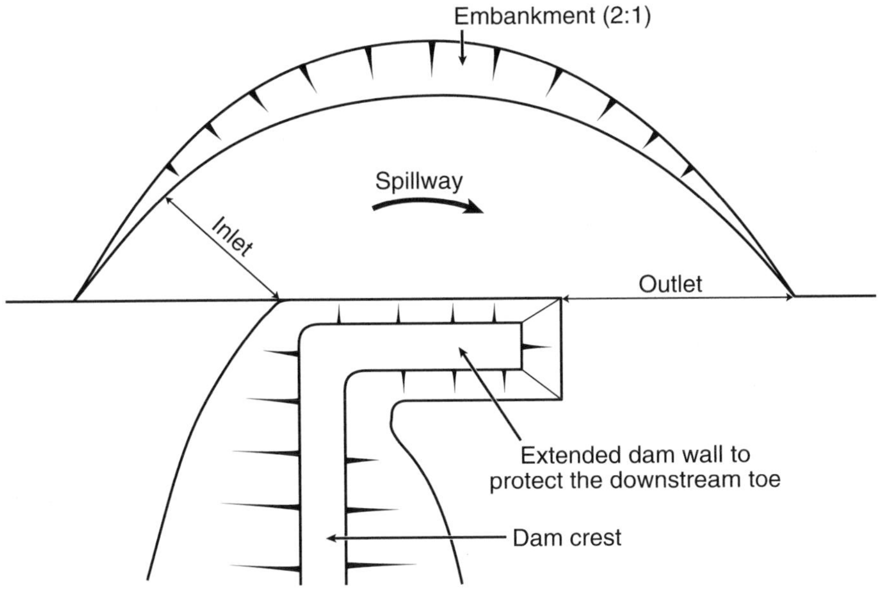

Figure 12.8 Plan view of a spillway
From Nelson, 1985

Assessment and repair of existing earth dams

- Remove any accumulated debris that could inhibit flow across the spillway. Repair any gulleys across the spillway. Check and level the spillway.
- Inspect the embankment for cracks. The most serious cracks develop transversely from the upstream slope to the downstream slope. Cracking can occur at the seepage line between the lower saturated layer and the upper dry section of the dam. Lower the water level behind the dam as soon as a transverse crack of this type is recognized. Attempt to close the crack by pumping water onto the crest of the dam to wet the soil and so induce settlement in the upper layer. Longitudinal cracks, parallel to the crest, can develop as heavy clays dry out and shrink. Fill these cracks with soil to prevent rainwater from opening them up and causing slippage.
- A settled dam crest should be built up again to its original level. Clay bags can be used temporarily.
- Piping occurs when seepage water creates a passage through the embankment. This is a very serious condition for which there is no straightforward remedy. Drain the water from the dam as soon as piping is detected.

- If slides develop on the downstream slope, reduce the water level and, if possible, create a flatter slope by using more earth.
- Clear the embankment and surrounding area of trees and bushes. Tree roots can cause weaknesses in the dam material. Bushes attract rodents and other animals which can burrow and cause serious damage. Rats and rabbits should be controlled. Encourage the growth of creeping grasses to stabilize the embankment slopes and spillway.

Other small gravity dams

Low-flowing dry-season water courses can be temporarily dammed to ensure a reservoir of water until the end of the dry season. Such dams may be important where displaced people settle around a flowing but receding water course during the early part of the dry season and no other water sources are available.

Temporary dams of about one metre in height can be quickly constructed from clay filled bags. Empty flour and grain bags are suitable. Choose a rocky outcrop if possible so that a natural rock spillway can be incorporated in the dam wall to take any trickle flows once the dam is full. At the beginning of the rains, the temporary dam will be washed away when the water course floods.

Rock fill dams of piled stone are similar in shape to earth embankment dams. Form a watertight barrier by incorporating a clay core in the centre of the dam. Use plastic sheeting plastered with clay on the upstream face. Gabions can be used to form a rock fill dam. Gabions are described in Appendix 17. The dimensions of a low masonry dam constructed in stone and cement mortar are shown in Figure 12.9.

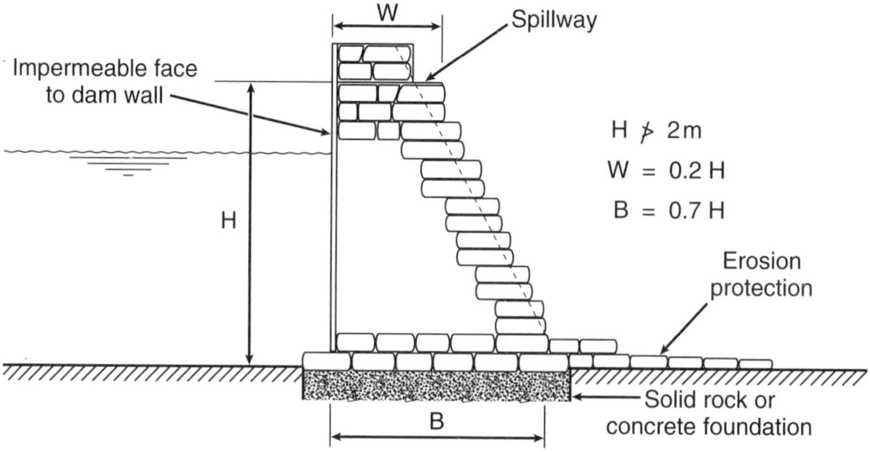

Figure 12.9 A typical low masonry dam

12.2.4 Sand-storage and sub-surface dams

Sand-storage and sub-surface dams may be used to retain and store water in ephemeral water courses.

Sand-storage dam A sand-storage dam accumulates sediment in which water can be stored. A sand-storage dam is built over several years, with the dam height gradually raised each year. The storage volume is initially very low. It increases over the years as sediment is deposited and the dam walls raised. A new sand-storage dam is, therefore, unlikely to be effective in a short-term emergency. However, if an existing sand-storage dam is encountered:

- Check for erosion around the end walls of the dam. Take action to halt actual or potential erosion which could lead to dam leakage or failure.
- The gravel filter and outlet pipe of a sand-storage dam can become blocked. If water is present in the sand upstream of the dam but there is no flow from the outlet, investigate and rectify the blockage.

Sub-surface dam A sub-surface dam is constructed below ground level and prevents the downstream passage of groundwater in the sand bed of ephemeral water courses. The advantages of a sub-surface dam are:

- Compared with surface dams, evaporation losses from the stored water are low and are almost eliminated where the water surface is at a depth of 60 cm or more below the sand surface. The presence of fine clay material, however, can increase losses through capillary transport of water to the ground surface.
- Siltation has little effect on the storage volume.
- The stored water is less open to pollution than a surface water source.
- The stored water does not provide breeding sites for mosquitoes or the intermediate hosts of human diseases.

In the right circumstances, a sub-surface dam can be constructed over a period of weeks and can help to solve a medium-term water supply problem. However, it is only practical to construct sub-surface dams in the dry season. Local hydrogeological conditions are critical and should be carefully investigated. Storage volumes depend on the underlying strata and are sometimes quite low. A good site for a sub-surface dam has the following features:

- A well defined valley.
- A water course with intermittent flows.
- Gentle slopes.
- Sand or gravel beds.

Use a hand auger or steel sounding rods hammered into the sand to investigate the profile of the underlying rock or soil. This will help to determine the potential storage volume and will influence the method of construction. Look for submerged natural rock bars and dykes which already provide some natural storage and can be exploited further by a sub-surface dam. Water courses tend to reflect fracture zones so beware of potential seepage points in fractured rock. Rock foundations are desirable but an impermeable soil layer may also be suitable.

A sub-surface dam is usually constructed in a trench dug across a valley or stream bed of sand. To ensure stable trench slopes, dig the trench relatively wide or use shuttering. Provide shuttering by driving down bush poles as the excavation proceeds (see Appendix 21). Dewater the excavation with a pump.

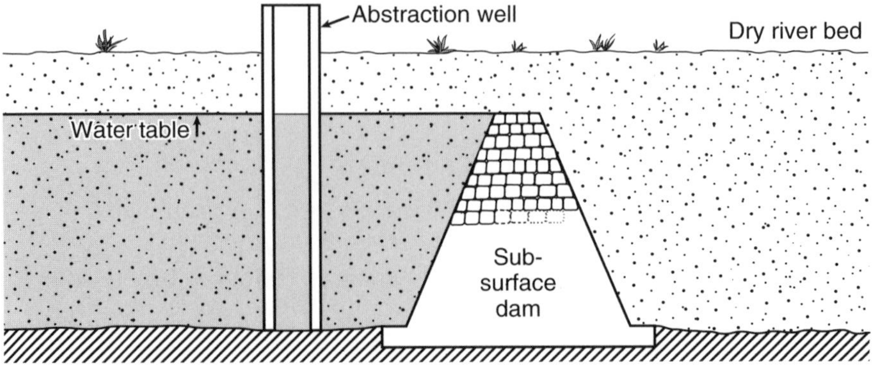

Figure 12.10 A sub-surface dam

After construction, backfill the dam wall carefully and wet the backfill with the pumped water to ensure good compaction. A wide variety of materials can be used to construct a sub-surface dam wall:

- Compacted clay.
- Stone masonry.
- Mass concrete cast within wooden shuttering or stone masonry.
- Reinforced concrete.
- Ferrocement.
- A plastered brick wall on a concrete or rock foundation.
- Galvanized corrugated steel or plain welded sheet steel.

The use of sheet piling and injection screens avoids the need to excavate a trench and dewater during construction. These methods are, perhaps, more suited to an emergency than other methods which require time-consuming excavation. However, both methods need equipment that may not be readily available. Use ordinary cement or bentonite as an injection grout. Bentonite has a fine particle size, about 10 microns or less, and is therefore suited to fine sands. Jet drilling (see 12.3.5) can be used to flush sand to the surface until the drill pipe reaches an impermeable layer. Pump a cement, bentonite or other clay slurry down an adjacent pipe as the jetting pipe is slowly withdrawn. Repeat this process across the valley to construct an impermeable screen.

Table 12.3 indicates different dam materials which have been used at various depths.

Water can be abstracted from behind a sub-surface dam by an infiltration gallery laid at the base of the dam wall, or by a conventional well or borehole. The depth and replenishment of stored water can be measured easily using perforated tubes inserted vertically into the sand bed.

12.3 Groundwater

12.3.1 Groundwater basics

Groundwater is water underground that fills the natural openings in rock and sediments. Recharge is the process whereby rainwater percolates through the

Table 12.3 Sub-surface dam materials and depth

Dam type	*Average depth, metres*
Injection screen	10
Brick wall	6
Concrete	6
Stone masonry	5
Reinforced concrete/ferrocement	4
Clay	3
Plastic sheets	2

From: Nilsson (1988)

soil, and through fractures and joints in rock, until it reaches the water table and joins the groundwater flow system (see Fig 12.1). Like surface water, water underground flows under the influence of gravity. Consequently, groundwater is likely to be closer to the ground surface in the bottom of a valley than at the top of a hill.

Groundwater movement is slower than the movement of water in streams and rivers under the same topographical gradient. This is because of the resistance to flow caused by the interconnected system of pore spaces, fractures or solution cavities in rock. The speed of movement is also dependent on the hydraulic gradient. In some alluvial aquifers and rock fractures the flow rate may be up to a few metres per day, but in other less permeable aquifers the flow rate is in the order of a few metres per year. See Appendix 10 for more information on the movement of water in aquifers.

A consequence of the slow movement of groundwater is that the water has time to dissolve chemicals from the soils and rock through which it passes. The longer the time spent underground, and the more soluble the rock, the higher will be the level of dissolved solids in the groundwater, indicated by the electrical conductivity (EC). Electrical conductivity can be measured with a hand-held, battery powered electrical conductivity (EC) meter. If water sampled from a spring or well source has a 'low salinity' (a low electrical conductivity of say 150 μS/cm) then the water may not have had much time to dissolve minerals in the rock. This could mean the water has moved relatively quickly through the aquifer and any pollution of the upstream groundwater could also move quickly to the spring or well. A slightly saline water (EC of, say, 1200–1800 μS/cm) may indicate that the groundwater has followed a long travel path. See 10.3.1 for guidelines on the risk of contamination of groundwater from latrines.

The yield of a well and water balance

The yield of a well depends on the amount of water stored in an aquifer and the rate at which the water can be extracted.

In hard rock, the rate at which water can be extracted depends on the size and number of fractures and the degree of interconnection. In granular material (sands and gravels), grain size and sorting will determine flow rate. For example, flow rate will be lower in smaller and poorly sorted grains because flow in the intergranular pore spaces will be restricted.

The amount of water stored underground will depend on the nature and extent of the aquifer. The amount of water stored per unit volume of aquifer is related to the porosity, which is the ratio of pore space to the total volume of material. For example, there will be relatively little storage in fractured bedrock with a porosity of less than 1 per cent. This can be compared to unconsolidated sediments which can have a porosity of up to 40 per cent and therefore have a much larger storage capacity.

There is a balance between the amount of water stored in an aquifer, the amount of water which leaves the aquifer through natural groundwater flow and through pumping, and the amount it receives through recharge. Therefore, care must be taken over the drilling of new boreholes and the rate of abstraction if a positive water balance is to be maintained. Water levels in new boreholes drilled during large scale emergencies must be closely monitored to detect the long term effects of continuous abstraction.

Groundwater terminology

Groundwater terms referring to the occurrence and flow of groundwater are explained below (see Figure 12.11). These terms are used in subsequent sections which describe well construction techniques and methods of spring protection.

- Aquifer. A geological formation or layer, made up of pervious materials, that transmits or yields water in appreciable quantities.
- Unconfined aquifer. An aquifer in which the upper water boundary – the water table – is at atmospheric pressure.
- Aquiclude. An impermeable layer of material such as clay or bedrock.
- Confined aquifer. A saturated aquifer between two aquicludes in which the water pressure is greater than atmospheric pressure.
- Perched aquifer. A local saturated lens held above a regional aquifer by a layer of impermeable material.
- Aquitard. A slightly permeable aquiclude such as sandy clay.
- Semi-confined aquifer. A completely saturated aquifer with an upper and/or lower aquitard boundary.
- Potentiometric surface (piezometric surface). The potentiometric surface is an imaginary surface whose height above a confined aquifer is determined by the pressure within the aquifer. The water in a well drilled into a confined, or semi-confined, aquifer will rise to the level of the potentiometric surface. If the potentiometric surface is above ground, water will flow out of the well, which is then known as an artesian well. The potentiometric surface of an unconfined aquifer is the water table. The slope of the potentiometric surface is the hydraulic gradient under which groundwater moves.
- Primary porosity. Primary porosity describes the voids that were created when a rock was formed, such as the intergranular pores in a sandstone.
- Secondary porosity. Secondary porosity relates to the voids that developed after a rock was formed; for instance, fissures and solution cavities.

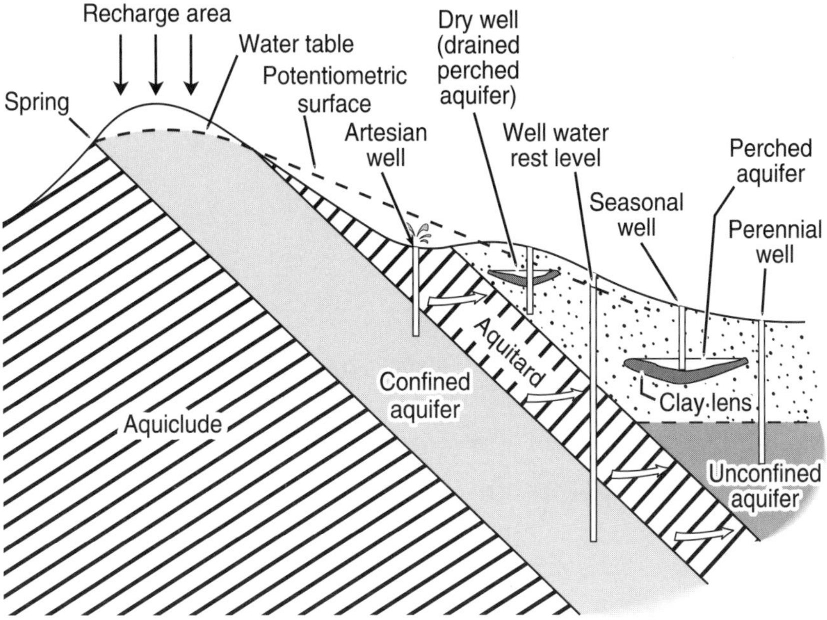

Figure 12.11 Groundwater terminology

12.3.2 Springs

Location and assessment of springs

A spring forms where groundwater meets the ground surface. Flow may be at an identifiable point, 'a spring eye', or from a more diffuse area, 'seepage'. Various types of spring are shown in Figures 12.12 to 12.15. Gravity springs can occur in highland regions where weathered rock provides both dry season storage and a fissured route for groundwater outflow on hillside slopes. A spring may occur where groundwater flow is blocked by an impermeable barrier. A fault plane or fissures can provide a route along which groundwater reaches the surface from a confined or unconfined aquifer (Figures 12.14 and 12.15).

Geological maps, if available, can help locate areas where springs may be found. Identify the dividing lines between outcropping permeable and impermeable layers. Look for gravity springs at these boundaries, where water may flow from an unconfined aquifer (Figure 12.13). The location of springs may change and the flow rates will change as the level of the water table varies from the wet to the dry season. Springs can often be seen at a distance due to greener areas of vegetation, which contrast with the surroundings.

Measure the yield of a low flow spring by channelling all the flow into a container of known volume (for instance, a jerrycan) and timing how long it takes to fill. Measure the flow from larger springs by diverting all the flow into a

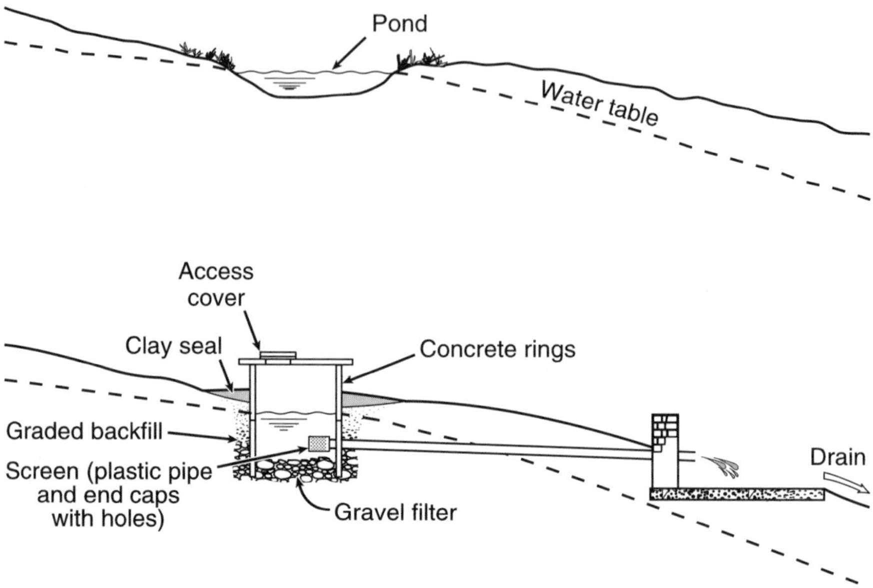

Figure 12.12 A simple depression spring and its protection

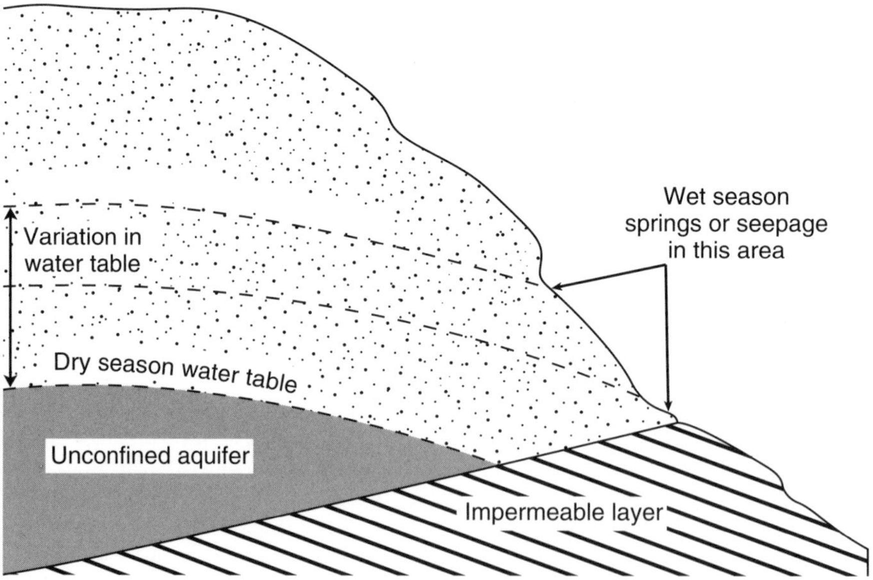

Figure 12.13 The variation in location and flow rate of gravity springs according to the seasons

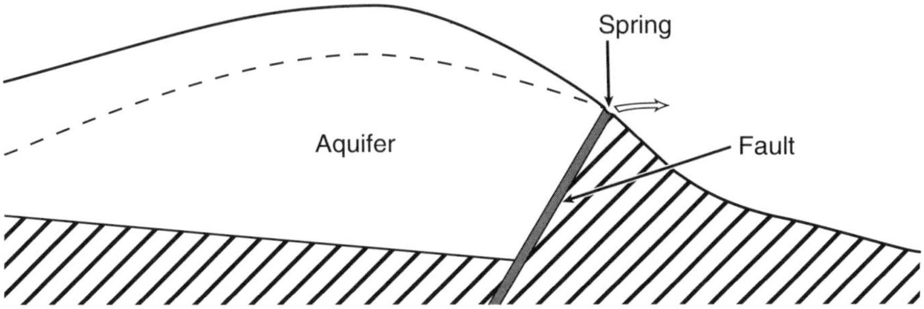

Figure 12.14 Spring flow from an unconfined aquifer due to an impermeable barrier to groundwater flow

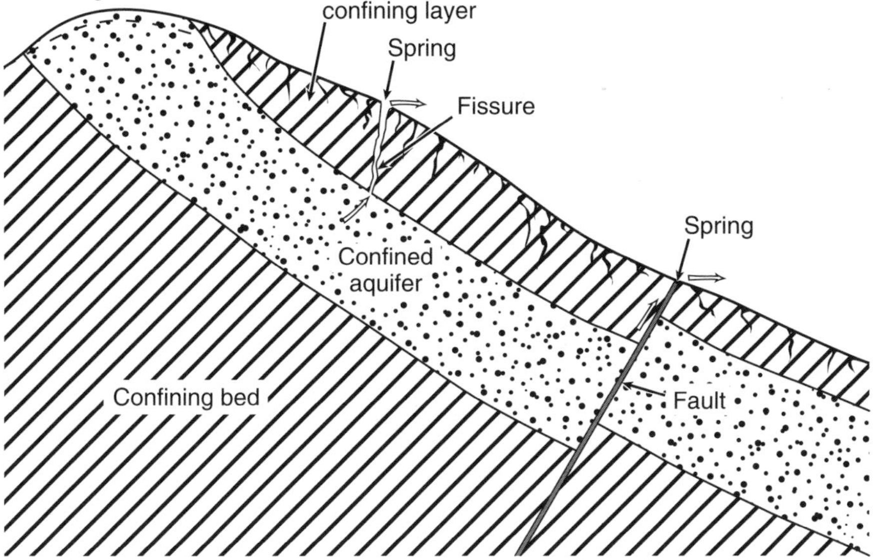

Figure 12.15 Spring flow from a confined aquifer

channel in which a V-notch weir is placed. Appendix 9 gives details of the measurement of flow over weirs.

Spring protection

Springs are usually a source of high quality water. Preserve this quality by protecting the spring source from pollution. The form of protection will depend on:

- The yield: low yield springs may require storage. High yield springs will need a more substantial structure.
- Whether the source is seepage or from identifiable spring eyes.
- Whether the water is to be collected directly from the spring or piped away.
- The time and materials available for the work.

When protecting a spring, do not allow a build-up of back-pressure on the spring. Back-pressure may cause the spring to divert to an alternative route outside the protected area. Therefore, size the outlet pipe, or pipes, to take the peak flow. If a tap is fitted to store water from low yield springs, a screened overflow must be fitted. The overflow must be sized to take the peak flow.

Information required for the design of a spring fed gravity piped water supply is given in 13.4.3.

Simple protection of springs

- Dig a cut-off drain above the spring to divert rainfall runoff away from the site. Mark the level of the water by driving a small bar horizontally into the ground before disturbing the site. Water will return to this level even if it drops during construction.
- Clean the spring site prior to protection. Clear all vegetation from the area to be enclosed. Be careful not to disturb the underlying impermeable layer or the spring may be lost through the diversion of groundwater away from the original eye. Ensure that there is good drainage from the spring collection point.
- Fence the area about 10 m above and around the spring to exclude animals and people.

In an emergency, a short construction time will be important. The method of spring protection shown in Figures 12.16 and 12.17 uses a 'Mini-filter' developed by SWS Filtration. Figure 12.16 shows no storage with an open outlet pipe. Figure 12.17 shows a deeper pit backfilled with large stones to provide some limited storage with a tap at the collection point.

Guide figures:

SWS 'Mini-filter':	size 50 mm (dia.) × 150 mm
	gravity feed capacity 2.3 m^3/h (0.6 l/s)
Plain well screen:	size 50 mm (dia.) × 300 mm
	gravity feed capacity 4.7 m^3/h (1.3 l/s)

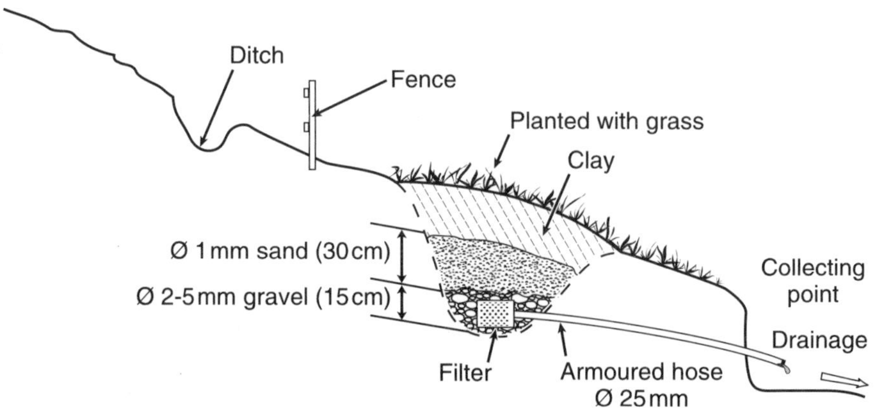

Figure 12.16 A free-flowing spring protected with a 'Mini-filter'

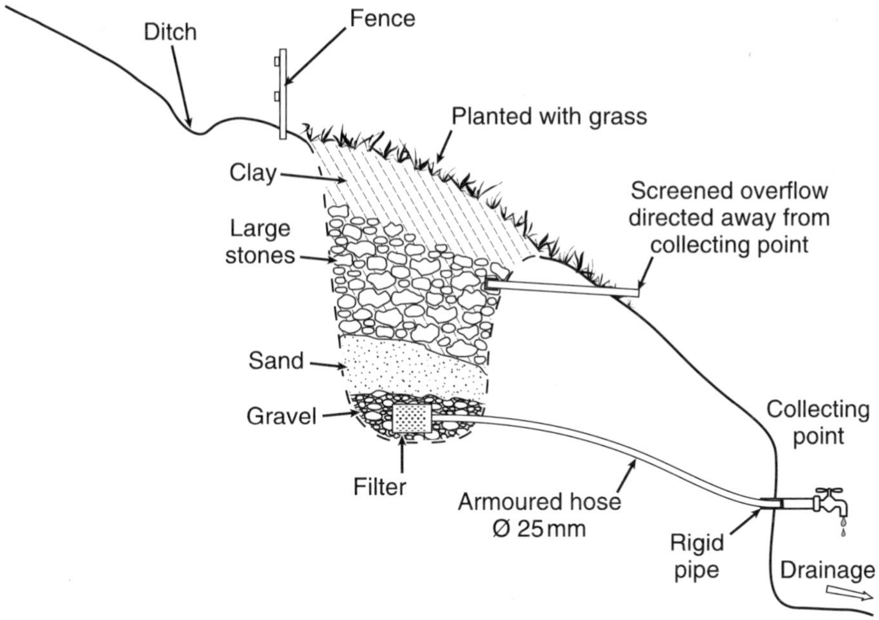

Figure 12.17 A spring protected with a 'Mini-filter' and a tap at the collection point for storage

The 'Mini-filter' could be improvised from standard well screen.

Figure 12.18 shows an alternative method of spring protection, where the site requires the construction of a retaining headwall. In this case, protect the spring as follows:

- Divert the spring water during construction of the spring walls. (If available, use anthill clay to form a small dam.)
- Construct a concrete or masonry wall and position the outlet pipe(s) at the same level, or slightly below, the spring eye. For spring flows greater than about 35 litres/minute it is advisable to have at least two outlet pipes.
- Plaster the spring side of the wall with clay to form a seal and guide the flow of spring water to the outlet pipes.
- Place large stones between the spring eye (or eyes) and the outlet pipes to give free passage of water from the eye to the pipes. Form a 'roof' with the different layers of backfill material. This is to prevent surface water and backfill material from reaching the spring water.
- Shape the final layer of earth to direct rainfall runoff into the cut-off drain. Encourage the growth of creeping grass to stabilize the earth above the spring.

Figure 12.18 shows a protected spring which allows for the collection of water at the spring site. The box, formed by the spring wall and the access steps, gives a stronger structure than a plain headwall. It also provides an area for collecting water that can be kept clean. However, if time or materials are lacking, a simple plain headwall and floor slab are sufficient.

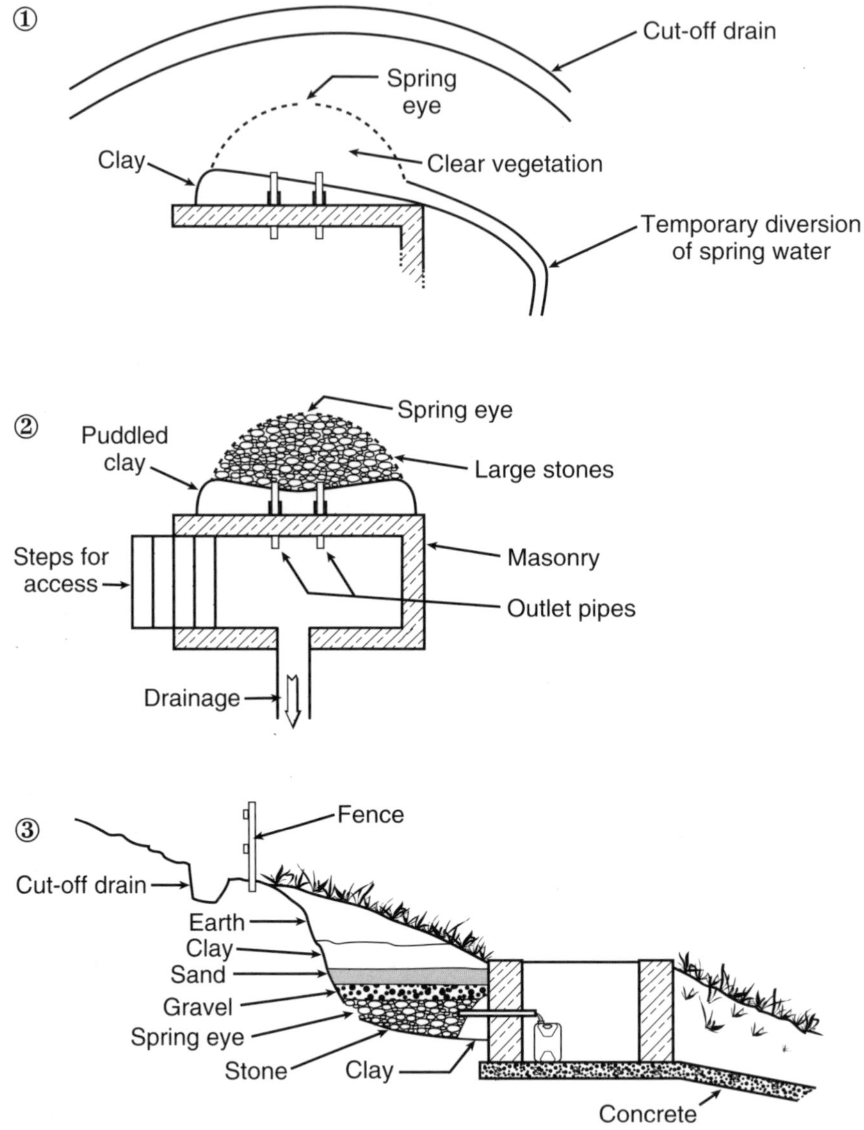

Figure 12.18 Stages in the protection of a spring

In areas of aggressive groundwater, protect the steel outlet pipe from corrosion by fitting a PVC pipe inside the steel pipe (cut the PVC pipe longitudinally to make a tight fit). The PVC pipe provides corrosion protection and the steel provides pipe rigidity.

Spring protection with a spring box Figure 12.19 shows one design of a spring box. A spring box need only be constructed where:

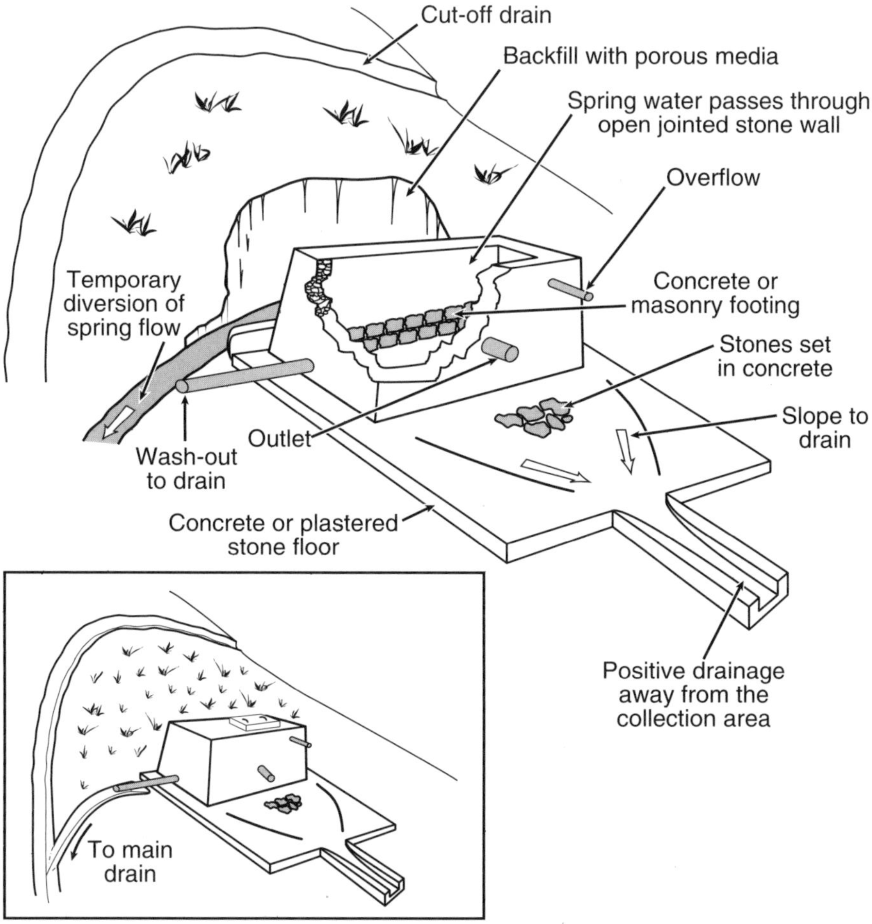

Figure 12.19 A spring box

- Storage of water from low yielding springs is necessary.
- A sedimentation chamber is necessary to settle out suspended solids.
- A more substantial structure is required for high spring yields.

Seepage springs

Diffuse seepage of water from the ground can sometimes provide an important water source.

To estimate the yield of a seepage spring, dig a trench across the slope to collect water seeping downhill and channel it into a measuring container. Time how long it takes to fill.

Collect and protect the seepage in carefully placed infiltration trenches. Fill the trenches with large stone and provide a 'roof' in the same way as shown for the spring in Figure 12.18. Channel the seepage into a collection chamber as shown in Figure 12.20.

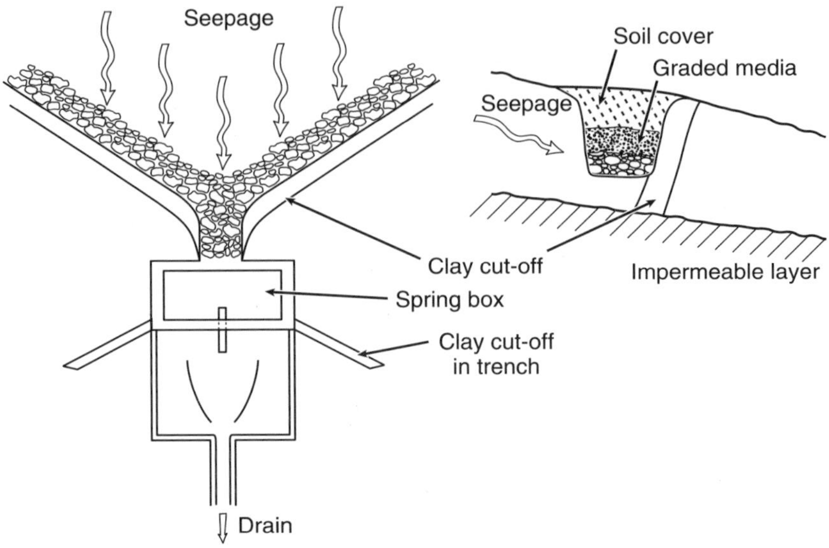

Figure 12.20 The collection of seepage

Spring use and maintenance

Flow from a spring need only be controlled if the spring is low-yielding and storage is necessary. It is common at peak collection times for the tap to be left running as water is collected almost continuously. Conventional taps generally break easily and do not last long. (See 13.4.2 for information on water saving taps.) Therefore, for springs which are heavily used at regular times, provide simple plugs, not taps, for opening and closing outlet pipes at the beginning and end of collection periods, ensuring that this does not cause a build-up of back-pressure (see discussion above). Springs run 24 hours a day, while water collection may be concentrated in just a few hours. Therefore, if water is scarce, it is worth considering piping the spring water to storage and thence to distribution.

Springs require little maintenance, but it is essential to:

- Keep the collection area and drainage channel clear of mud and accumulated debris (leaves, corn cobs, old containers, etc.).
- Keep the cut-off ditch and fence in good working order.
- Keep vegetation under control, so that it does not alter the spring flow or damage the structure.

Maintenance requires the co-operation and organization of the users to carry out the work necessary.

12.3.3 Wells: location and construction

A good well needs a good source of groundwater. The siting of wells requires considerable expertise and a fair amount of luck. Where possible, consult a hydrogeologist. An engineer or relief worker may have to collect information to help locate wells or, in some cases, may have to decide where a well is to be sited. This section gives some guidance on the information that is required to site a well and to select a well construction method.

Well design

This section gives an overview of characteristics common to many wells. More details on specific aspects of well design are given in later sections. Well design may vary greatly, depending on the nature of the aquifer and the methods of construction that are available. Figure 12.21 illustrates schematically the important features of a well. The well is basically a hole extending down to the water-bearing formation. The hole may need to be supported by a casing (borehole) or a lining (dug well). A screen is generally required in the water-bearing section to allow water to enter the well while excluding fine material. This screen is sometimes surrounded by an artificial gravel pack. At the surface, the well must be sealed, to prevent the entry of contaminated water. When water is pumped from the well, the water level drops from the static water level to the pumping or dynamic level – this drop is known as the 'drawdown'. In general, increasing the pumping rate increases the drawdown and an increased drawdown means an increased inflow into the well.

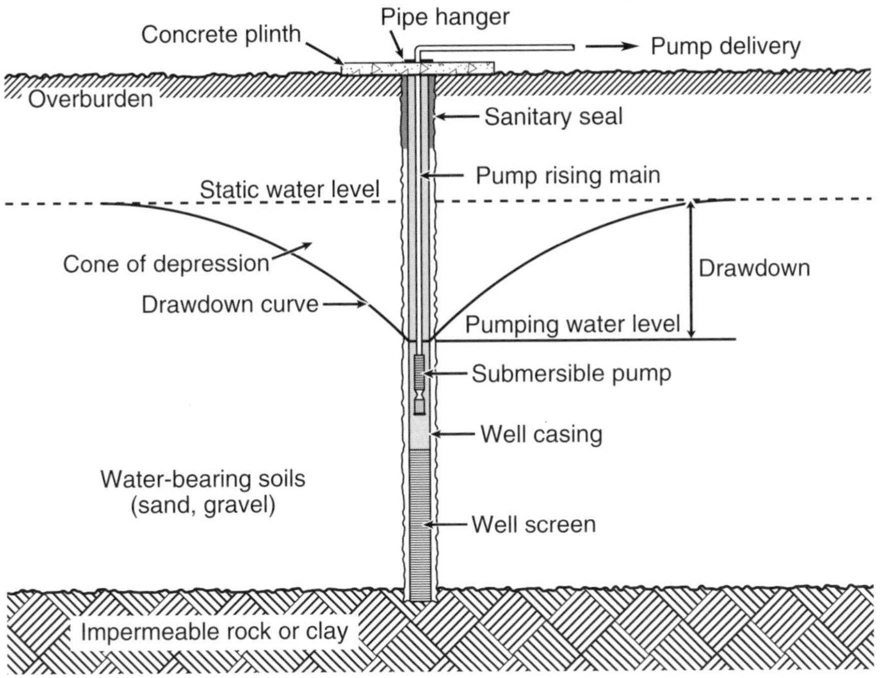

Figure 12.21 Schematic diagram of a typical well

Sources of groundwater

Groundwater yields are likely to be higher in aquifers of alluvium, unconsolidated sediments and weathered zones than in aquifers with bedrock fractures and joints. Yields may also be high in certain frothy lavas (pumice) and highly weathered limestone with large secondary solution cavities (see Table 12.4).

Table 12.4 Common examples of aquifers and aquicludes

Geological formation	*Aquifer*	*Aquiclude*
Unconsolidated sediments	Gravel and sand	Silt and clay
Sedimentary rocks	Partly cemented sandstone; Fractured hard sedimentary rocks; Limestone and dolomite with solution cavities (Karstic)	Mudstone, shale, siltstone; Dense sandstone; Non-fractured limestone
Igneous and metamorphic rocks	Weathered zones; Joints, porous zones between lava beds, lava tubes; Fractured dykes and contact zones	Unaltered rocks (schist, basalt granite); Volcanic ash, tuff deposits; Impermeable dykes
Faults	Faults in hard rock (sandstone, limestone, granite)	Faults in soft rock; Clay and precipitated minerals in faults
Joints	Open joints in tensile zone (syncline and anticline)	Closed joints in compressed zone

Nearly all genuine hard rocks are impermeable. In hard rocks, useful groundwater will only be found in open and interconnected fractures or partings. Unless local experience indicates otherwise, avoid drilling in hard rock as hitting interconnected open zones can be very difficult and can take several attempts. Therefore, first look at unconfined 'water table' aquifers of alluvium or weathered bedrock. They are more accessible, easier and cheaper to develop, and likely to have higher yields than bedrock.

Investigation procedure Information that can help in the location of groundwater can be obtained from various sources:

- Local expertise: are there local hydrogeologists who know the area? Ask at the local water department or check consultants in the nearest big town. If they are available, use them. It may be worth consulting traditional water diviners who have a considerable knowledge of the local environment.
- Existing records: borehole and dug well records indicating depth, yield and descriptions of the soil strata. Geological, hydrogeological and ordinary topographical maps. Sources of information include government departments (Water, Mining, Surveys, etc.), private consultants, and development agencies.

- Satellite imagery and aerial photographs: satellite imagery is usually useful in regional hydrogeological surveys rather than in detailed work. Aerial photographs are more suited to detailed fieldwork but training and experience are required in their interpretation. Seek local expertise.
- Site inspection and surveys: a practised eye can see linear features which indicate lines of weakness or faults in underlying strata. Typical features include lines of vegetation or trees, old or existing stream beds, and changes in soil colour. Promising well sites may be found where two linear features intersect and are often worth investigation. Follow up and compare the results of the information gathering process with the field investigations described in the following sections.

Figure 12.22 shows a range of possible well sites.

Surface geophysical surveys

Geophysical surveys can only give an indication of where groundwater may be found and how much there might be. Such surveys are only tools which add to the information available and improve the chances of drilling or digging a successful well. The choice or combination of techniques will be determined by hydrogeological conditions; seek advice from a hydrogeologist on their application for specific situations.

Electromagnetic (EM) surveys The electromagnetic (EM) method is based on the variation in electromagnetic conductivity of different rock formations. It is useful in quickly locating fractures and faults that may be water-bearing, in otherwise impermeable rock. Promising sites identified by the EM method can be verified by a grounded electrical survey. Electromagnetic surveys can be carried out using portable equipment.

Grounded electrical resistivity surveys The electrical resistivity method involves applying a current to the ground through electrodes. Any sub-surface variation in resistivities is measured and correlated with possible water bearing zones. The equipment used for this type of survey is relatively portable.

Seismic refraction surveys The seismic refraction method measures the reaction of geological bodies to artificially induced shock waves. Waves are induced by a small explosive charge or heavy weight and detected by an array of seismometers or geophones. This method can be used to identify the depth to bedrock, bedrock layering and, possibly, fracture occurrence that may contain water. Seismic refraction surveys are more time consuming, expensive and complex than the electromagnetic and electrical resistivity methods.

Magnetic surveys A magnetic survey detects the effect of certain minerals on the earth's magnetic field. Small, and relatively cheap, hand-held magnetometers are easy to use. They are especially useful in hard rock areas to detect metalliferous dykes (such as dolerite dykes) which can form natural barriers to groundwater flow.

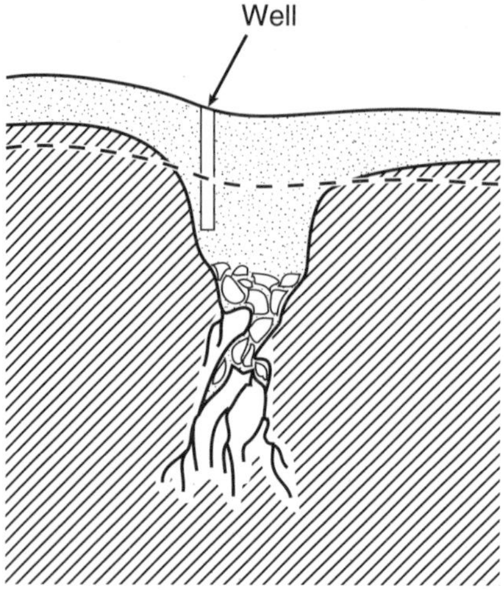

a. Fault zones
Natural drains and vegetation highlight fracture zones.

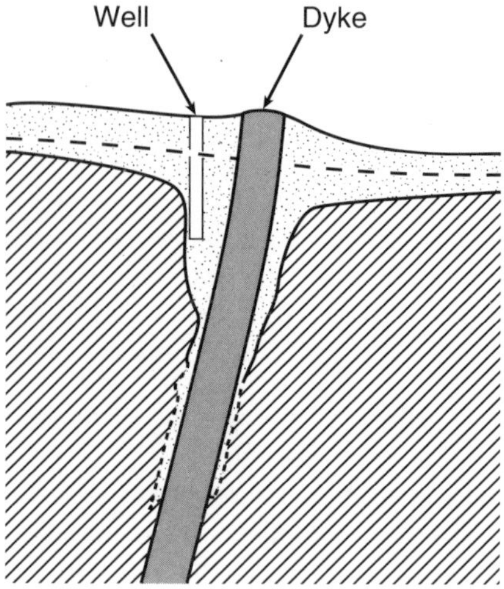

b. Dykes
Look for dykes which may form exposed ridges of a few metres height and show up on aerial photographs as linear features highlighted by bush growth.

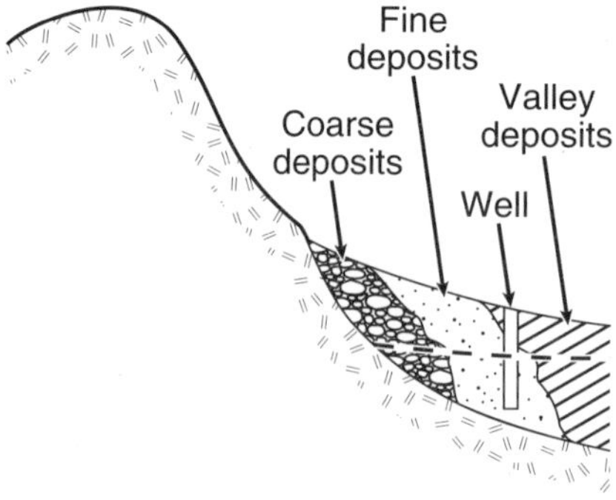

c. Inselbergs or rock domes
Well sites may be found at the base of inselbergs where the rock is often highly weathered and additional finer material has accumulated on top.

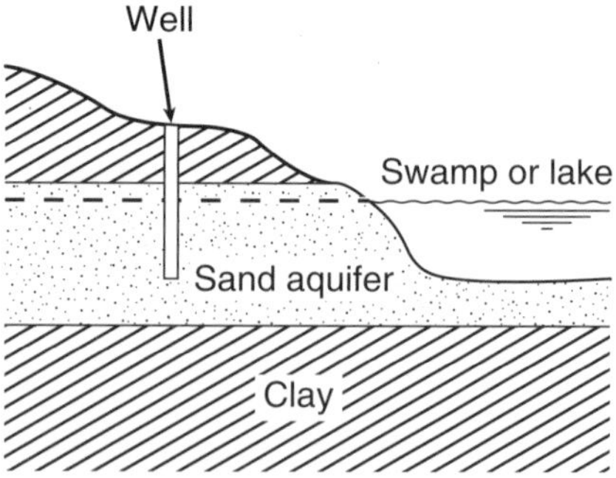

d. Above a swamp or lake
Swamps or lakes with constant levels which are not stream fed will be supplied by an aquifer. A well can be dug into the aquifer.

Figure 12.22 The siting of wells

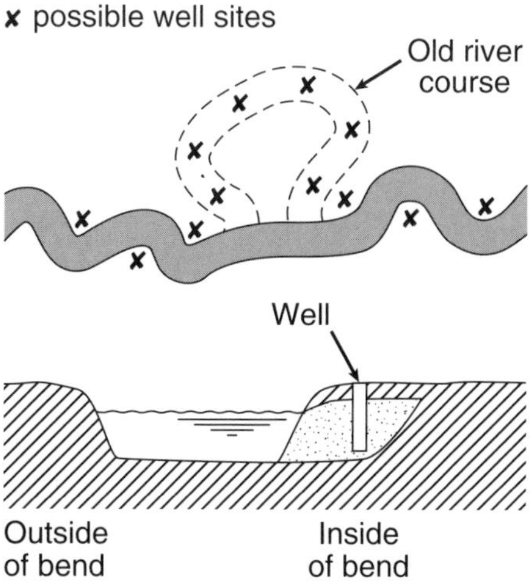

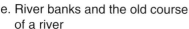

e. River banks and the old course of a river
A meandering river with a flat gradient may have changed course several times. Look for sites on the inside of the old and new courses of the river.

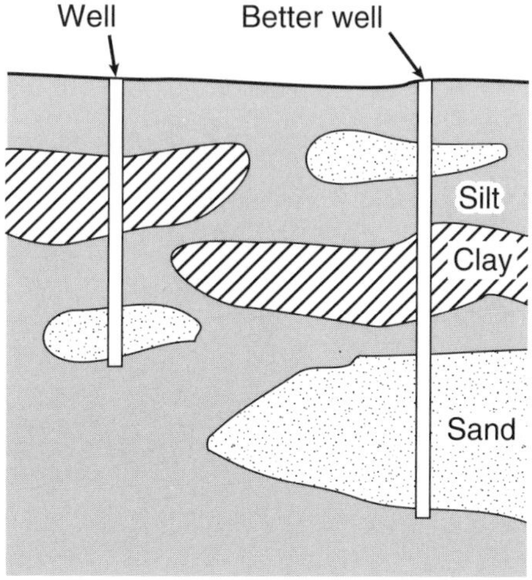

f. An alluvial plain
Find the best site by drilling with a hand auger in systematic lines across a plain.

Figure 12.22 (cont.) The siting of wells

Test drilling

The wasted effort of hand digging a dry well can be avoided by test drilling using a hand auger or a small powered drill.

A powered drill can penetrate hard ground far more rapidly than a hand auger. However, powered drills require a supply of fuel, oil and – in the circulation type – drilling fluids. They also require skilled maintenance and a range of spare parts. With rotary drilling, soil samples are intermixed, which reduces the amount of useful information that can be collected. Therefore, unless soil conditions preclude it, use a hand auger. See Appendix 11 for details of a typical hand auger set for survey drilling to a depth of 15 m. Petrol engine driven survey drills which can be operated by one or two people are available. They are mainly of two types: continuous flight auger or small direct circulation rotary drills.

Options for well construction

Having located a good source of groundwater, an appropriate well construction method must be chosen. Table 12.5 gives some guidelines on the choice of well construction method. Further guidance is given in the relevant sections.

Table 12.5 Well construction methods

*Method, well diameter and depth**	*Suitable formations for drilling or digging*	*Unsuitable formations for drilling or digging*	*Advantages*	*Disadvantages*
Dug wells Diameter: > 1 m Depth: < 30 m	Clays, sands, gravels, small boulders	Hard and soft rock Where depth to water > 30 m	Low capital costs Quick mobilization Uses local skills Possible to maintain at village level	Dangerous – large diameter hole Limited depth Time to dig and line
Hand-drilled wells Diameter: 100–200 mm Depth: < 30 m	Clays, sands, fine gravels	Rock formations, cobbles, boulders	Low capital cost Portable equipment	Limited depth Limited range of suitable formations
Jetted wells Diameter: 50–200 mm Depth: < 40 m	Clays, sands, fine gravels	Rock formations, cobbles, boulders	Very quick and easy in right conditions Low capital cost Portable	Limited depth and limited range of suitable formations Water required to drill
Percussion (cable tool) Diameter: 100–1100 mm Depth: up to 600 m	Soft rock, sands, gravels, silts and clays	Running sand, flint (or chert), hard rock, boulders	Reasonable capital and running costs Simple maintenance Good sampling during drilling Up to 30 m/day in soft rock	Experienced driller needed Temporary casings needed in loose formations Slow in hard rock, maybe 2 m/day
Direct circulation rotary drilling Diameter: 100–750 mm Depth: > 1000 m	Soft rock, metamorphic and igneous rock	Running sands, fractured rock, some shales, boulders	Little drill casing needed 100–150 m/day in soft ground 10–20 m/day in rock	High capital and operating costs High demand on skill, maintenance and spares Drilling fluid can damage aquifer
Reverse circulation rotary drilling Diameter: 400–1750 mm Depth: up to 350 m	Unconsolidated sediments, soft rock	Hard rock, boulders	80–100 m/day in unconsolidated sediments Drill casing not needed	Heavy drilling equipment Large quantity of water needed for drilling
Down-the-hole hammer Diameter: 100–450 mm Depth: up to 400 m	Hard rock	Sands, gravels, clays, soft rock, loose boulders	Up to 5 m/hr in hard rock Good sampling during drilling	High skill, capital and maintenance

*Depths indicated are those expected under normal conditions.
(Adapted from Hamill and Bell, 1986)

12.3.4 Dug wells

Appropriateness of dug wells in an emergency

In an emergency, dug wells are appropriate where they can be safely and quickly dug, where the yield can satisfy the demand and where there is a suitable means of drawing water from the wells. With proper planning and where conditions are suitable, a programme to install dug wells can be initiated very quickly. However, deep wells dug in difficult ground can take months to complete and are unlikely to be an option in the initial phase of an emergency. The extent to which dug wells can satisfy the demand for water will depend on:

- Well yield – which will depend on the aquifer characteristics, the well diameter and depth. The yield is likely to be less than for drilled boreholes due to the problems of sinking the dug well into the aquifer.
- The rate at which water can be abstracted – the available methods of lifting water such as bucket and rope, handpumps or powered pumps (see Chapter 14).

In a non-emergency situation, given sufficient yield, a village dug well can typically supply up to 300 people per day. In an emergency situation, given sufficient yield, one dug well might operate almost continuously throughout the day and supply 900 people. (At a pumping rate of 0.5 l/s operating for 75 per cent of the time over 10 hours, and supplying 15 litres/person/day.) The abstraction rate using handpumps can be increased by fitting more than one handpump, assuming the well yield is adequate.

The storage provided by a hand dug well is important in low yielding aquifers. Storage to meet peak demand may be replenished from seepage during off-peak periods. This would not be possible from a borehole, which has very little storage and only supplies the instantaneous aquifer yield. Where necessary, dug wells can be made deeper or wider to increase overnight storage.

In siting dug wells, follow the guidelines in 12.3.3. Many dug wells are sited by field observation and confirmed by hand or machine test drilling. Look for existing traditional wells and note where they are sited. Speak to local well diggers and find out how they site a well.

Safety

Before any work is started on the construction of a dug well, be aware of the safety measures that will need to be taken. Prepare both the well diggers and their equipment. Ensure that all those involved in construction understand the safe working methods to be adopted. This may require a reliable translator with a good understanding of the work. The establishment of trust within well construction teams is essential for safe co-operation. Try to choose people who know and get on well with each other.

The principal dangers in hand dug well construction are:

- Lack of knowledgeable supervision.
- Careless workers and work methods.
- Tiredness and lack of concentration.
- Faulty equipment.

- Falling materials.
- Collapsing soil.
- Poisonous gases from pump engines, explosives and naturally occurring gases.
- Incoming water.
- Excessive dust.
- Interference by casual onlookers and animals.
- Children playing on unattended well sites.

Key safety points include:

- Ensure that competent staff supervise construction.
- Agree signalling arrangements between diggers and the surface.
- Ensure that a minimum of four people work on a well at any one time. No person should dig alone.
- Provide safe and easy access to the well. Have available an additional standby method of well entry and exit.
- Protect the hole when digging is in progress, and make it safe when workers are not on site in order to prevent people, animals or materials falling in.
- Regularly check equipment: ropes, ladders, lifting gear, tripods, buckets, pick-axe and hammer handles and heads, and so on.
- Provide and use essential safety equipment, including safety helmets and protective footwear. Goggles should be worn when breaking rock.
- Include first aid training and equipment as part of the overall safety measures. Have available a harness for lifting injured personnel.
- Use safe and suitable dewatering equipment. A compressed-air powered pump is a relatively safe system. If electricity is used it should preferably be at 50 volts or 110 volts maximum.

Warning: *Do not lower combustion engines, petrol-powered or diesel powered pumps into wells for dewatering. Exhaust gases are heavier than air and will sink to the lowest levels. A lethal build-up of carbon monoxide will cause the death in seconds of anyone present in the well. At ground level, ensure petrol engines or diesel engines are positioned downwind of the well site.*

Ensure that there is a well-rehearsed and effective means of immediate evacuation of workers from the well.

If someone collapses while working at the bottom of a well, ventilate the well by using, for example, branches on ropes. Ensure that anyone lowered in to rescue them keeps talking to those at the top. If the talking stops, pull the rescuer out immediately. The rescuer should always have a rope permanently attached so that she or he can be withdrawn immediately if she or he collapses.

- Provide compressed-air tool operators with the following safety equipment in addition to the normal safety helmets: ear defenders, safety glasses, safety boots and gloves. Medical check-ups, especially for hearing and the respiratory system, are advisable if work extends over a prolonged period.
- Explosives must only be handled by competent and trained staff. Only licensed staff should place and detonate explosives. Purge the well of all toxic fumes after detonations. Leave fumes to dissipate over a period of 24 hours. Improvised explosives should not be used because of their erratic performance.
- Agree on sanitation procedures, to eliminate any risk of well diggers excreting or urinating anywhere near the well.
- Keep onlookers far away from the excavation and secure the site during non-working periods, especially at night. This is very important in a crowded environment such as a refugee camp. It may be necessary to employ guards.

Additional safety measures may be required, depending on the situation.

Excavation of dug wells

The local knowledge and expertise of the affected population can be very useful in many aspects of well digging – use it. Figure 12.23 shows the layout of a safe well construction site.

Basic tools and equipment Where excavation is by hand, diggers may prefer to use appropriate traditional tools. Standard shop-bought buckets are not strong enough and are unsafe. Do not use them. Arrange for strong buckets (kibbles) to be made locally. Make sure the handles are firmly attached and that they cannot slide off a hook. A bucket full of soil falling into the well could easily kill anyone below. Do not overfill buckets and kibbles.

A tripod and winch for use during excavation can be made from tree poles of adequate strength if they are available locally. Obtain smooth running, well engineered pulleys that match the rope sizes. A bad pulley can quickly wear a rope and shorten its useful life. Check pulleys regularly and keep them off the ground to prevent damage from dirt and grit. Thin rope may be strong enough for the task but difficult to handle. If available, use 24 mm diameter nylon rope for critical operations such as getting in and out of the well and for the removal of dug soil and rock.

Well digging It is difficult to dig inside a well of less than 1 m diameter. An optimum well diameter for digging and lining is 1.5 m. In unstable soil, line a well as the excavation proceeds. In some cases, only a temporary lining may be necessary to support loose soil at the surface.

Digging a well is very tiring work. Accidents happen when diggers are tired, so ensure a regular changeover of well diggers and surface workers. For efficiency and safety when digging in difficult soils and hot conditions, it may be necessary to change diggers every 15–30 minutes. The last thing a tired digger wants to do at the end of a digging session is to climb a long ladder to get out of the well. It is also unsafe. Therefore, except for very shallow wells, it is

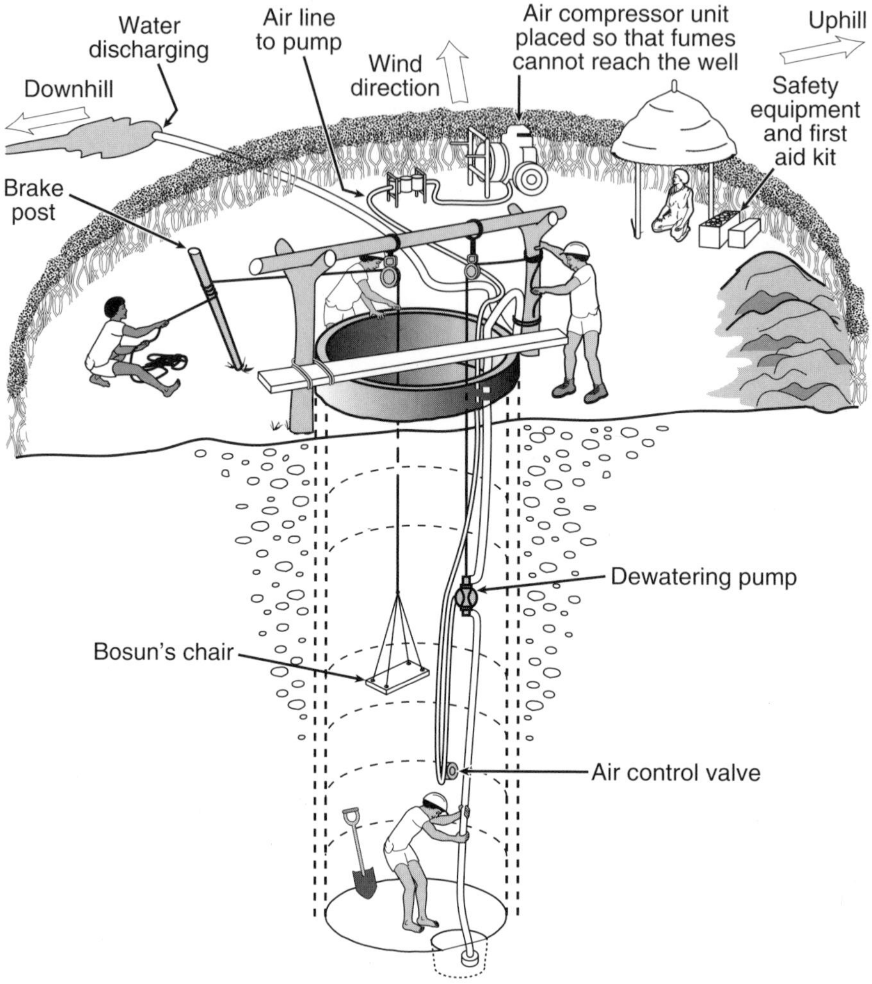

Figure 12.23 A safe well digging operation

advisable to use a form of 'bosun's chair' for entry and exit (Figure 12.23). This way the less tired surface workers raise the digger.

The well yield depends on several factors, but in particular: the aquifer type, the depth of the well, and the time of year. The diameter of the well has little effect on yield, but will increase the amount of storage. An emergency may not occur at the driest time and therefore measures must be taken to ensure that there is enough water at the end of the dry season.

- Use dewatering pumps to extract water and thus allow digging to a greater depth.
- If a well is not deep enough at the end of the dry season, deepen by means of a caisson column as shown in Figure 12.24. This method may be used to make the well deeper as the water table drops or to dig into an unstable sand layer.

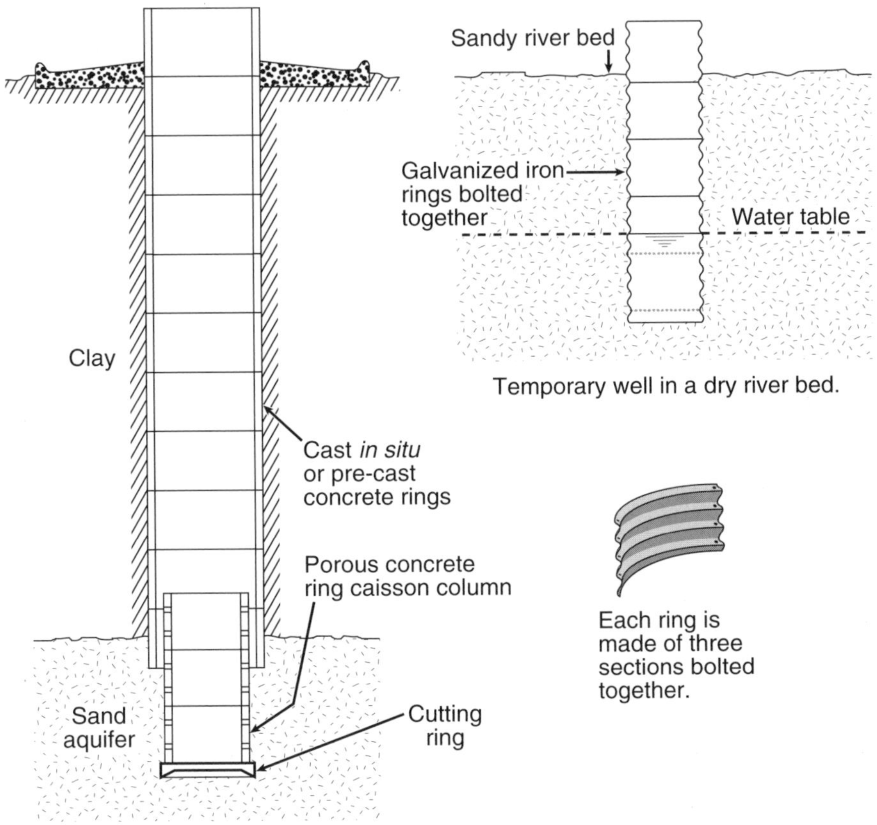

Figure 12.24 Well lining methods

The dangers of different pumps used in dewatering are listed above under 'Safety'. A handpump can be adapted for dewatering if it has a greater capacity than the pump to be installed. One of the safest methods of powered dewatering is by using an air-operated diaphragm pump supplied by a compressor from the surface. An air-operated pump is particularly appropriate where compressed air tools are already being used.

Compressed air tools Do not use powered rock breakers in small diameter wells over prolonged periods because of the adverse effect on operators of excessive noise and dust. Use compressed air tools primarily for drilling holes for explosives and for shaping a well after blasting. See Section 15.3.2 for general guidance on compressed air tools. See Appendix 12 for a recommended package of lightweight compressor, rock drill and rock breaker for use in dug wells.

Blasting The use of explosives in well excavation requires a skilled and licensed blaster. These notes provide a brief overview of well blasting for the engineer who may have to contract an experienced blaster for the work:

- Laws – Know the national laws and regulations concerning explosives.
- Purchase and transport – A licence is normally required to purchase explosives. Police permission and/or a guard may be required for the transport of explosives. Keep detonators and explosives apart.
- Storage – Store explosives in a licensed magazine. A store may require an official guard. Store detonators and explosives separately. Ensure that there is no smoking and that there are no metal tools in the store area. Handle cases with care.
- Control – Issue explosives in the sequence of dated manufacture. Do not open a new case until the previous case contents have been used. Do not open cases in a magazine. Keep accurate records.
- Safety – Ensure strict safety measures are followed on site.
  Before a blast:
  1. Clear the site of people and move them far away from the well.
  2. Post lookouts at all approaches.
  3. Give a clear warning before the blast.
  4. Ensure that everyone takes adequate cover.

  After a blast:
  5. Wait a period of time before returning to the site of a blast to allow for possible misfires and the dispersal of toxic fumes.
  6. Carefully check for undetonated explosives.

Toxic fumes are heavier than air and can stay in the bottom of a well for a long time. Forced ventilation should be considered as a well gets deeper.

The procedures for charging and stemming the shot holes and firing the blast are the responsibility of the blaster. Licensed blasters may be contracted from mines, quarries and appropriate government departments.

Well lining methods

There are many ways of lining a well and a summary of the main methods is shown in Figure 12.24. Find out what the local method is and use it if appropriate. The two basic methods are *in-situ* lining (from the top down or the bottom up) and caissoning.

In stable soils, wells are sometimes dug unlined down to the water table, and then lined *in situ* from the bottom up. This is a simpler process than the alternatives and has the advantage that lining materials are only used after water has been struck. The principal disadvantage is the danger of well collapse. *In-situ* lining from the top down is a safer although technically more difficult option.

Caissoning, illustrated in Figure 12.24, is the sinking of a lining column as excavation proceeds. This method is used when dealing with collapsing soil, and below the water table, to protect diggers as they work. It is important to use a 'cutting ring' with a slightly larger diameter than the lining column to ease and control the downward passage of the column. If a column moves out of the vertical, correct it immediately, as straightening later is extremely difficult. A corrugated lining cannot be caissoned as the corrugations inhibit downward movement.

Well lining materials

Concrete Refer to 19.3.2 for guidelines on concrete mixes. There are several methods of lining in concrete, using pre-cast rings, fixed *in-situ* lining or caissoned *in-situ* lining.

Concrete rings are widely used for well lining. Formwork developed by WIG Engineering in co-operation with Oxfam produces a concrete ring 600 mm deep by 1500 mm outside diameter and 100 mm thick walls. (Weight: approximately 630 kg. Cement required: 1.5 bags per ring or 2.5 bags per metre. See Figure 12.25.) Reinforcement may be needed for concrete rings which have to be transported but it is not essential for rings which are simply placed in position and are not going to be used for caissoning. All forces are compressive once the rings are in position. Concrete rings can be reinforced with steel, ferrocement and fibre. Chopped polypropylene strands, 75 mm long, have been used as reinforcement for the above rings at the rate of 1.2 kg per ring. If culvert and manhole rings (with step irons) are available locally, they are ideal for well lining.

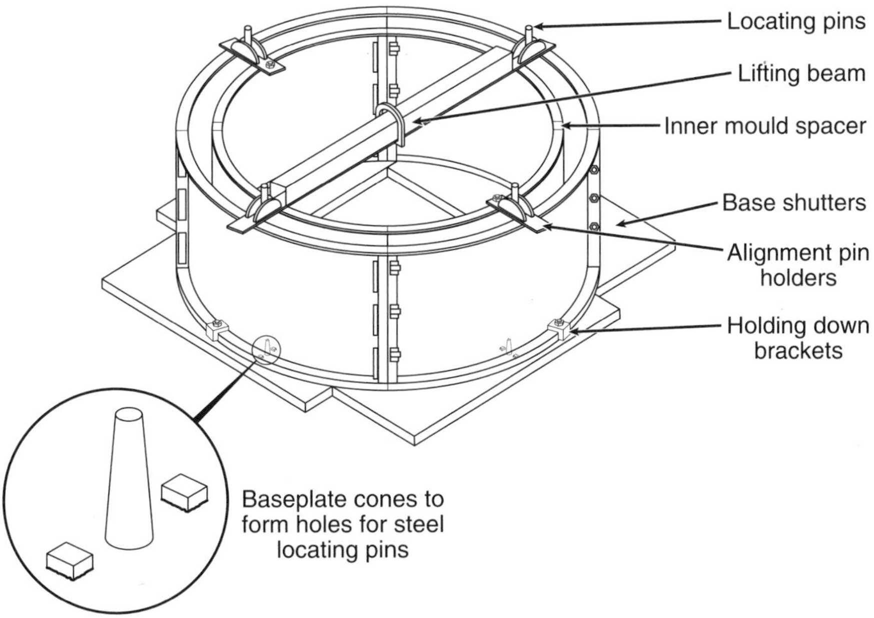

Figure 12.25 Formwork for pre-cast concrete well rings

In-situ concrete lining avoids the handling of heavy concrete rings on site. The accuracy of formwork is not so critical as for pre-cast rings and formwork could be made locally in a workshop with basic equipment (see Figure 12.26). Reinforcement is not necessary for cast *in-situ* concrete lining unless blasting is needed later on.

A concrete ring column can be caissoned by casting a stage at a time *in situ* as the column descends. This avoids the need to manoeuvre concrete rings into position (see Figure 12.24).

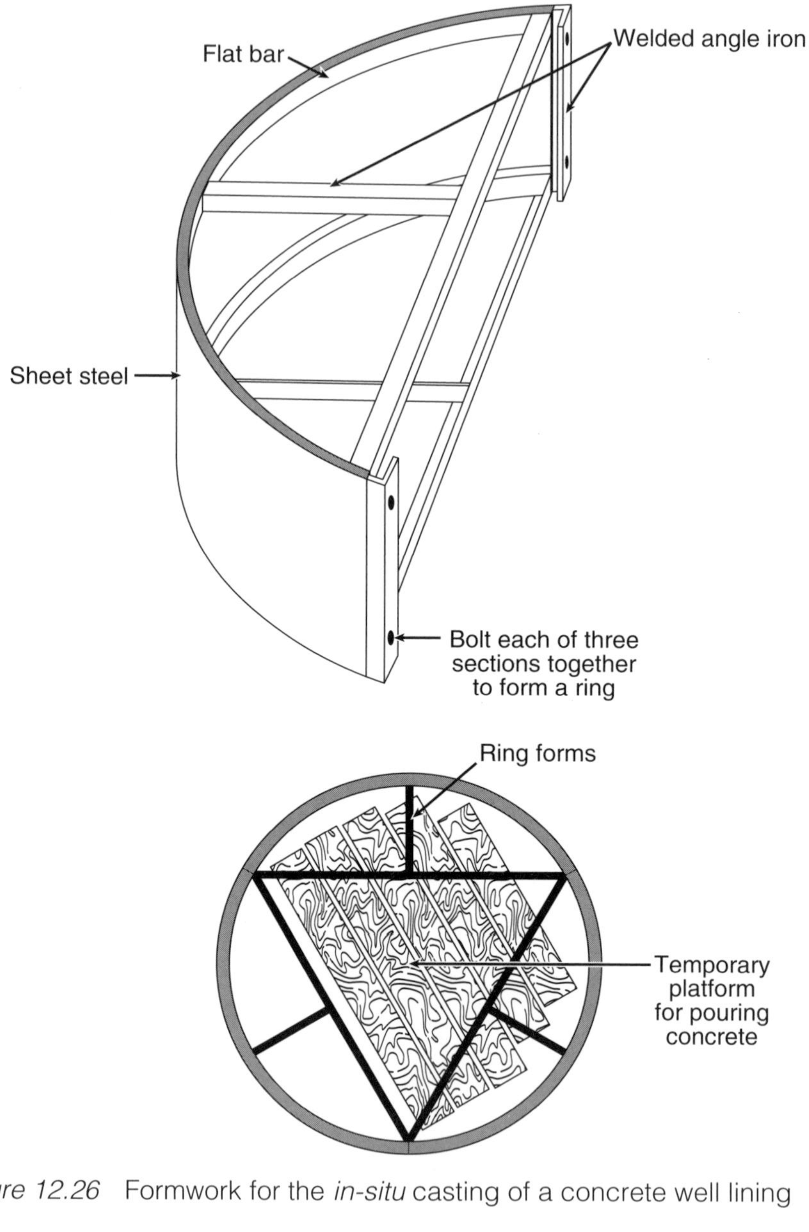

Figure 12.26 Formwork for the *in-situ* casting of a concrete well lining

Other well lining materials Moulded blocks, bricks and stone masonry are all suitable for *in-situ* lining of stable excavations. Unlike concrete rings, they can be handled easily with the minimum of equipment. A sand/cement block system used successfully in Ghana is shown in Figure 12.27. The blocks sit on 10 cm deep concrete rings which are situated at the base of the well and at every 10 m interval. The top three metres are sealed with cement mortar. Emergency rehabilitation work on older stone- and brick-lined wells often involves

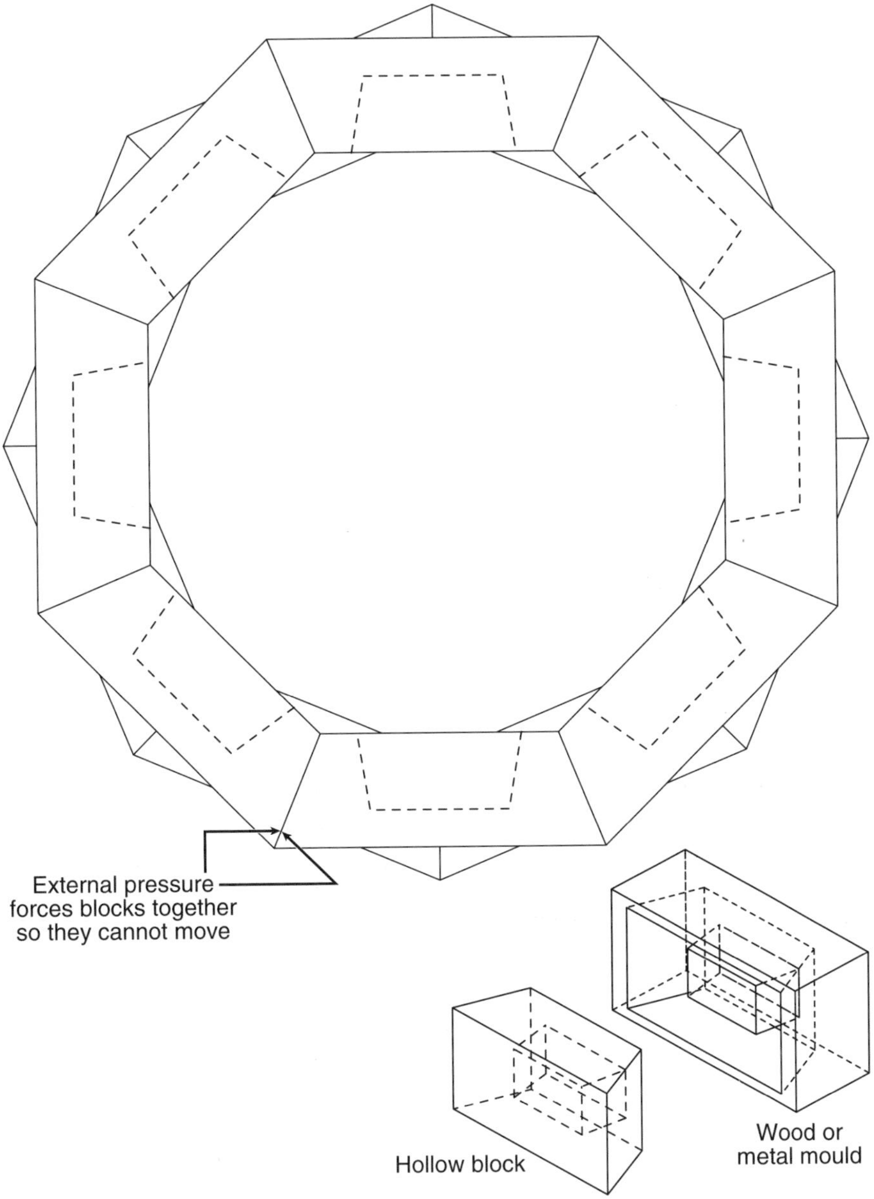

Figure 12.27 A method of lining with moulded sand/cement blocks

replacing missing stones and bricks where weathered mortar joints have caused them to fall out.

Corrugated steel culvert linings (for example, 'Armco' corrugated steel lining) can be used to line a dug well rapidly. Line it as digging proceeds or, in stable ground, line from the bottom (see Figure 12.24).

The potential for using plastic well liners in an emergency has not yet been fully tested but has certain attractions. The company, Van Reekum Materials, has produced a prototype system of polyethylene well liner sheets. The flat sheets are relatively easy to transport and can be formed into a circular shape on site. The sheets can be pre-slotted to give a permeable liner.

Completion

All wells must have:

- A sanitary seal at the surface to prevent pollution by surface water and seepage flowing into the well.
- A concrete apron and effective drainage which carries waste water away and does not leave pools of water around the well.

Wells dug in soft ground, especially fine sand, will need a permeable concrete plug or graded media in the bottom of the well to prevent the ingress of soils with the incoming water. See Appendix 20 for the correct sizing of the media.

It is especially important to consult with the users about the above-ground design of a well so that it suits people's needs and so that they are encouraged to maintain it in a hygienic condition. Figure 12.28a shows the design of a handpumped well which takes account of the local method of carrying water in clay pots. It also provides good access and animal watering facilities. Figure 12.28b shows a well design for drawing water by bucket and rope.

Rehabilitation of existing dug wells

Open dug wells may be damaged and contaminated during natural disasters (such as flooding) and during conflicts (by poisoning or by the bodies of animals or even people). In circumstances where developed urban supplies have been damaged or destroyed due to conflict or a natural disaster, it may be necessary to re-open old abandoned wells. Wells can be rehabilitated by cleaning, repair and deepening. Open wells, in particular, accumulate debris (buckets, ropes, cloth, etc.) and silt in the well bottom. Cleaning a well improves storage, recharge and water quality. To rehabilitate a well:

- Use dewatering pumps to lower the water level.
- Provide safety ropes, protective gear (hard hats, gloves, boots) for the workers who clean the well.
- Provide a safe means of entry and exit.
- Inspect the lining, headwall and apron for damage, cracks and missing bricks. Repair if necessary. Check to see if surface water can seep through the lining into the well by pouring water over the apron or around the top of the well at the junction with the ground. Patch the well lining and seal around the top of the well using puddled clay or a cement grout.
- After cleaning out the bottom of the well, clean the lining using a brush. Beware of using chlorine solution for washing inside the well as chlorine fumes and splashes to the skin and eyes can be very dangerous.

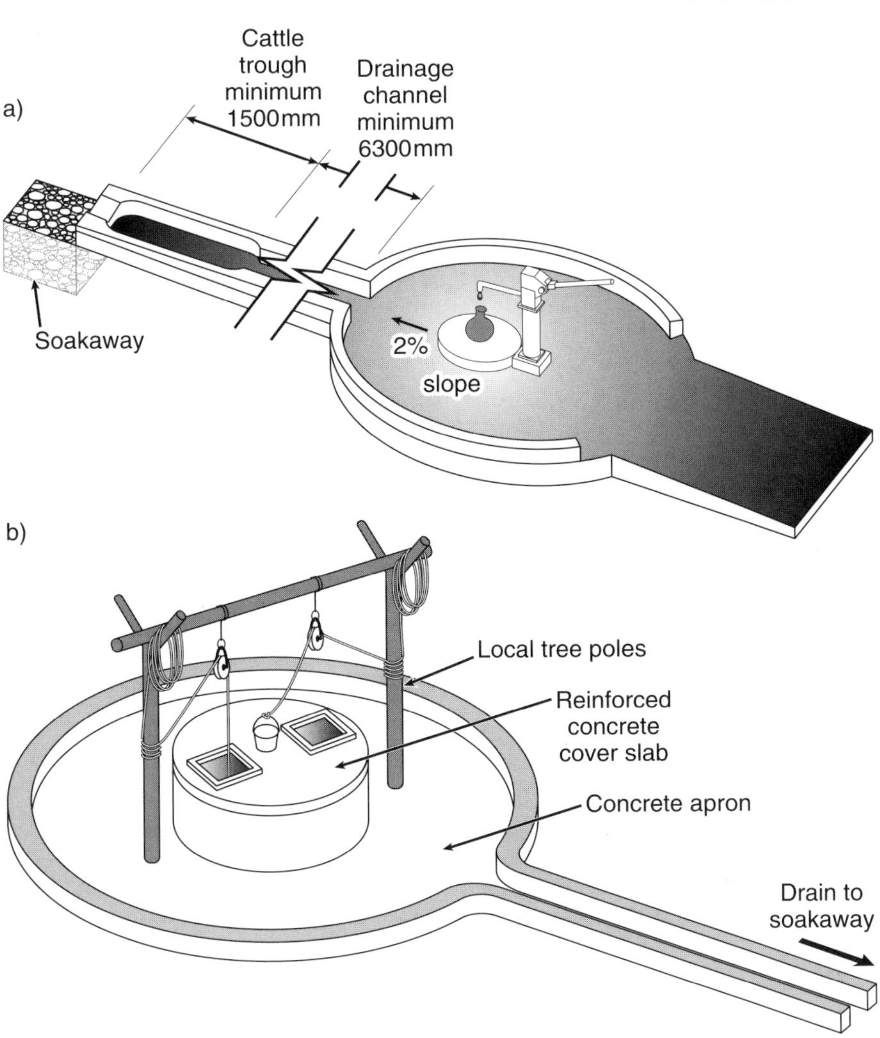

Figure 12.28 Above-ground design for dug wells

- Disinfect the well by estimating the volume of the well and adding sufficient chlorine to give a concentration of 50 mg/l (see 13.3.3). Leave it overnight before pumping out and putting the well into use.

Increasing the well yield Under drought conditions, the yield of many dug wells can be very low. In suitable aquifers, deepening a well may be the best way of increasing its yield. This can be achieved by further digging or by drilling horizontal or vertical holes in the well bottom.

Ensure diggers are well protected from the possible collapse of an old lining. Repair any damaged lining before deepening. Digging within a caisson column gives the best protection (see Figure 12.24). Deepening wells by digging and blasting in hard rock areas is arduous and takes time.

Specialized equipment is needed if holes are to be drilled in the bottom of a well. Vertical drilling is easier than horizontal drilling. Where water is confined below an impermeable or semi-permeable retarding layer, or where the aquifer is known to extend below the well bottom, drill holes vertically. In fractured rock, or in thin aquifers, drill holes horizontally for up to 30 m to try and intersect water-bearing fractures.

Compressed air rotary rock drills can be adapted to drill deep holes in hard rock. However, when drilling horizontally, the well diameter restricts the size of drill and length of drilling rods.

Management and maintenance of dug wells

- Ensure that spilt water drains away from the well and that the surroundings are kept clean. Fences will be necessary if animals are a problem.
- Monitor the condition of the well, using sanitary surveys (see Appendix 8).
- Initiate preventive maintenance to include the repair, replacement or reporting of worn or damaged ropes, buckets, pump parts, the well structure etc.
- Manage the use of the well. This may include a system of control and rationing if water is scarce. Fencing, a gate and a well supervisor will be necessary to allow only a manageable number of people to collect an agreed amount of water at any one time.
- Monitor water depth and well yield.

To obtain a rough estimate of the rate of inflow to the well: reduce the water level to the pump setting depth, or minimum collection depth, and time how long it takes for the level to rise a measured amount (such as 200 mm). Note that as the level of water in the well increases, the hydraulic gradient driving water into the well decreases and so the rate of inflow decreases.

12.3.5 Hand drilled and jetted wells

In certain circumstances, hand drilled or jetted wells can be appropriate.

The amount of water each hand drilled or jetted well can supply will depend on well yield and the rate at which water can be pumped out. Handpumps will supply about 12–36 litres/minute depending on the lift and the pump (see 14.5). So, even though hand drilled and jetted wells can be constructed quickly, there are clearly limitations on the amount of water that can be supplied from each well. There must also be enough pumps to match the number of wells. Therefore, carefully consider how many wells will be needed before embarking on either option in an emergency.

Hand drilled wells

In favourable soils, a hand drilled well can be drilled, screened and cased within a day. Typical augers for hand drilling and the associated equipment are dealt with in Appendix 11. The stages in the construction of a hand drilled well are shown in Figure 12.29. The type of aquifer, yield required, ease of drilling and

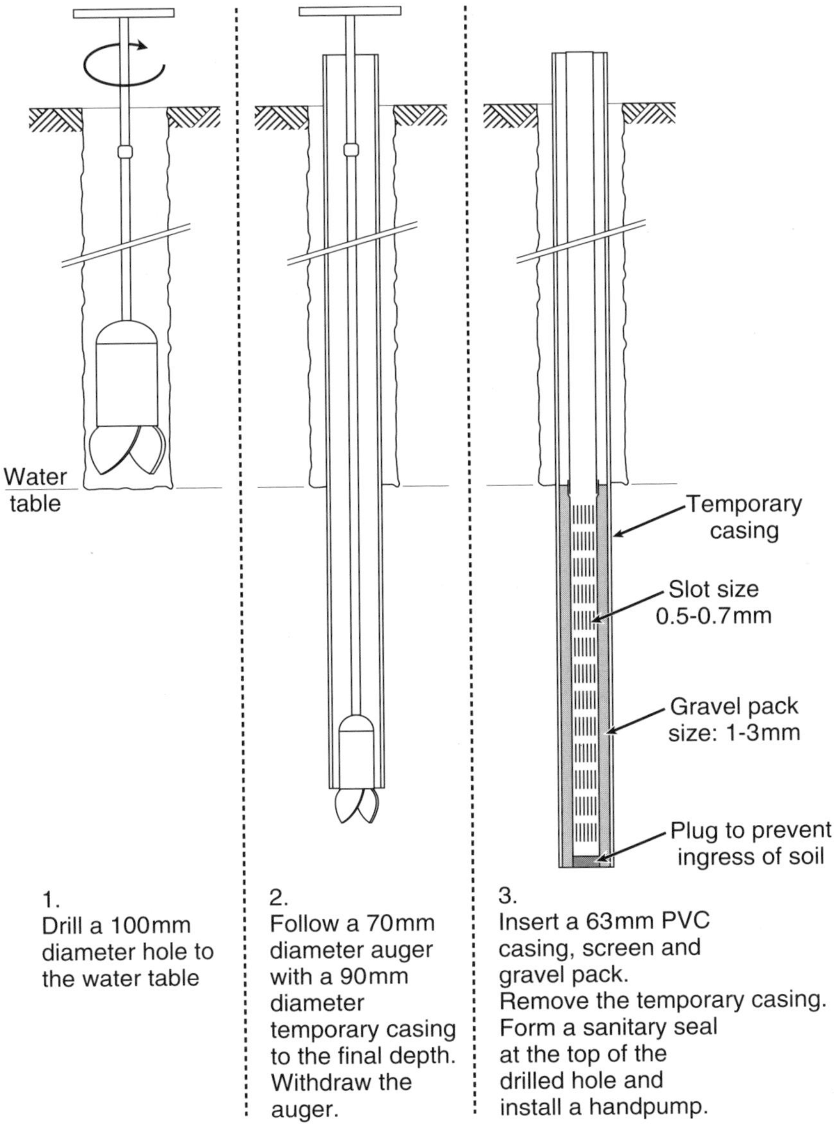
Water table
Temporary casing
Slot size 0.5-0.7mm
Gravel pack size: 1-3mm
Plug to prevent ingress of soil
1.
Drill a 100mm diameter hole to the water table
2.
Follow a 70mm diameter auger with a 90mm diameter temporary casing to the final depth. Withdraw the auger.
3.
Insert a 63mm PVC casing, screen and gravel pack.
Remove the temporary casing.
Form a sanitary seal at the top of the drilled hole and install a handpump.

Figure 12.29 Stages in the construction of a hand drilled well

the size of pump to be installed determine the diameter of each well. Standard drill sets are available for holes up to 180 mm diameter and depths of 25 m.

Key points:

- An adjustable cross-piece enables four people to turn the auger. Do not use more people than the equipment is designed for and do not use extension bars on the handles. In either case, the equipment could be damaged or get stuck in the hole.

- Always turn threaded equipment clockwise – even when removing the auger from the hole. Do not turn anticlockwise, as the extension rods will unscrew and the auger and rods will be left stranded down the hole! Heavier equipment uses lock-pins.
- Do not overfill the auger as it could become stuck, or excess material could damage the sides of the bored hole.
- Train the drilling team to use the rod catchers and pipe clamps habitually, to prevent equipment dropping down the hole. Equipment dropping is always dangerous.
- Keep screw threads clean and auger blades sharp. Replace or rebuild worn blades.
- Remember, the deeper the hole, the longer it takes to drill, as each time an auger is full the complete drill string of extension rods and auger must be withdrawn.

Jetted wells

Well-jetting is also known as wash-boring. Wells may be jetted in suitable formations such as sands, fine gravels, unconsolidated silts and clays. The method fails in permeable gravels as the circulating fluid is lost. It is not suitable in hard rock or where cobbles or boulders are present. Jetted wells may be particularly suited to the development of abstraction points in sand rivers or in alluvial deposits beside rivers. Jetting requires very little equipment and in the right conditions is an elegant, easy and rapid method of well construction. Figure 12.30 shows the basic technique of jetting which involves circulating water down a hand-held pipe. The process is as follows:

- Water issuing from the bottom of the steel jetting pipe fluidizes the soil, allowing the pipe to sink.
- The loosened soil is carried to the surface by water returning up the annulus formed between the jetting pipe and the wall of the hole. Where returning water is lost into the soil formation, clay or drilling fluid can be added to the water to maintain circulation and to help remove cuttings. If water is in short supply it can be recirculated via a pit where washings from the well are settled out.
- If required, to prevent the hole collapsing, temporary casing may be installed.
- When the hole is deep enough, permanent casing and screens may be installed as required.

Jetting pipes of 25–100 mm diameter will produce boreholes of 40–200 mm diameter. A centrifugal pump capable of handling solids will normally be required – typically, a small portable 50 mm pump powered by a 5 kW diesel or petrol engine. Well depth will be determined by the weight of jet pipe that can be safely handled. In fine to medium sands, depths of 30–40 m are possible. Where the hydrogeological conditions are suitable, small diameter boreholes may be jetted at the bottom of dug wells, through a confining layer of clay, into a confined aquifer of sand/gravel. Penetration of the confined aquifer allows

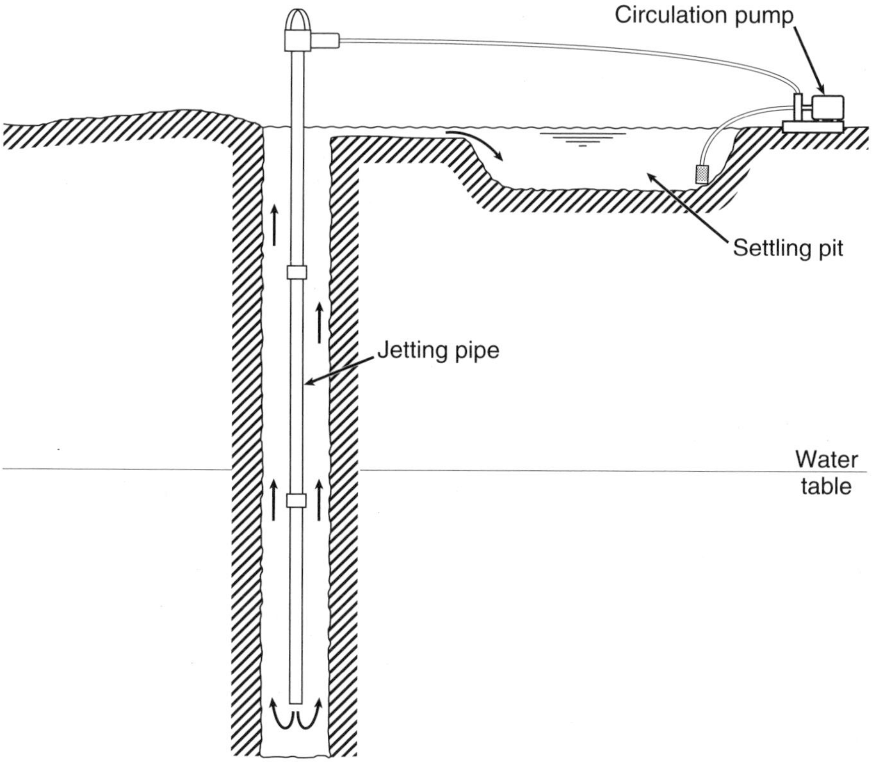

Figure 12.30 The basic technique of jetting wells

water to flow up into the dug well to the level of the potentiometric surface as shown in Figure 12.31.

12.3.6 Machine drilled boreholes

Borehole drilling is a vast subject. This section gives an overview of borehole drilling and design so that the engineer is aware of what is involved and of the various options available. For more comprehensive information on drilling practices consult the references on groundwater and wells in the Bibliography. A good practical manual is Ball (2001). Section 12.3.1 and Appendix 10 give definitions of aquifer and well terminology which are often used in groundwater and borehole development. Any extensive borehole programme should include a specialist hydrogeologist and an experienced driller. Wherever possible consult, or contract, specialists who are familiar with local aquifer formations and who can anticipate local drilling difficulties.

Factors to consider

The development of new groundwater sources, especially machine drilled boreholes, can take time and be expensive. This can be particularly significant in drought relief programmes. It is not uncommon, for example, for 'emergency

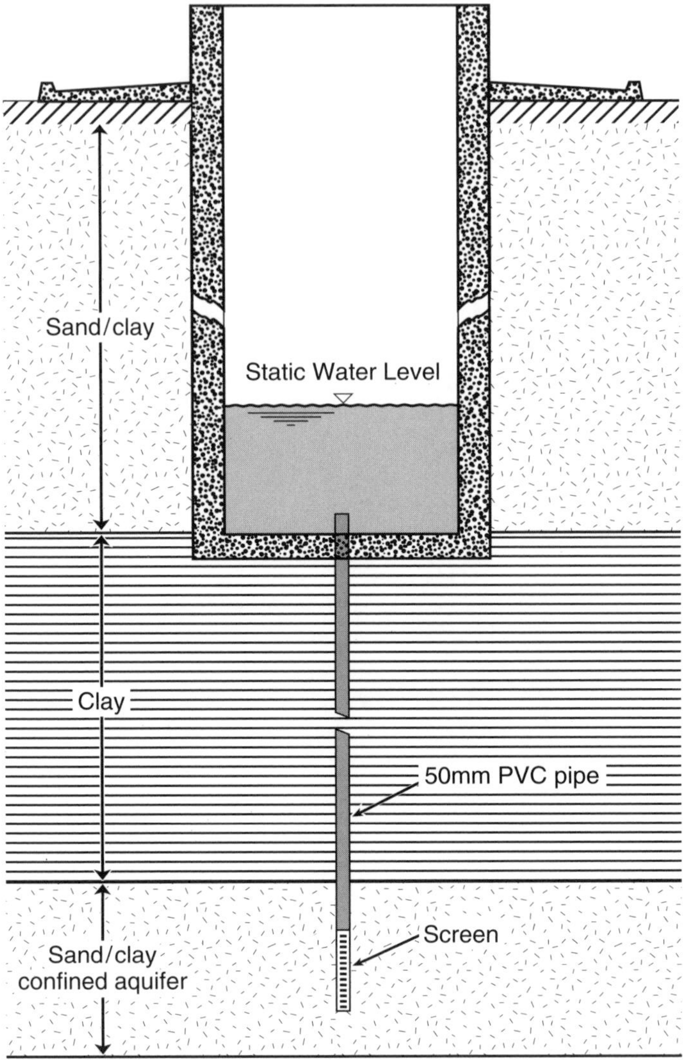

Figure 12.31 A dug and jetted combination well

boreholes' to be commissioned long after the rains have broken the drought. Therefore, before deciding on a machine drilled borehole programme, consider what it might entail:

- The potential for the development of groundwater needs to be assessed and sites for boreholes chosen. This requires specialist skills which take time to mobilize. Where possible utilize local experience.
- A drilling rig and crew need to be found, who are willing to do the job.
- A drilling contract usually needs to be negotiated.
- It can take several weeks to mobilize a drilling rig, even if locally available.

- The drilling rig crew need transport, somewhere to stay (even if it is a field camp) and food to eat. Someone has to organize this.
- Drilling rigs require support vehicles and all the ancillary equipment, fuel and materials to drill, case and screen boreholes of the required depth and diameter.
- Rigs are complex machines (even small rigs) and operation and maintenance problems regularly occur.
- Success rates can be very low in hard rock areas. Sometimes only one borehole in five has sufficient yield to be worth installing a pump.
- A borehole is no use without a pump. Pumps need to be matched to each borehole. Likely pumping needs can be anticipated, but it still takes time to acquire and install suitable pumps and power units (if powered).
- If the driller, who is critical to the operation, falls sick, wants to negotiate a pay rise, or needs to visit home, or other such contingency, the job can take a lot longer than expected.

The cost of drilling varies greatly. It will depend on the availability of drilling rigs, the soils and rock that need to be drilled, the size of a borehole, the level of competition, labour costs, the cost and availability of equipment and materials, etc. The number of boreholes to be drilled will affect the cost per borehole. For example, the considerable costs of mobilization will be similar whether it is one borehole or a number of boreholes to be drilled. A single borehole is going to be much more expensive, per borehole, than several drilled in the same locality. The cost of a borehole, therefore, can vary greatly, from a few thousand US dollars to tens of thousands of dollars.

A drilling rig and crew may be contracted from a private contractor or public utility (water department, ministry of agriculture, etc.). It may also be possible to arrange for the diversion of a drilling rig from an ongoing development programme. For example, UNICEF have extensive water programmes in several countries and they have in the past diverted crew and equipment for use in emergency programmes.

Stages in the construction of a borehole

When organizing borehole drilling bear the following stages in mind:

- Siting – see 12.3.3. Siting is usually carried out as a separate function or contract from the drilling.
- Drilling rig selection – See Table 12.6 and 12.3.3, Table 12.5.
- Drilling contract – with a water agency, private contractor or aid agency. See Appendix 6 for guidance on a water drilling contract.
- Mobilization – the organization of a drilling crew, rig and equipment with support vehicles, consumables (fuel, drilling fluids), living quarters and support for the crew.
- Construction and design – drilling hole(s) of a sufficient diameter and depth to obtain the required yield of water; the choice, installation and positioning of casing, gravel pack and screens.
- Development – obtaining an optimum yield of water.

- Test pumping – to confirm that the well yield and the capacity of the pump to be installed are compatible.
- Pump installation – construction and installation teams often follow up the drilling separately. They cast a concrete pad for the pump and install the hand or powered pump (see Figure 12.28).

Borehole drilling methods

Drilling methods are traditionally categorized into percussion drilling and rotary drilling. Each method, however, can involve a combination of both percussive and rotary actions. The methods differ according to how the hole is drilled, how drilled material is removed from the borehole and how the sides of the borehole are stabilized to prevent collapse during drilling. Table 12.5 (12.3.3) outlines some features of the different methods. Figures 12.32 to 12.35 illustrate the rigs used for the different methods.

Percussion drilling A percussion rig comprises a drill string, composed of a drill bit and a drill pipe, suspended on a cable which reciprocates at a rate and stroke controlled by the driller. The driller feeds out the cable so that the drill bit sharply strikes the bottom of the hole as drilling proceeds. The two common methods of achieving the reciprocating action are by a 'spudding arm' or, in a lightweight rig, by a clutch and brake-operated winch. Both are shown in Figure 12.32. The drilling procedure varies according to the formation being drilled.

In soft, unconsolidated formations, material is drilled and removed with a steel tube (shell) fitted with a cutting shoe and a flap valve or, in clay, an open tube clay cutter. The walls of the borehole are stabilized by temporary casings. The temporary casing is driven vertically into the borehole or it may follow the drill bit under its own weight. Layers of high permeability are noted during drilling so that, on completion, a screen to allow water into the borehole and permanent casing can be placed in the correct position. The temporary casing is then removed.

In hard rock formations, a heavy steel chisel is used to fracture the rock. The cable has a twist which rotates the drill string and chisel. This action helps to ensure a circular hole. If the hole is dry, a small amount of water is added to form a slurry with the crushed rock so that it can be removed with a bailer attached to a separate cable. There is no need for temporary casings when drilling in hard rock formations.

Rotary drilling Drilling is accomplished by the rotation of a weighted cutting tool. Rotation is achieved by one of two methods:

- By a hydraulic direct 'top drive' rotary head which travels vertically down the derrick as drilling proceeds (see Figure 12.33).
- By a square or hexagonal length of drill pipe (kelly) which passes in a vertical direction through a fixed rotary table (see Figure 12.34).

If necessary, drill collars can be placed immediately above the drill bit to provide weight to fragment the rock. Drilled material is continually flushed to the surface by fluid circulating through the hollow drill string. Drilling fluids include: air, water, bentonite clay, polymer, foam or a combination of these.

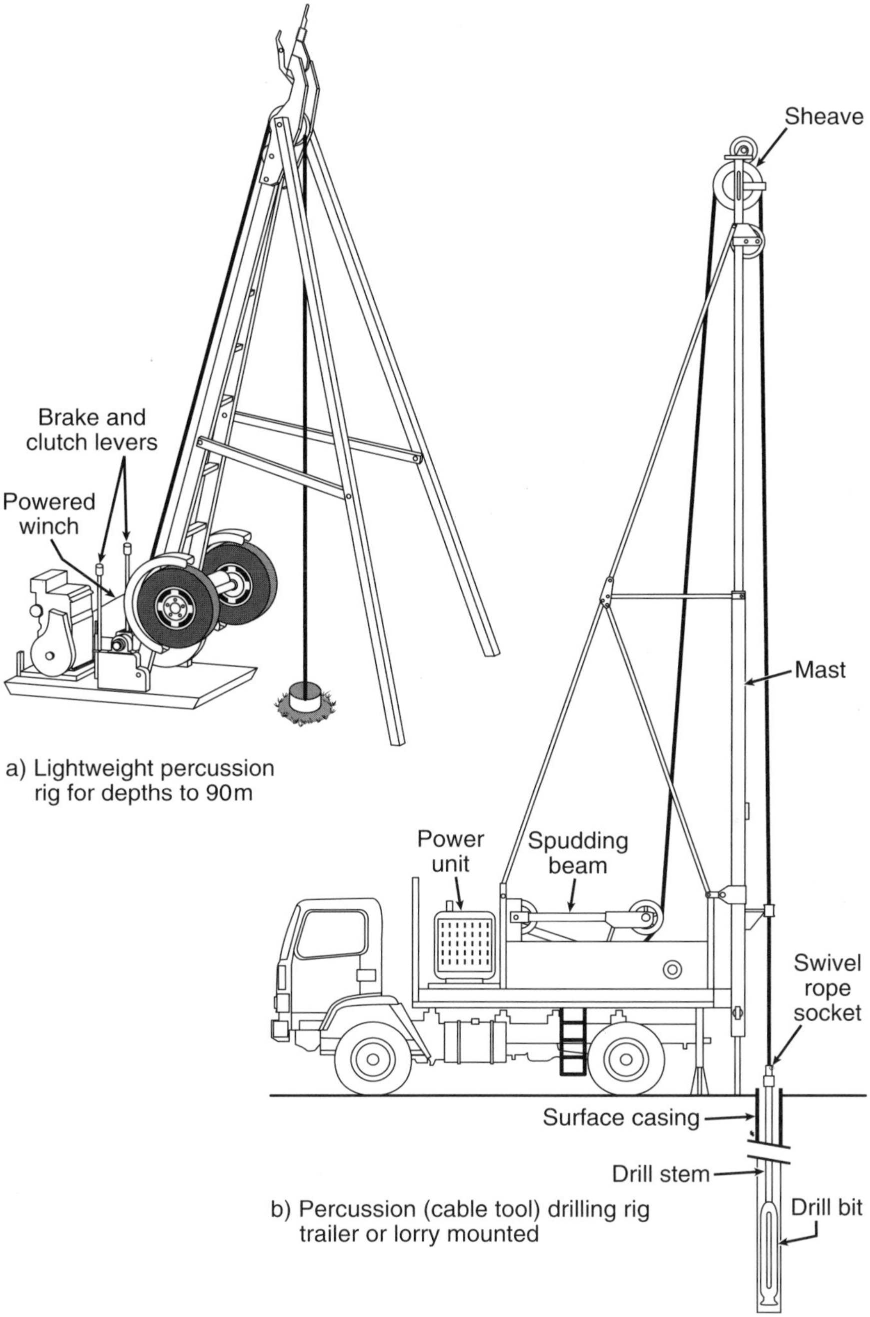

Figure 12.32 Percussion (cable tool) drilling

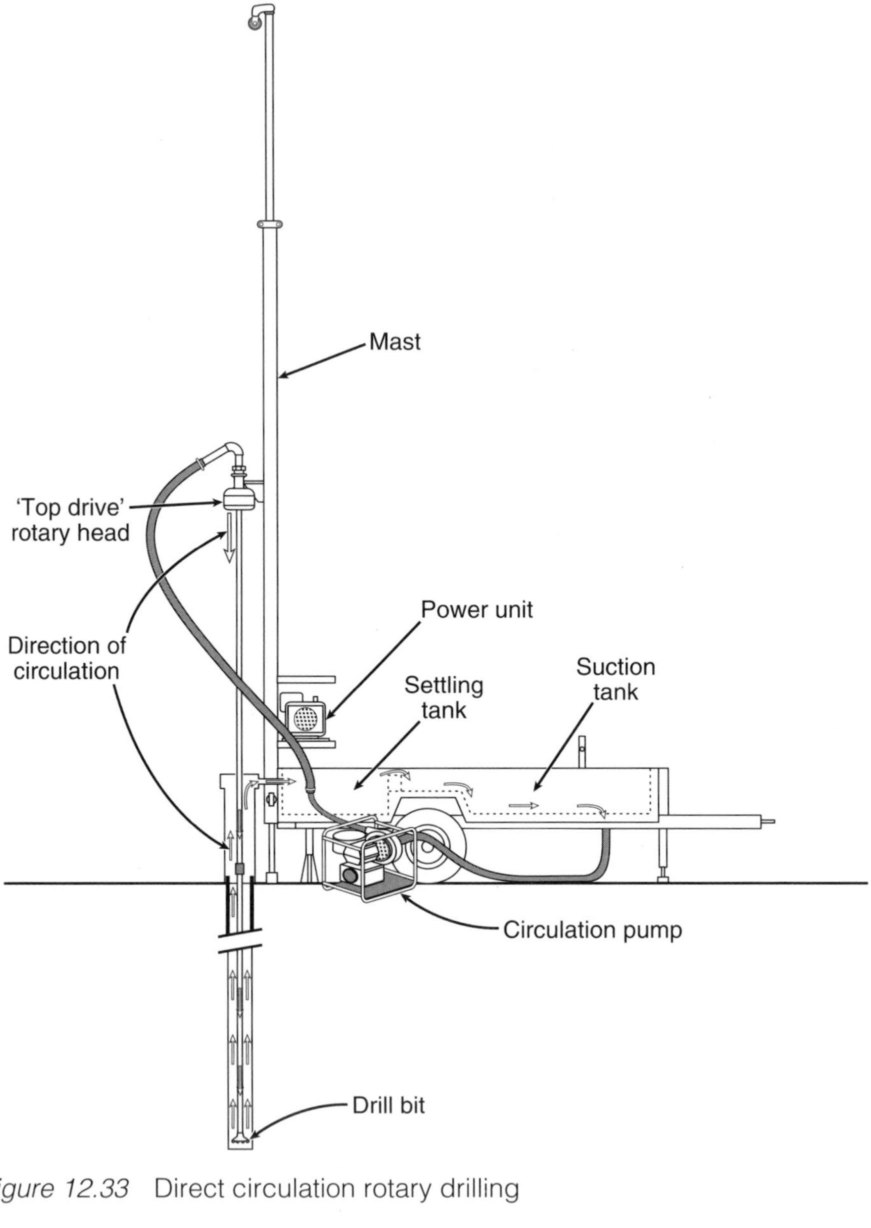

Figure 12.33 Direct circulation rotary drilling

The choice of drilling fluid depends on the conditions encountered and the type of drilling employed. In addition to flushing cuttings to the surface, some drilling fluids have other functions:

- Cooling and lubricating the drill bit and string.
- Stabilizing the borehole formation to stop it collapsing.
- Holding cuttings in suspension when drilling stops.

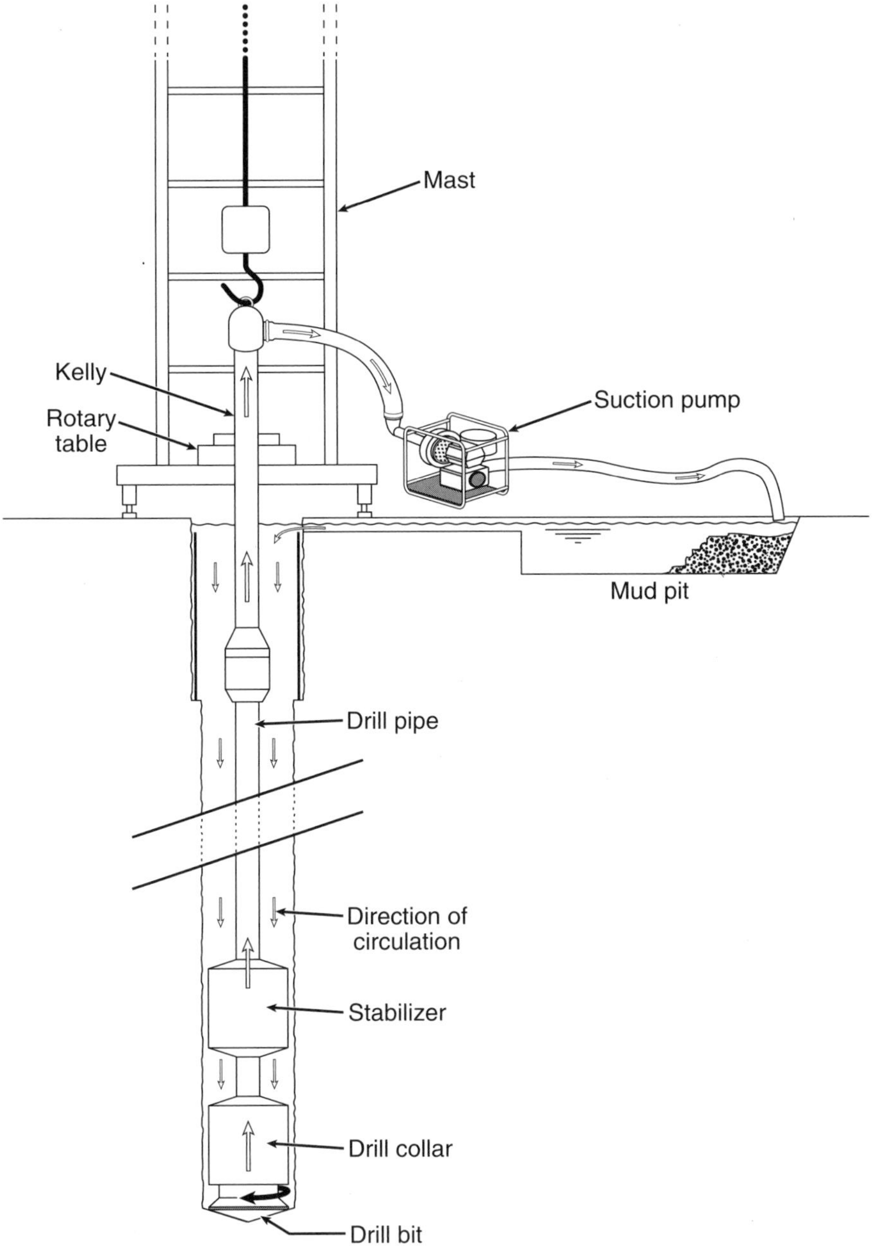

Figure 12.34 Reverse circulation rotary drilling

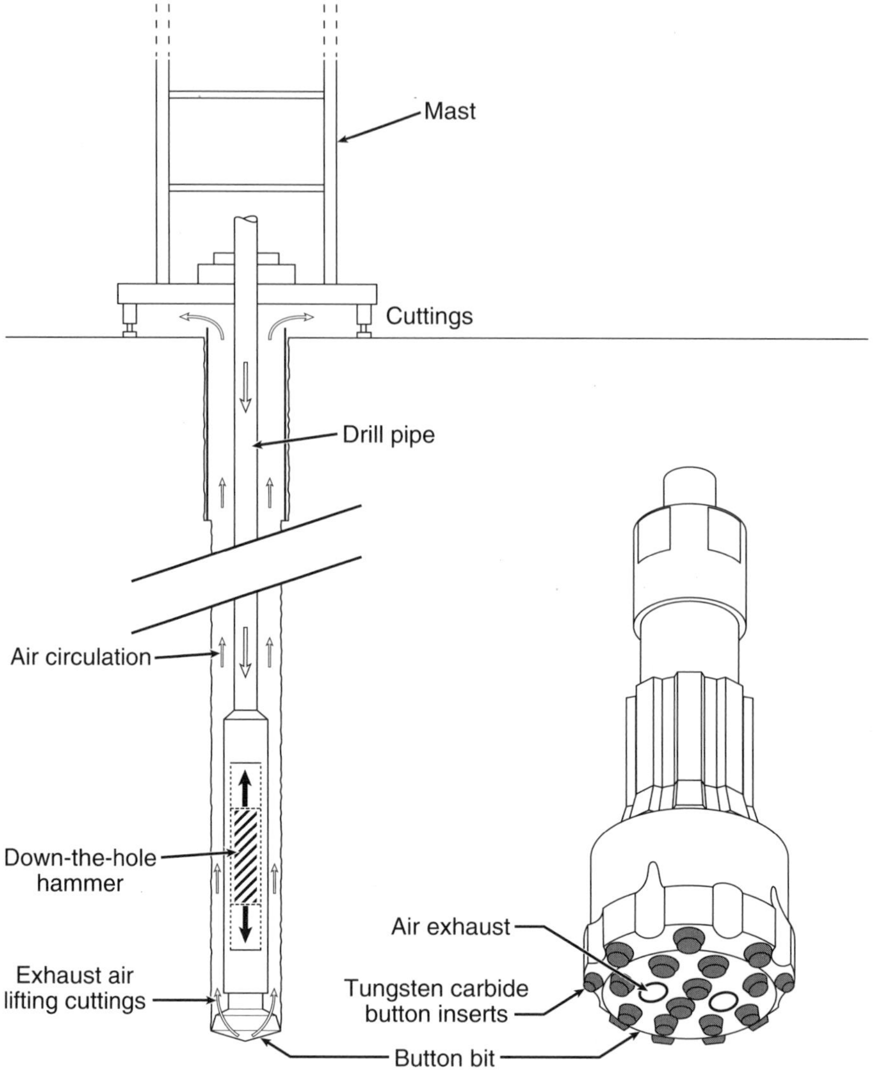

Figure 12.35 Down-the-hole (DTH) hammer drilling

Drilling liquids can be recirculated via settling pits to settle out the cuttings brought to the surface. Regular inspection of the cuttings indicates the formations being drilled. A log of the cuttings and the depth at which they change should be kept by the driller.

In direct circulation drilling, fluids are passed down the drill pipe and up the annular space between the pipe and the borehole wall. In drilling larger diameter boreholes (above 500 mm), the pumping power required for an annular uphole velocity to bring cuttings to the surface becomes excessive. Reverse circulation overcomes this problem. The internal diameter of the drill string (about 150–200 mm) allows the up-hole velocity to be maintained at a lower power. Fluid circulation can be achieved by a suction or air-lift pump.

Down-the-hole hammer (DTH) drilling In the DTH drilling system (see Figure 12.35), an air operated reciprocating hammer at the bottom of a slowly rotating drill string rapidly strikes the borehole face. The exhaust air immediately removes fractured rock and flushes it to the surface. The hammer face comprises tungsten carbide inserts which need sharpening or replacing as they wear. High drilling rates can be achieved in hard rock formations.

Size and complexity of drilling rigs

Table 12.6 gives some indication of the appropriateness of rig size and complexity in an emergency. Even though there may be few options in choosing who does the drilling and the equipment that is available in an emergency, do not accept the first offer of a drilling rig that comes along. Carefully consider the implications in terms of cost, the time lag before water is pumped out of the ground, and the logistical, technical and administrative support required to keep the programme running.

Table 12.6 A comparison of drilling rig size and complexity

Drilling rig size and complexity	*Advantages*	*Disadvantages*
Large and complex	Capacity in reserve to drill a range of formations and to overcome drilling difficulties. Can drill to depth, if necessary	Relatively more expensive to operate and maintain. Large rigs require more support vehicles and more people. In rough and/or wet terrain a large heavy rig may have problems moving about and getting access to sites
Lightweight	Cheaper and easier to operate and maintain. Easier to move about and get access to awkward sites. Feasible to airfreight	A lack of capacity: to drill deep boreholes (beyond about 100 m); to overcome drilling difficulties; to cope with hard rock drilling. Boreholes may not be truly vertical (but usually straight enough for most pump installations)

Lightweight drilling units A lightweight percussion rig is shown in Figure 12.32.

Lightweight rotary units range from continuous flight auger rigs (typically, 100 mm diameter holes to 25 m depth) to small versions of conventional direct circulation rigs. A typical lightweight drilling unit comprises a mast on which an engine, driving through a gearbox, rotates the drill pipe whilst travelling vertically, as shown in Figure 12.36. A portable pump circulates drilling fluid through a hydraulic swivel and down the drill pipe. Drilling depths of 60–75 m at a diameter of 100 mm are possible in favourable unconsolidated formations.

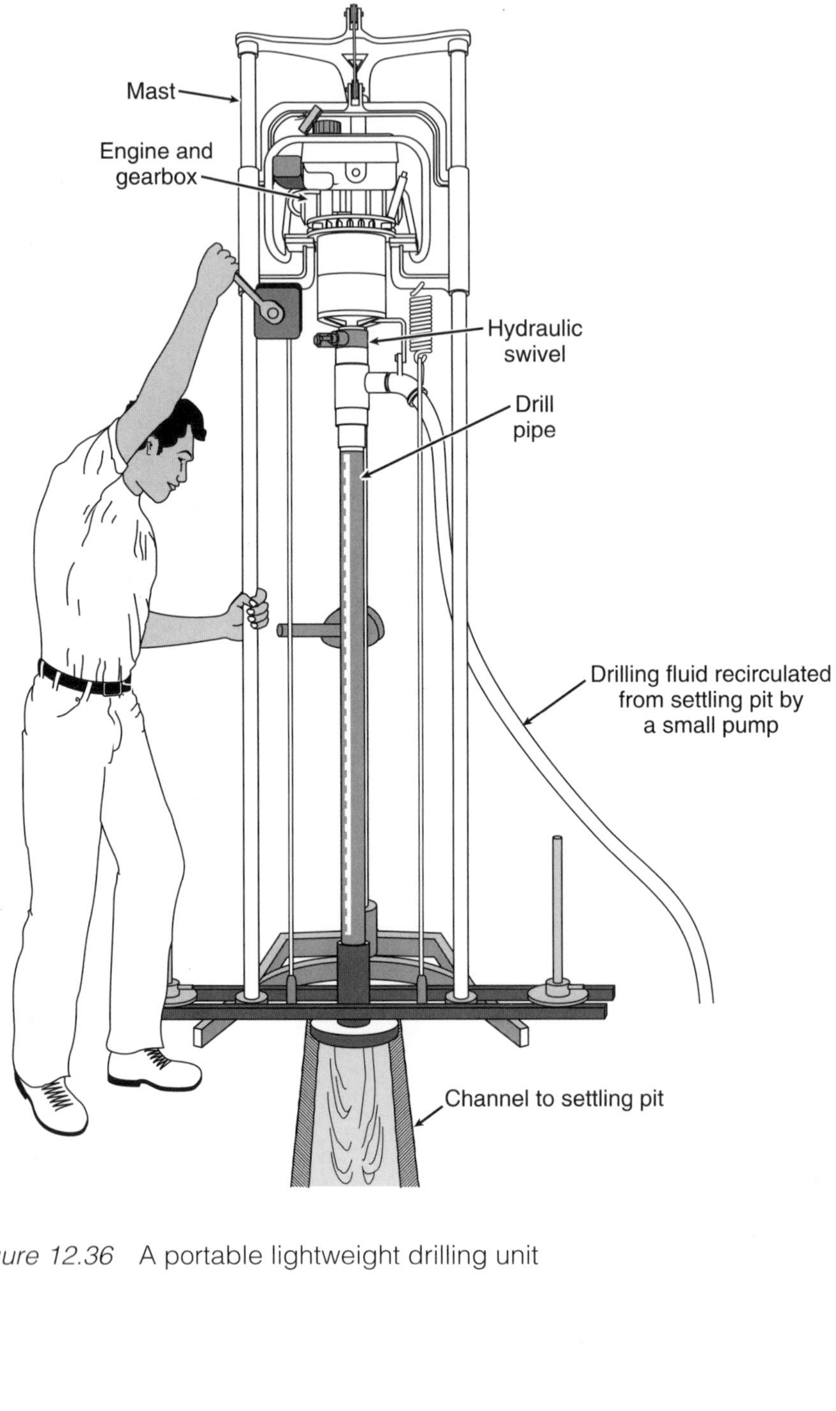

Figure 12.36 A portable lightweight drilling unit

Trailer or pick-up mounted rotary rigs (see Figure 12.33) can typically drill 100 mm diameter holes to 100 m depth in unconsolidated formations. They may also have the option of limited DTH drilling, which is advantageous where short sections of hard rock strata are encountered in otherwise unconsolidated sediments. However, DTH drilling requires a compressor which is often as large and expensive as the rig itself. Lightweight rigs can be airfreighted in an emergency.

Rating a drilling rig

The suitability of a rig for a particular job will partly depend on its lifting capacity and, for a rotary rig, the torque it can impart to the drill bit.

A key feature of a drilling rig is the weight of drill string that it can lift. The dimensions of the borehole (diameter and depth) and the method of drilling used will determine the weight of tools needed to drill and case it. Drilling rig manufacturers give capacity ratings for rigs based on 'average' or 'favourable' drilling conditions. A rig's lifting capacity is often referred to as 'pullback'. Rated capacity indicates the depth to which the rig can drill using particular drill rods and it incorporates an allowance for safety. The safety factor is normally 75–80 per cent and provides enough 'overpull' to extract a full string of tools if it becomes stuck.

DTH drilling is rated differently from conventional percussion and rotary drilling. The weight on a DTH bit should be enough to overcome the air pressure in the hammer to stop it 'bouncing', but not so much that the bit wears quickly or is damaged. The weight on a DTH bit is therefore relatively small. Little torque is required and rotational speeds are low.

Borehole design

Borehole design aims to achieve the following:

- Structural stability to prevent borehole collapse. The design will depend on the stability of the aquifer strata. For example, a borehole in fissured hard rock need only be cased over the thickness of the overburden. The remainder can be left open, as the formation will not require support. A borehole in unconsolidated formations will require casing and screens to prevent collapse. Figures 12.37 to 12.40 show common features of borehole design in different stable and unstable formations.
- Prevention of the ingress of fine material. Fine material (such as sand) in the water is undesirable. It may damage the pump and it will silt up the well. Therefore, a combination of screens, gravel packs and geotextiles are used to prevent material from the aquifer formation entering the borehole.
- Low hydraulic resistance to flow into the borehole. Resistance to flow into the well will restrict well yield. The correct screen length, size of aperture and material will minimize losses due to friction, encrustation and corrosion. (See 'Screens' and 'Gravel pack' below.)
- A reasonable lifespan. A borehole should last for 20–30 years, and many last longer. The correct selection of materials should ensure that the borehole will not collapse or severely corrode within that time.

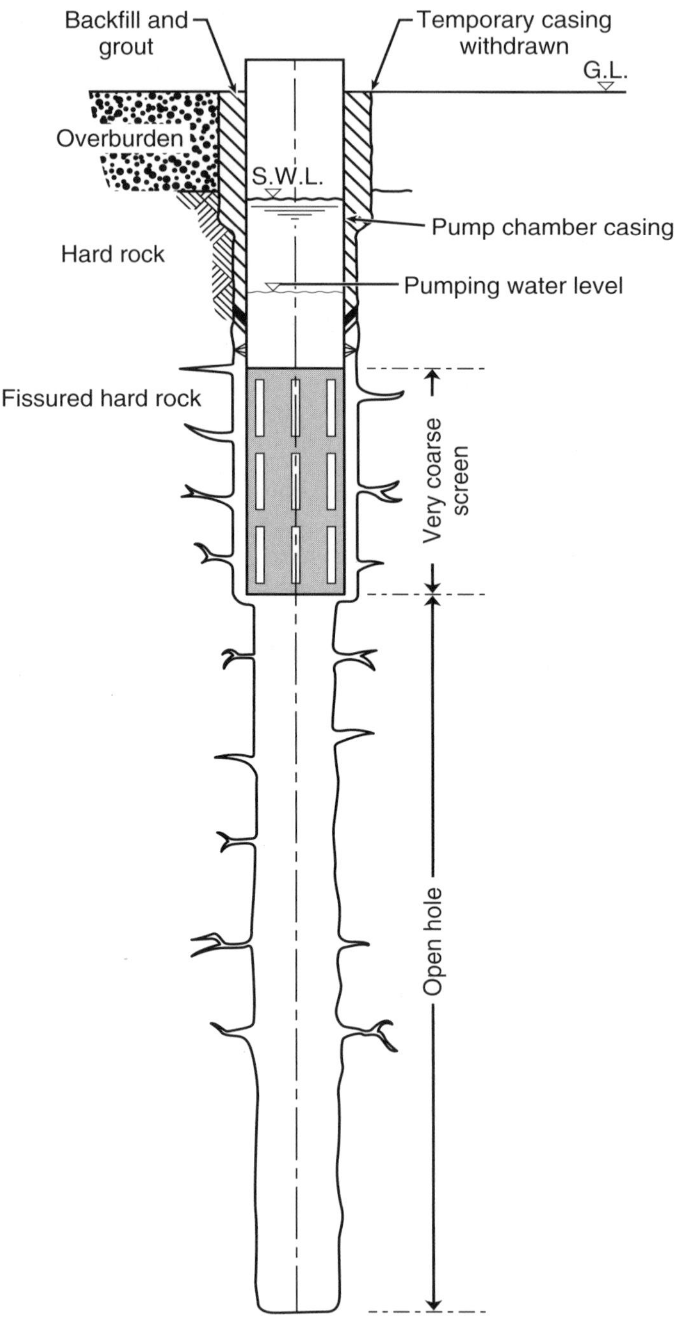

Figure 12.37 Design for a well in stable hard rock

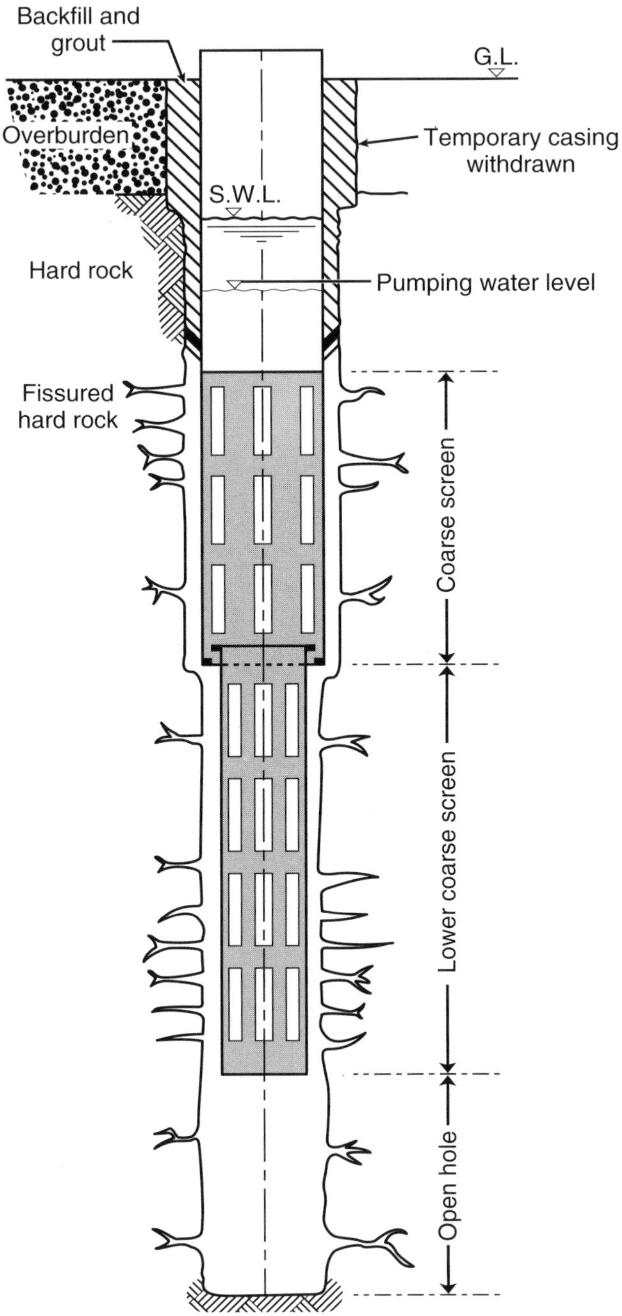

Figure 12.38 Design for a well in unstable hard rock

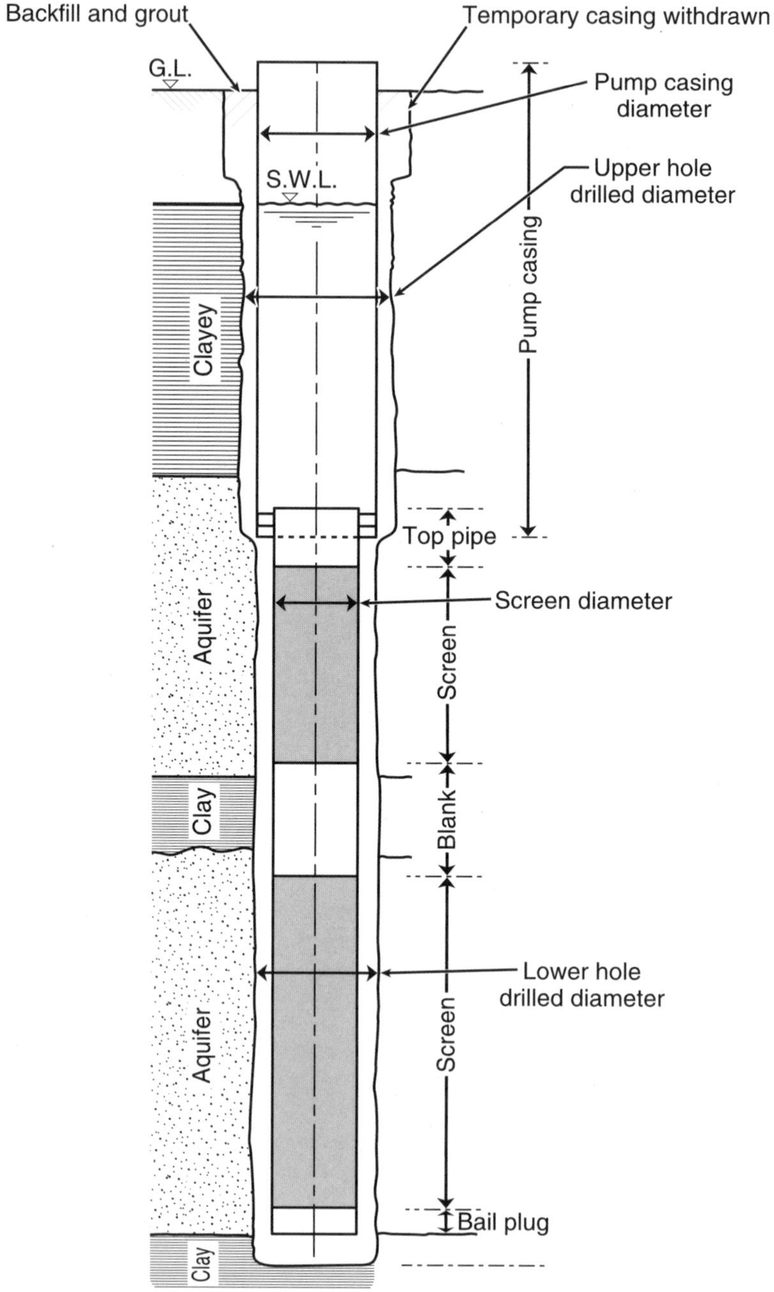

Figure 12.39 Design for a naturally developed well in an alluvial aquifer

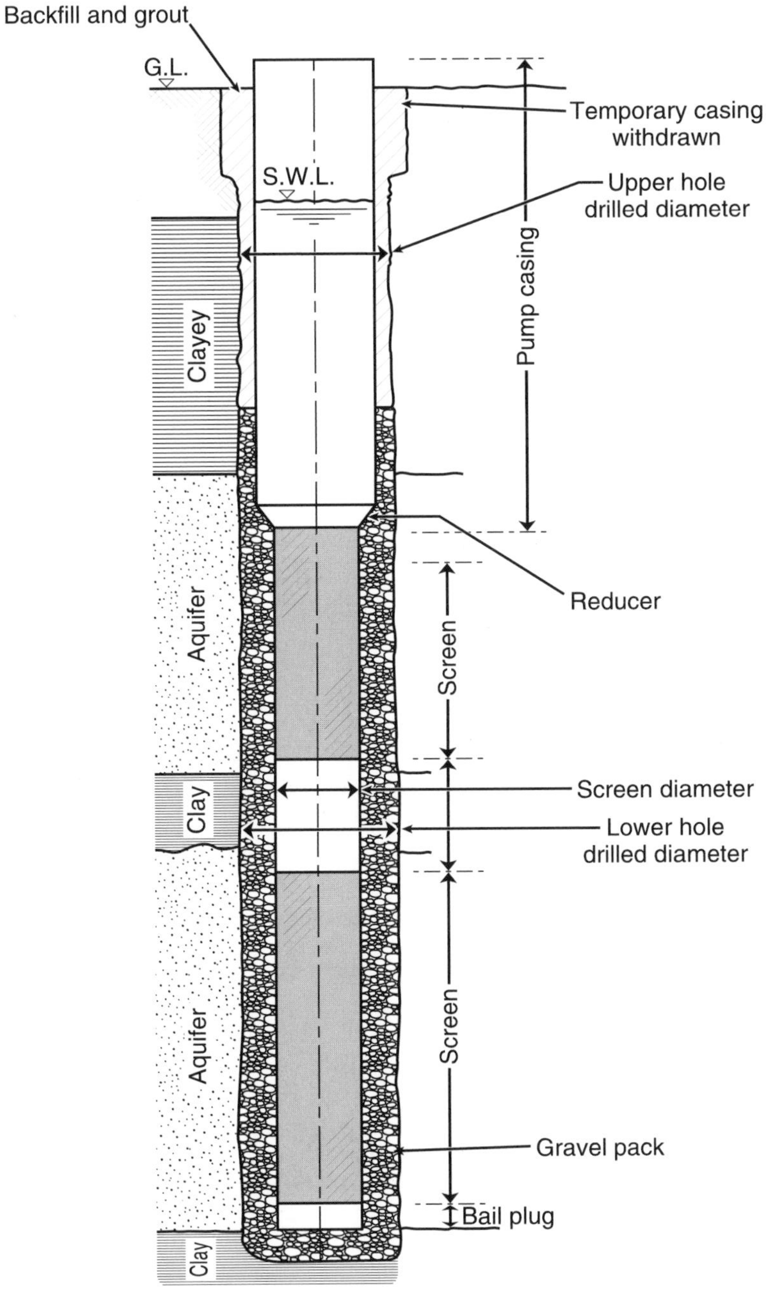

Figure 12.40 Design for a gravel packed well in an alluvial aquifer

- Good quality water. The borehole must be sealed at the top to prevent surface water contamination of the borehole water. This is usually achieved with a cement slurry or cement/bentonite grout seal.
- An optimum design. The design of a borehole affects the drawdown and hence the pumping costs. In normal circumstances, the choice of borehole diameter and depth, screen length, materials (stainless steel or plastic, etc.), and the projected design life are considered together to give the most economic design. This may not be a major consideration in an emergency, but nevertheless should be taken into account as far as possible.

Borehole diameter To minimize friction losses across a screen, encrustation and corrosion, the entrance velocity of water should not exceed 0.03 m/s. The entrance velocity is calculated by dividing the expected pumping rate by the open area of the screen. This gives a guide to the minimum borehole diameter and screen length. The borehole diameter should also aim to minimize upflow losses from the screened zones to the pump. As a guide, the casing diameter should not result in an uphole velocity greater than 1.5 m/s. The diameter of the borehole down to the setting depth of the pump must be large enough to accommodate a pump which can supply the required discharge. The casing diameter can be less below the anticipated pump setting depth but should comply with the screen requirements given above. These factors give a range of recommended borehole diameters for different pumping rates as indicated in Table 12.7.

Table 12.7 Recommended diameters of boreholes for different pumping rates

Anticipated pumping rate (l/s)	*Nominal pump diameter (mm)*	*Optimum internal diameter of borehole casing (mm)*
< 5	100	150
5–10	125	200
10–22	150	250
22–44	200	300

Casing Casing, usually in steel or plastic, provides support to the borehole wall. It may be temporary, for support during drilling, or provide a permanent lining in unstable formations. Table 12.8 gives further details.

Table 12.8 Borehole casing materials

Casing material	*Application*	*Joints*
Steel	Temporary or permanent lining	Flush threaded; threaded socket; butt welded
Plastic (PVC or ABS)	Permanent	Flush threaded; threaded socket; solvent welded

Screens Screens prevent fine material from entering the borehole, by straining the inflow of water. There are several types and the choice of screen depends on availability, cost, strength, corrosion resistance and the extraction area required. Screens are made of mild and stainless steel, various plastics and fibreglass. Screen 'openings' are formed in various ways (see Figure 12.41):

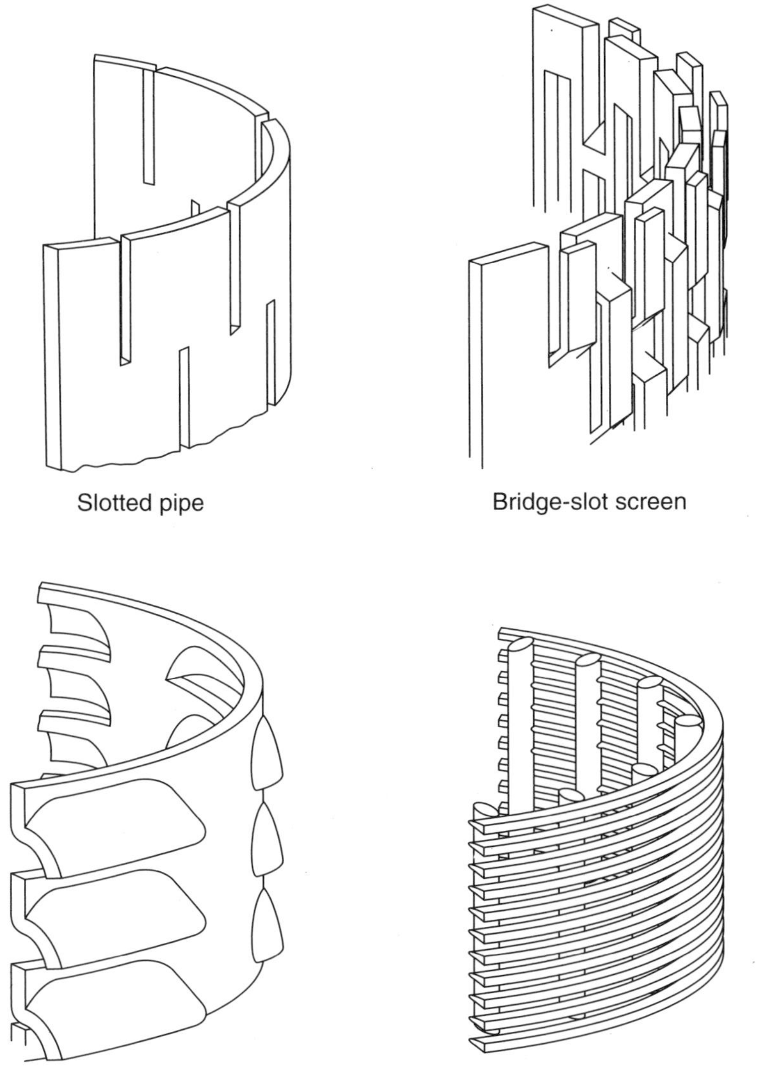

Slotted pipe

Bridge-slot screen

Louvred screen

Continuous-slot screen

Figure 12.41 Types of manufactured screen

- Bridge and louvre slots pressed from sheet metal.
- Wedge shaped wire wrapped in a continuous spiral.
- Slotted pipe.

If manufactured screen is not available it can be made on site. As longitudinal slots in thin walled plastic pipe can close under compression, use thick walled plastic pipe and cut it transversely with a hacksaw blade. This restricts the size of slot to about 1 mm. A screen made from PVC pipe is shown in Figure 12.42.

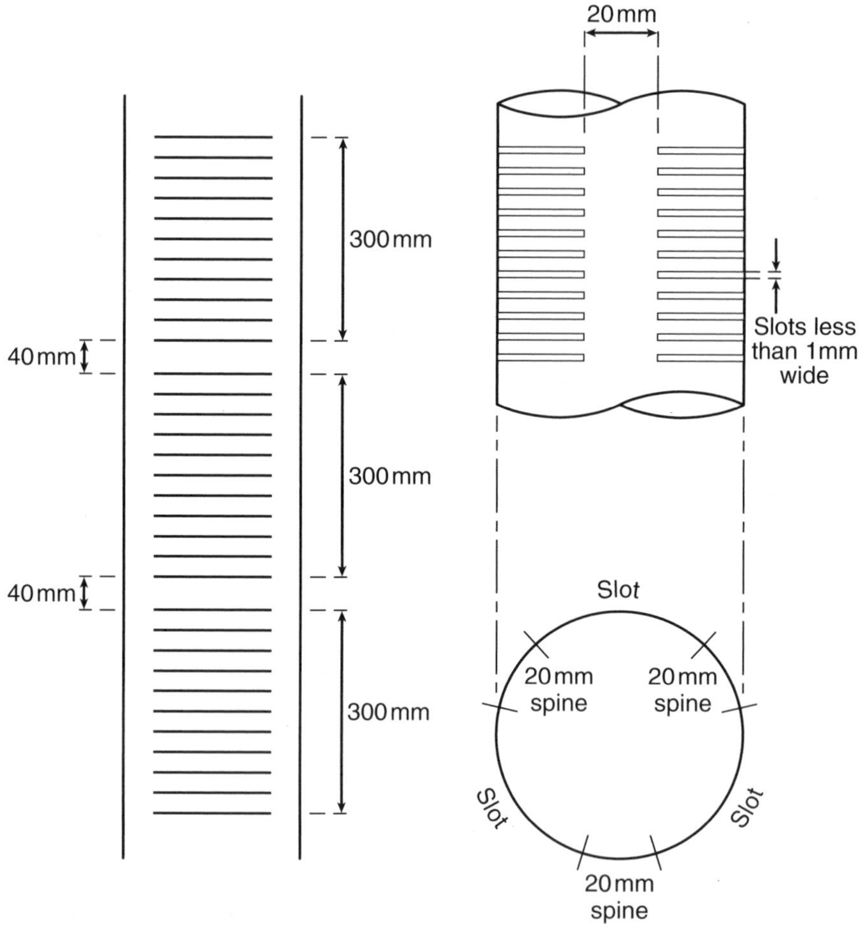

Figure 12.42 Screen made from PVC pipe

The screen opening size is chosen according to the grain size of the aquifer or gravel pack. Grain sizes can be determined by a sieve analysis of aquifer samples (see Appendix 20). In naturally developed strata, a slot size which will retain 40 per cent of the aquifer material is commonly chosen. Table 12.9 gives typical screen openings for different formation types.

Table 12.9 Typical screen openings for different formations

Formation	*Average size of screen opening, mm*
Clay and silt	0.056
Fine sand	0.167
Medium sand	0.442
Coarse sand	0.813
Very coarse sand	1.580
Very fine gravel	2.850
Fine gravel	6.700

Adapted from Driscoll, 1986

A screen must provide an open area large enough so that the entrance velocity is not greater than 0.03 m/s. The screen diameter or length can be increased to achieve this. Increasing the length of the screen improves the yield more than increasing the diameter. Screen manufacturers give the open area of a screen as a percentage of the screen surface. Table 12.10 compares 6-inch (150 mm) screens of different slot sizes as an illustration of the significant difference in open areas between screen types. The open area of a site-made screen, or screen of unknown open area, can be estimated from the pipe circumference, slot width and length.

Table 12.10 Open area comparison of different screen types

Screen diameter (ID) mm	*Slot size, mm*	*Continuous slot, %*	*Bridge slot, %*	*Plastic continuous, %*	*Slotted plastic, %*
150	0.5	18	–	10	5
150	1.0	31	6	18	9
150	1.5	40	8	25	13

Adapted from Driscoll, 1986

Screen length and position are determined by the aquifer thickness, drawdown, and the location of the most productive layers in the aquifer. Screen the zones of highest hydraulic conductivity, identified from the driller's log and from inspection of the drill samples. The borehole above the cone of depression should not be screened as this will contribute little to the yield. Table 12.11 is a guide to screen lengths for optimum yields in various types of aquifer. Screen lengths greater than those recommended will only marginally increase the yield. A borehole should not be screened more than is necessary for the required capacity of the borehole as screens are more expensive than casing. For example, a slotted plastic pipe screen of length 1.5 m should be sufficient for a borehole fitted with a handpump.

Artificial gravel packs A gravel pack may also be called a 'filter pack' or a 'sand pack'. The function of a gravel pack is either to prevent the ingress of fine material or to prevent the collapse of a borehole by giving it structural support.

Table 12.11 Recommended optimum screen length

Aquifer type	*Screen length*
Homogeneous unconfined aquifer < 45 m thick	33–50% of aquifer thickness: screen placed in the bottom section
Homogeneous unconfined aquifer > 45 m thick	80% of aquifer thickness: screen placed in the bottom section
Non-homogeneous unconfined aquifer	33% of aquifer thickness: screen placed in the most permeable part of the lower section
Homogeneous confined aquifer	80–90% of aquifer thickness: screen placed centrally
Non-homogeneous confined aquifer	80–90% of the most permeable layers

Source: Driscoll, 1986

In aquifers which are of fine, well sorted or heterogeneous material, an artificial gravel pack is installed to retain most of the aquifer material. The borehole is drilled at a diameter sufficient to accommodate both the gravel pack and the screen. The usual thickness of a gravel pack is in the range 50–150 mm. The advantages of a gravel pack are:

- The area around the screen is physically stabilized to prevent fine material from passing into the borehole.
- The area around the screen is of a higher permeability than the aquifer material.
- Screen slot sizes can be larger than if they were based on the natural aquifer material. Slot sizes are usually chosen to retain 90 per cent of the gravel pack material.

Borehole development

Construction is not complete until the borehole has been developed to give its maximum yield. Development is necessary to:

- Remove fine material from the aquifer in order to improve permeability in the immediate vicinity of the well screen.
- Remove the remains of any drilling fluid. (If a borehole is coated in bentonite mud, for example, its yield will be significantly reduced.)

A production pump should not be used to develop a borehole as it would be severely damaged by the abrasive material pumped. There are standard methods used in borehole development and these include surging and jetting.

Surging Surging creates rapid flow across screens to loosen the aquifer formation and to aid the removal of fine material and drilling fluid. It is achieved by using a modified air lift pump, by using surge blocks, or by intermittent pumping.

- Air lift pump. There are several ways of using the air lift pump to create surges of air and water in the borehole (see Figure 12.43):
  - The relative vertical positions of the air line and rising main are altered to give a pumping/non-pumping cycle.
  - The air supply is momentarily altered or shut off to vary the rate of pumping.
  - The discharge valve on the pump outlet is closed to allow pressure to build up and then it is suddenly opened.
- Surge blocks. A surge block acts like a piston in the borehole 'cylinder'. It is mounted on a drill stem and gently moved up and down. The surging action draws fine material and any remaining drilling fluid from the aquifer. This débris is removed intermittently with a bailer. Figure 12.44 shows a typical surge block, but any close fitting tool, such as a bailer, can also be used. Care should be exercised when using a surge block as vigorous use can damage a lightweight screen.

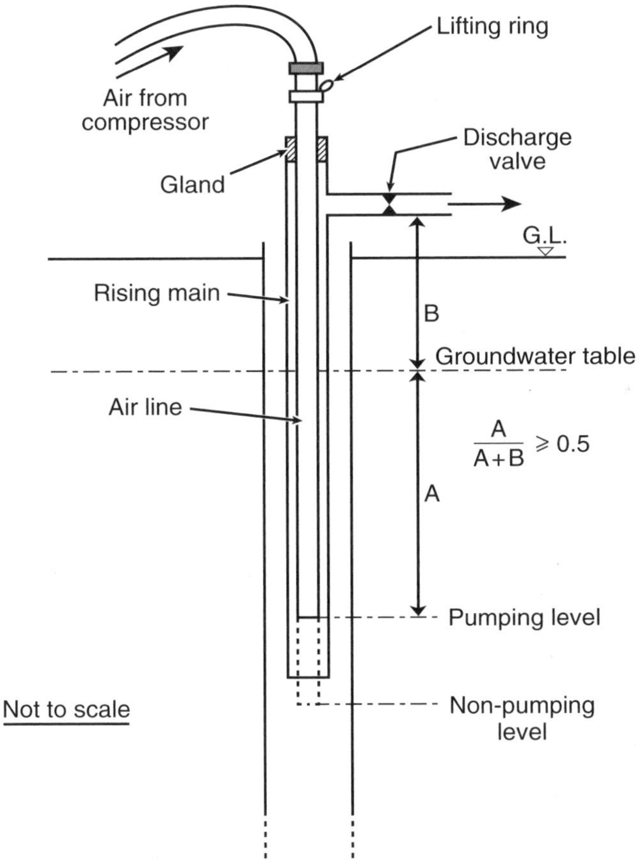

Figure 12.43 The arrangement of an air lift pump used in the development of a borehole
From Clark, 1988

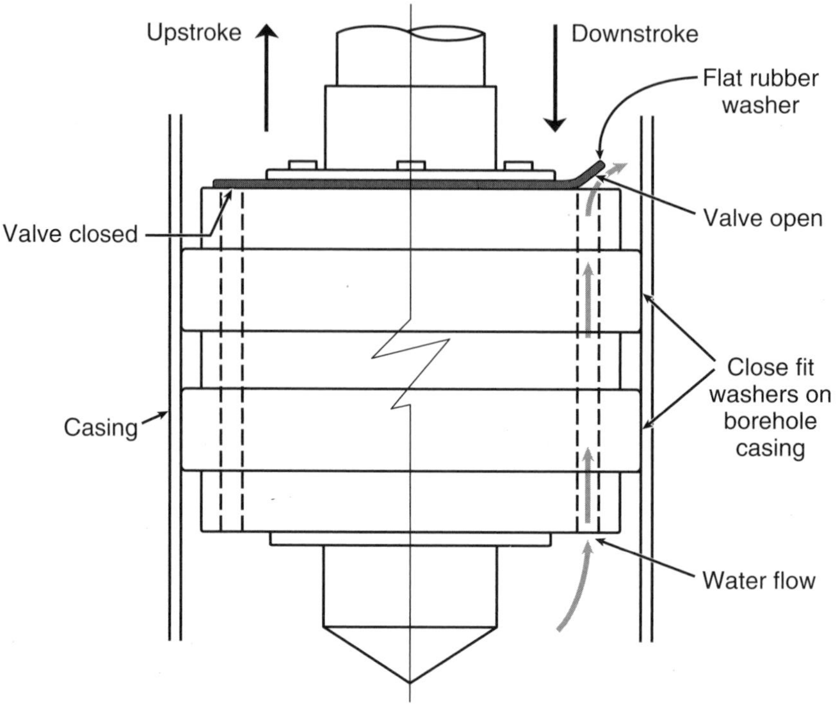

Figure 12.44 A surge block

- Intermittent pumping. Intermittent pumping is commenced at a relatively low flow rate and gradually increased to beyond the production rate. After each stage of pumping, the pump is stopped and water is allowed to flow back down the rising main into the borehole to create turbulence. A production centrifugal pump should not be used as fine particles will damage it.

Jetting Jetting is particularly effective in removing caked drilling mud from the borehole wall. A jetting tool (see Figure 12.45) is placed at the bottom of the drill pipe. Horizontal nozzles direct the jetting fluid, which has been pumped down the drill string, at the screen. The jetting tool is rotated as it is moved up and down over the length of screen. At the same time, the borehole is pumped at a greater flow rate than the jet inflow to remove the displaced particles.

Pumping tests

Pumping tests are carried out to assess borehole performance and to determine aquifer characteristics. A test involves pumping water from a borehole at a controlled rate and measuring the effect on drawdown in the well. A recovery test measures the drawdown after the pump is switched off. The recorded discharge, drawdown and recovery data can be used to determine various well and aquifer parameters. There are two main tests:

- Step-drawdown test – to measure the variation in well performance with the discharge rate.

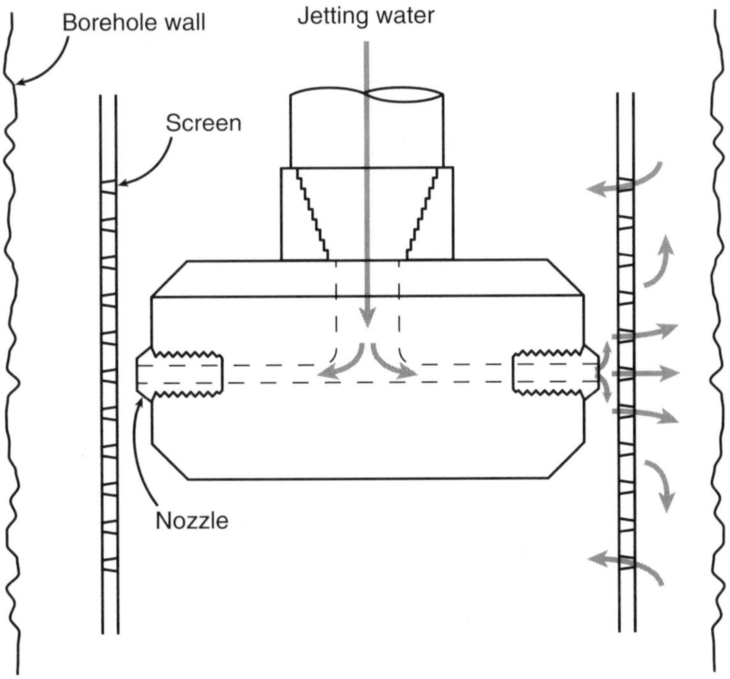

Figure 12.45 Jetting tool

- Constant discharge test – to measure well performance and aquifer characteristics.

The tests can be carried out with or without nearby observation boreholes. Measurements of drawdown in observation boreholes provide additional data for the determination of aquifer characteristics. Since most emergency situations involve single isolated boreholes, tests involving observation boreholes are not considered here. However, if two boreholes are located near each other, it is essential to monitor the drawdown in the borehole not being pumped (the observation borehole) when the other is pumping alone. If any drawdown in the observation borehole is detected, the boreholes are hydraulically connected and pumping from one borehole will affect the other. This interference means that if the two boreholes are pumped at the same time, they must be operated at a lower pumping rate than the rate indicated in the pumping test.

In an emergency, the main concern is to select a pump with a discharge which does not exceed the yield of the borehole and result in excessive drawdown. The investigation of aquifer parameters is time consuming and may be carried out later but it is not considered here. Appendix 10 defines storage coefficient, specific yield and transmissivity and gives representative figures. See the relevant references in the Bibliography for further guidance on their determination.

Step-drawdown test In a step-drawdown test, the drawdown is measured as the discharge is increased in steps. The discharge rate is held constant at each step. From the recorded data, the variation in specific capacity (the ratio of the discharge to the drawdown) with discharge rate can be measured. This information is used to decide the optimum pump size and pump setting depth. A step-drawdown test usually involves four steps. Each step is usually 30–120 minutes long. The final step should be at a discharge rate higher than the production rate. The other steps are chosen to give approximately equal increments. The driller should have carried out a rough test of well yield, which can be used to decide the maximum discharge and the steps to be used during the test. It is useful to continue the final step as a constant-discharge test – see below.

Continue to measure the residual drawdown at regular intervals following pump shut-off to monitor the recovery of the aquifer. The drawdown will at first quickly reduce and then gradually return to the static water level. It may take a long time to recover fully. Table 12.12 and Figure 12.46 give an example of results from a step-drawdown test.

Table 12.12 Example of results from a step-drawdown test

Discharge (Q) l/s	*Drawdown (s) mm*	*Specific capacity (Q/s) l/s/m*	*Specific drawdown (s/Q) m/l/s*
1.52	6.35	0.24	4.19
2.73	12.10	0.23	4.43
3.72	16.24	0.23	4.37
5.30	21.61	0.25	4.00

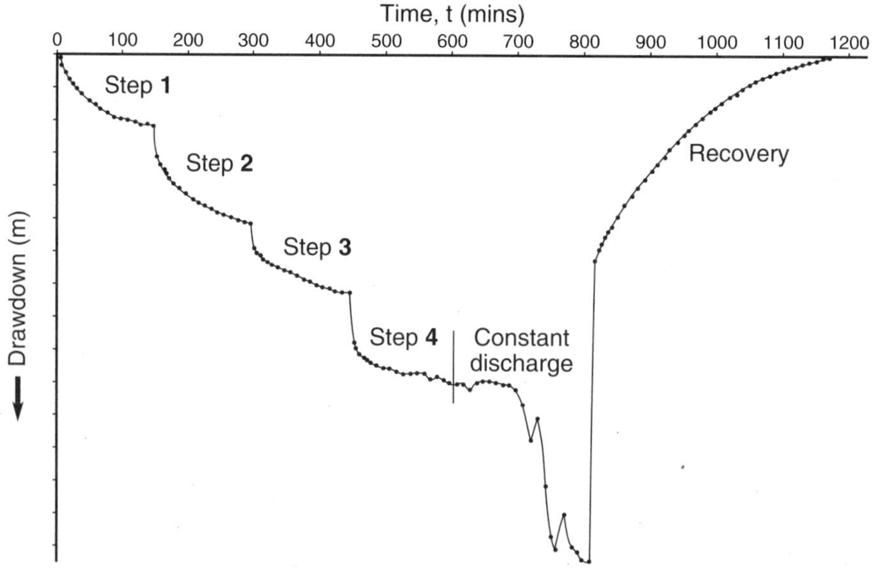

Figure 12.46 A time/drawdown graph plotted from a step-drawdown test

Constant-discharge test The length of time needed for a full constant-discharge test is at least 24 hours, or longer, if aquifer characteristics are to be determined. The interpretation of results from a constant-discharge test requires specialist knowledge and experience. Therefore, the value of a full test is limited if there is little time to carry out a proper test and if expertise in interpretation is lacking. However, a shorter constant-discharge test run at the end of a step-drawdown test can be valuable in showing up any obvious anomalies that might occur during pumping at or near the anticipated production rate. The procedure is to pump at a discharge rate higher than the production rate and for a time similar to the expected daily pumping period. Uneven or erratic variations in the drawdown can be monitored. See also Section 2.3.1 in Appendix 6.

Figure 12.46 shows erratic drawdown behaviour during the constant-discharge test run as the final step of a step-drawdown test. There could be several reasons for this, depending on the aquifer: the cone of depression reaching an aquifer boundary across which there is no flow; fractures in a hard rock aquifer; or other possibilities. The implication of the test for the engineer is that the production pumping rate should be chosen so that the sudden drawdown effects do not occur in daily operation.

Practicalities of pumping tests

- Ensure the borehole has been fully developed before testing.
- Check that everyone knows what to do. Prepare and test run the pump and equipment. Allow the well to recover before starting the actual test.
- During test pumping, ensure that the discharged water does not filter back into the well and affect the test results. Conduct the pumped water downhill and well away from the borehole.
- Measure the discharge by timing how long it takes to fill a drum of known volume. More accurate measurements can be obtained with a weir tank or orifice plate but a drum is usually accurate enough. Details of weirs and discharge values are given in Appendix 9.
- Because the initial drop in water level will be very rapid, be ready to monitor drawdown at short time intervals. The rate of change of drawdown will decrease as the test progresses. Time intervals can vary from 10 to 30 seconds in the first minutes to every 30 minutes after four hours.
- Make the change from one step of the pumping test to another as quickly as possible.
- Measure drawdown with an electric water level indicator (dip-tape). This consists of two electric wires connected to electrodes at one end of a measuring tape. When the electrodes touch the water surface, a closed circuit is indicated by a lamp or buzzer. If necessary, a level indicator can be made up locally using two insulated electrical wires and a tape.

Borehole monitoring Monitor the long-term effects of pumping by taking regular measurements of borehole water levels. Ensure that there is convenient access through each borehole pump base or pedestal so that a dip-tape can be used to measure the static water level and drawdown. A small diameter pipe (dip tube) is sometimes permanently inserted down the side of the borehole to facilitate insertion and removal of the dip tape without snagging.

If problems relating to well yield are subsequently encountered, it may be useful to carry out another step-drawdown test to compare with the original data. This can show up problems due to poor borehole development, blocking of screens, etc. The effectiveness of remedial actions on the rehabilitation of an old well can also be gauged by carrying out step-drawdown tests.

Borehole completion and pump positioning

- Contamination of a newly drilled borehole should be prevented by capping securely until the pump is installed. Place a cement grout around the top of the borehole casing to form a sanitary seal. This prevents the ingress of contaminated water.
- Disinfect the borehole with a 50 mg/l chlorine solution. Leave it in for at least four hours. Pump it clear before putting the borehole into operation.
- Follow a consistent system of marking a completed borehole on a nearby fixed steel plate or concrete pad. Typically, this may include a borehole number (perhaps allocated by the water department), the depth and the yield. Send all borehole records to the appropriate government department.
- Seal abandoned boreholes.

Positioning of pumps in a borehole The pump should be positioned so that the pump inlet is 2 m below the lowest pumping (dynamic) water level (not the static level). These water levels will fluctuate according to a number of factors, including seasonal variations and pumped extraction from other boreholes in the aquifer. Check these levels against available borehole and aquifer data. Any pump placed within a screened section is in danger of drawing fine material through the screen directly into the pump. If there is nowhere else to position the pump except within a screened zone, place a shroud over the pump (see 14.3.3). An electric submersible pump should be positioned above the screens to allow water to flow over the electric motor for cooling. If this is not possible, use a shroud to direct flow over the motor.

Rehabilitation of existing boreholes

Before drilling new boreholes, always consider rehabilitating old or damaged boreholes.

Physical damage to the well-head should be repaired to give a sanitary seal, an apron which drains away from the borehole, and a rigid mounting for the pump and rising main.

Damaged pumping equipment will need repair or replacement. Consider the time required to obtain spare parts and to do the repair work and set it against the advantages of installing a new pump. For emergency pumping from existing boreholes, consider using portable submersible pumps powered by a generator and with layflat pipe. It may be possible to remove pipes which have dropped down the borehole using borehole 'fishing tools' – consult a local driller or the water department.

Steel pipes corrode with age and at a rate which is dependent on the chemistry of the water. Pipes often corrode at pipe threads which are not galvanized. When this occurs, discharge rates will at first be lower and, as cracks widen, the losses increase until the pipe eventually drops away. Therefore, if a lowering of the discharge rate is detected, check the pipes and threads as soon as possible.

It may be possible to clear a borehole which has been blocked with debris using a percussion rig with a bailer (see 12.3.6 on percussion rigs). However, where this is not possible, it will be necessary to drill another borehole nearby or use another source.

Water which has been standing in a borehole for some time should be pumped clear and the borehole chlorinated as described in 'Borehole completion' above. Storage tanks and any pipes in the distribution system should also be flushed out and chlorinated.

The static water level will lower in a drought. This may result in dry pumping. Increasing the length of rising main to lower the pump may restore continuous pumping. Consult the original borehole records if they exist and can be found.

Screens in a borehole may become blocked. Some causes of blocked borehole screens and possible remedies are given in Table 12.13.

Table 12.13 Causes of blocked screens in boreholes

Problem	*Remedy*
Blocked well screen due to: poor well design; poor initial well development; corrosion; pumping rate too high	Re-develop the well using the methods outlined under 'Borehole development'
Chemical incrustation	Treat with a strong acid solution administered by specialist personnel under strict safety rules
Biofouling (iron bacteria)	Treat with a strong chlorine solution (50–500 ppm) agitated in the borehole and pumped

Low yielding boreholes drilled in fractured rock can be substantially improved by hydraulic fracturing. If purpose-made equipment is available, the technique is quick and straightforward. A packer is placed near the base of the borehole as shown in Figure 12.47. Water is pumped at high pressure beneath the packer to open up the fractures surrounding the borehole. The aim is to connect the borehole to the rock's fissure system or to increase permeability by opening up the cracks. For maximum effect, specific zones within the formation can be isolated between two packers.

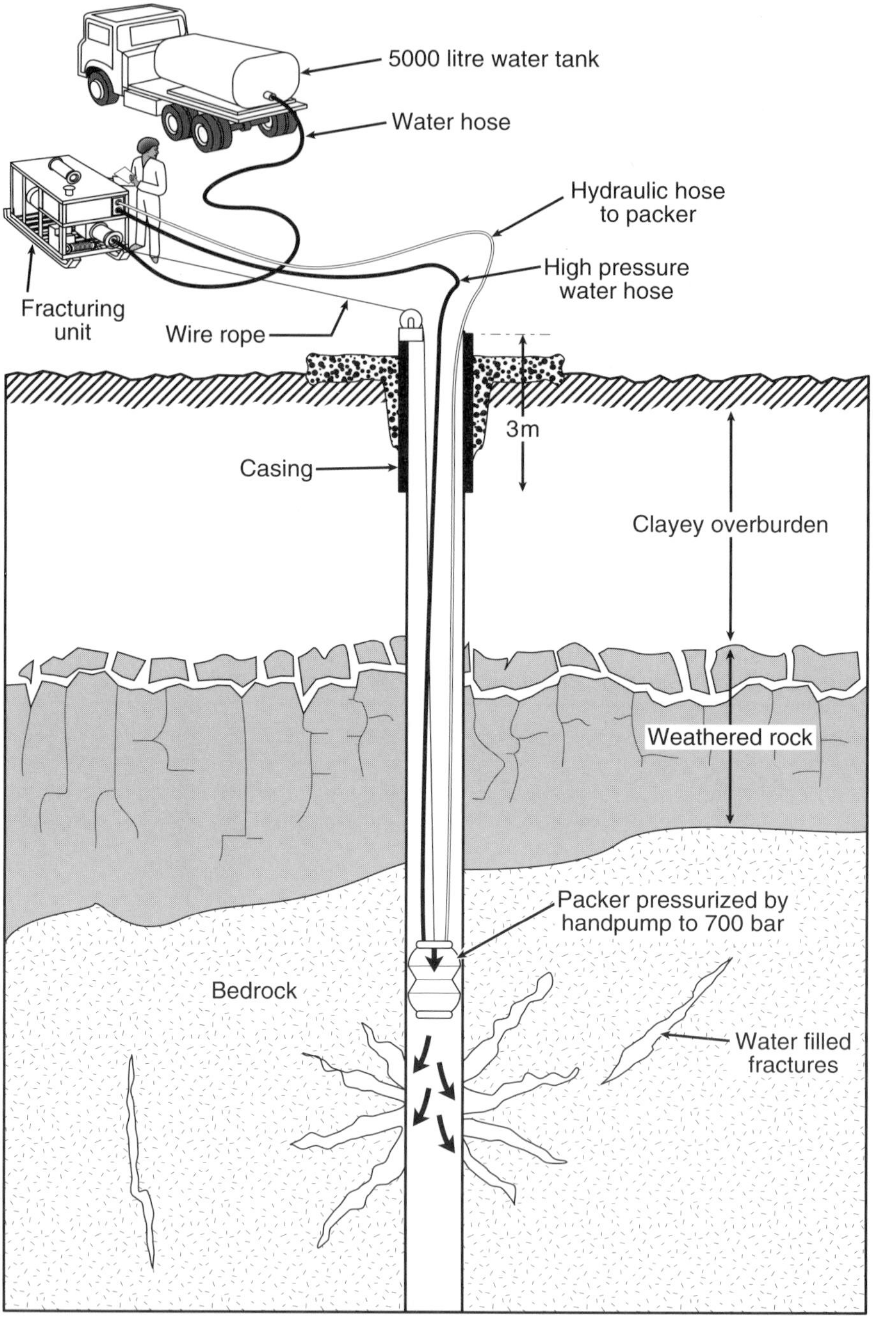

Figure 12.47 Hydraulic fracturing

12.4 Rainwater

The contribution rainwater can make to a water supply will depend on the regularity, reliability and quantity of rainfall in an area. In the wet season, directly collected rainwater can provide an important source of drinking water. Rainwater can be collected by:

- The family – roof and tent collection.
- Institutions – roof and surface runoff collection at clinics, hospitals, feeding centres, schools, churches.
- The community – ponds, small storage reservoirs.

12.4.1 Roof collection

Corrugated steel sheet, tiles, concrete, fabric and plastic sheets all provide surfaces suitable for rainwater collection. A thatched roof can discolour water and give it an unpleasant taste. At the family level, plastic sheeting can be shaped and arranged to collect useful amounts of rainwater for drinking during the wet season. The first flush of rainwater after a dry period should be allowed to run to waste as it will be contaminated with settled dust, bird droppings, and so on.

The rate at which water falls on a roof is a function of the rainfall intensity and the plan area of roof.

Consult rainfall records, if they exist and can be found, or make a rough 'guesstimate' of the likely intensity for the region and the plan area of the roof. Allow for some losses in intense rain. It is not practical to design for very intense rainfall – in the absence of good records, use a figure of 150 mm/h as a guide. In tropical areas, short duration rainfall intensities may be much higher. Gutters and downpipes need to be sized to take the design run-off (see Table 12.14). The capacity of a gutter will depend upon the cross-sectional area and the fall. The figures given in Table 12.14, based on free discharge from level gutters, can be used as a guide.

Table 12.14 Capacity of gutters and downpipes

Diameter of half round gutter, mm	*Capacity of half round gutter, l/s*	*Minimum diameter of downpipe, mm*
75	0.4	50
100	0.8	63
125	1.5	75
150	2.3	90

Gutters should have a fall of about 10 mm per metre to avoid standing water. Downpipes should be of a large enough diameter to prevent blockage by leaves. Guttering (see Figure 12.48) can be made from:

- Purpose-made pre-formed plastic.
- Half-sections of pipe.
- Galvanized steel roofing sheet, cut into strips and formed into a 'U' over a pipe or bent into a 'V' shape.
- Wooden planks, sealed at the joints.
- Split bamboo.

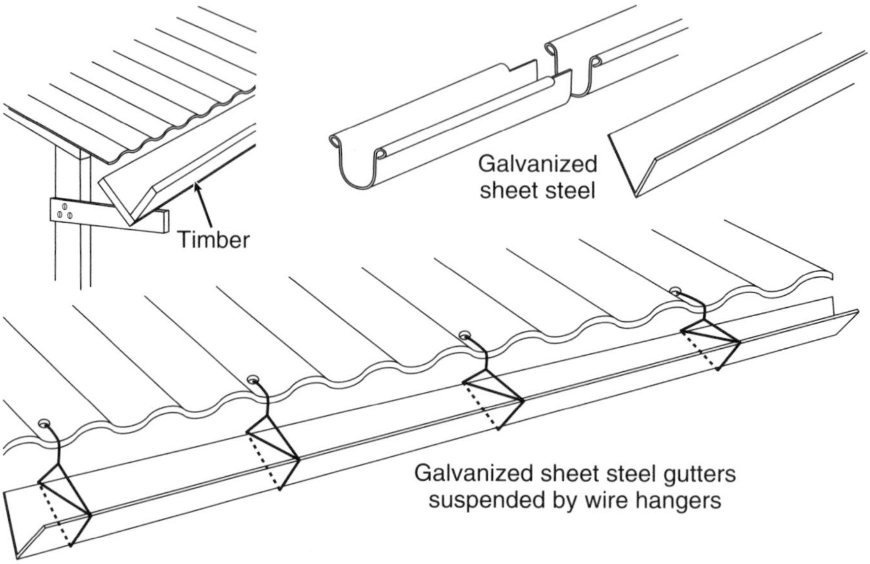

Figure 12.48 Different types of guttering

Rainwater storage

Storage can be provided by:

- Old oil drums that have been thoroughly cleaned several times with detergent.
- Conventional fabricated steel water tanks.
- Galvanized corrugated steel sheet, formed into a circular tank, riveted together and soldered at the joints; the tank has a flat galvanized steel bottom, lapped and soldered at the wall/floor joint.
- Unreinforced mortar jars (13.2.7, Figure 13.17).
- Granary bins lined and plastered with cement mortar or ferrocement.
- Concrete well rings, set on a concrete base and with cement mortar sealing the joints.
- Ferrocement water tanks (13.2.5).
- Rusted and damaged corrugated steel tanks, rehabilitated by using the old tank as formwork for a new ferrocement tank.
- Masonry tanks, either above or below ground.

Cover storage tanks to reduce evaporation losses, to prevent algae forming and to inhibit mosquito breeding.

12.4.2 Ground catchments

Rainfall running off the surface of the ground may be collected and diverted into a storage tank. Ground catchments to collect rainfall runoff are either small areas for use by families and institutions or extensive catchments in which water is channelled into large ground tanks. Small ground catchments are flat areas of ground cleared of vegetation. The ground is smoothed and compacted before covering with an impermeable material (such as stone or concrete). Plastic sheeting may be used in the short term. This type of catchment can be expensive and is clearly open to pollution. However, it may provide water for non-drinking purposes and therefore be a valuable supplement to other potable sources.

In collecting run-off from a surface catchment, keep the sediment load to a minimum. The soil in the immediate catchment area should be disturbed as little as possible. If feasible, plant stiff-stemmed vegetation in the vicinity of the ground tank inlet. A wide, shallow settling basin at the tank entrance reduces the flow velocity and encourages the settlement of solids.

Because of the poor quality of the water, some form of treatment will be required if the water is to be used for drinking. Roof runoff from buildings is usually of a higher quality than surface runoff and can often be used without treatment.

Tanks for the storage of runoff (ground tanks) are described in Section 13.2.3.

13 Water storage, treatment and distribution

13.1 Assessment and planning

This section gives information specific to water storage, treatment and distribution. Guidance is given on an appropriate planning strategy, on the assessment of treatment and storage requirements and on the day-to-day operation of a water supply system. For general information on assessment and planning, see Chapter 5. For more information on the planning of water supplies, see Chapters 9, 11 and 12.

13.1.1 Planning strategy

In planning a water supply and treatment system, use a staged approach. Consider what is necessary in the short term and what is desirable in the longer term. The system should supply water in sufficient quantity and of an acceptable quality. See Chapter 11 for more details on immediate actions to provide water in sufficient quantity and of adequate quality. Use a bar chart to plan your work and identify critical path activities (see Section 5.2.3).

For example, with highly turbid raw water it will be necessary to clarify the water before chlorination (see Section 13.3.1). In the short term, this can be achieved rapidly by coagulation and settlement. However, this process requires a continuous supply of chemicals and produces a contaminating sludge which requires safe disposal. It is a 'low-capital, high running cost' solution. In the longer term, it is desirable to have a system with low running costs and the minimum of external inputs. Roughing filters with, perhaps, slow sand filtration, can replace coagulation and settlement. However, constructing and commissioning roughing filters and slow sand filters may take weeks or perhaps months.

Therefore, plan to use coagulation and settlement in the initial stages but ensure that the plans allow for the development of roughing filters and slow sand filters in the longer term.

Similarly, with the construction of water storage tanks, the quick solution may be to use water storage packs or collapsible tanks which can be flown in and assembled very quickly. These could be replaced by more durable tanks, such as ferrocement tanks, with the temporary kits returned to the warehouse, held on site to cope with changing circumstances, or stored locally for future emergencies.

In designing a water supply system in emergencies, key principles to bear in mind are:

- Provide as much storage as possible. This ensures contingency storage in the event of breakdowns and helps to improve water quality.
- Enlist the aid of gravity to avoid pumping water. Pumping is dependent on fuel supplies, spare parts and skilled operators. Where pumps are involved, the system is vulnerable to mechanical breakdowns. Therefore, keep pumping to a minimum or avoid pumping altogether, if possible.
- Chlorinate water when supplying large numbers of people in crowded conditions (such as a refugee camp). Chlorination may not be so critical if there are many sources serving a dispersed population.

13.1.2 Stages in a water supply system

To deliver adequate amounts of safe potable water, a water supply system serving large numbers of people will normally involve the following stages (illustrated in Figure 13.1):

- Abstraction and transmission.
- Storage.
- Treatment.
- Distribution.

Actual systems will vary and they will not necessarily include every stage shown. Wherever possible, site stages to make use of gravity flow between them.

Table 13.1 gives an indication of the aims and possible processes involved in each stage. The precise combination of processes will depend on the characteristics of the raw water and the facilities available in each case.

Table 13.1 Stages of water treatment

Stage	*Principal aim of each stage*	*Possible processes*
Abstraction with treatment	Removal of suspended solids and micro-organisms	Natural filtration through riverside wells and infiltration galleries and wells
Pre-treatment	Removal of suspended solids to clarify the water sufficiently so that further treatment is effective	Storage. Correction of pH. Plain sedimentation. Coagulation and settlement. Roughing filtration
Main treatment	Improvement of the microbiological quality of the water by the removal of pathogens	Slow sand filtration. Disinfection, usually by chlorination

Water demand determines the size of the water supply system required. Raw water characteristics, notably turbidity and potability, determine the type and extent of treatment required. Careful design of abstraction and storage can improve quality and these stages should be regarded as part of the treatment system.

Elevation:
(ideal)

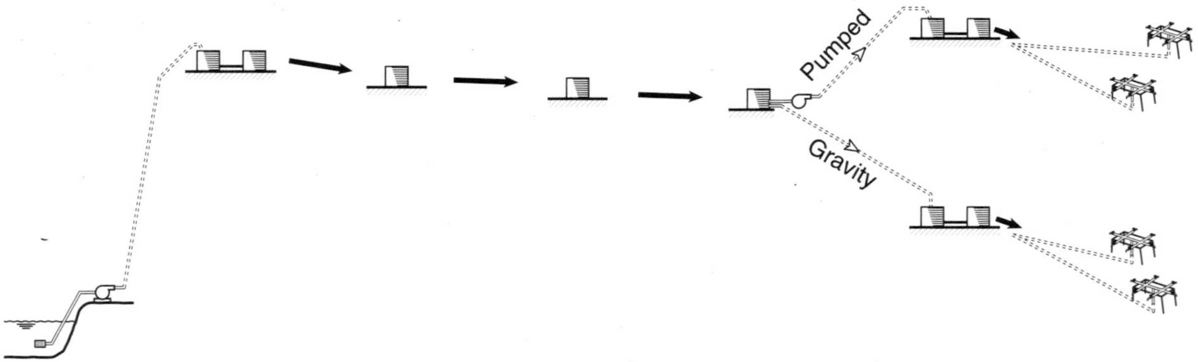

Stage:	**Water abstraction** Surface intake. Infiltration gallery or well(s). Spring(s). Large diameter well(s). Borehole(s).	**Raw water storage** Contingency reserve. May be combined with settlement and/or pH correction.	**Pre-treatment** Either: Settlement – plain or chemically assisted. Or: Roughing filtration.	**Slow sand filtration** Only include if filter can accept the turbidity of the influent.	**Chlorination** Final treatment stage. Safeguards downstream supplies.	**Storage** At strategic points on the distribution system. May be combined with chlorination contact tanks in simple systems.	**Distribution** To communal collection points – tapstands.
Design capacity:	Average flow rate over operating period.	Several tanks. Storage capacity will depend on reliability of the source (a few hours' to one day's supply).	Average flow rate over operating period.	Average flow rate over 24 hours.	Sufficient capacity to give the required contact time at the average flow rate.	Several tanks. A minimum of one day's storage.	Sized to meet peak demand flow rate.

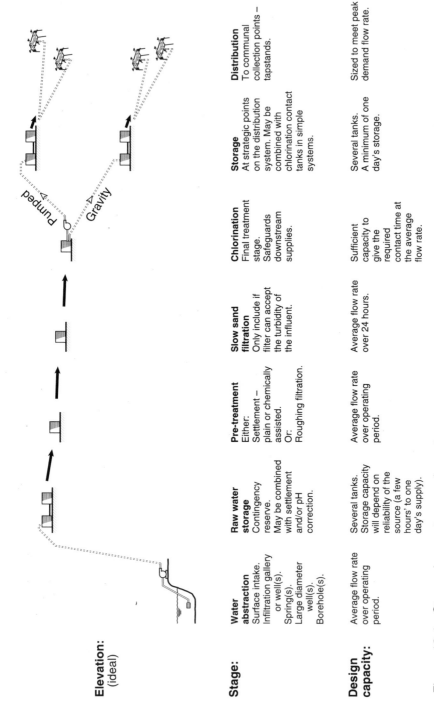

Figure 13.1 Stages in a water supply system

Highly turbid water containing mud in suspension requires a lot of treatment – clear water requires relatively little treatment other than disinfection. If the water is salty, people will not drink it and there is little that can be done to treat it (see 13.3.6). If the water is not immediately potable for other reasons, such as having a high iron content, then it may be susceptible to treatment.

While there are good reasons for protecting the water source from contamination by pathogens, such protection is not in itself sufficient to guarantee a safe supply. In the design of a treatment system for emergencies, safe water is achieved primarily by chlorination, possibly with the aid of slow sand filtration.

13.1.3 Assessment of treatment and storage requirements

Table 13.2 lists the treatment processes likely to be necessary for different sources of water.

Table 13.2 Water sources, their likely quality and their treatment

Source	*Quality*		*Treatment required*
	*Likely faecal contamination**	*Turbidity***	
Surface water			
Highland stream	Low to high	Low	SSF, chlorination
River	High or very high	High or very high	Either storage, coagulation and settlement and chlorination, or storage, RF, SSF, chlorination
Lake, reservoir, irrigation canal	High	Low	Storage, SSF, chlorination
Lake, reservoir, irrigation canal	High or very high	High or very high	As river (see above)
Rainfall collection	Low to high	Low	Storage, possibly SSF
Groundwater			
Protected spring	Nil or very low	Low	Either chlorination, if to a large densely settled population, or no treatment
Closed dug well	Nil or low	Low	As above
Open dug well	Medium to high	Low to medium	As above
Borehole	Nil or very low	Low	As above and possibly aeration

* Faecal contamination: (*E.coli*/100 ml)
Low, < 10; Medium, 10–100; High, 100–10 000; Very high, 10 000–100 000+

** Turbidity (NTU)
Low, < 20; Medium, 20–75; High, 76–250; Very high, 250–2000+

Note: SSF = Slow sand filtration, RF = Roughing filtration

Points to note:

- Where possible, make use of existing groundwater sources to avoid, or minimize, the need for water treatment. However, if a new system has to be installed, it is generally much quicker to install a water supply using surface sources than to drill boreholes. If they exist, spring sources can be developed rapidly and should be used.
- The use of chemicals (in coagulation and chlorination) should be kept to a minimum as they require significant financial, logistical and management support to supply, store and use safely.
- The use of mechanical equipment should be kept to a minimum because of its vulnerability to a breakdown in the supply of spare parts and fuel.
- Try to develop methods of treatment which can be operated and maintained with existing technical and managerial skills, especially after the initial emergency phase.

Assessment of storage requirements

Storage is required to:

- Provide a back-up when there is a break in upstream supply.
- Balance peaks in demand with the flow from the source or treatment works.
- Ensure a constant supply to a treatment process (for instance, a slow sand filter).
- Maintain pressure in a distribution system.
- Mitigate problems due to a deterioration in raw water quality (such as rapid peaks in the turbidity of river water).

Water abstraction pumps and pipes, treatment facilities and transmission pipes to the storage tanks need only be sized on the average flow rate (see Box 13.1). The treated water storage tanks and the distribution pipes are sized to cope

Box 13.1 Sample calculation of storage to cope with peak flow

For a population of 20 000 @ 15 litres/person/day, the daily water demand will be 300 000 litres/day (300 m^3).

To meet this daily demand, the average flow rate from source over a 14-hour operating day (5 a.m. to 7 p.m.) must be 21.4 m^3/h.

Assume peak flow will be concentrated into two, four-hour periods (morning, 6–10 a.m. and evening, 2–6 p.m.) and half the daily demand will need to be met during each period. That is, 150 m^3 in four hours or 37.5 m^3/h. The peak flow is thus 75% greater than the average flow. (Peak flow factor = 1.75). It is helpful to display this graphically. The graph in Figure 13.3 indicates:

- There needs to be 43 m^3 of water stored at the beginning of the day if the morning demand is to be met.
- The total storage required is 86 m^3.

In practice, the storage required to make up the deficit during the peak periods will be more than catered for by one day's contingency storage of 300 m^3.

with the peak flow rate. Therefore, locate treated water storage as far along the supply system as possible. This minimizes the impact of peak flows, so reducing the size of pipes and pumps required.

An emergency water supply will normally operate at full capacity during the immediate emergency phase. As the emergency stabilizes and moves into the recovery phase, the water supply system should be developed and expanded to provide sufficient capacity to cope with the peak demand. This will enable people to collect the water they need without having to queue at tapstands throughout the day. Water demand will then follow the classic morning and evening peaks (see Figure 13.2).

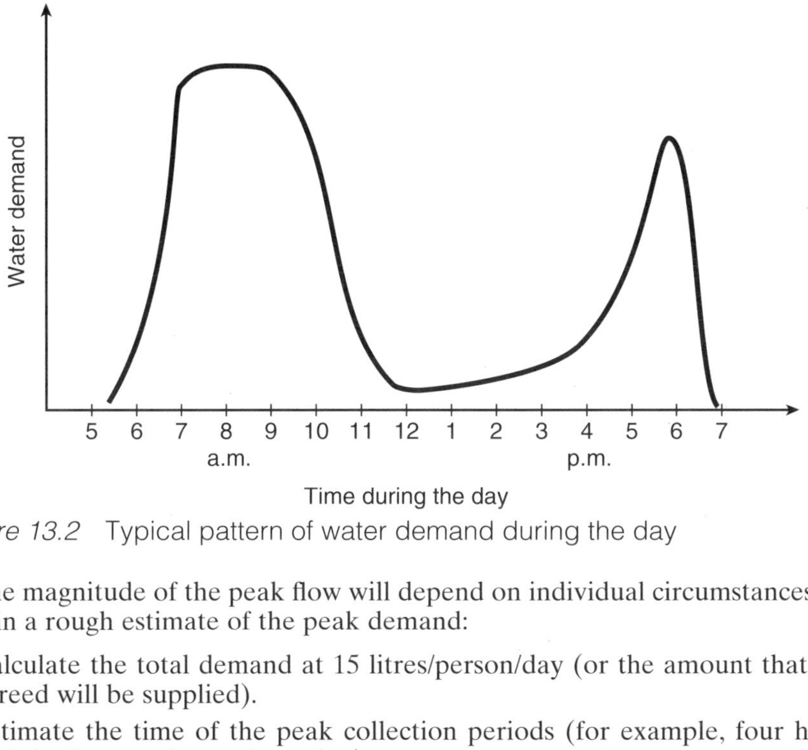

Figure 13.2 Typical pattern of water demand during the day

The magnitude of the peak flow will depend on individual circumstances. To obtain a rough estimate of the peak demand:

- Calculate the total demand at 15 litres/person/day (or the amount that it is agreed will be supplied).
- Estimate the time of the peak collection periods (for example, four hours each in the morning and evening).
- Assume half the total demand is collected during each four-hour period.

This procedure will tend to over-estimate the peak demand, which is preferable to an under-estimate, and allows for some increase in demand.

Aim to have sufficient contingency storage on distribution lines to continue the supply for at least one day in the event of an upstream break in supply. This will also be more than sufficient to balance the fluctuating daily demand (see Box 13.1).

13.1.4 Operation of a water supply system

In planning a water supply system, it is useful to have in mind the day to day operation of the system. The following is a typical sequence of daily operations:

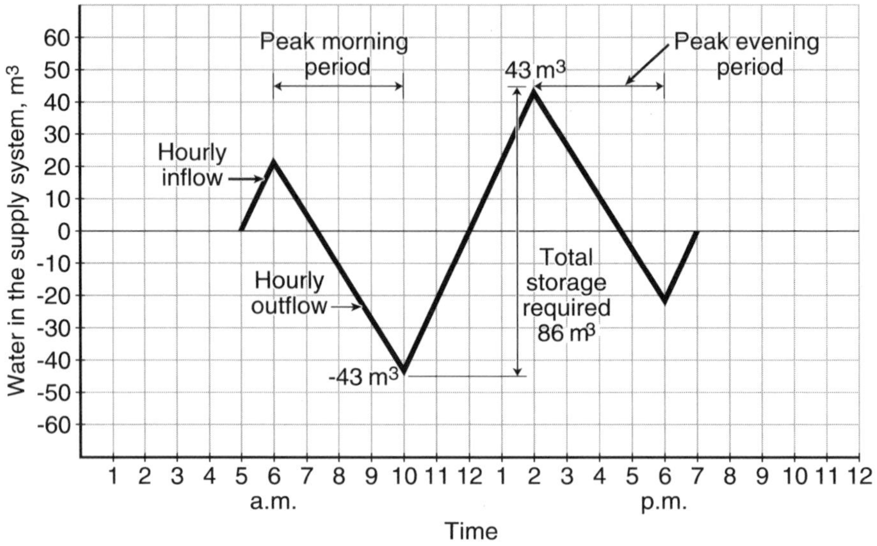

Figure 13.3 Variation of inflow and outflow during the day

- Night/early morning – delivery at the average flow rate from source and treatment to top-up the storage tanks in the distribution system.
- Morning – tank levels decline as the peak demand is met.
- Throughout the day – continued delivery from source and treatment at the average flow rate to replenish the storage tanks.
- Late afternoon/early evening – tanks are full to supply the peak demand.
- Late evening/night – continued delivery from source and treatment partially refills the depleted tanks and reduces the early morning top-up time.

The extent of night-time operations will depend on several factors:

- The need to keep some treatment processes running continuously (for instance, slow sand filters).
- The capacity of the system to meet the total demand for water.
- The type of source – boreholes should not be pumped continuously but given time to recover.
- Noise disturbance caused by pumping at night.
- The security of operators at night (in insecure or conflict situations).

Further operational details will be found in the following sections dealing with each stage of the supply system.

13.2 Water storage

13.2.1 Principal considerations

Water storage is primarily used as a means of ensuring that the correct quantities of water are available when needed in the water supply system. However,

Storage can also improve water quality. For the assessment of storage needs see Section 13.1.

The next section deals with tanks commonly used for water storage in emergencies and includes emergency tanks, ground tanks, water storage packs, ferrocement tanks, water jars for domestic storage and improvised water towers. Guidance is given on improvised water towers and on emergency tank repairs.

In planning water storage bear the following points in mind:

- *The more storage there is, the better.* It is essential to have an adequate reserve of water to cope with a breakdown in supply from the source. Aim to store at least one day's supply.
- If ordering tanks for a water supply system, always order plenty of smaller tanks (10 m^3) for use at service points such as clinics or for use in the later phases of the construction of the water treatment system (for instance, for use in roughing filters).
- Avoid large elevated tanks wherever possible because of the expense and time required for their erection. Site a tank on higher ground if a pressure head of water is required for gravity distribution. In flat terrain, despite the problems, pumped distribution may be the preferred option.
- Provide tanks with adequate overflow facilities to protect against erosion of the ground and the tank foundations.
- Ensure tank sites are well drained and not likely to flood.
- Cover storage tanks to prevent wind-blown debris and dust from settling in the water. Covers also prevent the growth of algae in strong sunlight.
- Fence tank sites where access to tanks, valves and equipment by unauthorized personnel, children and animals might be a problem.
- Masonry and reinforced concrete tanks take time to construct. Therefore, a more rapid means of tank construction must be used in an emergency.

Table 13.3 gives some comparative information on different types of tanks likely to be used in emergencies. Further details on each type of tank are given in the subsequent sections.

13.2.2 Rigid and flexible emergency tanks

Small capacity rigid tanks

Fabricated steel tanks intended for commercial and industrial establishments may be available locally and can be used as static tanks (see Figure 13.4) or temporarily fitted to a flat-bed truck for tankering. It may be possible to repair scrapped tanks from road tankers if they can be found locally. These can be mounted either on static supports or on a flat-bed truck.

Bulk containers manufactured in high-density polyethylene for the chemical industry can be used to convert a flat bed truck or pick-up into a water tanker. Tanks are enclosed in a galvanized steel framework which can be bolted together and lashed down with standard polyester webbing. Damage to polyethylene tanks can be made good with a heat gun and repair sticks or scrap polyethylene. Capacities range up to 1000 litres.

Table 13.3 Guide to tank selection

Type of tank	*Capacity*	*Comments*
Fabricated steel or plastic tanks	circa 1 m^3	Limited capacity. If available, use them
Pillow tanks	2.5–20 m^3	Very easy to transport and install. Can be used for water transport. Expensive and very difficult to clean out. Easy to puncture
Flotation collar tanks	2–80 m^3	Very easy to transport and install. Expensive. Seepage may be a problem
Ground tanks	5–1000+ m^3	Cheap. Can provide large amounts of storage. Can be used for other treatment processes. Time needed for construction, perhaps weeks
Water storage packs (Oxfam type)	10–100 m^3	Easy to transport and install. Reasonable cost. Durable. Standard item used in emergencies. Can be used for other treatment processes
Ferrocement tanks	10–100 m^3	Uses local materials and skills. Reasonable cost. Durable. Can be used for other treatment processes. Time needed for construction (weeks)

Collapsible fabric tanks

Collapsible fabric tanks have a low packed volume and are relatively easy to handle. There is no framework and they can be rapidly put into service. There are two main types: pillow tanks and flotation collar tanks.

Pillow tanks Pillow tanks (also called bladder tanks) are made from UV resistant high tensile EVA or PVC coated polyester fabric. They are available in capacities ranging from 2500 litres (2.5 m^3) to 20 000 litres (20 m^3).

When ordering, ensure that compatible fittings for the inlet and outlet connections and a repair kit are ordered and delivered with the tank. Tanks which have the inlet in the middle cause problems as it is difficult to get at the inlet when the tank is full. If given the opportunity, order or install tanks with the inlet to one end.

To obtain some head of water for distribution, place the tank on slightly elevated ground. Ensure that the ground is level. If the tank is erected on sloping ground, as it is filled, water will migrate to the lower side of the tank and the combined tank and water may start rolling downhill. Ten tonnes of rolling water is hard to stop and it can do a lot of damage. Remove all sharp objects – stones, roots, thorns – before putting the groundsheet and tank into position. If the tank comes wrapped in a fabric groundsheet, place the groundsheet underneath the tank for protection. Some tanks have restraining straps, or nets, and these can be pegged down if there is any likelihood of movement down an incline. Form an earth bund around the tank as a further precaution.

See Figure 13.5a for a typical arrangement of a pillow tank and its associated distribution pipe and taps.

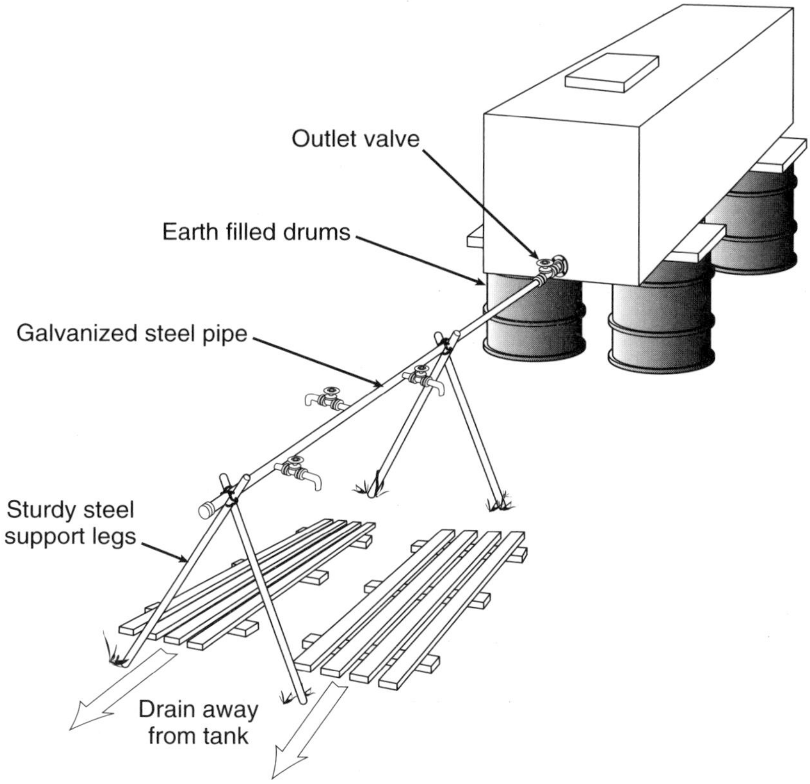

Figure 13.4 A temporary water distribution point

A pillow tank can also be used for transporting water by laying it on the flat bed of a trailer or truck (see Figure 13.5b). Use strong webbing or nets to secure it. As the tank is flexible, there can be considerable movement of tank and water on rough roads and when turning corners – drivers must be warned to drive slowly and take great care.

If silt or sludge accumulates in a pillow tank it is very difficult to remove.

Flotation collar tanks Flotation collar tanks are available in sizes from 1800 litres (1.8 m^3) to 90 000 litres (90 m^3). The tank (sometimes referred to as an 'onion tank') comprises an open-topped bag of synthetic rubber material with a self-supporting buoyant rim (Figure 13.5c). To achieve buoyancy, the rim may be either foam filled or inflatable. As the tank is open it cannot be used for transporting water. A loose cover is supported above the water by a spherical float. Unlike the pillow tank, the inflatable collar tank can be used on slopes.

13.2.3 Ground tanks

Large tanks excavated in the ground may provide large-scale storage for rain and stream water collected in the wet season and stored for use in the dry

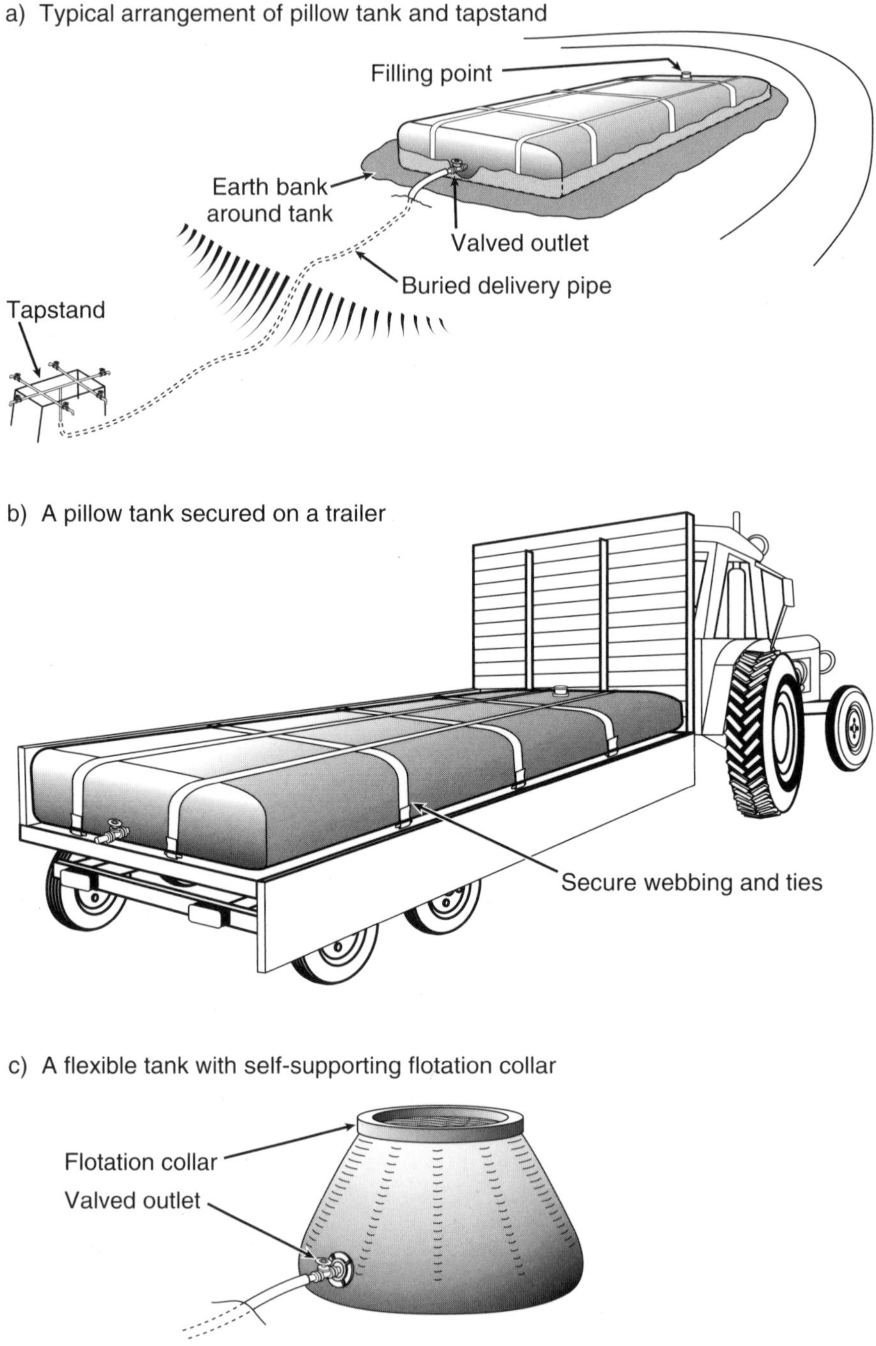

Figure 13.5 Collapsible fabric tanks

season. Ground tanks (see Figure 13.6) can also be used in water treatment as sedimentation or filtration tanks (see Section 13.3). In the Horn of Africa, large excavated ground tanks are called hafirs. They supply large numbers of people and animals during the dry season and have been used to store water as an emergency reserve supply for refugee camps. In Zimbabwe, commercial farmers use ground tanks lined with polyethylene sheet for the storage of irrigation water.

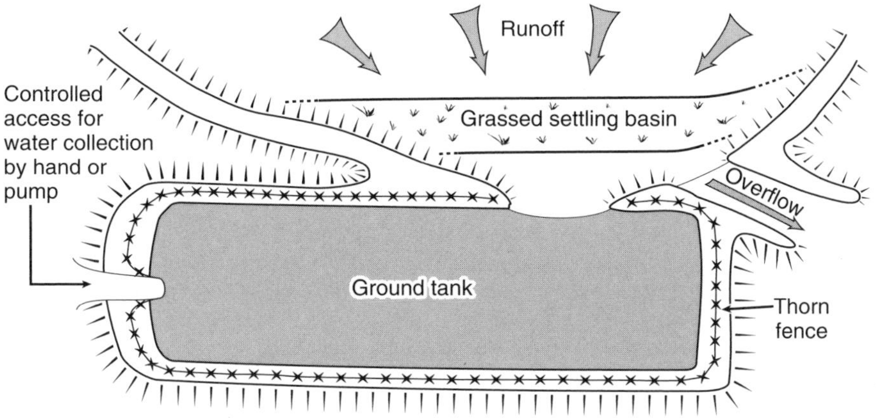

Figure 13.6 Plan view of a ground tank

Ground tanks vary greatly in size, from as little as 10 m^3 for tanks lined with masonry or ferrocement to several thousand cubic metres for tanks lined with clay or a geomembrane.

In suitable ground conditions, and if earthmoving machinery is available, ground tanks may be constructed in a matter of days. If human labour is to be used, a large tank may take several weeks. (See Section 18.3.6 for more information on earthworks.) However, once one tank has been constructed, then many more may be constructed using very little outside material.

Design

In the design of a ground tank, the key elements are the choice of lining material to minimize seepage losses and the stability of the tank walls. For long term storage, evaporation can cause significant losses (as much as 150 mm/month). See also Section 12.2.3 (small earth dams) for further information.

Evaluate the permeability of the soil by carrying out a permeability test – see Appendix 20. If the permeability of the soil is unacceptably high, look for clay soils which could be used for lining or, if clay is not available, consider using a synthetic liner – see Table 13.5.

The angle of tank side slopes will depend on the maximum slope the material can stand. Table 13.4 gives guideline slopes for tank lining. However, always look for local examples of natural slopes of the material concerned. Where there is uncertainty over a safe angle of slope and failure could be life threatening, limit the height of retaining walls to two metres. Steeper tank side slopes can be maintained by reinforcing the earth with local materials such as vegetation and bags filled with sand or earth or by using geotextiles, if they are available (see Appendix 20). Bags filled with earth taken from the tank floor can be used to construct tank walls (see 13.3.2, Figure 13.22 for an illustration).

Table 13.4 Slopes of soils (vertical : horizontal)

	Firm or stiff clay	*Granular soils*
Below ground	1 : 1	1 : 1
Above ground	1 : 3	1 : 1.5

Note: Where the slope is part excavation and part fill, either reduce the gradient of the excavated slope to the same as the filled slope, or leave a flat area at the top of the excavation so that the toe of the cutting aligns with the fill surface, as shown in Figure 13.7. Compact the fill in layers no greater than 300 mm thick.

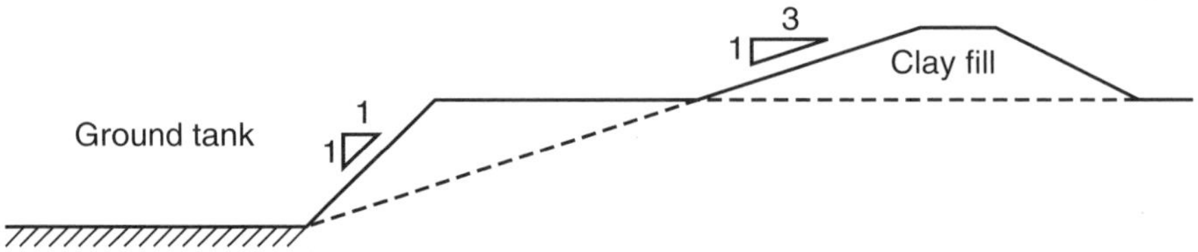

Figure 13.7 Recommended slopes for ground tank walls

Ensure that any overflow is channelled safely away from the tank, for example, with a spillway. To estimate the size of a spillway refer to 12.2.3. Ensure that diverted runoff or tank overflow will not create erosion gulleys. Construct fences, or establish some form of control, to prevent direct access to the tank by animals. Arrange a hygienic way of abstracting the water (see Chapter 14, Figure 14.8).

Tank lining

Tanks dug into permeable soils can be lined using a variety of materials: reinforced concrete, ferrocement, local clays, commercially available sodium bentonite/geotextile composite membranes, and synthetic membranes.

For emergency or temporary supplies, the factors deciding the choice of ground tank lining will include:

- The permeability of existing soils.
- The suitability of locally available materials.
- The combined freight and installation cost of imported materials.
- The skills and equipment available to handle and join synthetic lining materials.

Clay linings Soils with a clay content of 10 per cent or more can be used as a lining (see Appendix 20 for estimating the clay content of a soil). For a tank depth of three metres, scarify the soil at the bottom of the excavated tank to a depth of 200 mm, wet and compact. If there is a small amount of water in the tank, the soil can be compacted under water – 'puddled'. If the tank material has a clay content of below 10 per cent, seepage losses can be reduced by placing a clay blanket on the tank floor. The blanket material should have a wide range of particle size with a clay content of at least 20 per cent. Lay the blanket in 150–200 mm layers, wet and compact. A blanket at least 300 mm thick is recommended for a 3 m deep tank.

Commercially available Wyoming bentonite clay (85 per cent sodium montmorillonite) will swell up to 10 times its dry volume when wet. This is significantly more than the calcium montmorillonite constituent of 'black cotton soil'. Wyoming bentonite has been used for small reservoir and tank lining at an application rate of 5 to 15 kg/m^2.

Synthetic linings Table 13.5 gives guidelines on the choice of synthetic lining material for ground tanks. Synthetic linings can be protected by bags filled with earth or sand.

Table 13.5 Synthetic geomembranes for ground tank lining

Lining material	*Main features*
Low Density Polyethylene LDPE. Thickness for tank lining: reinforced 0.5–0.75 mm; unreinforced 0.5–1.5 mm; standard roll width 2 or 4 m	Inert; flexible – large sheets can be rolled up for transport; no specialist skills required for joining sheets on site using a double-sided sealing compound. Available in prewelded panels up to 1000 m^2
High Density Polyethylene HDPE. Available thickness: 0.5–2.5 mm. Standard roll width 5.6 m	As for LDPE but not so flexible – stress cracking can be induced if it is folded
PVC	Inert; flexible; requires specialist equipment for the ultrasonic welding of joints on site
Butyl rubber. Thickness for tank lining: 1mm. Available in sheet sizes up to 28 m × 40 m	Joints require skilled hot bond welding. Repairs can be made with a cold glue but this is not good enough for jointing

13.2.4 Water storage packs

Water storage packs have been used extensively by Oxfam and others in emergencies. A tank comprises corrugated steel sheets which form circular walls on which a synthetic rubber (EPDM) liner is hung. The PVC roof is supported by a central column and radial ropes. Each tank can be easily transported and assembled on levelled, smooth ground in a few hours using unskilled labour. Tanks are available in the capacities detailed in Table 13.6.

Oxfam includes comprehensive erection instructions with each tank.

The 10 500 litre tank is a convenient size to provide enough storage for service centres: clinics, feeding centres, food distribution points, etc. With a low weight of about 300 kg, it can be transported on the back of a pick-up. It may also be used for certain parts of a treatment system (such as roughing filters).

Table 13.6 Oxfam tank details

Oxfam ordering code	*Nominal storage capacity (litres)*	*Height (m)*	*Diameter (m)*
T11 S,L,R	10 500	2.3	2.5
T45 S,L,R	45 000	1.5	6.4
T70 S,L,R	70 000	2.3	6.4
T95 S,L,R	95 000	3.0	6.4

Codes refer to: S steel tank sheets, L liner, R roof

Allow a generous margin in estimating the number of these tanks you require. The pack can be ordered with a tapstand distribution kit and erected as shown in Figure 13.8.

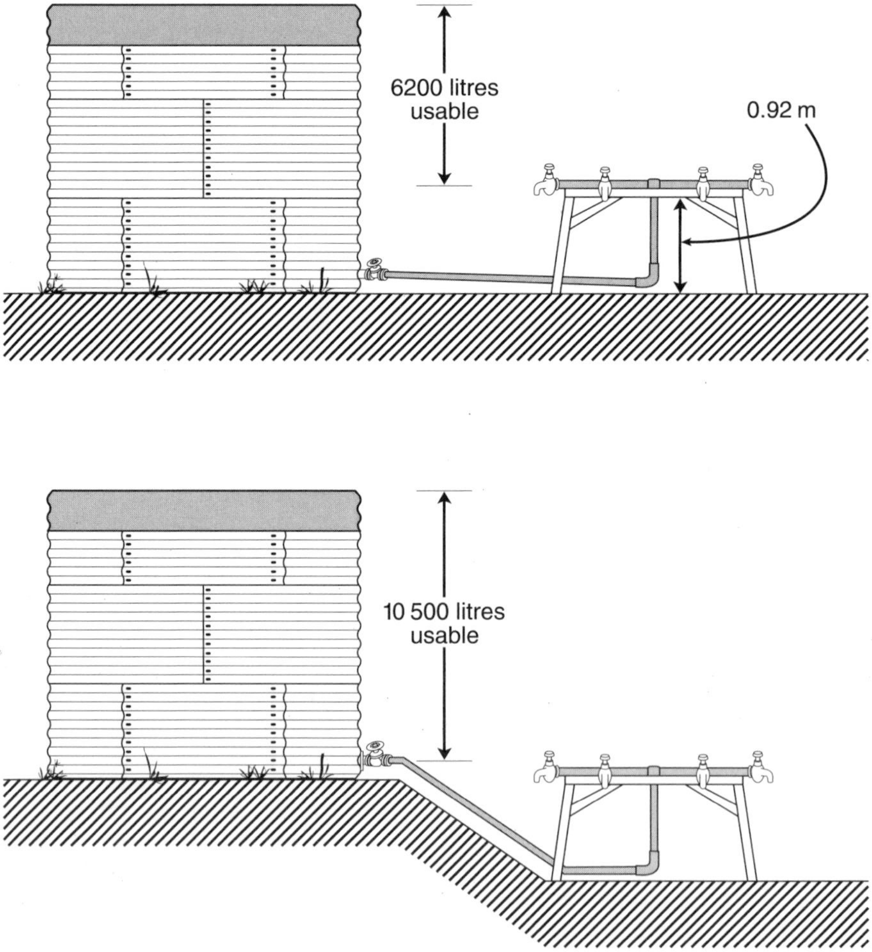

Figure 13.8 A 10 500 litre (10.5 m^3) 'Oxfam type' tank with tapstand

The components and stages in the construction of a 70 000 litre tank are shown in Figure 13.9. To erect the 10 500, 70 000 and 95 000 litre tanks, ladders or platforms (possibly made from empty fuel drums) of about half the final height of the tank are required.

Once erected, stabilize tanks by filling them with water and tying them down with guy ropes. Do not erect tanks in windy conditions.

In soft ground conditions or swelling soils (for instance, 'black cotton soil'), prepare suitable gravel or concrete ring foundations for tanks greater than 2.3 m high – and for all tanks if time allows.

Form earth banks around tanks where possible. This helps to prevent erosion around tank walls and provides stability against wind pressure when the tanks are empty.

When cleaning tanks, operators must take care to avoid damage to the synthetic rubber liners.

13.2.5 Ferrocement water tanks

Ferrocement water tanks are constructed from cement-rich mortar, plastered onto chicken wire reinforced with weld mesh or standard small diameter reinforcement bars. Tanks can be built with basic skills using commonly available equipment in a relatively short period. These are all advantages over reinforced concrete and masonry tanks.

Typically, they may be used to replace Oxfam tanks which can either be dismantled and stored for use elsewhere or used to develop water supplies rapidly in response to changing circumstances.

Table 13.7 gives comparative dimensions, material requirements and estimated construction time for tanks up to 50 000 litres (50 m^3). Tanks over 40 000 litres (40 m^3) require a central column to support the roof.

Table 13.7 Dimensions, materials and construction time for ferrocement tanks

Dimensions					
Tank volume, m^3	10	20	30	40	50
Base diameter, m	3.02	4.10	4.95	5.70	6.30
Mesh radius, m	1.36	1.91	2.33	2.70	3.01
Inside radius, m	1.33	1.88	2.30	2.67	2.98
Wall height, m	1.80	1.80	1.80	1.80	1.80
Materials					
Bags of cement, tank	11	18	27	41	51
roof	3	5	7	9	12
Weldmesh (2 m wide), length in m	20	30	40	50	66
Mesh size 150 × 150 mm					
Chicken wire: rolls of 1 m × 30 m	1	2	2.5	3	4
25 mm mesh chicken wire					
Binding wire, 16 gauge, kg	6	10	13	16	20
Clean sand, m^3	1.5	2.5	3	4	5
Gravel (< 25 mm) m^3	0.8	1.3	2.0	2.5	3
200-litre drums of water	13	20	25	30	35
Construction time, days	8	9	13	14	17

Source: UNICEF, undated

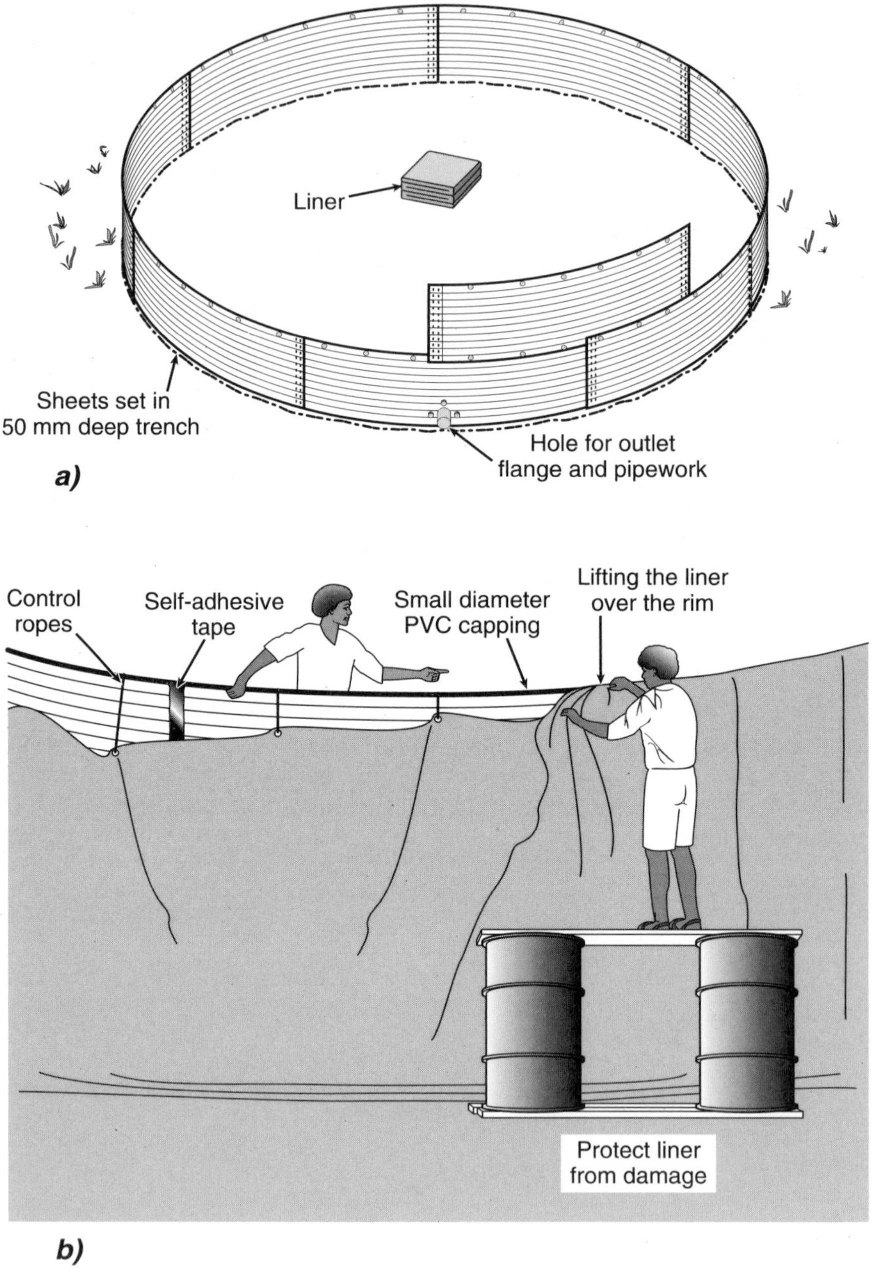

Figure 13.9 Stages in the erection of an 'Oxfam type' tank

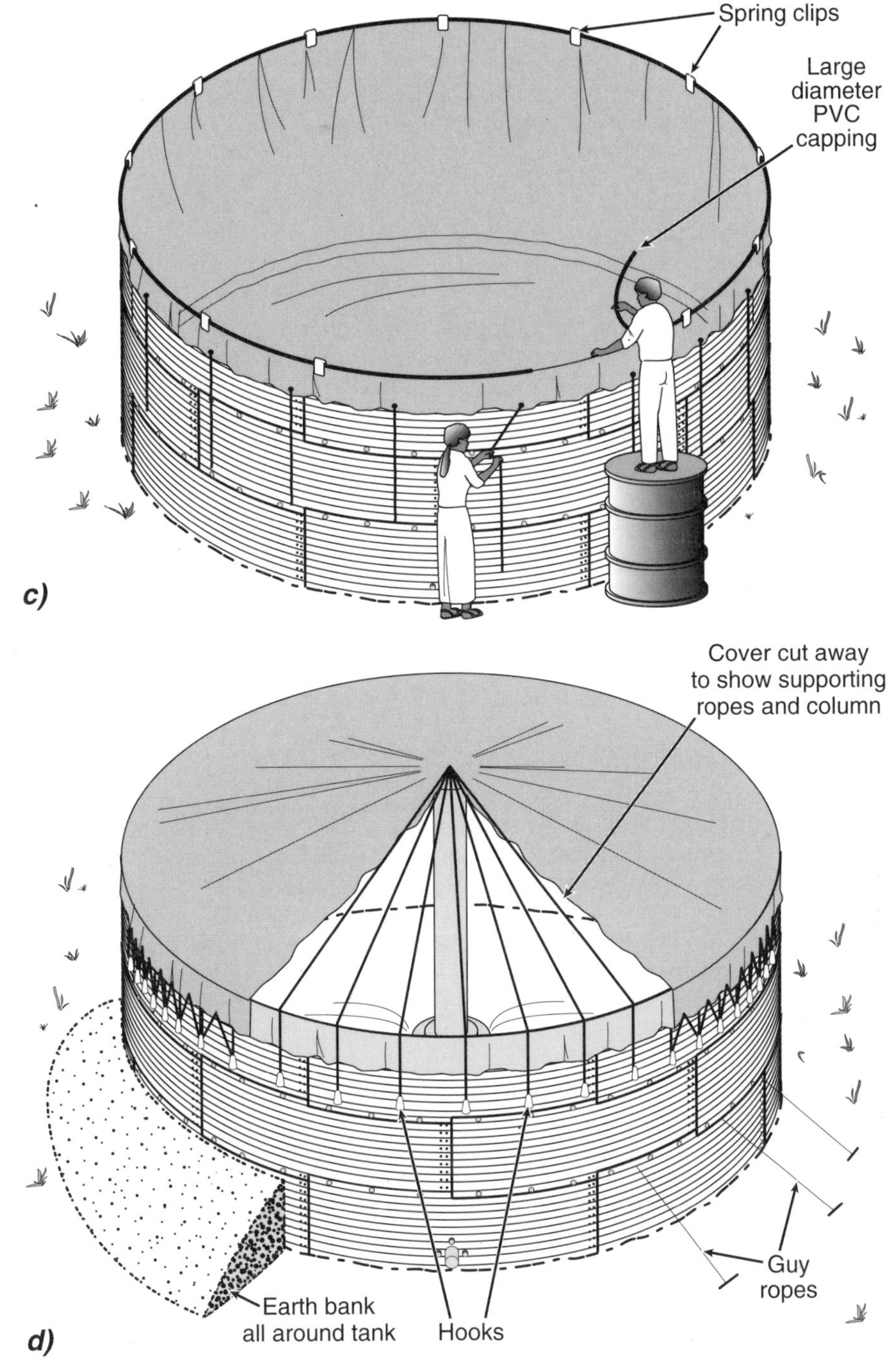

Figure 13.9 (cont.) Stages in the erection of an 'Oxfam type' tank

Box 13.2 outlines the construction procedure for ferrocement tanks based on a technique developed and successfully used in Kenya. A key aspect of the approach is that rigid shuttering is not required. Adapt the procedure for tank sizes up to 50 000 litres (50 m^3). This particular design is not suitable for tanks above this size. All concrete and mortar mix ratios are by volume. Use well graded clean sand (see Figure 13.25 for a method of washing sand).

13.2.6 Improvised water towers

(From MoD, 1981b)

Where an elevated tank is required in flat terrain, a water tower can be constructed from rough timber or tubular steel scaffolding. Figure 13.15 shows a tower supporting a 14 000-litre timber framed tank. The tank membrane can be butyl rubber, polyethylene or other suitable waterproof sheeting. Figure 13.16 shows a tubular steel scaffold tower supporting a steel tank.

The towers shown are designed for average wind and ground bearing conditions. To prevent overturning, the stabilizing moment of the weight of the structure must be greater than the moment of the wind pressure on the side of the tank (Figure 13.14). Calculate for the most critical time when the tank is empty and for the maximum expected wind speed (see example in Box 13.3). Arrange guy ropes and extra weight if necessary. Keep the tank topped up, if possible. Provide adequate baseplates compatible with the safe bearing pressure of the ground.

13.2.7 Domestic water storage

It is important to provide clean storage containers for storage in the home. There is little point in providing high quality water at a tapstand if people do not have the means to carry and store that water hygienically.

In the initial phases of an emergency, household storage is likely to be in plastic containers. Typically people may have a 10–15-litre plastic jerrycan for carrying and storing water and a bucket for washing. In later phases, it may be worthwhile considering improving household storage. One possibility is the use of concrete storage jars that can be made on site. In addition to improving storage, the skill of making the jars can be used after the emergency is over – one small way that the water engineer can make a contribution towards longer-term development.

Refer to Figure 13.17 on how to make cement (mortar) jars for domestic water storage. The jars may also be used for grain or flour storage. Cement water jars are heavy to transport and are liable to break. Therefore try to make them near their point of use.

13.2.8 Tank repairs

Before ordering new water tanks, check if existing tanks can be brought into service, perhaps with a little repair and rehabilitation.

Box 13.2 Construction procedure for a 20 m³ ferrocement tank

Day 1 Refer to Figure 13.10.

- Excavate a shallow circular level foundation, 100 mm deep and 2.05 m radius. Prepare weld mesh of 2.05 m radius for floor reinforcement.
- Prepare the wall reinforcement by forming a 12.30 m length of weld mesh into an upright cylinder, with overlap, to give a diameter of 3.82 m. Bend the bottom wires of the mesh at 90°. Bend the top wires inwards at an angle of 45°.
- Prepare the roof reinforcement by forming cut sections of weld mesh into a 1.90 m radius circle with a 450 mm high support at the centre.

Day 2

- Position any outlet or drain pipe in a narrow trench in the earth foundation under the floor and protruding through it as shown in Figure 13.10. Backfill the trench with concrete.
- Cast the concrete floor by laying a 50 mm thick concrete base (1:2:4 mix) in the prepared foundation. Place the floor reinforcement on the concrete. Cast another layer of concrete (1:2:4 mix) without delay on top of the reinforcement, working from the centre up to 400 mm from the perimeter.
- Position the wall reinforcement without disturbing the reinforcement already concreted. Pull into shape and bind. Place the remaining concrete and tamp firmly around the wall. Cover the concrete.
- Continue preparation of the roof reinforcement by cutting and placing chicken wire on the prepared roof weld mesh.

Day 3

- Keep the concrete wet throughout the day.
- Prepare the wall for plastering:
  - Tightly wrap the weld mesh from the top to the floor with chicken wire. Overlap the ends. Tie the chicken wire to the weld mesh in several places.
  - Tightly wrap 16 gauge binding wire around the wall as follows (see Figure 13.11) four times around the top weld mesh wire;
    every 100 mm for the top 600 mm;
    every 80 mm for the next 600 mm;
    every 50 mm for the next 700 mm;
    four times around the bottom and tie to the mesh.
  - Tie sacking to the outside wall. Firmly tie two ladders together to straddle the wall. Inspect the tank and pull it into a cylindrical shape using staked ropes or binding wire (Figure 13.12).
- If it is windy, postpone further work until the wind calms.
- Plaster the inside wall. Add water to a cement/sand mortar (1:3 mix) until it is just workable. The consistency of the mortar is critical. Experiment on a trial section first and note the water required for a successful mix. Start plastering at the bottom and push the plaster into the wire walls from the inside of the tank. Leave a space in the weld mesh for an overflow and any inlet pipe.
- Protect the walls with plastic sheeting.
- Splash the floor with water.

Day 4

- Remove the sheeting and wet the floor and walls. Keep the concrete wet throughout the day.
- Plaster a second layer of slightly wetter mortar on the inside wall. Remove the sacking and plaster a thin layer of mortar (< 10 mm thick) over the outside wall.

(Continued over)

Source: UNICEF, undated

Box 13.2 (continued)

- Cover both the inside and outside walls with plastic sheeting.
- Wet the floor.

Day 5

- Remove the sheeting and wet the floor and walls. Keep the concrete wet throughout the day.
- Cut the top overflow section of the weld mesh, bend outwards at 90° and wrap in chicken wire. Support and plaster the top of the overflow.
- Smooth a 10 mm thick layer of plaster on the outside wall and cover.
- Prepare the roof for plastering by sewing sacking to the underside of the roof mesh. This may be supported by poles as in a traditional hut.

Day 6

- Wet the floor and walls.
- Complete the inside wall: Plaster and smooth the inside wall to a total wall thickness of 50 mm. Make a mix of equal parts of cement and water. Smooth evenly onto the new plaster to within 150 mm of the floor.
- Complete the floor: Plaster the floor with cement mortar (1:3 mix) to create a slope towards the outlet. Finish the floor and remaining 150 mm of wall with a mix of equal parts of cement and water, and cover.

Day 7

- Position and plaster the roof: Place the roof reinforcement on the tank wall and bind it to the vertical wall wires. Cut an access hole (450 mm × 450 mm) in the roof wires. Support the roof on poles. Plaster the roof with cement mortar (1:3 mix) and cover. (See Figure 13.13).
- Cast an access cover in a shallow pit, reinforcing with weld mesh and chicken wire. Cure for a week.

Day 8

- Remove the roof sheeting and wet the roof, floor and walls.
- Plaster the roof (10 mm thick) and cover with plastic sheeting.
- The tank should now be strong enough to hold water.

Day 9

- Remove the roof poles and sacking. Plaster the underside of the roof. Plaster a piece of galvanized gauze over the overflow.

Afterwards

Keep the tank covered in plastic sheeting and/or fill it with water to cure for at least two weeks.

Steel tank repair

In an emergency, small leaks can be repaired with two-pack epoxy resin. Weld a steel plate over larger leaks and paint over the repair. Bullet holes in tanks can be temporarily repaired by sandwiching steel and rubber washers between a nut and bolt.

Concrete tank repair

Cracks in concrete tank walls should be repaired from the inside, if at all possible, by chiselling a cut in the cracked area and filling with a stiff cement mortar (1:3 mix by volume). Keep the repair wet for at least 24 hours before putting the tank back into operation. Remember to disinfect the tank if necessary.

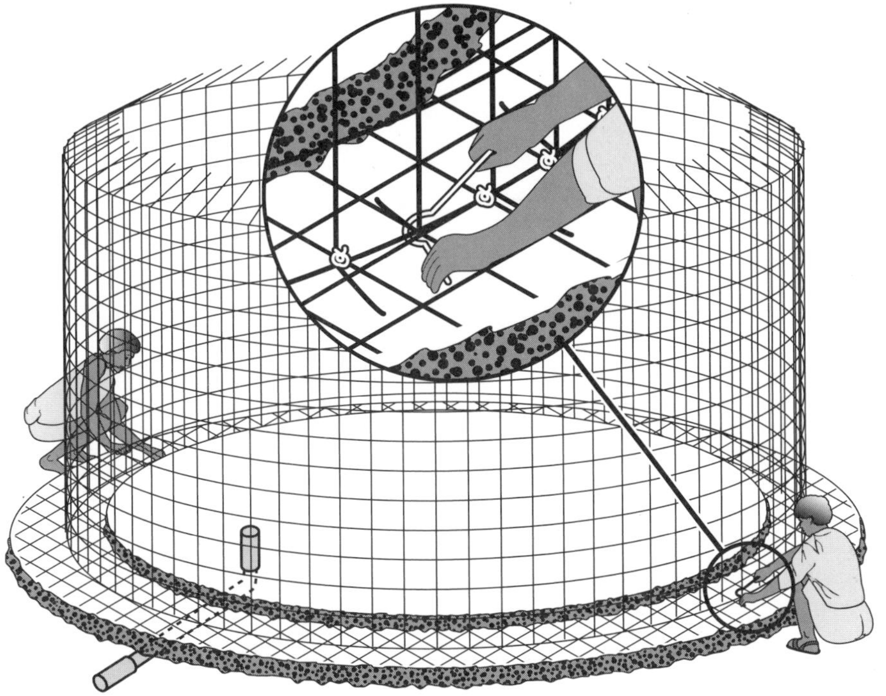

Figure 13.10 Foundation and wall preparation

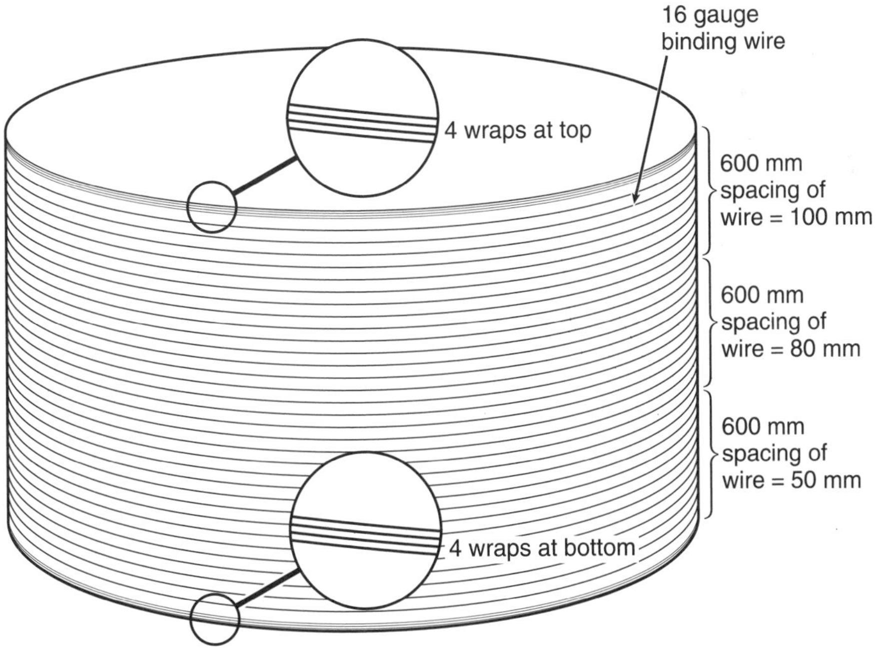

Figure 13.11 Wrapping the binding wire

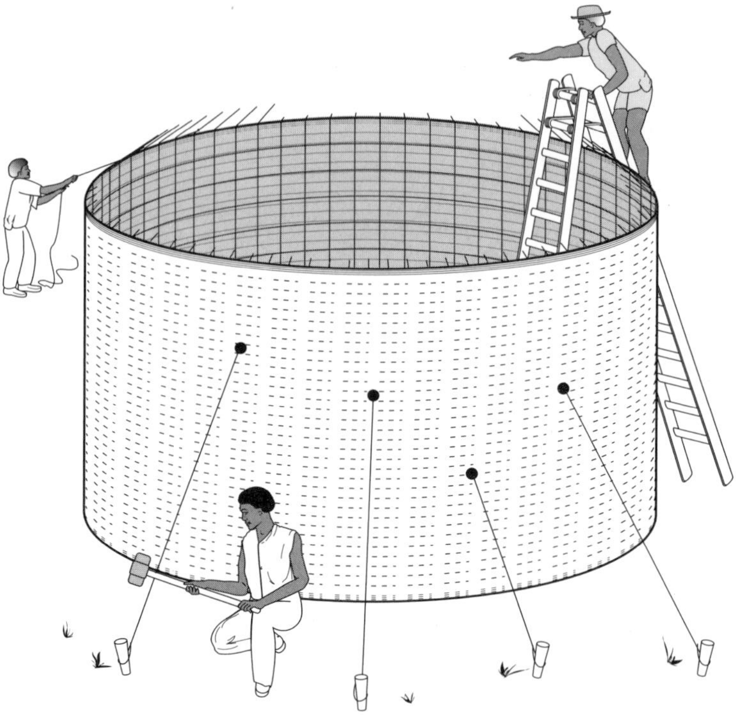

Figure 13.12 Pulling the tank into shape

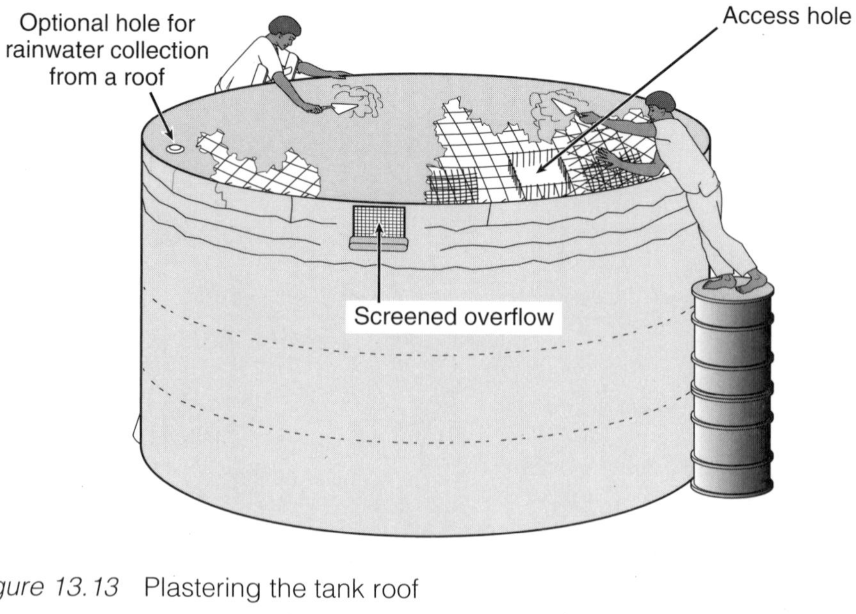

Figure 13.13 Plastering the tank roof

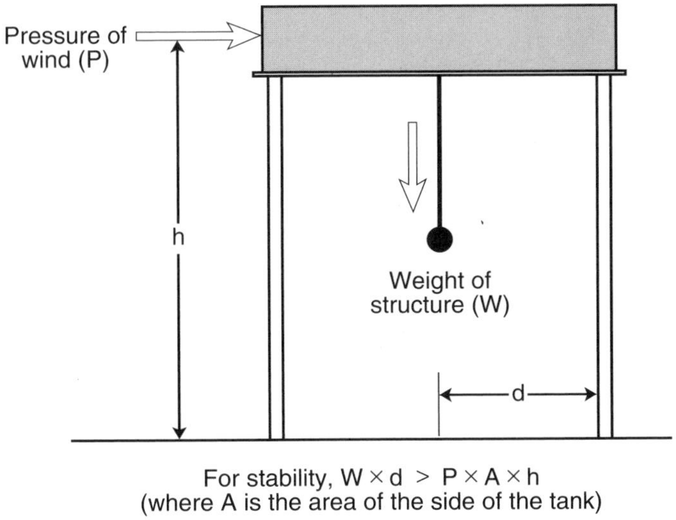

Figure 13.14 Overturning of water tower by wind pressure

If it is not possible to reach the inside of the tank easily, try undercutting (dovetailing) from the outside as follows:

- Drain to below the crack line.
- Chisel a cut in the cracked area as shown in Figure 13.18.
- Clean and wet the cut before applying a stiff mortar (1:3 mix).
- Keep the mortar wet for at least 24 hours before putting the tank back into operation.

Ferrocement tank repair

Repair cracks in ferrocement tank walls from the inside in a similar manner to that described above for concrete tanks. However, only cut away the plaster alongside the crack as far as the wire mesh.

13.2.9 Water tanks in freezing conditions

Ice can damage synthetic rubber tank linings and the structure of a tank. The snow load on the roof of a tank may also need to be taken into account. To keep water flowing and avoid ice damage to water tanks in freezing weather consider the following features (adapted from Buttle and Smith, 1999):

- Locate temporary water storage tanks, especially flexible fabric bladder and 'onion' tanks, inside buildings. It is likely that large buildings (e.g. warehouses) will also be needed for accommodation and, therefore, allow for tank space at the planning stage.
- Small volumes of water will lose heat more quickly than larger volumes and can be susceptible to snap freezes. Therefore, the larger the tank the better.
- Insulation will reduce heat loss and may prevent freezing. Spray-on polyurethane foam can be used to insulate a tank but this can be expensive

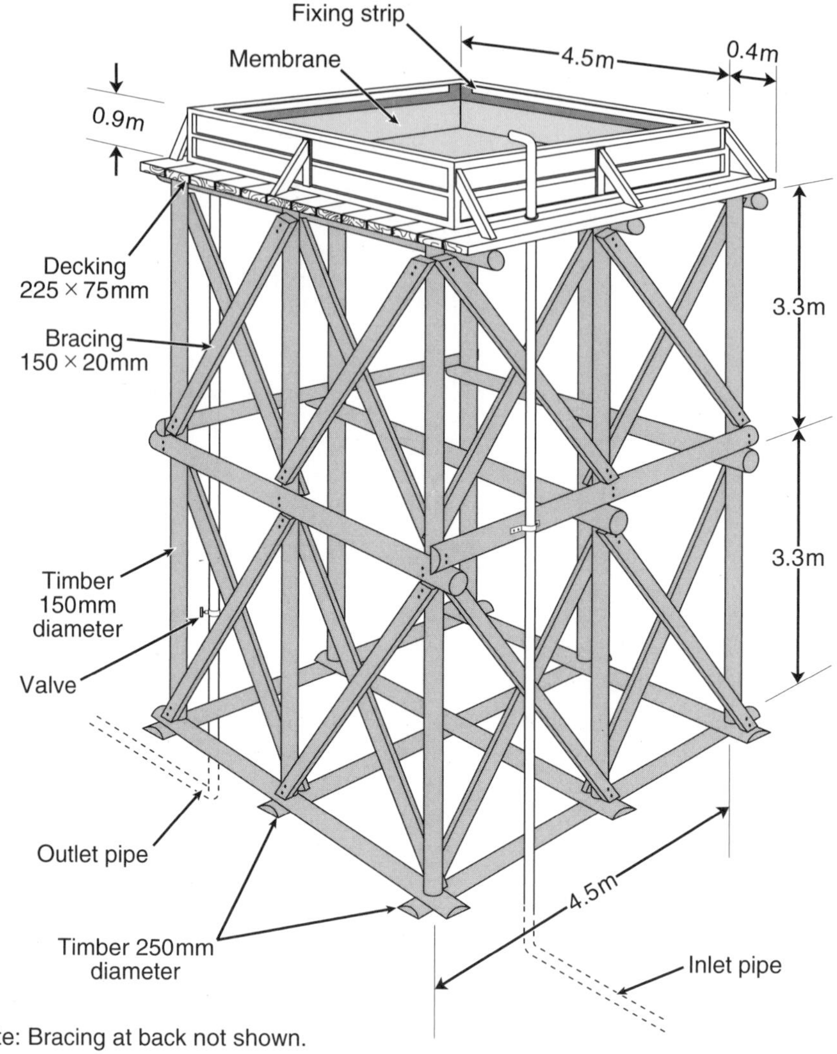

Figure 13.15 Improvised timber tower and membrane tank
British Crown Copyright, MOD, 1981b

compared to cut slabs of polystyrene insulation. Insulation must be kept dry as the insulation properties of wet material are severely reduced. Insulation on the outside of tanks must be protected from rain, wind, people and animals.

- Heat lost through the base of a tank may start to thaw frozen ground below. This can lead to structural instability and damage to the tank. Possible solutions to this problem are to mount the tank on a concrete base made from insulating concrete or gravel (i.e. with voids) or create air vents in the base at ground level to help the ground remain frozen.

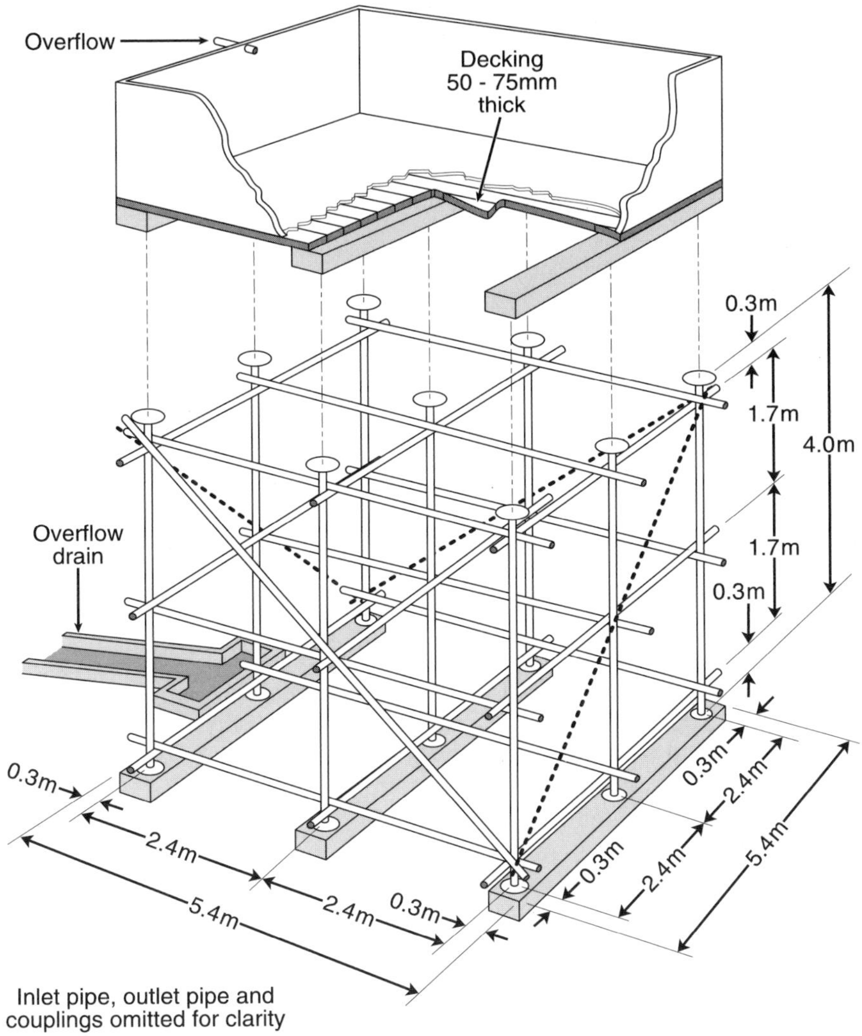

Figure 13.16 Tubular steel scaffold tower
British Crown Copyright, MOD, 1981b

- A tank roof may need to support snow. A steeply inclined roof will discourage the settling of snow and can be more easily brushed clear. Temporary tanks often have plastic sheet roofs which may not support the snow. It is preferable to make up a stronger steel sheet roof on which snow can settle. Snow is a good insulator and can help reduce heat loss.
- A rising and falling layer of surface ice can potentially damage internal fittings. Therefore, internal fittings (e.g. ladders) should be avoided.
- Protect valves inside insulated valve boxes (use polystyrene sheet) and, if possible, bury them beneath the frost penetration level. Box and insulate

Box 13.3 Calculation of weight of water tower to resist overturning by wind

Dynamic wind pressure, $P = 0.613\ V^2\ N/m^2$, where V = wind speed in m/s (1 mile per hour = 0.447m/s). Multiply V by 1.4 if situated in an exposed position (such as a hill top or where wind is funnelled down a narrow valley).

If wind speed is unknown then base estimates on a maximum wind pressure of 2.5 kN/m^2.

Example: What is the total weight of a water tower and tank needed to resist overturning by wind pressure if the tank tower is 3 m tall, the tank is 4.5 m square by 0.9 m high and the maximum wind speed is 120 mph (54 m/s)?

From formula above, wind pressure, $P = 1.8\ kN/m^2$

Weight of the structure required, W, (see Figure 13.14):

$$W > \frac{P \times A \times h}{d} = \frac{1.8 \times (4.5 \times 0.9) \times 3}{2.25} \qquad W > 9.72\ kN \text{ or } 991kg$$

(1 kg mass produces a force of 9.81 N)

Therefore, the structure must weigh at least 991 kg to prevent overturning in a wind of 120 mph.

exposed pipes or place them inside larger pipes with insulation placed in the annular space. Larger plastic pipe can be split lengthways, if necessary, to be placed around the smaller pipe to be insulated.

- Tapstands can be boxed and insulated. Place a valve at the base of the tapstand to drain at night.

13.3 Water treatment

A guide to the assessment of treatment requirements is given in Section 13.1 (see Table 13.2). This section gives details of the treatment processes:

- Pre-treatment aims to remove suspended solids in turbid water so that treatment to remove pathogens can be effective. Pre-treatment can also improve the potability of the water by removing unpalatable tastes. Pre-treatment includes abstraction, storage, sedimentation, aeration, roughing filtration and coagulation with settlement.
- Pathogen removal, which aims to remove all disease-causing organisms, includes slow sand filtration and chlorination.

13.3.1 Pre-treatment

Abstraction

Careful design of the abstraction system can reduce the amount of subsequent treatment required. At the very least, the method of abstraction should prevent

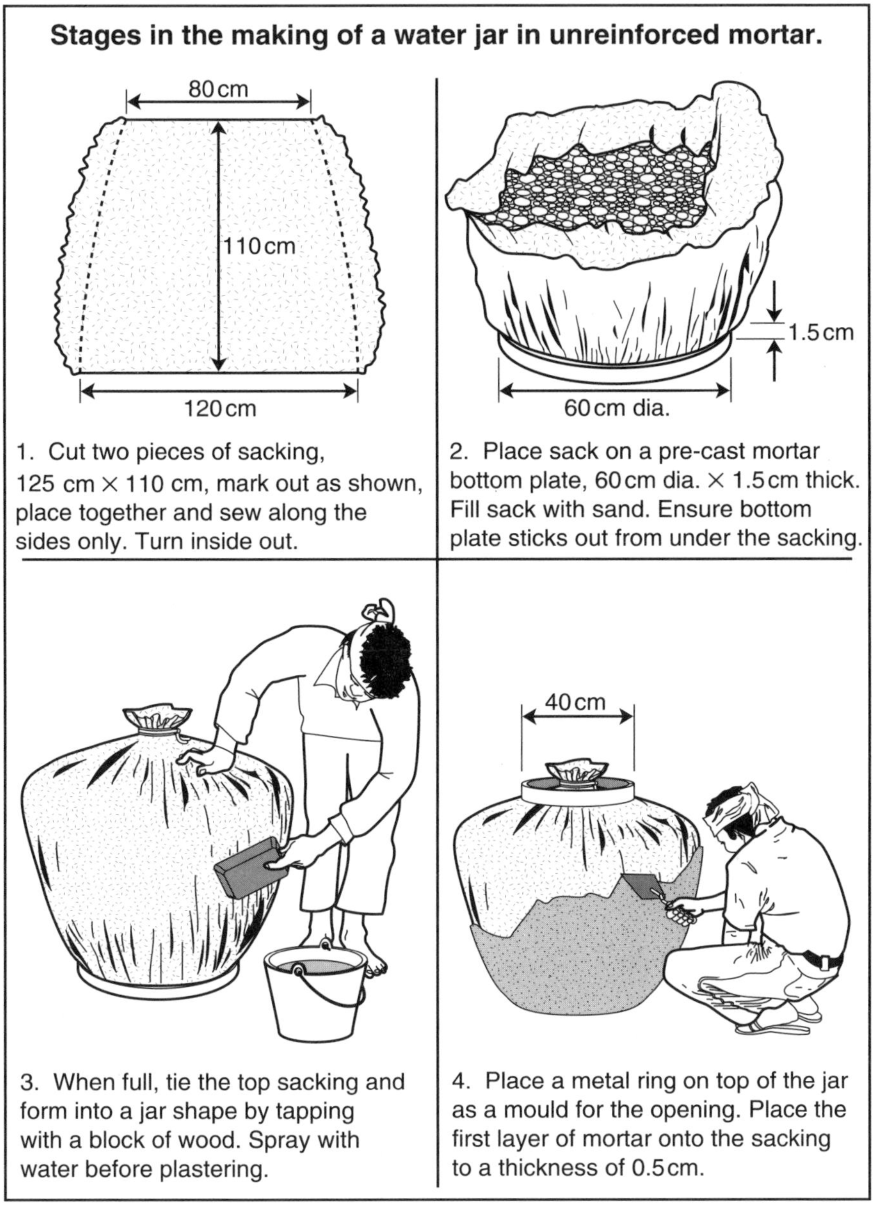
Stages in the making of a water jar in unreinforced mortar.
80 cm
110 cm
120 cm
1. Cut two pieces of sacking, 125 cm × 110 cm, mark out as shown, place together and sew along the sides only. Turn inside out.
1.5 cm
60 cm dia.
2. Place sack on a pre-cast mortar bottom plate, 60 cm dia. × 1.5 cm thick. Fill sack with sand. Ensure bottom plate sticks out from under the sacking.
3. When full, tie the top sacking and form into a jar shape by tapping with a block of wood. Spray with water before plastering.
40 cm
4. Place a metal ring on top of the jar as a mould for the opening. Place the first layer of mortar onto the sacking to a thickness of 0.5 cm.

Figure 13.17 Construction of household water storage jars (cont. over)

the ingress of silt into the system. The location of the abstraction point can affect both the level of suspended solids and the pathogen load in raw water. For example, siting the abstraction point upstream of a concentration of population can reduce the level of faecal contamination.

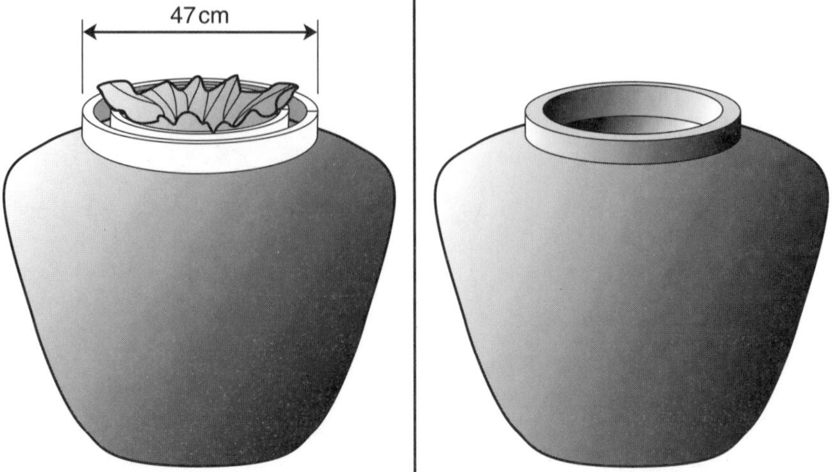

5. Add a second layer of mortar to give a total thickness of 1 cm. Check thickness of mortar by pushing in a nail. Form an opening at the top with a second metal ring.

6. Remove the sand, sacking and rings two days after plastering. Repair any defects with mortar. Paint the inside with cement slurry. Cure for two weeks.

The mortar is a 1:2 (cement:sand) dry mix, by volume.

A 250 litre jar requires 50 kg of sand and 25 kg cement.

Jars up to 1 m^3 have been made this way.
Unreinforced mortar jars can be considerably cheaper than clay jars.

The jars can be gradually filled starting four days after curing:

1st day of use – not more than half full
2nd day of use – not more than three-quarters full
3rd day of use – the jar can be filled.

A cover should be fitted to the jar when in use.

Figure 13.17 (cont.)
From Pickford, 1991, and Watt, 1978

Infiltration wells and galleries can reduce turbidity by filtration through the stream bed or river bank (see 12.2.2). It is only practical to construct a river bed infiltration gallery during periods of low flow in the river. Where an infiltration gallery is not immediately possible, consider the following phases:

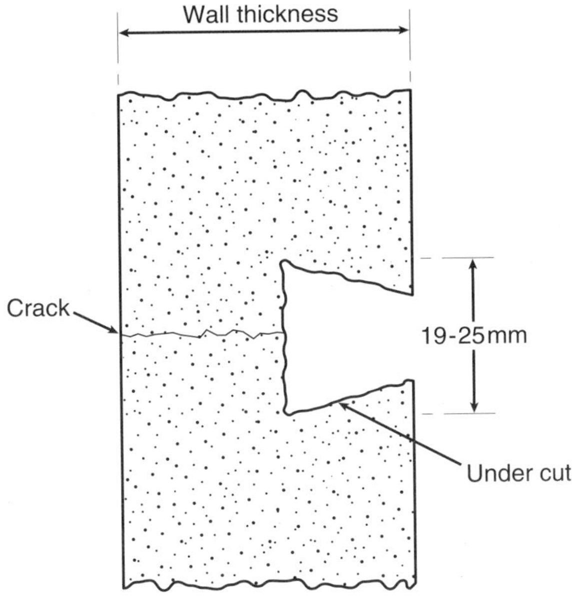

Figure 13.18 Repairing cracks in concrete tank walls

- Initial emergency treatment of pumped raw surface water with a coagulant to settle suspended solids followed by chlorination (see below and 13.3.3).
- In the dry season, continue the above treatment during the construction of an infiltration gallery.
- Complete the infiltration gallery before the river floods again. If working correctly, water from an infiltration gallery will only need chlorination before final distribution.

Storage

Storage can provide a reserve supply of water and is also a form of treatment. During storage:

- Turbidity levels may go down because of the natural settlement of suspended solids.
- Water quality can improve through the natural die-off of pathogenic bacteria.
- During periods when the raw water is highly turbid, stored water of lower turbidity can be supplied for treatment until the quality of the source water improves. Storage also attenuates the peaks in turbidity which might otherwise overwhelm the downstream treatment processes.

Connect raw water tanks in series to maximize residence time, and therefore settling time. Additional connections can be made to isolate tanks for cleaning or repair when necessary.

Draw water from a high level in a settlement tank, where water quality is better, using a floating off-take.

The sun's ultraviolet radiation will have some limited effect in reducing bacteria in open storage tanks. However, in the presence of organic matter and soluble nutrients such as nitrogen and phosphorus, sunlight will also encourage the growth of algae. The development of algae during storage can be a hindrance to effective water treatment. Observe the extent of algae in local ponds and river pools to assess likely algal growth in open tanks. If necessary, limit the growth of algae by covering tanks.

Details on different types of storage tanks can be found in Section 13.2.

Aeration

Tastes and smells are commonly due to the presence of hydrogen sulphide in groundwater or to decaying organic and bacterial matter in surface water. These tastes and smells can be reduced by aeration. Simple arrangements should maximize the air/water contact surface area and contact time. Arrange for gravity fed and pumped sources to discharge in a spray pattern into a tank. Where there is sufficient head, let the water fall down a cascade of steps or perforated tiles. This will also bring iron and manganese out of solution. The resulting particles can be settled out.

Plain sedimentation

Plain sedimentation removes some suspended particles in water by gravity without the use of chemicals.

In an emergency, it may not be possible, or desirable, to construct purpose-made sedimentation tanks. Several temporary storage tanks are often used on a rotational basis and the sludge removed periodically. The following is a guide to the design of a plain sedimentation tank and can be adapted to other forms of storage tank.

Design Sedimentation tanks either operate continuously or on a batch treatment basis.

A continuous flow sedimentation tank is designed to slow and spread the flow of water to allow time for particles to settle before the clarified water overflows an outlet weir to the next stage of treatment.

In the batch process, a tank is filled and the particles allowed to settle before the clarified water is drawn off. Further batches of water are treated until the sludge accumulating at the bottom of the tank needs to be removed.

The volume and depth of a sedimentation tank should allow for the build up of sludge. Conventional sedimentation tanks often have a mechanical means of de-sludging. In the absence of mechanical cleaning, batch treatment tanks must be run in parallel so that one tank can be taken out of service for the manual removal of sludge whilst the others continue operating.

The settling velocity of a particle in water depends on its relative density, size and the temperature of the water. As raw water particles exhibit a range of settling velocities, tank designs should ideally be based on local settlement field tests. In an emergency, it is only possible to carry out simple settlement tests in transparent parallel sided jars or a measuring cylinder. To carry out a settlement test (jar test):

Stir the sample of water to be tested, pour into a jar and start timing. A layer of clear water may form or the water generally becomes clearer. Time how long it takes for the water to clear sufficiently for the next stage of treatment – filtration or chlorination. The settling velocity is the depth of clear water divided by the settling time.

Jar tests can only give a rough indication of settlement rates. The rate of settlement is, in any case, influenced by settlement tank design and local environmental factors.

A larger settlement tank may be required in winter than in summer for two reasons. Firstly, increased rainfall will wash sediment into surface water sources, increasing the sludge load. Secondly, viscosity of water decreases with temperature resulting in a slower settling velocity in cold water.

Calculate the area of plain sedimentation tank required (m^2) by dividing the design flow rate, Q (m^3/day) by the settling velocity (m/day) as calculated in the jar test.

A commonly used term is the 'surface loading' which is equivalent to the settling velocity. It is defined as the ratio between the influent flow rate and the surface area of the tank: m^3/day/m^2 (This is also expressed as m^3/m^2/day or m/day).

Table 13.8 gives guideline design criteria for rectangular plain sedimentation tanks. For tanks with sloping sides, take the design width as the width at half the depth. Figure 13.19 shows a sedimentation tank excavated in the ground. (See 13.2.3 for details on the construction and lining of ground tanks.)

Table 13.8 Guideline design criteria for rectangular plain sedimentation tanks

Design parameter	*Guide range of values*
Detention time, hours	0.5–3
Surface loading, m^3/m^2/day	20–60
Depth of tank, m	1.5–2.5
Length : width ratio	4 : 1–6 : 1
Length : depth ratio	5 : 1–20 : 1

Adapted from: Schulz and Okun, 1992

Coagulation and flocculation

Many raw waters contain colloidal matter (particularly clays) in suspension. Colloids will not settle readily by plain sedimentation alone as their specific gravity is similar to that of water. Therefore, the colloidal particles must be encouraged to combine to form heavier particles before they can settle. This process is called coagulation and flocculation.

Colloidal particles can be brought together by the addition of chemicals or natural coagulant aids to form flocs of sufficient specific weight to settle. Suitable chemicals which cause the particles to agglomerate are called coagulants and the floc-forming process is called flocculation. The resulting flocs must be allowed to settle as a sludge. This sludge must subsequently be removed and disposed of safely.

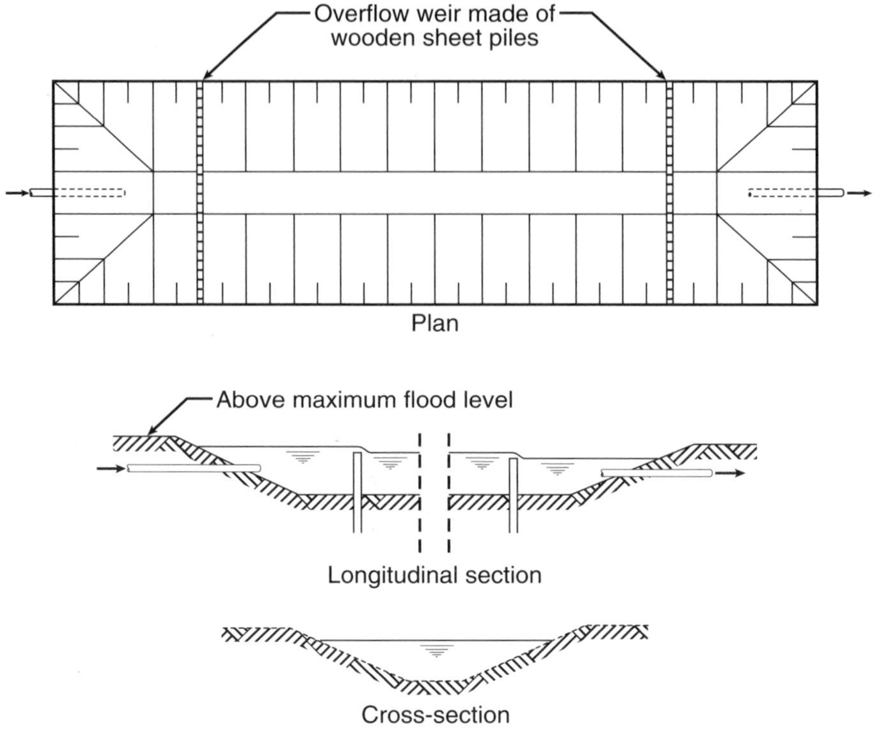

Figure 13.19 Excavated sedimentation tank
Source: IRC, 1983

In an emergency water supply, the process of coagulation can be instituted very rapidly (in a matter of hours), provided the chemicals are available. Therefore, where raw waters are turbid, coagulation should be considered for the initial phase of the emergency. However, because coagulation relies on chemicals and has associated problems of safe sludge disposal, plan to replace coagulation with other methods of turbidity reduction (such as the use of roughing filters) as soon as possible.

Chemical coagulants The most common coagulant is alum (aluminium sulphate, $Al_2(SO_4)_3.nH_2O$). The effective pH range for alum is between 6 and 8. Iron salts, such as ferric chloride, $FeCl_3$, and ferric sulphate, $Fe_2(SO_4)_3$, are effective above pH 4.5 up to about pH 9 but they are not as widely available as alum. Figure 13.20 shows the pH range and relative dosage requirements for alum and ferric sulphate, applied to a specific sample of water containing 50 mg/l of the clay, kaolin. For any given water, the optimum conditions will vary depending on factors such as pH, turbidity, chemical composition of the water, type of coagulant, temperature and the mixing conditions.

The alkalinity of the raw water can be increased by the addition of lime, $Ca(OH)_2$ or soda ash, Na_2CO_3, but this complicates the process and is not recommended in an emergency unless absolutely necessary. An alternative, if suitable materials are available, is to use a contact bed. Arrange for the water

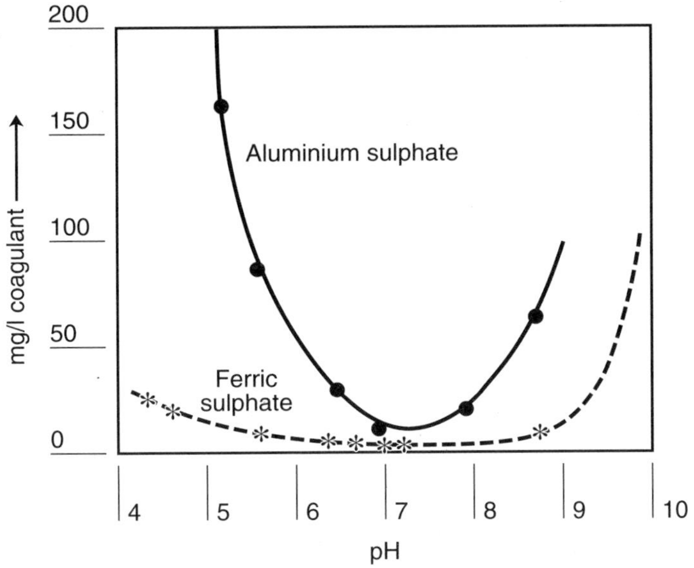

Points on the curves represent the coagulant dosage required to reduce the turbidity to half its original value.

Figure 13.20 Comparisons of pH range and coagulant dose for the coagulation of 50mg/l kaolin with aluminium sulphate and ferric sulphate
Source: AWWA, 1971

to flow through a bed or along a channel of granular alkaline material (such as chalk, limestone or marble chips). Include a system of periodic flushing to remove sediment.

Jar test The optimum coagulant dose will depend on the nature of the raw water. The optimum dose can be estimated by carrying out jar tests. Adjustments will need to be made in the light of operational experience.

To carry out a jar test to determine the correct dosing concentration for alum:

- Make up a 1% (10 000 mg/l) alum solution by dissolving 10 g of granular alum in one litre of clean water (one litre of granular alum weighs approximately 1100 g).
- Pour 1% alum solution and raw water into test jars to produce the required concentrations of coagulant. Initial recommended starting concentrations are 50, 60, 70, 80, 90, 100 mg/l (i.e. 5, 6, 7, 8, 9, 10 ml of 1% alum solution for each litre of raw water.
- Prepare to take turbidity readings for each jar at test times of 0, 2.5, 5, 10, 15, 25 and 40 minutes.
- Stir briskly with a dining fork for the length of time rapid mixing takes place in the full size system.

- Stir gently for the same length of time the water is resident in the settlement tank/clarifier. This may be for thirty minutes, or so. Periodic stirring will be necessary to keep the flocs gently moving. Allow to settle and then take samples from the top of each jar to measure turbidity.
- Plot turbidity results on a graph with 'Turbidity' (in NTU) as the y-axis and 'Alum dose' (in mg/l) as the x-axis. Plot for each 'Test run time' interval.
- The graph with the lowest turbidity value indicates the optimum coagulant concentration. If the highest or lowest concentration tested appears to be the optimum value, repeat the jar test which includes this value in the middle of the range of concentrations tested.
- Repeat the test to eliminate experimental errors.
- Test pH of the raw and product water to determine if pH adjustment is necessary. Use the jar test to determine the lime or acid dosing rates required for adjustment. Lime should be added to raise the pH into the optimum range of 6.5 to 7.5 for alum. Alternatively, if no lime is available, or for highly alkaline water, use extra alum to compensate but monitor alum carry over in the treated water. WHO recommends a maximum residual of 0.2 mg/l of aluminium sulphate in treated water although excessive aluminium should not be a major threat to health in the short term.

Although the jar test uses a 1% solution, dosing is normally made using 10% alum solution. This may have to be adjusted for larger or smaller volumes of water.

Natural and synthetic coagulants Natural and synthetic substances can aid the coagulation process and reduce the dose of primary coagulant required. Natural coagulant aids have traditionally been used in the household treatment of water (as is alum rock in some parts of the world) and in conventional treatment works. The crushed seeds of several plants have been found effective as both a coagulant aid and as a primary coagulant. Table 13.9 indicates dosing levels for three natural coagulants and alum. A potential disadvantage of natural water treatment aids is that they may provide organic matter for the growth of bacteria.

Table 13.9 Dosing levels for three natural coagulants and alum

Country	*Source of water*	*Raw water turbidity (NTU)*	*Alum dose mg/l*	*Residual turbidity (NTU)*	*Natural coagulant mg/l*	*Residual turbidity (NTU)*
Sudan	Hafir: pH 8.5	470	200	11 after 1 h	*Moringa oleifera* 200	16 after 1 h
Sudan	Nile river: pH 8.4	75	40	3 after 1 h	*Moringa stenopetala* 5	8 after 1 h
India	Yamuna river: pH 8.2	2200	65	40 after 2 h	*Strychnos potatorum* 3 to 3.5	16 to 17 after 1 h

Source: Jahn, 1981

Various synthetic polyelectrolytes are available which can be used as primary coagulants or coagulant aids. Their advantages include:

- Effective across a wide pH range.
- Low effective dosage (1–10 mg/l).
- Replacement or reduction in dosage of conventional inorganic coagulants such as alum.
- Lower sludge volumes.

A disadvantage is that synthetic polyelectrolytes are generally only available in a liquid form. In an emergency, the cost and convenience of freighting liquid synthetic polyelectrolyte must be assessed against the freighting of larger quantities of solid alum.

Stages in coagulation and flocculation: 1. rapid mixing; 2. flocculation Both hydraulic and mechanical methods of mixing and flocculation can be used. Hydraulic methods are preferred in an emergency as they do not rely on machinery or a power source.

1. Rapid mixing

The process of floc formation is very quick and therefore the coagulant must be dispersed rapidly and uniformly throughout the raw water. Dose at points of turbulent flow using one of the following methods:

- Dose at the overflow of weirs.
- Drip feed the coagulant from a drum into a T-piece pipe fitting through which the incoming water discharges into the flocculation tank.
- If a pump is used to deliver water to the flocculation tanks, the solution can be fed into the suction side of the pump from a header tank.

Further chemical dosing methods are described in 13.3.4.

2. Flocculation

Flocculation is the gentle stirring of the water to encourage the formation and settlement of flocs following rapid mixing. The guideline flocculation velocity of the water is in the range 0.1–0.3 m/s. Detention time is in the order of 30 minutes. In an emergency, if there is no time to build a purpose designed flocculator, experience has shown that swirling flow induced in circular tanks by directing the incoming water around the periphery can provide the gentle motion necessary for flocculation.

In a batch process, each tank must be regularly taken out of service for removal of sludge and cleaning. Therefore, ensure there are sufficient tanks in parallel to maintain throughput when a tank is taken out of service.

Upflow clarifier Oxfam and the University of Surrey have jointly developed a coiled pipe flocculator and upflow clarifier which uses standard emergency water equipment to improve on the batch system of chemically assisted sedimentation (Figure 13.21). A coil of pipe provides the conditions necessary to induce floc formation. The coagulant is dosed through the suction side of a

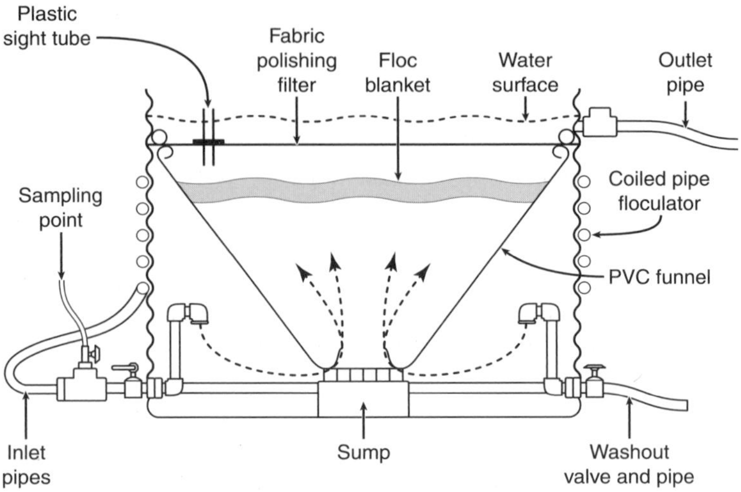

Figure 13.21 Upflow clarifier
Source: Oxfam, 2000

pump in which it is rapidly mixed. The water passes through two parallel coils of 75 mm layflat hose, each 30 m long coiled around the sedimentation tank. The pipes act as flocculators by gently stirring the water as it passes through the coils. Some flocs should be forming as the water enters the tank in which an upflow clarifier is built. The slow mixing water drops down to the bottom of the tank before rising inside a funnel. As the water rises up the widening funnel the velocity drops and the point will be reached whereby the upthrust on the floc will be balanced by the effect of gravity. The floc will stop moving and a floc blanket will be formed at this level. Further flocs will be trapped and thicken the blanket. Water passes through the blanket and a fabric polishing filter before leaving through the tank outlet. Eventually, the system must be drained down when the blanket becomes too thick. The polishing filter is periodically replaced and hosed down.

The clarifier must be operated to prevent breakthrough of the floc blanket and visual checking is important. Where possible, the clarifier is operated on a continuous basis overnight. If operated on a batch basis then the floc blanket will collapse and will need to be reformed. The system needs periodic desludging through the outlets at the bottom of the tank.

Sludge disposal The sludge should first be dewatered and dried before final disposal. Ensure that water from this process is safely drained away from any water sources. Sludge accumulated through the use of alum has a high metal content. In emergency situations, sludge disposal is likely to consist of dumping on the ground surface or in landfill. Whatever the disposal method care must be taken to ensure that the sludge does not contaminate water sources or agricultural land. Over a long period, sludge disposal may become a serious logistical and environmental problem. If this is likely to be the case, then alternatives to chemical coagulation should be considered, such as the use of roughing filters.

Roughing filtration

Roughing filtration (RF) is the removal of suspended solids by the passage of water through relatively coarse media (5–25 mm). Its main advantage is that it does not require the use of chemicals, and the resulting sludge, being free from the metals that are present for example in alum sludge, is relatively disposable. Its disadvantage is that it takes some time to install. Because of the time factor, it may be necessary to use coagulation with sedimentation as an immediate emergency measure whilst roughing filters are set up.

Despite the name of the process, the main removal mechanism is sedimentation. The coarse media offer a large surface area on which particles accumulate and, as the accumulated matter increases in size, it settles to the tank bottom. Roughing filters are divided into vertical-flow (downflow and upflow) filters and horizontal-flow filters.

The data that is available on roughing filters has mostly been collected from low-cost rural schemes. There is a wide variation in performance, depending on filter design and raw water characteristics. A general point to bear in mind is that the bigger a roughing filter, the longer it is likely to last without cleaning. However, the time to build a bigger filter will be longer and the volume of media needed will be greater.

Where roughing filters are being installed to replace coagulation, make an estimate of how many are needed, but leave provision for extra modules. If the performance of the first filters is not adequate, final clarification of the water can still be done using coagulants, until the required roughing filter units are installed.

Horizontal-flow roughing filter In a horizontal-flow roughing filter (HRF), water flows through a sequence of coarse, medium and fine filter material to discharge finally over an outlet weir. Periodic drainage of the filter will cause sediment to be washed to the filter bottom and flushed out with the accumulated sludge. (See Box 13.4 for an example of a horizontal roughing filter used in a refugee camp in Sudan.)

Designing a horizontal-flow roughing filter:

An HRF is usually required to produce water suitable for further treatment by slow sand filtration or chlorination. In each case, for the subsequent treatment to be effective, the water from an HRF must have a suspended solids concentration of 5 ppm, or less. Table 13.10 gives guidelines for the design of two filters, for raw waters above and below 150 ppm suspended solids, to give a filtered water of 5 ppm. The characteristics of the raw water strongly influence HRF performance, and in non-emergency situations pilot tests should first be carried out to determine the design parameters.

Filtration rate is measured in terms of the surface loading (also called overflow rate).

$$\text{Filtration rate or surface loading} = \frac{\text{flow}}{\text{filter surface area}} \quad \frac{(m^3/h)}{(m^2)}$$

This can be expressed as $m^3/m^2/h$ or m/h. Table 13.10 gives guideline figures on surface loading.

Table 13.10 Guideline figures for designing horizontal-flow roughing filters

Suspended solids concentration of raw water	*High* > *150 ppm*	*Low* <*150 ppm*
Filtration rate (m/h)	0.5–0.75	0.75–1.0
Individual filter lengths for grains with diameter:		
25–15 mm	3–4 m	2–3 m
15–10 mm	2–3 m	1–3 m
10–5 mm	1–2 m	1–2 m

Source: Wegelin, 1994

Box 13.4 Horizontal roughing filters (HRFs) in a refugee camp in Sudan

In 1985, Swiss Disaster Relief constructed a water treatment plant for Fau 5 refugee camp in Sudan. Raw water, of turbidity 1000–2000 NTU, was pumped from an irrigation canal to two sedimentation tanks which reduced turbidity by about a half. A combination of four HRFs further reduced turbidity to 5–20 NTU. The filtered water was then chlorinated before distribution.

The sedimentation tanks and roughing filters were dug in the local black cotton soil. Bags were filled with the excavated soil and used to form raised inclined tank walls. Each tank was then lined with plastic sheeting. Perforated pipes, for washing and drainage, were installed before backfilling with graded gravel as shown in Figure 13.22.

The treatment plant was constructed in six weeks by 100 labourers and a supervisor, using basic tools and the minimum of imported materials.

Table 13.11 HRF design figures for Fau 5 refugee camp, Sudan

Design capacity	240 m^3/day
Planned number of refugees	20 000
Maximum raw water turbidity	2000 NTU
Number of HRF units	4
Filtration rate	0.75 m/h
Individual filter lengths:	
coarse gravel	4 m
medium gravel	4 m
fine gravel	2 m
Filter width	2 m
Water depth	1.2 m

At least three sizes of medium are recommended for efficient filtration. The smallest size should not be less than 5 mm, otherwise high head losses and difficulty in cleaning will be experienced. The shape and texture of the media have little apparent influence on filter efficiency and a wide range of materials can be used. Examples of filter media include: gravel, broken burnt bricks, plastic rings or chippings, plastic matrix packs and charcoal. Vegetable matter has been used (coconut and palm fibre) but decomposition over time may be a problem.

Cover the filter chambers and/or keep the water level 100 mm below the top of the filter media to prevent the growth of algae.

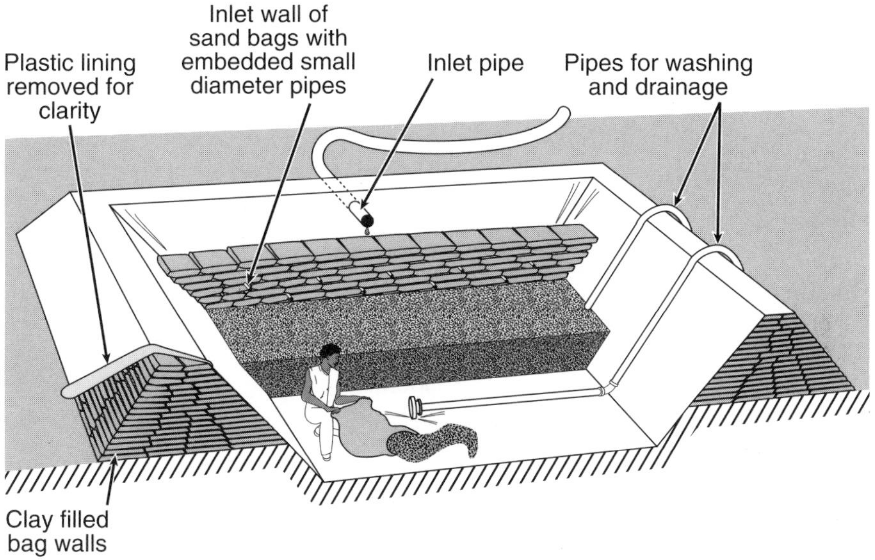

Figure 13.22 Cross-section of an excavated horizontal-flow roughing filter

Source: Wegelin, 1986

Vertical-flow roughing filters There are two ways of arranging the media for vertical-flow roughing filters:

- In series: separate tanks (or compartments) for each size of medium arranged in series.
- In layers: each size of medium layered on top of another within the same tank, in layers of equal thickness.

Separate compartments give better overall performance, but they are more costly, time consuming and complex to set up.

The water may enter the bottom of the tank and flow up through successive layers of media producing an upflow roughing filter in which the coarse media are in the bottom layer. Alternatively, water may enter through the top of the tank and flow down through the media; this is a downflow roughing filter in which the coarse media are in the top layer.

Oxfam have developed a vertical-flow roughing filter utilising a tank of 10.5 m^3 initial capacity (Oxfam tank T11) shown in Figure 13.23. The upflow design was chosen due to the cleaning efficiency which uses gravity flow to backwash accumulated solids. The number of roughing filters required depends upon raw

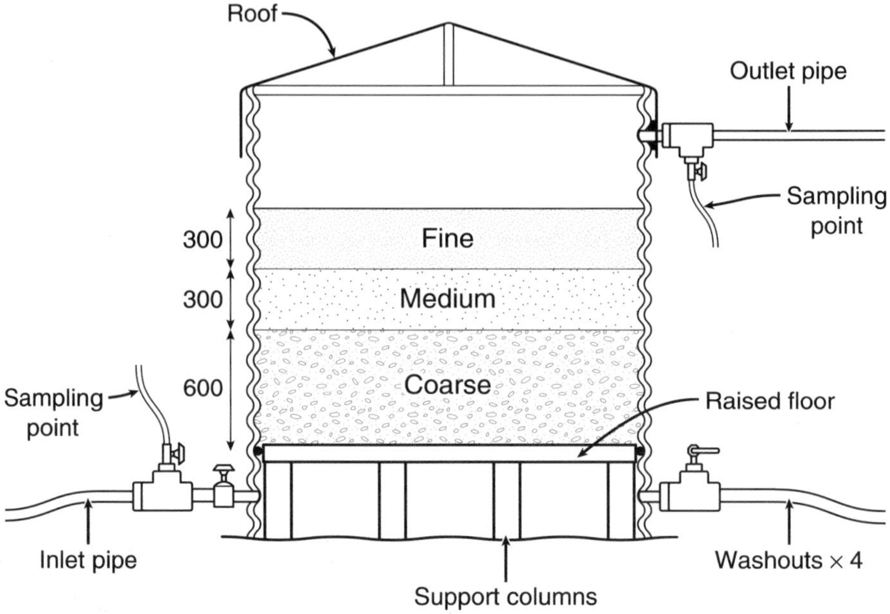

Figure 13.23 A vertical-flow roughing filter
Source: Oxfam, 2000

water quality and the production capacity. For optimum performance, the filters should be run at a maximum surface loading of 0.6 m^3/m^2/hour (m/h). This translates into a flow rate of 3.2 m^3/h for the T11 tank.

Roughing filters should aim to produce water with a turbidity less than 20 NTU if water is being passed through a slow sand filter or less than 5 NTU if it is to be chlorinated. Figures for a roughing filter based on three layers in one tank are suggested in Table 13.12. A roughing filter built of three layers in one tank has a removal efficiency of 85 per cent at 0.3 m^3/m^2/h and 75 per cent at 0.6 m^3/m^2/h. Three roughing filters in series, with one media size in each tank, have a removal efficiency of 87–92 per cent when operated at 0.3–0.6 m^3/m^2/h, in the turbidity range of 30–500 NTU (Oxfam, 2000). These figures can only be used as a rough guide for a particular application and pilot tests are recommended to develop the optimum arrangement.

A small-scale upward flow roughing filter contained in a 200 litre drum, to supply small institutions or a relief workers' compound, is shown in Figure 13.27.

Table 13.12 Tentative design guidelines for an upflow roughing filter

Media size	*Grading*	*Depth of layer*
5–10 mm	Fine	300 mm
10–15/20 mm	Medium	300 mm
15/20–25/30 mm	Coarse	600 mm

Source: Oxfam, 2000

13.3.2 Filtration

The two main types of filter are slow sand filters (SSF) and rapid filters. They are compared in Table 13.13.

Table 13.13 A comparison of slow sand filters and rapid filters

	Slow sand filter (SSF)	*Rapid filter*
Filter medium	Fine	Coarse
Filtration rate	Low: 0.1–0.3 m/h	High: 5–15 m/h
Mechanisms for the removal of impurities	Sedimentation, adsorption, straining, chemical and microbiological processes	Sedimentation, adsorption, straining, chemical and microbiological processes
Main mechanism for removal of impurities	Microbiological	Physical mechanisms, especially adsorption
Principal application	Treatment of low turbidity water (< 20 NTU) for distribution as potable water – post-chlorination may still be carried out	Treatment of low turbidity water – chlorination is required before distribution. Treatment of high turbidity raw water and following flocculation and sedimentation. Removal of iron and manganese
Principal advantages	Substantially reduces pathogenic bacteria, viruses and cysts, to produce a potable water without further treatment. No machinery required	Relatively small and compact
Principal disadvantages	Can only effectively treat low turbidity water	Cannot produce a potable water without further treatment. Backwashing water required to clean filter – this usually involves pumps

The drawbacks associated with a rapid filter make it generally unsuitable for emergency use. Therefore, only slow sand filtration is considered in this book. If the raw water is of high turbidity, it will be necessary to include some form of pre-treatment before passing the water to a slow sand filter.

Slow sand filtration is efficient at removing pathogens from water. Bacteria, viruses, protozoal cysts and helminth eggs are all substantially reduced. However, in an emergency, it is recommended that filtered water be chlorinated as a safety precaution.

Design and operation

In an emergency, the slow sand filtration pack supplied by Oxfam uses storage tanks (described in 13.2.4) which are adapted for use as a slow sand filter water treatment package. The following description of slow sand filtration will refer to the Oxfam package, but the basic processes involved are the same for all slow sand filters.

Operational experience The following data and comments have been obtained from operational experience of slow sand filters for refugee water supplies.

- A sand filter package can be erected by unskilled personnel and be running within 3–4 weeks. The critical time factor is the supply and preparation of sand – to speed up the process, sand preparation can be started even before the tanks are designed and ordered.
- Turbidities of water entering the SSF should be less than 20 NTU. Turbidities of up to 200 NTU can be tolerated for only a few days. If the turbidity of the incoming water is above 20 NTU, take measures to reduce turbidity level (roughing filters or coagulation).
- Storing raw water in tanks before filtering gives a significant reduction in turbidity and pathogen counts due to sedimentation and die-off.
- A properly operated slow sand filter gives safe, potable water but chlorination following SSF is recommended as a safety precaution.
- Recontamination of the treated water from the SSF can occur if any of the tanks or containers used to hold this water (including domestic containers) are not kept clean. Periodic chlorination of tanks used to store treated water may be needed.
- The filter run time (time between cleaning) varies widely, depending on the raw water turbidity (which varies according to the seasons) and filtration rate. Typical filter run times are between 2 and 20 weeks.
- Algae in the filter tank water above the sand does not necessarily adversely affect the operation of the filter.
- A tank must be drained completely when the flow is stopped for more than a day, otherwise anaerobic conditions in the filter sand are encouraged. This can give a lasting bad taste to the water even after resumption of flow. Avoid lengthy stoppages and draining of the filter if at all possible.
- One day operator and one night operator are required to operate each filter package.
- Operators must be trained to maintain a constant flow rate.

The Oxfam filter kit used to be operated with two filters in parallel so that a continuous supply could be maintained whilst one of the filters was being cleaned. However, the use of improved geotextile filter fabric on top of the sand reduces the cleaning interval and the time taken for filters to recover their biological treatment ability. Therefore, the old arrangement with two parallel lines has now been changed to have a single filter line. This arrangement is only acceptable, however, if there is a regular supply of chlorine for disinfecting the product water for the period immediately after filter cleaning when the filter is 'recovering'.

Design Figure 13.24 shows the main elements of the package, incorporating tanks in series: for receiving the raw water; for filtration and for receiving the treated water.

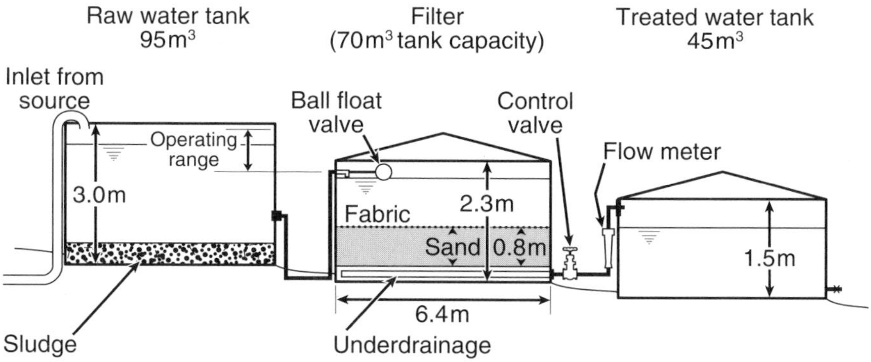

Figure 13.24 The Oxfam slow sand filtration treatment package

- If the raw water tanks are fed by pumps, try to arrange for a generous operating range (by locating raw water tanks at a higher level than the filter tank). This range should be calculated to give a convenient frequency and duration of pumping, plus a reserve for breakdowns and maintenance.
- Note the height of the inlet to the treated water tank (Figure 13.24), which should be slightly higher than the top of the filter sand – this helps prevent the filter being accidentally drained if the raw water tank is emptied. The difference in level between the water surface in the filter and the pipe inlet to the treated water tank is the head that drives the water through the filter. The flow rate through the filter can be controlled by throttling the control valve or by adjusting the level of the inlet pipe to the treated water tank.
- The sizing of the tanks required will depend on several factors:
  Raw water tank size – operating range, turbidity and settling rate.
  Filter size and number – filtration rate and water demand.
  Treated water tank size – contact time required for chlorination (see 13.3.3) and whether storage is to be provided here or further along the distribution system (see 13.1.1 for a more detailed discussion).
- Note that the standard Oxfam water treatment pack is designed to supply 3200 l/h. It includes two 95 000 litre raw water tanks and two 70 000 litre filter tanks with fittings but it does NOT include the treated water tanks. These must be ordered separately.
- The Oxfam SSF has been uprated to a surface loading (see below) of 0.2 $m^3/m^2/h$ to produce 3200 l/h with a single line filter.

The filtration process The most important mechanism for the removal of impurities is the formation of a biologically active layer of micro-organisms at the top of the filter bed – the *Schmutzdecke*. This thin layer is formed by the retention of particulate matter and starts to break down pathogens into inorganic compounds such as carbon dioxide, nitrates, sulphates and phosphates. The complete process involves the migration of bacteria into the sand layer to a depth of about 0.5 m. Therefore, the thickness of the filter bed should not be less than about 0.6 m for the process to be totally effective.

The filtration rate must be low enough to allow time for the microbiological processes to take place. Filtration rate is expressed as surface loading.

$$\text{Filtration rate or surface loading} = \frac{\text{flow}}{\text{filter surface area}} \quad \frac{(\text{m}^3/\text{h})}{(\text{m}^2)}$$

This can be expressed as $m^3/m^2/h$ or m/h.

The maximum recommended filtration rate is 0.3 m/h. Generally, the lower the rate, the more effective is the treatment and a rate of 0.2 m/h should give satisfactory results. The suspended solids strained out of the water on and near the filter surface increase the resistance to flow. Eventually, a thin top layer of sand and impurities must be scraped off to restore the flow to the required rate.

The Oxfam filter includes a synthetic fabric placed on top of the sand layer, which retains most of the strained matter. When the filter needs cleaning, the water is lowered to about 200 mm below the surface of the sand. The fabric is rolled up and removed from the tank. After washing, the fabric is placed back on to the filter. Depending on the conditions, it may also be necessary to remove a thin (10 mm) layer of sand. The use of the fabric greatly reduces the amount of sand removed at each cleaning.

The fabric can be very heavy when loaded. Therefore, the fabric is more manageable if cut into pieces, so that each piece can be rolled, lifted and washed by one person.

Conventional slow sand filters include an extra 0.3–0.5 m depth of sand on top of the minimum required for effective filtration. This allows for several sand scrapings before the filter sand must be replenished, which may be after 3 or 4 years. One of the main delays in getting a slow sand filter operational in an emergency is locating, transporting, washing and placing the sand. Therefore, if this is a problem, then a minimum depth of filter sand of 0.6 m plus the fabric may be sufficient in the short term to give effective treatment.

After cleaning, the filter microbiology needs time to completely re-establish itself. Therefore, it may take up to about two days for the quality of the filtered water to come up to normal operational standards. If acceptable in the circumstances and if alternative supplies of water are available, the filtered water can be run to waste and not distributed for drinking. But even a new filter, operating at a filtration rate of 0.2 m/h on start up will remove some bacteria.

Filter sand Look for suitable filter sand locally from accessible river sandbanks. Test samples by washing to remove fines and organic material. Dry and sieve the samples. An ideal sand specification is the following:

- Effective size (sieve size through which 10 per cent of the sand passes) is between 0.15 and 0.35 mm.
- Uniformity coefficient (the ratio of sieve sizes through which 60 per cent and 10 per cent of the sand passes) should be less than 3.

- Maximum size of 3 mm.
- Minimum size of 0.1 mm.

(see Appendix 20).

The above sand specification is for guidance. In practice, almost any sand will work, but fine sand will impose greater head losses. In many cases this extra head loss is acceptable and can be allowed for in the design. A quick test conducted in a 200-litre drum will provide head loss data for the required flow rate. Doing this could well save considerable time and expense in searching for and transporting ideal sand from a distance.

Wash the sand to remove fine and organic material before placing it in the filter. If the source of the sand is a river, this can be done at the river where there is a plentiful supply of water. Use a drum arrangement as shown in Figure 13.25. Fill the drum with sand. Allow water to flow into the bottom of the drum to fluidize the sand and wash the silt away in the overflow. Continue flushing until the overflow water becomes clear.

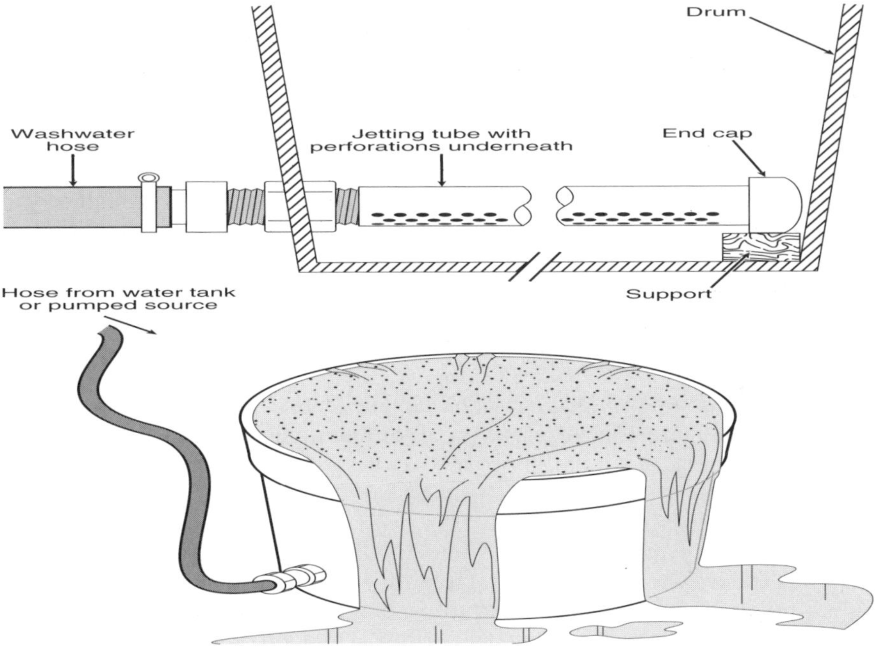

Figure 13.25 Washing the filter sand

Filter underdrainage A filter underdrainage collects water which has percolated through the filter and carries that water to the outlet pipe. The Oxfam filter underdrainage (see Figure 13.24) comprises a network of 100 mm slotted PVC pipes. Gravel above and around the underdrains prevents sand migrating to the slots (Figure 13.26). Use the 'filter rule' given in Appendix 20 to size the gravel layers. The gravel should be of a uniform size for the easy passage of water and large enough not to pass through the slots in the drains. An alternative to graded layers of gravel is to interpose a layer of synthetic fabric between the filter sand and gravel surrounding the underdrains. All gravel should be underlaid by a 50 mm layer of sand to protect the tank lining.

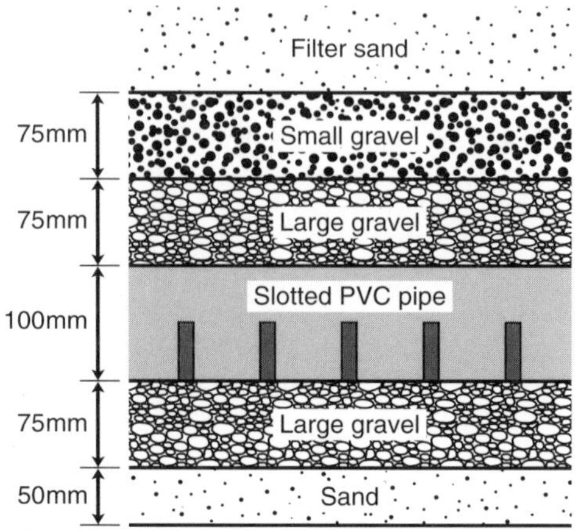

Figure 13.26 Filter underdrainage

The gravel and underdrainage should not be placed against the wall as water which 'short-circuits' down the wall sides will not pass through the filter sand. Leave at least 600mm of sand between the wall and underdrain for water to pass through before leaving the filter.

Other types of slow sand filter

A dug and lined slow sand filter The design of the horizontal-flow roughing filter shown in Figure 13.22 uses, as the filter chamber, an excavated basin lined with a plastic sheet. A similar approach can be adapted for the design of a slow sand filter.

Small-scale drum filters A simple slow sand filter can be made using a 200 litre drum, or similar. This can be an effective way of supplying small service centres (clinics, feeding centres, staff compounds, etc.) with a treated supply of water. Install a method of pre-treatment if the raw water turbidity is greater than 30 NTU. The drum filter and an upward flow pre-filter are shown in Figure 13.27. Backwash the pre-filter to clean it, as necessary, by periodically draining it down. Follow the same operation and management procedures for the drum filter as for a larger scale slow sand filter. Key points are:

- The filtration rate must not exceed 0.2 m/h. Therefore, for a 200 litre drum of diameter 600 mm, the flow rate must not exceed 60 litres/hour.
- Maintain a constant flow. This can be achieved by using gravity feed from a higher tank and collecting the filtered water in a storage tank. As the filter head loss increases, as suspended solids increase the resistance, adjust the height of the outlet to maintain the flow. This must not be misused to in-

crease the flow rate as water quality will suffer. If the level of the outlet is fixed, adjust the flow at an outlet valve.

- Sand specification – near single size 0.3–1.6 mm.
- Never allow the filter to run dry, unless the filter is not in use for longer than a day, in which case the filter should be drained.

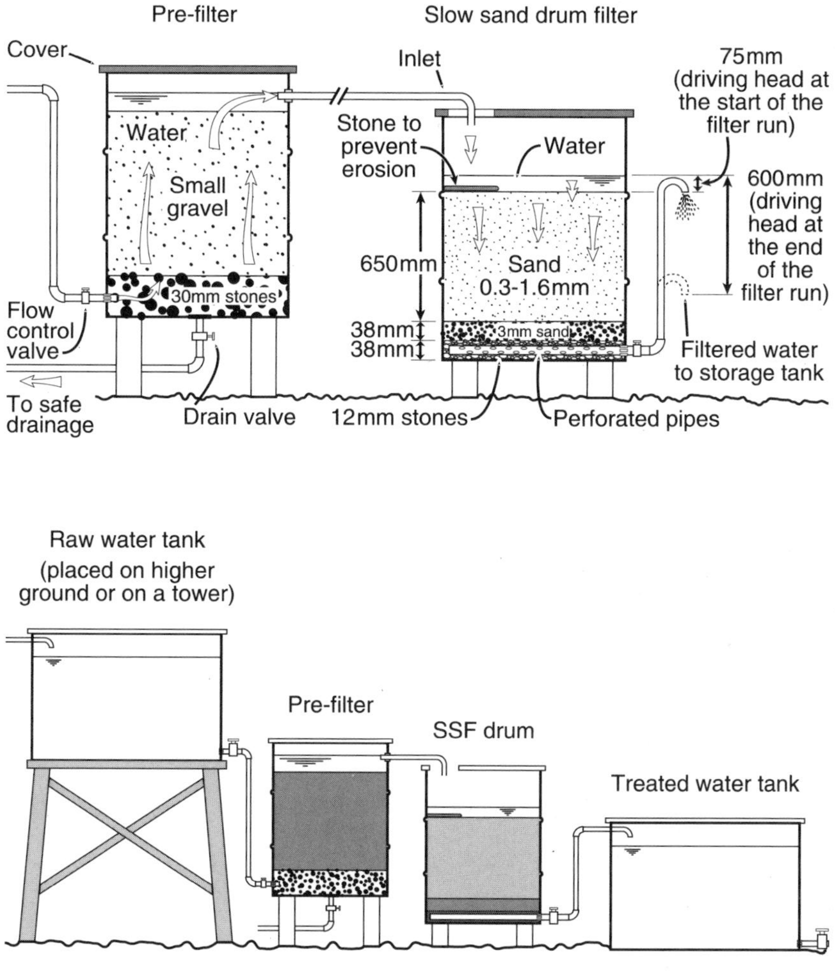

Figure 13.27 Slow sand drum filter and pre-filter

Ceramic candle filters Ceramic candle filters provide small volumes of water for household and clinic supplies. In small domestic units, flow through the filter is gravity driven. In package plants, where the yield is much higher, water is pumped through the filter.

A ceramic candle filter operating under gravity is shown in Figure 13.28. This arrangement can produce about one litre per hour per filter element. The upper raw water container can incorporate one or several filter elements depending on the flow required. The filters can also operate by siphonic action as shown in Figure 13.28. Complete units of upper and lower containers and filter elements can be purchased. Always order spare filter elements as they need replacing after long or heavy use. Spare filter elements can also be used to filter water in combination with a plastic bucket for the upper container and a jerry can for the filtered water.

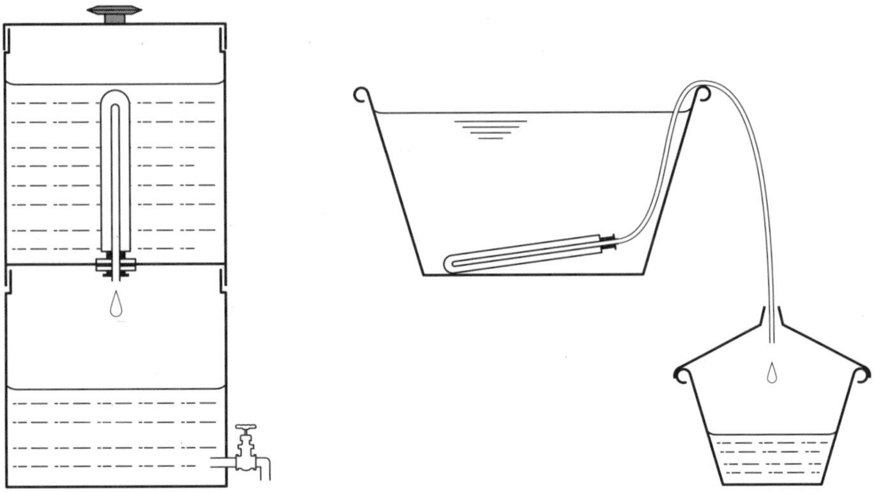

a) simple gravity system

b) a siphon

Figure 13.28 Ceramic candle filters

After some time the water flow diminishes as the candle becomes coated by the filtered out particles. The accumulated slime is cleaned off with a nylon brush in a bucket of water. Each brushing removes part of the ceramic candle so that the diameter of the candle is gradually reduced. A circular gauge should come with each filter – try not to lose it! The filter element needs replacing if the gauge can be slipped over the candle.

Silver acts as a bactericide, and candles are available which are silver impregnated for added protection.

13.3.3 Disinfection

Disinfection kills pathogenic organisms. It can be achieved by a variety of physical and chemical means. This section deals with the method most widely used in emergencies, chlorination. Some information is also given on two other methods: the use of iodine and boiling.

Chlorination

Chlorine is the most readily available and widely used chemical disinfectant for water supply. The aim of chlorination is the destruction of pathogens and the protection of the water supply. To achieve this, a chlorine dose must be sufficient to:

- Meet the chlorine demand of the water, that is, it must oxidize the contaminants (including reacting with any organic or inorganic substances).
- Leave a residual, in order to give protection against further contamination. This is achieved by ensuring a free residual of 0.2–0.5 mg/l of chlorine in the disinfected water, which inhibits any subsequent growth of organisms within the water supply system. Higher residuals may give an unpleasant taste.

A pre-condition for effective chlorination is that the turbidity of the water must be low. In an emergency water supply the aim is to have a turbidity of less than 5 NTU. Chlorination will function relatively effectively up to 20 NTU, but steps should be taken to reduce turbidities as soon as possible (see 13.3.1).

At high turbidity levels, large quantities of chlorine are needed to oxidize the organic matter present. This leaves a strong chlorine taste which may cause people to use other, possibly contaminated, sources of water for drinking. Furthermore, some pathogens inside particles of organic matter may survive the oxidizing effects of the chlorine.

Chlorine may be added to a water supply by:

- Dosing with a continuous flow of a one per cent solution of chlorine (see below and 13.3.4).
- Adding chlorine tablets or powder directly to a tank of water (for emergency chlorination only).

Table 13.14 outlines some of the advantages and disadvantages of using chlorine.

Chlorination and immunity to disease It has sometimes been suggested that the temporary provision of chlorinated water to people who normally have to

Table 13.14 Advantages and disadvantages of chlorine use as a disinfectant

Advantages	*Disadvantages*
It comes in several forms: powder, granules, liquid, gas	It is a powerful oxidizing agent which must be handled carefully – do not breathe chlorine fumes
It is usually readily available and relatively cheap in one form or another	It does not effectively penetrate particulate matter
It dissolves easily	It can give an unpleasant taste when slightly overdosed, which could dissuade people from drinking a safe water
Residual chlorine remaining in treated water provides some protection against further contamination	Its effectiveness against some pathogens – cysts, ova, viruses – requires higher chlorine concentrations and a longer contact time
It is effective against a wide range of pathogens	

drink polluted water can result in a reduction in immunity or resistance to disease, either because the chlorine affects the flora in the stomach or because the absence of pathogens in the water lowers subsequent immunity.

There is no evidence that any low level of residual chlorine that survives to the point of consumption is harmful. As an oxidizing agent, residual chlorine will react quickly with organic matter and it is therefore unlikely to survive long in the contents of the stomach (in which there are, in any case, high levels of naturally occurring hydrochloric acid). Current evidence suggests that there is very little likelihood that the absence of pathogens will have any effect on immunity to disease. Therefore, in crowded emergency situations, chlorination of the water supply is strongly recommended.

In other disaster situations, especially where populations are dispersed, chlorination of supplies may not be a priority. The decision on whether or not to chlorinate a water supply does not concern immunity. It concerns the balance of feasibility, cost and benefit to the health of the community as a whole (Feachem, 1993).

How much chlorine is required? Enough chlorine must be provided to meet the chlorine demand and to leave a free residual of 0.2–0.5 mg/l (WHO, 1984a) after a contact time of 30 minutes.

Chlorine residuals are of two kinds, combined residuals and free residuals. Combined residual chlorine is the proportion of the original chlorine dose which combines with ammonia and organic nitrogen compounds to form stable but less effective disinfectants than free chlorine. Free residual chlorine is that part of the chlorine dose which remains after the chlorine demand has been fully satisfied.

The actual dose will depend on the condition of the water. It can be expected to be in the range, 1–5 mg/l. Determine the optimum dose by trials on water samples.

To determine how much chlorine is required, it is necessary to analyse the water for the chlorine residuals. Simple colour comparator kits with reagents are available to indicate the free and combined residuals of chlorine in water.

The colour comparator shown in Figure 13.29 is used to indicate both chlorine residuals and pH concentrations.

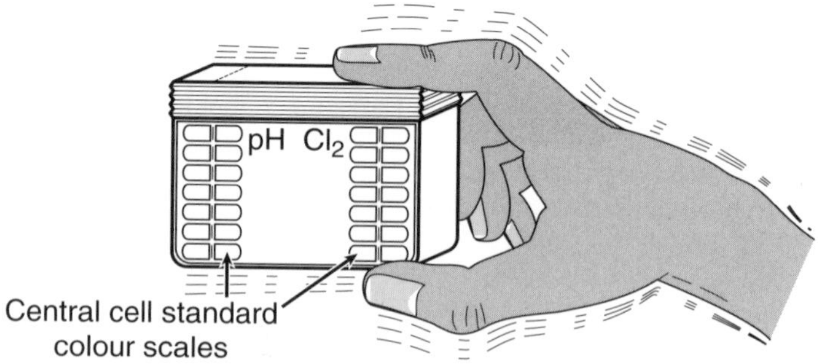

Figure 13.29 Colour comparator

Chlorine in water will form hypochlorous acid (HClO), at low pH values, or tend to dissociate into hydrogen (H^+) and chlorite (ClO^-) ions at higher pH values. Hypochlorous acid is the more active disinfectant and therefore chlorination is more effective in low pH (acidic) water. Chlorination is considerably less effective when the pH is greater than 8.

Disinfection using chlorine takes longer in cold than in warm water. Therefore, a normal contact time of 30 minutes may need to be increased to one hour. This implies that chlorination tanks may need to be increased in size or number to obtain the residence time for a particular throughput. Ensure all chlorination tests are conducted on samples that are at the correct temperature. For example, test samples in the outside temperature, not in a warm office or laboratory!

Box 13.5 gives a sample calculation for the chlorine requirement for a continuous process water supply system supplying a large community.

Box 13.5 Calculation of chlorine requirement

Task: to calculate how much chlorine is needed to chlorinate a water supply for 20 000 people receiving 15 litres/person/day of chlorinated water.

Water demand = 300 000 litres

If water is supplied by pump at a flow rate of 8 l/s then the total pumping time is about 10.5 hours/day.

In this case the water is of medium quality requiring a dose of 3mg/l of active chlorine to give a residual of 0.2 mg/l. This information was obtained by dosing small samples and analysing using a test kit.

For a pumping rate of 8 l/s the dosing rate must be $3 \times 8 = 24$ mg/s

Using a 1% chlorine solution, which contains 10 g chlorine/litre:
the rate of application required will be
$(24/1000) \times (100/1) = 2.4$ g/s (ml/s) or 144 ml/minute

For 10.5 hours pumping per day the amount of 1% chlorine solution required =
$144 \times 60 \times 10.5/1000 = 90.7$ litres/day

Therefore, a 200-litre drum of 1% chlorine solution would last two days.

Forms of chlorine Chlorine is available in the following forms:

- Chlorine gas is normally used in conventional water supply schemes of substantial size. Chlorine gas dosing equipment is expensive to install, complicated to operate and maintain, and it can be dangerous if not handled properly. Chlorine gas is unlikely to be used in an emergency water supply.
- High Test Hypochlorite (HTH) – calcium hypochlorite granules supplied in drums (70% available chlorine).
- Sodium hypochlorite – supplied in liquid form as:
  - Household disinfectant (Chloros, Parazone, Domestos, etc.) 5–15% available chlorine.
  - Laundry bleaches 3–5% available chlorine.

- Antiseptic solutions (Milton, Javel) 1% or 2% solution.
- Electrolytic generators are available which generate sodium hypochlorite from common salt. They are powered by electricity from mains AC or solar photovoltaic cells.
- Bleaching powder or chlorinated lime – about 30 per cent available chlorine when fresh.
- Chlorine tablets – various relatively expensive types:
  - Small calcium hypochlorite tablets (60–70 per cent available chlorine) used in tablet chlorinators.
  - 'Swimming pool' tablets containing trichloroisocyanuric acid: these tablets can be suspended in a tank with a purpose-made float to give a slow release of chlorine.

Antiseptic solutions (such as Milton or Javel) are usually of one per cent (or two per cent) concentration. If chlorine is required in bulk, it is more economical to make up a one per cent solution from stronger solutions.

Making a 1 per cent chlorine solution A comparatively stable working solution is of 1 per cent available chlorine. This can be used to dose water in a water treatment plant. A 1 per cent solution contains 10 g of chlorine per litre, i.e. 10 000 mg/litre or 10 000 ppm (parts per million).

Small quantities of 1 per cent solution are suitable for dosing supplies to service centres such as clinics, and for relief worker compounds.

Take care when mixing bleaching powder, as it will form lumps if simply added to water. Add just enough water to the powder to form a cream. Use a wooden stirrer and gradually add water to make the required solution. Allow the sediment which forms to settle and decant the liquid before use.

Table 13.15 is an approximate guide to making 1 litre of a 1 per cent solution from various sources. Remember that if the chlorine source has been stored for some time, its strength will have reduced.

A 1 per cent chlorine solution can be used to dose commonly used containers as indicated in Table 13.16. See Section 13.3.4 on methods of dosing.

Table 13.15 Preparation of 1 litre of 1 per cent chlorine solution

Chlorine source	*Available chlorine, %*	*Quantity required*	*Approx. measure*
High Test Hypochlorite (HTH) granules	70	14 g	1 heaped tablespoon
Bleaching powder	34	30 g	2 heaped tablespoons
Stabilized tropical bleach	25	40 g	3 heaped tablespoons
Liquid household disinfectant	10	100 ml	7 tablespoons
Liquid laundry bleach	5	200 ml	14 tablespoons
Antiseptic solution (e.g. Milton)	1	1 litre	No need to adjust as it is a 1% solution

Table 13.16 Chlorine doses for common containers

Container size	1 gallon (4.5 litres)	20 litres	45 gallon drum (200 litres)
Volume of 1% solution required	8 drops	Half-teaspoon	1 tablespoon + 1 teaspoon

Guide based on the approximate measures: 1 teaspoon = 5 ml; 1 tablespoon = 15 ml

Storage and handling Both the liquid and powdered forms of chlorine reduce in strength over time, especially once containers are opened. Therefore, store dry chlorine in sealed containers, away from heat and out of sunlight, and keep liquid solutions in dark coloured bottles.

Chlorine is corrosive – handle with care, avoid skin contact and, when mixing a chlorine solution, wear protective clothes and gloves, protect the eyes and do not breathe the fumes.

Some other methods of disinfection

Iodine Iodine is an effective bactericide and kills spores, cysts and viruses. The recommended dose is 2 mg/l with a contact time of 30 minutes (WHO, 1989). It appears to be more effective than chlorine in penetrating suspended solids in water. This may be significant in an emergency in the absence of pre-treatment, and where iodine is available for small-scale use in clinics, etc. However, iodine is not appropriate for large scale use as it is far more expensive than chlorine and not so widely available.

Boiling Boiling is an effective physical method of complete sterilization. It is more reliable than chemical disinfection as it will destroy pathogens within suspended particulate matter. However, there are significant disadvantages:

- Energy is required to boil the water (about 1 kg of wood is needed to boil 1 litre of water).
- Boiling must continue for 5–10 minutes.
- Boiled water is de-aerated and has a flat, unattractive taste.
- There is a delay between boiling and cooling before the water can be drunk.
- There is nothing to hinder post-boiling re-contamination through poor handling and storage.
- It is only practical for small quantities of water.

13.3.4 Chemical dosing equipment

Methods for the dosing of liquid chlorine and coagulant solutions fall into the following categories:

- Batch dosing to a fixed volume of water.
- Constant rate dosing into water flowing at a steady rate.
- Proportional dosing at a rate proportional to a variable flow rate.

Figure 13.30 shows an improvised, gravity fed, constant rate method of chlorine dosing. The dose rate from the floating bowl is controlled by the driving head to the glass jet, which is controlled by the weight of the floating bowl. This driving head, and hence the dosing rate, may be adjusted by adding or removing stones from the floating bowl.

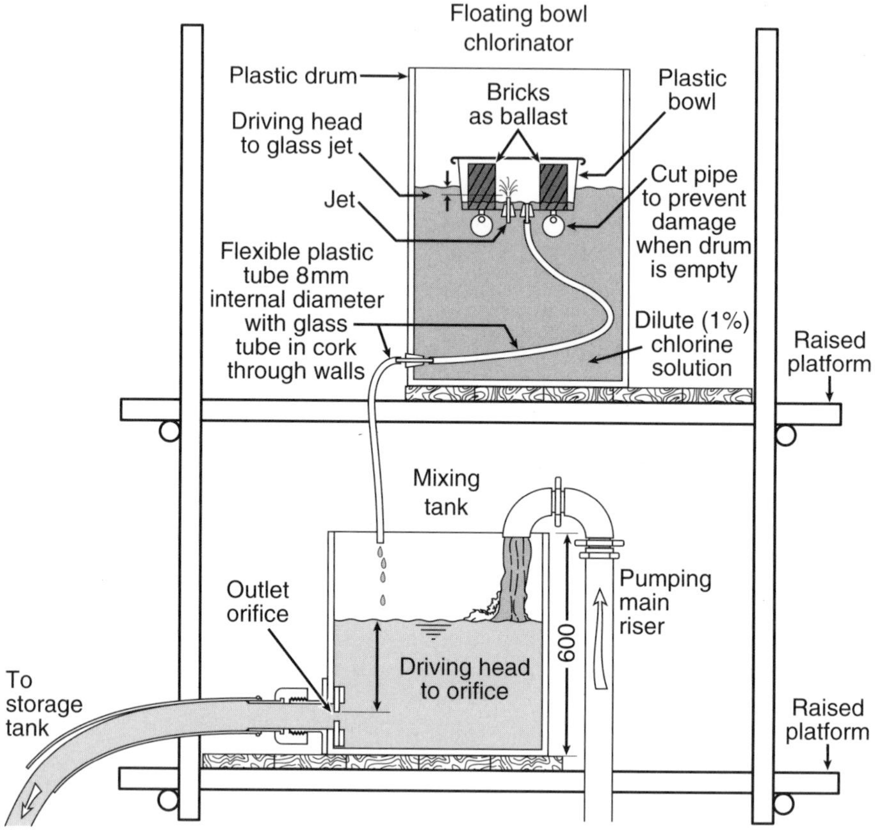

Figure 13.30 Gravity fed, constant rate chlorine solution dosing

The displacement doser (Figure 13.31) is a common method of proportional dosing used for small-scale community and institution supplies (such as hospitals). The differential pressure created across the orifice (or alternatively a venturi) displaces solution from the flexible bag and injects it into the flow.

13.3.5 Packaged water treatment plant

Portable packaged plants may be suitable in certain cases where appropriate expertise and a supply of consumables (fuel and chemicals) are available. They have been used to supply relief personnel during the installation of a larger system for the population as a whole. They are not normally appropriate for supplying water to large populations in an emergency because of the supply of

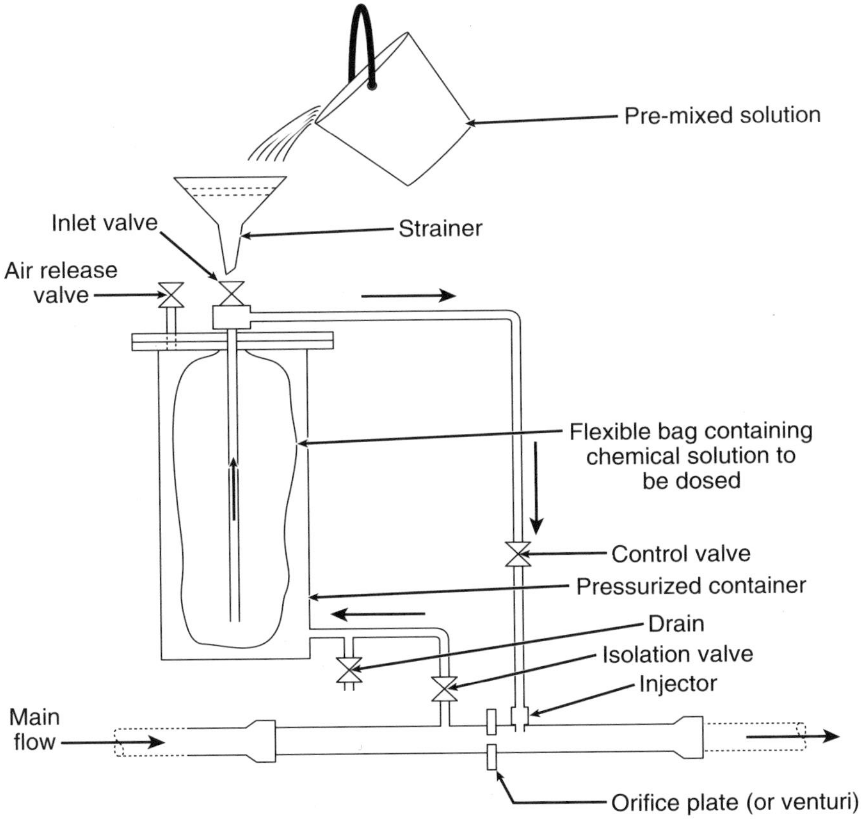

Figure 13.31 A displacement doser

consumables, and skilled operation and maintenance required. Units may be available from the military.

Portable treatment units generally consist of a water pump, a filtration unit and a method of chlorine dosing. Each section of the package may be supplied as a module, for ease of handling and independent use, or supplied as a self-contained unit for mounting on a trailer or skid. Typical capacities range from 2 to 22 m^3/h. Larger units are installed in standard freight (ISO) containers. When ordering, obtain guideline operational data from the supplier so that sufficient consumables (chemicals and fuel) can be ordered in advance.

Disinfection may be by superchlorination. The addition of a large dose of chlorine can rapidly disinfect water without the need for a long residence time. Excess residual chlorine is removed by a carbon filter and the water is then ready for immediate supply. A carbon filter may also remove bad tastes and odours.

Package filtration plant

There are several systems available:

- Small, high rate, pressurized sand filter with backwash. A carbon filter may also be incorporated.

- Ceramic candle filter, in which raw water is pumped through a chamber containing a number of porous ceramic candles. Ceramic candles can silt up quickly and have to be regularly cleaned, and eventually replaced.
- Diatomaceous earth (DE) filter.

The diatomaceous earth (DE) filter is a widely used system comprising stainless steel wire-wound candles enclosed in a cylindrical filter chamber. The raw water to be filtered is injected with a diatomaceous earth, or cellulose powder, which forms a thin filter coating on each candle. Water is pumped across the filter coating and exits up the inside of each candle. The flow rate gradually diminishes as the filter becomes blocked. The candles are then cleaned by either backwashing with filtered water or by the sudden release of air compressed in the filter head. To establish a new filter bed, more filter powder is added to the incoming raw water. A typical DE consumption of 0.28 kg/m^3 for low turbidity water has been reported by one supplier. The filtration run time between cleaning depends on the raw water turbidity, but is typically a period of hours.

Pre-treatment, such as the settlement of suspended solids in storage tanks, can significantly increase package plant filtration runs.

Package plant chlorination

The common chlorination method used in package plants is to dose with hypochlorite solution, using a diaphragm displacer of the type shown in Figure 13.31.

13.3.6 Desalination

Desalination processes for the removal of salt from sea water are very expensive, employ high technology and require skilled operation and maintenance personnel. Desalination is therefore impractical for most emergencies and it is not considered further in this book.

13.4 Water transmission and distribution

In a water supply system, water has to be moved from the source to the point of consumption, usually via storage and treatment. This requires pipes and, when gravity cannot be used, pumps. This section covers the selection and installation of pipes; valve and pipe fittings; and the different methods of gravity and pumped water transmission and distribution. Chapter 14 describes pump hydraulics, selection, installation, operation and maintenance. In emergencies, water may be transported, disinfected and distributed in mobile tankers. Water tankering is covered in Section 11.5.

13.4.1 Pipes

If locally available pipe can do the job required then use it, even though it may not be the ideal solution. Pipe may be stocked locally either by a water agency or by contractors. Ask if you can take pipe from existing stocks with a guarantee to replace them later by placing an immediate order. This kind of arrangement has helped in previous emergencies to speed up pipeline installation.

If pipe is not available locally it will have to be imported. When ordering pipe:

- Restrict the lengths of pipe to what can be easily transported and handled with the available trucks and equipment. Do not order 9 m lengths of pipe if trucks have a maximum flat bed length of 6 m!
- Similarly, only order coiled polyethylene pipe which can be lifted by available equipment.
- Smaller diameter pipes can be 'nested' inside larger diameter pipe for transportation.
- Order more than enough jointing materials and fittings – more are always needed and, if spare, can be kept in stock for future repairs.

Details on polyethylene, PVC-u and steel pipe, which are commonly used in emergencies, are given below.

Polyethylene pipe

Polyethylene (PE) pipe is particularly suitable for emergency work due to the variety and ease of jointing methods and the flexibility of the pipe.

Fusion welded PE pipe joints are as strong as the pipe itself. As a consequence, the pipe is able to withstand hydraulic end thrust from internal pipeline pressure as the joints will not be forced apart. This is a major advantage over push-fit PVC pipe, which cannot withstand end loading. Thrust blocks are not required at changes of direction for PE pipe, which saves installation time.

PE pipe can be quickly fusion welded on the surface, pressurized and put into service. The pipe is flexible and strong enough even after welding to be fed into a trench, once it has cooled.

Polyethylene pipe is available in several forms:

- LDPE – Low Density Polyethylene
- MDPE – Medium Density Polyethylene
- HDPE – High Density Polyethylene
- HPPE – High Performance Polyethylene

The earliest PE pipes were made of LDPE, for smaller service pipe diameters, and HDPE. In many countries MDPE is replacing both LDPE and HDPE. HPPE is the most recent material to be developed. HPPE is made of a higher density polyethylene than MDPE, which gives higher pressure ratings, or thinner pipe walls for the same pressure ratings. HPPE should not be confused with the older HDPE pipe as the plastic has a different molecular structure and so the pressure characteristics are different.

PE pipe sizing and pressure ratings Polyethylene pipe sizes are specified in terms of nominal outside diameter (OD) – not by the internal diameter. For all PE pipe greater than 25 mm, the ratio between wall thickness and outside diameter is constant for a specific pressure rating. This is the standard dimensional ratio, SDR.

$$\text{SDR} = \frac{\text{Outside diameter}}{\text{Minimum wall thickness}}$$

Knowing the SDR and OD will give the minimum wall thickness and hence the approximate bore size. Pressure ratings are related to SDR categories and are usually quoted for a temperature of 20°C. The pressure ratings must be significantly adjusted as temperature rises, (for instance, they decrease by 60 per cent at 40°C).

Table 13.17 Pressure ratings of polyethylene pipe (at 20°C)

	OD, mm	*SDR*	*Pressure, bar*
MDPE	20–63	11	12
	90–315	11	10
	90–1000	17.6	6
HPPE	90–500	11	16
	90–500	17.6	10
	160–1000	26	6

PE has advantages over other materials at low temperatures as it retains ductility down to -60°C. In freezing conditions the pipe will remain flexible, providing greater ease of installation. The low thermal conductivity of MDPE slows the freezing of water in the pipe and, if the water does freeze, the ductile PE will cope with the expansion without pipe failure.

PE pipe can be supplied in lengths of 6 or 12 m, for diameters greater than 90 mm, or in coils of varying length. Check the relevant national standards and manufacturer's literature for locally purchased LDPE and HDPE pipe.

See Appendix 13 for dimensions of selected MDPE pipe.

Joining PE pipe The common method of joining PE pipe is by fusion welding, either electrofusion or butt fusion. Other joining methods include push-fit systems and mechanical couplings.

Electrofusion uses socket type fittings with integral heating wires connected to surface mounted terminals. Electric current from a generator and control box is applied through the terminals. The heating wire melts the polyethylene and welds the fitting or coupling to the pipe wall.

In butt fusion, the two parallel ends of pipe to be joined are heated until molten and then pushed together and allowed to cool.

Custom made butt fusion machines incorporate a jig for holding and bringing the pipe ends together under pressure, a non-stick heater plate for heating the pipe ends, a trimmer for trimming the pipe ends parallel, and a hydraulic power pack. The use of a machine ensures all joints are aligned and made at the correct temperature and pressure.

Welding machines are specific to a range of pipe diameters and they are relatively expensive. They are only worth obtaining if several kilometres of PE pipe are to be laid.

Experience in recent emergencies has indicated that, even where butt fusion machines are available, on pipes up to about 100 mm diameter pipelayers tend to discard the specialized jig after some time and only use the heating plate. With practice, pipelayers heat the pipe ends and push them together by hand to make an adequate joint.

A purpose made heating plate is not absolutely essential. A 25 mm thick steel plate, 150 mm square, with a long handle welded on, has been used satisfactorily when heated in an open fire. When using this method, maintain the quality of the joints by taking the following measures:

- Designate a suitably skilled person as the 'pipe joiner' and allow him/her some time to practise.
- Cut the pipe ends straight and parallel and trim rough edges with a knife. Ensure there are no gaps bigger than a millimetre when the ends are brought together.
- Heat the plate in an open fire (a few minutes in the centre of the hot embers).
- Touch each end of the pipe to be joined on opposite sides of the hot plate until an even layer of molten plastic forms on each rim.
- Remove the plate and push the pipe ends together, slightly rotating them until an even bead of molten plastic is formed all around the rim. Hold the joint steady and allow it to cool for a few minutes.
- After 10–15 minutes, the joints may be given a crude test – they should be able to withstand any attempt to break them by hand. Proper pressure testing will be required at a later stage.

Fittings for butt fusion are 'pupped' (a short length of pipe attached) to allow for butt fusion jointing.

Polyethylene flange adaptors allow jointing of PE pipe to other pipe materials and flanged fittings (using a steel backing ring and gasket).

Push-fit connectors and fittings are available for small diameter (20–63 mm) service pipe joints. Push-fit adaptors allow jointing with other materials such as threaded steel pipe.

Compression joints are available for the jointing of PE pipe up to 110 mm. Compression adaptors allow jointing to other materials.

For low pressure applications, it is possible to screw PE pipe on to GI threaded pipe and fittings. Jointing can be aided by heating the PE pipe end.

PE pipe installation PE pipe can be laid directly in a trench if the soil is uniform and without sharp stones. Coarse sand, fine gravel and soft soil are suitable bedding and backfilling materials. It is difficult to join pipes in a narrow trench. Therefore, to keep the width of the trench to a minimum, join the pipes on the surface and 'snake' the pipe into the trench.

Fusion jointed PE pipe can be installed above ground. Protect it from direct sunlight and insulate if possible. Black MDPE pipe is protected from ultraviolet with carbon black and, therefore, for above ground use, should be used in preference to blue MDPE. The high coefficient of linear expansion (0.15 mm/m/°C) means that significant length changes can be expected where there are wide temperature variations. For example, the increase in length of a 6 m MDPE pipe is 9 mm per 10°C rise in temperature. It may be necessary to snake the pipeline along the ground to take up any movement.

When laying PE pipe in hot climates, let the pipe cool in the trench before connecting to anchored fittings, to allow for contraction.

PE pipe can be suspended (for instance, from bridges at river crossings) but it must be adequately supported along its length (see Table 13.18).

Table 13.18 Spacing of supports for polyethylene pipe

Nominal size, mm	*Recommended support spacing, m, at 20 °C*
25	0.5
90	0.85
180	1.4

With specific gravity values from 0.916 (LDPE) to 0.965 (HDPE), PE pipe will float in water. Pipes filled with water will float just under the surface. Pipes filled with air will float on the surface. Underwater pipe crossings must, therefore, be adequately anchored.

If necessary, it is possible to float a fusion welded length of PE pipe across a stretch of water and sink it into position with weights. A pipeline can be better manoeuvred into position if it is only partially filled with water.

Handling and storage of PE pipe Polyethylene pipe is tough and lightweight, but it must be handled correctly to avoid damage and deformation, especially in hot climates.

Pipes must be supported along their full length during transport. Firmly secure pipes as they can slip easily, especially in wet and freezing conditions.

In storage, do not stack pipes more than 1.5 m high, and provide adequate support battens and lateral restraints. In hot and sunny climates, keep pipes under cover and well ventilated. Avoid storage in containers.

PVC-u pipe

PVC-u pipe is lightweight and can be easily installed. However, it is not as flexible or versatile as PE pipe and therefore the applications to which PVC-u pipe is suited are restricted. PVC-u pipe becomes brittle at low temperatures and should not be laid in freezing conditions.

PVC pipe sizing and pressure ratings PVC-u pipe is available in both imperial and metric diameters in standard 4 m and 6 m pipe lengths. The older imperial sized pipe is available in four pressure classes, as shown in Table 13.19.

Table 13.19 Working pressures for PVC-u pipe

Class		*Maximum working pressure*
BS3505	*ISO*	*at 20 °C*
B	NP 6	6 bar
C	NP 9	9 bar
D	NP 12	12 bar
E	NP 15	15 bar

The newer metric sized pipe is available in two pressure classes of 8 bar and 12.5 bar.

For ambient temperatures above 20°C, allow a pressure reduction of 2 per cent per 1°C rise in temperature.

See Appendix 13 for dimensions of selected PVC-u pipe.

Joining PVC pipe PVC-u pipe can be joined by push-fit insertion joints or with solvent cement.

Push-fit joints comprise a socket containing a rubber sealing ring. Lubricate the sealing ring with pipe lubricant, soap or detergent. Push the clean pipe spigot into the socket up to the insertion mark on the pipe. It is especially important to allow for expansion and contraction at the joint by reference to the insertion mark. If pipe is laid in hot weather, it will contract when cooler water flows through it. Therefore the pipe must be inserted at least as far as the insertion mark to give sufficient length of inserted pipe to prevent it pulling out of the socket when it is cooled by the water. If pipe is laid in cold weather, it will expand when warmer water flows through it. If the pipe is inserted no further than the insertion mark, there will be sufficient space in the socket to take the expansion of the pipe. Hot pipe left in the sun will contract appreciably when buried and, over a long length, may pull out of a socket.

Push-fit joints cannot sustain end-loads. Pipe must therefore be anchored in position by backfilling before pressurizing. Bends, blank ends and fittings must also be adequately anchored.

Solvent cement joints may have to be used, but they are not recommended in an emergency due to various difficulties associated with the joint. The procedure involves abrading the pipe surfaces, marking the socket depth on the spigot, cleaning the mating surfaces with cleaning fluid, careful application of the solvent cement and a clean and firm insertion of the spigot in the socket. Joints must remain undisturbed for 30 minutes and, at 20°C, 24 hours must elapse before the pipe is pressurized.

A hot climate makes solvent cementing even more difficult as solvent can evaporate from stored tins, and jointing must be performed quickly.

Compression joints of up to 110 mm are available for the jointing of PVC pipe. Flanged and threaded compression joint adaptors are also available for joining to steel pipe and fittings.

PVC pipe installation and commissioning PVC-u pipe can be laid directly in a trench if the soil is fine-grained, uniform and without sharp stones. Pipes should preferably be joined in the trench, to avoid separation of the joints by subsequent movement during laying.

As stated previously, push-fit joints cannot withstand end-loads. Therefore, all bends, valves, fittings and blank ends must be firmly anchored (See 'Pipe laying' below).

Most push-fit joints are able to accommodate an angular deflection of about 1° per joint. This translates into a deflection of about 100 mm per 6 m length of pipe.

Above 5°C, PVC-u pipe up to OD 150 mm can be cold bent to a radius not less than 200 × ODmax.

In an emergency, it is possible to form bends in PVC pipe by filling the pipe with sand and heating the area to be bent. However, the pressure characteristics of the pipe will be adversely affected.

PVC-u pipe installed above ground should be solvent cemented to support end loads at bends and blank ends. In an immediate emergency, it is possible to use push-fit pipe above ground temporarily, but this is precarious. Pipes must be anchored at each joint. Replace the pipe with a more suitable pipe and jointing system as soon as possible.

Pipe installed above ground should be protected from sunlight and supports should allow for expansion and contraction. Keep restraining clamps loose.

Handling and storage of PVC-u pipe PVC pipe is light and therefore easy to mishandle. Pipe ends can be easily damaged. The soundness of PVC pipe joints depends on the condition of both spigot and socket. Therefore, take extra care in the handling and storage of PVC pipe.

PVC pipe can distort if transported or stored incorrectly. High temperatures exacerbate distortion and, apart from the adverse effect on the pipe properties, laying banana shaped pipe can be very frustrating.

Stack pipe with sockets protruding and placed at alternate ends of the stack. Do not stack higher than 2 m; less in a hot climate or if pipes are nested. Support pipes along their length. Dig a shallow recess trench to take the sockets of pipes placed on the ground. In hot and sunny climates keep pipes under cover and well ventilated. Avoid storage in containers. In very high temperatures, pipe and plastic fittings can be stored under water.

Galvanized steel (GI) pipe

In most emergency situations, plastic pipe is the clear choice for pumping mains and distribution. However, there are cases where galvanized steel pipe is appropriate:

- Pipe sections subject to high pressure.
- Pipe sections that cannot be buried such as hard rock areas.
- Short gully, stream or road crossings.
- Across cultivated farmland.
- Exposed pipework at tapstands, tanks, etc.

Galvanized steel (GI) pipe is commonly available in 3 or 6 m lengths in diameters of up to 4 inches (100 mm). Maximum pressure rating of GI pipe depends on the pipe wall thickness. For medium wall GI pipe the maximum pressure rating is 25 bar (see Appendix 13).

Joining GI pipe GI pipe is usually supplied with tapered pipe threads at both ends with one straight connector per pipe. It is preferable to cut pipe to length with a pipe cutter, if available, rather than a hacksaw. Pipe cutters give a neat straight cut ready for threading, whereas a hacksaw cut must be filed smooth and it is often not straight. If threaded GI pipe is to be laid, it will be necessary to obtain pipe threading equipment of the correct diameter.

To join threaded steel pipe:

- Clean the threads to remove surface rust, dirt and any previously-used jointing compound.
- Check that the threads are not damaged – small imperfections may be corrected with a file. Crushed or broken thread, and deformed pipe ends, must be cut off and the pipe re-threaded.
- The joint can be made watertight using a variety of materials. Wrap hemp or several layers of white PTFE tape around the thread in a clockwise direction before screwing the pipes together. Use a jointing compound with the hemp. If these are not available, use teased out string, rope or rags and any thick paint (preferably not lead paint).
- The use of PTFE on poorly cut threads (> 3-inch diameter) is not recommended as the gaps in the thread are too great. Use jointing compound and hemp.
- Do not overtighten threaded joints as they can be damaged or, worse, a fitting can be cracked.

To enable pipes and fittings to be removed for repair, join threaded GI pipe with screwed unions on at least one side of a valve or fitting and in long lengths of steel pipe (> 100 m).

Steel pipe can have flanged joints. Flange dimensions can vary widely, so new fittings must be carefully matched to existing pipework. It is sometimes worth making a dummy flange out of card and using it to check new flanges before purchase. Ensure there are sufficient gaskets for each flange joint.

Steel pipe can be welded, but this should be reserved for critical joints and for making up adaptors and special fittings.

Steel pipe installation and commissioning Firmly anchor exposed steel pipe using pipe anchors of steel and concrete.

Exposed empty steel pipe can become very hot in a warm and sunny climate. Be careful when filling hot pipes with cold water, as the sudden contraction can damage threaded joints causing them to leak.

Handling and storage of steel pipe Steel threads can be easily damaged. Protect them in transit and when loading and unloading. New steel pipe is normally bundled with a straight connector on one end and a thread protector on the other.

In transit, ensure connectors are firmly screwed on to each pipe as they can vibrate loose.

In hot and sunny climates, store steel pipe under cover as the pipe can literally become too hot to handle.

Hoses

Flexible hose can be useful in the early part of an emergency both to distribute water to tapstands and to provide the links between pumps, tanks and other components of a rapidly established water system. Hoses are light, making them easy to transport and handle. They can be quickly rolled out and joined to a variety of pipework and fittings. Hoses allow for movement between fixed tanks and pipework. They can also be used to make changes in pipeline direction. Always try to bury or cover hoses used for temporary tank connections, as heat and sunlight can significantly weaken the hose material. Replace hoses as soon as possible with more permanent buried pipe.

Types of hose:

- Lay-flat hose is made of rubber lined canvas ('firehose'), unreinforced PVC or polyester reinforced PVC. It is commonly available in diameters from 19 to 200 mm and in coils up to 100 m. The main advantage of lay-flat is that it collapses when not in use, making it easy to handle for a variety of uses. Lay-flat is not as tough as semi-rigid hose or pipe. It can kink and throttle flow at changes of direction. Pipe flow losses are relatively high. Lay-flat hose cannot be used on the suction side of a pump where a rigid pipe able to sustain a partial vacuum is required. Lay-flat is often referred to as 'flat delivery hose'.
- PVC suction and delivery hose is made of flexible smooth bore PVC, reinforced with a semi-rigid PVC spiral. It is available in a variety of pressure ratings for different applications in the temperature range –10°C to 55°C. See Appendix 13 for typical specifications.

See Appendix 14 for descriptions of hose fittings.

Pipe laying

Do not open a trench too far in advance of laying pipe. Backfill as soon as possible. This is especially important where pipe is being laid in clay soil during the rains. A flooded trench can complicate pipe laying and use up valuable time. However, do not completely backfill a trench after laying a pipeline but leave the joints exposed. Any joint leaks can be clearly seen on pressurizing the pipe. Repair any leaks before completing the backfilling.

In non-freezing conditions, pipe only needs to be buried sufficiently deep to afford physical protection and to keep the pipe and water cool. A depth of 300 mm is often adequate, but check the depth of frost penetration with local engineers.

Clearly mark out trenches with pegs and string. If manually dug, allocate digging teams to pipeline sections. Provide each team leader with depth and width gauge sticks. See Chapter 6 for details on the organization and management of labour-based construction.

Information on pipe laying specific to each type of pipe material is included in the relevant preceding sections. See Appendix 23 for notes on basic surveying and setting out.

Pipe anchors Pipe anchors are necessary to resist pipe movement due to unbalanced forces at changes in diameter and direction, and at valves, junctions and blank ends. They are especially important in the case of push-fit PVC pipe. Figure 13.32 is a guide to the design and positioning of pipe anchors. Figure 13.33 is a guide to anchor block size.

Pipe fittings

Pipe fittings include elbows, tees, and reducers. Appendices 13 and 14 give guidance on the correct specification of fittings.

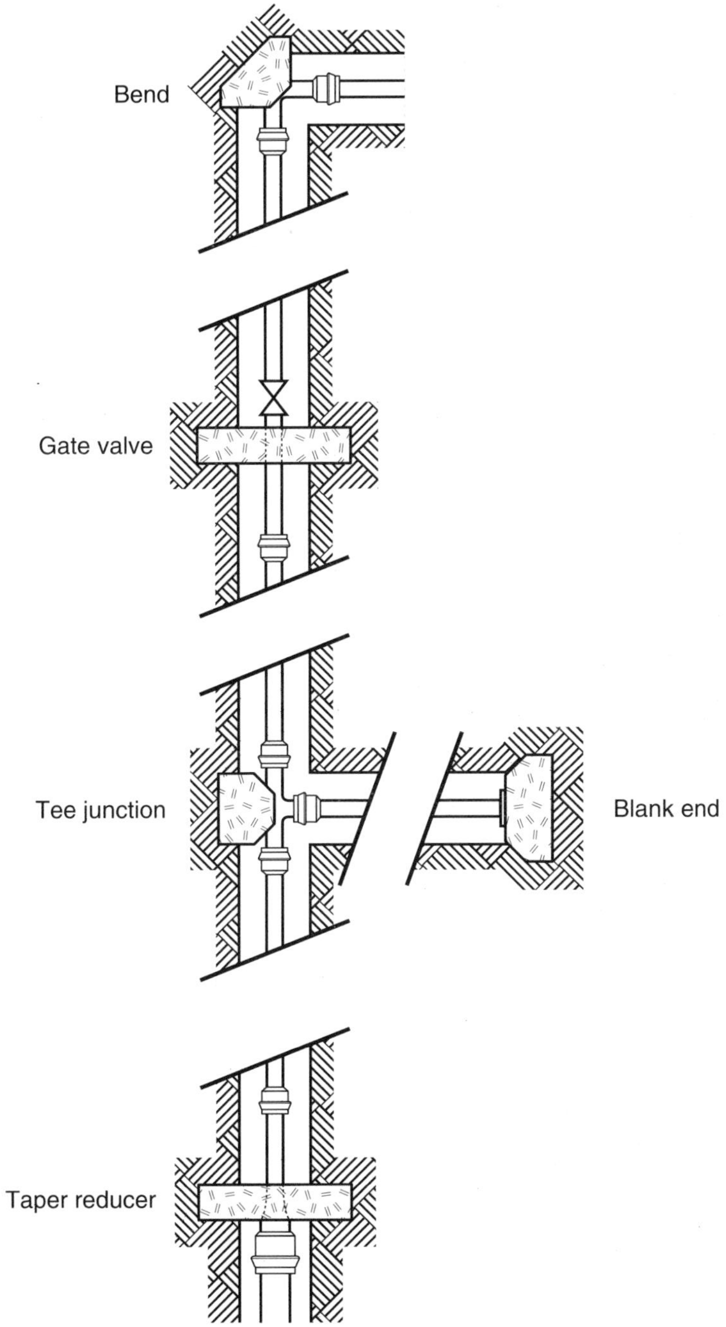

Figure 13.32 Pipe anchors

Anchor block dimensions are based on the following conditions:

- Dry ground conditions.
- Soil density of 1800 kg/m^3.
- Pipe pressure of 6 bar.
- Anchor block bases and faces are cast against undisturbed ground.

In the presence of rock, block sizes can be reduced.
In waterlogged soils, the plan area of blocks should be increased by about 50%.

Anchor blocks at bends:

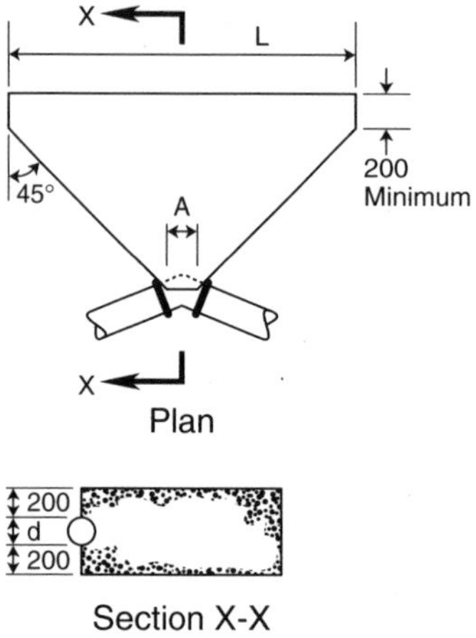

Pipe diameter mm	Bend (degrees)	A mm	L mm
80	$11\frac{1}{4}$ & $22\frac{1}{2}$	200	300
	45	200	300
	90	250	300
100-150	$11\frac{1}{4}$ & $22\frac{1}{2}$	200	400
	45	250	500
	90	300	750

Anchor blocks at Tee-junctions and dead ends:

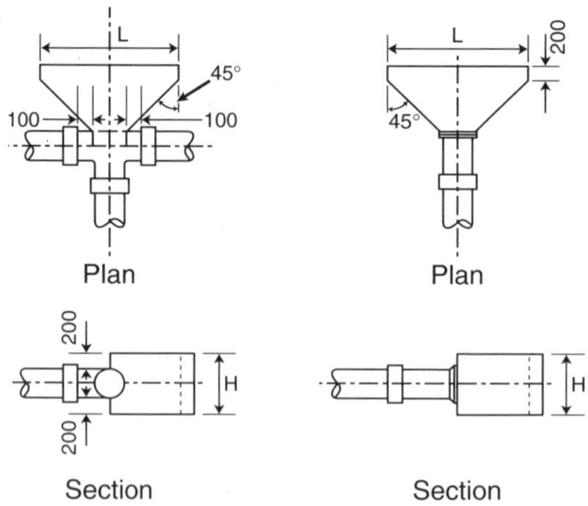

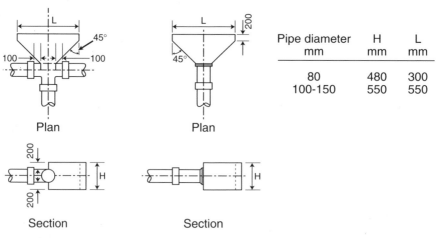

Pipe diameter mm	H mm	L mm
80	480	300
100-150	550	550

Figure 13.33 Anchor block dimensions

13.4.2 Valves and tapstands

Valves

Refer to Appendix 15 for descriptions and diagrams of the following main valve types commonly used in emergency water supplies:

- Gate valves (also called sluice valves) for the isolation of flow. This is the most commonly used valve.
- Globe valves (also called screw-down stop valves) for the isolation and control of flow in small diameter (up to 50 mm) branch pipes.
- Butterfly valves for flow control.
- Non-return valves (also called reflux or check valves) to allow the flow of water in only one direction. A foot valve is a non-return valve placed on the end of a pump suction pipe. It prevents water running back through the pump and emptying the suction pipe.
- Air valves are usually placed at high points in a pipeline to release accumulated air automatically in a pressurized pipe, to allow air to escape when the pipe is filling and to allow air to enter a pipe when it is emptying.
- Float valves automatically maintain the level of water in a tank to prevent overflowing.

All buried valves should be marked and protected during installation, or as soon after as possible. Quick and temporary protection can be provided by wooden boxes or short lengths of plastic or steel (GI) pipe. Stand the pipe vertically over the valve and cover with a screwed down end cap. Valve handles may need to be removed, to prevent unauthorized operation.

Tapstands

A tapstand (also called a standpost) must be quick and easy to erect and sufficiently sturdy to withstand constant use. A simple tapstand can be made from 2 or 3 inch (50–75 mm) GI pipe as shown in Figure 13.34a. This design can be improved later by encasing the uprights in masonry or concrete pillars. The Oxfam water distribution pack includes pre-fabricated water collection points which could be copied locally (Figure 13.34b). A single or double tapstand can be quickly made from strapping GI pipe to a wooden post (Figure 13.34c). (See also Section 13.2.2, Figure 13.4).

Some spillage is inevitable at tapstands and adequate drainage is essential, otherwise water collection points become very unhealthy places. Soakaways are appropriate where the soils are sufficiently permeable (refer to Section 10.5). Gardens can help to use up surplus water but they may also encourage excessive use of water for non-essential activities. Drainage to animal drinking troughs could be controversial, as it may not be desirable to attract animals to the tapstand areas. In impermeable clay soils it may be necessary to direct wastewater to vegetation plots (evapotranspiration beds) to return water to the atmosphere.

Service pipes

Service pipes are branches from the main pipeline to each tapstand. The pipes are usually 25 mm or 32 mm diameter and the branch connection may be made

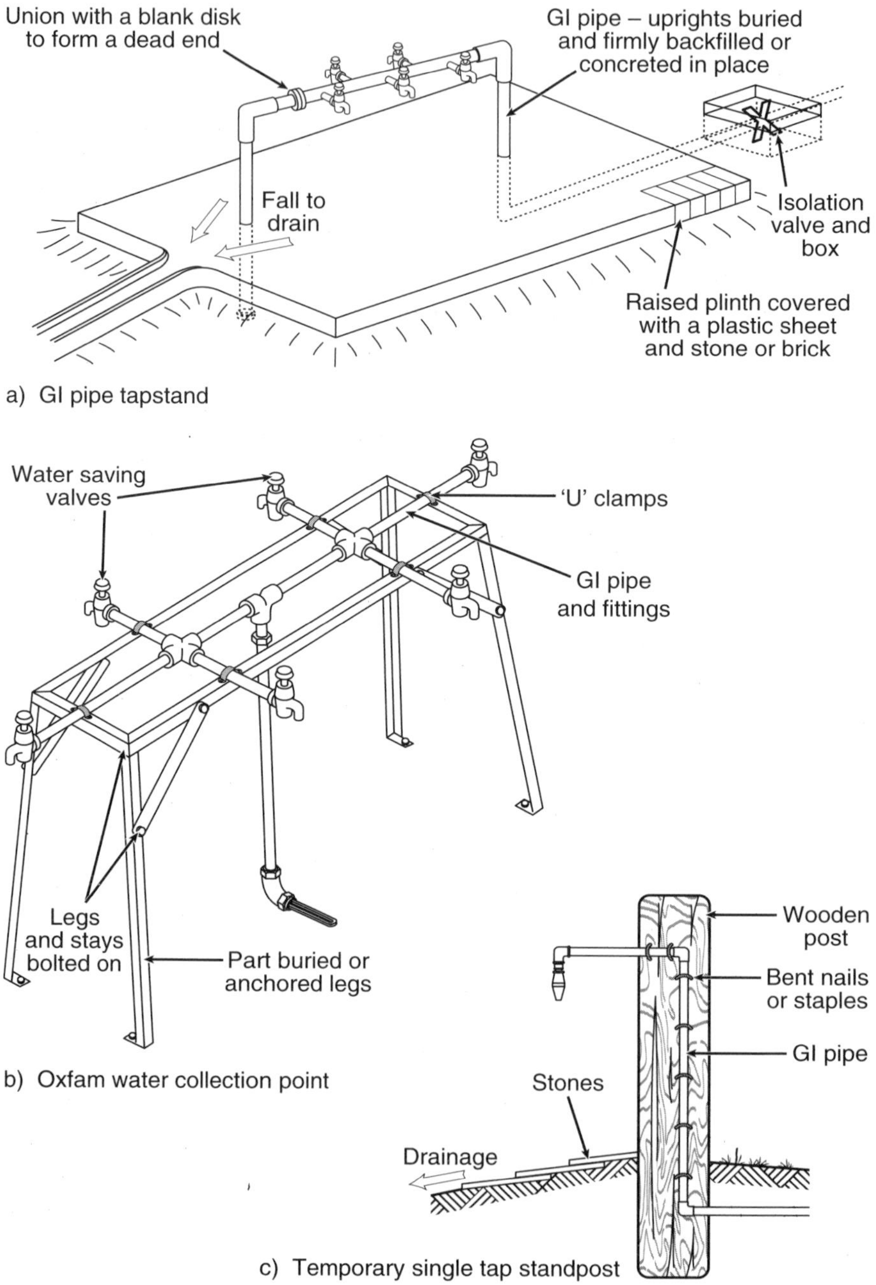

Figure 13.34 Emergency tapstand designs

with a T-junction and reducer or by ferrule straps (see Appendix 14). Self-tapping ferrule straps enable under-pressure and dry connections to be made very quickly to PE and PVC pipe. The ferrule strap is bolted on the pipe and the integral cutter drilled through the pipe wall by turning a key. The connection can be made in a matter of minutes. Once made, it can also be used to isolate flow to the tapstand. On a T-branch, include a valve (stop-cock) on the service pipe to control flow to a tapstand and to stop the flow for the maintenance of taps. A globe valve is normally used.

Taps

Leakage at tapstands from open, worn or broken taps can waste valuable water and create muddy and insanitary pools. Therefore, taps must be constantly maintained and immediately repaired when faulty. Encourage users to monitor their own taps. Initiate a system of reporting faults.

The common bib-tap is not the best type of tap for a communal tapstand. The seat washer and threads tend to wear quickly when in constant use. Bib-tap handles often come away easily, making the taps difficult to operate. Taps can be left open during periods when there is no flow so that when flow is restored a lot of water can be wasted.

Water saving taps attempt to overcome these problems. They are either self-closing when released or only deliver a set amount of water when operated. A simple and effective water saving tap is the 'Talflo' (Figure 13.36).

The flow rate of a tap, and therefore the number of people served, will depend on the residual head at the tapstand and the head loss across the tap. Figure 13.35 indicates typical discharge rates for different taps. It is normally desirable to aim for a residual head of 5–10 m. However, some water-saving devices, such as the 'Talflo' valve, experience water hammer 'bounce' above certain pressures which can lead to excessive wear and possible damage. Therefore, from field experience, it is recommended that these valves are operated at pressures as low as 2 m.

13.4.3 Pipeline design

Flow in pipes

A basic equation relating to flow in pipes is Bernoulli's equation:

$$H = \frac{P}{\rho g} + \frac{v^2}{2g} + z$$

where:

- H = total energy
- P = pressure of the water
- ρ = density of water
- g = gravitational acceleration
- v = flow velocity of water
- z = height of water above a datum

The equation reflects the three components of total energy possessed by unit mass of water flowing in a pipe: pressure energy, kinetic energy, and potential energy due to its position above a datum. The form of the equation has been

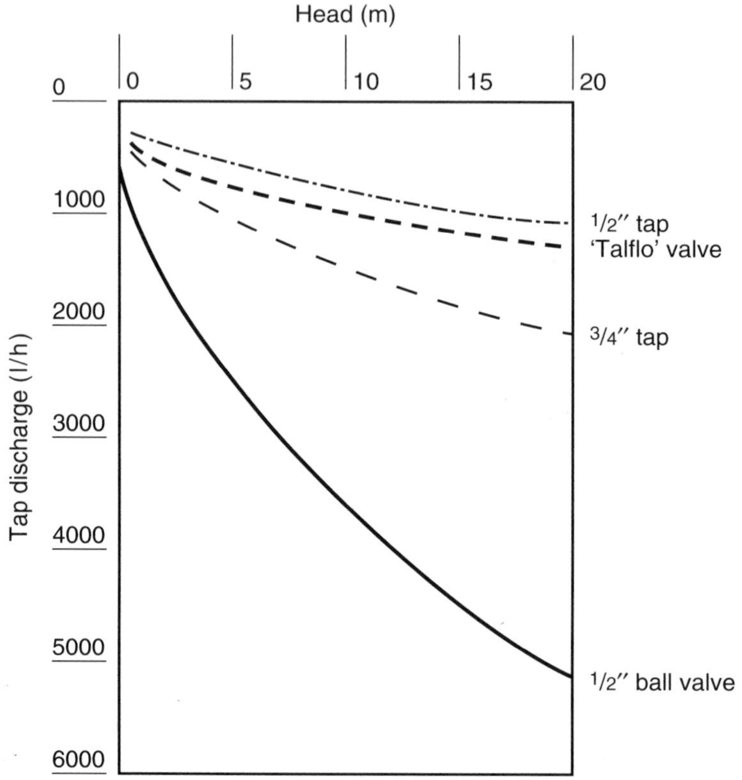

Figure 13.35 Typical tap discharge rates

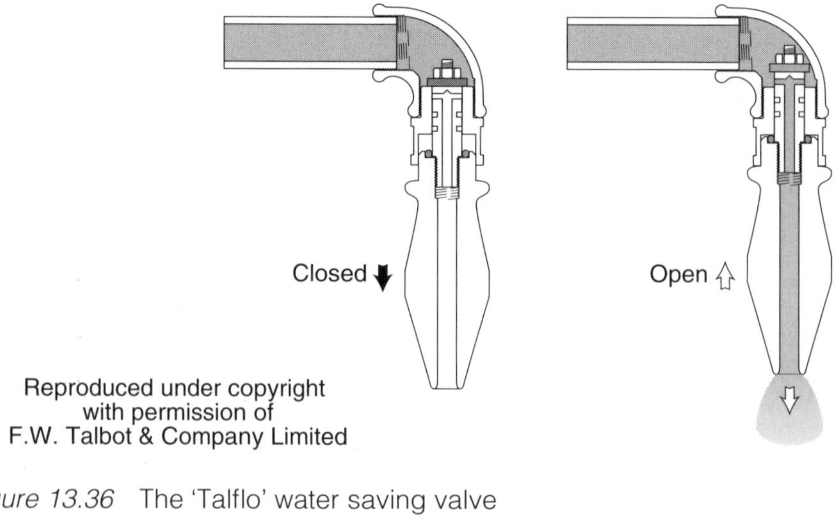

Figure 13.36 The 'Talflo' water saving valve

chosen so that all the components can be expressed in terms of 'head of water', usually in metres. This can be visualized by representing the energy components in a diagram as shown in Figure 13.37. The slope of the energy lines is called the hydraulic gradient. As water flows from one position to another it loses energy through friction with the pipe wall.

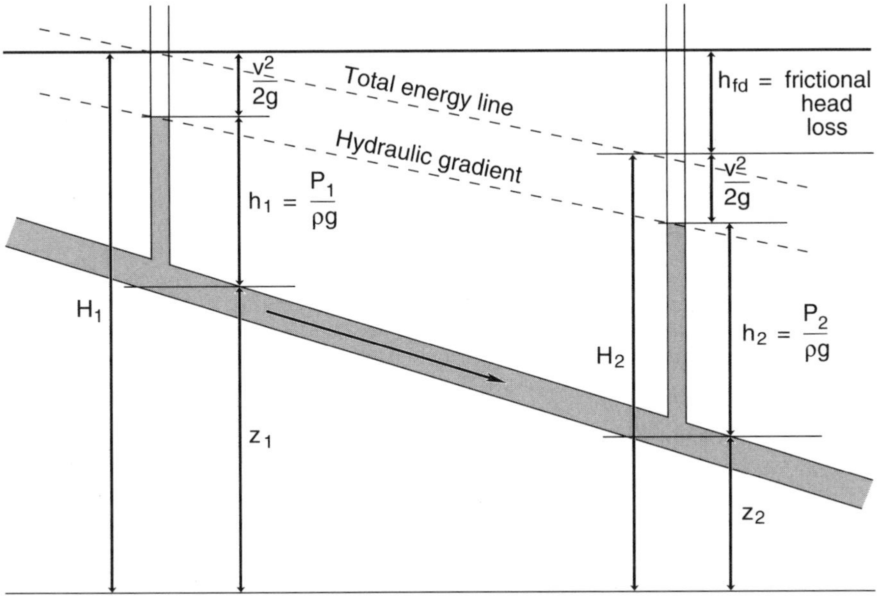

Figure 13.37 Variation in energy as water flows through a pipeline

Frictional head loss in pipes A key element in pipeline design is determining the frictional head loss in the pipe. There are various formulae for calculating the head loss and the most accurate is the Colebrook-White formula. However, this is complex and difficult to use in the field. Therefore, charts and tables have been produced, using the Colebrook-White formula, which greatly simplify calculations.

Manufacturers often include pipe flow charts based on the Colebrook-White formula in their literature. For a particular pipe material, flow rate (l/s or m^3/h) is plotted against loss of head (in m/1000m) for various pipe sizes.

Tables are an alternative to charts. Tables are produced which relate frictional head loss to pipe diameter and pipe roughness. The roughness of a pipe depends on the pipe material, method of jointing, age and condition. Many emergency water supplies involve small diameter plastic pipes and Appendix 16 includes hydraulic tables for plastic pipe in the range 20–150 mm.

It is useful to have more than one method of calculating pipe losses as a double-check, and in case tables and graphs are left behind, or are lost or defaced in some way.

The Hazen-Williams formula is an alternative method of calculating frictional head loss if a scientific calculator is available. The following forms of the Hazen-Williams formula are the most useful.

$$h_f = \frac{10.9\ L\ Q^{1.85}}{C^{1.85}\ D^{4.87}}$$

$$Q = 0.275\ (h_f/L)^{0.54}\ C\ D^{2.63}$$

where:

h_f = head loss in metres
L = length of pipe in metres
Q = flow in m^3/s
C = Hazen-Williams coefficient
D = internal pipe diameter in metres

Values for C, the Hazen-Williams coefficient are:

for PE and PVC pipe	150
for new galvanized steel (GI) pipe	130

Secondary losses In addition to friction losses, energy is lost at pipe entry and exit, changes of diameter and direction, pipe fittings and at obstructions. These 'secondary losses' or 'minor losses' cause a further drop in the total energy line. There are various methods of estimating the losses:

- A reasonably accurate method is to express secondary losses in terms of the velocity head in the pipe:

$$h_L = k_L \frac{v^2}{2\,g}$$

  Values of k_L for various conditions are given in Appendix 16.
- A less accurate method, but one which is sufficient in many cases, is to express secondary losses in terms of 'equivalent pipe length'. That is, the length of pipe which would result in a friction loss equivalent to the secondary loss. This can be expressed as the length:diameter ratio. Ratios for various fittings are given in Appendix 16.
- In long pipelines, a rough estimate of secondary losses can be allowed for by adding a small percentage, say 5 per cent, to the actual pipe length before proceeding with the calculations. In long pipelines with few fittings, secondary losses can be neglected.

Water flow velocities in pipes Low flow velocities will allow sediment to settle in the pipe. High velocities will enhance erosion by suspended particles in the water and, if pumping, will require higher head pumps. Desirable flow velocities are 0.7 m/s to 2 m/s. However, higher velocities may be unavoidable in an emergency.

Gravity flow design

In many situations, it will be necessary to calculate the pipe diameter required to carry a certain rate of flow at a given head between two points. The following examples provide a basic guide to the design of gravity flow pipelines. Adapt the approach as required.

Case 1 A long single pipe and even sloping terrain For a long single pipe (> 1000 × diameter) of uniform diameter flowing full, the loss of energy (mainly frictional) will be the difference between the water level in the supply tank and the level of free discharge to the atmosphere at the receiving tank (Figure 13.38). In a long pipe with few fittings the secondary losses will be small and are neglected. That is, the difference in head, h, will equal the frictional head loss in the pipe, h_f. Use hydraulic tables, charts or a formula to calculate the diameter of pipe required for a specified flow.

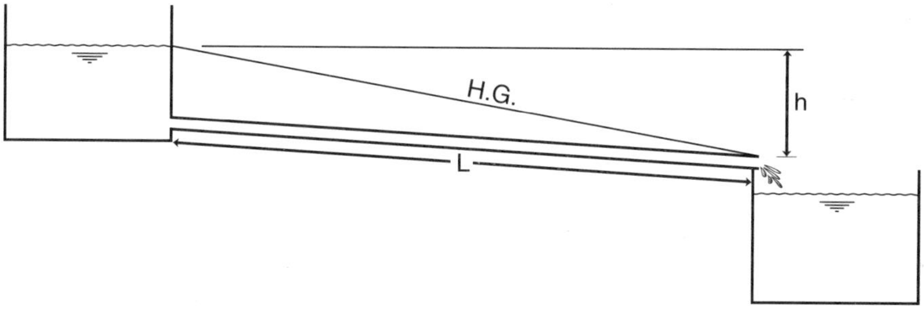

Figure 13.38 Flow through a long pipe between two tanks

A stock of PVC pipe is available. What diameter of pipe is required for the following case?

Flow required	= 5 l/s
Length of pipeline	= 100 m
Difference in head	= 1.5 m

Two different methods are shown below.

- By hydraulic tables (Appendix 16)

The hydraulic gradient, s, is calculated from the data supplied and is 1.5/100 = 0.015. From the table, a 3-inch (75 mm) PVC pipe will give a flow of 5 l/s under a hydraulic gradient of 0.0130. Therefore, the slightly higher hydraulic gradient of 0.015 will satisfy the required flow rate. The next smaller sized pipe of 2.5-inch (62 mm) will give a flow of 3.8 l/s at a gradient of 0.0173 and so it would be undersized for the flow required.

- By Hazen-Williams

$$Q = 0.275\ (h_f/L)^{0.54}\ C\ D^{2.63}$$

where:

h_f = 1.5
L = 100 m
Q = 0.005 m^3/s
C = 150
D = internal pipe diameter in metres

i.e. $Q = 4.271\ D^{2.63}$

1st trial, D = 0.069 m (2-inch PVC pipe), Q = 3.77 l/s
The flow is not sufficient to give 5 l/s.

2nd trial, D = 0.081 m (3-inch PVC pipe), Q = 5.75 l/s
Therefore, choose a 3-inch PVC pipe to give the desired flow of 5 l/s.

Case 2 Uneven terrain In practice, terrain is often uneven and design is less straightforward. It is often necessary to try several possible designs to find a workable solution. There are no set rules on where to start the design of a pipeline as each situation is different. It could be from either end or from a critical point identified in the route survey. The following example illustrates some important considerations.

The requirement is to deliver water at a flow rate of 3 l/s from one tank to another over a distance of 1200 m. The pipe freely discharges into the receiving tank. The route has been surveyed and the profile plotted as shown in Figure 13.39.

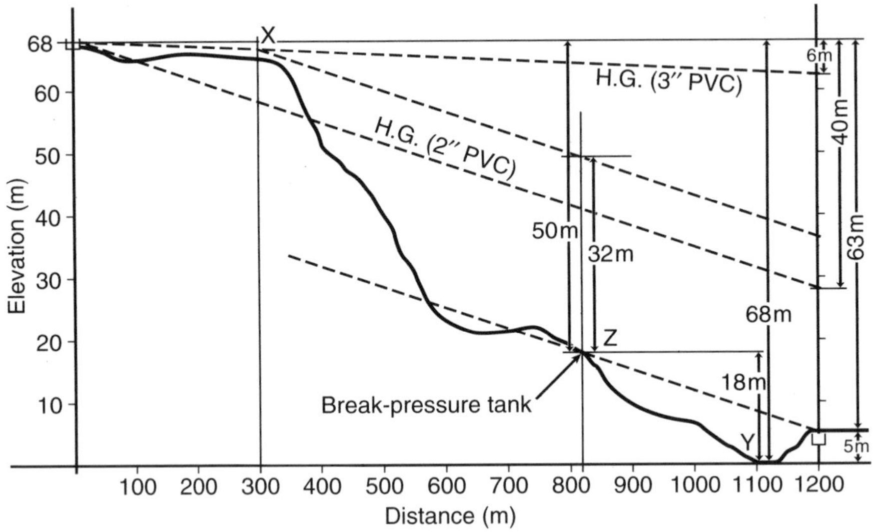

Figure 13.39 The design of a gravity-flow pipeline

The difference in elevation between the level of water in the top tank and the pipe outlet is 63 m. The maximum difference in elevation between the tank and the lowest point of the pipe is 68 m.

The hydraulic gradient for a flow of 3 l/s in a 2-inch PVC pipe has been plotted on Figure 13.39 using figures from the table in Appendix 16.

Pipe	Head loss m/1000 m	H.G.	Head loss over 1200 m
2-inch	33	0.033	40 m

The 2-inch PVC pipeline will give a residual head at the end of the pipe of:
63 m – 40 m = 23 m

This is the head loss across a valve located at the pipe outlet and adjusted to give a flow of 3 l/s.

Negative pressure The hydraulic gradient (H.G.) line dips below the pipe profile within the first 400 m of the route. This will result in negative pressure in the pipe which is undesirable because:

- Dissolved air can come out of solution and become trapped causing air-locks and a reduction, or stoppage, of flow.
- Polluted groundwater can be sucked into the pipe at leaking joints.

It is essential to avoid negative pressures. This can be achieved by careful design. One solution is to choose a larger diameter pipe. Try a 3-inch PVC pipe. From tables:

Pipe size	Head loss m/1000 m	H.G.	Head loss over 1200 m
3-inch	5	0.005	6 m

The H.G. line for a 3-inch PVC pipe has been plotted on Figure 13.39. The H.G. line is always above the pipe profile and therefore negative pressures do not arise.

But the residual head at outlet is: 63 m – 6 m = 57 m. This is very high and unacceptable. Another solution must be found which avoids negative pressures and results in a reasonable residual head.

One solution is to combine 2 and 3-inch pipes. It is clear that over the first section of the pipeline a 3-inch pipe avoids the negative pressure problem. A 2-inch pipe over the latter section of the pipeline will reduce the residual head to an acceptable level.

Draw the H.G. line for the lower section of 2-inch pipe high enough to just remain above the pipe profile. The 2-inch H.G. line intersects the 3-inch H.G. line at X to indicate the length of 3-inch pipe required. From Figure 13.39, the length of 3-inch pipe required is 300 m.

Head loss over the 300 m of 3-inch pipe	= 1.5 m
Head loss over the remaining 900 m of 2-inch pipe	= 29.7 m
Total head loss over the length of the pipe	= 31 m

Then, the residual head is: 63 m – 31 m = 32 m

Maximum pressures and break-pressure tanks

The maximum pressure that a pipe will be subjected to is the static head – when the bottom valve is closed in the above example. The pipe profile shows that the maximum static pressure on the pipe is 68 m at Y – i.e. the static pressure exceeds the maximum working pressure of Class B, PVC-u pipes, which is 6 bar. High pressures require suitably rated pipes which may not be available. If possible, it is best to avoid high pressures by careful design.

A break-pressure tank allows the pipe to freely discharge to atmosphere. Flow down the pipe then recommences at atmospheric pressure. There are many different designs of break-pressure tanks. Some are not 'tanks' at all but a combination of pipes within pipes. Figure 13.40 is one design of break-pressure tank. The only limiting factor on size is that it has to be big enough for the valves and fittings to fit inside and, therefore, tanks can be quite small (0.5 m square and deep is often sufficient).

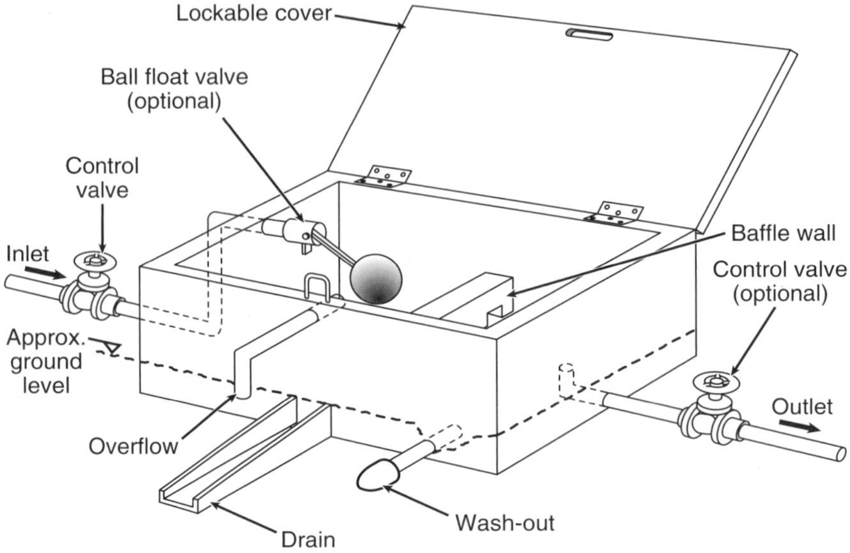

Figure 13.40 A typical break-pressure tank

Site a break-pressure tank as follows:

- Decide on the residual head required. In the example, the pipe freely discharges into the tank and the residual head is zero.
- Determine the hydraulic gradient for the flow required. In the example, the gradient for a flow rate of 3 l/s down a 2-inch PVC pipe is 0.033.
- Draw the H.G. line back from the discharge point until it intersects the pipe profile. It may intersect the profile at more than one place as in Figure 13.39.
- The conditions for the siting of a break-pressure tank are:
  - It should lie on or above the H.G. line.
  - The pipe downstream should not rise above the H.G. line.
  - The inlet valve must be rated for the static pressure at no-flow.

Therefore, for the example shown in Figure 13.39, site the break-pressure tank (b.p.t.) at Z. The difference in head between the hydraulic gradients of the upstream and downstream sections at Z represents the pressure break.

In the example:

Working head broken at Z	= 32 m
Static head broken at Z	= 50 m
Static head at Y without b.p.t.	= 68 m
Static head at Y with b.p.t.	= 18 m

Maximum static head on pipeline without b.p.t	= 68 m
Maximum static head on pipeline with b.p.t	= 50 m

Residual heads

If flow freely discharges into a tank, the residual head is zero and the pipe will be carrying its maximum flow. Where a tap or tapstand is supplied directly, then a residual head (normally 5–10 m) is required to obtain a reasonable flow at the taps. See Figure 13.35 for residual heads required for various typical tap discharge rates.

Air-blocks

Beware of air-blocks at all high points in the pipeline. Air-blocks can stop the flow altogether or, perhaps even worse, can be the cause of lower flow which may not be recognized. Arrange for the release of air at all high points and where a reduction in pressure may result in the release of air – check the hydraulic gradient. In the case of short undulations, avoid the crest in the pipeline by deepening the trench, if possible. See Appendix 15 for a description of air-valves. If no air-valve is available, install a small valve to release air by hand periodically. A very small hole in the pipe (which wastes a little water) is better than nothing, and prevents any problems with the accumulation of air.

Wash-outs

It is useful, but not essential, to include wash-out valves at low points, especially if the pipe is conveying raw surface water. Make up a wash-out from a T-branch fitting and a gate valve.

Spring supplies

The above example has assumed flow from a tank, such that the pipe inflow is sufficient to meet the natural pipe flow rate. Flow from a spring may be piped directly if the spring yield equals or is greater than the natural rate of flow in the pipe. The spring protection must include an overflow in this case.

If the spring yield is less than the natural flow, the pipe will not flow full. This may create problems: air-locks, water hammer and variable flow. It is best to feed the pipeline from a storage tank which stores spring water during periods of low demand. Alternatively, the flow in the pipe can be throttled at the discharge point so that it equals the spring supply.

Additional considerations

- Analyse complex pipe systems as a sequence of individual pipe lengths between critical points on the line: between taps, break-pressure tanks, junctions.
- It may not be possible in an emergency to design a pipeline and to wait whilst the correct pipe can be obtained. As a consequence, the emergency engineer may have no choice but to design the pipeline for pipe that is immediately available. Pipes run in parallel may overcome some of these restrictions: calculate flows for each pipe.
- In very short lengths of pipe (for instance, between tanks and gravity discharge from tankers) the secondary losses at inlet, outlet and valves will be significant and must be taken into account when calculating flow.
- A recommended reference for further guidance on gravity-flow water systems is Jordan (1984).

Pumping main design

A pump transfers energy to water to increase its kinetic energy (flow rate) and pressure energy (head) as shown diagrammatically in Figure 13.41. Details of the characteristics of different pumps and their application, installation, operation and maintenance are given in Chapter 14.

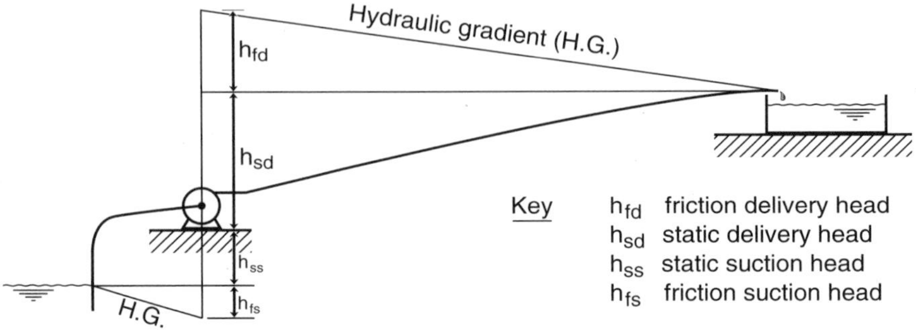

Figure 13.41 Change of head at a pump

Negative head often occurs in pump suction pipes and this must be checked against the pump's net positive suction head requirement. (see 14.2.1; net positive suction head).

In designing a pumping main, a pump must be selected which will match the characteristics of the pipe system to give the flow rate required. The procedure is as follows:

- First consider the pipe system (Figure 13.42).
- Then determine the total head requirements for a range of flow rates.

Total head = static head + friction loss + secondary losses

The losses will increase with increasing flow rate. The frictional head loss for varying flows can be read from charts or tables, or calculated using a suitable formula such as Hazen-Williams (see 'Frictional head loss in pipes' earlier in this section). Secondary losses can be neglected in a long pipeline with few fittings.

The procedure is demonstrated in the example given below.

Example of calculation to size pump for pumping main: Select a pump which will deliver 24 l/s from tank A to tank B (B higher than A).

Situation: a 4-inch PVC pipe of length 300 m freely discharges into tank B. The static head between the mean water level in tank A and the point of discharge is 20 m.

- You need to draw the system curve for a range of flows, including the required flow of 24 l/s.

Use the table in Appendix 16 to read off the head loss for a range of flows and tabulate as shown in Table 13.20. Alternatively, use the Hazen-Williams formula to calculate the head loss for a range of flows and tabulate.

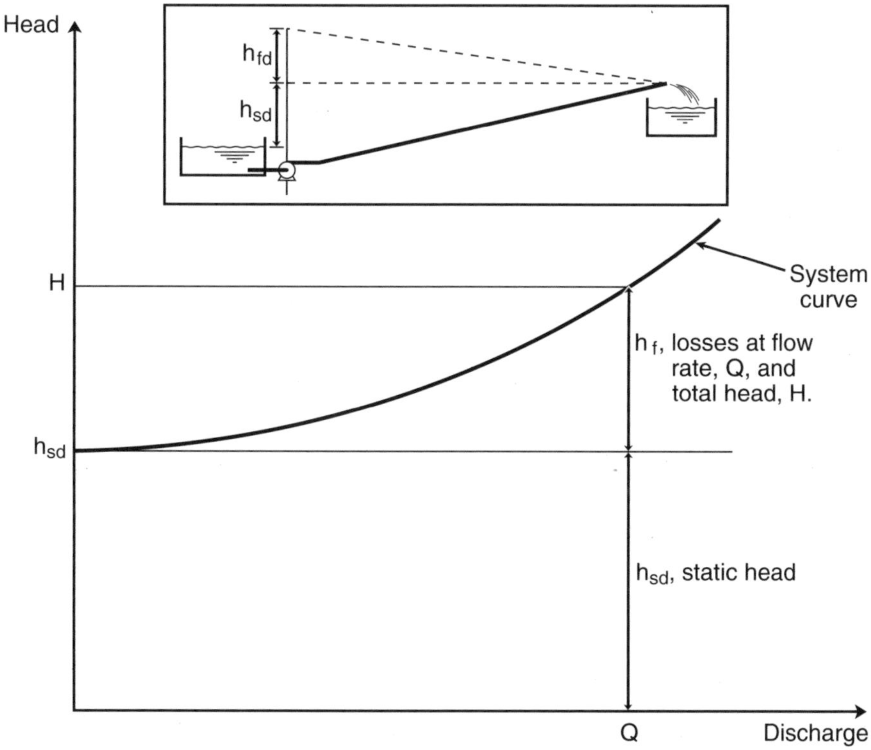

Figure 13.42 The head requirement for a pumping main

Table 13.20 Calculated head discharge data in a pumping main

Q, l/s	*Q, m³/h*	*Friction head, m*	*Static head, m*	*Total head, m*
5	18	1.0	20	21.0
10	36	3.6	20	23.6
15	54	7.6	20	27.6
20	72	13.0	20	33.0
25	90	19.6	20	39.6
30	108	27.4	20	47.4

In this case, the values in the Hazen-Williams formula are:

For PVC pipe, C = 150
Pipe length, L = 300 m
Pipe diameter, D = 0.105 m (N.B. internal diameter)

Tabulate the figures for discharge and total head (Table 13.20) and plot the H/Q system curve (Figure 13.43).

- Next, select a pump from manufacturers' pump charts which matches the duty required, and obtain the pump's characteristic curves. If there is only a limited range of pumps available for immediate use they will have to be matched as closely as possible to the flow requirements by a judicious selection of pump and pipe sizes. (In this example, it is assumed that an end-suction, single-stage, centrifugal pump will be chosen. This is the most common type of pump for this application and most likely to be available in an emergency.)

- Superimpose the H/Q pump characteristic curve on the pipe system curve (Figure 13.43).

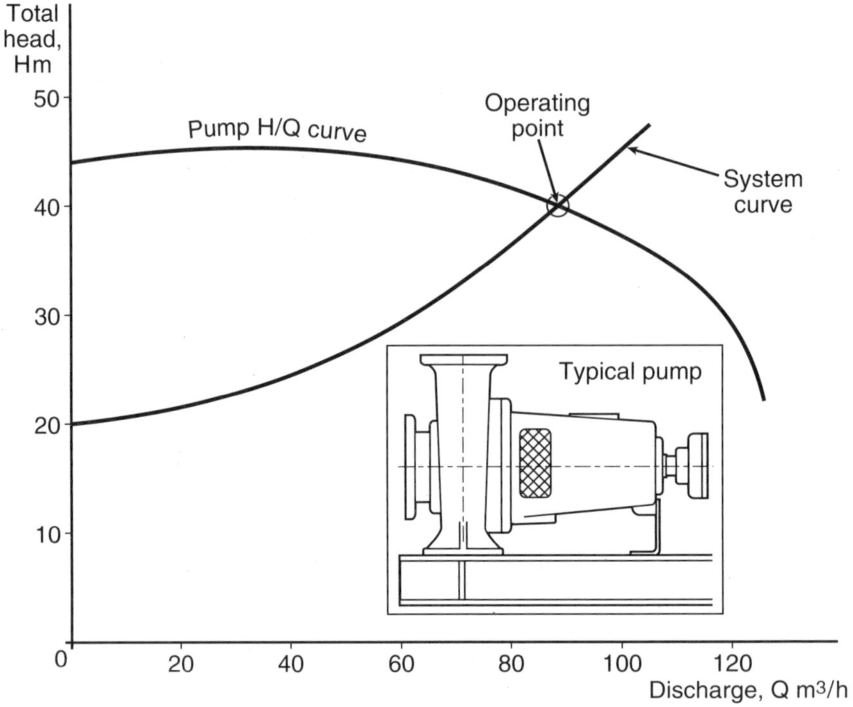

Figure 13.43 Matching a centrifugal pump to a pumping system curve

The operating point is where the curves intersect. This indicates the only possible discharge for the particular pump and system. If the discharge is not the flow rate required, and no changes to the rising main dimensions are possible, consider the following options:

- Vary the speed of the pump. If the speed of the pump can be varied (such as when driven by a diesel engine) a centrifugal pump characteristic will move along the system curve, and within limits, will vary as follows:
  Flow – varies with Speed
  Head – varies with $(\text{Speed})^2$
  Power – varies with $(\text{Speed})^3$
- Try a different pump. Superimpose several H/Q pump characteristics on the pipe system curve to find the best match. Any one pump model will have several

variations. In the case of a centrifugal pump, manufacturers alter the characteristics by varying the diameter of the impeller. Always check the chosen pump has the impeller diameter corresponding to the curve used in design.

- Throttle the pipe system. The effect of throttling the system is to increase the pipe losses thereby increasing the gradient of the system curve. This is only going to be of use if, for some reason, a lower flow rate is required.

Note that the diameter of a pump discharge outlet does not mean that the rising main should be of the same size. The rising main should be sized to minimize losses and is often one or two sizes larger than the pump outlet (for example, a 75 mm outlet may discharge into a 100 mm rising main).

Combinations of pumps

Where no single available pump can match the duty required, it may be necessary to consider combinations of two, or more, pumps. Positive displacement pumps should not be run in series although they can be run in parallel.

Centrifugal pumps in series The effect of running two centrifugal pumps in series is to increase the head as shown in Figure 13.44. Use the combined H/Q curve and follow the same procedure as for one pump.

Check the following when running pumps in series:

- Both the second pump in series, the pipe fittings and pipeline must be able to withstand the higher pressures developed.
- As flow rate is increased the net positive suction head (NPSH) required will increase. Check the first pump in series is able to pump under the new suction conditions. (See 13.2.1).

Centrifugal pumps in parallel The effect of running two centrifugal pumps in parallel is to increase the discharge as shown in Figure 13.45. Use the combined H/Q curve and follow the same procedure as for one pump. Check the following when running pumps in parallel:

- Pumps run in parallel must have stable H/Q characteristics such that there is only one possible point on the characteristic curves at which both pumps can operate.
- The division of flow may need to be adjusted for balanced running.
- As flow rate is increased, the net positive suction head (NPSH) required will increase. Check the pumps are able to operate under the new suction conditions. (See 14.2.1).

Distribution systems

The two main types of distribution system likely to be installed are: branched (also called dendritic) and ring main systems. More complex networks are normally confined to developed urban systems.

The choice of distribution system will be determined by several factors: location and type of the source or sources, optimum system design, system reliability, the terrain, the equipment and materials available, stages of development and the time required for installation.

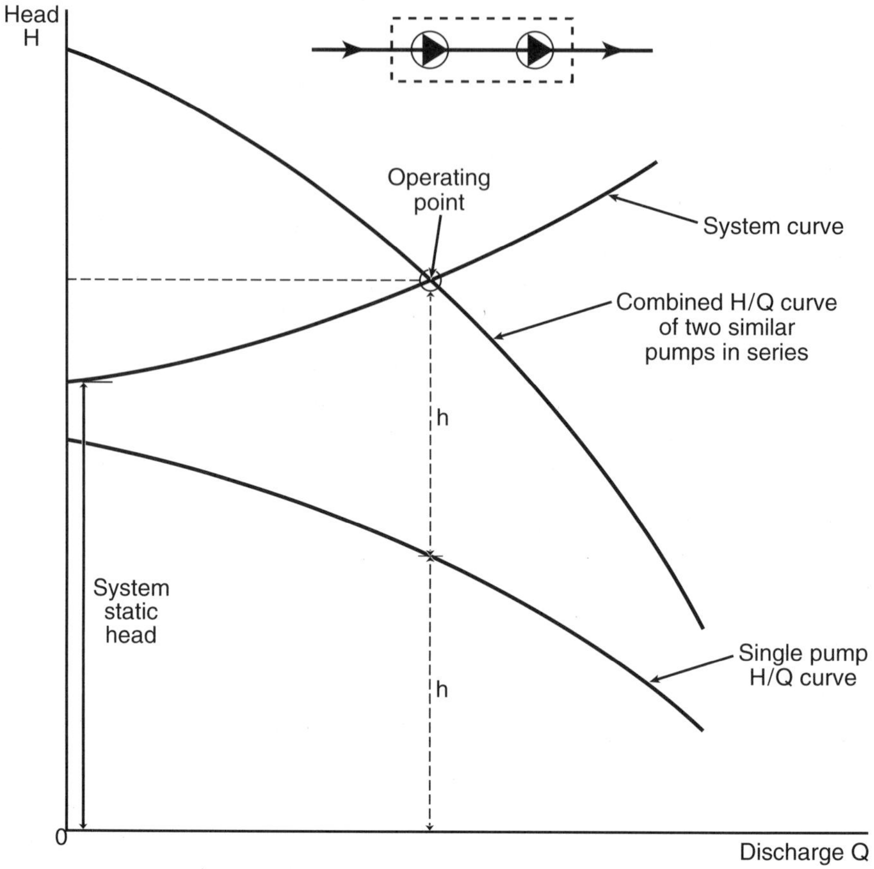

Figure 13.44 Centrifugal pumps in series

The development of an emergency supply to a refugee camp, for example, may involve several stages:

- A simple single pipeline serving several tapstands for the immediate collection of water.
- The addition of several branches and new sources (such as boreholes) as they are developed.
- The linking of branches and interlinking of sources for back-up to form a ring main with branches.

This process is similar to the development of a typical urban water supply, except that the process takes only a few months instead of being spread over years. Wherever possible, the initial simple branched system should be designed and sized to take account of possible future upgrading and the higher water demand that will follow.

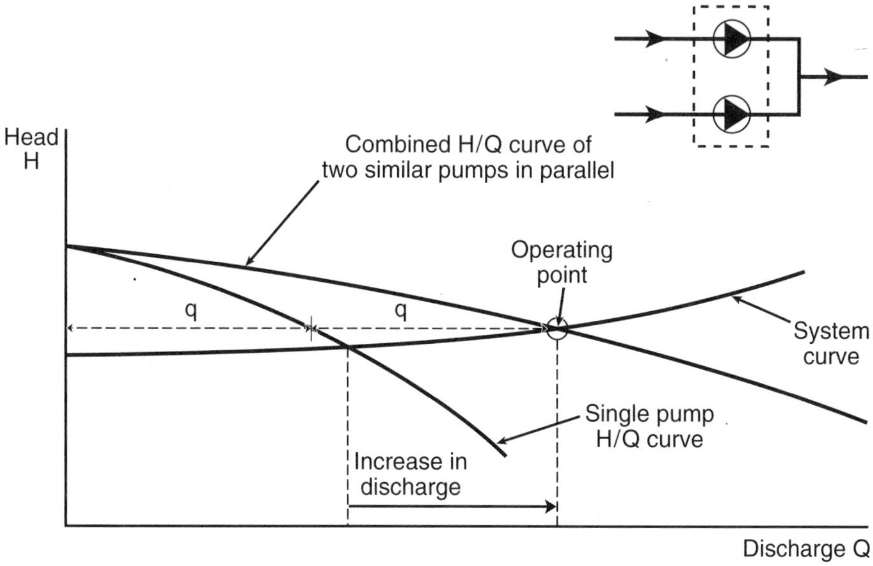

Figure 13.45 Centrifugal pumps in parallel

Design for the peak demand The design of the abstraction and treatment stages of a supply system is based on the average daily water demand. The distribution system, and associated storage, should be designed for the peak water demand (see Section 13.1).

Pumping controls Storage tanks are often some distance from the pumps which are pumping to them. Adequate systems of control must be introduced so that tanks are filled but do not overflow. If the tank, or tanks, can be seen by the pump operator, then a simple float which indicates the water level may be all that is needed. For example, make a float out of three Coke bottles tied together, and attach a cane with a flag or ball on top.

More elaborate systems may need to be devised if pumps and tanks are far apart or out of sight. Bells or horns within hearing range, or even two-way radios, may have to be considered.

Branched systems Typical arrangements of branched systems are shown in Figure 13.46 although many different combinations of source, treatment, storage and distribution are possible. There are four basic types of branched system:

- Gravity system.
- Indirect pumping system.
- Direct pumping system.
- Combination or indirect-direct pumping system (also known as the 'rise and fall' system).

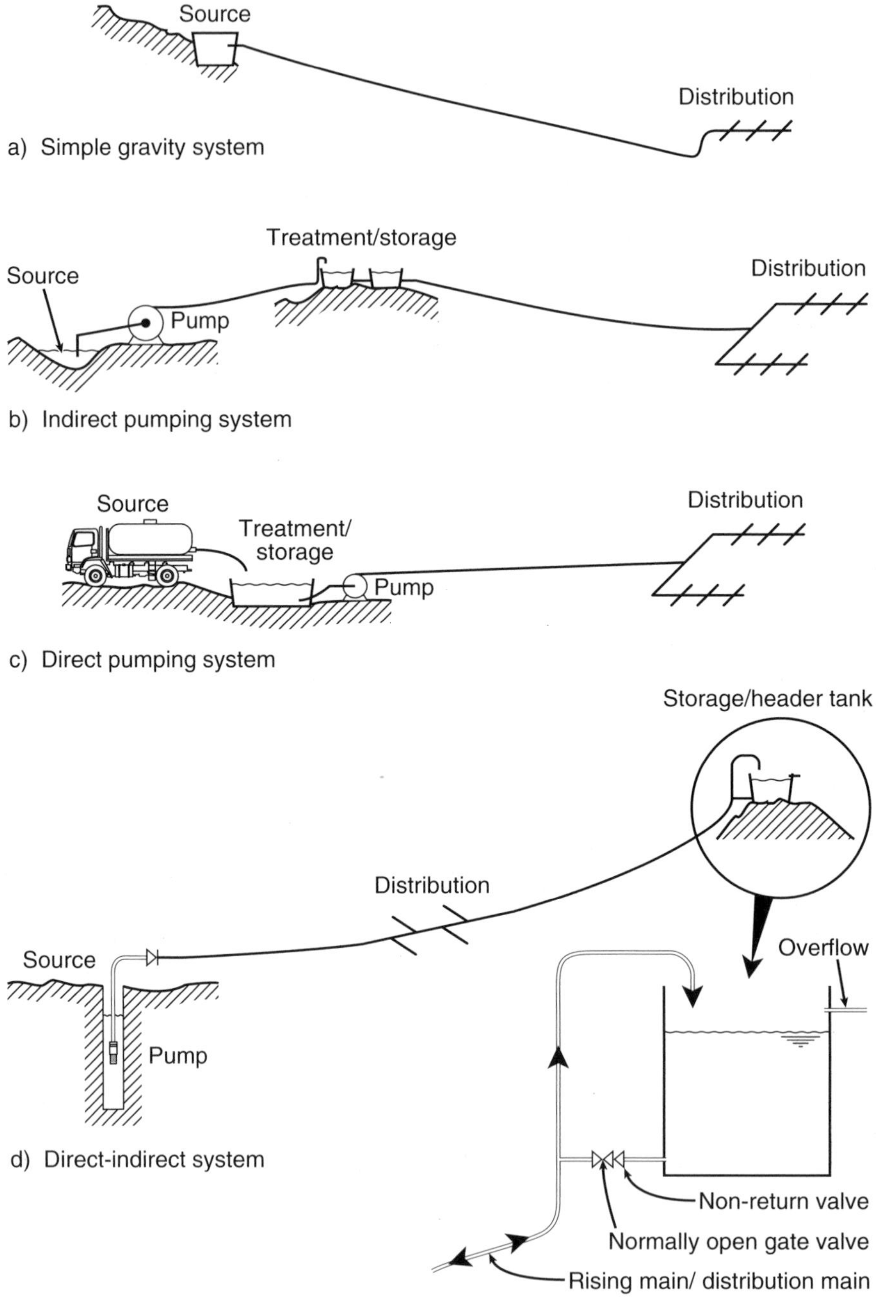

Figure 13.46 Branched distribution systems

Practical considerations in the design of branched systems:

- Water tanks provide storage to even out the demand and to provide a reserve if there is a break in supply. Tanks also ensure a relatively constant head on distribution lines.
- Pumps can be quickly installed to pressurize the system as a temporary measure until header tanks can be erected. Pumps should be backed up with adequate standby pumping capacity.
- Positive displacement pumps cannot be used in a direct system as they require some form of pressure release when all taps are shut. Do not use helical rotor pumps, for example, to supply tapstands directly; use centrifugal pumps instead.
- The direct-indirect system can be used where the area to be supplied is between a safe source and high ground. Pipe can be saved, and time in laying reduced, by using the rising main as the gravity distribution main. It is also a more reliable method as a pipe burst or a breakdown in any one section of pipe either side of the supply area will not mean that the supply is totally cut-off. Careful management of pumping and collection times is necessary if the system is to work as designed.

The inset in Figure 13.46d shows one arrangement for the piping at the header tank. There are several possible arrangements depending on the circumstances. It is not necessary for the inlet pipe to discharge over the top of the tank. If the non-return valve is not included, it can enter the bottom, or side, directly. The advantage of having the pipe over the top is that the water can be seen, and heard, entering the tank. A ball float valve should only be installed on the inlet if there is reliable pressure control of the pumps or a method of pressure relief is incorporated in the delivery main.

For a method of calculating flows in a branch line, see the calculations for a ring main given in Box 13.6 which includes the sizing of a branch line.

Ring main

A ring main is illustrated in Figure 13.47. One principal advantage of a ring main is that flow is apportioned in two directions and can, therefore, better meet peak demand. In addition, it is a more reliable system than a single branch, because, if there is a break in the ring, water can still flow to all points.

Design of a simple ring main Two key conditions apply in calculating flow and head losses in pipe networks:

- Continuity of flow must be satisfied at all junctions – what flows into a junction must flow out.
- The pipe friction losses between any two points in a ring are the same, irrespective of the route taken.

Box 13.6 Sample calculation for ring main design

A refugee camp with a population of 7500 people is to be supplied with 15 litres/person/day through a number of tapstands distributed around the camp. The daily demand is 7500 × 15 = 112 500 l/day. One tap serves 250 people, therefore a total of 30 taps are required. Each tapstand contains six taps, so five tapstands are required at B, C, D, E and F.

Let the tapstands be distributed on a ring main ABCDE and a branch line DF as shown in Figure 13.47. The lengths of pipe and relative ground levels at each tapstand are shown. The ring is supplied with water at A from a tank elevated by 2 m at a ground elevation of 12 m to give a total head of 14 m. A residual head of 8 m at each tapstand will give a flow of 0.25 l/s from each tap (see Figure 13.35).

Design to meet the peak flow. Assume all taps will be open at peak collection periods so the total flow to each tapstand, 6 × 0.25 = 1.5 l/s and peak flow around the ring main = 7.5 l/s.

To choose a suitable size of pipe for the ring main it is necessary to identify, by inspection, the point in the ring most difficult to supply (a combination of least available head, longest pipe route and highest flows giving highest losses). In this case, point D seems the critical point to supply. If the wrong point is chosen then the flows calculated will either be meaningless or highly unlikely to work in practice and the process must be repeated choosing another point.

To determine the flows in each section of pipe it is assumed that flow is in two directions (ABCD and AED). The friction losses in one direction can then be equated to the losses in the other direction and the flow calculated. Knowing the flows, a suitable pipe diameter can be determined to give the required residual heads at each tapstand.

Let the flow in AB be Q. Then the flow in each section of the ring will be:

AB = Q; BC = (Q – 1.5); CD = (Q – 3);
AE = (7.5 – Q); ED = (6 – Q)

Equate the friction losses ($h_f \propto l\, q^2$).

Losses in ABCD:

AB $60Q^2$
BC $250(Q - 1.5)^2 = 250Q^2 - 750Q + 562.5$
CD $75(Q - 3)^2 = 75Q^2 - 450Q + 675$
Sum of losses in ABCD = $385Q^2 - 1200Q + 1237.5$

Losses in AED:

AE $55(7.5 - Q)^2 = 55Q^2 - 825Q + 3093.75$
ED $170(6 - Q)^2 = 170Q^2 - 2040Q + 6120$
Sum of losses in AED = $225Q^2 - 2865Q + 9213.75$

Losses in ABCD = Losses in AED

$385Q^2 - 1200Q + 1237.5 = 225Q^2 - 2865Q + 9213.75$ giving
$160Q^2 + 1665Q - 7976.25 = 0$ or
$Q^2 + 10.4Q - 49.85 = 0$

Solving for Q

$$[\, x = \frac{-b \pm \sqrt{(b^2 - 4ac)}}{2a} \,]$$

$$Q = \frac{-10.4 \pm \sqrt{(108.16 + 199.4)}}{2}$$

Q = 3.6 l/s

Flows in each section of pipe are:
AB (3.6l/s); BC (2.1 l/s); CD (0.6 l/s); AE (3.9 l/s); ED (2.4 l/s)

The diameter of the ring main must now be determined to give the required residual heads at each tapstand. It is convenient to tabulate results as shown in Table 13.21.

Columns **b**, **c**, and **h** are filled in from known data. A pipe diameter, **d**, is tried based on the known flows and the allowable losses. In this case a 3-inch PVC pipe (ID 81mm) is selected. Use head loss data from Appendix 16 to estimate head losses in columns **e** and **f**. Obtain column **g** by subtracting the friction losses from the total head available at the previous point. The residual head in column **i** is obtained by subtracting the ground level, **h**, from the total head, **g**. For the required flow from the taps the residual head must be at least 8m.

The table indicates that a 3-inch PVC ring main will give sufficient residual head for the required flow plus a 'reserve' to overcome losses through fittings. If significant, losses in fittings can be included by allowing an extra 5 per cent pipe length or by subtracting calculated losses (using $kv^2/2g$) from the total head available.

The flow in the branch DF can be accommodated by choosing a smaller diameter pipe than used in the ring main. In this case, losses for a 50mm OD (40mm ID) pipe have been tabulated.

A distribution main with several branches is designed by sizing the main for the most difficult point to supply (furthest from the supply point, least available head, etc.) and then sizing each branch separately. Tabulate calculations in a similar format to that shown in Table 13.21.

Table 13.21 Tabulation of ring main design calculations

Point	Pipe length m	Flow l/s	Pipe ID mm	Friction loss m/100m	Friction loss Total m	Elevation Total head m	Elevation Ground level m	Residual head m
a	**b**	**c**	**d**	**e**	**f**	**g**	**h**	**i**
A						14	12	
	60	3.6	81	0.7	0.4			
B						13.6	4	9.6
	250	2.1	81	0.3	0.75			
C						12.9	2	10.9
	75	0.6	81	neg	neg			
D						12.9	4	8.9
A						14	12	
	55	3.9	81	0.8	0.4			
E						13.6	4.5	9.1
	170	2.4	81	0.45	0.8			
D						12.8	4	8.8
	50	1.5	40	4.4	2.2			
F						10.6	2	8.6

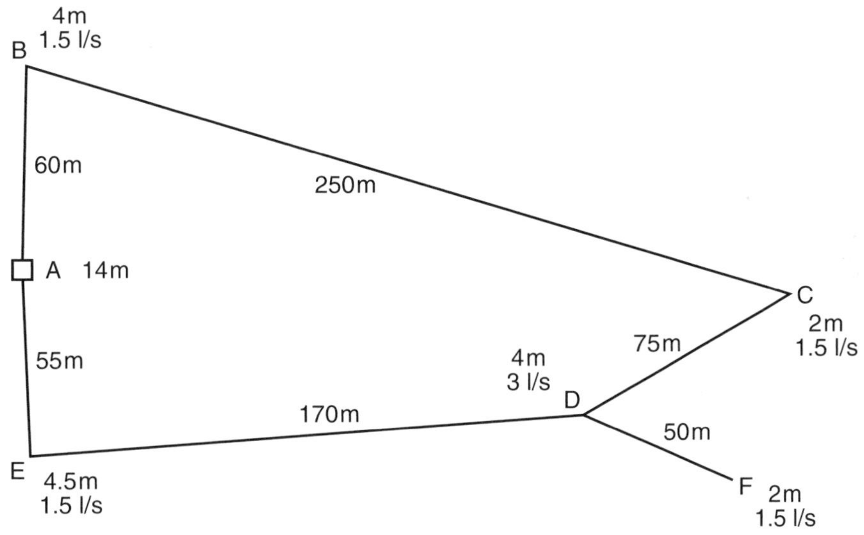

Figure 13.47 A ring main

For a simple ring main laid in an emergency, where the direction of flow is fairly obvious, the flows can be found algebraically. It is convenient to refer to the Darcy equation for flow in pipes which gives the head loss due to friction, h_f, as:

$$h_f = \frac{4\,f\,l}{d}\,\frac{v^2}{2g}$$

where: f is a friction coefficient
l is the length of the pipeline
v is the flow velocity
d is the internal diameter of the pipe
g is the acceleration due to gravity

For a simple ring main of one size of pipe, f, g and d are constants.

giving $h_f \alpha lv^2$

But flow, q = vA, where A is the cross-sectional area of pipe and is constant

so $h_f \alpha lq^2$

As friction losses between two points in a ring are the same they can be equated as shown in the worked example in Box 13.6.

14 Pumps

The purpose of this chapter is to give guidance on the selection, installation and operation of pumps in emergency relief. Chapter 13 deals with the use of pumps in the treatment, storage and distribution of water. The prime movers (engines and motors) that drive the pumps are dealt with in Chapters 15 and 16.

14.1 Pump types and applications

Pumps are used to lift water against gravity or to pressurize water sufficiently to move it through a pipeline at a desired rate. Pumps should only be used where gravity cannot be enlisted to do the job. Common areas where pumping may be reduced or eliminated are in water abstraction and distribution, water treatment and tanker offloading. In hilly, well-watered country, careful design can reduce the need for pumping. In flat arid terrain with deep groundwater, pumping will be essential.

The pumps (or water lifting devices) covered in this chapter are: surface mounted centrifugal, electric submersible multi-stage centrifugal, helical rotor and handpumps. Surface mounted centrifugal pumps are typically used in emergencies for pumping water from a surface source, such as a river or lake, and for pressurizing water in a distribution system. Electric submersible and helical rotor pumps are typically used for pumping water from boreholes or wells. Helical rotor pumps are generally more reliable, can deal with poorer quality water and can cope better with a range of pumping heads. Handpumps and windlass and buckets are commonly used in community water supply in developing countries and may be important in emergency relief where there may be many individual well sources.

Table 14.1 gives a summary of pump type and application and gives preliminary guidance on the selection of pump type. Detailed guidance on selecting and specifying pumps is given in 14.6.2.

14.2 Pumping head, discharge and power

14.2.1 Pumping rates, head and suction lift

Pumping rates

Pumps are rated according to the flow rate of water which can be pumped against a certain pressure, or 'head', at a given operating speed. A pump is usually rated at its most efficient output even though it may operate over a

Table 14.1 A summary of pump types and their application in emergency relief

Application / *Pump type*	*Lifting from wells or boreholes*	*Abstraction from surface sources (lakes, rivers)*	*Distribution through pipeline*	*Flow circulation in treatment system*
Surface mounted centrifugal	●	●●●	●●●	●●
Electric submersible multi-stage centrifugal	●●●	●	●	n
Helical rotor (Mono)	●●●	●	n	n
Handpump	●●●	n	n	n
Windlass and bucket	●●●	n	n	n

●●● = most suited; n = not suited.

range of flows and heads. It is preferable to install a pump that operates at, or near, its most efficient operating point. Pump flow rates are commonly expressed as m^3/h, m^3/s or l/s. Pressure is normally expressed as metres head of water (1 m head is equivalent to a pressure of 9.81 kN/m^2).

Pumping head

When pumping water through a pipeline, the total pressure head which a pump must overcome is composed of static, friction and velocity heads as shown in Figure 14.1. See 13.4.3 for more details.

Static head The static head is the total vertical height through which the water is to be pumped. This is made up of the static suction head, h_{ss}, and the static delivery head, h_{sd}. Note that the static suction head is the vertical height from the pump inlet to the surface of water, not to the bottom of the pipe, whereas the static delivery head is the vertical height from the pump outlet to the outlet of the delivery pipe.

Friction head The head required to overcome friction in the system (pipes and fittings) is the friction head loss. This can be divided into friction losses on the suction side of the pump, h_{fs}, and on the delivery side, h_{fd} (see 13.4.3 for how to calculate friction losses).

Velocity head A certain amount of pressure head is needed to accelerate the water from zero to its flow velocity, v. This is termed the velocity head (= $v^2/2g$, with g being gravitational acceleration, 9.81 m/s^2). In most practical pumping applications the flow velocity is small enough for the velocity head to be neglected. For example, with a high flow velocity of 4 m/s the velocity head is approximately 0.25 m, whereas static and friction heads may be many tens of metres.

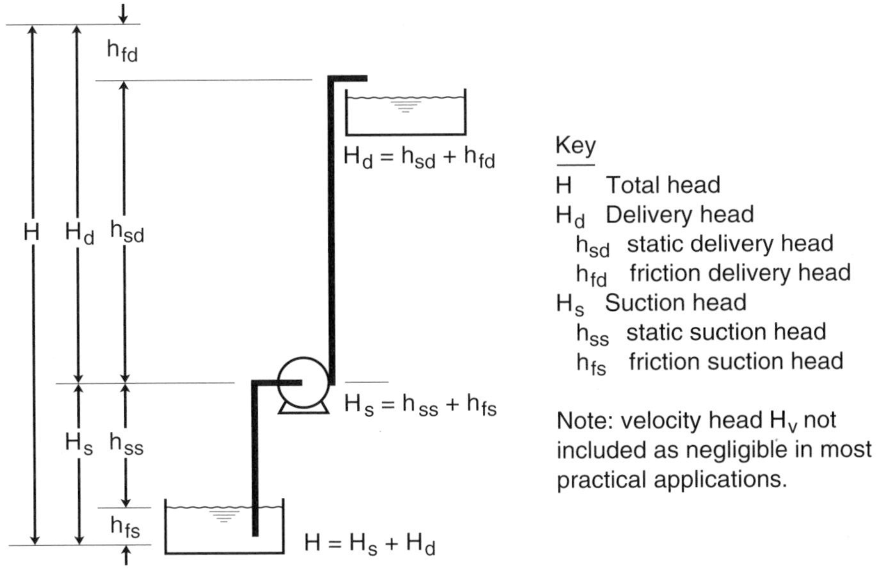

Figure 14.1 Components of the total pressure head generated by a pump

Thus, ignoring the velocity head, the total pumping head is given by

$$\text{Total head} = \text{static head} + \text{friction head}$$

Suction lift

To raise water from below the level of a pump, a partial vacuum (a pressure less than atmospheric) must be created in the suction pipe. When the pipe is inserted in an open body of water, atmospheric pressure causes the water to flow into the pipe. The theoretical maximum lift for a perfect vacuum is 10.35 m (atmospheric pressure at 0°C and sea level). This is reduced by about 1 m for every 1000 m above sea level. However, the actual maximum suction lift is less, because energy is used to move the water and to overcome resistance to flow. There will also be a minimum pressure requirement at the pump inlet which will depend on the individual pump.

Net positive suction head (NPSH) The term 'net positive suction head' (NPSH) refers to the head that causes water to flow into the pump. This can be divided into available NPSH – a feature of the pump location relative to the water source and of the suction pipe characteristics – and required NPSH – a characteristic of the pump. Increasing the pump discharge rate decreases the available NPSH.

The available NPSH is:

$$\text{available NPSH} = h_a - h_{vp} - h_{fs} - h_{ss}$$

where:

h_a atmospheric pressure (equivalent to 10.35 m water at 0°C and sea level, decreasing with altitude by about 1 m for every 1000 m altitude)

h_{vp} vapour pressure of water, negligible in this context (about 0.23 m at 20°C)
h_{fs} friction losses in the suction pipe
h_{ss} static suction head below pump inlet

For example:
If the surface of the water is 4.4 m below the pump inlet, atmospheric pressure is 7.8 m (at about 2500 m altitude) and the friction losses through the strainer, foot valve, bends and connections are estimated at 0.5 m for the anticipated flow rate:

$$\text{available NPSH} = 7.8 - 0.5 - 4.4 = 2.9 \text{ m}$$

The required NPSH is the minimum pressure requirement at the pump inlet and depends on the pump design. Consult the manufacturers' data for these figures. For water to be able to flow into the pump inlet:

$$\text{available NPSH} \geq \text{required NPSH}$$

Check that this is the case at expected operational peak flow rates.

Actual suction lift varies for different pumps. Some pumps are unable to lift water and, in order to pump, require a positive head at the inlet. Even a pump with good suction capability is unlikely to lift more than about 6–7 m at sea level.

Reduce friction losses on the suction pipe as far as possible:

- Select a suction pipe of the recommended diameter. The suction pipe should never have a smaller diameter than the pump inlet. It is often larger.
- Keep the suction pipe as short as possible. Arrange pump platforms or pontoons to pump from as close to the water surface as possible.
- Keep the number of fittings on the suction side to a minimum and avoid sharp bends and elbows.

14.2.2 Pump power and efficiency

The power output measured in watts (W) of a pump, P_w, sometimes called the water power, is given by:

$$P_w = Q \rho g h$$

where:

Q is the flow rate of water, m^3/s
ρ is the density of water, (1000 kg/m^3 or 1 kg/l)
g is gravitational acceleration, 9.81 m/s^2
h is the operating pressure head against which the pump must discharge (see 13.4.3)

For ease of calculation the flow rate in litres/second is equivalent to the quantity 'Qρ'. A pump delivering 5 l/s against a 50 m operating head would have a power output of $P_w = 5 \times 9.81 \times 50 = 2452.5$ W or about 2.5k W. The required input power to the pump, P_p is given by

$$P_p = P_w/\eta$$

where η is the overall efficiency with which power from the prime mover is converted into water power. This will depend on power transmission efficiencies and pump efficiencies.

Transmission efficiencies may be up to 90 per cent for close coupled electric motors and may be about 65 per cent for belt drives from internal combustion (IC) engines. Maximum centrifugal pump efficiencies are about 70–80 per cent but may be much lower than this. Combining the transmission losses and pump losses gives typical overall efficiencies of 40–60 per cent. These are only approximate figures and overall efficiencies will vary depending on how closely the pump operation matches its design duty point and on the type and mechanical state of the transmission system. A centrifugal pump delivering 2.5 kW and powered by an IC engine will typically require 5.0 kW from the engine.

14.2.3 Pump classification and characteristics

Most pumps can be classified as rotodynamic or positive displacement pumps.

Rotodynamic pumps use a rotor or impeller rotating inside a casing. The rotor and casing shape further divides rotodynamic pumps into:

- Centrifugal – either single-stage surface mounted or multi-stage submersibles in boreholes. These are the most common types of pump and are considered in detail below.
- Axial flow and mixed flow pumps – rarely used in disaster relief, not discussed further here.

Positive displacement pumps involve a pumping element (such as a piston or helical rotor) displacing a fixed amount for each cycle of the pump. Positive displacement pumps can be designed to pump against very high heads. They can be subdivided into:

- Positive rotary – the helical rotor pump is widely used for water supply from boreholes (see Section 14.4).
- Reciprocating – a plunger reciprocating inside a cylinder or a reciprocating diaphragm. Many handpumps on wells and boreholes use pistons in cylinders (Section 14.5).

For rotodynamic pumps, pump discharge rates vary considerably with the head against which the water is being pumped (see Figure 14.2). Both pumping head and discharge rate increase as the speed of the pump increases. Since discharge varies with speed, head varies with $(\text{speed})^2$ and power varies with $(\text{speed})^3$, when specifying a centrifugal pump it is important to have an accurate assessment of the pumping head.

With positive displacement pumps, the pumping head is independent of pump speed. The discharge rate is not affected by the operating head to the same extent as rotodynamic pumps. Thus a positive displacement pump, such as the helical rotor, can operate satisfactorily over a wide range of heads and pump speeds. This characteristic is particularly useful in an emergency where precise pumping heads are not known in advance and supplies need to be brought on-line quickly. A limited stock of helical rotor pumps can cover a broad range of borehole depths.

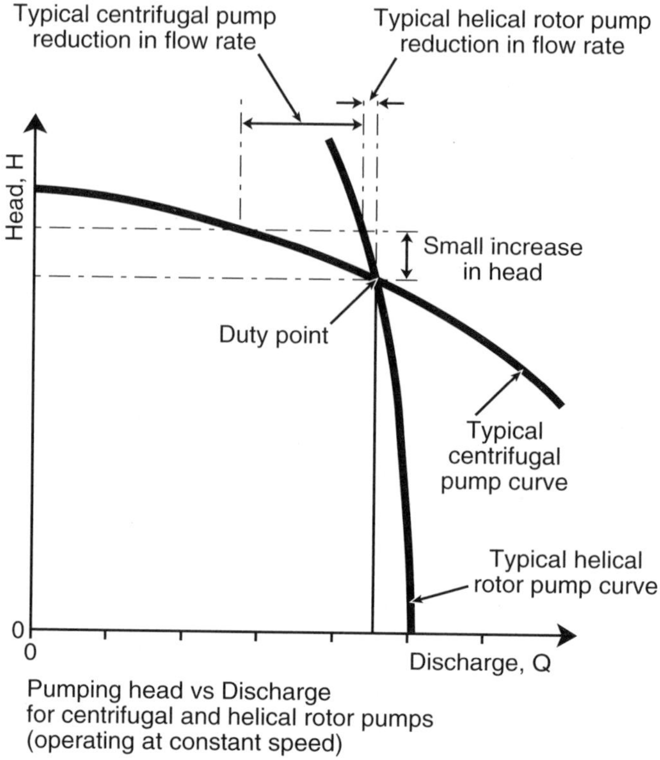

Figure 14.2 A comparison of head–discharge relationships for centrifugal and helical rotor pumps

Figures 14.2 and 14.3 illustrate the different pumping characteristics of centrifugal and helical rotor pumps.

14.3 Centrifugal pumps

14.3.1 General

Centrifugal pumps are by far the most common type of rotodynamic pump, and they are used in many different applications. A single impeller inside a chamber forms the basic single-stage centrifugal pump as shown in Figure 14.4. High-speed rotation of the impeller causes water to be sucked into the eye and thrown radially, emerging through the outlet under pressure.

Figure 14.5 shows how head, discharge, power and efficiency are related for a typical centrifugal pump. Ideally the pump should be chosen to operate at or near maximum efficiency.

A multi-stage pump consists of several stages placed one after the other on the same shaft. The arrangement is equivalent to a number of individual centrifugal pumps in series. The flow remains constant, but the pressure head

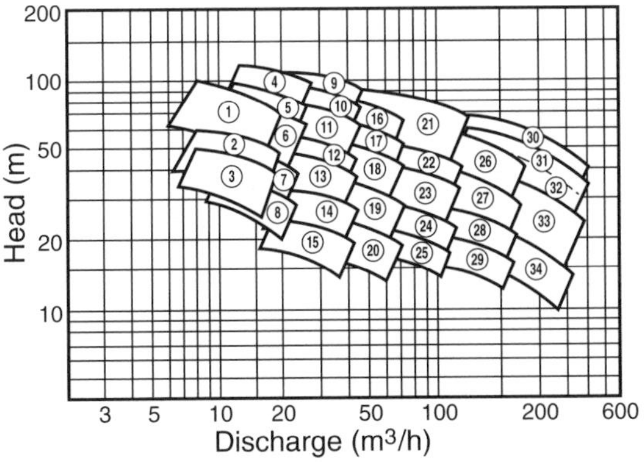

End-suction, single stage centrifugal pumps
(Atalanta Engineering Ltd)

Performances shown are from engine-driven pump sets at varying engine speeds at a normal suction lift of 5m.

Consult individual performance curves for other conditions.

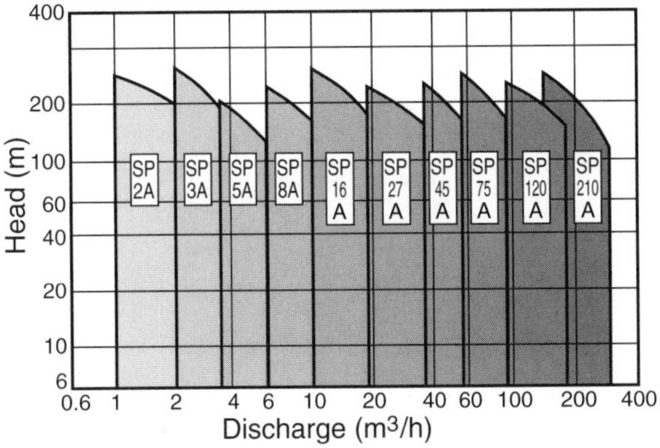

Centrifugal electric submersible borehole pumps
(Grundfos Pumps Ltd)

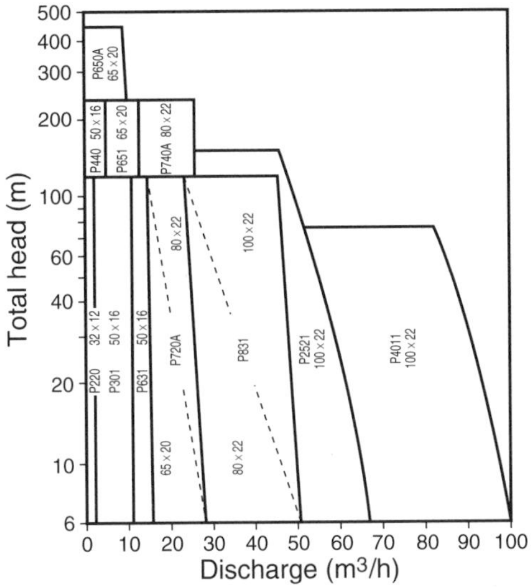

Helical rotor, 'Mono' type borehole pumps
(H_2O Waste-Tec,
a division of Mono Pumps Ltd)

Key to coding:

Pump			P4011
Column pipe diameter	×	Drive shaft diameter	100 × 22

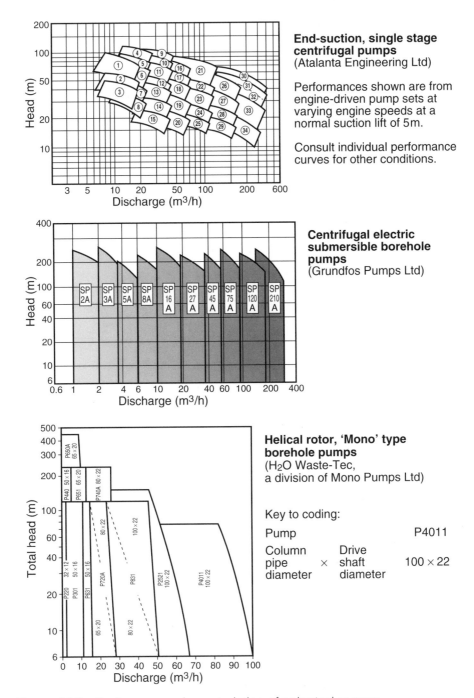

Figure 14.3 Performance characteristics of selected pumps

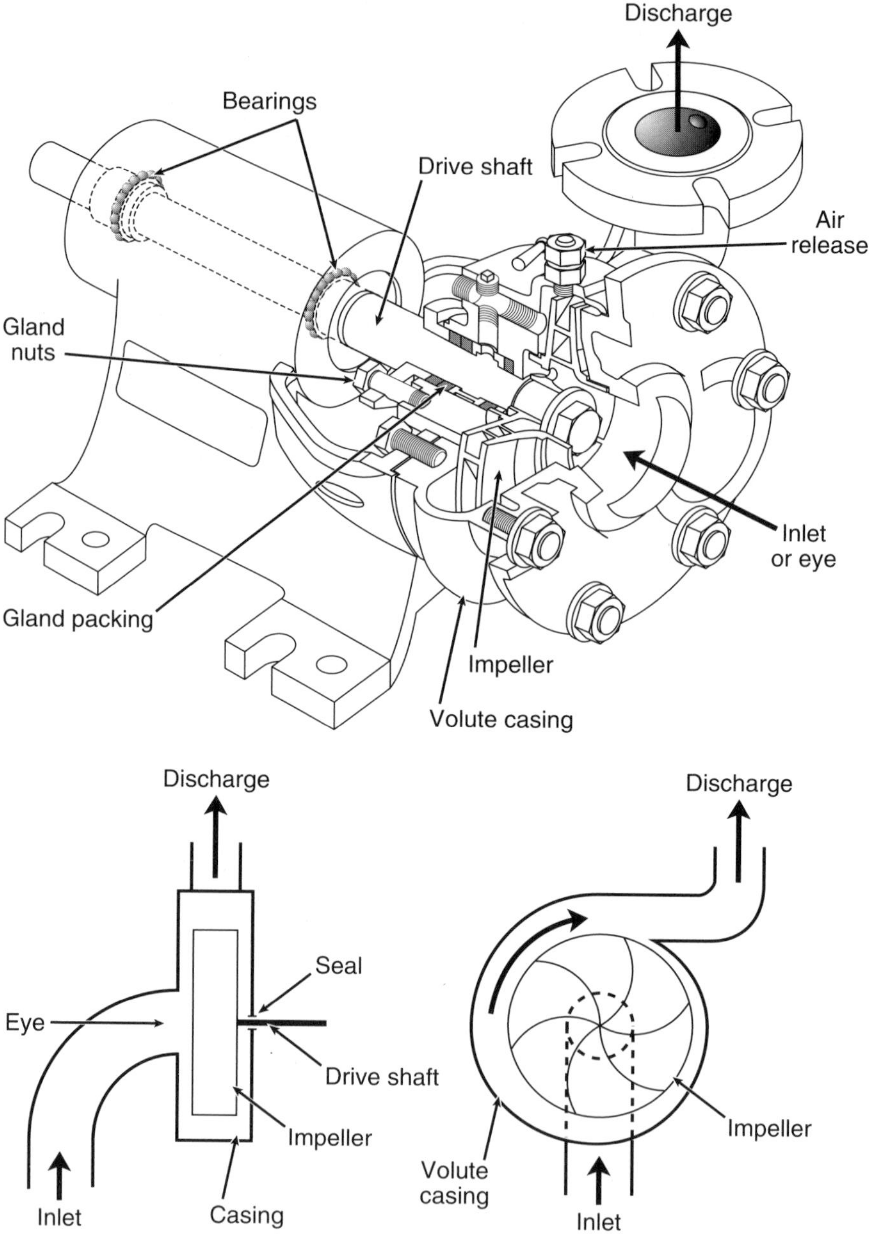

Figure 14.4 End suction, single-stage centrifugal pump

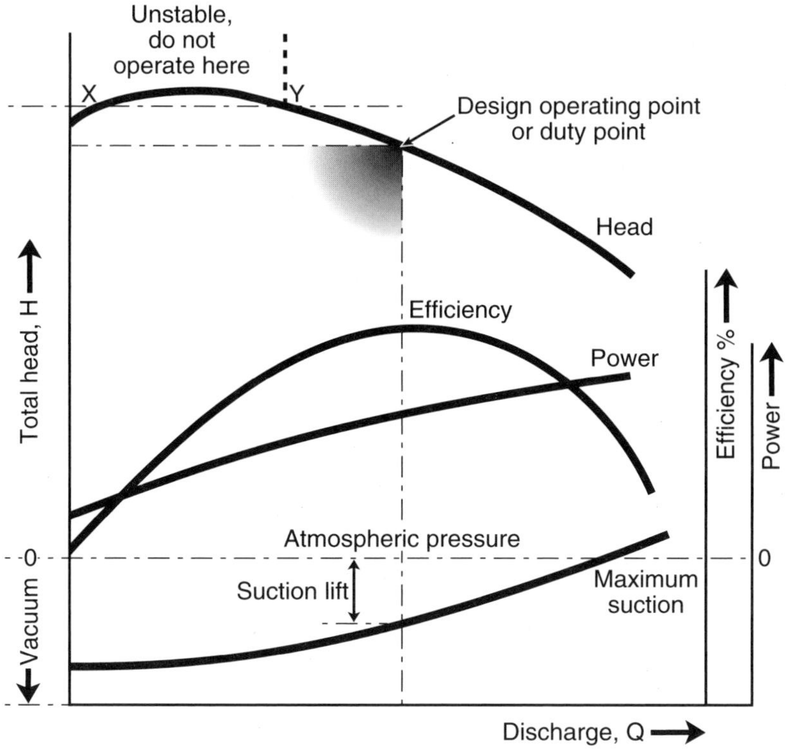

Figure 14.5 Centrifugal pump characteristic curves

developed is increased at each stage. Multi-stage pumps are commonly used for the boosting of water pressure and in submersible borehole pumps. Figure 14.6 shows a multi-stage, submersible borehole pump. The slim design of several stages mounted together allows the pump to fit inside a small diameter borehole. Higher heads can be attained by adding more stages and uprating the motor. Borehole pumps may be shaft driven from the surface or, as shown in Figure 14.6, close-coupled to a submersible electric motor.

Multi-stage centrifugal pumps, particularly submersibles, are manufactured to very close tolerances, and can be easily damaged and will block very easily. They will only pump very clean water.

14.3.2 Surface mounted centrifugal pump

This section focuses on the installation of a centrifugal pump at a surface water source such as a river bank. Similar principles apply to other locations. Figure 14.7 shows a typical arrangement of auxiliary fittings for a standard surface-mounted centrifugal pump, pumping from a surface water source. Refer to 14.6.1 for general guidelines on installation and maintenance.

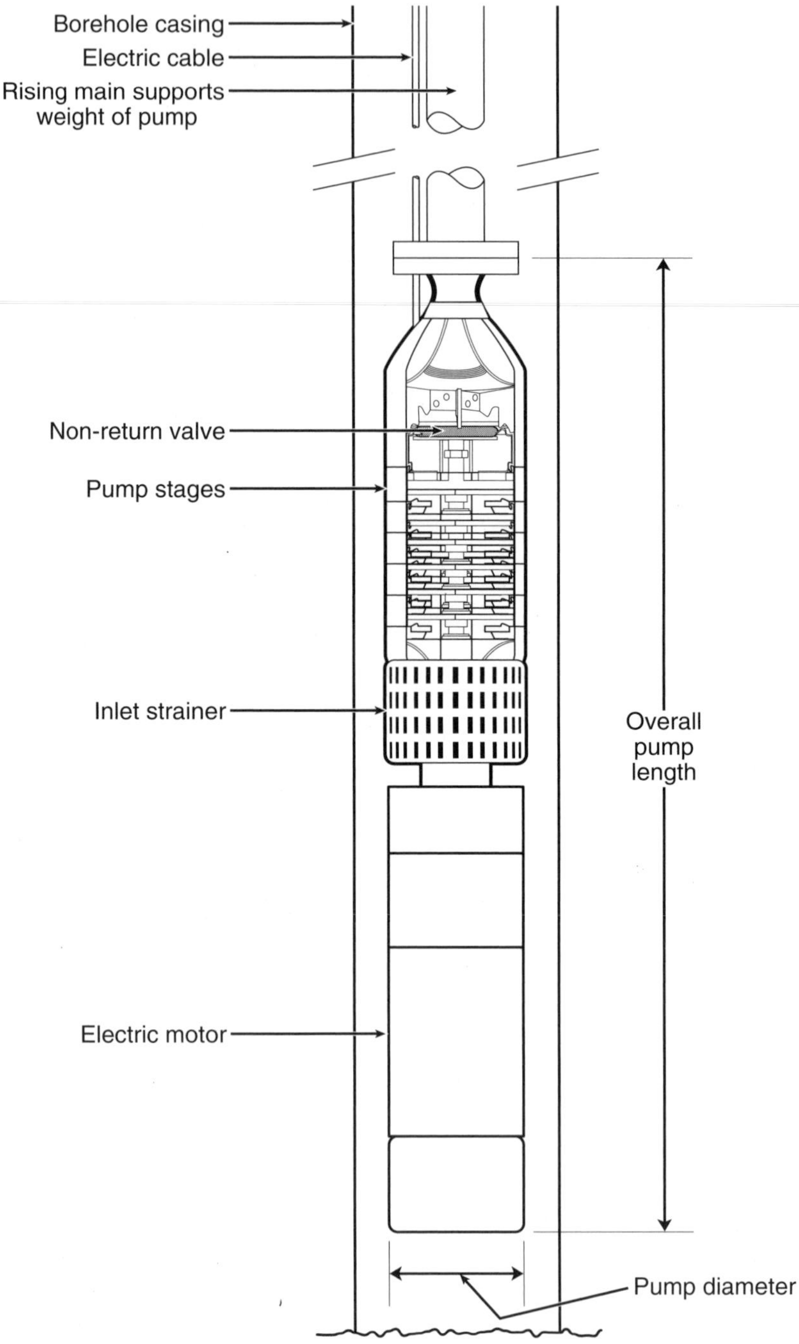

Figure 14.6 Multi-stage electric submersible borehole pump

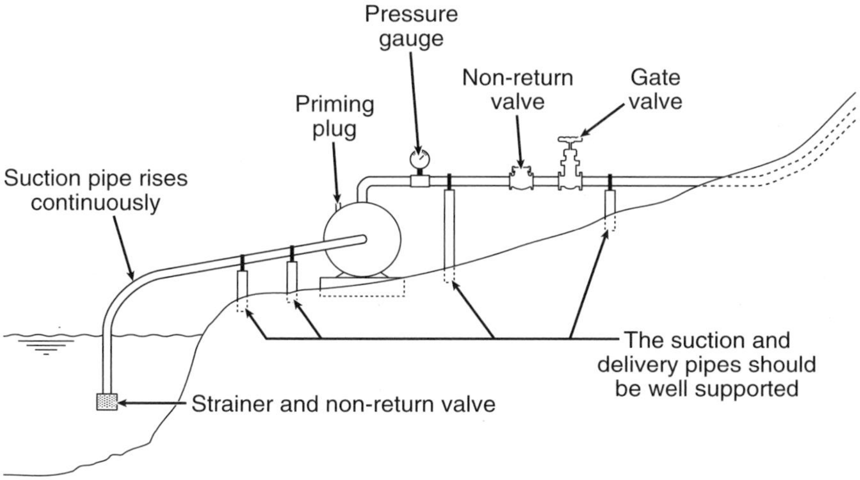

Figure 14.7 Typical arrangement of centrifugal pump fittings

Installation

Location Site pumps upstream of bathing, washing and animal watering areas. A good pump site has:

- A reasonable depth of water close to the bank.
- A firm bank that is not likely to be washed away.
- A bankside which is free of silt, weed and grass.

Choose a pump site which keeps the length of the pumping main to a minimum and provides a gradual incline to the storage tanks. Avoid dips and peaks in a pipeline. Silt can settle out in a dip when water in the pipe is stationary. Air can become trapped in a peak and cause pumping problems. See 13.4.3 for the design of pumping mains.

The position and arrangement of the suction inlet is critical to avoid pumping silt and to prevent the ingress of weeds, leaves and debris. Figure 14.8 shows some arrangements of pump suction inlets. There are limitations on how far a pump can lift water (see 14.2.1). So keep suction lifts and lengths of suction pipe to a minimum. Submerge the inlet of the suction pipe a sufficient depth (at least 0.3 m) to prevent the formation of vortices, which can entrain air and adversely affect pump performance. When the pump is running at full speed, check for such vortices.

Sand or silt will rapidly damage most pumps irreparably. Therefore, take great care to minimize sand or silt ingress into the pump:

- Never allow a suction inlet to sit on the bottom of a lake or river bed.
- Fit a means of excluding silt (see Figure 14.8), or suspend the inlet at least 0.3 m above the bottom of the source, or at the minimum, position it on rock, a board or similar.

To prevent blockage of the suction pipe by vegetation, fit a strainer or, for large pumps, pass the water through a screen before the suction inlet.

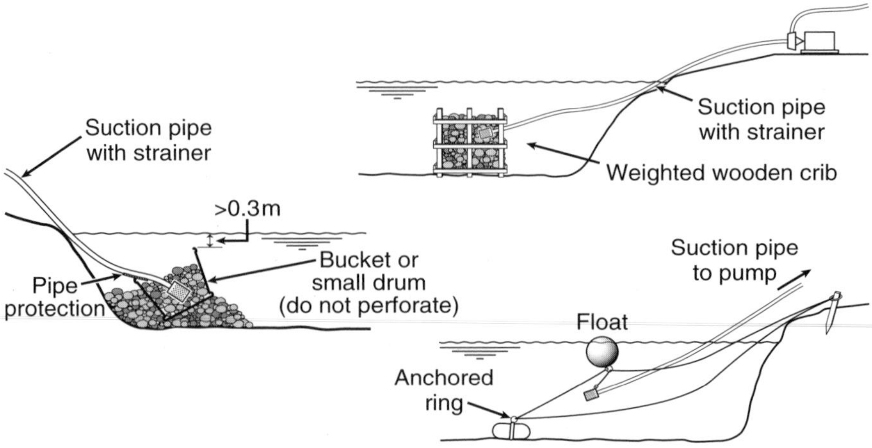

Figure 14.8 Simple arrangements of pump suction inlets

In areas liable to flooding, mount pumps on a floating platform such as that shown in Figure 14.9. Alternatively, arrange a means of quick removal from the flood zone on a winch and rail system, or similar.

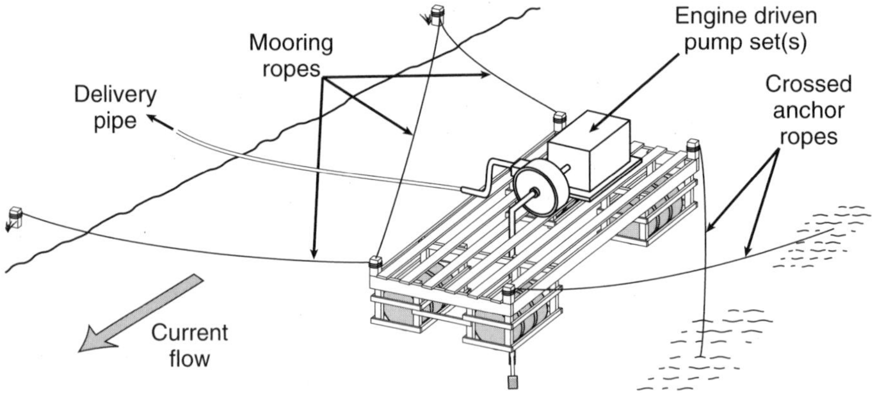

Figure 14.9 A temporary floating pump platform

Foundations A pumping set mounted with its prime mover on a rigid steel bed-plate can be temporarily installed on prepared level ground. On soft soils, place the frame on a bed of level gravel or on thick timbers set on level gravel. Anchor the set with spikes passed through the holding-down holes in the frame.

For more permanent installations cast a concrete plinth. If there are no manufacturer's instructions, use the following rough guide:

- For petrol or diesel engine driven sets
  Weight of concrete = 3 × weight of the pump set.
- For electric motor driven sets
  Weight of concrete = 1.5 × weight of the pump set.

(density of concrete is about 1800–2400 kg/m^3)

Locate the foundation holes for the anchor bolts in the concrete using a template made up on site. Make the depth of the holes at least fifteen times the bolt diameter or half the depth of the plinth and make them large enough to allow for the correct positioning of the bolts.

Firmly support, position and level the pumpset with wedges about 25 mm above the plinth with the anchor bolts suspended on their nuts through the holes in the bed-plate. Grout the bolts into the holes. Allow the concrete to set, finally level and tighten the nuts. To stabilize the pump set and reduce vibration, fill the bed-plate with freely flowing grout (1 part cement : 2 parts sand).

Operation of surface mounted centrifugal pumps

When installing and operating a surface mounted centrifugal pump:

- Prime the pump before starting.
- Never run the pump dry.
- Start against a closed valve.
- Check you have enough spares in case the pump breaks down.

More details on these points are given below. Box 14.1 gives guidance on fault-finding.

Prime a centrifugal pump before starting A centrifugal pump cannot pump air alone and therefore, where the suction head is negative, it must be primed with water before it can function as a pump. To prime, remove the priming plug and fill the pump chamber and suction pipe with water. Some centrifugal pumps are 'self-priming'. Foot valves, designed to prevent water flowing out of the suction pipe so that the pump remains primed when stopped, are usually supplied. However, foot valves are rarely watertight and, after a period of shut-down, a pump may need to be re-primed.

Never run a pump dry Pump seals, and some bearings, can be damaged if they run without water. Therefore, always pour water into the pump chamber and run a pump 'wet', even when testing prior to installation.

Start against a closed valve The power required by a centrifugal pump is at a minimum when there is no flow (refer to Figure 14.5). Therefore, although it may not be immediately obvious, it is better to start a centrifugal pump against a closed valve to reduce the power required on start-up. No harm will come to the pump if it is run against a closed valve in the delivery pipe for a short period of time as it only churns the water in the pump. However, if the pump remains in this state for a prolonged period it will eventually overheat, so open the valve in the delivery pipe as soon as the pump is running.

It is good practice for the operator to close the delivery valve just before the pump is stopped so that the pump is ready to re-start against a closed valve. This also has the advantage of relieving the pressure of the head of water in the main on the non-return valve and pump components.

In some arrangements, a bypass pipe with valve may be fitted around the non-return valve in the rising main. By opening the valve in the bypass pipe, water from the rising main may be allowed to flow back into the pump for priming. Close this valve once the pump is primed.

Box 14.1 Surface mounted centrifugal pump: troubleshooting

- **Little or no water delivered on starting**
  Pump not primed.
  Leak(s) in suction pipe, pipe connections, foot valve, seals.
  Air-lock on suction side due to pipe not continuously rising.
  Blocked strainer, foot-valve, suction pipe or pump.
  A valve (isolation, flow control or non-return) not fully open or damaged.
  Low speed of rotation of pump due to: slipping drive belts, electric motor under-voltage, incorrect speed setting of IC engine.
  Pump rotating in the wrong direction.
  Pumping head too high for pump.
  Suction lift too high – see NPSH 14.2.1.
  Air entrained at the suction pipe inlet – lower the inlet.
- **Loss of delivery after successful pumping**
  Leak in suction pipe, pipe connections or seals.
  A fall in the level of water on the suction side has exposed the end of the suction pipe or increased the suction lift beyond the capability of the pump.
- **Excessive power absorbed** (straining engine and high fuel consumption)
  For positive displacement pumps, check for throttled valves in delivery pipe.
  For centrifugal pumps, check for abnormally low heads in system and check against pump characteristic.
  Transmission problems: misalignment of shafts/pulleys; over-tight drive belts.
  Solids in pump.
- **Noise/vibration**
  Delivery head too high.
  Suction lift too high.
  Blocked suction pipe or impeller.
  Air in the system.
  Transmission misalignment.
  Worn or damaged bearings.
  Loose holding-down bolts or cracked baseplate.
- **Prime mover problems**
  Refer to Sections 15.2 and 16.6 for problems with prime movers.

Spares Few spares should be required for a short term emergency, but gland packing or mechanical seals (with an extraction and installation tool set) are advisable.

14.3.3 Electric submersible centrifugal pump

Figure 14.10 shows an electric submersible centrifugal pump borehole installation. See also 14.6.1 for general guidelines on installation and maintenance.

Installation

Before installing the pump:

- Make a note of the data on the pump name plate. If a spare name plate is included with the pump, attach it to the pump control panel.

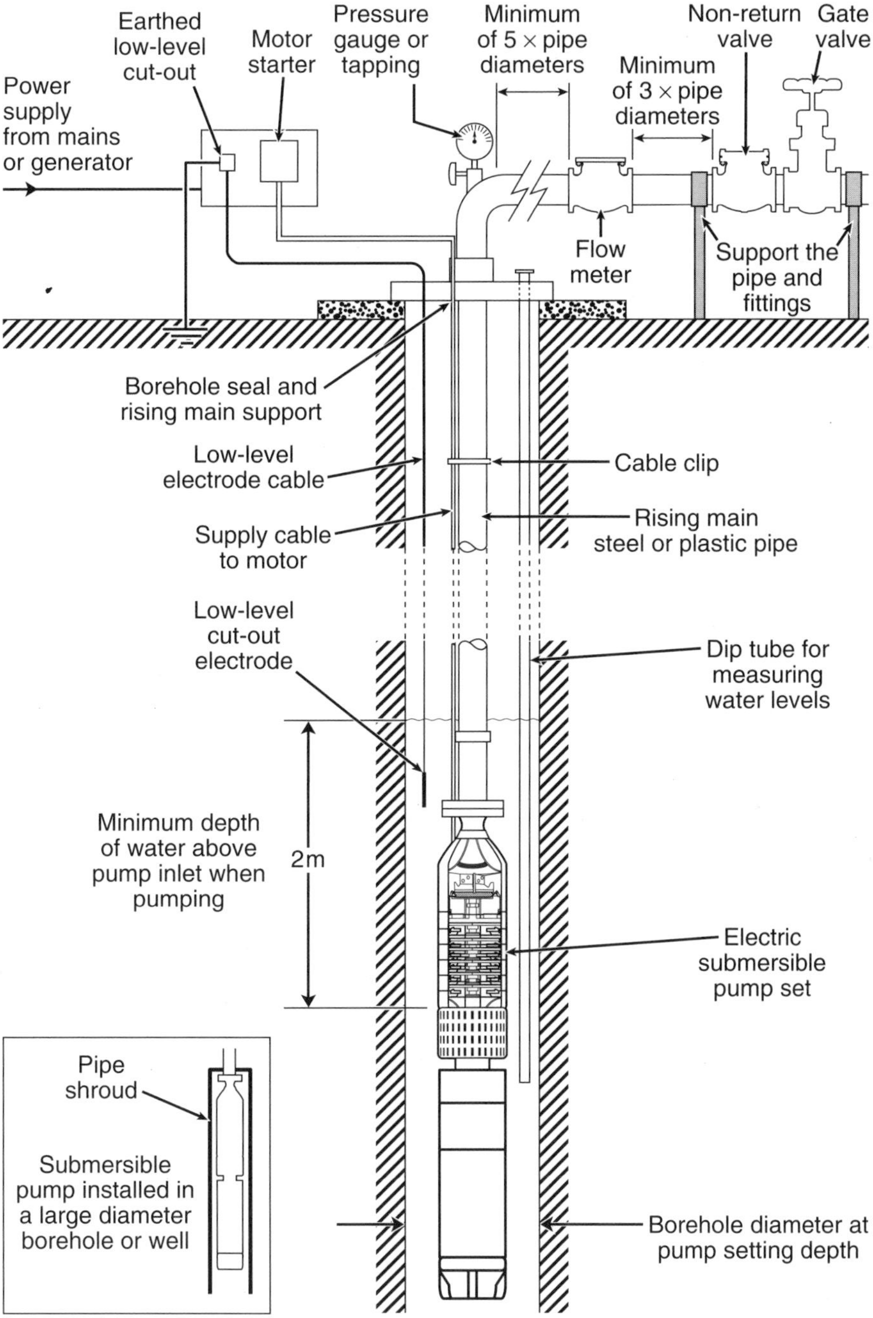

Figure 14.10 Electric submersible borehole pump installation

- Ensure that you have a suitable gantry and adequate lifting tackle (including pipe clamps) on the site. Pumps and pipes can be very heavy.
- Check that the voltage, phase and frequency are compatible with the power supply available.
- Check all cables:
  - The motor cable and supply cable for damage.
  - That the cables are adequately sized to ensure the correct voltage at the motor (see Section 16.4).
  - The low-level cable and connection to the electrode for damage and continuity.
  - The low-level unit has a good earth return through a steel borehole casing, earthed rising main or separate earth return.
- Carry out insulation tests with a 500V insulation resistance and continuity tester (commonly known as a 'megger') on the motor and on the supply cable (see Section 16.6.3):
  - The resistance between any motor lead and the motor frame should be greater than 1 MΩ (Megohm).
  - The resistance between the individual cores of the supply cable should be greater than 1 MΩ.

  If a 'megger' is not available, carry out a careful visual check on all cable insulation material.
- Check that the borehole has a large enough diameter all the way to the pump setting depth to accommodate the pump, the riser pipe and the joint between the motor and supply cables.
- Check that the non-return valve in the pump is in working order.
- Check that the pump setting depth is such that the pumping (not the static) water level will be 2 m, or more, above the pump inlet (check against the borehole pumping test data). See Section 12.3.6.
- Check that the pump drive shaft turns freely. This can only be checked if the motor coupling is exposed and it can be turned by hand or spanner.

Note: A flow of water across the electric motor is necessary to cool it, so do not install the pump at the very bottom of a borehole, where water may enter the pump from above without flowing past the motor. If the pump is located where flow over the pump body may not occur (such as in a surface water source or large diameter well) it must be surrounded by a pump shroud (see Figure 14.10) which ensures that water first passes over the motor before entering the pump. Provided such a shroud is fitted, the pump can be installed horizontally if needed, but check pump manual before purchase.

Procedure for installation (see Figure 14.13 for the type of lifting tackle commonly used):

- Insert the pump, riser pipe and cable into the borehole using lifting tackle and at least two pipe clamps to prevent accidental loss of the pump and pipe work. Never clamp the pump body.
- As the pump is lowered into the borehole, attach the supply cable and low-level cut-out electrode cable(s) to the riser pipe at 3 m intervals. Leave some

slack in the cables if the riser pipe is plastic, as the pipe will stretch slightly under load.

- If the pump and rising main do not sink easily, it may be because of the buoyancy of the empty rising main – fill the rising main pipe with water as you lower it.
- Some pumps have a connection for the attachment of a straining wire. The wire takes the weight of the pump for lowering and lifting. Attach the wire according to the instructions and secure it firmly at the top of the borehole after installation.
- When the pump is submerged, repeat the insulation test between the cores of the supply cable and an earth. If both the rising main and casing are plastic, use an earthing rod driven into damp earth.
- Clamp and support the rising main at the top of the borehole.
- Cover the top of the borehole to prevent the ingress of any contaminants.

Consult Chapter 16 for the wiring of motor starters and controls, and the measures which must be taken to provide adequate motor protection.

Operation of electric submersible centrifugal pumps

For the initial start-up, disconnect the pipework beyond the delivery valve so that the pumped water can be clearly seen and the flow rate measured when the valve is opened. Before starting the pump, set the motor overload to 90 per cent of the motor full load current.

Check the direction of rotation of the pump as follows:

- Start the pump and open the valve until the water delivered is about one-third of the rated maximum output of the pump.
- Measure the flow rate and pressure. Use a temporary gauge if a permanent gauge is not included in the installation. In some cases the highest flow rates and pressures may be clear from observation, obviating the need for a pressure gauge.
- Stop the pump and interchange two of the phases supplying the pump motor (see Chapter 16 for more information on the wiring of electric motors).
- Start the pump and again measure flow rate and pressure.
- Stop the pump.

The connections which give the highest flow give the correct direction of rotation. Carry out the rotation check as quickly as possible so that the pump is not run in the reverse direction for any length of time.

Continue the commissioning procedure:

- Run the pump in the correct direction until the discharged water is clear.
- Re-connect the pipework to the discharge valve.
- Start the pump against a closed valve and slowly open the valve until fully open. Check the drawdown to ensure that the pump does not run dry and remains submerged under normal operation.

- Check the ammeter reading on the control panel when running at the design duty and adjust the motor overload down until it trips out. Re-adjust the motor overload to the trip out value plus 5 per cent.

The pump installation is now ready for regular operation.

Do not run the pump against a closed or severely throttled valve as the motor needs a minimum flow of water for cooling. Maintain a check on the ammeter reading, as an increase in current drawn or fluctuations in current can indicate pump or motor mechanical problems. See Box 14.2 for a guide to fault-finding.

Box 14.2 Electric submersible centrifugal pump: troubleshooting

- **Pump motor fails to start**
  Broken or loose electrical connections.
  Blown fuse – check the installation before replacing fuses.
  Motor overload – see 'Overloads trip' below.
  Low voltage.
  Damaged supply cable insulation – check insulation resistance.
  Cable, cable joint or motor windings may be wet or earthed.
  Pump blocked with sand.
- **Little or no water delivered**
  Pump not submerged.
  Pump rotating in the wrong direction.
  Leak(s) in riser pipe joints or corroded pipe.
  Riser pipe joint threads corroded and disconnected.
  Non-return valve in pump blocked or corroded.
  Valves on discharge line blocked, damaged or not fully open.
  Worn pump due to pumping sand or other particles.
  Strainer or impellers blocked with sand or chemical deposits.
  Blocked or damaged borehole screen.
  Pumping head too high for pump.
- **Loss of delivery**
  Pump runs dry due to excessive drawdown (only if not protected by a low-level cut-out).
  Leak in riser pipe – pull out and repair pipe.
- **Overloads trip**
  Current overload/motor temperature sensor – possible causes: blockage, insufficient flow of water over motor, overload due to mechanical problems, low voltage.
  Under-voltage – low voltage on supply system.
  Incorrect oil level in dashpot operated overloads.
  Low-level cut-out – excessive drawdown.
  Incorrectly set overloads – check settings.

Spares

There are no spares to stock for the maintenance of an electrical submersible pump during the period of an emergency. Pump repairs cannot be carried out on site. A specialist workshop is required. However, stock spare submersible cable joints and spares for the control panel and for the generator (if the pump is not run on mains supply).

14.4 Positive displacement pumps

14.4.1 Helical rotor pumps

This section deals with helical rotor pumps, as they are the most likely form of mechanically powered positive displacement pump to be encountered. Positive displacement handpumps are dealt with in Section 14.5. When installing or operating positive displacement pumps, bear the following points in mind:

- Never operate positive displacement pumps against a closed valve. The pump or fittings will be damaged, or the motor will stall, as there will be nowhere for the displaced water to flow.
- Do not directly connect positive displacement pumps in series. Positive displacement pumps can operate in parallel.

Output is directly proportional to the speed of the pump and, within limits, it is not greatly affected by variations in the head (see 14.2.3, Figure 14.2). The pumping head is directly proportional to the power input.

The fine clearances and/or the arrangement of valves in some positive displacement pumps (such as the diaphragm pump) allow air to be pumped, which makes them self-priming.

14.4.2 Installation and operation

The main type of rotary positive displacement pump used in emergency water supply is the helical rotor pump shown in Figure 14.11 which is commonly used as a borehole pump. The rotor is in constant contact with the rubber stator and as it rotates water is positively displaced from the suction end to the discharge end of the pump. The pump may be shaft driven from the surface (Figure 14.12) or close-coupled to a submersible electric motor.

High heads can be achieved with small variations in discharge. The simple mechanical design of the pump makes it very reliable and, compared with a multi-stage submersible centrifugal pump, it can cope well with abrasive or dirty waters.

With a shaft driven helical rotor pump, the engine transmits power to a drivehead by V-belts. The drive-belt pulley may be mounted on a horizontal or vertical drive shaft, depending on the drivehead design. The vertical drive shaft will require a 90° twist in the V-belts (see Figure 14.12). The submerged pump element is then driven by a vertical shaft from the drivehead. This vertical shaft runs in water-lubricated rubber 'bobbin' bearings which centre the shaft inside the rising main. Rubber stabilizers centre the rising main inside the borehole.

The engine and drivehead are mounted either on an integral base frame or on separate base frames supplied with an angle iron spacer bar to align the pulleys correctly. The V-belt tension is adjusted after assembly.

The characteristic head/discharge curve of a helical rotor pump is illustrated in 14.2.3, Figure 14.2.

Installation of shaft driven helical rotor pumps

(See also Section 14.6.1) Before installing the pump:

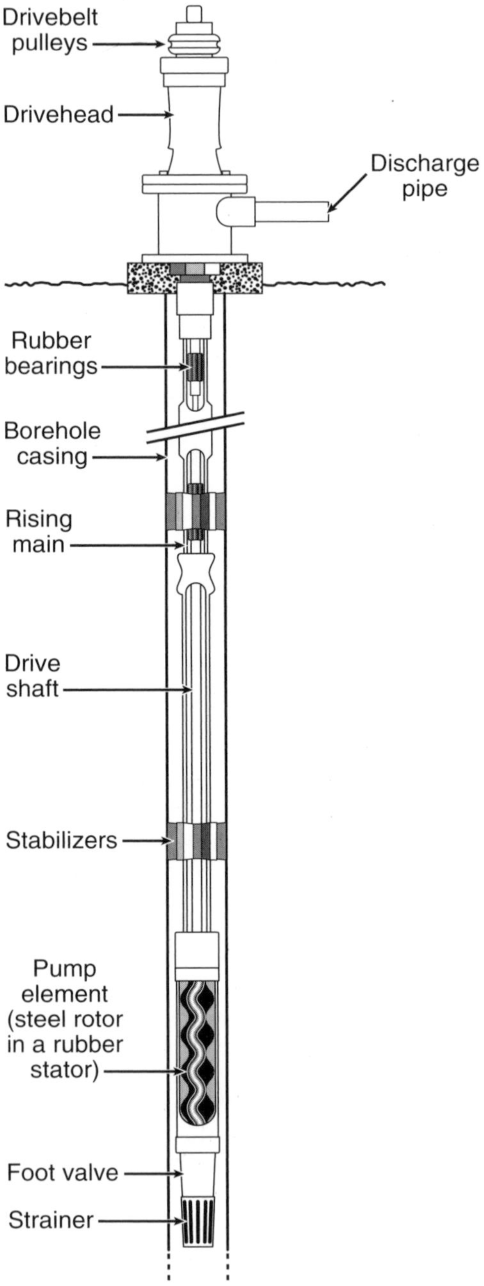

Figure 14.11 Shaft driven helical rotor pump mounted on a borehole

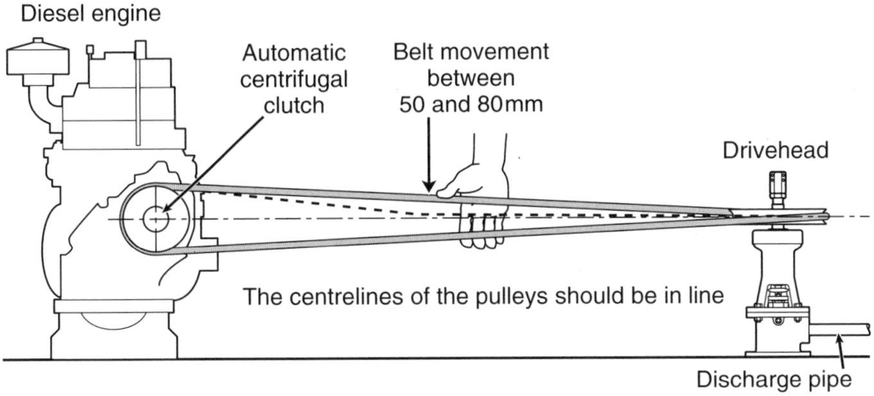

Figure 14.12 The alignment and tension of V-belts driving a 'Mono pump'

- Check that the borehole has a large enough diameter all the way to the pump setting depth to accommodate the pump and rising main.
- The pump drive shaft needs to fall vertically from the drivehead to the pump – check that the borehole is vertical and straight to allow this.
- Make a note of the pump data and display a record of the pump details in the pump house.
- Ensure that there is a suitable gantry (tripod) and adequate lifting tackle (including pipe clamps) available. Pumps and pipes can be very heavy.
- Make sure that the pump foot-valve is in good working order.
- Set the pump at a depth such that the dynamic (not static) water level will be 1 m, or more, above the pump inlet (check against the borehole pumping test data).

Installation procedure (Refer to Figure 14.13):

- Insert the pump and riser pipe with the drive shaft into the borehole using lifting tackle and pipe clamps. Never clamp the pump body.
- Ensure that the shaft 'bobbin' bearings are installed correctly, so that the rubber 'spider' used to centre the shaft locks firmly against the inside of the riser pipe to prevent the bearing rotating with the shaft. There is usually an arrow pointing to the top of the 'bobbin' bearing. (Note: drive shafts have left-hand threads and riser pipes have right-hand threads.)
- If the rubber stabilizers used to centre the rising main are slightly oversize, they can be trimmed to fit inside the borehole with a water-lubricated knife or hacksaw.
- Ensure that the rising main is tightly screwed into the discharge head and that the drive shaft is securely attached to the drivehead at the top of the borehole.
- Tighten the holding down nuts of the base plate for the drive and discharge head to a prepared concrete foundation.

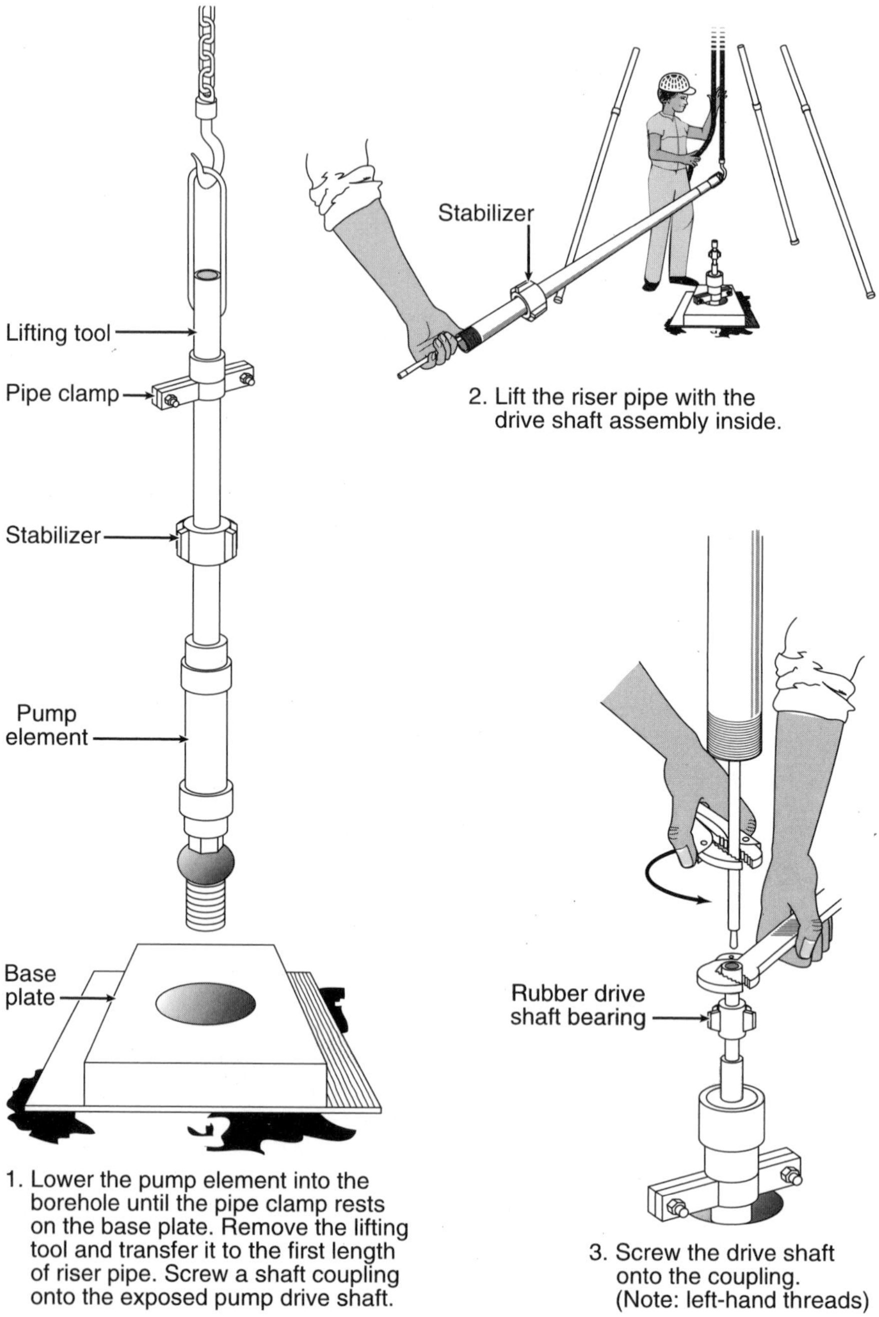
Lifting tool
Pipe clamp
Stabilizer
Pump element
Base plate
1. Lower the pump element into the borehole until the pipe clamp rests on the base plate. Remove the lifting tool and transfer it to the first length of riser pipe. Screw a shaft coupling onto the exposed pump drive shaft.
Stabilizer
2. Lift the riser pipe with the drive shaft assembly inside.
Rubber drive shaft bearing
3. Screw the drive shaft onto the coupling. (Note: left-hand threads)

Figure 14.13 Installation of a helical rotor pump

Based on the Monolift borehole pump

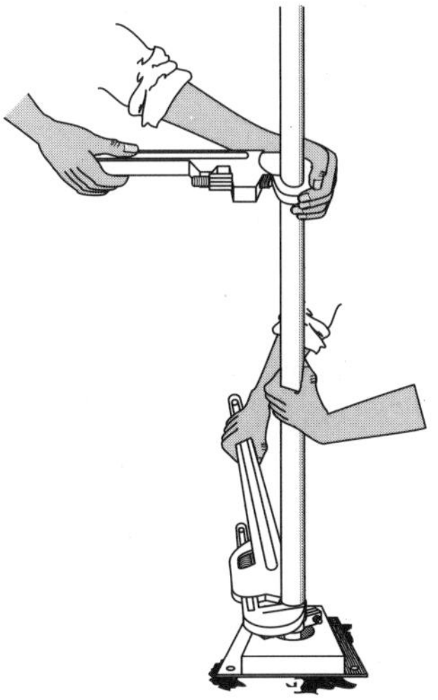

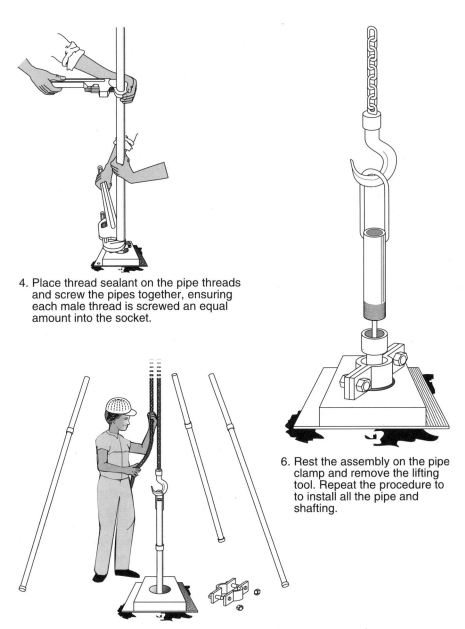

4. Place thread sealant on the pipe threads and screw the pipes together, ensuring each male thread is screwed an equal amount into the socket.

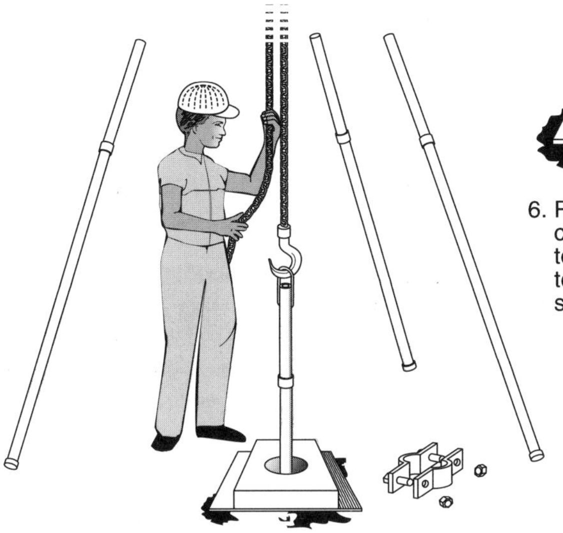

5. Take the weight of the pump assembly on the lifting gear. Remove the pipe clamp and lower the pump down the borehole. Replace the pipe clamp below the socket on the top of the riser pipe.

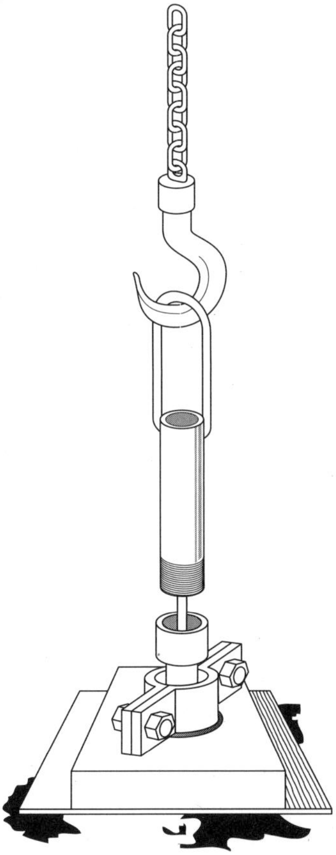

6. Rest the assembly on the pipe clamp and remove the lifting tool. Repeat the procedure to to install all the pipe and shafting.

Figure 14.13 (cont.) Installation of a helical rotor pump (part 2)

Commissioning

For the initial start-up, disconnect the pipework beyond the drivehead so that pumped water can be clearly seen and the flow rate measured when the pump is running.

Figure 14.12 indicates the usual alignment and tensioning of the drive belts with a 90° twist. Before starting the engine, remove the drive belts and check that the drivehead pulley will rotate in the correct direction when the engine is running. Note that there is a ratchet in the drivehead to prevent the pump from rotating backwards. Replace the drive belts and check the tension of the belts half-way between the engine and the drivehead. The belts are correctly tensioned if the movement is between 50 and 80mm. Adjust the position of the engine to alter the tension and ensure that the pulley centres remain in line.

Ensure that the clutch is disengaged and start the engine. Allow the engine to run up to speed before engaging the clutch. Some drive arrangements include a centrifugal clutch which is automatically engaged when the operating speed is reached.

Observe the water and measure the flow rate. A bucket and stop watch is sufficient to check the flow rate is correct for the particular running speed. Do not stop the pump if the water is dirty or sandy as sand will settle onto the rotor and the pump may not restart. Pump until the water becomes clear. If air is discharged with the water, the borehole is being over-pumped. Reduce the engine speed or change the pulley to reduce the pump speed.

The drivehead has a soft-packed stuffing box to seal against the vertical drive shaft. With the pump running, adjust the gland to give a gradual leak past the shaft and packing. A slack gland will result in excessive leakage and a wet pump surround. If there is no leakage the gland is too tight and the packing and shaft will get hot and wear quickly (see 14.6.1). Box 14.3 gives guidance on fault-finding.

Operation of helical rotor pumps

- Check the condition and tension of the drive belts each day and adjust or replace as necessary.
- Before starting the pump, ensure the delivery valve is OPEN and that pumped water may discharge at some point in the pipeline. Attempting to pump into a closed pipeline may damage the pump or transmission system.
- Start the engine, allow to run up to speed and engage the clutch.
- Check that there is gradual leakage at the gland of the stuffing box on the drivehead.

14.5 Lifting water by hand

In large parts of the developing world, water is lifted by hand using buckets and rope, perhaps with a windlass, or by handpump. In some disaster situations, such as drought, and where refugees are widely dispersed among the host community, lifting by hand may be the most appropriate method of obtaining water. For a practical manual on water lifting see Baumann (2000).

Box 14.3 Submersible helical rotor pump: troubleshooting

- **No water delivered**
  Leak(s) in riser pipe.
  Drive shaft disconnected.
  Low speed of rotation of pump due to: slipping drive belts, clutch not fully engaged, electric motor under-voltage, incorrect speed setting of IC engines.
  Pump rotating in the wrong direction.
  Worn or damaged pump element.
- **Low discharge**
  Leaks in riser pipe.
  Blockage in pipes.
  Low speed of rotation of pump due to: slipping drive belts, clutch not fully engaged, electric motor under-voltage, incorrect speed setting of IC engines.
  Pump intermittently runs dry due to excessive drawdown and entrains air into the pumped water.
  Worn or damaged pump stator or rotor.
- **Loss of delivery**
  Drive shaft disconnected.
  Leak in riser pipe.
  Slipping or broken drive belt(s).
- **Excessive power absorbed**
  Transmission problems: misalignment of shafts/pulleys; over-tight drive belts.
- **Noise/vibration**
  Air in the system.
  Transmission misalignment.
  Worn or damaged drivehead bearings.
  Loose holding-down bolts or cracked base frame.

Handpumps can be used on either boreholes or hand-dug wells. A conventional windlass and bucket requires a large diameter well, to accommodate the bucket. The Zimbabwe 'bucket-pump' is an example of a specially adapted windlass and bucket suitable for boreholes or tubewells. It is more reliable than a handpump, although it has a lower discharge rate because of the small capacity of the bucket. It is suited to groups of households, supplying a maximum of perhaps 100 people. Where hand drilled or jetted wells are feasible, the bucket-pump is very appropriate.

A handpump allows the well to be sealed against contamination and may increase the amount of water that can be lifted. However, a good windlass mounted on a properly protected well may be adequate in the short term and easier to maintain in the longer term. Even if the 'official' rope or chain and bucket breaks, people are very adept at improvising their own rope and bucket. Ensure that a maintenance system is set up to clean open wells regularly.

Before installing large numbers of handpumps or windlasses, consider how they are going to be maintained and repaired. Without an effective maintenance and repair programme, the handpumps and windlasses will very quickly break down with the heavy use they are likely to encounter in an emergency. If handpumps are to be installed on dug wells, ensure that when the handpump breaks down, people may still draw water from the well with a bucket and rope (for example through a removable manhole cover).

In an emergency, one handpump or windlass can supply water for up to 500–1000 people (see Table 14.2 for typical depths and discharge rates). For further discussion on the use of low technology solutions, such as dug wells, see 12.3.4.

Table 14.2 Typical lifts and discharges of handpumps

Pump category	*Lift, m*	*Typical discharge rates*, l/min*
Shallow or suction lift	0–7	36
Medium lift	7–15	24
High lift	15–45+	16
Windlass and bucket	0–40	5–15

* Rate varies with lift and strength of pump operator. With 12 hours of continuous pumping and a discharge rate of 20 l/min, enough water can be pumped for 720 people at 20 litres/person/day.

Description of handpumps

The majority of handpumps for lifting water from wells are reciprocating piston or plunger pumps. The key components of piston pumps are a piston or plunger with a sliding seal inside a cylinder and two non-return check valves. On the piston upstroke (see Figure 14.14), water is drawn by the piston up the pipe and into the cylinder through a non-return valve (sometimes called a foot valve). At the same time the piston displaces water, which is already in the cylinder above the piston, up into the rising main (high or medium lift pumps) or out through the pump's outlet (suction pumps). On the piston downstroke, the cylinder check valve closes, preventing the water in the cylinder returning down the pipe, and the check valve in the piston opens, so allowing the piston to move down through the water in the cylinder.

At shallow lifts the piston and cylinder unit can be above ground, with the water raised by suction (see Figure 14.14). The maximum practical suction lift is about 7 m (see Section 14.2.1).

At medium lifts (7–15 m) lifting by suction is not possible, but the force required to lift water is small enough for a person to operate the pump by directly lifting the connecting rods and water that is being pumped. This direct action avoids the need for pump linkages and bearings (see Figure 14.15). This makes the pump cheaper, simpler and easier to maintain.

For high lifts, the weight of pump rods and the column of water in the rising main is too much to be lifted directly. A mechanism to increase the mechanical advantage is required. This can be achieved by a lever, flywheel or pedal (see Figure 14.16). With a helical rotor handpump, a crank and gearbox is needed, making it quite an expensive handpump. To withstand the higher operating stresses, high lift pumps must be of sturdier construction than the shallow or medium lift pumps.

Research and development has concentrated on making the maintenance of handpumps easier for the village pump caretaker, the 'village level operation

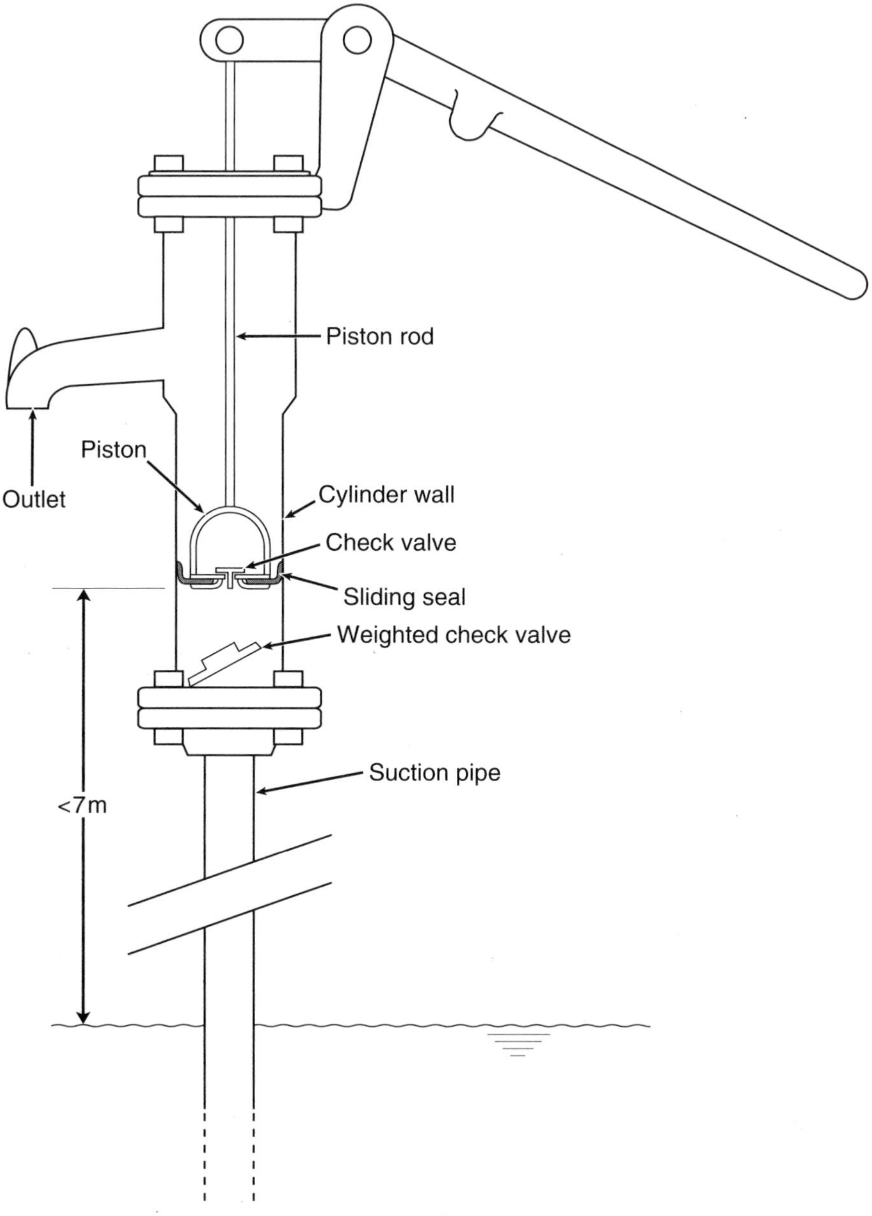

Figure 14.14 Shallow well suction lift handpump

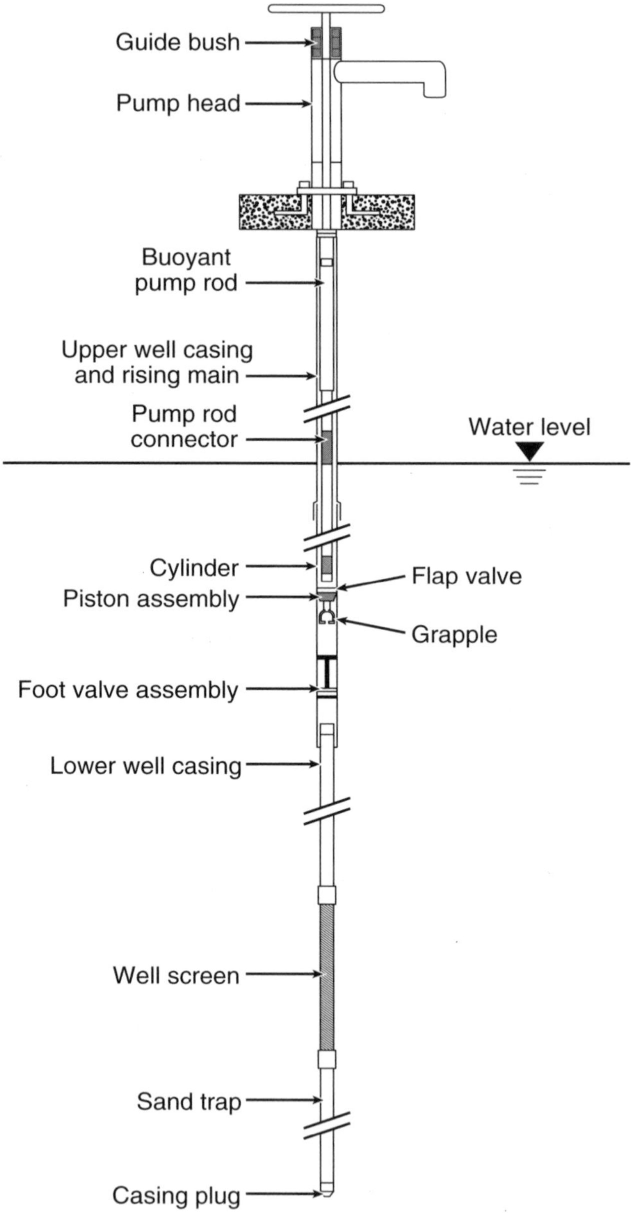

Figure 14.15 Medium lift 'Tara' direct action handpump

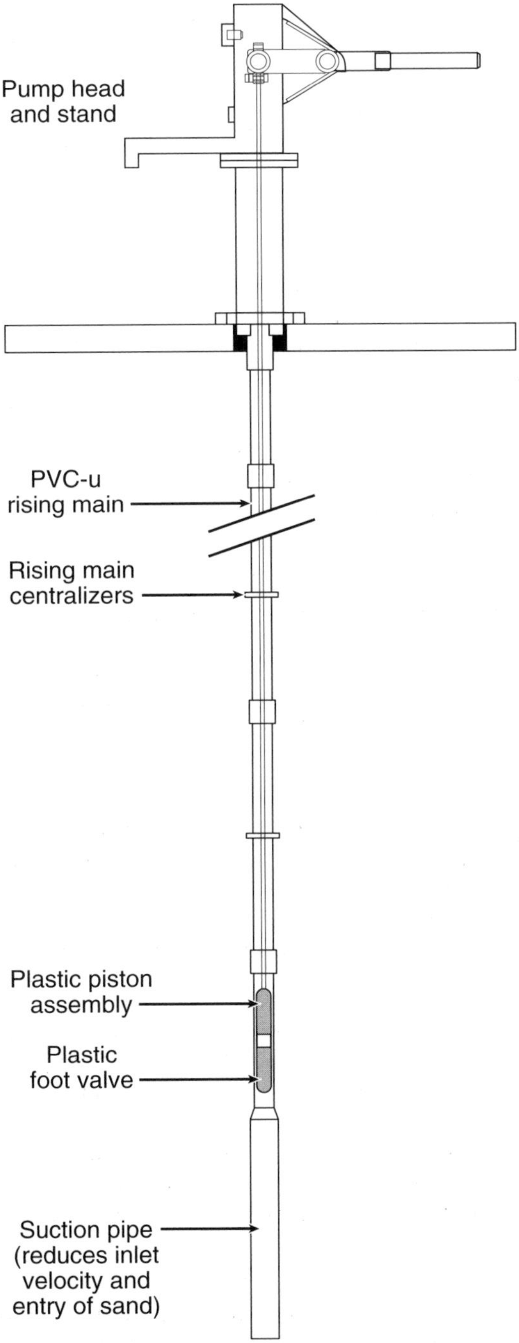

Figure 14.16 High lift 'Afridev' handpump

and management of maintenance' (VLOM) principle. This has led to the design of pumps in which the piston assembly and foot valve can be withdrawn without removal of the rising main. Servicing and repair work can be carried out with only a few tools and by unskilled personnel. This system also suits the needs of emergency programmes.

Table 14.2 gives data on typical lifts and discharge rates for shallow, medium and high lift handpumps.

When selecting handpumps, consider the following points:

- Select pumps based on the expected depth to the dynamic water level during pumping (the dynamic, not the static water level). In some aquifers of low hydraulic conductivity the drawdown can be significant, which results in the dynamic water level being considerably lower than the static water level.
- The installation and maintenance of shallow and medium lift handpumps is less complicated than that required for high lift handpumps.
- Some high lift handpumps do not work well in low lift applications because they rely on the weight of the pump rods to assist the downstroke.
- High lift handpumps are relatively expensive.

Suction lift handpump A typical suction lift handpump is shown in Figure 14.14. A new, or repaired, pump must be primed by pouring water into the cylinder.

Suction lift pump problems are commonly due to worn bearings, linkages and valves. However, they are usually easy to repair because all moving parts are above ground and accessible. Spare parts can often be fabricated locally without specialized materials or equipment.

Medium lift handpump Whereas the moving parts of suction lift handpumps are all above ground, the piston, cylinder and valves of deeper lift force pumps are submerged below the water level in the well. Figure 14.15 shows a typical direct action handpump developed in Bangladesh: the Tara. There are several design features which aid operation and maintenance which may also be found in other pumps of this type:

- The pump rod and rising main are made of standard PVC-u pipe. The buoyancy effect of the submerged air-filled PVC-u pump rod helps to reduce the effort needed on the upstroke. Some force has to be applied on the downstroke.
- The piston and foot valve may be directly withdrawn from the well without removing the rising main. The foot valve is withdrawn using the grapple extension attached to the piston. This greatly reduces the complexity of maintenance.

High lift handpump Figure 14.16 shows a typical high lift pump: the 'Afridev'. Most high lift handpumps are designed to raise water from depths of up to 45 m. Some can pump from greater depths, but a considerable physical effort is required and the flow rate is low.

14.6 Selection and operation of pumps

14.6.1 General guidelines on pump installation and maintenance

In a water supply system, key pumping installations should have adequate standby capacity. That is, for a single pump there should be one standby pump connected in parallel. For two or more pumps operating in parallel there should be at least one standby pump also connected in parallel. In practice, the duty and standby pumps are rotated so that every pump is periodically run. However, it is advantageous to allow some pumps to run more often than others so that they do not all start wearing out at the same time. The wear and maintenance needs of the pumps run for the longest periods can be used to adjust maintenance schedules and to order spare parts to ensure that the other pumps are kept serviceable.

For information on belt and shaft drive units, refer to Section 15.5.

Installation

Details on the installation of specific pumps are given in Sections 14.3 and 14.4.

Borehole pump installation and removal equipment Figure 14.13 shows the installation procedure for a shaft driven helical rotor borehole pump. Similar equipment and tools are used for the installation of an electric submersible pump and for some deep lift handpumps with a heavy column of riser pipe and connecting rods. The equipment includes:

- Tripod – construct a tripod from galvanized steel pipe, using, for example, spare riser pipe.
- A block and tackle or chain block – only use pulleys and blocks in good condition. Check them frequently for wear and breakage. Clean and grease regularly.
- Pipe lifting tool – this can be made up from a piece of riser pipe of compatible diameter (with good threads) and reinforcement bar welded to the pipe. Use it for lifting and lowering riser pipe into the borehole.
- Pipe clamps – always use a pipe clamp and lowering tool, or two sets of pipe clamps, when installing a column of riser pipe into a borehole. Fit clamps below pipe sockets for extra safety. In the absence of factory made pipe clamps, the clamps shown in Figure 14.13 can be made up locally. Saw a pipe socket of suitable diameter in half along the length of the pipe. Weld thick mild steel bar to the socket halves and drill holes to take 12 mm diameter bolts to form the clamp.

Pipework should be supported independently of the pump and not by the pump flanges.

General servicing and maintenance of pumps

Pipework One of the commonest causes of pumping failure is an air leak in the suction line. Therefore, ensure all joints in the suction pipework are airtight. In an emergency, use a temporary airtight bandage made from a one metre length (× 25 mm) of tyre inner tube wrapped tightly around the joint (see Figure 14.17). The joint should be repaired properly as soon as possible.

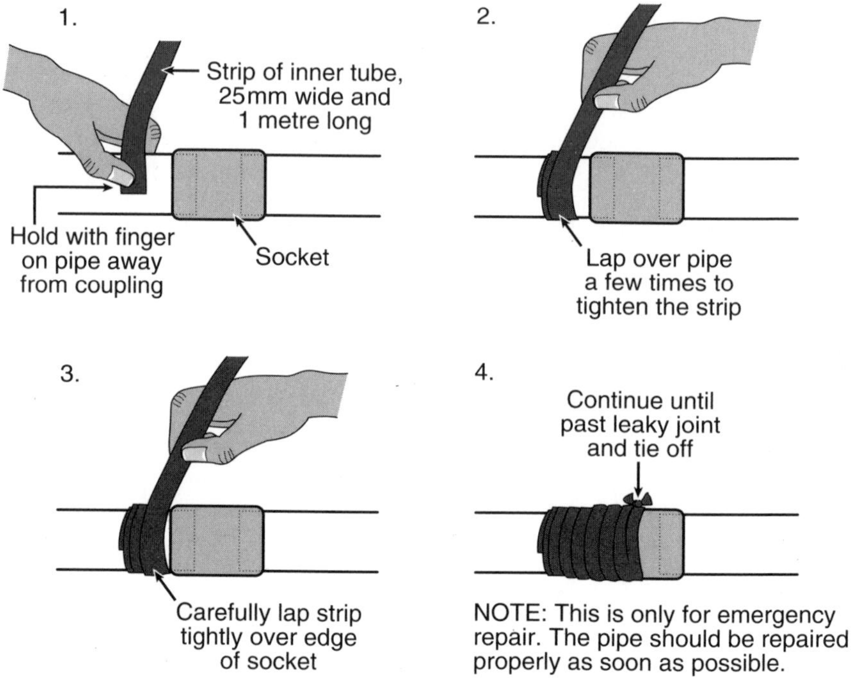

Figure 14.17 Temporary repair of a leaking pipe

Bearings Bearings are lubricated by grease, oil or water. After installation, check that the bearings are lubricated before starting up and turn the shafts by hand to ensure they are free to rotate.

In addition to providing lubrication, greased bearings seal against the ingress of dirt. Store and use grease carefully to keep it clean. Under difficult conditions, such as a damp, humid atmosphere, greased bearings may need to be replenished at least once a month. Be careful not to overgrease by applying too much pressure with a grease gun, as this can cause the bearings to run hot. A bearing is too hot if a hand cannot be comfortably placed on the bearing housing. Normally, grease does not require complete renewal until after about 10 000 hours' running.

Sealed bearings are charged with grease and cannot be replenished.

Shaft seals The drive shaft connecting the pump impeller to the prime mover must pass through the pump housing (see Figure 14.4). Seals prevent the escape of pressurized water from inside the pump along the rotating drive shaft. The seal is the most vulnerable part of a pump. The two common methods of sealing a rotating pump shaft are either by soft packing or by mechanical seals. A soft packing seal can be adjusted, while a mechanical seal may be in the form of a cartridge and cannot be adjusted.

Soft packings A stuffing box with a soft packing is shown in Figure 14.18. A soft packing should leak slightly to ensure that the packing and shaft are adequately cooled and lubricated. The leakage rate will vary, but about 10 drips per minute is common for many pumps. If the leakage is too much, tighten each gland nut a flat at a time (1/6th of a turn) and check the leakage after about 10 minutes. Repeat until the acceptable leakage rate is achieved.

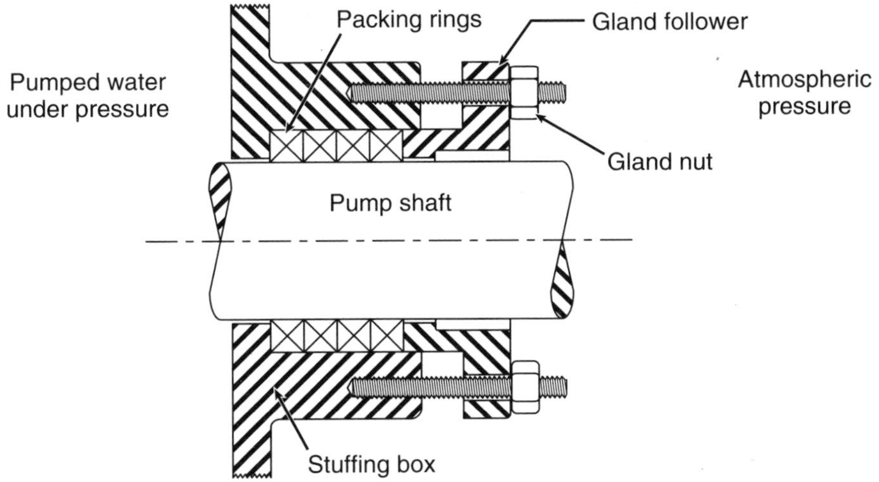

Figure 14.18 A soft packed stuffing box

An old packing will lose lubricant and shrink. One or two new rings of packing can be inserted to 'top-up' the stuffing box, but no more. When the leakage from the packing is excessive, remove all the old packing and re-pack the stuffing box.

To re-pack the stuffing box, close the valves either side of the pump, if necessary, to prevent the pump from flooding when the packing is removed. Remove the gland nuts and gland. Carefully remove the old packing and clean out the stuffing box without damaging the shaft.

Packing may be ready cut to the correct size in formed rings or rings may have to be cut from rolls. Check that the new packing is of the correct size – a slightly larger packing can usually be tolerated in an emergency. Roll out oversized packing using a pipe on a clean surface. Do not hammer packing.

To cut packing rings with matching ends, wind the packing around an old shaft or pipe of the same diameter as the shaft until there are a sufficient number of rings. Cut parallel to the line of the shaft with a sharp knife to give individual rings. Keep the rings clean. Do not simply open the rings, as they could crack, but insert them by twisting open as shown in Figure 14.19. Stagger

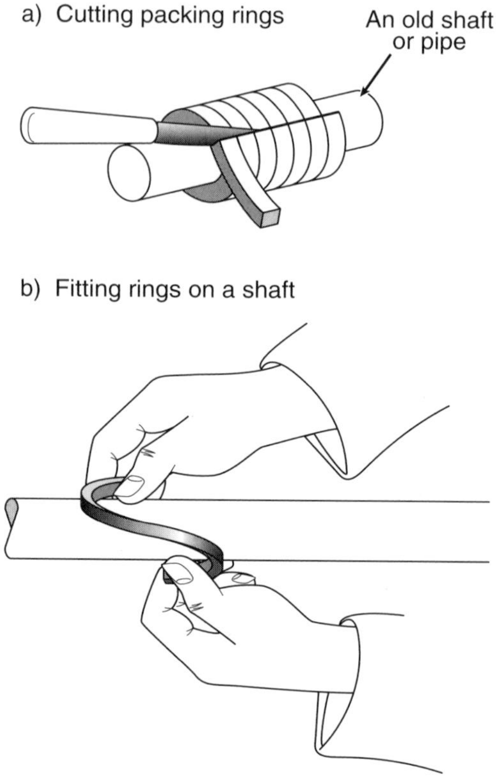

Figure 14.19 Cutting and fitting packing rings

each successive joint at right-angles to the previous one and tap the rings down with the gland. The 'V' pattern of plaited packing should point in the direction of rotation when viewed from the shaft end.

Screw on the gland nuts until finger tight and check that the shaft turns freely. Start the pump and, although there may be considerable leakage from the gland, let the pump run for some time. Gradually tighten the gland nuts one flat at a time until the gland drips at the required rate. Check the gland remains cool.

Note that there is a risk of a gland on the suction side of a pump leaking air and this can result in the failure of a pump.

Mechanical seals A mechanical seal consists of two ceramic disks, one of which rotates. The seal is formed by a film of water between them. Mechanical seals cannot be repaired in the field. If they fail, they must be replaced.

Leakage through the seal is very low and there should be no drips. The low leakage is lost in the form of water vapour. A newly installed mechanical seal which initially drips slightly may wear itself in over a short period of time. A mechanical seal should never be run dry as it may crack and result in a large leak. Check a mechanical seal for leaks regularly (at least once a week). After the first signs of slight leakage, a seal may last for a week or so before it must be replaced. Secondary damage (for instance, to the shaft) can be caused if a faulty or worn seal is not replaced. Note that a mechanical seal can be damaged by very worn or failed bearings.

Some pumps have a sealed cartridge. Replacement as a complete unit may require special tools and/or a puller. Check with the supplier and obtain the tools in advance of needing to use them.

14.6.2 Selecting and specifying pumps

Refer to 13.4.3 for information on how to select pumps for a particular pumping duty using the pump and pipeline characteristics. Section 7.2 gives general guidelines on procurement. Some general guidelines on pump selection are:

- Operation and maintenance. It takes a great deal of careful planning to get pumps operational and only a little negligence to put them out of order. Ensure that the pumps are protected, particularly against silt and sand, and properly operated and maintained. This means trained operators, regular servicing, a reliable energy source and spare parts.
- Local pumps – wherever possible, install pumps which are known to operators and mechanics and which are supplied locally so that they can be purchased and installed quickly. This has the advantage that ancillary fittings, spare parts and replacement units are available at relatively short notice.
- Compatibility – when ordering or purchasing pumps, ensure that they are compatible with the pipework and other fittings. If they are not, specify adaptors.
- Pumps are operated by hand or mechanically by engine or motor (prime mover). Select the prime mover (diesel engine, electric motor, etc.) so that it is compatible with other equipment, existing fuel supplies, operator and mechanic skills, spare parts supply and so on. The prime mover must be specified as carefully as the pump.
- Size and weight should be considered, to facilitate handling, transport and installation.

Box 14.4 (overleaf) gives a checklist of information to supply when specifying or ordering a pump. When requesting a pump, ask for the pump installation instructions to be sent as soon as possible, in advance of the pump. This allows time to obtain and check all the ancillary equipment and it enables the pump foundation to be prepared for quick installation of the pump on arrival. This can save vital time in an emergency.

Box 14.4 Information required for specifying a pump

- The number and type of pumps.
- The application (abstraction, distribution, etc.).
- Surface mounted or submersible.
- Site conditions: temperature, altitude, humidity.
- The nature of the water to be pumped (clear, sandy, muddy, corrosive, etc.).
- The flow rate – whether total or per pump.
- The total working head, the suction lift or head of water above the pump inlet. If suction lift, whether the pump is to be self-priming.
- If required to run in parallel or series with other pumps and if so, give details.
- Pump arrangement:
  - Stationary or portable/mobile.
  - Horizontal or vertical shaft.
  - Close coupled, long shaft, gear or belt driven.
  - Space restrictions; for example, borehole diameter.
- Drive: diesel/petrol engine or electric motor.
- If electric, specify:
  - Mains, generator or solar power.
  - If mains, is supply via a dedicated transformer?
  - Is the supply shared with other users?
  - Voltage, single or three phase, frequency (Hz) – the distance of the pump from the power source.
  - Reliability of the supply (blackouts? voltage fluctuations?)
  - Details of type of starter and control panel.
  - Give the supplier the hydraulic design and power source data and let them size the motor – do not size it yourself, but check the offer.
- For an electric submersible borehole pump give the following additional information:
  - Borehole data – diameter at pump setting level.
  - Static and dynamic water levels.
  - Pump setting depth.
  - Length of power cable and rising main required.
  - If low-level cut-out required.
  - If pump shroud required.
- Mounting: skid, baseplate, etc.
- Ancillaries required:
  - Couplings, pulleys, drive belts to be included.
  - Service kit such as gland packing, etc.
  - Spare parts such as seals, bearings, etc.
  - Associated valves, pressure gauges.
  - Pipe adaptors/couplings, etc. (some fittings may not be supplied directly by a manufacturer; however, ensure compatible fittings are specified in an order to the emergency support office).

15 Mechanical plant

This chapter gives guidance on the selection, operation and maintenance of mechanical plant commonly used in emergency relief. Fault-finding guides are included to help the non-specialist to understand what maintenance and repair may be needed. Detailed guidance on the maintenance and repair of individual items is beyond the scope of this book. For such guidance, refer to the relevant equipment manuals.

15.1 Assessment and planning

Support to a temporary settlement and the rehabilitation of existing plant following conflict and natural disasters can be divided into two main phases:

- Initial assessment of needs; procurement; installation or repair of equipment.
- Operation and maintenance.

15.1.1 Selection of equipment

The correct selection and specification of equipment in the initial phase is critical to the longer-term operation and maintenance phase. Frequent breakdowns and maintenance can be avoided if equipment is chosen which is suited to the task and the environment in which it operates. In many emergencies, however, quick decisions are made initially by non-specialist engineers and these decisions have long-term repercussions in terms of plant suitability, reliability and cost. It therefore pays many times over to seek specialist knowledge and advice where it is clear that major inputs of equipment will be required. One source of such specialist advice is RedR (see Introduction). For further guidance on procurement of equipment see Chapter 7. Chapters 14 and 17 deal with the specification of pumps and vehicles.

Reference manuals

Manuals are invaluable and they should always be specified when ordering equipment. If a manual cannot be found for existing equipment, check around the site and in offices. The value of a manual is not always recognized by non-engineers and it can often be hidden away in a packing case or a filing cabinet. If it cannot be found, order several copies from the supplier: at least order one for yourself, one for the workshop, and one extra.

Spare parts books or lists are also invaluable as they give the manufacturer's description of a part and the part number. Part numbers are important when ordering spares, especially over a long distance, with information passing through several different people, many of whom will be non-technical and all of whom will be in a hurry.

15.1.2 Operation and maintenance

Operation and maintenance must be planned and managed if plant is to continue doing the job for which it was intended. This will involve establishing operation and maintenance schedules and the training of suitable staff, if they do not already have the expertise. Alternatively, it may involve negotiating and letting operation and maintenance contracts. Contracts can be for maintenance alone or they can also include operational activities.

Maintenance is a term which is used broadly to refer to a wide range of activities from servicing to major repair work. Servicing is the regular, planned inspection and preventive maintenance of essential equipment to keep plant in good running order and so minimize breakdowns. Many routine servicing tasks (such as daily checks) can be carried out by operators. Corrective maintenance refers to the repair and replacement of worn out and broken parts to keep plant in a reliable operating condition. Corrective maintenance, involving fault diagnosis, is carried out by skilled mechanics. The exact division of preventive maintenance tasks between operators and mechanics will depend on operator skills and competence. This will have to be assessed in the field and tasks allocated accordingly.

It is helpful to plan an operation and maintenance programme in stages:

- An inventory of major plant should have been carried out in the assessment of existing plant or compiled as new plant was installed. If it is not available, compile it. List all the equipment (the inventory) which requires regular maintenance. Establish servicing and maintenance schedules (frequencies of tasks) based on the running hours of plant. As plant is commissioned, relevant operational data can be added to the inventory for the future monitoring of performance (such as fuel consumption).
- Determine routine servicing tasks to be carried out by operational staff (including lubrication, cleaning radiators, adjusting gland packing) and preventive maintenance tasks to be carried out by skilled mechanics.
- Determine the tools, spares and consumables required by operations and maintenance staff (such as spanners, oil, fuel, and filter elements).
- Ensure a safe operational environment (for example, guards on pulley belts and shaft drives).
- Give operations and maintenance staff appropriate training.
- Establish a system for keeping operation and maintenance records. These are vital for the monitoring of performance and costs, for planning, and to identify common problems which need particular attention.

The servicing periods of stationary plant is measured in running hours. Vehicle servicing periods are measured in distance travelled (kilometres or miles) or time (months), whichever is the sooner. In some situations where there are a number of engines operating on the same site, in a large temporary settlement for example, it may be more convenient to arrange for the servicing of all engines at the same set interval. This will mean some engines are serviced early, but supervision of servicing is made easier and this arrangement ensures all engines are serviced regularly.

Hours-run meters should be specified when ordering new stationary plant. Individual hours-run meters which detect run times based on vibration can be attached to most plant. If hours-run meters are not fitted, if they are faulty, or if they are not available then a method of recording start and stop times must be instituted. If this is a problem, then run times can be estimated from the fuel consumption.

Fuel consumption should be monitored to prevent the theft of fuel and to detect engine problems. This involves measuring fuel consumption soon after installation and instigating regular checks, say every month, to compare current figures with the initial consumption figures. To measure engine fuel consumption:

- Transfer the fuel line to a graduated litre container of fuel. Note: in the case of diesel engines, arrange for the spillway pipe from the injector pump and injectors to return to the container (see 15.2.3, Figure 15.4).
- Run the engine up to normal working temperature under its normal working load.
- Start timing when the fuel reaches a predetermined measuring mark on the container. Time using a watch with a stop-watch facility.
- Time how long it takes to consume a reasonable amount of fuel for the test, say 0.5 litre.
- Convert to fuel consumption in litres per hour.

See 17.2.4 for information on fuel handling and storage.

Supervisors and mechanics should keep regular logs of each service carried out, recording the date, hours run, and tasks undertaken. Encourage staff to look out for, and report, changes in performance and recurring problems. Tabulate water production rates on a monthly basis as shown in Table 15.1.

Table 15.1 Tabulation of water production rates for pumps

Pumping station	*Start date*	*Hours-run reading*	*End date*	*Hours-run reading*	*Total hours run*	*Flow rate m^3/h*	*Total pumped m^3*	*Average daily flow m^3/d*
P.S. 1								
P.S. 2								
				Totals:				

15.2 Internal combustion (IC) engines

This section gives general guidelines on maintenance and fault finding applicable to petrol and diesel engines. It is assumed that the basic principles and operation of internal combustion engines are understood. The fault finding charts are intended to help the non-specialist to recognize faults and potential problems so that remedial action and repairs can be taken by skilled mechanics.

15.2.1 Maintenance of internal combustion engines

Precise servicing intervals and tasks will vary and must be checked against the manufacturer's recommendations. In the absence of specific information, see Box 15.1 for guidance on the servicing of stationary plant. (Refer to 17.3.4 for guidance on the servicing of vehicles.) Box 15.1 gives guidance on diesel engines and light single cylinder petrol engines. These are the only stationary petrol engines likely to be encountered, and are used for powering small portable generators or dewatering pumps.

Service intervals are usually stated for average running conditions. If the running conditions are severe then adjust the servicing schedule accordingly. The following cases, which apply to diesel engines, are typical, but adjust according to local circumstances and experience.

- Change oil and oil filters more frequently in hot conditions. For example:

below 35°C	every 250 hours
above 35°C	every 125 hours

- Clean or change air filters more frequently in dusty conditions. For example:

clear air	every 500 hours
moderate dust	every 125 hours
severe dust	clean and check every day

- Drain and change fuel filters more frequently if the fuel quality is poor. For example:

clean fuel	every 500 hours
dirty fuel	every 250 hours

If the fuel is very dirty, install an extra filter in series with the existing filter.

Notes on key aspects of IC engines

Engine oil

- Check the oil level at the beginning of each working day and top up if required.
- Oil will drain more completely and quickly if the engine is warm and the filler cap is removed.
- Inspect drained waste oil for the presence of the following:
  - Metallic debris; indicates possible internal damage or excessive wear.
  - Water will appear as separate globules or as a creamy oil/water mix; this can indicate leakage from the cooling system.
  - Fuel (check by smell); indicates internal leakage from the fuel system.

Box 15.1 Guideline servicing periods for stationary diesel and petrol engines

Actual servicing periods will vary between engines. Consult the relevant handbook wherever possible. The following is a guide in the absence of specific information.

Diesel engines

Daily
(to be carried out by the operator)
Check fuel and oil levels.
Check for oil and fuel leaks.
Check coolant level (water-cooled engines).
Check battery water level, if applicable.
Check for loose nuts and bolts.
Check fan belt tension, if applicable.
Drain water from fuel filter/agglomerator.
In very dusty conditions, empty dust cap/bowl of dry air cleaners.

All subsequent servicing to be carried out by skilled mechanics.

Every 125 hours

The maintenance described above and the following:
Check the condition of the battery, if fitted.
Check for coolant leaks (water cooled).
When moderately dusty, empty dust cap/bowl and clean or replace the air cleaner element.
In high ambient temperatures (above 35°C) change the engine oil and oil filter.

Every 250 hours
Change the engine oil and oil filter element.
Check the valve clearances.
Clean or replace the injectors if the exhaust smoke is black.
Renew fuel filter element if using dirty fuel.
Check condition and tension of drive belts (alternator, fan, etc.), if applicable.

Every 500 hours
Replace air cleaner element.
Renew fuel filter element.
Check exhaust and air intake for leaks, damage or restrictions.
Check the battery charging system, if applicable.
Replace the fan belt, if applicable.

Every 1000 hours
Decarbonize only if engine performance is poor.
Clean wire gauze in engine breather, where applicable.

Every 2000 hours
Decarbonize.
Check fuel injection timing.
Check lubricating oil pressure.

Every 6000 hours
Carry out a major overhaul.

Every year
(water cooled engines)
Drain, flush and refill the cooling system.

Small, single-cylinder stationary petrol engines

Daily
(To be carried out by the operator)
Check fuel and oil levels.
Check for fuel and oil leaks.
Check battery water level, if applicable.
Check for loose nuts and bolts.
Check fan belt tension, if applicable.
In very dusty conditions, check and clean/wash the air filter element.

All subsequent servicing to be carried out by skilled mechanics.

Every 50 hours
The above checks and the following:
Change the engine oil.
Check and clean/wash the air filter element.
Check and clean the spark plug with a wire brush.

Every 200 hours
Check and clean the fuel filter.
Check and adjust the spark plug gap, if necessary.

Every 500 hours
Clean the fuel tank.
Replace the air filter element (oil soaked foam element type).

Every 1000 hours
Check the exhaust and inlet valve clearances and seating.

- Change the oil filter at the recommended intervals.
- Use the correct grade of oil. The viscosity of an oil is indicated by its SAE number. The higher the SAE number (increasing in steps of five) the thicker or heavier the oil at ambient temperature. A 'W' in the number indicates a guaranteed oil performance at a given temperature. A disadvantage of single number monograde oils (for example, SAE 30) is that an oil specified for the operating temperature may be too thick for the starter to turn the engine at ambient temperature. Multigrade oils overcome this problem. A multigrade SAE 20W/40 oil, for example, has a 20W ambient temperature viscosity and the viscosity of an SAE 40 oil at normal engine running temperature. Ensure the quality of the oil is to a recognized standard such as API or ACEA.

Air cleaner Restricted air flow, caused by a blocked air cleaner, can cause a loss of engine power, overheating, dirty exhaust and cylinder wear. Therefore, clean or change air cleaner elements frequently in dusty conditions. In a very dusty environment specify or, where possible, fit a heavy duty cleaner or pre-cleaner and check/empty daily. Check all filter elements for holes or cracks before re-using. Three types of air cleaner commonly used are: foam element, paper element and oil bath. The paper and foam types are sometimes combined in one unit.

- Foam element. Clean in warm soapy water, rinse and allow to dry. Alternatively, clean in kerosene and allow to dry. When dry, soak the element in clean engine oil and then squeeze to remove excess oil before replacing.
- Paper element. Paper element filters may be for once-only use or reusable – see the engine manual. Tap reusable paper element filters on a hard surface to remove dust. Compressed air can be used to blow away dust, but only from the inside out. Do not brush a filter as dirt can become embedded in the element. Visual inspection of paper elements cannot give a good indication of their condition as it is not always possible to see if the pores are blocked with dust.
- Oil bath. Incoming air picks up clean engine oil, contained in a bowl, and then passes through a gauze mesh. The oil entrained in the air picks up the dust and adheres to the gauze. The passage of the air and oil washes dirty oil to the bottom of the cleaner bowl and keeps the gauze oiled. Replenish the oil bath with the same clean oil as used in the engine. Do not fill beyond the mark in the bowl as this will restrict the air flow. Oil from an overfilled oil bath can be carried over into an engine. This is potentially very dangerous as it is possible for a diesel engine to run off this oil and run out of control.

Fuel and fuel filters Condensation can cause water and rust to accumulate in a fuel tank or drum, even when only clean fuel has been placed inside. Condensation forms when warm air cools during the night and water condenses on the sides of the tank or drum. Tanks may need to be drained occasionally to remove the water. Prevent condensation by filling fuel tanks at the end of the day. Refer to 17.2.4 for the safe handling and storage of fuel.

A fuel filter is much more critical to the functioning of a diesel engine than it is to a petrol engine. Diesel fuel systems are considered in more detail in 15.2.3.

Batteries The level of electrolyte in a lead-acid battery should be just above the battery plates. Water is lost during charging and through evaporation and this loss must be made up with distilled water. Check frequently in hot climates.

The specific gravity of the electrolyte decreases as a lead-acid battery is discharged, so a measurement of the specific gravity of the battery electrolyte indicates its state of charge. The specific gravity of a fully charged battery, measured using a hydrometer, varies with temperature; in a temperate climate it is 1.28; in a tropical climate it is 1.24.

Oxygen and hydrogen are evolved during battery charging. Therefore, charge batteries where there is good ventilation and do not allow naked flames or smoking near a battery, especially when it is on charge.

Battery terminals should be checked regularly to ensure that they are tight. It is easy to overtighten a battery terminal and crack it, so beware. Terminals should be protected with petroleum jelly to prevent corrosion. If battery terminals do become corroded with a copper sulphate gel, it should be removed with boiling water and washed away from all parts of the machine.

When disconnecting a battery, remove the earth terminal first. When connecting a battery connect the earth terminal last. Do not disconnect a battery from a machine when it is running, as the charging circuit can be damaged. Disconnect and remove a machine's battery when carrying out any electric arc welding on that machine or its base frame.

Jump starting batteries An engine which will not start because of a flat battery may be 'jump started' using a second charged battery.

Warning

The incorrect connection of jump leads can seriously damage electronic components. Follow the correct procedure, referring to Figure 15.1.

- Check that the batteries are of the same voltage and earthed (usually the negative terminal is connected to earth).
- Connect the red lead to the positive terminals of each battery. Connect the black lead to the negative terminal of the charged battery and to an earthed part of the chassis of the engine with the flat battery 0.5 m away from the battery. This is to reduce the risk of a spark igniting any hydrogen gas that may be given off by the batteries when the final connection is made.
- If the charged battery is connected to another engine, start this engine and run it at a fast idle. The engine with the flat battery should now start. If it does not – check the connections and try again. If it still will not start, refer to Tables 15.3 or 15.6 below.
- Stop the engine with the charged battery and disconnect the jump leads in the reverse order to the way they were connected. Make sure the loose ends do not touch each other or either machine.

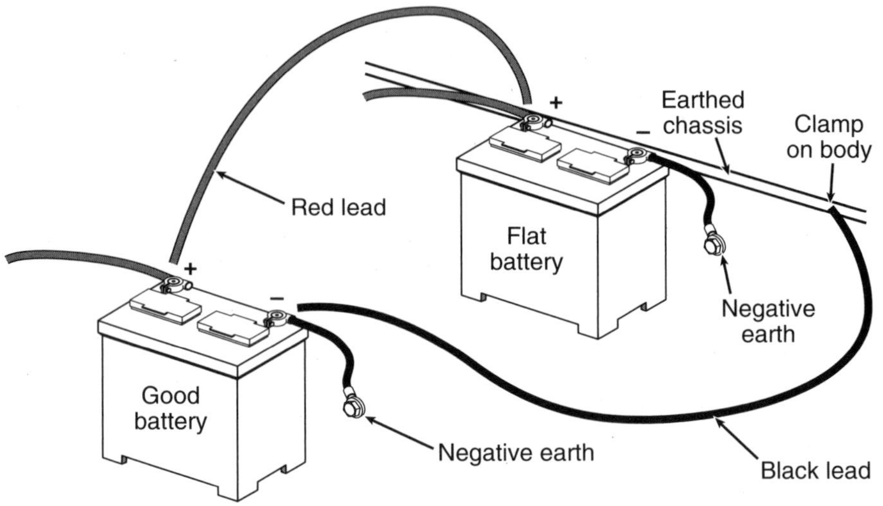

Figure 15.1 Jump lead battery connection

Internal combustion engine derating

The power output from petrol and diesel engines declines with increasing altitude and temperature so a suitable engine must be selected. Give the operating conditions (altitude and ambient temperature) when specifying plant powered by IC engines, especially for the sizing of generators. See Table 15.2 for derating factors.

Table 15.2 Diesel engine derating values

Standard conditions (ISO 3046)	25°C and atmospheric pressure of 100 kPa approximately at altitude of 100 m
Temperature derating	derate by 2% per 5°C above 25°C
Altitude derating	derate by 1.3% for every 100 m above 100 m

Refer to manufacturers' literature for the derating of turbo-charged engines. For precise derating values, check individual manufacturer's recommendations.

15.2.2 Petrol engines

Fault finding

Use Table 15.3 to identify the possible causes of a fault and refer to Table 15.4 for possible remedies. Use the charts together with whatever other reference material may be available on specific machines – operator's handbooks, maintenance manuals and spare parts books – to identify components that may be at fault.

Table 15.3 Symptoms and possible causes of faults in petrol engines

Symptom	*Possible causes (see Table 15.4)*
Difficulty starting:	
Engine will not turn over or only slowly – electrical problem	1,2,3
Engine will not turn over – cranking problem	4,5
Engine turns over but will not fire – fuel problem or	8,9,10,11
ignition problem	6,7
Engine turns over but will not fire or engine fires but cuts out – poor compression	12,13,14,15
Poor idling	6,7,9,13,14,15,16,17, 18,19
Lack of power	6,7,9,10,11,13,14,15, 16,17,20
Engine misfires	6,7,16
Engine stops after a short running period or when load is engaged	6,9(iii), 10,11, 16, 17
Engine stops suddenly – probably an electrical problem	2,6,7
Engine dies out gradually – probably a fuel problem	8,9,10
High fuel consumption	6,7,9,11,13,14,15,16, 17,20
Excessive exhaust smoke	13,15,16,17
Overheating	20,21,22
Mechanical noises	21,23

Tracing an ignition fault A high proportion of petrol engine faults are connected with the ignition system. A conventional contact breaker ignition system and a solid state electronic ignition system for a small single cylinder engine are illustrated (Figures 15.2 and 15.3). These complement the fault tracing guide. For a contact breaker ignition system use Table 15.5. Test after each stage. If the fault persists, go to the next stage or the stage indicated.

Warning

Ignition systems produce high voltages.

Hold cables with insulated pliers when testing.

Beware of fans and pulleys when the engine is running.

Beware of electric motor-driven thermostatically controlled radiator fans which may suddenly start even when an engine is not running.

Table 15.4 Possible causes and remedies for faults in petrol engines (see Table 15.3)

	Possible causes	*Possible remedies*
1	Flat battery	Check tension of alternator drive belt. Recharge or use jump leads
2	Loose or corroded terminals	Check, clean and tighten all terminals
3	Starter does not turn: i) Defective starter solenoid or switch. ii) Worn or damaged starter motor brushes or commutator	i) Check connections and change solenoid or switch. ii) Clean or replace
4	Starter tries to turn but gearing jams	Turn the end of the starter shaft with a spanner, if accessible; or crank engine by turning crankshaft with spanner
5	Starter turns but does not engage	Check for worn or dirty starter gear. Clean or renew
6	Ignition fault	See 'Tracing an ignition fault', p.421
7	Ignition timing incorrect: i) Distributor clamp loose. ii) Advance/retard mechanism faulty. iii) Distributor drive faulty	Check/repair and set the correct timing
8	No fuel reaching carburettor: i) Fuel tank empty. ii) Fuel pipes or filter blocked or leaking. iii) Fuel tank vent blocked. iv) Fuel lift pump faulty (check the pump by removing outlet pipe and observe fuel flow)	i) Do not rely on the fuel gauge, if fitted. Check by sight or a dipstick. ii) Inspect, clear and/or repair. iii) Check and clear with pin or wire. iv) Mechanical pump – inspect diaphragm and replace if punctured. Electric pump – check contacts and clean or tighten as necessary
9	Fuel reaching carburettor but fault in carburettor: i) Water and/or dirt in fuel. ii) Float chamber needle valve stuck closed – no fuel flow. iii) Float chamber needle valve not closing properly – flooded. iv) Float punctured – flooded. v) Air leak into manifold	i) Empty and clean bowl. Drain fuel tank. ii) and iii) Tap carburettor float chamber lightly on outside to try to loosen needle valve. If problem persists, open up carburettor to release valve. iv) Replace float. v) Manifold loose – tighten; or leaking gasket – replace
10	Carburettor jets blocked	Blow through jets to clear
11	Choked air filter	Clean or renew air filter
12	Cylinder head gasket leaking	Replace gasket
13	Sticking or leaking valve	Check, clean/regrind or replace
14	Valve timing or clearance incorrect	Check – adjust clearances and/or timing
15	Blue smoke: i) Piston rings stuck or worn. ii) Cylinder worn	i) Replace rings and piston if also worn. ii) Rebore and fit oversized piston and rings
16	Fuel mixture not set correctly: Mixture too rich – engine hunts and gives black exhaust smoke. Mixture too weak – engine may misfire	Adjust mixture settings in carburettor
17	Choke stuck on	Release choke

(Continued)

Table 15.4 (cont.)

	Possible causes	*Possible remedies*
18	Slow running adjustment incorrect	Adjust setting in carburettor
19	Slow running jet blocked	Blow clear
20	Choked exhaust	Clear/replace exhaust system
21	Bent fan or slipping fan belt	Correct shape and/or fan belt tension. Check belt for wear/damage
22	Faulty cooling system: i) Air cooled – blocked passages or lack of air flow. ii) Water cooled – lack of water, blocked radiator or faulty water pump	i) Clear passages and improve air flow. ii) Top up water/clear radiator. Replace water pump
23	i) Medium low pitch knock – big end bearing wear. ii) High pitch tap – worn gudgeon pins. iii) Low pitch thud – main bearing slack. iv) Intermittent thud – loose flywheel or end play on crankshaft. v) Whistling or hissing – air leaks in fuel induction system. vi) Continuous tapping – excessive valve clearance	i) Engine overhaul. ii) Replace and check pin sleeves. iii) Engine overhaul. iv) Tighten/adjust. v) Inspect and rectify. vi) Adjust

Solid-state electronic ignition system For more complex electronic ignition systems, the checks in stages 1, 2, 4, 5 and 6 of Table 15.5 are applicable, but for checks on the distributor and other components it will be necessary to refer to the specific manufacturer's handbook.

Figure 15.3 shows a solid state ignition system for a small single cylinder petrol engine. Engines of this type commonly power small hand-portable generators, small portable water pumps and other lightweight machinery. They are usually fitted with a rope recoil starter and do not include a battery. If a fault in the ignition system is suspected, trace the fault as described in stages 1 and 2 of Table 15.5. If the fault is not identified, go on to the following stage:

By-pass the ignition switch (if fitted). If the plug sparks: faulty ignition switch. If there is still no spark: defective transistorized trigger switch or ignition coil.

Without specialist equipment, the fault can only be rectified by replacing one part at a time to identify the defective component.

15.2.3 Diesel engines

Fault finding

Use Table 15.6 to identify the possible causes of a fault and refer to Table 15.7 for possible remedies. Refer to the following section on 'Diesel engine fuel systems'. In addition, consult whatever reference material is available on specific machines – operator's handbooks, maintenance manuals and spare parts books.

Standard diesel engine fuel system Figure 15.4 is a schematic layout of a typical diesel engine fuel system.

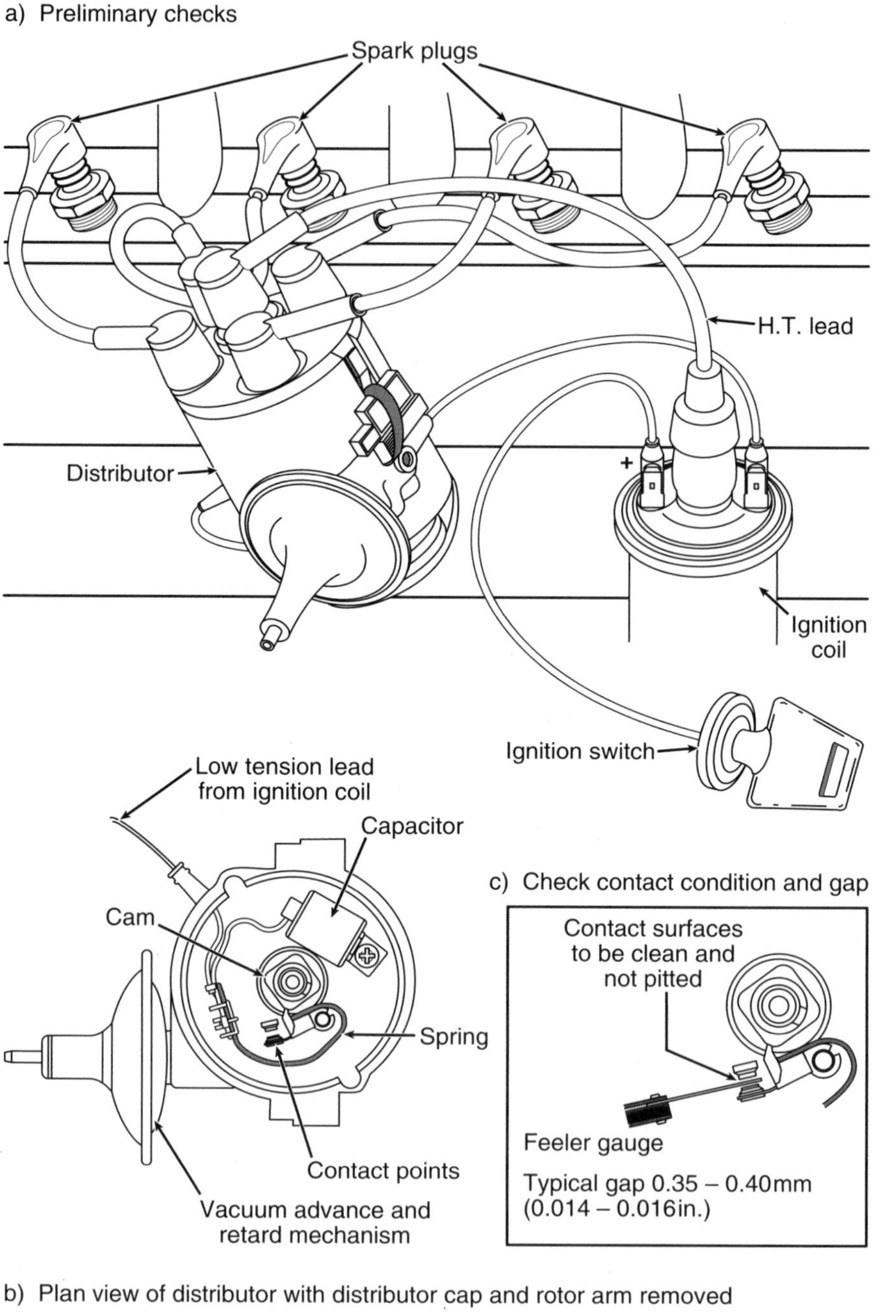

Figure 15.2 Schematic layout of a contact breaker ignition system

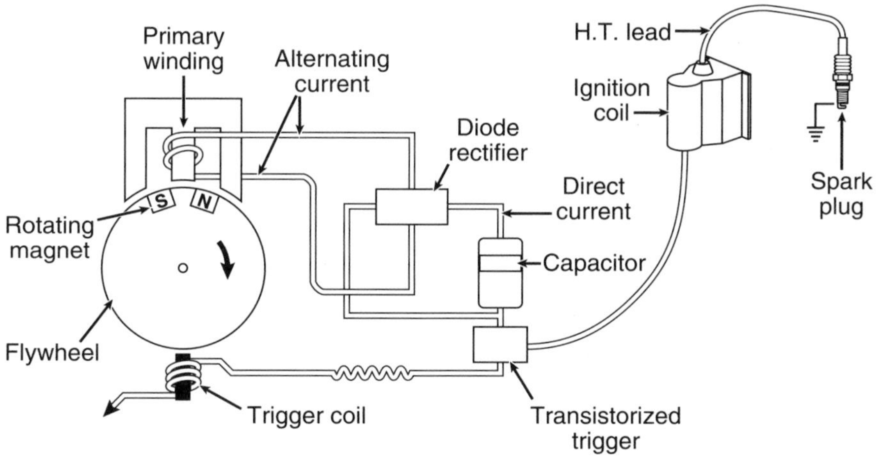

Figure 15.3 Schematic layout of a solid-state ignition system for a small single cylinder engine

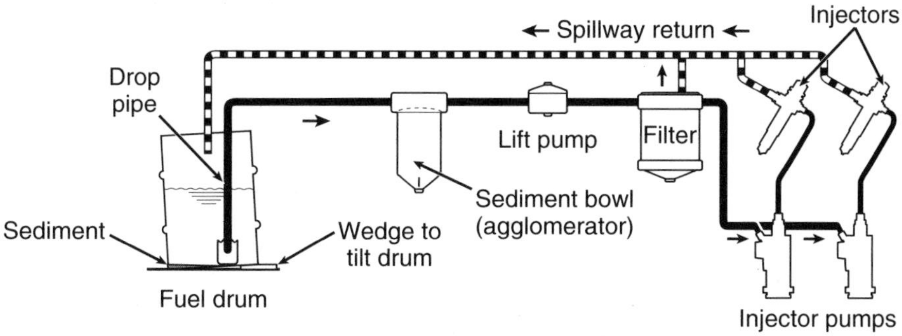

Figure 15.4 Diesel fuel system (not to scale)

Warning

Diesel fuel must be clean and free from water when it reaches the fuel injection pump or serious damage can be caused to the fuel injection system and to the engine.

Fuel storage Skid-mounted diesel engine sets often have their own small fuel tank attached to the engine or fabricated into the base frame. Fuel is often used directly from drums where there is no bulk fuel storage. Ensure drums are clean and allow fuel to stand (preferably for 12 hours) to allow sediment and water to settle before use. Tilt the drum to keep water and sediment away from the pipe end. Lead excess fuel from the filter and injectors (used for injector lubrication) via the spillway back to the fuel drum/tank. Only change the fuel

Table 15.5 Tracing faults in an ignition system

Stage 1 Check for:
- Damp ignition system – wipe dry the ignition leads and inside the distributor cap.
- Damage to wiring and loose connections.
- Ignition cables attached to the spark plugs in the wrong firing order – adjust. Cylinders are numbered from the front (timing belt) end of an engine. The most common firing orders for engines are as follows (with the alternatives given in brackets):

4-cylinder engine 1342 (1243)
6-cylinder engine 153624 (142635)

Smooth running of the engine will indicate the correct order.

Stage 2 Remove and visually inspect the spark plug(s):
- Incorrect plug (heat range and reach) – check the operator's handbook or compare with another similar engine – replace if incorrect.
- Cracked insulation – replace plug.
- Deposits across electrodes – clean with wire brush.
- Burnt out electrodes – replace plug.
- Electrodes wet with petrol (engine flooded) – dry out and crank engine with the spark plug removed to exhaust fuel.
- Incorrect plug gap – check with feeler gauge (typically 0.7–0.8 mm) and adjust.

Carry out a spark test:

With the spark plug removed from the engine, attach it to the plug lead. Earth the metal side of the spark plug by holding it with a pair of insulated pliers against the cylinder head away from the plug hole. Crank the engine (turn, pull the recoil rope or switch on the starter) and check to see if there is regular sparking across the electrodes. If there are good healthy sparks go on to stage 3. If unsure about spark, compare with a spark plug in an engine in good order. If no spark, or a weak spark, carry out the same test with the end of the plug lead held about 6 mm from the cylinder head (spark plug removed). If there is a good spark from the plug lead but no spark from the spark plug – change the spark plug. If there is no spark, or a weak spark from the plug lead, go on to stage 3.

Stage 3 Remove the distributor cap and check the contact breaker:
- Contact breaker points do not open and close when engine turned – check screw holding the fixed contact and adjust to the correct contact point gap (typically 0.35–0.40 mm at maximum opening).
- Contact points spring broken – replace points.

If the contact breaker points do open and close, continue with this stage.
- Incorrect contact point gap – reset (typically 0.35–0.40 mm at maximum opening).
- Broken lead – repair.
- Shorting or insulating washers broken down – adjust/replace.
- Contact breaker points pitted – clean or renew – then reset.

Stage 4 H.T. (High Tension) sparking:
- Disconnect, at the distributor cap, the central H.T. lead coming from the coil. Carry out spark test by holding the end of the lead 6mm from the engine with insulated pliers. Flick the points quickly open with an insulated screwdriver or crank the engine and watch for a spark between the lead and the engine.

If there is a spark then the fault is likely to be in the distributor or plug leads – go to stage 5.
If there is no spark go to stage 6.

Stage 5 Check distributor cap:
- If cap cracked – replace or, in an emergency, bind tightly with adhesive tape.
- Burnt/corroded connections – cleaning the cap will get the engine going for a while but if badly burnt/corroded replace cap as soon as possible.

Check rotor arm:
- Clean if necessary.
- Sprung central pick-up contact does not reach the rotor arm – replace spring and/or contact. (In an emergency, try packing between spring and contact with conducting material – nuts/washers/metal foil).
- Hold central distributor cap lead close (about 3 mm) to centre of rotor arm. Flick contact points open. No spark is normal. If it is a powerful spark, the rotor arm insulation may have broken down – replace the rotor arm.

Stage 6 Check ignition switch circuit:
- Loose or faulty low tension lead to coil – rectify.
- Remove low tension lead from ignition switch (thin wire to coil marked +). Switch on ignition and hold close to metal part of engine. No spark – problem with ignition switch and wiring. In emergency by-pass switch. Spark – go to stage 7.

(Continued)

Table 15.5 (cont.) Tracing faults in an ignition system

Stage 7 Check for faulty capacitor or H.T. coil: Connect a spare capacitor between an earth on the engine and the moving contact connection. Carry out the spark test with the distributor H.T. lead as in Stage 4. If sparking is improved, the original capacitor is	faulty – replace. If weak or no spark – defective ignition coil. Reconnect capacitor and replace coil. Note: capacitor deterioration can often be anticipated when an engine idles normally but struggles on load.

drop pipe to another drum when the engine is stopped. During changeover, keep the pipe submerged in fuel in a small container on the end of the pipe or air will get into the system. See 17.2.4 for more details on fuel storage.

Sedimentor and fuel filter The sedimentor (also called an agglomerator or sediment bowl) is designed to intercept dirt and water in the fuel before it reaches the injector pump. Check and drain the sedimentor regularly. The frequency of checks depends on fuel quality and must be based on experience. The frequency at which the fuel filter element has to be changed must also be based on experience (about every 500 hours for clean fuel, 250 hours or less for dirty fuel). Include two fuel filters in series if the fuel is particularly dirty.

Fuel injection pumps A fuel injection pump raises the pressure of the diesel fuel to open a needle valve in the injectors and inject the correct amount of fuel at precisely the right moment for efficient combustion. To achieve this function a fuel injection pump is accurately engineered to very fine tolerances; hence the need for clean fuel. A single element injector pump supplies one injector. A multi-cylinder engine may have one single element pump per injector or one distributor fuel pump which supplies all the injectors. Fuel injection timing is set correctly for new machines and it should not be adjusted.

Fuel injectors The function of a fuel injector is to atomize the fuel into a fine directed spray for efficient mixing and combustion with the hot compressed air. A needle valve in the injector nozzle must open and shut at a prescribed injection pressure (breaking pressure) for correct operation. A fuel injector gives a characteristic 'crack' when functioning. This can be used to ascertain if fuel is reaching the injectors and is being injected into the combustion chamber. Place the fuel control in the start position, operate the decompressor and crank the engine. The injector(s) should be heard to 'crack' when injecting fuel. If an engine runs erratically or loses power whilst running, check each injector as described below.

Warning

Diesel injector tests in air are a last resort. Injection pressures are very high. Take great care when carrying out tests to keep eyes and other parts of the body well out of the line of any fuel spray. Diesel fuel under pressure can easily penetrate the skin.

Table 15.6 Symptoms and possible causes of faults in a diesel engine

Symptom	*Possible causes (see Table 15.7)*
Difficult starting:	
Engine turns over but will not fire – fuel problem	1,2,3,4,5,6,7,8,9,10,11
Engine will not turn over or only slowly – cranking problem	12,15,16,17,18
Engine turns easily – poor compression	19,20,21,22,23,24,25, 26,30
Engine will not bring load up to speed – lack of power	Poor compression, fuel problems and overheating plus 27,28,29,30,56
Engine misfires	Poor compression and overheating plus 4,5,6,8,9,28,29
Engine runs then stops	Fuel problems, poor compression, overheating plus 14,31
Engine fails to attain running speed	6,10,15,31,53
Engine hunts (speed varies up and down around a mean)	6,8,9,53
High fuel consumption	Poor compression plus 1,8,9,11,20,23,24,26, 27,28,29,30,56
High oil consumption	21,23,24
Dark blue exhaust smoke	23,24
White exhaust smoke	7,32
Black exhaust smoke	1,8,11,31,33
Excessive carbon deposits on piston head, cylinder head and in exhaust	1,8,11,27,28,54,55,56
Overheating: i) Air cooled engines ii) Water cooled engines	i) 14,28,31,34,35,44 ii) 14,28,31,36,37,38,39
Low oil pressure	13,14,40,41,42,43
High oil pressure	43
Vibration	Poor compression plus 8,9,20,24,44,45,46,47
Knocking (detonation)	Overheating plus 1,8,28,52
Mechanical noises	23,26,46,47,48,49,50, 51,52

Table 15.7 Possible causes and remedies of faults in diesel engines

	Possible causes (see Table 15.6)	*Possible remedies*
1	Incorrect grade or poor quality fuel	Change fuel
2	Fuel tank empty	Fill and bleed fuel system of air
3	Stop/start lever in wrong position	Adjust
4	Choked fuel filter – visually inspect	Poor servicing – change filter
5	Faulty fuel lift pump	Inspect and repair
6	Air in fuel system	Bleed air from system
7	Water in fuel system	Drain fuel system including filter bowl, agglomerator and tank
8	Faulty injector nozzle	Test spray and clean/change nozzle
9	Faulty fuel injection pump	Have checked by competent workshop
10	Retarded injection	Check and adjust
11	Choked air filter	Poor servicing – clean or replace
12	Lubricating oil too heavy	Change oil
13	Lubricating oil too thin	Change oil
14	Lubricating oil level low	Poor servicing – top up
15	Engine started under load	Disengage load at clutch
16	Battery not charged (electric start)	Charge or 'jump start' (see Figure 15.1)
17	Loose or corroded terminals	Check, clean and tighten
18	Faulty starter motor (electric start)	Check terminals, solenoid switch, starter gear, brushes
19	Loose injector	Check and tighten
20	Valves leaking or sticking	Clean and regrind. Reset tappets
21	Valve guides worn	Replace guides
22	Broken or defective valve spring	Replace spring
23	Worn cylinder bore: excessive piston clearance gives a continuous slapping	Rebore and fit with oversized piston and rings
24	Broken, worn or sticking piston rings	Clean and free rings. Check cylinder liner is not scored
25	Incorrect decompressor clearance	Inspect and adjust
26	Incorrect tappet clearance	Check and adjust
27	Choked exhaust system	Clear or replace
28	Incorrect injection pump timing	Check and time
29	Incorrect valve timing	Reset valve timing
30	Cylinder head gasket leaking	Check and replace
31	Engine overloaded	Reduce load
32	Water leaking from the cooling system into the cylinder combustion area	Check and replace gasket
33	Inlet air temperature high	Improve ventilation to engine housing and air flow to and from engine

(Continued over)

Table 15.7 (cont.)

	Possible causes	*Possible remedies*
34	Poor circulation of cooling air: i) Recirculated cooling air ii) Air inlet and/or outlet obstructed	as 33 above
35	Cylinder cooling fins blocked	Clean
36	Water cooling system thermostat faulty	Check and replace
37	Cooling water level too low	Top up
38	Slack water pump drive belt	Inspect drive belt for wear. Tighten or replace
39	Blockage in water cooling system	Clear with cleaning fluid additive
40	Choked oil strainer or filter	Clean strainer or change filter
41	Badly worn bearings	Overhaul
42	Worn oil pump or damaged drive	Check and replace
43	Defective oil pressure relief valve	Repair or replace
44	Piston seizure	Stop engine immediately
45	Damaged cooling fan	Reshape or replace
46	Loose or damaged engine mountings	Inspect, tighten or change
47	Loose flywheel – intermittent thuds	Check and tighten
48	Worn connecting rod bush or bearing – low pitch knock	Overhaul
49	Worn gudgeon pin or small end bearing – high pitch tap	Overhaul
50	Main bearing worn – low pitch thud	Overhaul
51	Crankshaft end play – intermittent thuds	Adjust
52	Excessive carbon build up on piston	Decarbonize
53	Incorrectly adjusted governor or tight governor linkages	Adjust
54	Continuous idling	Shut down instead of idle
55	Regular running on low load	Match engine to load by choosing a lower powered engine
56	Low temperature running	Check sizing and operation of cooling system, especially water-cooled engines

With the engine running, loosen the fuel feed pipe union at the injector and check that fuel spurts from the pipe joint. Repeat the check on each injector. If the sound of the engine alters, there is no problem with the injector and fuel supply to that particular cylinder. However, no change in the sound and running speed indicates that either the injector is blocked/faulty or, if no fuel is seen, there is probably air in the injection pump and it needs removing – see below.

Bench tests using a hand operated injector tester can be carried out to check and set injector breaking pressure and spray pattern. These tests can be carried out by skilled mechanics with the appropriate tester. Wherever there are a large number of diesel trucks operating, there is likely to be a workshop where injector tests can be carried out. Breaking pressures will vary between engines. Consult the handbook for the correct breaking pressures of new and used injectors.

In the absence of test equipment, injectors can be tested to some extent on the engine. Remove and refit the injectors to spray into the air. Bleed the fuel system. Crank the engine and, at a safe distance, observe the spray patterns. All injectors should have the same spray pattern and depth of penetration. A comparatively short or weak spray indicates a defective injector nozzle. A good spray should not appear streaky or dribble fuel.

Removing air from the fuel system (bleeding) Air can enter a diesel fuel system through leaking pipe joints, gaskets, fuel change-over taps, or by running out of fuel. If air enters the system, the engine will stop as the air will prevent fuel reaching the injectors. Some systems are self-venting and they will automatically expel trapped air. In other cases the air must be bled from the system. Engines which are self-venting have to be cranked several times before the air is expelled. If cranking is a problem due to a weak or flat battery, then the air may be bled as described below.

Bleeding air is also called priming the fuel system. To prime the fuel system (refer to Figure 15.4):

- Ensure there is fuel in the tank.
- Place the engine control lever in the run position.
- Loosen the bleed screw on each fuel filter and, if the fuel is not gravity fed, manually operate the fuel lift pump by the priming lever, or crank the engine. Pump until air bubbles no longer accompany the fuel being expelled and a smooth flow of diesel is seen. Tighten the bleed screw and repeat the procedure on each successive sedimentor and filter.
- Loosen the vent screw on the injection pump. Crank the engine until bubble-free fuel flows continuously. Tighten the vent screw and crank the engine to start. Several turns may be required before the injectors can be heard to 'crack' open. The engine should then start.
- If the engine fails to start, prime the injection pipes. Loosen each injector feed pipe union (two turns only). Crank the engine until bubble-free fuel flows. Tighten unions and start the engine.

Governor systems and positive stop Without a governor there would be no check on the speed of a diesel engine and it would eventually overspeed and break up. A governor maintains a set engine speed by regulating the amount of fuel delivered by the fuel injection pump(s). If an engine fails to reach its required running speed or it is unable to maintain a steady engine speed (the engine 'hunts') then the governor will need checking by a skilled mechanic.

A spark ignition (petrol) engine can be stopped simply by switching off the electrical supply to the ignition circuit. But a compression ignition (diesel) engine does not rely on electrical power for combustion and once started will continue to run until the fuel supply is cut-off. A positive means of shutting off the fuel supply is usually provided by either a manual 'Stop' lever or an electrically operated fuel solenoid valve. Failure of the fuel solenoid valve can prevent an engine starting. Check that the electrical leads have not become loose or disconnected before consulting a skilled mechanic.

Decarbonizing

Carbon deposits may build up in a diesel engine after a period of running and this can adversely affect performance. With modern fuels and oils, an engine will run almost indefinitely without the need for decarbonization. However, poor quality fuel and oil may result in the deposition of carbon inside the engine and removal of the carbon will be necessary.

Decarbonizing an engine is a job for a skilled mechanic. An engineer with responsibility for a programme should be aware of the possible need for decarbonizing and consult with a mechanic. Find out if decarbonizing will be necessary, when and how this can be scheduled (because plant will be out of action for a while), and what spares will be required so that they can be purchased well in advance. Minimize the time that plant is out of action.

15.3 Compressed air plant

Emergency work can entail the use of compressed air plant in the following areas:

- Portable compressed air plant in general construction work and in water well drilling and digging.
- Stationary compressors and compressed air tools in motor vehicle workshops.

This section gives a brief overview of the plant likely to be encountered.

15.3.1 Compressors

The compressor pressurizes the air and delivers it to the air tool via a receiver and supply pipe. Compressors are categorized into two main types: reciprocating and rotary.

Reciprocating compressors

Reciprocating compressors are either single-stage or multi-stage. In the single-stage compressor, air is compressed by one stroke of a piston in a single cylinder. Single-stage compressors are suited to low working pressures of less than 7 bar. In a multi-stage compressor, air passes from one cylinder to the next, increasing in pressure at each stage. Two-stage compressors are more efficient than single-stage compressors allowing a smaller engine to be used for the same output. Inter-cooling between the stages enables higher pressures to be achieved very efficiently.

Rotary air compressors

Sliding vane and rotary screw compressors are the two main types of rotary compressor.

The sliding vane compressor consists of a cylindrical rotor mounted eccentrically in a cylinder. Rotation causes blades set radially into slots in the rotor to be thrown to the cylinder wall by centrifugal force. Due to the eccentric mounting, the space between the vanes decreases as the rotor moves from the suction inlet to the delivery and the trapped air is compressed. The vanes are sealed, lubricated and cooled by oil which circulates in the system.

The rotary screw compressor consists of two finely matched helical rotors within a casing. The lobes of a male rotor match the flutes of a female rotor. The rotation of the two rotors is synchronized so that air trapped between them is compressed as it progresses from the inlet to the outlet port.

Receivers

Air usually passes from a compressor to a cylindrical receiver which has the following functions:

- To smooth out pressure fluctuations.
- To serve as a reservoir of pressurized air to meet intermittent high demands for air.
- To cool the air and remove moisture and carried-over compressor oil before entry into the supply lines.

Check and ensure that collected liquids and deposits due to atmospheric dust, rust, etc. are periodically removed from the receiver, otherwise they will build up and eventually carry over into the supply lines. Automatic drainage is often provided, but check that it functions correctly. A receiver may not follow a rotary compressor as there is no pulsation to dampen. If there is no receiver, fit a coalescing filter in the delivery line. A coalescing filter removes fine particles by filtration and encourages aerosols of air and water to coalesce and fall out by gravity.

Compressed air requirements

The operating duty of a compressor and the air demand of equipment is usually expressed in l/s (dm^3/s) of free air delivered (F.A.D) or air delivered at atmospheric pressure (1 bar). When compressed, the volume will be less – for example, 25 l/s F.A.D. is equivalent to a volume of 3.61 l/s when compressed to a working pressure of 6 bar.

15.3.2 Compressed air plant for construction work

Choice of equipment

Most pneumatic tools used in construction work are designed for a working pressure of 6–7 bar. Therefore, a compressor with a normal working pressure of 7 bar is suitable. To calculate the capacity of the compressor required, list the pneumatic equipment that will be operating at any one time and sum their individual air requirements. Allow a margin for worn equipment and leaks. This gives the compressor capacity required.

Percussion tools

A percussion tool consists of a piston reciprocating in a cylinder delivering a series of rapid blows to a matching tool. A two-handed pneumatic breaker suitable for breaking heavy rock and concrete weighs from 20–35 kg. Typical air consumption is 25 l/s F.A.D. at a working pressure of 6 bar. Picks are similar but lighter than concrete breakers at 8–12 kg with a typical air consumption of 17 l/s F.A.D. at a working pressure of 6 bar. They are suitable for both vertical and horizontal work. Chipping hammers are even lighter. Breakers and picks commonly use moil point tools and chisel bits for breaking and splitting work.

Rotary tools

Rotary rock drills incorporate both rotary and percussive actions to give rapid penetration rates. For efficient operation, the correct shape of drill steels must be maintained. Drills may have built-in lubricators or rely on in-line lubrication. Check that the lubrication system functions and is topped up with the correct oil. A lightweight hand-held rock drill weighs about 12 kg and typical air consumption is about 24 l/s F.A.D. at a working pressure of 6 bar.

Ancillaries and spares

Pneumatic tools need to be continuously lubricated. Hand held tools may have their own integral lubricator (which must be topped up each day) or an in-line lubricator installed in the air line between compressor and tool. Check on the form of lubrication and, if required, obtain, or specify when ordering, a portable lubricator and sufficient lubricant for the tools to be operated.

Include all the necessary air line accessories when placing an initial order. Hose, couplings, tool shanks and so on differ in size, so ensure that all the fittings are compatible. Do not skimp on hose but obtain a sufficient length of hose for the jobs anticipated. Order spare claw couplings, coupling packing, and hose and hose clamps.

Key points to observe when using compressed air equipment:

- Provide adequate safety equipment – hard hats, footwear, gloves, goggles, ear defenders and air filter masks.
- Check all nuts are tight on breakers and drills.
- Blow out air hoses to remove dust and condensation before coupling to tools.
- Ensure that a tool is lubricated by placing a hand over the tool exhaust and feeling for spent oil.
- If no specialist air-tool lubricant is available, use ordinary engine oil. DO NOT use diesel, as it may ignite in the rock drill like a diesel engine!
- Keep all dust, sand, grit, etc. out of air lines and tools when not in use by connecting hoses to themselves and covering tool connections with claw coupling covers.
- Regularly monitor and service the compressor as recommended by the manufacturer. Service more frequently in hot, humid and dusty conditions.
- Progress from larger to smaller diameter drill steels as a hole is drilled deeper.
- Keep drill and breaker tools well dressed. Arrangements can often be made with mines, quarries and government workshops for the re-grinding of tools.

See Appendix 12 for a small compressed-air-tool rock breaking and drilling package for dug well construction. This can be adapted to other construction work.

15.4 Grinding mills

Grinding mills are often required in a relief operation, to process grain into flour. They vary from small vertical plate mills of 200–400 kg/h output to large container-sized hammermills of 8000 kg/h capacity. They can be driven by electric, diesel or petrol engines. Table 15.8 is intended as a preliminary guide for ordering equipment.

Table 15.8 Data on hammermills for maize

Power drive	*Maize flour output (1mm screen), kg/h*	*Nominal shipping details, m³ (kg)*
Diesel engine, 7.3 kW	250	1.7 (450)
Diesel engine, 23.4 kW	750	2.0 (640)

From Alvan Blanch Development Co. Ltd

Containerized grain milling system

A containerized mill has the same dimensions as a standard 20 ft freight container and therefore it can be handled as a normal container for ease of transport. This type of mill is designed for quick erection and operation within a few hours.

Typical power requirements are:

Output of 6 tonne/h of maize flour   2 × 90 kW mill motors (240 kVA)

Output of 8 tonne/h of maize flour   2 x 100 kW mill motors (325 kVA)

15.5 Belt and shaft drives

Mechanically powered equipment generally consists of a prime mover (IC engine or electric motor) which drives a tool or piece of equipment such as a pump. The following discussion refers to pumps, but the same principles apply to similar equipment powered by a motor.

Power from the prime mover has to be transferred through some form of power transmission system, commonly belt or shaft drives. Poor alignment of pump and motor shafts or of pulleys can lead to power losses in transmission, the overheating of bearings, and the wear of couplings, pulleys and belts. Therefore, always check alignment when the pump and motor are separate units. It is also good practice to check factory assembled sets before commissioning.

Shafts Pump and motor shafts must be both concentric and parallel. The most common form of drive is through a flexible flange coupling. Check and adjust as follows (Figure 15.5):

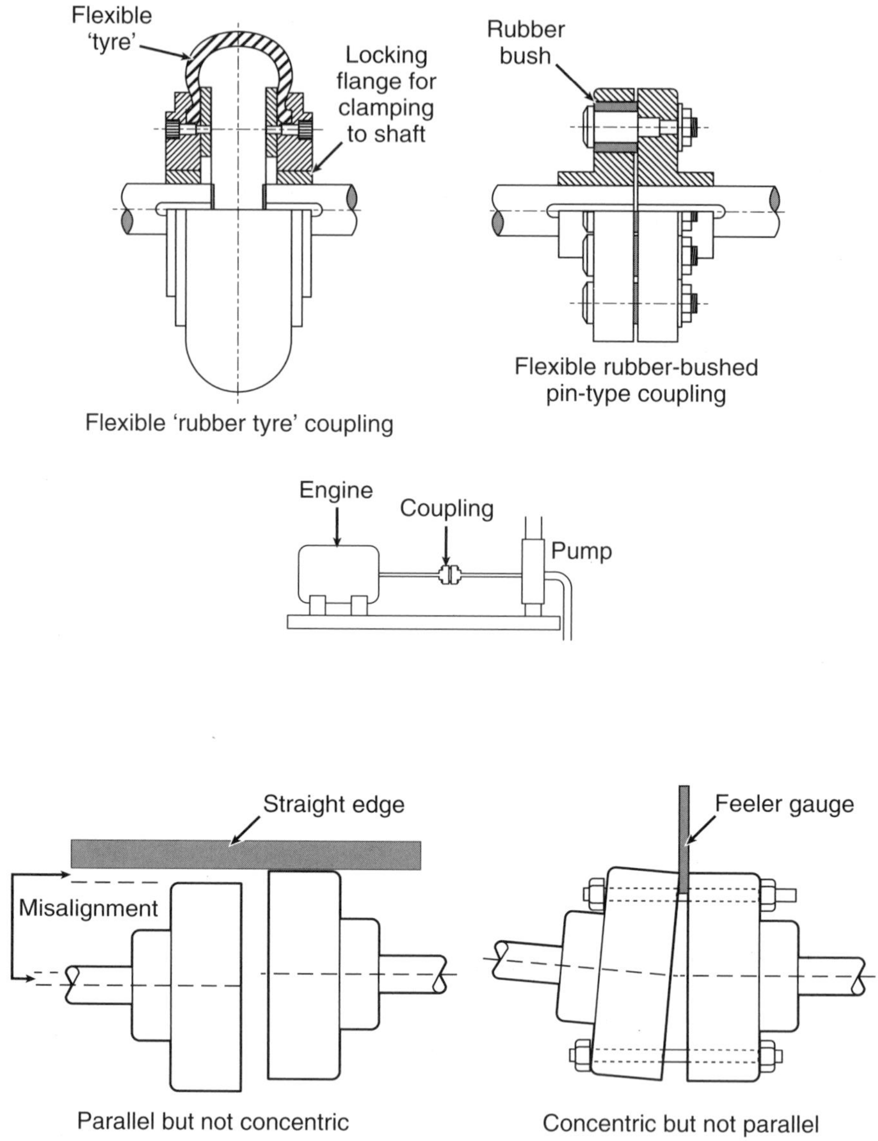

Figure 15.5 Couplings and shaft alignment

- To check that shafts are parallel: mark measuring points on the couplings so that the shafts may be kept aligned as they are turned. Measure any misalignment with a feeler gauge. Turn both shafts at the same time and check at every quarter turn. Use a ruler as shown in Figure 15.5 to check that the shafts are concentric.

- Adjust as necessary. To move the pump or prime mover in a horizontal direction use the bolts in the base frame slots. Use shims or adjustments if fitted to raise or lower the pump or prime mover vertically.

Pulleys and drive belts Ensure the angle of a 'V' belt and the width match the pulley. Check the alignment of drive pulleys by using a long straight edge or taut string (Figure 15.6). The string should lie flat across the face of each pulley if they are correctly aligned.

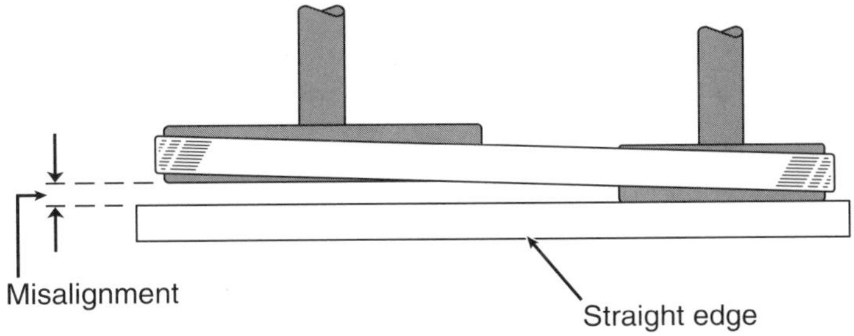

Figure 15.6 Checking the alignment of pulleys

A loose drive belt will slip causing power loss, overheating and rapid wear of the belt. A tight drive belt will consume extra power, rapidly wear the belt and damage the pump or engine bearings. Therefore, ensure drive belts are adjusted to the manufacturer's recommended tension. Rule of thumb: there should be some give in the belt under firm finger pressure. Better a belt which is too loose (it wears itself out) than too tight (it may damage bearings).

It is recommended to carry a 'link belt' in stock as it can be adjusted, or 'linked', to any required length so reducing the number of spare belts in the store.

16 Electrical plant

In an emergency, the two most important uses of electrical power are usually lighting and pumping water. Simple electrical lighting systems may be used in facilities providing night-time services, such as hospitals and clinics, or for security lighting. Electric submersible pumps are often powered from a generator.

This chapter provides basic knowledge and guidelines for the non-specialist who may have to install a simple lighting circuit, or order, install and operate generators and electric motor driven pumps.

Always seek professional advice!

Working with electricity is very hazardous.

Consult local electricians – look for electricians in the displaced community. The information in this chapter is for guidance in emergencies when decisions may have to be taken without the benefit of appropriate professional advice.

16.1 Simple electrical systems

16.1.1 A typical electrical installation

A typical, small electrical installation is illustrated schematically in Figure 16.1. Electricity is supplied from a generator via fuses and isolators to a distribution board. From the distribution board, the supply is directed to an electric water pump and to lighting and socket outlet circuits. This example might be found in a pumping station where the distribution board directs the supply to an electric motor driven pump, and to lighting and socket circuits. An emergency supply to a single pump is unlikely to have lighting and socket circuits and will, therefore, be supplied directly from the generator via an isolator and pump motor starter. The isolator and starter may be separate or combined in a control panel. Figure 16.2 shows a simple 'loop-in' lighting circuit.

This chapter gives details on the following:

- Safety precautions when dealing with electrical apparatus.
- Basic background information on electricity to enable the non-specialist to understand the terminology used and standard practices described.
- The generator which produces the electricity.

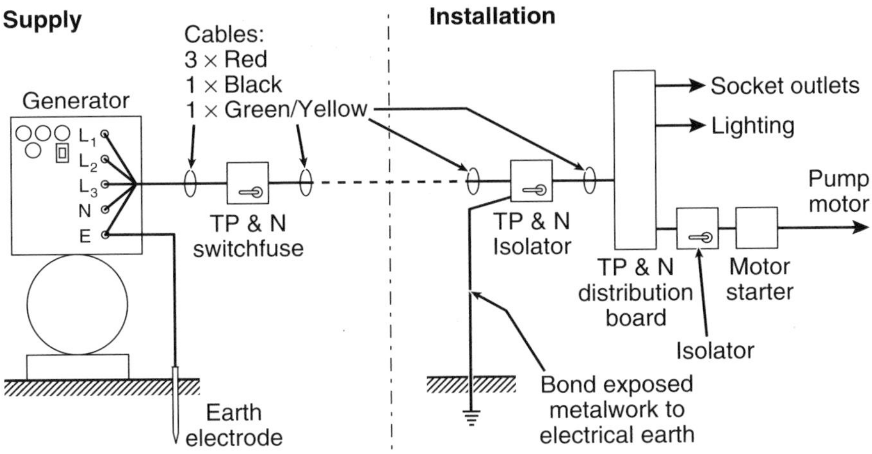

Figure 16.1 A typical electrical supply from generator to pump

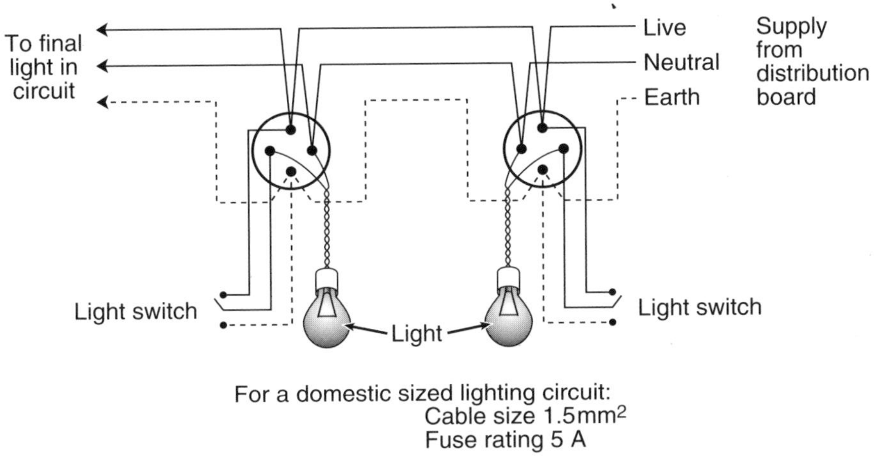

Figure 16.2 A simple lighting circuit

- Cables which carry the current from the generator to the pump. Information is given on how to size cables.
- Protection; this covers: earthing, fuses and circuit breakers, distribution boards and protection from the outside environment.
- The electric induction motor which drives the pump.

Pumps are dealt with in Chapter 14.

16.1.2 Safety

An electric 'shock' rapidly overwhelms the normal signals of the nervous system. The resulting lack of muscle control often prevents a conscious person from letting go of the live conductor which is causing the shock. The consequences are instantaneous, painful and often fatal.

Electricity can kill!

If a person is receiving an electric shock:

- Do not touch them – or you will also receive an electric shock.
- Switch off the power.
- If the power cannot be switched off quickly, pull the person clear using dry non-conducting material such as thick clothing or a loop of rope. Alternatively, push them clear using a dry stick.
- Carry out artificial respiration if the person is not breathing – and keep going: people have been revived after more than half an hour of artificial respiration.
- Obtain medical help as soon as possible.

Safety rules

Ensure that workers understand and follow simple safety rules, and follow them yourself:

- If the work is remote from a distribution board or generator, disconnect the supply at the isolator (some isolators can be padlocked or the handle can be removed), remove the fuses and leave a notice explaining what is happening.
- Never assume wires, equipment or electrical enclosures or panels are dead – always check first. When using a tester, check that the tester is working correctly by trying it on a known live circuit first.
- If in doubt, do not 'try' something to see if it works – always ask first.
- Damp or sweaty skin reduces resistance, so keep hands dry when working.
- Before switching on after installation or maintenance work, ensure that everyone concerned has completed their work and that everyone knows the power is coming on again.
- When installing electrical equipment, ensure that all cables are properly insulated and protected and that proper earthing is provided. Fuses and circuit breakers are an essential safety feature – do not try to override them.

16.2 Some basic electrical principles

16.2.1 Electrical power generation

An electromotive force (emf) is generated in a conductor, such as a metal wire or cable, when it cuts across a magnetic field or when a moving magnetic field cuts across the conductor. This phenomenon can be used to convert mechanical energy to electrical energy (in electric generators) or to convert electrical energy to mechanical energy (in electric motors).

A current will flow in the conductor which crosses a magnetic field if the conductor is connected in a closed electrical circuit. The direction of current flow depends on the relative direction of movement of the conductor and the magnetic field. If the conductor is rotated, the direction in which it cuts the magnetic field will change during each revolution and hence the direction of current flow in the conductor will change, giving rise to an alternating current (Figure 16.3).

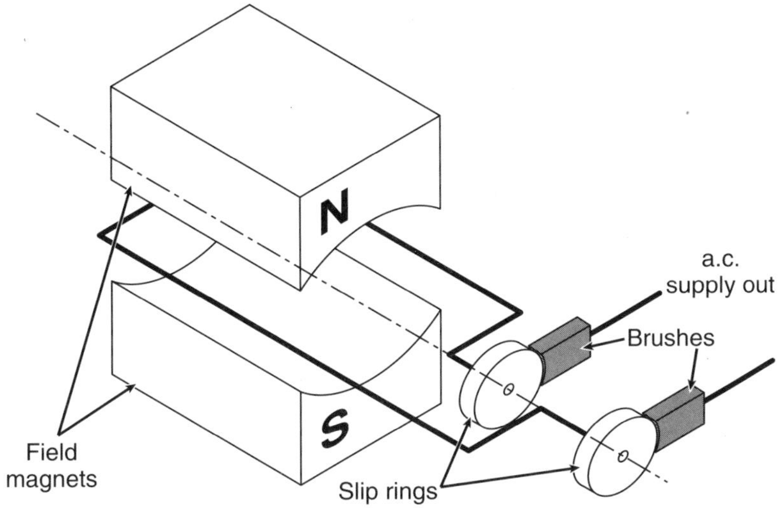

Figure 16.3 A simplified brush-type a.c. generator

In practice, the conductor armature is kept stationary (and termed the stator) and the field magnets are rotated (and termed the rotor). In a brush-type alternator (Figure 16.4), the electromagnets on the rotor are supplied by a low voltage direct current (d.c.) through slip rings. In a brushless alternator, the d.c. field current is provided by rectifying an alternating exciter current generated by the alternator itself. In both the brush-type and brushless alternator the initial exciter current is produced on start-up by permanent magnets on the rotor or by a residual magnetism field system. The magnetic field is produced by electromagnets on the rotor. The rotor may have more than one magnet each with a pair of magnetic poles. The rotor, stator and associated components are collectively called an alternator. Three separate stators spaced out equally around a magnetic rotor will each produce alternating current with a phase difference of 120°. Each current flows in a separate circuit and the cables in the circuit are called phase cables. This is termed a three-phase supply. A single phase supply utilizes one phase only.

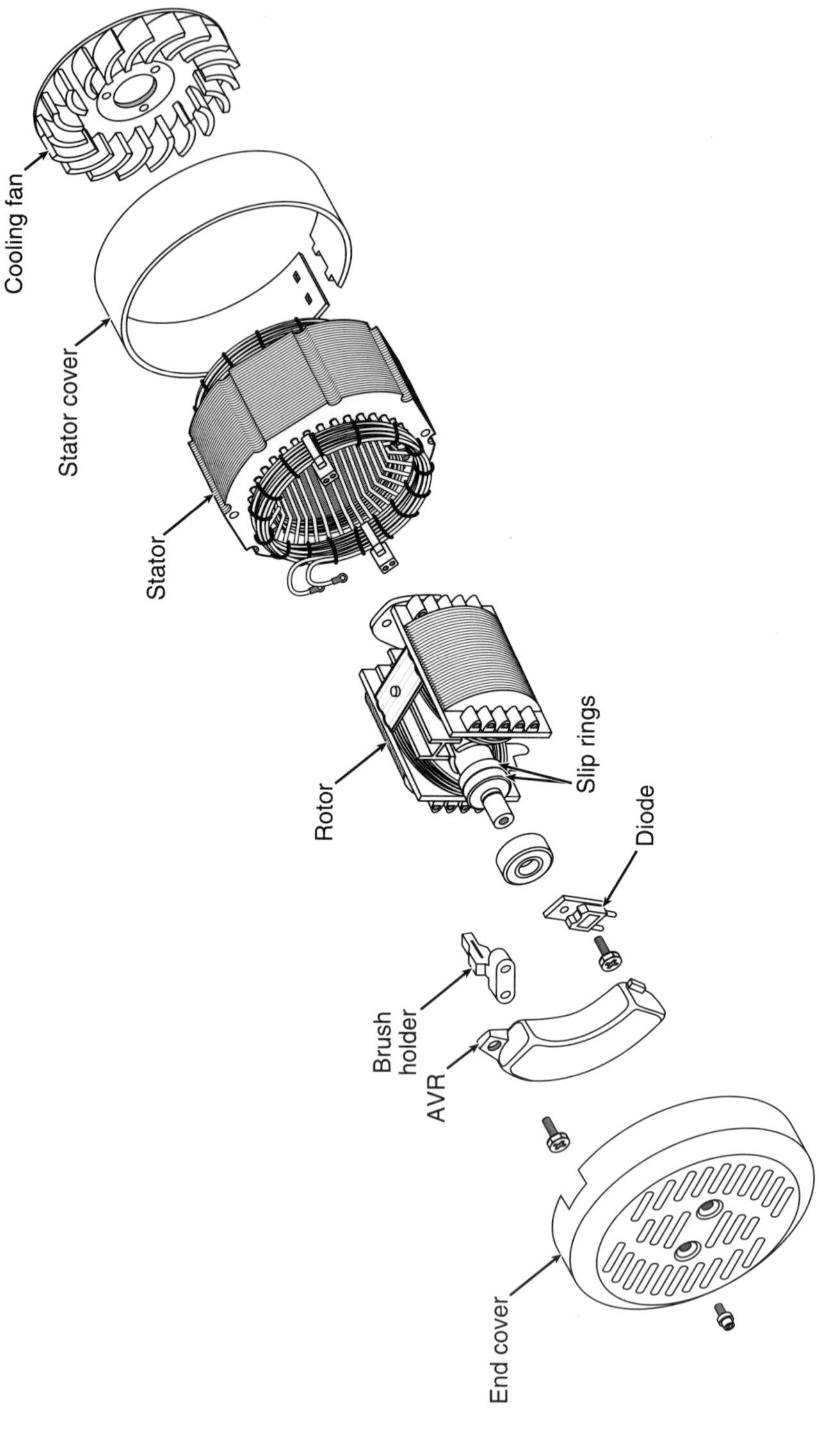

Figure 16.4 A brush-type alternator

The number of pairs of poles and the speed of rotation determine the frequency of the emf induced.

$$f = p \times n$$

where: f is the frequency in hertz (Hz)
p is the number of pairs of poles
n is the speed of rotation (revs/second)

The magnitude of the emf (voltage) produced also depends on the number of poles and the rotational speed.

To maintain a constant specified frequency and voltage, the rotation of the alternator must be kept at a constant specified speed. Electricity is commonly supplied from a generator as three-phase alternating current (a.c.) with a frequency of 50 Hz or 60 Hz (cycles per second). The line voltage (see Box 16.1) is typically 415V (phase voltage 240V) or 380V (phase voltage 220V).

Box 16.1 Standard cable coding

Phases			Neutral	Earth
Red Brown U R L_1	Blue Brown V S L_2	Yellow Black W T L_3	Black Light blue N N N	Green/Yellow Green/Yellow E E E

16.2.2 Cabling configurations

Figure 16.5 summarizes the terminology used when referring to a three-phase electricity supply.

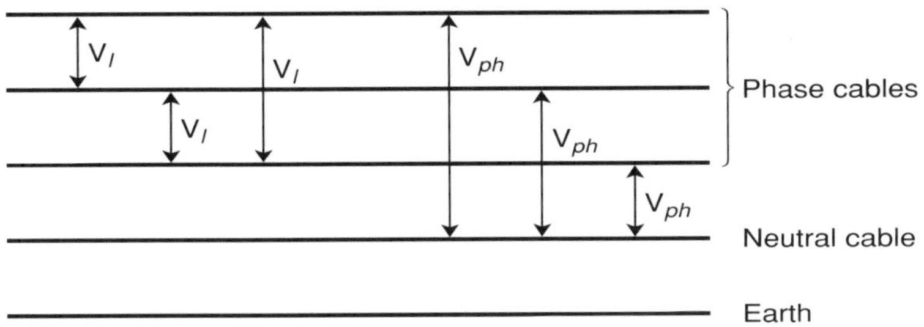

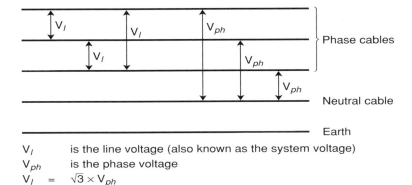

V_l is the line voltage (also known as the system voltage)
V_{ph} is the phase voltage
$V_l = \sqrt{3} \times V_{ph}$

Example: If $V_l = 415V$, then $V_{ph} = 240V$ and the system is designated 415/240V

Figure 16.5 A typical three-phase electricity supply

Cable coding

There are standard codings for cables used in three-phase, neutral and earth supply (see Box 16.1). Keeping to the standard colour codes makes subsequent fault-finding easier. Codes may be indicated by coloured core insulation, sleeving or tapes.

16.2.3 Electrical power and power factor

In a simple d.c. system, the power supplied, P, is:

$$P = V \times I \text{ (watts, W)}$$

where V is the voltage (volts, V) and I is the current (amps, A).

In a.c. circuits, life is more complicated. The power supplied which is capable of doing work is termed the 'active power' and is denoted in units of kilowatts (kW) or for very small motors in watts (W). In a.c. circuits with inductive equipment (such as motors, transformers) the active power will be less than the apparent power supplied, which is measured as the product of voltage and current. The apparent power is denoted in units of kVA. The difference between the active and the apparent power is the reactive power. The total of the active and reactive power is termed the apparent power and is measured in kilovolt-amperes (kVA). The power factor is defined as:

$$\text{Power factor} = \frac{\text{Active power (kW)}}{\text{Apparent power (kVA)}}$$

The value of the power factor (p.f.) depends on the type of electrical installation and machinery supplied. Electric motors generally have a power factor of between 0.8 and 0.9.

In a single-phase a.c. supply: Active power, $P = V_{ph} \times I \times \text{p.f. (kW)}$

In a three-phase a.c. supply: Active power, $P = V_l \times I \times \sqrt{3} \times \text{p.f. (kW)}$

16.3 Generators

The principles of electrical power generation are dealt with in 16.2.1.

16.3.1 Basic types

Generators likely to be encountered in an emergency are of two main types:

- Small, portable, single-cylinder petrol or diesel driven generator sets for emergency lighting, giving a single-phase supply up to about 5 kVA.
- Skid mounted, single and multi-cylinder diesel driven generator sets for the supply of electric submersible and surface mounted pumps. These sets give a three-phase supply from 2 kVA to over 30 kVA.

The rated output of an a.c. generator is the apparent power in units of kVA, calculated at the rated current and voltage. The rated current is the current capacity under continuous operation. The apparent power is used in preference to the active power (in kW) as the active power will vary depending on the power factor of the connected load (see 16.2.1). In addition to the rated current, most generators are able to manage a large momentary current – useful to allow for the high starting currents of electric motors.

An automatic voltage regulator (AVR) maintains the output voltage at a specified value despite load variations. Overcurrent protection automatically breaks the circuit if the load exceeds the generator rating or if a short circuit occurs. Protective devices include automatic circuit breakers and fuses.

16.3.2 Sizing and specifying generators

Sizing for electric motors

A generator supplying an electric motor must be able to cope with both the peak running load (the full load) and the increased load due to starting (starting load). If the generator is only just big enough to run the motor at full load, the extra load on starting may result in the motor failing to start. The magnitude of the starting load depends on the type of motor and the method of starting. See Section 16.6 for a fuller description of electric motors and starters. Competent suppliers will be able to match and supply a suitable generator if they are given basic information on the load to be supplied (see Table 16.1).

In an emergency, and in the absence of full information about a generator, the following general rules can be used to ensure that the generator is able to meet the load requirements on start-up:

- Generator full load kVA (P_f above) should be $\geq 2 \times$ output motor power (in kW).
- Check the full load current (FLC) of the pump motor and ensure that the rated current capacity of the generator is able to supply the FLC plus 15 per cent.

Beware of greatly oversizing a generator. If a diesel engine is run continuously on a light load, there is a risk of the injectors becoming clogged with carbon deposits of unburnt fuel. Regular light loading can lead to excessive fuel and oil consumption.

Sizing for lighting

Conventional resistive lighting and heating impose no extra load on start up and have a power factor of unity (p.f. = 1). Therefore, choose a generator which is able to supply the maximum load at any time of all the individual lighting and heating appliances plus a 10–15 per cent safety margin.

Fluorescent lamps have a power factor of about 0.6. Therefore, the expected maximum capacitive load of this type (in kW) must be divided by 0.6 to obtain the size of generator required in kVA. Add a 10–15 per cent safety margin.

Specifying a generator

Use Table 16.1 as a guide when specifying a generator. Small portable sets are often supplied with very little instrumentation, if any, as standard. Specifying non-standard items may delay delivery. Therefore, balance the value of extra equipment and instrumentation against the urgency of the need. As with all

Table 16.1 Information needed to specify a generator

Essential information	*Recommended information*
It is essential to specify the following information to ensure that the generator will give the correct output: • The supply required. Either: Single phase, 2-wire (phase and neutral), and system voltage, for example: 110V, 220V or 240V. Or: Three-phase, 4-wire (three-phase and neutral), and system voltage, for example: 380/220V, 415/240V. • Supply frequency: 50 Hz or 60 Hz. • Continuous output kVA. List the pieces of equipment to be supplied by the generator and their power requirements. In the case of motors, give the method of starting. For example: One electric submersible pump with a motor size of 5.5 kW (6.6 kVA) started direct-on-line (DOL). One booster pump with a motor size of 4 kW (4.8 kVA) started DOL. Total is 9.5 kW (11.4 kVA). • Site conditions. Temperature (maximum and minimum), altitude, and humidity. Note any particular problems, such as dust.	In addition, it is recommended to specify the following: • Skid mounted or mobile. • Weather protection and IP rating (see 16.5.2). State whether the generator should be supplied as an open or weather protected set. • Engine – any generator set of size will be diesel driven. State the following options: Air or water-cooled. Hand and/or electric start. (Even with electric start, it is useful to have a hand-start facility for when the battery is flat, or missing.) Engine monitoring facilities – over-heating, low oil pressure, battery charging ammeter or indicator. Automatic engine shut down in the event of over-heating, low oil pressure, or broken fan belt. Base fuel tank and/or separate service tank. • Control panel. Integral (set-mounted) or free-standing control panel. Integral control panels must be mounted on anti-vibration mountings. Instrumentation to include: One ammeter per phase. One voltmeter and selector switch (to monitor each phase-phase and phase-neutral voltage). Frequency meter. Hours-run meter. Engine monitoring meters and indicators may be mounted in the control panel. • Exhaust pipework – run length and any bends.

machinery, specify an operation and maintenance manual and a spare parts book.

16.3.3 Installation of generators

The following installation guidelines refer to permanently or semi-permanently installed stationary sets.

On delivery and before installation check that the generator output (voltage, frequency, power), control gear (switches, contactors, protective devices) and load (pump motors) are all compatible.

Table 16.2 Symptoms and possible faults in generators

Symptom	*Possible causes*
No generator output	i) Faulty or loose terminals, disconnected wiring or dirty contacts ii) Blown fuse or tripped circuit breaker – Overloaded generator – Short circuit due to a breakdown in cable insulation iii) Break in stator output coil iv) Demagnetized permanent magnet v) A faulty automatic voltage regulator (AVR) Brush type generators only: vi) Worn or dirty brushes and slip rings
Output voltage is very low (only a few volts)	i) A faulty AVR Brush type generators only: ii) Disconnected rotor coil iii) Worn brushes or faulty contact
Output voltage is low but more than just a few volts	i) Engine speed too low: adjust ii) Short circuit in a coil iii) A faulty AVR
Output voltage is high at normal engine speed	A faulty AVR
Output voltage is normal when the set is cold but varies when the set warms up	A faulty AVR
Generator trips out or rated generator output not available and the speed of the engine fluctuates significantly (> 10%) between no-load and load conditions	i) Excessive initial current on start up. Reduce starting load by: starting higher loads first; fitting reduced voltage starting ii) Output of engine below rated engine power: service and/or repair engine iii) A faulty engine governor
Engine problems	See Section 15.2

- A generator must not be run inside a building without adequate ventilation and removal of the exhaust gases.
- A generator must not be operated unprotected in the rain unless contained within a purpose made weatherproof enclosure.

If necessary, construct a basic shelter to protect against strong sunlight, rain and excessive dust. In tropical climates, support a corrugated GI roof on a simple angle iron frame with the uprights set in concrete. Hang chain link fencing wire to form temporary walls – this allows for ample air-flow. Upgrade as soon as practicable. See Section 16.5.2 and Figure 16.6.

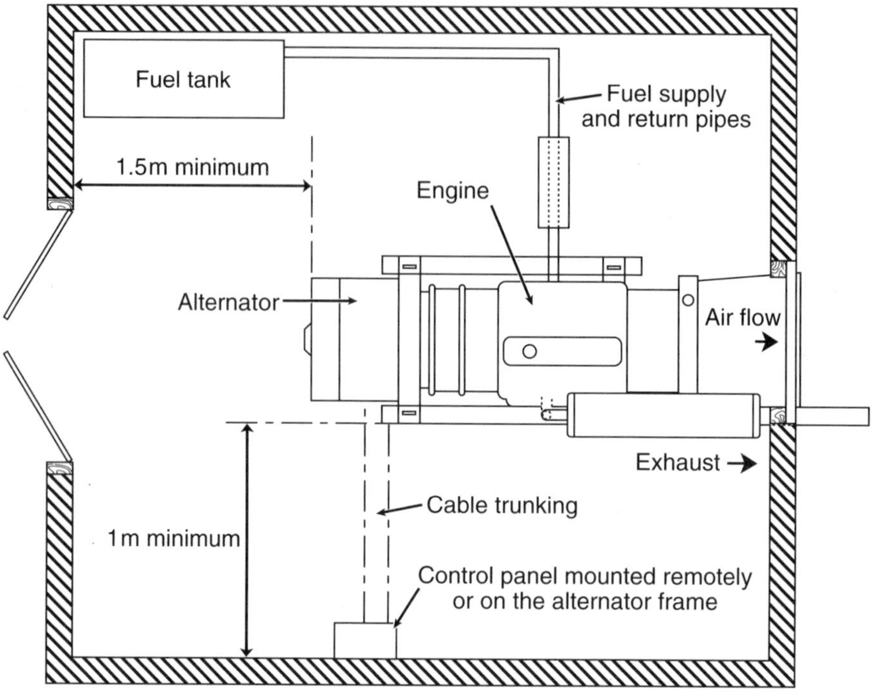

Figure 16.6 Plan of a typical generator house

A skid mounted generator set can be temporarily mounted level on a bed of gravel. When time permits, cast a concrete slab described in 14.3.2.

Adequate air-flow is necessary to supply the engine with air for both combustion and cooling. In a solid-walled housing it is essential that hot discharged cooling air does not recirculate to the cooling air inlet or the engine inlet. It is good practice to install flexible ducting of canvas, or similar material, to direct the hot cooling air out of the generator house.

Provide cooling air intake holes near the bottom of the walls. Provide another air intake in the wall nearest to the air filter to ensure a good supply of cooler air for combustion. Include air holes or a gap around the top of the walls to release accumulated hot air above the generator set.

Direct the exhaust pipe over the cooling air outlet to exhaust in the same direction. Keep the exhaust system as short as possible, with the minimum of bends to keep back-pressure within limits. A build-up of back-pressure prevents efficient removal of exhaust from the cylinders with a consequent loss of engine power.

Leave at least 1 m access space on each side of the generator. Leave 1.5 m at the alternator end. Protect the cables in some form of conduit (such as PVC pipe) both between the generator and remote control panel (if not set-mounted) and from the generator to the load supplied.

All generator sets should be earthed through a suitable protective conductor and earth electrode. See Section 16.5.1 'Protection against electric shock and fire (earth leakage protection)'. If there is no generator earth terminal, connect the earth to the neutral terminal. The earth must be protected against damage and corrosion.

Operation and maintenance

The following points refer to the operation of all generator sets.

- Always start and stop a generator off-load. The generator engine should be started with the alternator isolator switch in the 'OFF' position.
- Where the generator is supplying several items of equipment, do not switch them all on at the same time. Switch the loads on one at a time. Start with large motors first, followed by small motors. Finish with pure resistive loads such as resistive lighting circuits. If a problem is experienced in starting an electric motor, try starting that motor first, before switching in any other circuits. This enables the full capacity of the generator to be used in starting the motor.

Refer to Section 15.2, 'Internal combustion engines' for the operation, servicing and maintenance of generator set prime movers (diesel and petrol engines).

Keep daily records of hours run, to monitor usage and to plan servicing and maintenance schedules. In the absence of an hours-run meter, run times can be estimated from the fuel consumption. See Section 15.1.2 for how to measure fuel consumption and for further details on the operation and maintenance of stationary engines. As a guide, diesel engine fuel consumption on full load is about 0.3 l/kWh. Some manufacturers quote fuel consumption in g/kWh. One litre of diesel fuel weighs about 850 g.

Alternators and switchgear require limited attention, but carry out extra and more frequent inspections in extreme temperatures or dusty conditions. Consult the manufacturer's handbook for guidance. Check the following:

- Keep alternator ventilation openings clear. Use a dry air supply to clean internally.
- Grease alternator bearings as required.
- Check the functioning and condition of the switchgear: relays, contactors and protection devices.
- Check and tighten all machinery nuts and bolts, and terminals.
- Check the condition of the mountings and frame.
- In brush type generators, check the brushes and slip rings for wear, and replace if necessary.

A common problem associated with electric start generator sets is the misuse of the battery. Batteries are always in great demand. They may go missing temporarily to start someone's vehicle or they may disappear altogether. The charging circuit in a generator set can be damaged if it is run without a battery connected. Electronic protection modules can be damaged by 'jump-starting' sets with jump-start leads the wrong way around (see 15.2.1, Figure 15.1 for the correct procedure). Therefore, impress upon operators and supervisors the importance of keeping the battery in good condition and connected in circuit. Electronic protection modules should be 'diode protected' to prevent damage in the event of incorrect polarity at jump-starts.

WARNING

Do not change fuses or re-set circuit breakers without first isolating the supply, stopping the generator and correcting the fault.
Do not attempt to start a generator with an electrical load connected.

Take care when testing insulation resistance as electronic components (such as the AVR) may be damaged if not disconnected prior to the test. Check the manual.

Recommended spares

Where a major breakdown of a generator would cause critical problems (causing, for instance, severe reduction in water supplied) it will be necessary to have a complete standby generator available as an immediate replacement for a failed unit. The type and number of spares required for alternators and associated switchgear will depend on the number of installed generators of the same model. Recommended spares for individual alternators include: fuses and/or circuit breakers of the appropriate ratings; an isolator switch; spare sets of brushes for brush type generators; diodes for d.c. circuits; a spare AVR.

16.3.4 Solar power

Solar power may be appropriate for low-power applications, especially in remote locations where fuel supply is problematic. For example, it could be used to power refrigerators for storing drugs and vaccines in remote health clinics. Other applications include radio transceivers, lighting systems and water pumps. Photovoltaic (PV) solar panels require no spare parts, no fuel and only simple maintenance.

A solar panel consists of silicon solar cells connected in groups called modules. The unit used for rating a module is the 'peak watt' (W_p) and is the power produced by the module under peak sunshine conditions of 1000 W/m^2 solar irradiance (insolation) at 25°C. This approximately corresponds to mid-day conditions in tropical countries. In most tropical locations the average insolation is 5 kWh/m^2/day (equivalent to five hours of sunshine at 1000 W/m^2) A common module rating is 50 W_p. The actual power output of a module will depend on sunshine intensity. To maximize input, modules should be tilted towards the sun at the same angle as the latitude of the location. However, it is recommended to tilt panels at a minimum angle of 15°, even on the equator, to ensure the panels do not collect excessive dust and are partially self-cleaning.

Modules commonly give a nominal 12V d.c. output. An inverter may be used to convert to a.c. output. Several modules may be connected in series or parallel to form an array and give various outputs according to the load requirement. A typical module rated at 50 W_p would give about 3.5 A when charging a lead-acid battery at 14V.

Solar panels may be connected directly to the load (such as pumping applications) or the electrical energy they produce can be stored in a battery. Regular maintenance is important if a battery is included in the system. A lead-acid battery must be kept topped up with distilled water, as it is this simple action which, if omitted, can result in system failure.

Table 16.3 gives guidelines on the information to supply when ordering solar equipment. Vaccine refrigerators should be specified to comply with WHO/UNICEF/EPI cold chain specifications.

Table 16.3 Information to supply when ordering solar equipment

Application	*Information to supply*
Solar pump	Water source: well, borehole, river, lake, etc. Well/borehole characteristics: diameter, yield Head: total static lift Water demand: average and peak requirements Water storage and distribution system
Solar refrigerator	Internal volume required Maximum amount of goods or ice to be frozen each day Normal ambient temperature
Lighting	Number of lights Wattage of each light Average hourly usage of each light
Telecommunications	Continuous standby power requirement Transmitting/receiving power Number of hours of transmitting and receiving

From Hulscher and Fraenkel, 1994

16.4 Cables

Cables carry electric current from the generator to the point of use. A cable has an electrical resistance and, when current flows, some of the electrical energy is lost as heat. The magnitude of the temperature rise caused by this heat depends on the magnitude of the current and the ability of the cable to dissipate heat. This ability is affected by the proximity of other cables – avoid bunching of cables. Temperature rise increases cable resistance. Therefore, in very hot climates, shield surface run cables from direct sunlight to prevent an excessive temperature rise. PVC degrades over time when regularly exposed to sunlight and so it is particularly important to shield PVC insulated cables.

Cable resistance produces a voltage drop along its length. Long thin cables produce greater voltage drops than short thick ones. A large voltage drop along a cable may prevent an electric motor from starting. For cables supplying electric motors, the voltage drop at full load should preferably not exceed 4 per cent of the rated supply voltage although for other installations higher voltage drops may be acceptable.

Thus, two key factors determine cable size: the current carrying capacity and the allowable voltage drop along the cable. Many of the situations for which the emergency engineer may need to size cables involve single electric submersible pump installations. Refer to Table 16.4 for maximum recommended cable lengths with a maximum voltage drop of 4 per cent.

Table 16.4 Sizing cables for electric pumps

	3 × 415V, 50 Hz (4% voltage drop)								
Motor kW	*Maximum cable length (metres) for cables of the following cross-sectional area*								
	1.5 mm^2	2.5 mm^2	4 mm^2	6 mm^2	10 mm^2	16 mm^2	25 mm^2	35 mm^2	50 mm^2
0.37	700								
0.55	530								
0.75	400								
1.1	285								
1.5	220								
2.2	150	260							
3.7	90	160	260						
5.5	70	130	200						
7.5		100	150	230	330				
11.0			100	150	260				
15.0				120	200				
18.5					160	250			
22.0					130	200			
30.0						160	250		
37.0						130	210	290	
45.0							170	240	
55.0								200	
75.0									200

	1 × 240V, 50 Hz (4% voltage drop)				
Motor kW	*Maximum cable length (metres) for cables of the following cross-sectional area*				
	1.5 mm^2	2.5 mm^2	4 mm^2	6 mm^2	10 mm^2
0.37	125	210	330		
0.55	90	155	235		
0.75	65	115	175		
1.1	50	85	135	205	310
1.5	35	60	95	140	235
2.2		45	70	110	175

Source: Grundfos Pumps Ltd

If cables of the appropriate size cannot be obtained, then larger cables can be used. If only smaller cables are available, two or more cables can be run in parallel to give the required cross-sectional area.

Cables should be protected from physical damage by burying in trenches, putting them overhead or running them through conduits, such as pipes.

16.5 Electrical protection

The protection of electrical installations can be divided into:

- Circuit protection, whereby people and equipment are protected from the adverse effects of electric current.
- Equipment protection, whereby the equipment is protected from the adverse effects of moisture, dust, and so on.

16.5.1 Circuit protection

Isolators

All electrical circuits should have a means of isolation. An isolator switch is used to isolate a circuit when it is not carrying a current so that, for example, it cannot become live when taken out of service for maintenance. All motors and motor starters should have an isolator. Some isolators can be locked with a padlock in the 'OFF' position for safety whilst carrying out maintenance or to prevent unauthorized operation. The keys to the padlock should be kept in the pocket of the person working on the isolated equipment. See Figure 16.1.

Protective switchgear

Protective switchgear has the dual function of isolating a circuit and providing an automatic means of breaking a circuit when there is a fault. Manual switchgear is of several types:

- Switch-fuses, where the fuses are included in the switch box (see Figure 16.1).
- Separate switch boxes and fuse boxes.
- Fuse-switches, where fuses are part of the moving switch.

Protective devices

Protective devices must be rated to carry the full load current but the rating must be no greater than the current carrying capacity of the smallest cable protected. Protective devices must never be fitted in the neutral line.

Protection against electric shock and fire (earth leakage protection) All live parts must be insulated and enclosed to prevent accidental contact in normal operation. Earth leakage occurs when, due to a fault, an electric current flows to earth through a person or a piece of equipment. This may cause an electric shock and possibly be fatal. An earthed conductor cable provides a relatively safe path to earth for the fault current (see Table 16.5 for the sizing of earth conductor cables). The fault can then be detected and the circuit automatically broken. In all circuits, provide earth protection by bonding all exposed metalwork (switchgear boxes, conduit, cable trays, etc.) to an earthed protective conductor cable. Ensure that the earthed conductor cable is well connected to an earth electrode.

Suitable materials for earth electrodes include copper rods, steel pipes or rods, reinforcing bar, steel borehole casing, and the protective sheath of a steel

Table 16.5 Relative sizes of phase cable and earthing conductors of the same material

Size of phase conductor cross-sectional area (c.s.a.)	*Size of earthing conductor minimum c.s.a.*
up to 16 mm^2	same size as the phase conductor
16–35 mm^2	16 mm^2
over 35 mm^2	at least half the c.s.a. of the phase conductor

wire armoured cable. The minimum cross-section for an earth electrode is 25 mm^2 for copper and 50 mm^2 for steel.

The resistance of the earthing system must be low enough for the protective devices to operate quickly. The effectiveness of an earth electrode will depend on the soils and their moisture content. Damp ground provides a better earth. However, it will also encourage the eventual corrosion of steel electrodes. When placing earth electrodes in the ground it is advisable to liberally wet the area around the electrode, or electrodes, to ensure a good initial contact with the surrounding soils. Table 16.5 gives the recommended minimum sizes of earthing conductors for various sizes of phase conductors of the same material.

Fuses protect against certain earth leakages but miniature circuit breakers can give better protection.

Residual current devices (RCDs) If the resistance of the earthing system is high, then when a fault occurs, the fault current may be too low to activate the protective device (such as a fuse). A residual current device (RCD) overcomes this problem. When a fault occurs, some of the current flows to earth before it returns to the supply terminals through the neutral line. An RCD detects the imbalance between the phase and neutral currents (the residual current) and when this exceeds a pre-set value, breaks the circuit. RCDs with a rated residual operating current of 30mA are commonly used with outdoor portable equipment. RCDs may fail to operate over time, due to the accumulation of dust and dirt. Therefore, they are provided with a facility for regular testing. It is advisable to press the test button periodically to enable the mechanical operation of the RCD to be checked.

Overcurrent protection Overcurrent protection devices protect against currents which are higher than the equipment, conductors and components are designed to handle. High currents may be caused by excessive loads or by short circuits. Protection is provided by:

- Automatic circuit breakers – miniature circuit breakers (MCBs) or moulded case circuit breakers (MCCBs).
- High breaking capacity (HBC) fuses, also known as high rupturing capacity (HRC) fuses.

Miniature circuit breakers (MCBs) have fixed ratings and moulded case circuit breakers (MCCBs) are adjustable. Circuit breakers are particularly advantageous in the field because, unlike fuses, they can be reset after removing the fault. MCBs may be combined with RCDs (making RCBOs) to provide both earth leakage and overcurrent protection. There are several types of MCBs and RCBOs with a variety of ratings which must be correctly matched to each application.

In general, miniature circuit breakers by themselves can provide only short circuit protection for motor loads. Motor start-up currents may be as high as 12 times the normal running current. MCBs in general cannot accommodate this and provide the close thermal protection required by motors. They can, however, be used to protect lightly loaded motors or motors started off-load, or they can be used in conjunction with thermal overload relays. In this case the MCB will protect the cable to the motor and protect the motor against short circuit faults, and the motor will be protected by a second thermal device. Table 16.6 gives recommended type D MCB ratings for protecting motors up to 30 kW.

Table 16.6 Miniature circuit breakers for motor protection

MCBs for the protection of single-phase 240V a.c. motors				
Motor power		*Normal running current*	*Starting current*	*Type D MCB current rating*
HP	*kW*	*A*	*A*	*A*
1	0.75	5.5	66	10
2	1.5	10.5	126	16
4	3.0	20.0	240	32
7.5	5.5	34.0	408	40
10	7.5	45.0	540	63
MCBs for the protection of three-phase 415V a.c. motors				
Motor power		*Normal running current*	*Starting current*	*Type D MCB current rating*
HP	*kW*	*A*	*A*	*A*
3	2.2	4.8	57.6	6
4	3.0	6.4	76.8	10
7.5	5.5	11.0	132.0	16
10	7.5	14.4	172.8	20
15	11.0	21.0	252.0	32
25	18.5	35.0	420.0	50
40	30.0	54.0	648.0	63

Source: Crabtree Electrical Industries Ltd

HBC fuses protect motor circuits from short circuit faults. They should be selected to rupture rapidly when there is a major short circuit fault, while being able to carry the normal full load current and momentary motor starting current. They should be used in conjunction with overload relays to protect the motor from unacceptably high currents. Semi-enclosed rewirable fuses (as used in domestic consumer units) and cartridge fuses (as used in domestic plugs) also break a circuit in the event of an overload but they are not recommended for the protection of motor circuits. Table 16.8 gives recommended HBC fuse ratings for direct-on-line and assisted starting (see Section 16.6.2). Estimate the full load current of the motor from Table 16.7 and then select the fuse from Table 16.8.

Phase failure protection 'Single-phasing' occurs when one phase supplying a motor becomes disconnected or it experiences an open circuit for some reason.

Table 16.7 Approximate full load currents of a.c. electric motors

Motor rating		*Single-phase*	*Three-phase*		
kW	*HP*	*240V*	*220V*	*380V*	*415V*
0.75	1.0	6.2	3.3	2.1	2.0
1.5	2.0	11.8	6.2	3.6	3.5
3.0	4.0	20	11.6	6.6	6.5
4.0	5.5	29	15.3	8.5	7.7
5.5	7.5	36	21	11.5	11
7.5	10	45	27	15.5	14
15	20	91	53	30	29
20	27		70	40	38
25	34		85	50	45
30	40		101	60	54

Table 16.8 HBC fuse ratings for direct-on-line and assisted starting

Direct-on-line starting (to withstand 7 × full load current for 10 seconds)			*Assisted starting: Star-Delta, auto-transformer, rotor resistance starters (to withstand 3 × full load current for 20 seconds)*		
Motor full load current, A		*Standard fuse rating, A*	*Motor full load current, A*		*Standard fuse rating, A*
From	*To*		*From*	*To*	
0	0.7	2	5.5	10.0	16
0.8	1.1	4	10.1	14.3	20
1.2	1.6	6	14.4	18.3	25
1.7	2.6	10	18.4	22.6	32
2.7	5.2	16	22.7	29.2	35
5.3	7.5	20	29.3	35.0	40
7.6	9.9	25	35.1	42.8	50
10.0	11.6	32	42.9	55.0	63
11.7	15.7	35	55.1	74.2	80
15.8	19.3	40	74.3	97.3	100
19.4	22.9	50	97.4	125	125
23.0	28.6	63	125	160	160
28.7	41.4	80	160	180	200
41.5	54.3	100			
54.4	71.5	125			

The motor may continue to run, but a winding will become overheated as the current rises to compensate for the loss of the phase. Protection devices, if fitted, should detect the temperature rise (thermal cut-outs in the windings) or the loss of a phase and they should act to disconnect the whole supply.

Over-voltage An over-voltage protection device protects the motor from voltage surges in power lines due to lightning. It should be connected on the supply side of the motor starter. After a lightning strike, change the over-voltage protection device as it may have been damaged.

Circuits and distribution boards

An installation comprising several circuits must have a means of separating the circuits so that they each have their own protective devices. This is so that a fault in one circuit does not affect all the circuits. It also means that part of the installation can be isolated for maintenance and inspection without disconnecting the whole installation. A distribution board receives the incoming supply and distributes it to the final circuits via suitably rated protection devices – fuses, RCDs and MCBs.

The connection to a mains electricity supply will be governed by the requirements of the local supply authority. Earthing arrangements vary and the supply authority may, or may not, provide an earth terminal. An installation fed from a three-phase and neutral (TP&N) supply will require earthing through a separate earth electrode. This is similar to providing a separate earth for a generator supply and a typical arrangement for this situation is shown in Figure 16.1.

16.5.2 Protection of electrical enclosures

Electrical equipment will only operate properly if protected from the adverse effects of moisture and dust. In an emergency, there may be little time to construct adequate shelters for equipment. It is particularly important, therefore, that control panels, motors and generators are adequately specified to cope with the field conditions.

An internationally recognized system of degrees of protection provided by an enclosure is the IP rating system. The IP (internal protection) rating shown in Table 16.9 classifies the extent to which an enclosure will resist the ingress of solid bodies and water. The classification consists of the identifying letters, IP, followed by two numbers. The first number indicates the degree of protection against the ingress of solid objects and the second against water. So, for example, specifying a rating of IP54 should ensure the equipment enclosure is protected against the ingress of dust and splashing water. When one of the forms of protection is not specified, the number is replaced with a X (e.g. IPX4). Other letters may be included as follows: **IP W 54 S**

W: Optional letter for application in specified weather conditions

5: Indicates resistance to the ingress of solid bodies

4: Indicates resistance to ingress of water

S: Optional letter for equipment tested against water penetration when not in use (S) or in use (M)

Table 16.9 Electrical equipment internal protection (IP) ratings

1st numeral *Degree of protection with respect to persons and solid objects.* *Protected against:*		*2nd numeral* *Degree of protection with respect to harmful ingress of water.* *Protected against:*	
0	Non-protected	0	Non-protected
1	Solid objects > 50 mm	1	Dripping water
2	Solid objects > 12 mm	2	Dripping water when tilted up to 15°
3	Solid objects > 2.5 mm	3	Spraying water
4	Solid objects > 1.0 mm	4	Splashing water
5	Dust protected	5	Water jets
6	Dust tight	6	Heavy seas
		7	Effects of immersion
		8	Submersion

The classification system should be used with some care when specifying equipment. A high IP rating does not necessarily mean it is weatherproof. To be sure, specify the environmental and weather conditions against which the equipment should be protected.

Condensation can be a problem and there may need to be a compromise to allow sufficient ventilation without allowing the ingress of dust and water. Holes in the enclosure bottom can aid ventilation and drainage without necessarily impairing protection against the weather.

Any protection can be destroyed by poor cabling into a control panel. Use cable ('stuffing') glands for proper sealing of enclosures. When ordering, ask for them to be fitted to the control panel/enclosure or, if this is not possible, ask for them to be supplied for fitting during installation. If glands are not available, use anything to hand which will close the gaps around cable entry points. Silicone sealant and even paper and rags are better than nothing.

16.6 Induction motors

16.6.1 Sizing motors

The standard a.c. motor used for constant speed applications, such as water pumping, is the induction motor. Although other types of a.c. motor operate on single or three-phase supplies, only induction motors are considered in this book. The induction motor consists of two main parts: the stator and the rotor. The principle of operation is similar to that of a generator and is described in 16.2.1.

The stator windings are connected to the three-phase supply such that when a current flows, a rotating magnetic field is produced. The rotating magnetic field induces a current in the rotor which produces its own magnetic field. Rotation of the rotor is caused by the rotor magnetic field 'chasing' the stator magnetic field. There is always a difference in the speed of rotation of the rotor and the stator field (called slip) caused by the torque produced by the load.

There are two types of rotor: cage or wound rotor. A cage rotor is often referred to as a 'squirrel cage rotor'. A wound rotor motor is also referred to as a 'slip ring motor'. Standard electric submersible pumps use a squirrel cage motor.

Speed of a.c. induction motors

The speed at which induction motors rotate is determined by the supply frequency and the number of poles on the stator. Standard induction motors are usually manufactured with two, four or six poles. The synchronous speed (the speed of rotation of the stator field) is given by:

$$\text{Synchronous speed (rev/min)} = \frac{\text{a.c. frequency (Hz)} \times 60}{\text{No. of pairs of poles}}$$

For example: A 4-pole motor operating off a 50 Hz supply has a synchronous speed of 1500 rev/min. The same motor operating off a 60 Hz supply would have a synchronous speed of 1800 rev/min. The actual motor speed will be less than the synchronous speed because of the slip (about 4 per cent). Thus, a motor with four poles running off a 50 Hz supply will have a speed of about 1440 rev/min. The exact speed will depend on the motor power rating and loading.

Electric motor efficiency, power and current consumption

The efficiency of an electric motor is given by:

$$\text{Motor efficiency} = \frac{\text{Power output}}{\text{Power input}}$$

The efficiency of electric motors varies from about 80 per cent for small motors (1.5 kW) to 90 per cent for larger motors (15 kW and above).

For a three-phase a.c. supply : Active power, $P = V_l \times I \times \sqrt{3} \times \text{p.f.}$ kW (see 16.2.3). If the required shaft power of a pump is P_p kW and the efficiency of the electric motor driving it is η_m, then the current taken at full load is:

$$I = \frac{P_p \times 1000}{V_l \times \sqrt{3} \times \text{p.f.} \times \eta_m}$$

If the power factor is not known, use a value of p.f. = 0.8 for approximate calculations. Approximate full load currents of single and three-phase motors are given in 16.5.1, Table 16.8. Box 16.2 gives an example of how to calculate motor size and current consumption.

16.6.2 Induction motor starters

This section provides an overview and guideline information on starters and associated protective devices. Most suppliers should be able to supply the correct equipment based on information about the motor (type, rating), the duty (for instance, the centrifugal pump head and flow), the site conditions, the type of supply (three-phase, 415V, 50 Hz), and any specific requirements.

Only the smallest motors (0.1 kW +/-) can be started with a hand operated switch. This is because the starting load for motors is much higher than the

Box 16.2 Calculating motor size and current consumption

Example: Calculate the motor size and operating current of an electric motor required to drive a centrifugal pump delivering 10 l/s at 20 m head (static delivery plus losses in the system). Take the overall efficiency of pump and direct-coupled transmission as 70%, i.e. $\eta_m = 0.7$.

Pump shaft power requirement (see 14.2.2), P_p:

$$P_p = \frac{Q \rho g H}{\eta_p} = \frac{10 \times 9.81 \times 20}{0.7} W = 2.8 \text{ kW}$$

Assume 80% efficiency for a three-phase cage motor of this size. The shaft power demand is 2.8 kW so the motor input power, P_i, is 2.8/0.8 = 3.5 kW. To provide a safety margin, the motor should be able to supply about 10–15% more shaft power than the theoretical requirement. Therefore, motor size should be a minimum of 4 kW. Although the motor size is 4 kW the actual power consumed will be 3.5 kW as calculated above.

The current requirement of the motor is given by:

$$I = \frac{P_i \times 1000}{V_l \times \sqrt{3} \times \text{p.f.}} = \frac{3.5 \times 1000}{415 \times \sqrt{3} \times 0.8} = 6.1, \text{ say } 6A$$

Current consumption under the given operating conditions will be 6A and can be checked with an ammeter. Note that the current may vary:

- On start-up.
- If the hydraulic conditions change.
- If the conditions have not been estimated correctly.
- If there is a mechanical or electrical fault (see 16.6.3).

normal full operating load. Electric motor starters normally comprise electro-magnetic controlled contactors, overload and fault protection devices, and monitoring meters. The various types of starter are selected according to site specific requirements. In most cases, a standard motor starter can be supplied matched to a pump. However, extra protection and metering devices may have to be specified. An isolator should be included in the supply to isolate the starter when carrying no load current. A starter provides the following:

- A safe means of stopping and starting the motor.
- A method of overload protection in the motor and/or in the starting circuit.
- A means to prevent automatic re-starting following an intermittent failure of the supply.

A starter may be self-contained or the starter components may be enclosed in a larger control panel. All the non-conducting metal parts in a starter enclosure must be earthed. A control panel may include further protection devices, indicator lights and monitoring meters (ammeters, voltmeter, frequency meter). Monitoring meters can give an indication of problems with the motor circuit and are very useful in fault-finding. An ammeter should be included as a minimum, even for small motors. A pump control panel may also include water level controls (low-level cut-out and/or high level cut-in).

A starter consists of two separate circuits:

- A main circuit to connect the supply to the motor.
- An auxiliary control circuit to operate contactors (main circuit switches), protection devices, interlocks and timers. The voltage of the control circuit can differ from the main circuit and a transformer may be included. Typical control voltages are:
  - At 50 Hz: 110V, 220V, 240V, 380V, 415V.
  - At 60 Hz: 110V, 220V, 280V, 480V.

A contactor is a solenoid-operated switch. When the control circuit is closed, the solenoid coil is energized. This 'pulls in' the main contacts to complete the main circuit. The coil automatically opens the main circuit when no current flows through the control circuit. This safety device is called a no-volt release (NVR) coil. The control circuit may be broken by operation of the 'stop' button or by the activation of a protection device (such as a current overload circuit breaker). In certain circumstances, sparking can burn or pit the contacts over time. In particular, if the starter enclosure is not properly protected, small particles of dust trapped between the contacts can quickly cause the contactor to burn out. If a contactor fault is suspected, isolate the starter and check the contacts. Change the contactor if the contacts are badly burnt. It may be possible to clean the contacts for a temporary repair to keep the installation operating. Check the contactor coil voltage and specify it when re-ordering.

Three-phase motors

A typical arrangement for the starting of three-phase motors is shown in Figure 16.7. Three-phase cage motors commonly employ one of the following types of starter:

- Direct-on-line (DOL).
- Star-Delta.
- Auto-transformer.

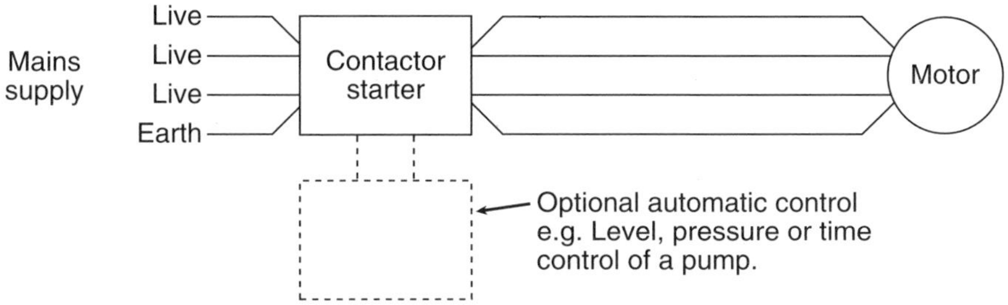

Figure 16.7 Schematic layout of a three-phase motor and starter

The choice of starter depends on the voltage drop allowable in the supply system and the torque required to accelerate the load to normal running speed. Three-phase starters are described below.

Direct-on-line (DOL) starters The initial starting current of a squirrel cage motor connected direct-on-line is six to eight times the full load current. This current surge can affect other plant connected to the supply. If the supply is from a generator, the generator must be sufficiently sized to meet the starting demand. Therefore, the size of motor which can be started direct-on-line may be limited by the supply.

The limit will depend on circumstances. A supply authority may not allow the connection of motors greater than about 4 kW. However, the characteristics of some electric submersible pumps are such that the run-up time to full speed is very short (typically 0.1 second) and much higher ratings can be accepted. Starting on a generator supply will depend on the size and characteristics of the generator which must be matched to the starting demand (see 16.3.2).

Star-Delta starter A Star-Delta starter limits the initial starting current to about 2.5 times the full load current. However, it also limits the starting torque to a similar degree. (Note: reduced current starters, such as the Star-Delta starter, give what is known as a 'soft start'). A Star-Delta starter can only be connected to motors in which both ends of the three windings (i.e. six cables) are brought out to the motor terminals. Submersible borehole pumps are unlikely to employ Star-Delta starting because of the need for six cables. Therefore, submersible borehole pumps are normally started direct-on-line or by an auto-transformer starter.

Auto-transformer starter If the motor only has three terminals, an auto-transformer starter can be used for reduced voltage starting. An auto-transformer starter may also be preferred to a Star-Delta starter if a higher starting torque is required. A reduced voltage is applied to the stator windings through a three-phase auto-transformer to give a reduced current on starting. Automatic starters switch from one transformer tapping to the next on a timed sequence of progressively less voltage reduction until the transformer is bypassed when the motor reaches full running speed.

Rotor resistance starter A rotor resistance starter is only used to start a wound rotor (slip-ring) induction motor. The connection to the stator is direct-on-line. When the stator windings are connected, an emf is induced in the rotor windings in the same way as in a cage motor. However, the rotor windings are each connected in circuit to a variable resistor through the slip rings. On start up, all the resistances are fully in circuit and this limits the induced currents in the rotor windings which, in turn, reduces the starting current drawn in the stator windings. The resistances are gradually reduced as the motor speeds up until they are cut out completely at full speed. The motor then runs in the same way as a cage motor. On some motors, the slip rings can be short-circuited at full speed and the brushes lifted off the slip rings to minimize wear.

Rotor resistance starting gives the motor a high starting torque capable of starting against high inertia loads.

Single-phase motor starters

To be self-starting, an electric motor must have a rotating magnetic field. The displacement of phases in a three-phase supply provides the rotating field. But a single-phase motor requires an auxiliary winding to give a displacement on starting. The auxiliary 'start' winding is automatically switched out of circuit when the motor has run up to speed. There are various arrangements for starting single-phase motors and the starter and/or control box must be correctly matched to the motor. Figure 16.8 shows a typical layout of motor, control box and contactor starter.

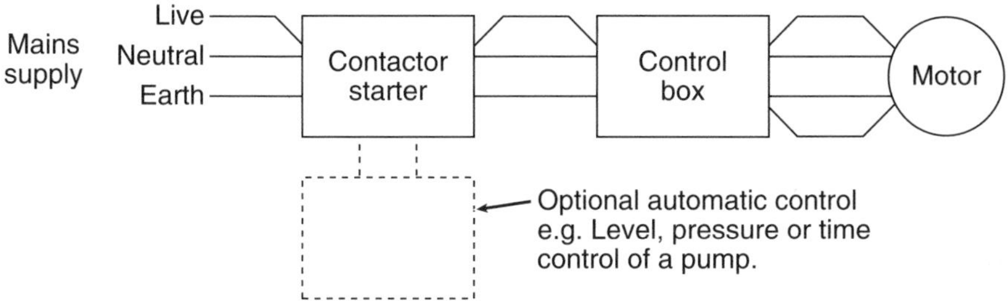

Figure 16.8 Schematic layout of a single-phase motor, control box and starter (Grundfos Pumps Ltd)

Reversing the rotation of induction motors

If a three-phase induction motor runs in the wrong direction: stop the motor, switch off the supply and change over any two phases supplying the motor. This will reverse the direction of rotation. See also 14.3.3.

Note that the incorrect connection of a single-phase motor can cause the motor to fail.

Motor circuit protection

Refer to Section 16.5 for further information on circuit protection. Motor circuits should have an isolator and be protected by a circuit breaker and a fuse. In addition, phase failure and over-voltage protection can be provided if desired.

16.6.3 Operating electric motor driven pumps

Typical starting procedure The following procedure assumes a supply from a generator powering a water pump, but operation from a mains supply is similar. It also assumes that initial daily checks have been carried out on the generator engine as described in Section 15.2.

- Ensure the delivery valve is in the correct position for the particular pump (see Sections 14.3 and 14.4). If in doubt, open the valve slightly.
- Check that the isolator on the supply to the starter is 'OFF'.
- Start the generator and allow it to attain normal running temperature.
- Check that the generator is indicating the correct voltage and frequency (for example, 415V, 50 Hz). Note: the frequency meter may show a slightly

higher reading than the running frequency, as the frequency should have been set for the normal full load condition.

- Turn on the main power switch on the generator.
- Turn on the main isolator to the starter (usually on the control panel).
- Turn the START switch (or press the START button) and release.
- If an ammeter(s) is fitted, check that the starting and running currents are normal.
- If suitable meters are fitted, check that the supply frequency and voltage are normal.
- If water flow meters are fitted, check that the correct amount of water is being pumped.

If there are any abnormal readings, switch off the pump, turn the starter isolator to 'OFF' and then close down the generator. Investigate the problem (see next section). Expected meter readings when a pump motor is running normally are listed below.

After stopping the pump at the end of a period of running, remember to isolate the supply to the starter by turning off the main isolator to the control panel before stopping the generator. This ensures that the isolator is off when the generator is started again.

Meter readings For DOL starting, ammeter readings should indicate an initial, momentary current surge (about 7 × full load current) which quickly settles to the normal running current. Ensure the ammeter rating is sufficient to cover the initial starting current by specifying the duty to the supplier. The voltage will dip and recover very quickly on starting.

For 'soft start' (Star-Delta or Auto-transformer starters), ammeter readings should indicate a high starting current and then, after a few seconds, the lower normal running current will be indicated. The voltage will dip slightly and recover very quickly on starting.

During normal running, the voltage should be constant at the system voltage. The frequency of the supply should be correct for the system and constant under constant load conditions. The current reading should be constant at the full load current.

Monitoring electric motor performance

It pays to monitor the running of electric motors regularly to give advance warning of potential problems and possible failure. Therefore, regularly check the current, voltage and frequency readings by establishing a programme of regular monitoring carried out by trained personnel.

Recommended monitoring and fault finding equipment:

- Clamp-on ammeter.
- 500V insulation resistance and continuity tester (a 'megger').
- Frequency meter.
- Electrical screwdriver and tester.
- Multi-meter.

A comprehensive clamp multi-meter can be used for a range of measurements on a.c. and d.c. circuits: voltage, current, resistance, frequency, and continuity.

Current drawn If the control panel does not include ammeters, use a clamp-on ammeter to measure current consumed. Clamp around one phase at a time to measure the current in each phase while the pump is running. Compare the reading with the normal operating current (see previous readings or the pump data sheet). Table 16.7 gives the full load current for motors of various sizes. If the current reading is low:

- Check the frequency of the supply and, if necessary, correct the generator output if it is a generator supply.
- If a voltmeter is not fitted, determine the voltage as described below.
- Check the flow from the pump. If the flow from a centrifugal pump is restricted by a blockage or a nearly closed valve, it will not be working so hard and the current reading will be low.
- Possible leakage in the rising main or air entrainment. Check to see if the flow is normal.

If the current reading is high:

- Check the frequency of the supply and, if necessary, correct the generator output, if it is a generator supply.
- If a voltmeter is not fitted, check the voltage as described below.
- Possible electrical overload due to a damaged pump.
- If the current reading is high, or if the highest phase current exceeds the lowest phase current by more than 10 per cent there are the following possible faults:
  - The contacts of the motor starter contactor are burnt: replace contactor.
  - There is either a break in the circuit of one phase or a poor connection, possibly at the cable joint: test for continuity and resistance as described for the winding resistance check (see below).
  - The motor windings are short-circuited or partly disjointed: measure the winding resistance (see below).

Voltage Measure the voltage between the phases of a three-phase system or between the phase and neutral of a single-phase system. To measure the voltage with a voltmeter, connect the voltmeter across the terminals in the motor starter. A poor electricity supply can give significant variations in voltage. When the motor is running on load, the voltage should not vary beyond more than 10 per cent of the system voltage. Larger variations may damage the motor.

Insulation resistance

SWITCH OFF AND ISOLATE THE SUPPLY

Make a note of the wiring coding for each terminal before removing the phase leads from the motor starter that lead to the pump. Use a 500V insulation resistance tester ('megger') to measure the insulation resistance between each phase and earth. For each phase, attach the live lead of the megger to a phase and ensure the earth lead of the megger is well earthed (for instance, fastened to a steel rising main or borehole casing). If the insulation resistance is lower than previously recorded:

- Check the supply cable for damage. In the case of a submersible pump, first check the overground cable for abrasion.
- If the reading is lower than before, but still above 0.5 MΩ then monitor regularly.
- If the reading is below 0.5 MΩ then the cabling, motor and components must be inspected and tested individually to locate the fault. In the case of a submersible pump, remove the pump and separate it from the cable. Test the cable, joint and pump separately. Submersible pump cable joints can fail due to the ingress of water. The remedy is to make a new joint.
- If the insulation resistance is higher than previously recorded then monitor frequently.

Winding resistance

SWITCH OFF AND ISOLATE THE SUPPLY

Make a note of the wiring coding for each terminal before removing the phase leads from the motor starter that lead to the pump. Measure the winding resistance by attaching the leads of a multi-meter to two phases at a time. Compare readings with the manufacturer's data sheet. If there is a discrepancy, disconnect the cable from the pump and measure the resistance of motor windings and cable separately. (In the case of a submersible pump, this will mean lifting the pump out of the borehole.) The additional check identifies where the fault lies – in the windings or in the cable. This is also a cable continuity check.

Electrical connections

SWITCH OFF AND ISOLATE THE SUPPLY

Inspect and check that all terminal connections are tight, clean and dry. Terminal connections can work loose due to machinery vibration and the expansion and contraction of copper components. Simple preventive maintenance checks of this kind can save future down-time and component damage.

Recommended spares for motor control panels

The type and number of spares to keep in stock will depend on the range and number of electric motor driven pumps installed. For large sites (such as a large refugee camp) it is advisable to stock spare pumps, and complete starters or control panels in case of complete unit failure. This enables faulty equipment to be replaced for major repairs.

Typical spares for individual starters and control panels include: main switches, contactors, overload relays, circuit breakers and fuses. When ordering, ensure contactors and relays are rated for the correct control circuit voltage.

17 Vehicles

The careful selection, management and maintenance of vehicles is critical to the effectiveness of most relief programmes. These guidelines are for anyone who has to manage a small vehicle fleet (up to about 15 light vehicles) as one of several management responsibilities in a relief programme. The fleet may be supplemented by individual trucks and special purpose vehicles. Large truck fleets for the transport of food and other bulk items and detailed guidance on vehicle repairs are beyond the scope of this book.

17.1 Vehicle selection and specification

17.1.1 Sources of vehicles

Although sometimes necessary in relief operations, air-freighting of vehicles is very expensive. Bear in mind that the emergency may be of a short or uncertain duration. Consider all other options first:

- Hire personnel vehicles and pick-up trucks locally. Avoid using motor-cycles if at all possible – at the best of times they are dangerous. In emergency conditions when the standard of driving is frequently low they can be a liability. If it is necessary to use motor-cycles ensure that protective clothing is worn (helmets, gloves, strong trousers and boots).
- Contract trucks from local hauliers for the transport of goods.
- Enter into an arrangement with another agency or government department to second, share, contract or hire for the duration of the emergency.
- Borrow vehicles for a short interim period from the agency's existing development programme (if there is one) until new vehicles arrive.
- Purchase in-country, either new or second-hand, provided the condition of the vehicle can be assessed.

Good vehicles are essential. It can be counter-productive, and dangerous, to persevere with unreliable vehicles and poor back-up.

17.1.2 Vehicle selection

Key points to consider in the selection of appropriate vehicles:

- The availability of fuel. What kind of fuel is available – petrol or diesel?
- Vehicles operating locally. Select similar vehicles to those that are being used locally. Spares are likely to be available and drivers and mechanics

will be familiar with them. Note any local modifications to standard specifications.

- Standardize the vehicle fleet wherever possible. A variety of different makes and models means the stocking of a wide range of spares, tyres and special tools. Standardization makes fleet management and vehicle maintenance simpler.
- Diesel engines are usually preferable, even for light vehicles. Diesel engines are generally more economical and reliable than petrol engines. Diesel fuel has a low fire risk compared to petrol. Petrol engines may be preferred where diesel is not available or is of poor quality.
- Select an engine size suitable for the job. An oversized engine may result in speeding and dangerous driving in the hands of inexperienced drivers. Avoid turbo-charged diesels unless absolutely required for the conditions (such as high altitude). Turbo-charged engines require extra spare parts and require careful operation when warming up and cooling down because of turbo-lubrication.
- Two- or four-wheel drive? In many emergencies, a four-wheel drive (4×4) vehicle is essential. However, in dry conditions and where there are predominantly good tarmac roads, a sturdy two-wheel drive vehicle may be adequate. Two-wheel drive vehicles are cheaper and may consume half as much fuel as the equivalent 4×4 model. 4×4 vehicles also require more specialized maintenance and extra spare parts.
- Long or short wheelbase? A long-wheelbase vehicle is more stable on poor roads and in off-road conditions. A longer wheelbase gives more carrying capacity. Space for the fitting of long range fuel tanks may be restricted in short-wheelbase vehicles.

Features to avoid:

Automatic transmission	Specialized; not for off-road use; cannot start without a battery.
Electric windows	Cannot open or close when the electrical system fails.
Central door-locking	Too dependent on the electrical system, unless there is a manual override.
Alloy or aluminium wheels	Too fragile.

Donations

Use the above selection guidelines to assess offers of free vehicles. Donated vehicles which are non-standard use different fuel to the current fleet and require specialized servicing, spare parts support and maintenance are likely to be a liability rather than an asset. Treat the donation of used vehicles with even greater caution. It is often better to decline offers.

17.1.3 Vehicle specification

Use Table 17.1 as a specification checklist. See Section 7.2 for general guidelines on specifying and ordering.

Table 17.1 Vehicle specification guide

Model	Left/right hand drive; long/short wheelbase.
Body	Saloon, station wagon, pick-up, twin cab, soft or hard top. Number of doors.
Seats	Number and arrangement of seats. Cloth upholstery, not plastic, especially for vehicles operating in hot climates. Lap-and-shoulder seat belts.
Colour	Avoid military type colours. Normally choose white for tropical conditions and conflict areas.
Engine	Diesel or petrol. Size (cm^3 or cc). Number of cylinders. Normally aspirated or turbo-charged. Engine cooling: standard or heavy duty. Include oil cooler, if required. Air cleaner: standard, heavy duty, pre-filter or raised.
Electrical system	Voltage (12/24V); type of battery – standard or heavy duty.
Transmission	Number of gears; high/low dual range gearbox; floor or column shift two-wheel (2x4) or four-wheel (4x4) drive; freewheel hubs.
Tyres	Specify according to the terrain: tarmac, off-road, sand, snow. Tube or tubeless. Number of spare wheels and tyres (at least two). Type of spare wheel mounting on vehicle – specify at least one internal anchor point for spare wheel (spare wheels attached to doors or bonnets may cause damage on rough roads and are more prone to theft).
Steering	Manual or powered steering.
Suspension	Standard or heavy duty springs and shock absorbers.
Fuel tank(s)	Standard or long range tanks and capacities.
Protection	Front/rear lamp guards. Steering protection guards. Front protection 'bull bar'.
Security	Anti-theft devices – lockable wheel nuts and fuel filler cap(s) (usually opened with the ignition key); heavy duty steering lock.
Winch	Electric or driven by an engine power take-off (PTO).
Spares and tools	Vehicle tool kit, fast moving and additional spares, owner's manual, spares catalogue and workshop manual (specify language).
Towing kit	Pintle, 50 mm ball, adjustable height, electrical equipment for lights.
Climate	Air-conditioning; heating; tinted windscreen; rear window washer/wiper; heated rear window.
Terrain	Sand ladders and shovels; mud flaps on all wheels; chaff guard for radiator (for extensive bush work); set of low-pressure tyres (for muddy terrain); tyre chains (for snow or mud).
Additional items	Roof rack, fire extinguisher, first aid kit, tow rope, warning triangle, high lift jack, tyre pump and repair kit, battery 'jump' leads, 20 litre metal jerrycans with pourer for fuel, 20 litre plastic jerry can for water, rear canopy and frame (for pick-ups), security flags with mounting pole, short wave, AM or other specified radio (FM of limited use).
Pre-delivery checks	Pre-delivery inspection (PDI); road test and first oil change.

17.1.4 Trucks

This section is confined to the use of a truck or small numbers of trucks to support the work of engineers in the field. Trucks for bulk transport are beyond the scope of this book.

Only buy a truck if it really is the most efficient and cost-effective option, or sole option, and there is enough time for the order to be processed. It can take from three to six months for the delivery of a truck from an international truck manufacturer. Consider:

- Using government trucks, repairing out-of-service trucks if necessary. Ensure that, if they are repaired, they will be made available for the intended emergency work.
- Borrowing/hiring/sharing from other agencies.
- Hiring from local contractors. Hire rates are likely to increase in an emergency. Liaise closely with other agencies to ensure rates are kept at a reasonable level. If hiring, draw up a proper contract. This could be in the form of: an agreed rate for a delivery; a daily or weekly rental; or a formula based on the 'tonne–kilometre' actually carried (65 tonnes over 100 km = 6500 t-km). See Section 6.3 for more guidance on working with contractors.

Truck selection

The most suitable type of truck will be determined by the goods to be carried and the kinds of terrain, roads, bridges and ferries over which the truck will have to operate. One large truck causes proportionately far more damage than many small vehicles. This is especially important where road access and crossings may be a problem (see 18.1.1). Large trucks require more competent drivers, larger workshop facilities, better roads and more specialized spares. One large truck out of service has a greater impact on fleet carrying capacity than the breakdown of one small truck. Therefore, in many relief situations, it is better to use several small trucks than a few large trucks. An exception is long-distance bulk transport between main centres along good roads.

The most appropriate size for local distribution over poor roads is a rigid 5–8 tonne capacity truck. In severe conditions – wet earth roads, hilly terrain, sand – four-wheel drive may be necessary. Short and medium length high-sided trucks are preferable. Longer beds may be necessary for carrying pipes and some construction materials. More adaptable trucks have removable sideboards, pillars and tailboard for loading from the top, rear or sides, and for conversion to a flat-bed to carry containers. Hire tipper trucks locally, wherever possible, and leave the problems of faulty tipper hydraulics to a contractor. Table 17.2 gives guidelines on the selection of trucks.

Trailers increase carrying capacity but they can be hazardous on pot-holed, hilly roads, especially if they are unloaded and if drivers are inexperienced. Empty trailers of convenient size can be carried on the back of a truck for return journeys if local laws allow it.

Table 17.2 Truck selection guide

Define the requirements	
Carrying capacity	Weight, volume, shape (bulk/packaged), stacking requirements.
Distance	Long or short (local distribution) distance.
Location	Flat or hilly. Weather conditions. Tarmac, gravel or earth roads. Load limits – roads, bridges, ferries.
Loading/unloading	Access from side/rear/top. Sidewalls – high, low, removable, drop-down. Open or closed platform. Load support. Tarpaulin, ropes and fastenings. Auxiliary equipment – hydraulic loader, tailboard elevator.
Assess the suitability of available truck options	
Size of vehicle	Utility weight (load carrying capacity) and total weight. Number of axles. Distance between axles (weight distribution). Weight per axle (load limits). Ground clearance. Usable area and volume. Overall truck dimensions. Suitability for operation with trailer.
Technical data	Engine power/total weight ratio = 6–8 h.p./tonne for diesel engines. Add 15–20% more power for poor roads and high altitudes. Four-wheel, front-wheel or rear-wheel drive. Gears (high/low). Suspension. Suitability for off-road driving. Size, number and type of tyres. Size and location of fuel tank. Spare wheel. Mechanical and electrical connections for trailer. Power assisted steering (necessary for trucks above 10 tonnes gross weight).
Operation and maintenance	Fuel type, availability and consumption rate. Lubricants required. Spare parts availability. Workshop requirements – equipment and skills. Ease of servicing in the field. Cost of operation – fuel, lubricants, maintenance and repairs. Registration and insurance. Class of driver's licence required.
Purchasing considerations	Vehicle standardization. Optional equipment. Local operational experience. Lead-time for purchase and delivery. Purchase price and expected life span.

Adapted from UNHCR, 1989

Additional truck equipment

Provide tarpaulins and ropes for trucks to protect vulnerable loads (such as cement bags) from wet weather. Trucks should have lashing rings or cleats for securing rope and webbing.

A hydraulic loader fitted to one truck in a small fleet can be very useful where only manual labour is available for the handling of goods. Typical lifting capacities range from 1 to 5 tonnes. The capacity is often given in tonne–metres (tm). For example: a loader with an overall capacity of 5 tm has a lifting capacity of 1 t at a maximum reach of 5 m or a lifting capacity of 2.9 t at a reach of 1.7 m.

> *CAUTION: As with all lifting operations, take safety precautions when lifting heavy loads. Keep within the loader's limits and always lift vertically. Use steadying ropes to guide a load where necessary. Keep everyone clear of the lift area during all lift operations.*

17.1.5 Tyres

Radial-ply tyres generally have a higher tread life than cross-ply tyres. However, the sidewalls of a radial tyre are prone to damage. Many radial tyres used off road have to be replaced long before the tread wears out because of a damaged sidewall. It is often better to drive over sharp objects than around them. Never mix radial and cross-ply tyres on the same vehicle as handling can be adversely affected. Tyres are designated by the nominal size of their cross-sectional width and of the rim diameter on which the tyre is mounted. For example, a 7.50 × 16 tyre has a nominal cross-section width of 7.5 inches when fitted to a wheel rim of recommended diameter 16 inches, measured at the tyre seat position. See Figure 17.1 for an explanation of a full tyre coding. A minimum 8-ply rating is recommended for 4×4 light vehicle off-road use.

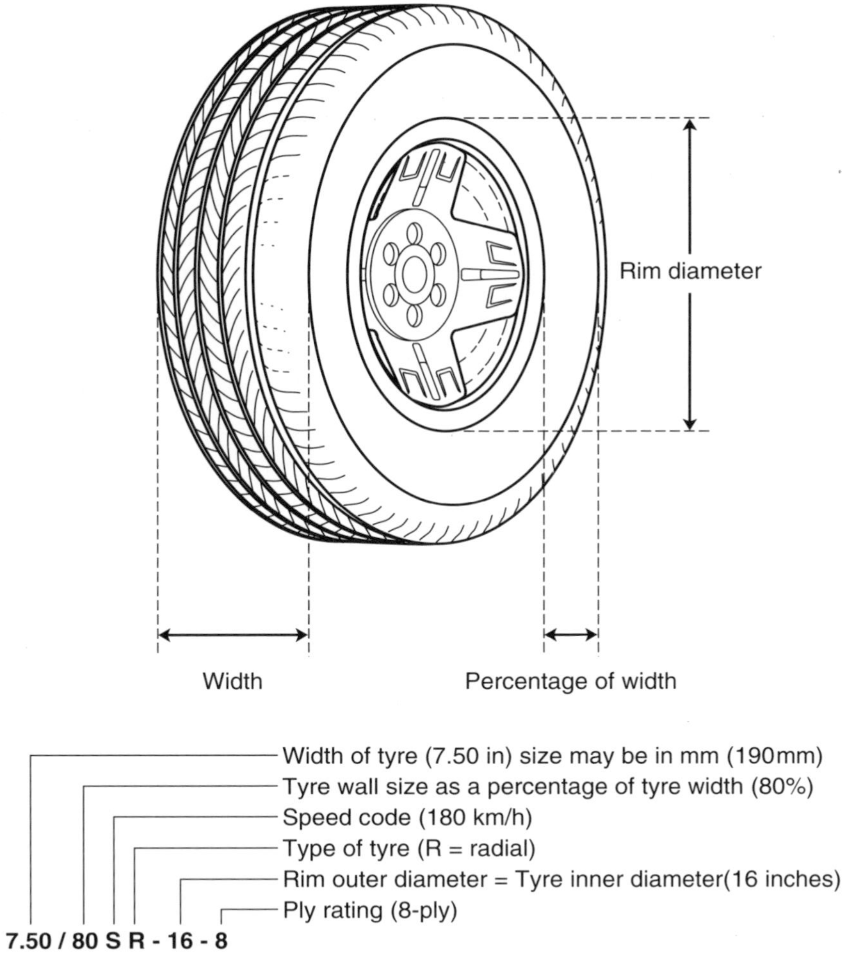

Figure 17.1 Tyre coding

Tube-type tyres are preferable to tubeless tyres. Tubeless tyres rely on an airtight seal at the wheel rim. Any damage, corrosion or dents to the rim can affect the seal. Stock and carry an adequate supply of tyre repair kits, tyre changing tools and spare inner tubes. Always replace an inner tube with a tube of the same type. Ensure the valve's tube is not too long or it may be damaged as the tyre passes objects. Ensure valve cap is in place. Tyres on the same axle should be of the same brand, type, wear and pressure. This improves vehicle stability and safety, especially when braking.

The flotation characteristics of a tyre determine the ground bearing pressure for a particular load. The footprint is the area of the tyre in contact with the ground. The bigger the footprint the better the flotation characteristics and traction. No tyre can suit all conditions. If a variety of conditions is likely to be encountered then choose an 'all-purpose' or 'dual-purpose' tyre. If the principal conditions are likely to be of a particular type, choose accordingly.

- Mud – A knobbly tread 'mud' tyre is designed to be self-cleaning. The mud is thrown off to continue to give grip. A disadvantage is that the tyre only gives fair grip on a wet road. Tyre chains can be used effectively on a standard road tyre but they are messy and time consuming to fit. A set of extra-wide, low ground pressure tyres may be worth having for very muddy locations (such as off-road in the wet season).
- Sand – Hot, dry sand requires a tyre which has high flotation characteristics and good high temperature performance. The tyre should also have a high enough ply rating to withstand sharp stones and thorns. Reducing the pressure in tyres to improve flotation can be effective in crossing soft sand and other soft terrain. However, it is important to keep speeds low (not more than 40 km/h) and re-inflate as soon as possible. For sandy conditions, include in the specification (and put it in the vehicle!) electric tyre inflators powered by the vehicle battery.
- Snow – For driving in fresh snow, use a 'mud' tyre. However, the usual type of snow driving is over compacted snow for which 'snow tyres' or tyre chains are used.

17.2 Vehicle management

A typical vehicle management arrangement is for the team leader to take responsibility for overall fleet management. Each vehicle is assigned to an individual staff member and a driver and these two people are collectively responsible for the correct use of the vehicle. In a large team, vehicle management may be assigned to a transport and/or workshop manager, especially in the case of a combined truck and light field vehicle fleet. Vehicle management responsibilities include:

- Meeting transport needs as they arise.
- Fulfilment of legal vehicle requirements.
- Ensuring the optimum, correct and safe use of the vehicle.
- Arranging adequate vehicle servicing and maintenance.

Work schedules will have to be planned so that a vehicle can return to the workshop for a service on a day agreed between the staff member, driver and workshop manager/mechanic. It is no good if all the vehicles arrive on drivers' pay day at the end of the month!

17.2.1 Vehicle administration

Vehicle registration, tax and insurance

The manager should ensure that there is a system to keep vehicle registration, tax and insurance up to date. In large organizations this may be done by an administrative department. Avoid any vehicles having to be taken out of service due to administrative lapses. Clarify the extent of passenger insurance, especially as regards the carrying of non-agency personnel such as government officials, staff of other agencies, or refugees.

Vehicle records

Keep records of vehicle details (serial numbers, etc.) and of all vehicle journeys, servicing and maintenance. Details are then to hand if a vehicle is stolen or involved in an accident. Good records help in planning maintenance. Allocate a fleet number to each vehicle for ease of identification.

The usual system of vehicle monitoring utilizes vehicle log books. Each driver makes an entry in the log book for every trip made. Pages for entering the vehicle's servicing and repair history are also often included. It is useful to include basic vehicle details in the front of each log book. Keep duplicate log book records of a vehicle's service and repair history in the vehicle file.

Open a separate file for each vehicle and record basic vehicle details and its operational history. It is recommended to keep the following in the file:

- A copy of the 'vehicle record form' from the vehicle log book in the front of each file, for easy reference.
- A list of tools and equipment assigned to the vehicle.
- Completed vehicle log sheets (see Figure 17.2).
- Vehicle servicing and maintenance history (see 17.3.4 and Figure 17.3).
- Vehicle allocation and transfers.
- Details of any accidents.

Collate data from each vehicle log sheet to show distances travelled and vehicle fuel consumption. Comparisons can be made and anomalies seen. Fuel consumption can be high due to bad driving, poor vehicle condition and servicing, and the condition of the roads. Theft of fuel may show up in the summary as an increase in fuel consumption.

17.2.2 Drivers

Recruit competent local drivers and assign one driver to a specific vehicle wherever possible. Individual responsibility encourages care and attention to a vehicle. Select drivers carefully according to a system that is seen to be fair and impartial (see 6.2.2). A driving licence does not necessarily indicate that the driver is competent. Therefore, a proper assessment of a driver is an essential

Vehicle Reg no.											Page no.
Date	Journey details		Kilometre reading		Kms travelled		Fuel		Oil	Driver's signature
	From	To	Start	End	Off	Per	litres	cost	litres	

Figure 17.2 A typical vehicle log sheet

Workshop dates In	Workshop dates Out	Days off road	Defect/ Service	Kilometre reading	Checked by	Next service due

Figure 17.3 A typical service and repair history form

part of the recruitment process. Where competent drivers are in short supply, it may be necessary to provide training. The avoidance of one bad vehicle crash pays for a lot of training time. Always employ drivers on a trial basis, say for one month, before an appointment is confirmed.

Select drivers according to a two-stage process. Assess candidates' sight, knowledge of vehicles and ability to complete logs. Give candidates who pass this first stage a test drive.

Rules for drivers can be included as part of a driver's contract of employment. The topics covered will depend on local circumstances but may include:

- Grounds for dismissal – consumption of intoxicating substances (alcohol, drugs); falling asleep at the wheel; theft of fuel, oil or equipment; negligence resulting in an accident; use of vehicle for private commercial purposes.
- Driver responsibilities – daily and weekly checks; reporting defects; completing the log book; keeping the vehicle clean.
- Vehicle refuelling – when and how.
- Breakdown and accident procedures – what to do, who to inform.
- Maximum driving time – for example, eight hours per day followed by a minimum rest period of six hours.
- Safety rules – the wearing of seat belts by all occupants; observance of speed limits; no unauthorized passengers; maximum loading, etc. (see 'Safety and accident procedures').
- Security procedures when leaving a vehicle unattended - detail what the driver is not responsible for, such as other people's belongings.

- Special security procedures in sensitive or dangerous areas.
- Daily and weekly checks. Include check lists in the front of each log book as a reminder to drivers.
- Tyres should be maintained at the pressures recommended in the vehicle manual for the appropriate road speed and vehicle loading. Incorrect pressures can adversely affect tyre and vehicle life, and the comfort and safety of driver and passengers. See Appendix 25 for pressure conversion tables.

A list of driver responsibilities can be kept in each log book.

Drivers can share information about road conditions, vehicle performance and procedures at drivers' meetings. This helps each driver and the workshop manager to better understand any problems. It can also be an opportunity for the manager to reiterate drivers' rules, safety guidelines, and accident, refuelling and servicing procedures. If possible, provide a staff room with tea/coffee where drivers can relax.

Convoy driving

Avoid convoy driving if possible. Individual and small group vehicle movements are preferable for flexibility and efficiency. However, it may be necessary to drive in convoy for security reasons or for long distance driving in remote locations. Establish rules for travelling in convoy and stress the need for convoy discipline. Convoy rules will depend on each situation and the support available. Examples follow:

- The driver in front should always keep the vehicle behind in view. In dusty conditions, frequent stops may need to be made at agreed intervals to ensure that everyone is still together. Driving with lights may assist in keeping visual contact.
- The convoy control vehicle travels at the rear.
- The front vehicles keep to an agreed convoy speed.
- Expect breakdowns and agree procedures to deal with them. All vehicles must stop whilst repairs are carried out. Alternative decisions: tow, recover by base workshop, temporarily abandon.
- If a truck convoy is delivering to locations along a route, agree a waiting system so that unloading truck drivers do not have to 'catch up' or return to base on their own.
- One vehicle (the control vehicle) plus at least one other should have radio contact with base.

17.2.3 Safety and accident procedures

Vehicle related accidents pose the greatest danger in emergency programmes. Implement and follow safety guidelines to minimize the risks. Consider the viability of a safe driving bonus scheme. In addition to the drivers' rules discussed above, the following points should be emphasized:

- Speeding should be a disciplinary offence.
- If seat belts are fitted they should be worn.

- Driving more than eight hours per day with reasonable breaks should be the exception, not the rule.
- Avoid night driving wherever possible.
- Every vehicle should carry a first aid kit and drivers should be trained to use it.
- Reversing: use a guide if the view is restricted, especially when driving trucks.
- Ensure drivers are aware of the maximum load carrying capacity – not in figures but in some practical way, for instance, 'a space of four fingers between the axle and the bump stop'.
  - Heavy items, such as spare wheels, even if carried inside the vehicle, should be well secured: in the event of an accident, unsecured heavy items may cause serious injury.
  - Loads should be evenly distributed and placed as low as possible.
  - Place a heavy individual weight to the middle of a vehicle.
  - Roof rack carrying capacity is very limited – only carry light items on a roof rack.

Important safety guidelines relating to fuel are covered in 17.2.4.

Follow the daily and weekly checks in preparation for long journeys. Do not assume everything has been checked beforehand. It is worth the extra few minutes to double-check with the driver. Ensure sufficient quantities of fuel, drinking water and, possibly, food are included in case of delays, breakdowns and detours.

Establish a procedure to follow when an accident occurs and ensure all drivers understand it. Sample guidelines in the event of an accident would include:

- Assist any injured persons.
- Report the accident to the police/local authorities and inform the programme manager.
- Do not become involved in any instant settlement at the scene of the accident.
- Record all relevant details of the accident:
  - Location, date and time of the day, weather conditions.
  - Names, addresses/contacts of those involved and witnesses.
  - Driver licence, vehicle registration and insurance details.
  - Description of the accident (draw a sketch).
  - Record any injuries to people and animals and damage to property.

17.2.4 Fuel and lubricants

Fuel management

Fuel is a valuable and easily traded commodity. Keep close control and account of fuel purchase and consumption. The temptation to steal fuel is often high – do not increase it by making theft easier. Check fuel consumption periodically using the figures from the log book entries. Cross-check with fuel and oil receipts where drivers purchase fuel. Immediately investigate high fuel consumption and any similar discrepancies, such as the frequent topping-up of oil. An oil consumption of 1% of the fuel consumption can be regarded as fair. Check current and expected fuel consumption against the future availability of fuel. Local fuel supplies may be erratic and vary from reliable to non-existent. Plan ahead to cope with potential fuel shortages. Consider ordering in bulk and establishing safe and secure storage facilities.

There are advantages and disadvantages between obtaining fuel from local filling stations or arranging agency purchase and storage:

Local fuel supply	**Own fuel supply**
No capital outlay for facilities	Immediate local availability
Less administration	Better control
Lower security and theft risk	Lower fuel cost

In some cases, a lead agency (such as UNHCR) may provide fuel supply facilities for use by other agencies and this is usually the best option if it is available.

Ensure that the legal requirements for the storage of fuel, especially petrol, are met. In most countries, the volume of petrol which can be stored above ground is limited by law.

If you have to store fuel, observe the following guidelines:

- To reduce the risk of confusion, do not store petrol and diesel together.
- Store fuel as far from any office and accommodation as possible.
- Display a clear notice in relevant languages – 'DANGER, NO SMOKING'.
- Minimize the use of drums. See guidelines below.
- Petrol: Do not store petrol in small, vented above ground tanks as it is a major fire risk. Petrol can deteriorate quickly in high ambient temperatures. Therefore, arrange systematic use of all petrol stored and organize low volume, frequent deliveries.
- Diesel can be safely stored above ground for up to six months before it shows signs of deterioration, even in high ambient temperatures. Beware of diesels which do not contain anti-waxing additives as they may form wax globules and block supply lines when stored below freezing. Figure 17.4 shows a typical diesel storage tank arrangement. The mild steel tank may be cylindrical or rectangular. Do not use internally galvanized steel for diesel tanks or pipework as the diesel will attack the zinc.
- Ensure that suitable fire fighting equipment is always available and that staff know how to use it. Do not use water to control a fire, as the water will turn to steam, creating a fire ball which spreads the blaze. Have earth or sand available to extinguish the flames and a blanket in which to smother someone on fire.
- Avoid refuelling from a storage tank that has been filled in the last 24 hours as filling creates turbulence stirring up sediment. Allow time for the sediment to settle.

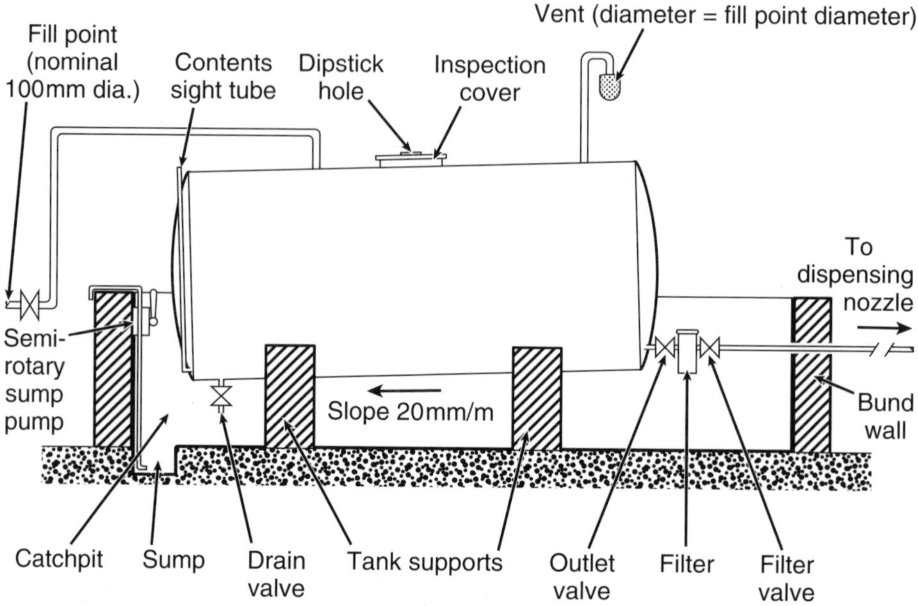

Figure 17.4 Typical diesel storage tank arrangement

- If possible, provide shade for fuel tanks to avoid temperature differences to reduce condensation.

Oversee fuel deliveries and prepare in advance for the tanker arrival. Check volume of fuel in tank before and after delivery. Sample fuel and check quality (see below for method). Ensure tanker delivery hoses are well earthed to prevent a build up of static electricity which could cause a spark.

Drum storage

In many circumstances there is no alternative but to store fuel in drums. Guidelines for safe storage include:

- Store drums in a secure, ventilated, shaded and accessible area.
- Erect 'DANGER, NO SMOKING' signs in relevant languages.
- Clearly separate diesel, petrol, lubricants and other fluids. Mark all drums to show contents and date of purchase, or arrival in store. Use the oldest drums first. Mark drums with recognizable coloured symbols.
- If a vehicle tank is filled with the wrong fuel or fluid, always completely drain and clean the tank. Petrol supplied to a diesel engine is dangerous and will cause severe damage to the engine.
- Do not stack drums more than two high.
- Wear gloves when handling drums.

- Keep drums tightly sealed except when drawing contents.
- Clean and dry drums before opening to avoid contamination. Open hot drums slowly to avoid the rapid release of pressurized contents.
- Avoid pumping from the bottom of a drum where contaminants collect. Pump fuel through a filter or, if not available, a cloth. Use separate pumps, hoses, filters and funnels for each fluid.

Handle drums with care. Roll drums off trucks down a plank. If this is not possible, old tyres can be used to cushion the fall. Figure 17.5 shows an improvised method of handling fuel and oil drums, or any other awkward or heavy object.

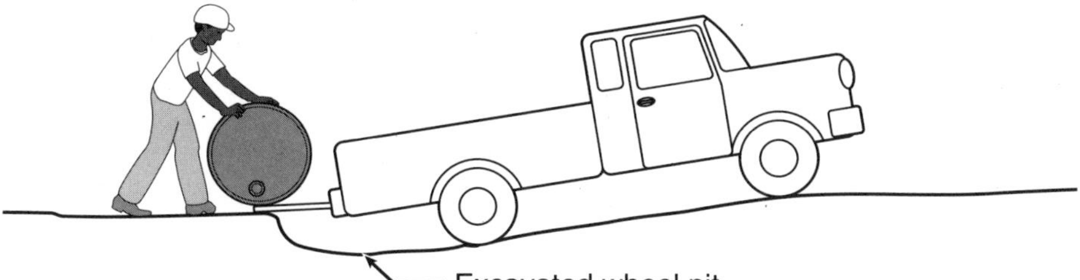

Figure 17.5 Handling fuel and oil drums

Use a no-spark dipstick – a length of wood – to check the volume of fluid in a drum (18 mm ~ 1 gallon). A full drum should reach to about 30 mm from the top. Check delivered drums for water. Condensation can cause water and rust to accumulate in a fuel drum or tank even when only clean fuel has been placed inside. Tanks may need to be drained to remove the water occasionally. To prevent condensation in vehicle tanks, fill them nearly full (allow space for expansion) at the end of the day.

Use a semi-rotary or diaphragm barrel pump to remove the contents of a drum. Check the compatibility of pump materials with the fluid before use. A nitrile rubber diaphragm is suitable for pumping diesel. To avoid the mixing of sediment, water and other contaminants, do not move a drum prior to dispensing.

To take a sample from a drum without disturbing the contents use a 'drum thief'. This can be made up from a length of clear plastic hose as shown in Figure 17.6. To take a full length 'section', dip the hose to the bottom of the drum, place a thumb or stopper over the top end and withdraw. Look at the sample and note the fluid layers. Discharge each fluid layer into a container and try to identify it by smell. If necessary, and if equipment is available, weigh measured volumes of each liquid and identify it by the specific gravity.

Using a longer flexible tube, this method can be adapted to siphon fuel from a variety of tanks. This avoids the need to suck the end of the pipe and the danger of getting a mouthful of fuel.

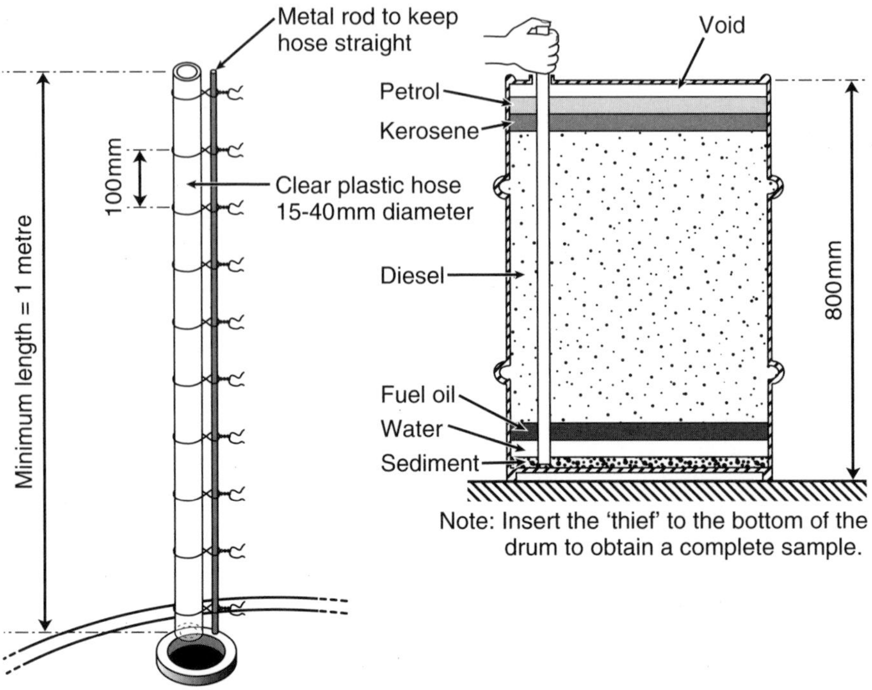

Figure 17.6 Sampling using a 'drum thief'

17.3 Vehicle workshops

17.3.1 Workshop requirements

Although in the early stages of an emergency it is often necessary to 'make do and mend', as soon as possible, establish a servicing and maintenance strategy. The workshop facilities and staff required will depend on factors such as the type of vehicle, driver competence, road conditions, availability of skilled mechanics, spares and equipment. The establishment of any effective vehicle workshop will need substantial investment. This should be brought to the attention of agency managers allocating funds for emergency operations.

Workshop location, site and services

Locate a workshop close to the agency's main office to aid communication and management, and near to a main road for access to major support services – dealers, specialist workshops, local administration, and so on. Locate it away from dwellings and livestock.

The site should be level, with an existing hardstanding, it should be free from flooding and excessive dust and with sufficient space for workshop facilities. Secure the site with a fence.

Services such as water, electricity and telephones are needed.

Workshop design

The following recommendations are based on designs used in tropical climates. They will need to be adapted for colder weather, although size and equipment will be similar.

Ensure that the workshop area is properly drained away from the workshop entrance. In high and intense rainfall areas, it may be necessary to have a substantial overhang on the roof and large storm drains to prevent flooding of the working area. Soakaways may be necessary depending on local drainage and the type of soil (see Section 10.5). Areas of high rainfall are also prone to high winds. Obtain local advice and orientate the workshop to protect the roof against strong winds whilst still ensuring good drainage. Use roll-down plastic sheeting (heavy canvas is better if available) to protect the working area from wind-blown rain, dust and sand. The sheeting can be rolled up to give ventilation when required (see Chapter 19 for more information on construction).

The size of a workshop and the facilities it will contain will depend on the number of vehicles in the fleet. As a guide for new vehicles, plan on 10 per cent of the vehicle fleet being in the workshop at any one time.

A small workshop formed from a standard freight container is shown in Figure 17.7. If a second container is available it can be positioned on the other side of the pit to give support to the working bay roof and to provide further storage. Containers used for transporting emergency equipment can be converted into workshop stores and offices. They are robust, secure and fire resistant. Corrosion to the underside of containers can be minimized by raising them slightly on simple supports of timber, stone or concrete. In hot climates, erect a raised roof above the container to keep it cool. A thatched roof is ideal. The layout of a workshop for up to 15 vehicles is shown in Figure 17.8. An alternative to a pit is a ramp/pit which gives more ventilation in a hot climate (Figure 17.9). Line pits to prevent collapse.

Workshop equipment and tools

New vehicles will initially require standard tools for servicing and routine preventive maintenance. Older vehicles will require more specialized equipment and special tools for the replacement and repair of components. Box 17.1 gives recommended equipment and tools for a small workshop to cater for a fleet of up to 15 4×4 vehicles. Adapt this list to suit the situation.

Vehicle tool kit

In addition to the standard vehicle tool kit – which is assumed to include a wheel spanner and jack – Box 17.2 lists tools that it would be advisable to carry in vehicles working remote from a workshop.

17.3.2 Workshop staff

A single mechanic, with both mechanical and basic administrative skills, with an assistant, or assisted by the drivers, should be able to run a small workshop. For fleet sizes above six vehicles it is advisable to employ a workshop manager to supervise a mechanic, assistant mechanics and drivers (Table 17.3). There may be great local pressure to recruit particular candidates for jobs in the workshop. As with drivers, devise an open and fair system of recruitment,

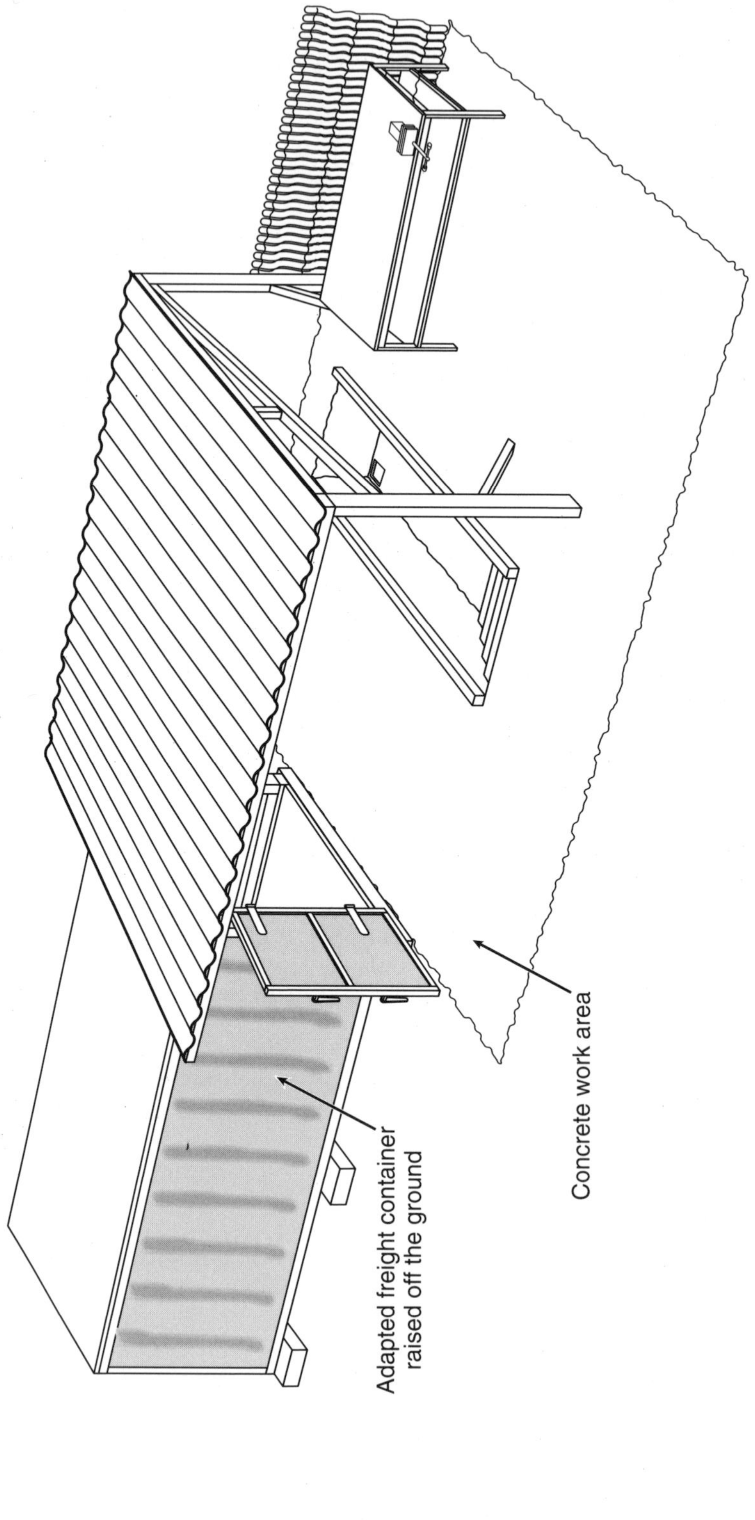

Figure 17.7 A small emergency workshop

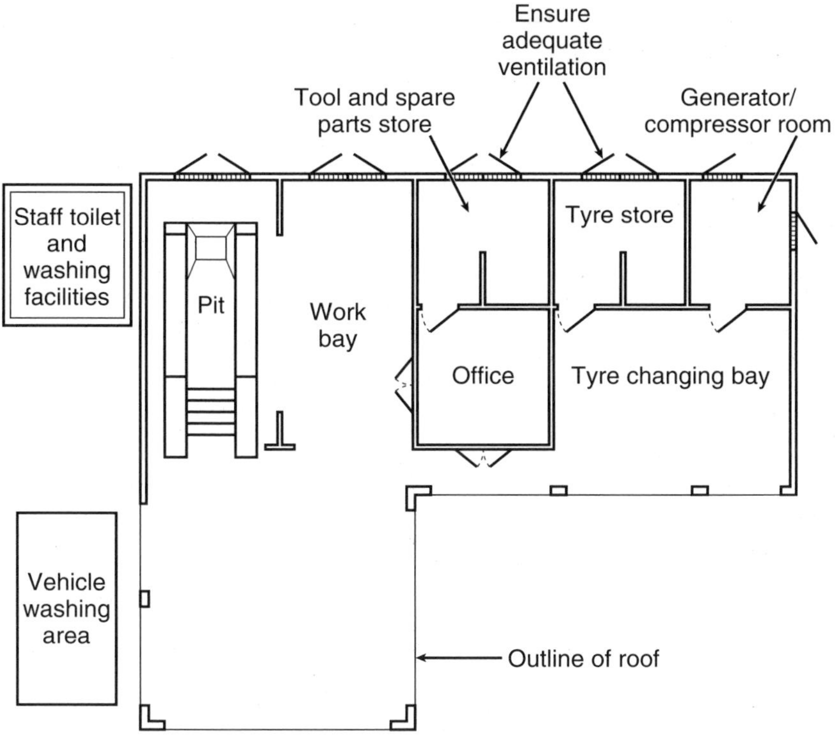

Figure 17.8 An emergency workshop for up to 15 vehicles
Adapted from Land Rover, 1989

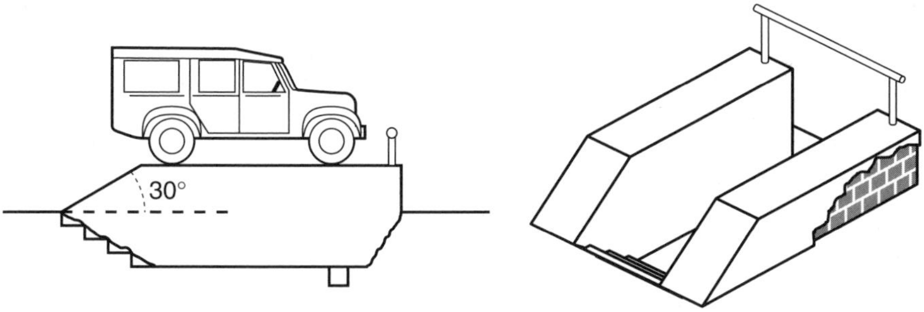

Figure 17.9 A ramp/pit alternative to a simple pit
Source: Land Rover, 1989

involving vehicle knowledge and practical tests. Recruit on an initial trial basis and on the potential of candidates to improve through coaching on-the-job during the probationary period.

Workshop management

(See also Chapter 6.) There are considerable pressures on a well equipped vehicle workshop and its staff. Local external pressures may include requests to

Box 17.1 Equipment and tools for a vehicle workshop to maintain a fleet of about 15 vehicles

Equipment

- Portable diesel engine driven generator and electric arc-welder mounted on a two-wheeled trolley. Welder rating (100% duty): 80A/23V a.c. and d.c. Generator: 5 kVA, 240V, 50 Hz, single-phase. Welder to be suppled with 5 m of electrode and return leads, electrode holder, welder's mask and spare glass, chipping hammer, welder's gauntlet gloves, wire brush and an assortment of coated mild steel electrodes (2.5 mm and 3 mm).
- Portable diesel engine driven compressor, 300 l/min FAD (Free Air Delivered) @ 7 bar, complete with receiver, air filter, regulator, pressure gauge, safety valve and outlet valve, mounted on a two-wheeled trolley.
- Schrader tyre inflator complete with pressure gauge to 10 bar and high pressure hose with dual foot connector.
- Light commercial tyre changing equipment, compressed air operated, with capacity for 7.50 × 16 tyres.
- Battery charger suitable for slow and fast charging of 6, 12 and 24-volt batteries, 20A charge rate with 140A boost for starting, complete with ammeter and charging leads.
- Battery hydrometer.
- Manual chain hoist with a lifting capacity of 1.5 tonnes and lifting height of 3 m, complete with automatic brake and forged steel safety hook.
- Lifting sling of 3 m length and 2 tonne lifting capacity.
- Hydraulic trolley jack of 2 tonne capacity.
- Four tripod axle stands of 2 tonne capacity.
- Four manual barrel pumps – one each for petrol, diesel, lubricating oil and one spare; each with thread to suit standard drums (M64 × 4mm and/ or 2-inch BSP).
- Lever operated grease gun, complete with hydraulic flexible connectors.
- Hand-held, multi-speed, electric drill, 13 mm, complete with metric and Imperial H.S.S. drill sets. Include extra small diameter drills.
- Two 100 mm bench vices.
- Bench pillar drill, 13 mm capacity.
- Bench grinder, 125 mm diameter wheel.
- Hand grinder with 100 mm grinder and cutter wheels.
- Hydraulic press, 10–14 tonne capacity.
- Water power wash, diesel engine driven, 15l/min @ 150 bar.
- 'Multi-tester', voltage, current and resistance test equipment.
- Fire extinguisher(s).

Hand tools

- Combination spanner set, 6 to 24 mm.
- Combination spanner set, ⅜" to 1¼" AF.
- Ring and open end spanner sets, ¼" to 1¼" and 6 to 27 mm.
- Socket sets:
  ½" drive sets, 8 to 32 mm and 5⁄16" to 1¼".
  ⅜" drive sets, 6 to 10 mm and ¼" to 9⁄16".
- Socket ratchets, ¼" and ⅜" drive; socket extensions; socket adaptors and knuckle bar.
- Sockets and adaptors to suit vehicles. For example; 42 mm, ¾" drive for Land Rover crank pulley nut.
- Torque wrench, 0 to 200 Nm.
- Adjustable spanners, 100, 200, 450 mm.
- Two 450 mm pipe wrenches.
- Filter strap wrench.

(Cont. over)

Box 17.1 (cont.)

- 'Mole' grip, 250 mm.
- Pliers: 200 mm combination; 200 mm long nose; 150 mm side cutters.
- 'Water pump' pliers, 250 mm.
- Circlip pliers: internal straight and bent; external straight and bent.
- Crimping pliers.
- Screwdriver sets, flat (nos. 1–6) and posidrive (nos. 1–3).
- Impact driver.
- Allen key sets, metric and imperial.
- A set of 'Torx' keys.
- Feeler gauges, metric and imperial.
- Vernier calliper, 150 mm.
- Steel rule, 300 mm.
- Ball pein hammers, 1 lb and 2 lb.
- Mallet, 1 lb copper/leather.
- Adjustable hacksaw frame, 250–350 mm.
- Sets of H.S.S. 13 × 0.65 mm hacksaw blades: coarse (18 teeth per inch, t.p.i.); medium (24 t.p.i.); fine (32 t.p.i).
- Junior hacksaw frame and set of blades.
- Files, 300 mm flat; bastard, second-cut and smooth.
- Cold chisels, flat and cross-cut.
- Parallel punch set, 2–10 mm.
- Centre punch.
- Wire brushes.
- Oil can.
- Scissors, 250 mm.
- Paint brushes, 13, 25 and 50 mm.
- Pop rivet gun with selection of rivets, ⅛" to 3/16".
- Set of standard metric taps and dies.
- Stud extractor.
- Set of tyre levers, 500 mm.
- Two 550 × 200 × 200 mm tool boxes with padlocks.
- Pullers and special tools appropriate to the vehicles concerned, e.g. steering ball pullers.

repair non-agency vehicles; to carry out 'little jobs' for influential people; to lend tools, equipment and spare parts and so on. The requests may come directly to the manager or to individual staff members. The manager must try to understand the pressures on individual members of staff and limit them wherever possible. Goodwill actions must be tempered by the potentially adverse effects on agency operations. It is often better to severely limit external jobs at the beginning of an operation – even when there may be a felt need to create a good impression – or it may become even more difficult to decline them later.

In some countries, a box of tools may be worth several times the monthly salary of a mechanic. The theft of high-value spare parts and tools is often a great temptation. Firm and fair workshop procedures can help to minimize losses using one of two methods:

- Issue tools from a central tool store at the beginning of the day which must be returned when no longer required before the end of the day.
- Issue each mechanic with a lockable box of tools for the duration of their employment. Carry out a monthly tool box inventory check and ensure missing tools are replaced at the mechanic's expense. It may be necessary to provide a secure store in which to keep all tool boxes overnight.

Make all drivers similarly responsible for the tools and equipment carried in each vehicle and carry out monthly checks. Make regular checks part of

Box 17.2 Vehicle tool kit

- Ensure the original tool kit is with the vehicle.
- Set of combination spanners, 6–24 mm.
- Set of Flat and Posidrive screwdrivers.
- Combination pliers, 150 mm.
- Adjustable spanner, 150 mm.
- Set of tyre levers, 500 mm.
- Puncture repair kit: Inner tube vulcanizing clamp, assorted vulcanizing hot patches. Valve spanner.
- Roll of insulated electrical wire.
- Assorted electrical spade connectors.
- PVC insulating tape.
- One set of jump-leads (battery cables).
- 30 m of man-made fibre rope (such as polypropylene), for vehicle recovery, plus two D-shackles.
- Pulley block for use in vehicle recovery.
- Torch and/or 12V lamp with battery clips or plug to suit cigarette lighter socket.
- Foot pump.
- 'Hi-lift' jack.
- Precautionary spare parts: fan belt, inner tube.
- Roll of metal wire for emergency repairs.

For a petrol-engined vehicle, ensure the following are also carried:

- Spark plug spanner.
- Brass spark plug brush.
- Spare spark plug.
- Fine emery paper.

Table 17.3 Workshop staffing

For up to 6 vehicles	*For 6–15 vehicles*
Mechanic Service and maintain vehicles. Basic vehicle administration – vehicle records, stock control and ordering spares.	**Workshop manager** Overall management of workshop. Allocate and supervise work. Administer workshop – keep vehicle records; order and allocate fuel, tools and spare parts; check log book returns.
Drivers Daily and weekly checks. Complete log book. Report problems and assist mechanic.	**Mechanic** Service and maintain vehicles.
Administrator The administrator may be responsible for all the agency's administration, not just the workshop. Therefore, the administrative responsibilities should be divided between the mechanic and administrator based on the ability of each and their respective workloads.	**Assistant mechanic** Assist in servicing and maintenance.
Guard Provide night-time security.	**Storekeeper** Issue and keep records of tools and spare parts.
	Guard Provide night-time security.

accepted management routine. This may be awkward at first but it should become normal and reassuring to all involved.

Workshops are busy places and it would be unfair to impose close controls on mechanics if others were allowed free access. Therefore, restrict access to those who have a reason to be there. In large workshops, it may be necessary to institute a system of control using a security guard and signed passes. This is often the case, for example, in central fuel depots managed by a lead agency. Management staff should ensure that they follow the agreed procedures as an example to others. Avoid putting security staff under pressure by trying to bypass the system 'because it saves time'.

Staff training

Only in the later stages of an emergency will it be possible to institute a planned training programme. But it should be possible at any time to coach staff on-the-job to improve specific skills. Allocating half an hour or so each week, to go through a specific task, can often give valuable returns in terms of time saved and improved quality of work. Look out for recurrent problems and programme short sessions to overcome them. Pay particular attention to workshop safety.

17.3.3 Spares and stores

Ordering spares

The most important spares to obtain at the beginning of an emergency are the fast-moving spares for regular servicing and maintenance. These should be purchased and should arrive at the same time as the vehicles. Fast-moving spares include: air, oil and fuel filters; suspension bushes (for example, shock absorber mounting bushes); brake linings and pads; fuses; spark plugs; light bulbs and headlights; tyres; inner tubes; V-belts; wipers and mirrors.

A common guideline for initial budgeting is to order appropriate spares on the basis of 10–15 per cent of total vehicle cost. Suppliers will put together a package of spares for the conditions specified based on their experience. Specify difficult conditions, such as sandy roads.

For a number of similar vehicles, order spare parts on a fleet basis rather than the same set of spares for each vehicle. Large items can then be included (for instance, a complete gearbox) and the cost spread over several vehicles. Remember to include batteries and tyres in the imported spares if they are not available locally. Consider including extra wheels, tyres, inner tubes and small tool kits in vehicle consignments as it may be quicker to clear them through customs than to have them sent separately as 'spares'. However, check with experienced importers as this may have the reverse effect of holding up the importation of vehicles in some countries.

One of the most frustrating and time consuming tasks in an emergency is sorting out misunderstandings over equipment and spare parts orders. See Chapter 7 for guidelines on specifying and ordering procedures. If possible, refer to the manufacturer's spare parts catalogue as shown in Figure 17.10. Quote the exact description used in the catalogue, even if it may not sound precise. The people who will deal with the order are likely to be purchasing officers and despatchers. They will be using the catalogue so do not confuse them with extra technical jargon. If it is necessary to give additional information on an order, make a note on the order form and attach a covering letter.

Specify the packing required on the order form. Multi-packed filters are susceptible to contamination once the first one is taken out of the package.

SPARE PARTS ORDER

Project number: *SDN 304* Date:--/--/--
Order number: *94/05*
Vehicle type: *Land Rover 110, pick-up*
Chassis number: *SALLD6CD 700385*
Engine number: *QWERTY 12345*
Spare part catalogue number/date: *RTC 9863 October 90*

No. off	Part number	Catalogue description	Page	Office check
2	*NRC 8455*	*SHOCK ABSORBER – FRONT*	*E 30*	
10	*90517711*	*FUEL FILTER ELEMENT*	*H 36*	

Figure 17.10 An example of a spare parts order form

Therefore, give instructions for parts to be packed individually or in resealable boxes. Specify that all parts must be clearly labelled on the outside of individual packaging by part number and/or description.

Request that spares should be wrapped in shock absorbent packing material and arranged in strong boxes. Ensure a packing list is attached to each box for the quick and easy identification of the contents. There is nothing more frustrating than having to open up several boxes to find out what is inside. All crates should be labelled with the total weight, organization name and destination address. It is often useful to have the name of an individual in the address, such as the workshop manager. State a maximum crate weight so that they can be handled on arrival by the available mechanical handling equipment or manual labour. See Chapter 7 for more details.

Storing and issuing spares

Store spares securely and protect them from rain, damp, dust and extremes of temperature. Storage may need to take into account local wildlife: rats gnaw through wooden boxes and plastic bags and they damage rubber bushes, inner tubes, and so on. Termites can destroy wooden crates from beneath with little sign of outside damage until it is too late. Only issue a new part if the old broken or worn part is handed in. Dispose of old parts so that they cannot be re-cycled, especially used filters which should be crushed before disposal.

See Section 7.5 for details on stores management.

17.3.4 Servicing and maintenance

Servicing is the regular, planned inspection and preventive maintenance of essential equipment to keep a vehicle in good running order and so minimize breakdowns. Maintenance refers to the repair and replacement of broken and worn out parts, to keep a vehicle in a reliable operational condition.

Servicing and maintenance records

Establish a workshop file for each vehicle to record all relevant servicing and maintenance work. Use a simple form as described in 17.2.1 (Figure 17.3). Include the form in both the vehicle log book and the vehicle workshop file. If the form is simple it will be used. If it requires too much time to complete, it may not be used at all.

On completion of a service, place a sticky label on the dashboard in front of the driver with either the kilometre reading or the date for the next service. Use a label such as: NEXT SERVICE DUE 20 000km OR 30/10/01.

Servicing procedures

Frequent 'mini-services' entail minor mechanical checks. They help to identify potential problems between each complete service. A 'filter service' entails changing filters and oil, and more rigorous checks. A 'complete service' is just that. The manufacturer usually gives servicing recommendations based on 'average conditions'. Shorten service intervals to take account of more severe conditions, such as extremes of temperature, very dusty terrain, frequent wading, harsh terrain or poor quality lubricants.

Suggested variations in service periods according to the conditions are outlined in Table 17.4.

Table 17.4 Vehicle service intervals according to driving conditions

Service interval	*Typical conditions*
2000 km Very severe conditions	Regular off-road driving over harsh terrain, sand/mud/dust, frequent use of 4-wheel drive, slow speeds, extremes of temperature, poor quality oil.
3000 km Severe conditions	75% off-road driving over rough tracks, sand/mud/dust, intermittent use of 4-wheel drive, medium speeds, medium quality oil.
5000 km Easier conditions	Surfaced roads and good tracks, occasional use of 4-wheel drive, high average speeds, good quality fuel and oils.

In severe conditions the servicing pattern would be: 3000 km – mini-service; 6000 km – filter service; 9000 km – mini-service; 12000 km – complete service. Use a checklist at each service to ensure that everything is covered. Box 17.3 gives an example for a diesel-engined Toyota Land Cruiser. Adapt this checklist for other vehicles, according to manufacturer's recommendations and local experience.

For more details on the servicing of petrol and diesel engines and fault finding refer to Section 15.2.

Box 17.3 Service pattern for a Toyota Land Cruiser

'Mini-service'

- Clean the engine and suspension area.
- Change the engine oil.
- Check the air cleaner and clean, if necessary.
- Check oil levels: main gearbox, transfer box, axles.
- Check for water in the axle oil – emulsified oil is recognized by its creamy appearance.
- Check axle breathers can operate.
- Drain the sedimentor (agglomerator) of any water and dirt.
- Grease the transmission and steering.
- Check springs, spring mountings and shock-absorbers.
- Check engine and gearbox mountings.
- Check exhaust pipe mounting brackets.
- Check fan/alternator belt(s).
- Check all warning lights operate.

'Filter service'

Include everything in the 'mini-service' and in addition:

- Change the diesel fuel filter.
- Change the oil filter.
- Check axle hub freeplay.
- Check freeplay in the steering.
- Check brake pads and/or shoes.

'Complete service'

Include everything in the 'filter service' and in addition:

- Change the gearbox oil.
- Change the transfer box oil.
- Change the front and rear axle oil.
- Grease door locks and hinges.

17.4 Driving techniques and vehicle recovery

17.4.1 Driving techniques

The following is a basic guide to off-road driving and driving on poor unsurfaced roads. Watch and learn from experienced drivers.

If in doubt about a route: stop – think – inspect on foot before proceeding.

Basic rules

- Keep thumbs outside the steering wheel as the wheel can snatch at a thumb and damage it if the front wheel hits a bump.
- Control vehicle speed by selecting the correct gear. Do not rely on the clutch as it can become overheated and severely damaged.
- Use all the gears according to the terrain. If a slow route over rough terrain involves very frequent gear changes, try driving in the low gear range.
- Always wait for a spinning wheel to stop before engaging another gear, four-wheel drive, or differential lock.

- Only use differential lock when traction is lost or in anticipation of poor traction. Disengage differential lock as soon as it is no longer needed. The transmission can be damaged if differential lock is engaged when driving on a hard road surface.
- If free-wheel hubs have been fitted to the front wheels, lock them before engaging four-wheel drive and unlock them afterwards.
- Do not engage low gear range when the vehicle is moving.
- Use the engine as a brake to retard motion when necessary.
- Crossing an obstacle:
  - Stop and inspect the route ahead on foot.
  - Select the correct gear (high/low) and differential lock (if fitted) before proceeding.
- Use a passenger positioned some distance ahead of the vehicle to guide the vehicle around and over obstacles that the driver cannot easily see.

Corrugations

Corrugations are a series of ridges formed at right-angles to the direction of travel. This washboard effect is created on well-travelled, unsurfaced, gravel roads in the dry season. Regular grading of a road limits their development.

Corrugations can be extremely uncomfortable and hard on the vehicle. They can be dangerous to travel on and driving requires concentration and some skill. For each vehicle there is an optimum speed at which the vehicle skims across the peaks of each ridge. Accelerating to reach this speed takes a little nerve, but having reached it the ride is improved. Typical optimum speed for light field vehicles is in the 50–70 km/h range. Take care at speed, as braking is impaired and steering less precise, due to intermittent contact with the running surface.

Soft ground (sand and mud)

Choose the correct gear (and differential lock if fitted) in advance of the soft ground and move forward, keeping the speed of the engine high. Do not subsequently change gear as the loss of momentum can bog down the vehicle.

Lowering tyre pressures increases flotation and therefore traction. But reducing tyre pressures also reduces ground clearance. Always re-inflate to the correct pressure at the end of the soft ground.

Sand is variable. It may, or may not, be better to follow in the tracks of previous vehicles. Undisturbed sand can form a crust which helps to support the vehicle; disturbed sand can retard the progress of a following vehicle. In other circumstances, the passage of several vehicles can help to compact the sand and it is better to follow the tracks formed. Check with local drivers and learn to recognize the differences in ground behaviour.

In slippery and muddy conditions, select gears carefully to keep control and to avoid wheel spin. If too low a gear is selected, the torque transmitted to the wheels may be too high, resulting in wheel spin. Use the accelerator gently and do not attempt to change gear in the middle of a mud patch or it will bog down.

If stationary and the wheels start spinning – stop. Continued wheel spin will merely dig the wheels deeper into the sand or mud. As soon as the wheels start to spin reverse out while it is still possible.

Steep or slippery slopes

On descending steep or slippery slopes, engage a very low gear to control the speed of descent.

If a vehicle fails to reach the top of a slope, or the engine stalls when climbing, reverse back down using the engine as a brake:

- Apply the foot brake (do not use the handbrake as it is unlikely to hold).
- Ensure the front wheels are straight (check out of the window, do not rely on the alignment of the steering wheel.
- Check that the area behind the vehicle is clear of people or other obstructions.
- Keeping your foot on the brake, select reverse gear low range and completely release the clutch and brake pedals.
- If the engine stalled, start the engine in gear with the starter. Never try to start the vehicle by rolling backwards and 'bump' starting as the wheels may loose grip and control of the vehicle will be lost.
- Let the braking action of the engine limit the speed of descent.

Flat terrain

Driving off-road across a large expanse of flat terrain can entail particular hazards. It can sometimes be difficult to see sudden dips in what may appear to be continuous flat land. Therefore, resist the temptation to travel at high speed or a serious accident may result.

It can be difficult to concentrate and it is easy to become disorientated. Therefore, carry a compass, know the correct heading and check it regularly.

Rutted wheel tracks

Avoid over-steering in existing deep rutted wheel tracks. The vehicle can swerve alarmingly if the front wheels are positioned at an angle to the direction of travel and they suddenly grip when reaching level ground or jump out of the rut.

Crossing ditches

To cross a ditch, select low gear and differential lock (if fitted) and cross at an angle. Avoid the wheels at opposite corners of the vehicle becoming suspended over the ditch at the same time as all the power will go to the suspended wheels. If this does happen, push the vehicle forwards or backwards until one of the free wheels is able to grip.

Wading

Before plunging a vehicle into water check the route first. Do not wade into fast-flowing water, but if it is safe wade across on foot, checking the depth of water and the bed surface for firmness, rocks and dips. Check the exit bank for slope and grip. Choose a route and fix on a landmark on the opposite bank as a guide.

Each vehicle will have its own restrictions and requirements regarding wading. Some vehicles (such as the Land Rover) have a wading plug which must be screwed into the clutch housing. A plug can be easily lost, so check where it is before setting out and ensure a suitable spanner is also kept in the vehicle. Plug the axle breathers to prevent the ingress of water into the axles. If the vehicle frequently wades, regularly check the axle oil for water contamination and change it when necessary. Emulsified oil is recognized by its creamy appearance.

If the water is deep enough for the fan to spray water over the engine, disconnect the fan or protect the electrics and air cleaner with plastic sheeting. Keep the air intake well clear of the water. It is advisable to fit a raised air intake when wading through water deeper than 0.5 m.

Maintain steady progress by selecting a suitable gear and keep a constant engine speed. Do not decelerate or change gear. Do not allow the engine to stall as this will allow water up the exhaust pipe.

After wading, remove the plugs and check the brakes. Dry out the brakes by driving slowly with the foot brake lightly applied.

Towing

Take the following measures when towing:

- Check and adjust vehicle and trailer tyres to the pressures recommended.
- Check that there are both vehicle and trailer spare tyres and that they are inflated to the correct pressures.
- Check that the trailer drawbar is at the same height as the hitching point on the vehicle.
- Be aware that the towed vehicle has neither power-assisted braking or steering.
- Refer to the towed vehicle manual for towing information, especially maximum speed and distance to prevent damage to the transmission due to lack of lubrication.
- Passengers are safer in the towing vehicle.
- Drivers should make clear signal arrangements.

17.4.2 Vehicle recovery

There are various techniques for recovering a vehicle when it is stuck. Most recoveries use shovels, local vegetation for traction and people pushing. The following basic recovery equipment will help:

- Shovels
- Sand ladders (also used in mud), about 2 m × 0.3 m and a rung spacing of 0.15 m.
- Hand or powered winch.
- Towing rope and D-shackles.
- Pulley block.

Self recovery

Try to reverse out of the problem. If this fails, dig around and under the vehicle until the wheels and axles are clear. Pack sand ladders or brushwood under the wheels and lay a path for the vehicle to follow. Select low gear and ease out the clutch to avoid wheel spin, while feeling for some grip. With the aid of people

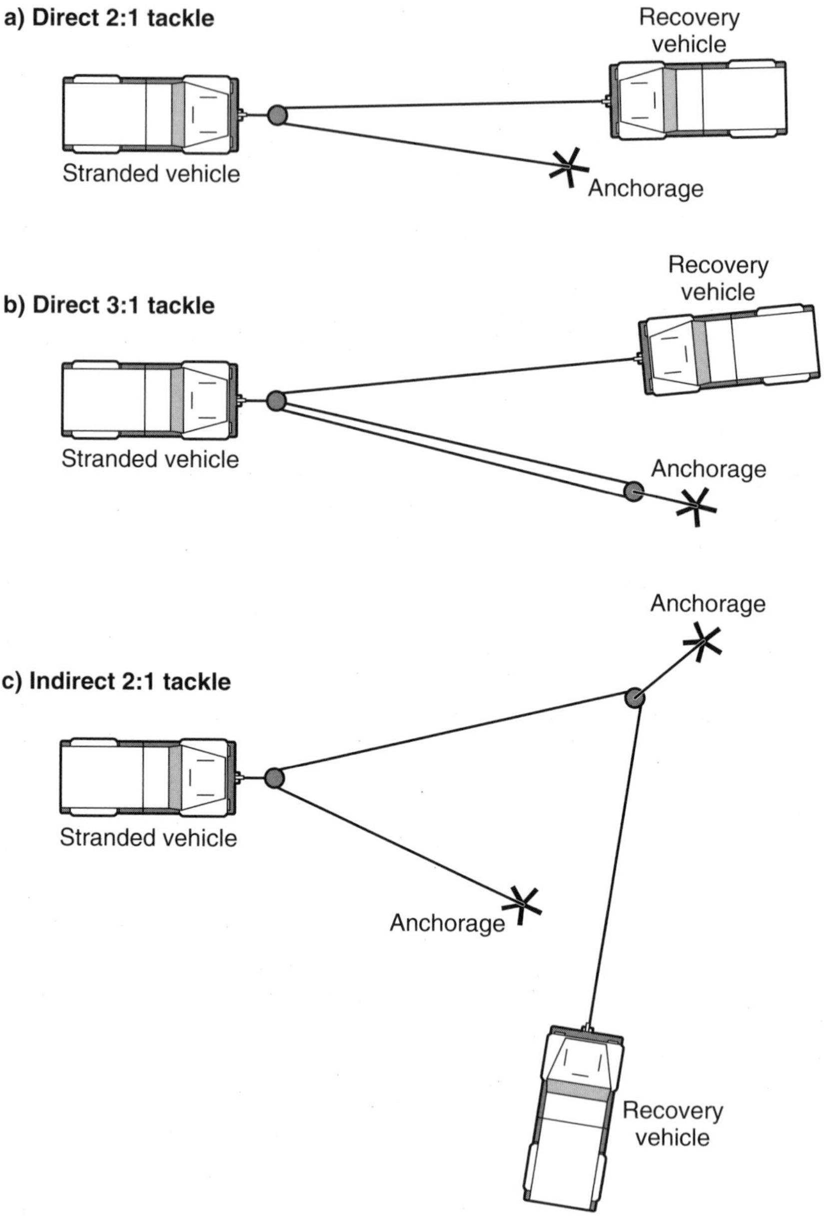

Figure 17.11 Typical vehicle recovery arrangements

pushing, the wheels may grip and the vehicle attain sufficient motion to clear the soft ground.

Tell the people pushing to keep out of the line of potential wheel spin or they may be hit by flying brushwood as well as sand or mud. Try not to use stone as it may be dangerous to those pushing and it can also damage tyre sidewalls. Ensure that helpers stand clear of sand ladders as they can quickly shift at alarming angles.

If the load of a jack can be spread sufficiently and safely using timbers it may be possible to lift a wheel sufficiently to pack brushwood or a ladder underneath.

If the vehicle has its own winch, use a convenient tree or trees as a rope anchor. If no suitable anchor exists, a ground anchor can be formed by burying a length of timber or the spare wheel. However, this takes time and considerable effort. (See Appendix 18 for anchorages).

Assisted recovery

There are several ways of making an assisted recovery:

- Another vehicle can be used as an anchor for the stranded vehicle's winch provided that the resistance to movement of the assisting vehicle is greater than the pull required to extract the stranded vehicle.
- A simple tow and/or winch from another vehicle. Be careful to pull from firm ground!
- A tandem tow from two vehicles roped together in line.

Ensure that all pulls are in straight lines to avoid undue strain on the chassis.

Winching

Ideally, a winch should be used in conjunction with a vehicle's own means of improving traction: four-wheel drive and differential lock. Winch maintenance and driver training in winch use go a long way towards successfully recovering a vehicle.

Use gloves when handling steel wire rope. Damaged wire rope can cause severe cuts. Do not kink wire rope and always wind rope back onto the winch drum after use so that there is no slack and it is ready for use again. When back at base, it is advisable to unwind the cable, clean it and check for any damage.

Ideally, the winch pull should always be in line with the vehicle. Keep all helpers and onlookers away from the line of pull in case the rope, shackles or mountings fail. Refer to Figure 17.11 for typical vehicle recovery arrangements.

18 Roads, crossings and airstrips

People affected by disasters, whether refugees or displaced people, are frequently forced to flee into inaccessible areas. Suitable access to the victims of a disaster is vital so that they can be supplied with basic humanitarian assistance. This chapter focuses on the physical infrastructure (roads, crossings and airstrips) required to ensure access is secured and maintained. Related chapters are Chapter 7, which deals with the overall logistics system and Chapter 17, which deals with vehicle selection, management and maintenance.

18.1 Introduction

18.1.1 Planning improved access

To plan improved access:

- Assess the access needs, establish priorities and initiate a staged approach.
- Match the vehicles to the road.
- To deal with the problem of periods of interrupted access, consider more storage as well as an improved road.

To establish needs and priorities, liaise with the local highway department and the agencies responsible for logistics and food delivery. Identify essential immediate actions in the context of a longer-term plan. Anticipate future access problems and take appropriate measures in time (prior to the wet season, for example). See Chapter 5 for the principles of assessment and planning. It is usually easier to build more storage or order smaller trucks than it is to build or improve roads.

In remote areas, a light-duty earth or gravel road may be all that is available or all that is possible to build at short notice. On this type of road, one large vehicle does proportionately far more damage than many smaller vehicles. Access may be better guaranteed through the provision of a large number of small trucks than a small number of large ones. Find out who decides on maximum truck size. The general rule is to avoid trucks larger than 10 tonnes.

Generally, the more storage there is, the longer the period of interrupted access that can be tolerated. Storage is particularly important in areas which experience sustained seasonal rainfall.

Make an outline plan

Refer to Chapter 5 for general guidelines on planning a response. In making an outline plan, consider the following:

- Identify the problems. Is a new or improved road the answer to the access problem? What about changing the vehicle types used? For interruptions to access, what about increasing storage?
- Establish the priorities and design a staged approach. Which routes and which sections are the highest priority?
- Assess the resources and constraints. Political issues often surround access to land and the choice of route. Find out what these constraints might be and the likelihood of obtaining the necessary permission to cross land. Avoid compensation wherever possible. Contact the local authorities and work with them.
- Assess seasonal factors: availability of labour; soil condition and moisture content; access for construction (for instance, cross-drainage and river crossings).
- Survey and select the route (see Section 18.3.3).
- Plan a staged approach. Look at improving the worst sections of road first – spot improvements – and gradually upgrade the route where necessary.
- Liaise. Continually liaise throughout the planning, implementation and maintenance stages with local people, the local government administration and the department responsible for roads (the Ministry of Works or the Public Works Department), the political establishment, other agencies, and relief co-ordinating bodies.

Detailed planning can then be carried out for each solution (for example, see Section 18.3.2 for road construction planning).

18.1.2 Choice and design of road

The engineer working in emergency relief will frequently be required to construct or repair an unpaved road using labour intensive methods. Where the road surface was paved but has become badly damaged, it may be appropriate to convert the damaged section of the road into an unpaved road.

Machine-based road construction, using heavy earth moving equipment, is a specialized job requiring experience in road engineering. Machinery takes time to mobilize, requires trained operators, mechanics and spare parts, and consumes large quantities of fuel which may not be readily available. Where feasible and appropriate, it may be possible to contract work to a highways contractor with an established workforce and equipment. In this case, follow the guidelines in Chapter 6 on working with contractors.

As in most emergency work, follow a staged approach, gradually improving on the immediate response. For example, a road may be formed initially by the clearing and widening of a path, with only short difficult stretches improved along the route. The road may be designed initially for one-way traffic only, with passing places, and upgraded later.

Adequate drainage and the selection of the correct materials are key aspects of road design. Drainage is by far the most important because uncontrolled water can cause erosion and waterlogging. Uncontrolled runoff from intense rainfall can erode an unpaved road in minutes, leaving it permanently impassable unless repaired. Standing water can cause waterlogging and stop traffic until the water drains and the soil dries out.

Box 18.1 Road drainage principles (refer to Figure 18.1)

Keep water off the running surface and clear of the road by:

Preventing water getting on the road (catchwater drains).

Getting the water off the road (suitable camber or diversion banks).

Getting water away from the road (side drainage).

Getting the water across the road (cross-drainage).

Control erosion of the road; of the ditches; of culverts and of adjacent land.

Control siltation in ditches and culverts.

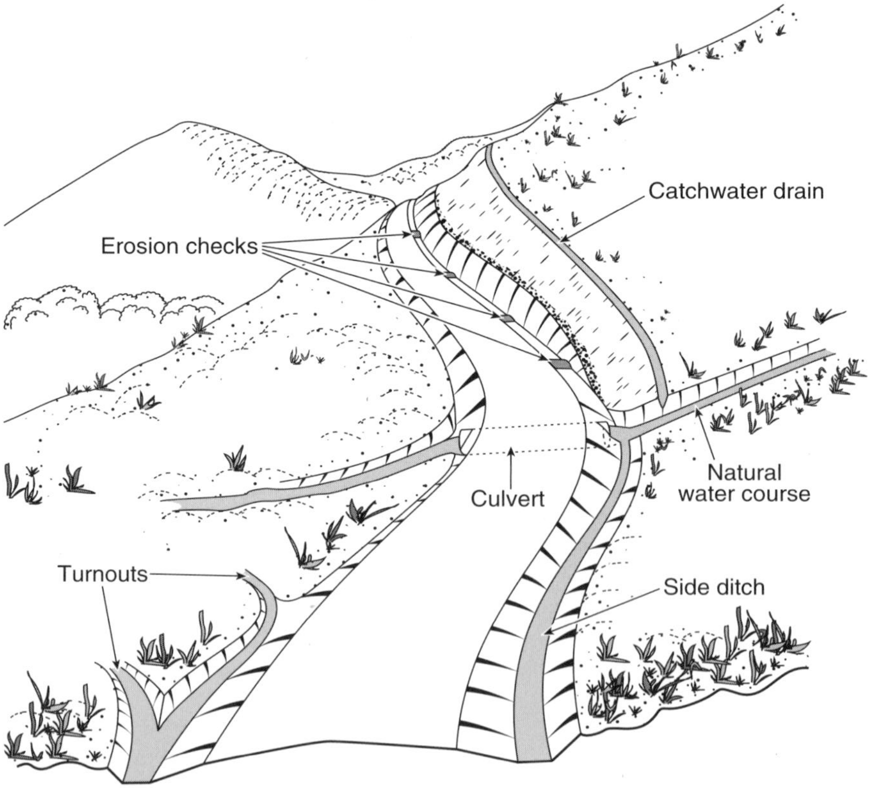

Figure 18.1 Typical road drainage features
Adapted from PIARC 1994

Most soils when dry form a satisfactory road. Appropriate materials for road construction may be obtained by routing the road through the right material (and avoiding the wrong ones) or by haulage. Haulage is time-consuming and expensive and should be avoided if possible.

Section 18.3 deals with the details of road design and construction.

18.2 Assessing existing roads and crossings

In many relief operations, especially in remote rural areas, roads and crossings will take loads which are heavier and more frequent than the traffic to which they are normally subjected. Therefore, assess the capacity of the roads, bridges, culverts, fords and drifts to ensure that they can consistently take the loads required. The early detection of defects or potential problems, together with prompt remedial action, can sustain a lifeline which may otherwise be broken.

18.2.1 Inspection and inventory

Assess the condition of an existing road by travelling along the route. Draw a strip map inventory as a record of the assessment (Figure 18.2). Draw from the bottom of the page and keep a record of the kilometre reading. This orientation is easier to read and follow when travelling along the road.

Add to the information by asking the drivers where they get stuck and which sections are the most difficult or dangerous to travel according to the season or weather conditions. Ask local people about their experience of access in the region and what they see as the main problems with the road.

If possible, rather than simply noting the symptoms, identify the cause of deterioration in a road.

Use the inventory to draw up a priority list of works so that the road can be incrementally reinstated by concentrating on the worst areas first – spot improvement. Table 18.1 indicates road features to check.

Follow up the inventory with further searches. Enlist the help of local residents to locate particular soils. Investigate the local supply outlets for manufactured or processed materials (cement, reinforcement bar, sawn timber, gabion baskets – or wire for making them) and obtain prices for budgeting purposes.

18.2.2 Local capacity

Local government departments

Find out the existing responsibility and capability for road construction and maintenance by speaking with the local authority responsible for highways such as the Public Works Department (PWD), Ministry of Works (MoW), or Highway Authority. Local authorities may not have a budget for extensive emergency work but they may have the staff, equipment and capability to carry it out. Consider funding them to do the work. Check that this is politically acceptable before making definite arrangements locally. Building an access road for recently arrived refugees may mean the diversion of scarce resources away from ongoing development work and may cause resentment among local people. Even if the local authorities cannot be directly involved, continue to liaise with them and make use of their local knowledge and advice. They are likely to be responsible, eventually, for the maintenance of what is constructed.

In some cases, governments establish their own refugee agency, with their own personnel responsible for the different sectors. A disadvantage of this is that the local authority departments may be bypassed.

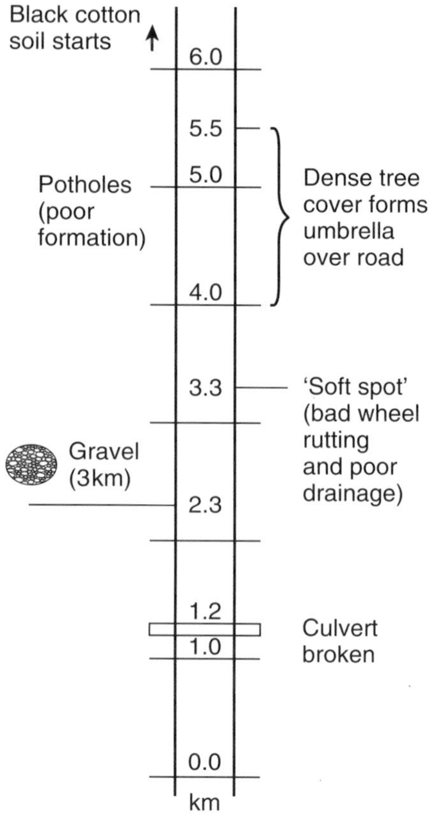

Figure 18.2 A road inventory

Contractors

Investigate the possibility of letting specific work to contractors. Assess their capability by visiting examples of their work and inspect their equipment (refer to Section 6.3).

Local development work, labour and skilled staff

Check with local development agencies on local development issues and on their approach to labouring work. Emergency activities can often undermine existing development initiatives. Check any minimum (or maximum) wages and the relevant labour laws. Roads are sometimes constructed on a food-for-work (FFW) basis, but it is not always appropriate. FFW may not be compatible with existing development approaches and the system gives the engineer little control over the labour force.

Establish the range of skills which could be recruited through local government departments, contractors and local development agencies. This will give an indication of the level and amount of training which may be required.

Ownership and access to materials

Find out what the laws are regarding access to and ownership of land and materials. There will be both legal and traditional procedures and, although they may take valuable time, they must be followed. For example, some person, or a traditional spirit, may have control over river sand and gravel. They may simply require a token offering, or appeasement, before the materials can be extracted. Failure to observe such a practice may result in protracted negotiations, the denial of access or subsequent labour problems.

Table 18.1 Features to check on a road inventory

Feature	*Notes*
Alignment	Are there alternative routes, or detours, to avoid soft spots and hazards? Can the road be re-routed along the watershed to avoid troublesome low-lying areas? (see 18.3.3).
Road width	Is it acceptable to reinstate only a narrow (say, 4 m wide) strip with passing places? It can be widened later if necessary.
Gradient	Is the road too steep (>8%) in any section for the expected vehicles and loads?
Drainage	Will the existing drainage be sufficient, when reinstated, or are further drainage works necessary or advisable? Check road profile, side drains and cross drainage (see relevant sections below).
Crossings	Check all bridges (18.2.3), culverts, fords and drifts.
Load bearing capacity	Is the road capable of taking the expected traffic (such as regular convoys of heavy food trucks)?
Running surface	Dust, corrugations, potholes, soft spots?
Materials	Include information on the type and location of soils (sand, stone, gravel) and timber.

18.2.3 Bridge assessment

Bridge assessment and inspection is needed to:

- Assess the load bearing capacity of the bridge.
- If capacity is not sufficient – provide information to a specialist for determining what (if any) temporary remedial work is needed to increase the capacity.
- Supply information needed for longer-term maintenance and repair.

Load bearing assessment

In a disaster situation, there is usually little time, and often no specialist, to carry out a precise engineering assessment of the load carrying capacity of a bridge. This section introduces two approaches to bridge assessment, which can be used when a quick decision must be made on whether to allow a load to cross a bridge: the Military Load Classification system, and inspection and trial. Guidelines are given on how to consult a specialist remote from the emergency. Figure 18.3 shows the principal components of a bridge and Figure 18.4 gives the critical dimensions of I-beams.

The Military Load Classification of bridges The methods adopted for the load classification of bridges by the military in Europe may also be applicable in relief operations. The procedures involve the allocation of a Military Load Class (MLC) number to the bridges and vehicles concerned. If the MLC of a

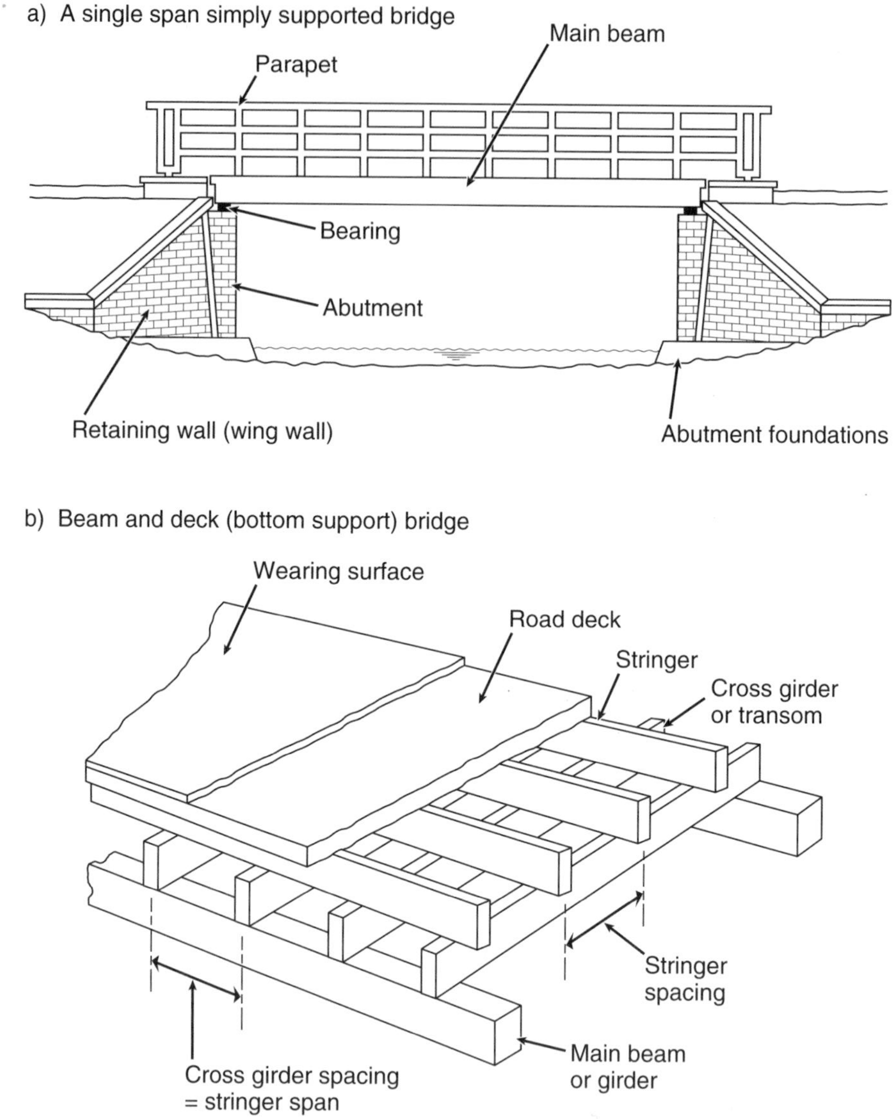

Figure 18.3 Components of a bridge

vehicle is less than, or equal to, the bridge classification, the vehicle can safely cross the bridge. The methods are quick (less than one hour) and involve only simple measurements. Tables and graphs are used to avoid the need for complex calculations. The approach is limited to bridges with a clear span of less than 40 metres. Certain bridges are not covered (such as suspension bridges, arches in metal or concrete, portal spans, trusses) but they can still be classified, based on the strength of the deck, stringer and girder systems only.

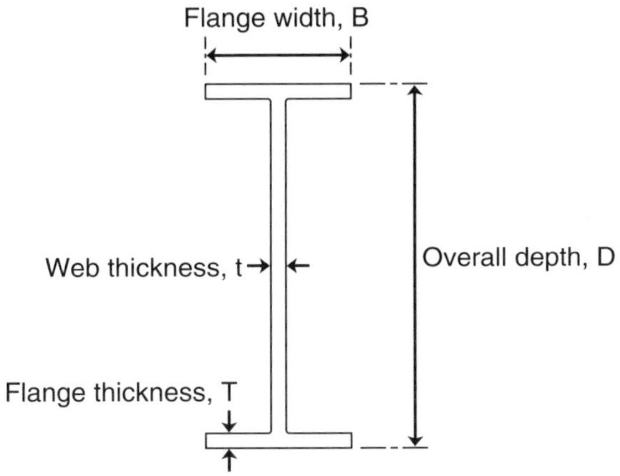

Figure 18.4 Critical dimensions of steel I-beams

The classification methods are too extensive to include in this book and brief extracts are unhelpful without guidance and the accompanying tables for both bridges and vehicles. It is therefore recommended that if bridge assessment is likely to be an aspect of relief work in a particular situation, a copy of the Military Load Classification Manual used by the British Army (MoD, 1994) should be obtained. RedR holds a number of manuals in its London office for use by relief workers.

Inspection and trial In the absence of an experienced bridge engineer or the Military Load Classification manual referred to above, an assessment should follow a logical sequence of inspection and trial loading. Referring to Figure 18.3, consider the following:

- Is there any locally available information? (from the Highway Department or Public Works Department).
- Is the bridge in current use:
  - By vehicles? (what gross weight, axle load, wheel load?)
  - By animals, animal carts or pedestrians?
- How does the bridge work:
  - What are the main structural members?
  - What are the secondary members?
- Are the main members damaged, missing, rotten, corroded, poorly maintained or in good condition?
- Are the secondary members sound and secure in their fixings to the main members?
- Is the deck surface sound and in place?
- Are the foundations, abutments and piers showing signs of failure? (Refer to the later section on 'Bridge inspection').
- What is the degree of risk in the event of a collapse and is a test under a vehicle load feasible:

- Low risk over a shallow drainage channel?
- High risk over a deep gorge?

If the initial inspection shows that the structure is sound in all significant respects, base your assessment of its capacity on local knowledge of loads previously carried and monitor the crossing of a typical load:

- Look carefully for signs of cracking or distortion of the deck.
- Look at the secondary and main members for signs of deflection.
- Any deflection should not exceed 1/300 of the span of the member under any loading.

Trials should be carried out on beam bridges (as shown in Figure 18.3) which will fail gradually by deflections or cracking in the structure. Never carry out a trial loading on a truss structure (including 'Bailey bridges') as these structures can collapse suddenly without any indication that maximum load has been reached.

Restrict the loading on any suspect bridge to one vehicle at a time to avoid excessive convoy loads and braking forces.

Consult a specialist when in doubt

Consulting a specialist With modern communications by telephone, e-mail and fax, a rapid response can be obtained from a specialist provided sufficient essential information can be given:

- Provide a sketch of the bridge with key dimensions: span; depth of cross members; spacing of main beams; depth (and shape) of main beams; width of main beams; web thickness (I-beam); flange thickness (I-beam). The sketch need not be to scale but should be in proportion.
- Draw key elements in greater detail to identify sizes in every aspect.
- Where possible, take photographs of the bridge and fax or e-mail copies to the specialist.
- Send as much information as possible on the condition of the bridge (see the detailed inspection checklist in Box 18.2).

Bridge inspection

Both the initial assessment and the longer-term monitoring of a bridge will require an inspection of critical features. The checklist in Box 18.2 provides basic bridge inspection guidelines (adapted from TRRL, 1988). Refer to Figure 18.3 to identify some of the terms used.

18.3 Design and construction of unpaved roads

18.3.1 First considerations

The design and construction of paved roads is unlikely to be a priority in an emergency response. Therefore this section deals solely with unpaved road

Box 18.2 Detailed inspection checklist for bridge assessment

Bridge approaches, deck and parapets

- Bumps in approach road (increases potential impact load).
- Road drainage near bridge.
- Standing water on the deck – blocked or damaged deck drains.
- Damaged, loose or worn deck surface.
- Timber deck: gap between planks; decay or insect attack; missing, loose or damaged running strips.
- Parapets loose or otherwise in a dangerous condition.

Superstructure

- Impact damage to beams, girders, trusses or bracings.
- Concrete beams: cracking; spalling; reinforcement corrosion; poor concrete.
- Steel girders or trusses and bracings: corrosion; bent or damaged joints or bracings; bends in webs, flanges, stiffeners, truss members or bracings; loose bolts or rivets; cracking of steel members.
- Timber beams: decay or insect attack; splitting timber; separation of laminations (if beams laminated); loose or corroded nails, screws or other fixings.
- Timber trusses: decay or insect attack; splitting timber; loose deck to truss connections; loose or corroded bolts or pins at joints; bends in truss members; damaged or corroded steel parts.
- Underside of deck: check similar features as for those listed above.

Bearings

- Drainage onto bearing shelf.
- Room for the bridge span to move.
- Bearing seated properly.
- Bridge span seated properly on bearing.
- Damaged bedding mortar.
- Rubber bearings: splitting, tearing or cracking of rubber; damaged or loose fixed bearing bolts or pins.
- Metal bearings: parts properly seated and free to move; sliding surfaces and lubrication system; corrosion, cracks or bends in metal parts.

Abutment, wing walls and retaining walls

- Erosion or scour near abutment or retaining walls.
- Damage to caissons or piles.
- Movement of abutment or retaining walls.
- Debris against abutment.
- Vegetation growing on or in an abutment.
- Water leaking through expansion joints.
- Weepholes working or water seeping through the abutment.
- Concrete: cracking; spalling; reinforcement corrosion; poor concrete.
- Masonry: cracking; bulging; poor pointing; deterioration of bricks or stones.
- Gabions: settlement or bulging; damage to gabion wires or ties.
- Timber: decay; insect attack; splitting timber; loose or corroded binding cables or fixing spikes.

Embankments and fill in front of abutments

- Scour at base of slopes.
- Slip or erosion of fill.
- Cracking of road or embankment edge.
- Piping through fill.
- Movement or deterioration of piled walls.
- Stone pitching slope protection: cracking; poor pointing; scour or erosion at edge; pieces broken off.
- Gabion slope protection: movement of gabions; damage to gabion wires or ties.

(Continued)

- Rip-rap slope protection: in place or washed away; bed settlement.

Piers
- Scour or damage to base of piers.
- Movement of pier.
- Impact damage.
- Debris against pier.
- Vegetation growing on pier.
- Water leaking past expansion joint.
- Concrete piers: cracking; spalling; reinforcement corrosion; poor concrete.
- Masonry piers: deterioration; cracking; poor pointing.
- Steel piers: debris; corrosion; bent members; loose bolts or rivets; cracking.
- Timber piers: debris; decay; insect attack; splitting timber; loose bolts or pins at joints; bent pier timbers; damaged or corroded steel parts.

The river
- Blockages in the waterway: debris or growth under the bridge.
- Change of river course upstream.
- River training works: damage to bank beyond upstream works; damage to piles, gabions or loss of rip-rap.
- Scour holes in the river bed.
- Bed protection and aprons: as for slope protection above.

Bailey bridges (refer to Figure 18.25)
- Missing: safety pins; panel pins; bolts; rakers or tie plates; sway braces; horizontal bracing frames; transom clamps.
- Loose: bolts; sway braces; horizontal bracing frames; transom clamps.
- Wear at stringer to transom seating.
- Cracking.
- Bends in members.
- Corrosion.
- Settlement of bearings.
- Damage to bearings or baseplates.
- Maximum vertical sag.
- Maximum horizontal bend.

Culverts
- Debris, vegetation, etc. in or near culvert.
- Settlement of the culvert.
- Scour at ends of culvert or at edge of the apron.
- Concrete culvert: cracking; spalling; reinforcement corrosion; poor concrete.
- Corrugated steel culvert: change of shape; corrosion; loose or corroded bolts.
- Damage to culvert aprons or headwall.
- Movement of headwall.

Adapted from TRRL, 1988

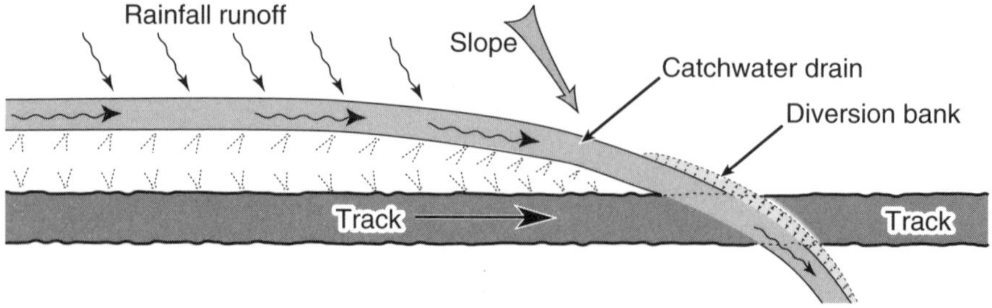

Figure 18.5 A catchwater drain diverting rainfall runoff across a track

construction using labour-based methods. Refer to Chapter 6 for guidelines on the management of labour-based construction. If working with contractors, see also Appendix 5 for sample contract documents. Three types of unpaved roads are covered:

- Earth roads: good for less than 50 vehicles/day. If road passes over poor soils (such as slippery clay of poor load bearing capacity) gravelling may be necessary.
- Gravelled roads: up to 200 vehicles/day.
- Improved tracks: intermittent light traffic. Improved tracks are suitable where an engineered road is not absolutely necessary or as a first stage in the improvement of access. Tracks for light and intermittent traffic can provide access to facilities such as water abstraction and treatment sites, food distribution centres and clinics.

The key design parameter in emergency road construction is the maintenance of access – essentially, the maintenance of good drainage to prevent erosion or waterlogging. Allowing high vehicle speeds is a much lower priority, so there is much less emphasis on the correct geometric alignment to allow such speeds. In designing and constructing unpaved earth and gravelled roads you will need to consider the following:

- Planning and monitoring.
- Route selection and clearance.
- Drainage and erosion control.
- Road building materials.
- Equipment and tools.
- Earthworks.

Details on these items are given below.

Safety on site

As with all engineering activities, safety should be a key consideration. For the basic principles of safety management see Section 6.1.4. The main cause of accidents in labour-based road construction is people working too closely together; for example, a misdirected pick-axe into someone's hand. Allow a distance of at least 2 m between workers involved in excavation. Plan work so that gangs are not working too closely to each other or following behind too quickly.

Beware of employing the very old or the very young, who may not be able to cope safely with the work, and who may pose a risk to other workers.

Drivers should drive carefully near labour-intensive works and settlements, especially among rural people unused to traffic. Ensure that there is a first aid kit available at each site. Ensure that all accidents are treated and reported.

18.3.2 Planning road construction

In the planning of road construction:

- Look at improving the worst sections of road first – spot improvements – and gradually upgrade the route where necessary.

- Mobilize resources. Recruit and train staff and labour. Procure tools and equipment. Obtain materials through purchase and negotiation.
- Design detailed solutions based on the available resources.
- Establish depots, stores, staff quarters (if required) and security.
- Implement construction activities. See the 'detailed work plan' below.
- Implement a maintenance operation.
- Liaise with: local people, the local government administration and the department responsible for roads (MoW, PWD), the political establishment, other agencies, and relief co-ordinating bodies.

Detailed work plan

The engineer cannot closely manage all aspects of labour-based road construction as there are too many people involved. Delegate day-to-day supervision to adequately trained technical assistants and supervisors. Plan the detailed work and expected work output with the supervisory staff and adjust the timetable on the basis of experience. The following is a typical sequence of activities:

- Clear bush and trees.
- Clear scrub.
- Remove topsoil.
- Dig catchwater drains as required.
- Remove/bury/break boulders.
- Dig side ditches and begin to form road profile.
- Slope side ditches.
- Camber the profile and compact the earth (compaction is recommended but is frequently neglected).
- Dig turnouts (see Section 18.3.4).
- Construct cross-drainage (start with 'dips' in the road and improve in stages).
- Carry out erosion protection work (drains and slopes).
- Finish details – masonry headwalls, etc.
- Establish a maintenance programme.
- Replace dips with culverts or improved crossings.
- Gravel the running surface (at a later date, after natural settlement and compaction).

Allocate set tasks for individuals or a gang to complete – a length of drain to be dug or a quantity of soil to be excavated. The incentive in task work is that when the task is complete, and the quality of work has been approved by the supervisor, the worker can finish for the day. Encourage the recruitment of women. Experience has shown that, generally, women are more likely to complete a task well than men.

Table 18.2 provides guidelines on typical task rates. Remember that they must be adapted to the climate, soils, and the health and fitness of the labourers. Base planning and the setting of tasks on locally measured task rates wherever possible. For planning purposes, use half the value of the rates shown. On the job, set the workers the standard task rate quoted in Table 18.2 and adapt with experience. Tasks cannot easily be increased once they are set too

Table 18.2 A typical work plan or production record

Site:__________ Date of work:____ Supervisor:_____ Date of form:_____

Activity	*Standard task rate*	*Gang*	*Output (O) m^3*	*Actual task rate (O/I)*	*Input (I) wd*	*Comments*
Clear bush	m/^{3}wd					
Excavate topsoil	5.0 m^3/wd					
Excavate ordinary soil	2.5 m^3/wd					
Excavate hard soil or gravel	2.5 m^3/wd					
Excavate and load common fill	5.0 m^3/wd					
Haul common fill up to 200 m	5.0 m^3/wd					
Spread gravel or common fill	20 m^3/wd					
Install 600 mm culvert	1.5 m/wd					
Install 900 mm culvert	1.0 m/wd					
Erosion checks	10/wd					
Mix and place concrete	1.0 m^3/wd					
Erect concrete masonry	1.0 m^3/wd					
Haul gravel	m^3/td					
Dayworks	/wd					

wd = worker day; td = tractor or tipper day. Where rates not given, measure on site.
Location of each activity:
Clearing_________ Formation________ Ditches_________ Gravelling_________
From Antoniou *et al.*, 1990

low. Give supervisors a daily work plan based on task rates. They should then keep a record of actual work output.

Monitoring: reporting and record keeping

Refer to Chapter 6 for general points about record keeping and reporting. In particular, supervisors should keep accurate records of the large numbers of people who may be employed and paid in labour-based construction. Providing the supervisors with clear, simple forms will ease this task. Table 18.2 can be adapted for production records. The table can be used for daily, weekly or monthly periods. Establish a reporting routine so that supervisors report to the engineer regularly.

18.3.3 Route selection and clearance

Selection and setting out

Roads often develop from footpaths between villages and are improved along a similar route. Do not deviate from existing routes unless necessary – the alignment is probably as good as you will get and the track will be well compacted. Where the existing route is clearly inappropriate, a new route should be selected. Care in the choice of route can greatly reduce the amount of work required for construction and maintenance. In selecting a new route consider the following:

- Drainage – a route which runs along a ridge benefits from natural drainage. Look where rainfall runoff water might come from (such as areas of exposed rock) and where it might drain to. Consider the effect of drainage onto farmers' land – drainage from roads can initiate severe erosion.
- Soil type: avoid black cotton, heavy clay soils or deep sandy areas.
- Gradient: try not to exceed a maximum gradient of 8 per cent.
- Clearance: consider the amount of bush clearance needed – this can be a time consuming task if there are many large trees and rocks. Check the ownership of trees as compensation may need to be paid if they are to be felled.

An existing road may follow high ground for part of the route but dip into lowland to serve villages along the route. Look at the possibility of joining up the highland sections to form a 'high-way' by following the watershed. When surveying the route, try to get an overall view of the terrain by viewing the route from higher ground. It is often easier to see important features at a distance. For larger road projects, dig trial pits along the route to assess the characteristics and suitability of subsoil materials. Identify the sources of road building materials along the route. Use existing quarries or establish borrow pits or new quarries.

To set out the road or track, simply peg the centre line. Supervisors then peg the edges of the track from the central pegs using a measuring stick cut to the length of half the carriageway width.

Clearing the route

Clear bush either side of the track to allow for working space and drainage. Wherever possible, preserve trees and vegetation to bind soils against erosion. But remove trees and overhanging branches close to the road to allow the track to dry out quickly after rain, especially for a road in a north-south orientation. If possible, remove small trees by their roots using draught animals and a rope. Fell large trees and remove the tree stumps. Tree stumps can be removed by burning or by digging and pulling with hand winches, draught animal or tractor power. Tree roots and hidden stumps which remain on unpaved tracks will be exposed through erosion and cause tyre punctures.

Large rocks can be awkward to move and time consuming to break up. If a large rock cannot easily be broken by hand tools, move it by winch and crow bar. If this fails, carefully dig a hole next to the rock (take care it does not slip), roll it into the hole using crow bars and backfill. As a last resort, rocks may be cracked by heating with fire and quenching with water. This needs a lot of fuel, water and time to be successful. The cracked rock will still have to be broken with sledgehammers.

18.3.4 Drainage and erosion control

As the route is being cleared, install some form of water control. One heavy downpour of rain can wash away whole sections of unprotected track in a matter of minutes. Control erosion and waterlogging by good drainage (see Figure 18.1). Remember:

- Prevent water getting on the road (catchwater drains).
- Get the water off the road (surface drainage).
- Get water away from the road (side drainage).
- Get the water across the road (cross drainage).

Catchwater drains Where the runoff from higher ground causes substantial flooding of the track or road, excavate a catchwater drain to divert the water at a diversion bank or other cross-drain (see Figure 18.5). To avoid failure of the edge of the road, dig the catchwater drain 3–5 m from the road edge if possible.

Surface drainage on tracks – diversion banks To get water off a track, use diversion banks. This is a small rise across a track which diverts water from the track to a side drain (see Figure 18.6) which channels the water safely away. Banks should be 250 m apart on flat ground and as close as 30 m apart in steep terrain in a wet climate (Hindson, 1983). Use natural diversion banks wherever possible: the remains or edges of ant hills and slight rises in the ground. Diversion banks force vehicles to slow down, which can be frustrating to drivers but may improve safety.

Where water crosses a track, site diversion banks immediately downhill on the track to discourage any flow along the track. Much runoff water is channelled on to a track by footpaths, animal and farm tracks which feed into the main track. Therefore, place small diversion banks across the feeder tracks to dissipate flow from higher ground into the surrounding vegetation.

On steep inclines in a cutting (such as an approach to a stream) divert the water into side drains running along the edge of the track. This prevents gulley erosion in the main section of the track.

Fill natural dips in the track to prevent the ponding of water. Regularly fill wheel ruts before they create impassable 'soft spots'.

Road surface drainage – road profiling To drain the water off the road, the surface is given the profile shown in Figure 18.7. For earth and gravel roads, choose a camber or crossfall of 7 per cent. Unless compacted, this will often bed down to a slope of about 5 per cent. In flat terrain, the road is given an equal

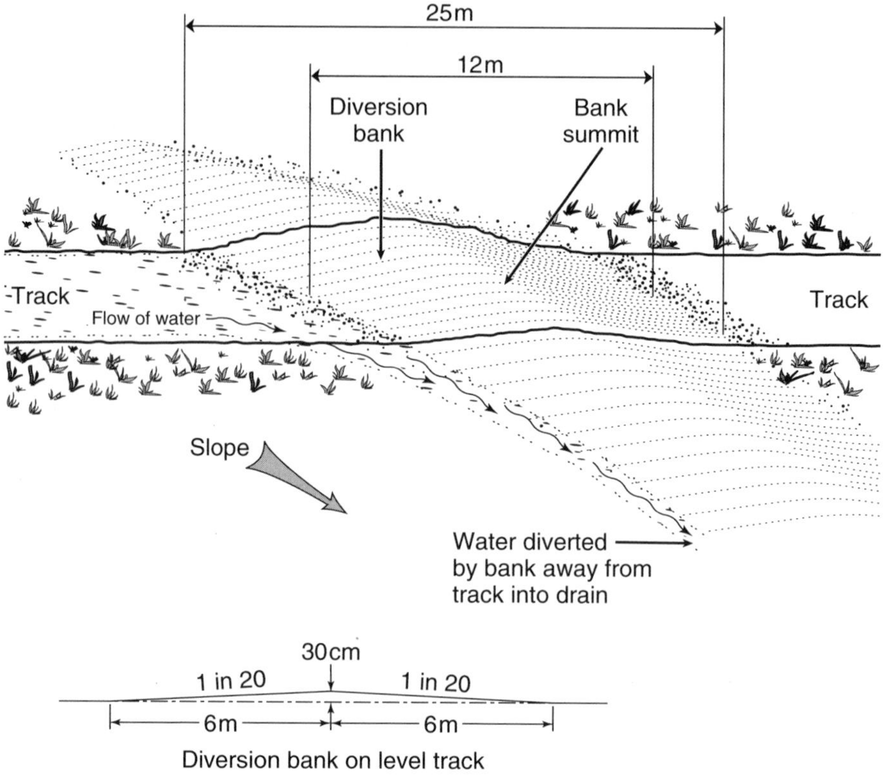

Figure 18.6 A diversion bank and drain
From Hindson, 1983

camber on both sides of the centre line. Once the route has been cleared and set out, the procedure for constructing the road profile is:

- Remove topsoil if it is highly organic and there is a better load bearing soil close to the surface.
- Spread soil dug from the ditches on to the road surface to give the correct profile.
- Choose a ditch size which will give sufficient soil for the camber required.
- Check the profile using a camber board and spirit level (Figure 18.7).

In hilly terrain, do not go directly up a gradient greater than 8 per cent but traverse the side of the hillside. Drain towards an inner ditch to avoid erosion of the outside of the road. The excavation of an inner ditch can take time so if time is short do not excavate this ditch as runoff from the road will erode its own ditch over time. Return later and upgrade. Arrange adequate cross-drainage (see Section 18.5) from the inner ditch and control erosion at cross-drainage discharges. Try to drain into natural water courses. In steep terrain (gradient > 10 per cent), cut the whole road into the hillside. Do not cut and fill, as the fill on the outside of the road will be unstable. Consider the need for a

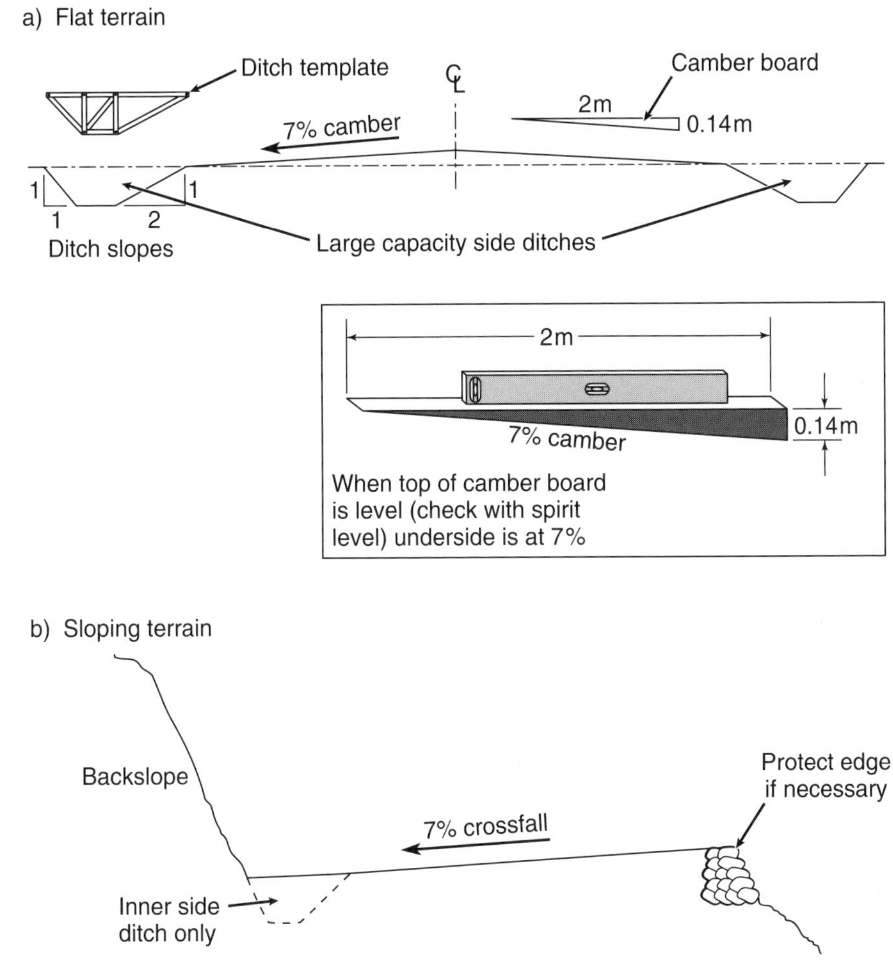

Figure 18.7 Road profiles in flat and sloping terrain

wide road against the increased excavation required and the time available. To increase access quickly, first construct a single lane road with passing places. Widen the road later.

In very uneven rocky terrain, the road profile can be formed by filling within masonry walls. However, this is very time consuming and laborious. Rocky sections will remain passable, even though they may be uncomfortable and slow, so avoid improving until more vulnerable sections have been constructed first.

Side drainage Provide side drainage by excavating ditches or drains. The size of the ditch is determined by the amount of soil required to form the surface profile and the amount of water drained from the road surface and the adjacent land. Estimate the adequacy of the drain, after sizing for the road surface material, by observation of the terrain and similar drains, and seeking local knowledge of flooding. Calculations based on rainfall intensity and runoff coefficients may be unreliable and impractical in the circumstances. See Figure 18.8 for a typical ditch profile.

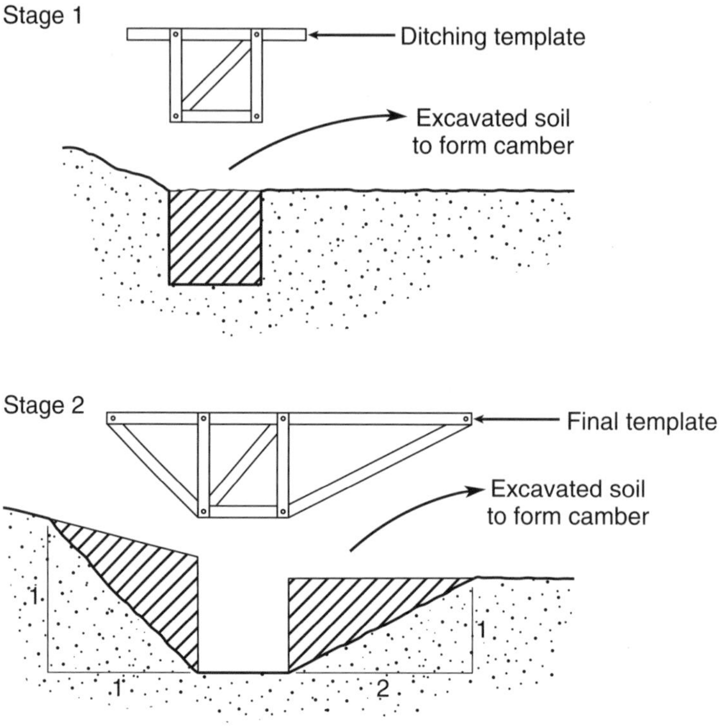

Figure 18.8 Typical side ditch profile

To excavate the side drains or ditches:

- Each digger should have measuring sticks for the depth and width of the ditch.
- Dig a rectangular ditch to the correct depth.
- Shape the ditch to the correct slopes.
- Supervisors check the finished ditch with a template.

The recommended gradients for side drainage are:
Minimum 2 per cent; Maximum 3 per cent without scour (erosion) protection.

Make simple erosion checks using lines of large single stones or wooden stakes (Figure 18.9). Silt will build up behind the checks and reduce the gradient. Place smaller stones below each check to prevent erosion downstream. Encourage grass growth along drains to help bind the soil together. Grass can also be encouraged on the road surface if it can be kept short. Table 18.3 gives guidelines on the spacing of erosion checks.

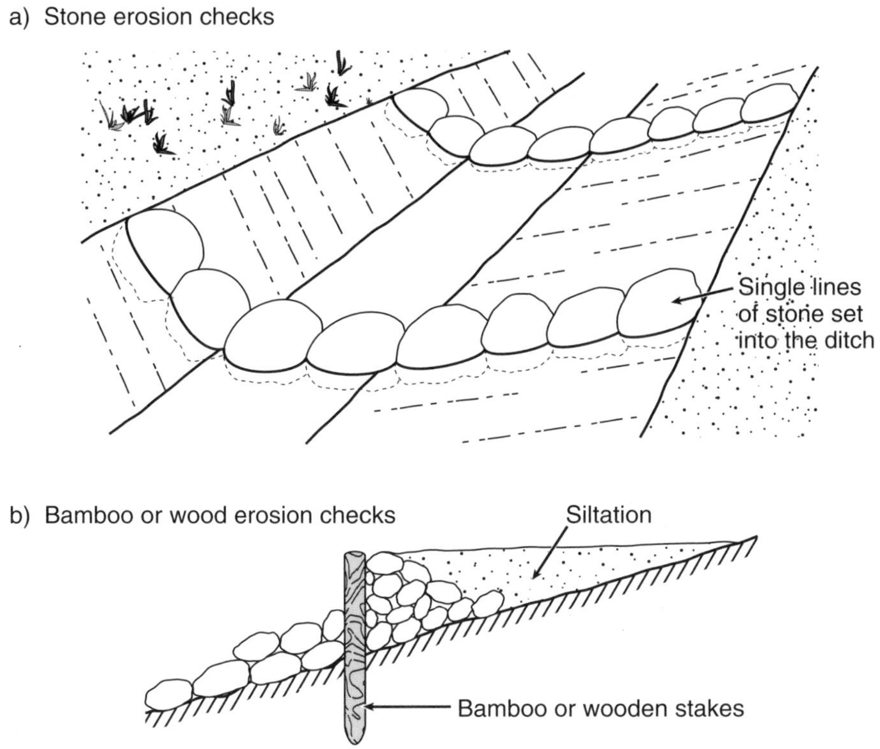

Figure 18.9 Simple erosion checks

Table 18.3 Guidelines for the spacing of erosion checks

Gradient, %	*Spacing, m*
> 10	5
5–10	10
3–5	20
< 3	Not necessary

From Antoniou *et al.*, 1990

Turnouts (mitre drains) Turnouts or mitre drains take water away from the side drains. They are normally set at an angle of about 30° (see Figure 18.10). They should have a minimum gradient of 2 per cent to prevent silting but not be too steep to cause erosion. To avoid erosion damage to farmland, look for well protected areas on which to discharge (such as thick bush), fan out the flow and, if necessary, discharge onto stones. Include turnouts as often as possible (see Table 18.4).

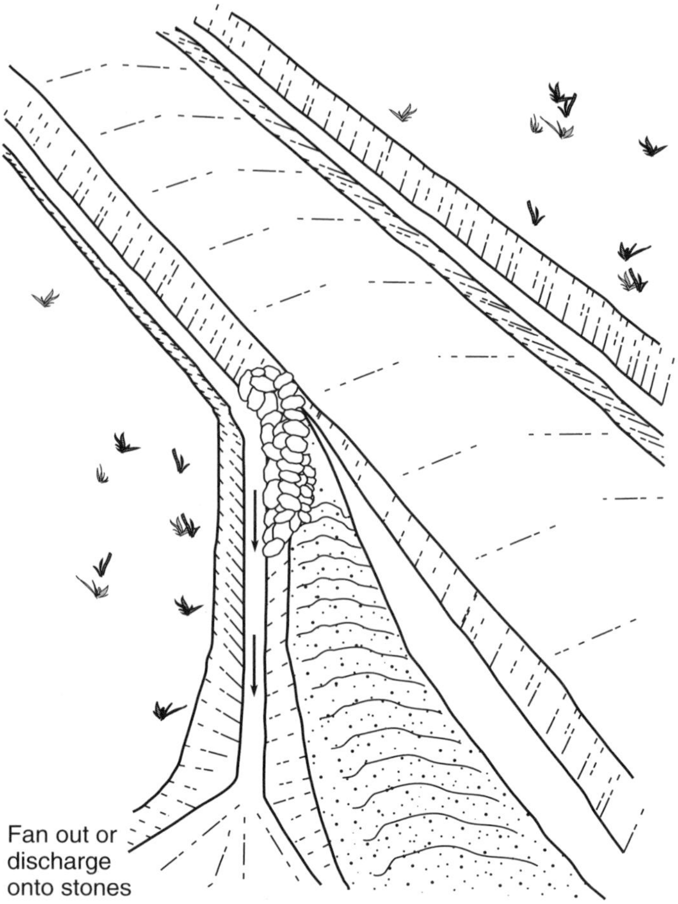

Figure 18.10 Turnouts

Table 18.4 Guidelines for the spacing of turnouts

Road gradient, %	*Maximum turnout spacing, m*	*Remarks*
12	40	If exceeded,
10	80	scouring
8	120	will
6	160	occur
4	200	
1–2	50	If exceeded, silting will occur

From Antoniou *et al.*, 1990

Cross-drainage It is essential to provide adequate cross-drainage to prevent the build-up of runoff water in the side ditches. An unrelieved build-up of water could quickly damage a road. A raised road can also act as a dam, and in flat terrain, the tailback of water can cause serious local flooding. Therefore, make provision for adequate cross-drainage as the road is constructed and do not leave it until a later date because of the emergency. Cross-drainage is a major subject and is referred to separately in Section 18.5.

18.3.5 Road building materials

There are two ways in which you can obtain suitable materials for road construction: either transport them to the road, or route the road over suitable materials. Transporting road building materials is a major operation and unlikely to be applicable on a large scale in an emergency. Similarly, the use of concrete or asphalt is unlikely to be appropriate.

Table 18.5 gives some information on the suitability of different road materials.

Table 18.5 Some comments on road building materials

Material	*Comments*
Organic topsoil (usually removed)	Usually removed before forming a road surface but do not remove if subsoil is the same material or if it is undisturbed sandy soil which can form a strong layer
Black cotton soil (avoid)	Very firm when dry but expands greatly when wet and becomes slurry-like. Very difficult to travel over when wet
Well drained clayey loam (good)	Where possible route the road over a well drained, clayey loam with a good sand content
Clay (avoid)	Good running surface when dry but slippery and maybe impassable when wet
River gravel (needs surfacing)	Good road base but a very poor running surface. Cover a river gravel base with a 150mm layer of good surface material
Deep sand (avoid)	Very difficult to stabilize. Either mix the sand with clay and gravel or turn over with cement. Both methods are arduous and take time
Mixed gravel (good)	A good gravel for road surfaces contains about 50% stone for strength , 40% sand to fill voids and 10% clay to bind the rest. Moisture content should be 10–16%, moist but not wet
Laterite (good)	Use it if available but avoid mixing with clays which are often associated with thin layers of laterite pebbles
Consolidated shale (poor in wet)	Good running surface when dry but slippery when wet.

Refer to Appendix 20 for simple soil tests

If possible, divert a route to avoid black cotton soil. If a diversion is not possible, attempt to form a protected dry crust above the water table. There are various ways of doing this:

- Construct and gravel an embankment using a suitable geotextile (such as Terram 2000) for drainage covered with a butyl rubber seal (see Figure 18.11).

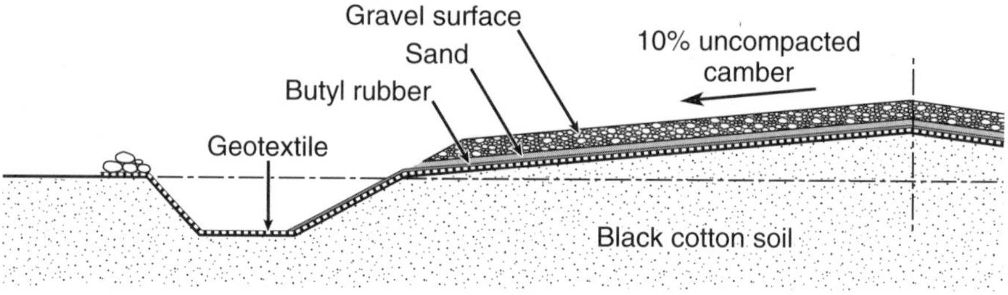

Figure 18.11 Road formation over black cotton soil

- If a suitable geotextile and butyl rubber are not available, try constructing an embankment using a gravel and coarse sand drainage layer on a mattress of woven timber and brushwood. A 150 mm minimum layer of gravel is essential. Construct to a 10 per cent (uncompacted) camber.

If vehicles are stuck in black cotton soil, drier clay to improve traction can be found just below the wet surface.

18.3.6 Earthworks

Digging, moving and compacting

For most emergency situations, road construction will involve manual excavation, haulage and spreading of the road building material. Institute good safety practices (see 18.3.1) Use task rates, as indicated in Table 18.2, to estimate the number of workers required for excavating, hauling and spreading earth but adjust estimate based on local experience. In sloping ground, use slotting to calculate the volume of work involved in excavation. Cut a narrow slot to the depth required and determine the volume of excavation and the type of soil before setting the task rate.

Where side slopes have to be excavated, excavate in two stages. First excavate to a vertical face. Then excavate the back slope at an angle of 2:1 (vertical:horizontal). Step the back slope if it is greater than 2 m high.

Labour cannot haul any great distance – it is demoralizing to haul further than 50–100 m regularly. To haul gravel, use a tractor and trailer. Use simple, robust, non-tipping trailers. Where available hire tipper trucks. Table 18.6 gives hauling distance guidelines using light haulage equipment. The output per worker of hauling and unloading will vary according to the haulage distance.

People cannot physically concentrate enough energy to compact well. Therefore, use passing vehicles and construction vehicles to compact the road or leave it to the natural processes of settlement and compaction. A self-powered

Table 18.6 Haulage guidelines for road construction

Method of hauling	*Materials hauled*	*Hauling distance, m*
Shovelling	Soil, sand	0–10
Stretchers	Stones, soil, sand	0–50
Wheelbarrows	Soil, stone, sand	10–150
Animal carts	Soil, stone, sand, water	150–500
Tractors	Soil, stone, sand, water	500–800

From Antoniou *et al., 1990*

vibrating (dynamic) roller can be used. For example, a motorized, hand-controlled vibrating compactor can be carried in the back of a Land Rover. If using a compacting roller:

- Each layer to be compacted should not be greater than 150 mm thick.
- The roller should make about 10 passes along the line of the road.
- Where water is not available to aid compaction, spread and compact immediately after transporting the fill. Try to compact in the morning when material may still be damp.

Equipment and tools

Keep everything in scale. Do not mix heavy plant with labour. It can be demoralizing for a gang of labourers to see a machine achieve in one hour what they have been struggling to achieve all week. Machines work to different profiles (e.g. ditch shapes) and therefore it is often impractical to mix plant and labour.

As a general rule, resist donations of heavy plant, as they can become time consuming to manage and deploy. They can also consume large quantities of fuel, which may be in short supply. Without specialist servicing they will quickly deteriorate or break down. However, sufficient supervision vehicles (stable pick-ups) are important.

Hand tools will be used in large quantities. It is important to establish a rigid stores procedure, to be followed by everyone for the storage, replacement ordering, issue and return of hand tools (see Chapter 7 for stores procedures). The choice and number of hand tools will depend on their cost, strength, fitness for purpose, type of terrain and soil, the size of the work force, cultural suitability, appropriateness for use by both men and women, and availability. Find out what tools people like to use and buy good quality tools. It is false economy to try to save money by purchasing cheap tools. Table 18.7 is a guide to the tools that may be required for a small road project employing about 80 people. For rock breaking, tools such as wedges, tongs, plugs and feathers may be needed (see Figure 18.12) in addition to sledgehammers. Safety glasses should be provided for use when breaking rock.

18.4 Road repair and maintenance

This section deals mainly with labour-based remedial works and maintenance. However, there may be the opportunity to hire plant, such as a grader, from a

Table 18.7 Tools required for a small road project

Tools	*Number*	*Spare handles*
Hoes	50	5
Mattocks	10	2
Forked hoes	25	5
Pick-axes	15	2
Shovels	50	5
Miners' bars	5	–
Wheelbarrows	10	–
Bush knives	30	–
Slashers	10	–
Axes	10	5
Earth rammers	10	2
Rakes	10	2
Buckets	3	–

From Antoniou *et al.*, 1990

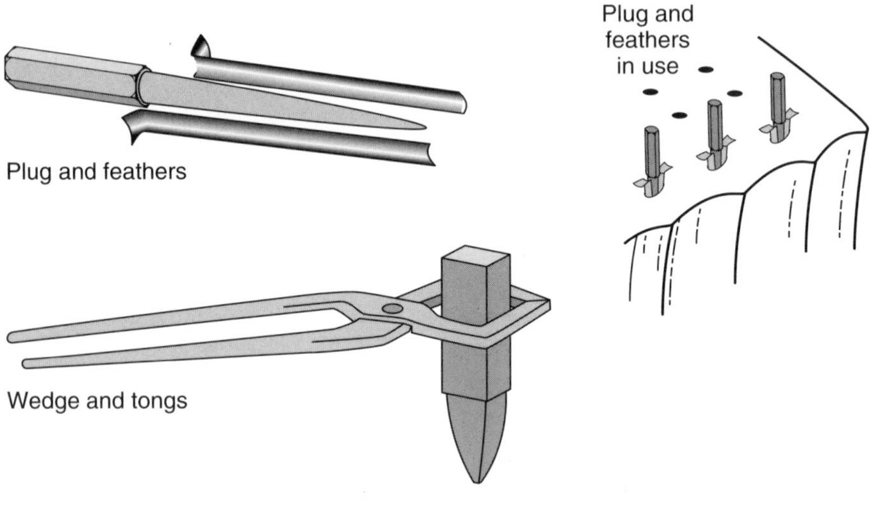

Figure 18.12 Stone and rock breaking tools

local contractor or local authority, so brief reference is also made to basic remedial and maintenance work using a motor grader.

Organization of routine maintenance

Appoint a technical assistant to plan, execute, monitor and report on maintenance activities. Organize routine maintenance by allocating sections of road to individual labourers. Appoint a senior labourer for daily supervision. A typical ratio is 1 supervisor to 10 labourers. Mark each section of road, typically 1.5 km per labourer, and issue each labourer with: a wheelbarrow, pickaxe, shovel, rake, hand rammer and watering can. Train the labourers to carry out the following maintenance activities, as required:

- Clean and re-form ditches.
- Repair and rebuild erosion checks.
- Clean culverts and vented fords.
- Repair headwalls.
- Patch potholes, ruts and gullies.
- Maintain the correct road camber and crossfall.

Repairs

Culverts Culverts must be kept clear and in good structural condition or the road may be washed out. Culvert maintenance involves clearing silt and debris from the waterway, controlling erosion and doing any necessary structural repairs. As soon as erosion at the outlet of the culvert is noticed, take action to prevent it by:

- Fanning out the discharge to reduce the velocity. This will involve some excavation and spreading of earth.
- Installing stone or gabions to dissipate the erosive energy of the water.

Further work to reduce the discharge velocity involves the addition or enlargement of culverts, a reduction in the drainage gradient or the construction of drop inlets or outlets. All these require reconstruction work.

Concrete culvert pipes may be damaged due to settlement and cracking. Grout minor cracks. Inspect culverts fabricated with corrugated steel rings for weakness due to rusting. See Section 18.5.2 for further guidelines.

In the absence of materials or time to rebuild culverts, convert them into drifts (see Section 18.5.3).

Masonry walls Inspect and repair or rebuild suspect masonry retaining walls before they completely collapse.

Soft spots Dig out and fill soft spots. If possible, drain them and allow them to dry out. In urgent cases, it is possible to form a temporary matting from felled trees and saplings placed at right angles to each other and bound together to form a raft. Where the road is wide and time is short, consider the repair of just a narrow section, rather than the complete width.

Potholes, ruts and road surface gullies Brush loose material and water from the area to be repaired. Cut away until sound material is reached and the sides are vertical. The fill should be similar to the existing surface material. Check the moisture content of the fill simply by squeezing the material in the hand. If it sticks together it is suitable but it should be discarded if water can be squeezed out. If the material is dry, wet both the material and the pothole with sprinkled water. Build up the pothole in layers about 70 mm deep. Compact each layer with a hand rammer so that the finished patch stands slightly above the surrounding surface.

Corrugations In the dry season, dragging can help to prevent the formation of corrugations and can remove light corrugations. Different types of drag are shown in Figure 18.13. Experiment to find the best way of dragging.

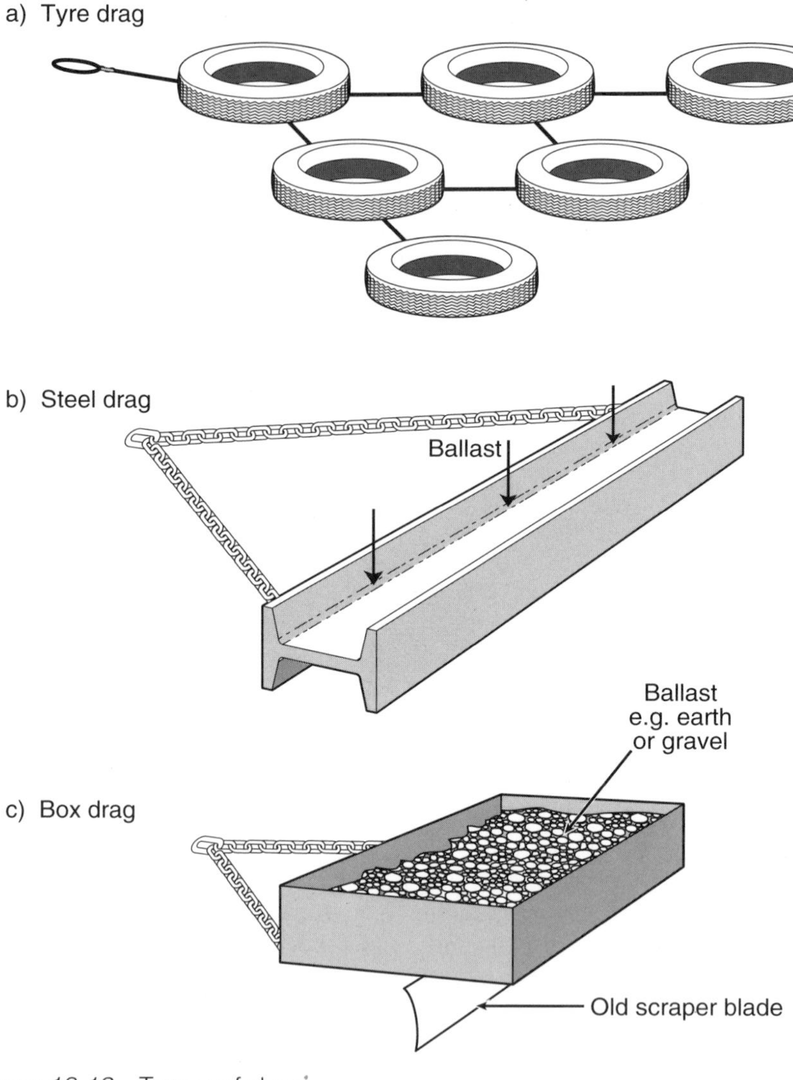

Figure 18.13 Types of drag

Make the tyre sledge from old heavy truck or tractor tyres. Tow at about 30 km/h with a tractor to remove light corrugations.

Make the box drag from an old grader blade firmly bolted to a wooden box. Make the steel drag from an old RSJ or length of rail – concrete blocks may be attached to add weight.

Vary the blade angle and the drag weight. Offsetting the weight to one end of the drag helps to maintain the camber. Tow at 5–30 km/h depending on the conditions. Several passes will be required.

In the dry season, a grader may be used as a drag to remove severe corrugations. When dragging, the grader starts at the middle of the road and drags to the side.

Grading

In moist conditions, the surface can be re-formed or graded. Water may be required if the soils are insufficiently moist for binding and compaction. Water and the necessary tankers must, therefore, be available. Grading is carried out in the following sequence:

- Use the grader's tines to loosen a hard surface.
- Use the grader's blade to cut to the bottom of the corrugations and leave a windrow of loose material in the centre of the road.
- If water is available, spray the graded section of the road (if it is still too dry) before spreading the windrow back across the road to give the correct camber.
- On completion, grade the other side of the road. Grade a bend flat, without a crown, with the outside of the bend higher than the inside. Typically, a grader works on a 200 m length of one side of the road at a time (TRRL, 1985).

A grader, which forms side ditches as shown in Figure 18.14, cannot maintain the shape of labour-constructed side ditches or turnouts and these must be maintained by hand.

Relocation of a sunken road

In flat terrain roads which are poorly constructed or maintained may be below the surface of the surrounding land. This can be a major problem as the road can immediately flood when it rains. A solution is to reroute the new road alongside the sunken road, using the sunken road as a drainage and seepage channel.

18.5 Crossings

This section deals with methods of crossing gaps or obstacles such as drainage channels, streams or rivers. It includes culverts, drifts and fords, emergency bridges and aerial ropeways.

18.5.1 Choice of crossing

The choice of crossing will depend on the time, skills, materials and equipment available for construction and the time period for which a lack of access can be tolerated. In selecting a crossing over a stream or river, a critical parameter is the level to which the water will rise at peak flow. This is related to the discharge of water and to the profile of the stream or river bed in the vicinity of

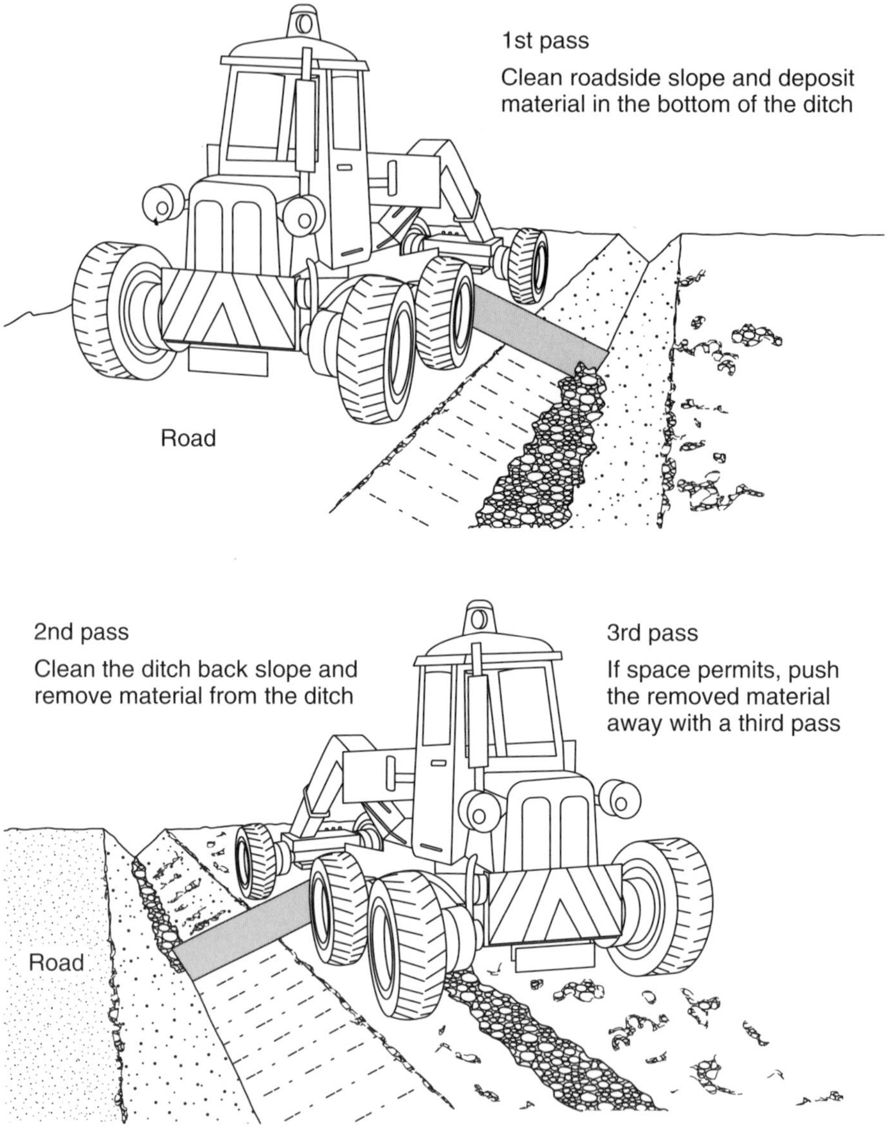
1st pass
Clean roadside slope and deposit material in the bottom of the ditch
Road
2nd pass
Clean the ditch back slope and remove material from the ditch
3rd pass
If space permits, push the removed material away with a third pass
Road

Figure 18.14 Maintaining side ditches with a grader

the crossing. The discharge will depend on the catchment area, the intensity and duration of the rainfall, the nature of the soils and the terrain. The most reliable method of estimating high water levels is to look for indicators of flood levels. Look at the river banks, note changes in vegetation and ask local people.

Culverts may carry a natural watercourse or convey water under the road from side ditches situated on the uphill side of the road. Culverts require materials of sufficient strength to support the road above and they can take time to put in place. In an emergency, fords, drifts and simple dips in the road are often a better first stage option. Culverts can be constructed at a later date if necessary.

Fords, drifts and dips (submersible crossings) are often adequate where only short duration floods are expected. Small emergency bridges can be constructed over permanent streams. For larger rivers, a prefabricated modular bridge (such as a Bailey bridge) or a temporary floating causeway may be appropriate. To erect these, an engineer without significant bridge experience should, if at all possible, request outside help. This can often be provided by e-mail, phone and fax. If such help is required contact RedR or the supplier of the bridging system. If a major bridge has to be constructed, a bridge specialist should be called in.

Aerial ropeways are easy to erect and can be very useful in getting people or equipment across a gap, often a problem in the initial stages of bridge construction.

18.5.2 Culverts

If timber is available, a culvert can be made from sawn logs as shown in Figure 18.15. Factory made spun concrete pipes or concrete pipes cast on site are commonly used for culverts. Corrugated steel culverts are lighter than concrete and therefore easier to handle and transport to site. The choice of materials will probably be decided by availability. A typical pipe culvert installation is shown in Figure 18.16.

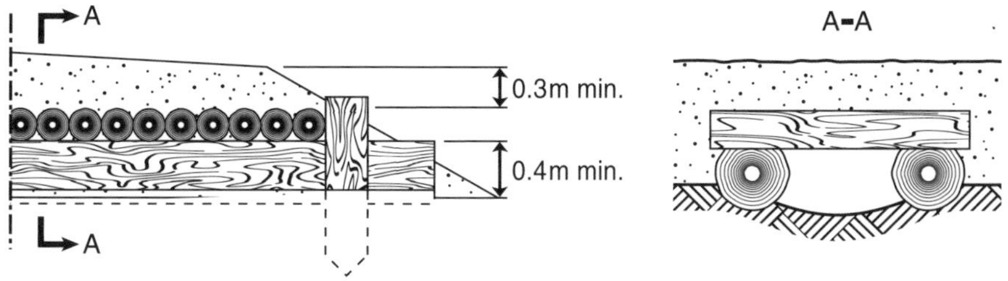

Figure 18.15 A log culvert
From Beenhakker *et al.*, 1987

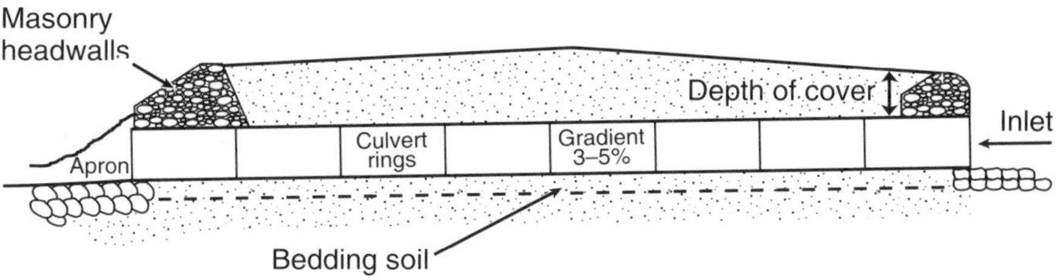

Figure 18.16 A typical pipe culvert
From Antoniou *et al.*, 1990

Ensure culverts have sufficient soil cover to spread the traffic load (see Table 18.8). Ensure that erosion near the culvert is controlled, particularly on the discharge side.

Table 18.8 Depth of cover for culvert pipes

Type of pipe	*Diameter, mm*	*Depth of cover, mm*
Spun concrete	600	300
	900	450
Concrete cast on site	600	450
	900	700
Corrugated steel	600	300

From Antoniou *et al.*, 1990

18.5.3 Fords and drifts

There is little time in an emergency to construct anything but the simplest of bridges. Even pre-fabricated modular bridges take time to purchase, transport to site and erect. An alternative to a bridge is a submersible crossing. There are two basic types:

- Bed-level fords and drifts.
- Vented fords and submersible bridges raised above bed-level.

Submersible crossings are generally simpler and quicker to construct than bridges and are often adequate for many small crossing points which experience intermittent short-term flooding. Always consider submersible crossings before opting for a bridge.

The siting of submersible crossings differs from the siting of a bridge as a wide crossing often provides slower, shallower water and a gentler approach. If the banks are steep (>10 per cent), reduce the gradient by approaching at an angle. Try to ensure that, on the approach, drivers have a clear view of the crossing.

Where crossings disrupt the natural flow of the river, scour may be induced, which, if left uncontrolled, can rapidly damage the crossing. Take appropriate control measures.

Fords

Fords, as defined here, are unpaved crossings. The simplest ford is a crossing at a shallow river section over a naturally supportive stream bed. A natural ford can be improved by reducing the approach gradient and strengthening the vehicle running surface.

Large stones placed across the ford to retain a gravel surface suffer two problems. Scour may occur downstream if they are too large or placed too high. Conversely, if they are not large enough they will be swept away under flood conditions.

Figure 18.17 shows three methods of retaining natural river gravel, or imported fill, and a method of scour prevention (from TRRL, 1992).

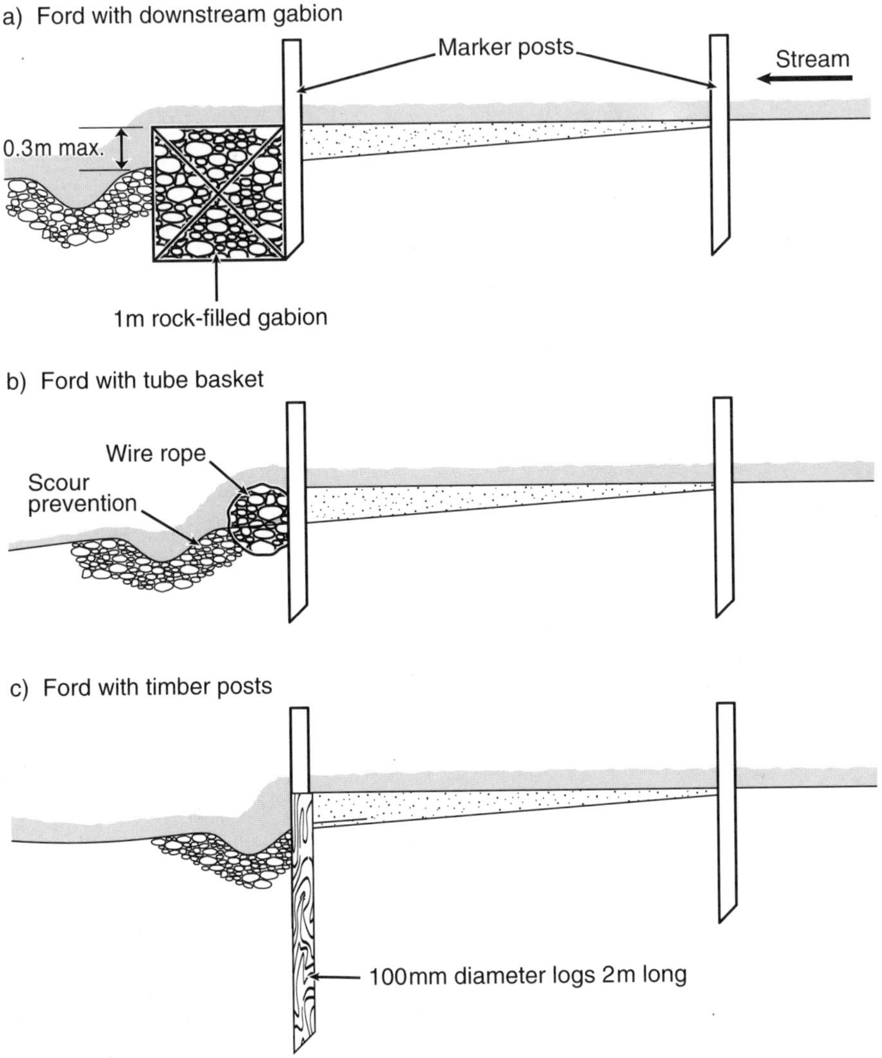

Figure 18.17 Three methods of improving fords
From TRRL, 1992

To ford a stream using gabions (Figure 18.17a), place a line of gabion baskets in a trench, 0.2–0.3 m deep, dug across the stream so that they protrude no more than 0.3 m above the level of the stream bed. Fill the middle basket to act as an anchor and tension the baskets with a rope before filling as shown in Figure 18.18. See Appendix 17 for information on gabions.

If gabions are not available, make a wire tube by rolling chain link fencing mesh (Figure 18.17b). After filling, tie the tube at the top and tension with a wire rope anchored at each end.

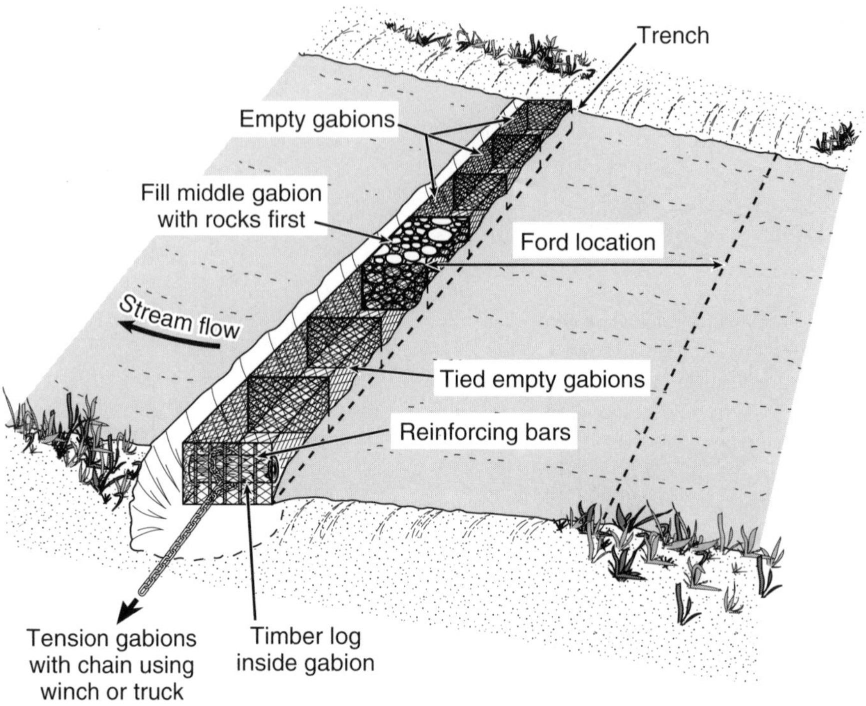

Figure 18.18 Placing gabions to improve a ford

Figure 18.17c shows how timber piles can be used if suitable timber is available and piles can be driven into the stream bed.

Drifts

Drifts, as defined here, are paved fords. A drift may also be known as a bed-level causeway, paved dip, ford or Irish bridge. Figure 18.19 shows alternative designs. Curtain walls and aprons protect the vehicle running surface from scour. Remember that concrete requires time to gain strength and, being inflexible, it is liable to cracking. Gabions provide an instant and flexible structure and may be appropriate for hurriedly constructed crossings or for sandy crossings subject to intense flash flooding. Choose a combination of design features suited to each set of circumstances.

Vented fords

A vented ford (also known as a vented causeway) raises the vehicle running surface above the level of the stream bed. It is passable in normal flood conditions but submerged and impassable under high flood conditions. The resistance offered by a vented ford to the natural flow of a stream or river means that it must be built to withstand both the water pressure and the impact of debris carried in the flow. Construction takes considerably longer than a simple drift, and should be carried out during periods of low stream flow. A vented ford may

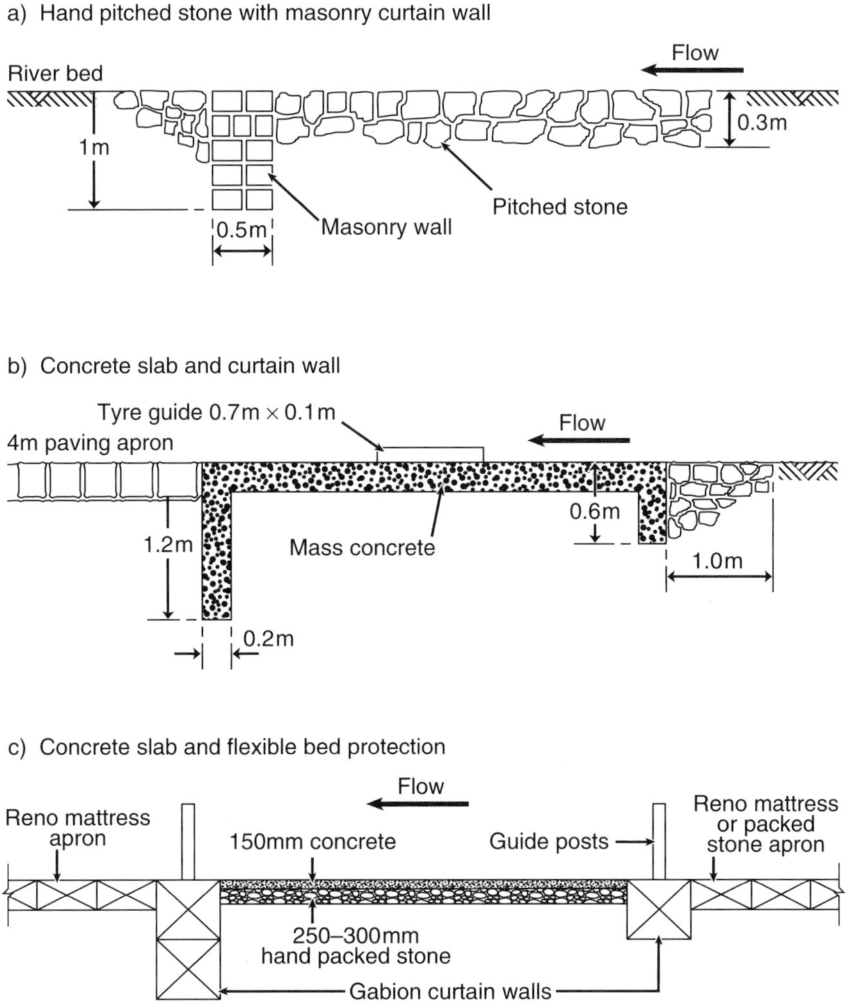

Figure 18.19 Alternative drift designs
From TRRL, 1992

be an appropriate alternative to a bridge where access for food and relief supplies can be improved in the dry season in anticipation of the wet season.

Figure 18.20 shows a temporary vented earth ford. Protect the earth fill from erosion with stone and/or gabions. If time and materials are available, a more permanent structure can be constructed in concrete or cemented masonry. The vents are standard concrete or corrugated steel culvert pipes. Pipes spaced too far apart can induce water flow parallel to the road which could result in scour. Set the vents level with the stream bed, and at the same gradient, to avoid siltation.

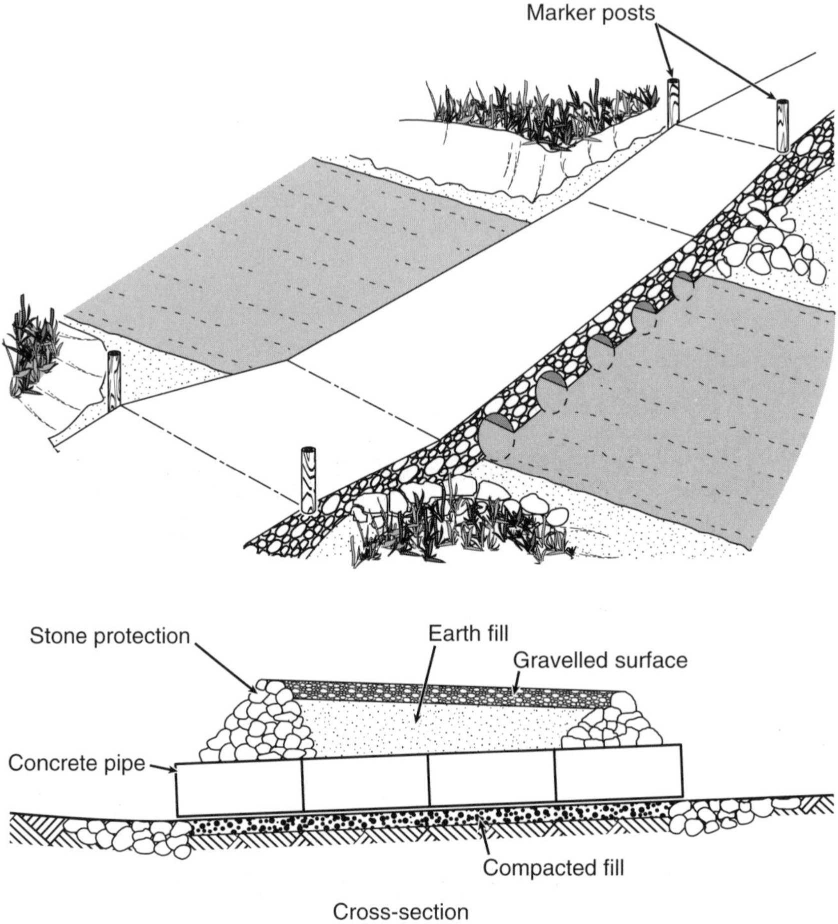

Figure 18.20 A vented earth ford

18.5.4 Small emergency timber bridges

This section is confined to small bridges (up to about 12 m span) which can be erected within a reasonably short period of time (a matter of weeks) using locally available materials. In most cases, this excludes the extensive use of concrete and steel beams.

The following sections give standard bridge designs based on three categories of timber: heavy hardwood, lighter hardwood, and softwood, used either as logs or as sawn beams. Density is measured when the wood has an 18 per cent moisture content. The three categories are:

Heavy hardwood	density >650 kg/m^3
Light hardwood	density <650 kg/m^3
Softwood	density >420 kg/m^3

Figures 18.21 and 18.22 show a standard design for a single lane log bridge. Table 18.9 indicates the number and diameter of logs in the three timber categories needed to carry a vehicle of 20 tonne maximum gross weight. Use seasoned logs, if available, stripped of bark. Match and position the logs so that the deck planking is in contact with all the logs. If the logs need to be levelled, notch the underside of logs at the abutment rather than removing material from the upper surface of the log.

Figures 18.21 and 18.23 show a standard design for a single lane sawn timber beam bridge. Table 18.10 indicates the size of the five beams in the three timber categories needed to carry a vehicle of 20 tonne maximum gross weight.

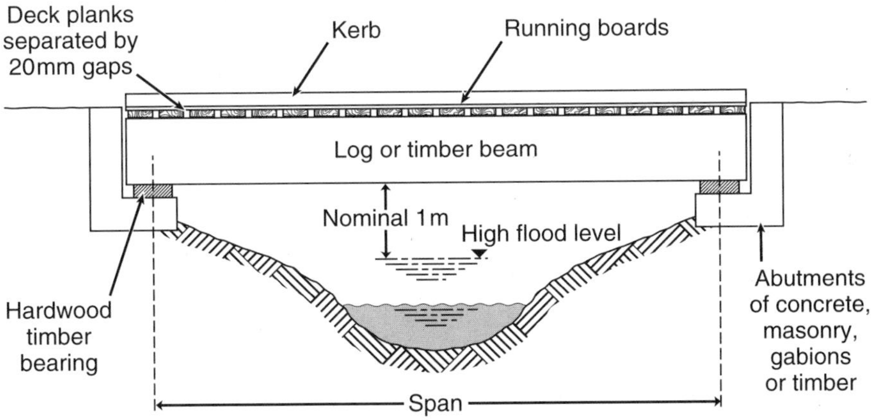

Figure 18.21 Longitudinal section of a log or timber beam bridge
From TRRL, 1992

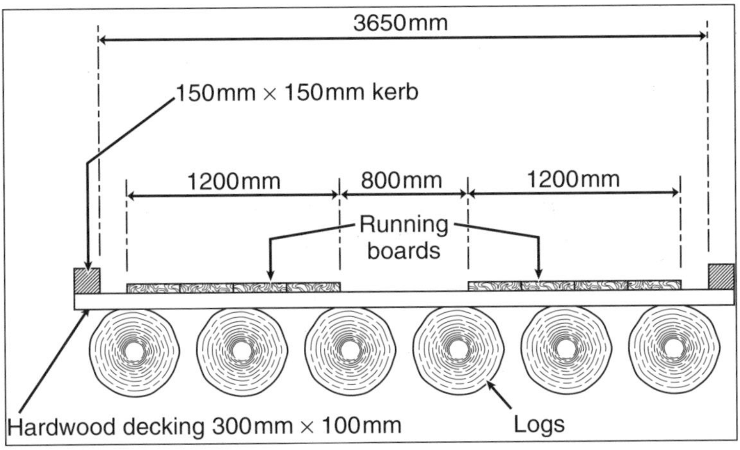

Figure 18.22 Cross-section of a log bridge (for log diameters, refer to Table 18.9)
From TRRL, 1992

Table 18.9 The diameter of logs for a bridge for vehicles of 20 tonne maximum gross weight

Span (m)	*Number of logs*	*Diameter (mm) of logs for:*		
		Heavy hardwood	*Light hardwood*	*Softwood*
4	7	325	400	475
6	6	375	475	550
8	6	450	525	625
10	5	500	600	725
12	5	550	675	800

NOTE: Diameter given is minimum along central third of span and refers to logs stripped of bark; see Figure 18.22.

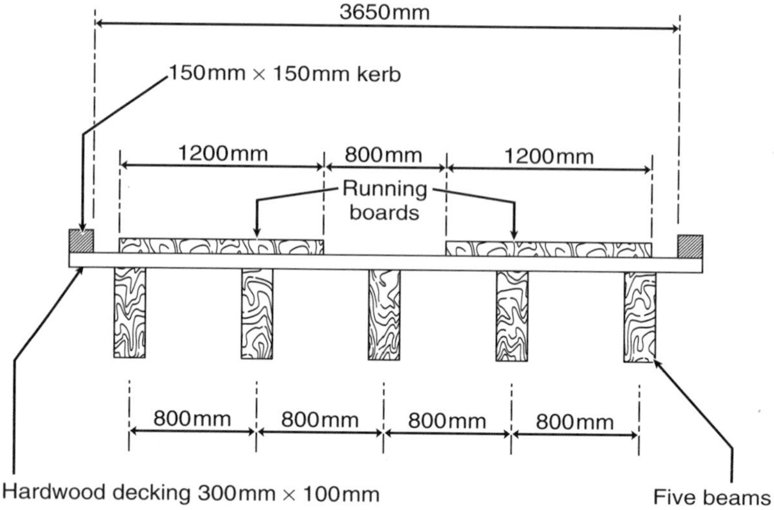

Figure 18.23 Cross-section of a timber beam bridge (for timber dimensions, see Table 18.10).
From TRRL, 1992

Table 18.10 The dimensions of sawn timber beams for a bridge for vehicles of 20 tonne maximum gross weight

Span (m)	*Beam size (mm × mm) for:*		
	Heavy hardwood	*Light hardwood*	*Softwood*
4	150 × 375	150 × 500	200 × 550
6	150 × 475	200 × 550	200 × 700
8	200 × 500	200 × 650	250 × 750
10	200 × 600	250 × 725	300 × 850
12	200 × 700	250 × 850	300 × 1000

Timber decking

Construct the deck with 100 mm thick timber planks. Pack any gaps between planks and logs with timber packing pieces. Space the planks to leave a 20 mm gap between them to drain water and avoid the accumulation of dirt and moisture.

Fix two strips of running board to suit the wheel spacing of the vehicles using the bridge. This protects the deck planks and guides the vehicles centrally across the bridge.

If available, use galvanized screws or coach bolts to secure the decking and running strips as nails tend to work loose.

Abutments

If the bridge deck is replacing a damaged or collapsed bridge, use the existing abutments and piers if they are still in a serviceable condition. Temporary abutments can be constructed from gabions, timber planks or logs. They need to be above the flood level or securely anchored to the bank to withstand scour (see Figure 18.24).

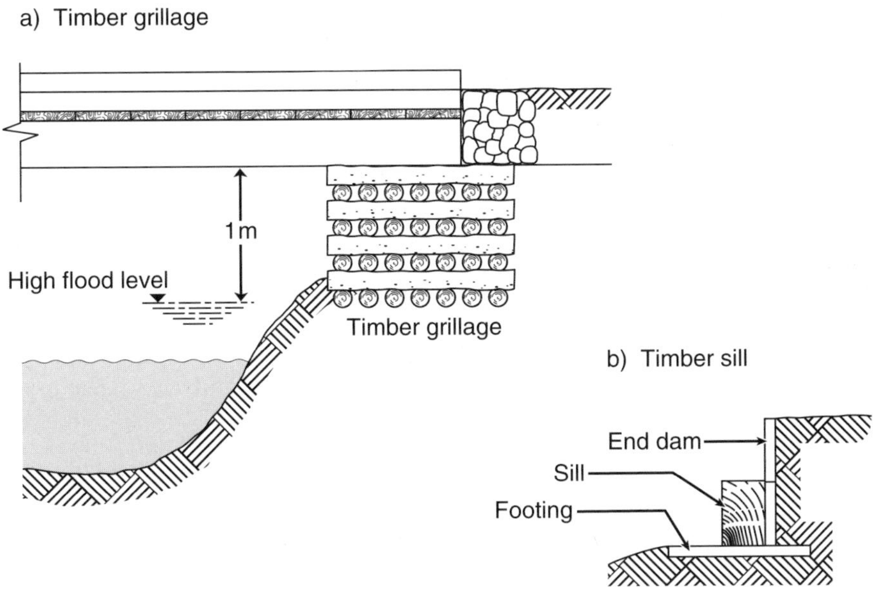

Figure 18.24 Two types of temporary abutment

Piers

Piers for multi-span bridges permit an increase in the total distance bridged or a reduction in the section of load bearing beams.

Timber piled piers may be possible where a means of piling is readily available. Concrete rings can be used where the stream or river bed is firm enough to support them. In the dry season, a column of concrete rings can be caissoned onto firm material beneath the bed surface. For stability, a height to diameter ratio not greater than 3:1 is recommended. Provide scour protection around the base of ring piers.

Scour protection

Inspection of the site and other local bridge structures will aid in the assessment of the type and extent of scour protection that banks, bridge abutments and piers will require. Useful materials for protection are gabion and Reno mattresses. Details on the use of gabion and Reno mattresses are given in Appendix 17.

Rip-rap, which comprises large stones, can be placed against a slope for scour protection. Stones found in the river will not be heavy enough to withstand being washed away. Larger stones must be found if the rip-rap is to provide effective protection in a flood. Very large stones will be difficult to handle without lifting gear and gabions may be more practical.

Fine, non-cohesive bank soils, which may be washed through the gaps in rip-rap and gabions, may be retained by placing a gravel filter layer or geotextile layer between the bank and the protection.

Stone pitching is made of stones set in mortar. It can protect slopes from erosion by rainfall runoff but is susceptible to scour at the edges.

18.5.5 Prefabricated modular bridges

Prefabricated modular bridges are quick to erect once on site, but they may take a considerable period of time to specify, order and transport to site. In addition, suitable abutments and piers (necessary for a multi-span bridge) need to be constructed, and the total cost including air-freight, in an emergency, is relatively high. Therefore, although modular bridges can look an attractive solution at first sight, it may pay to seriously consider other alternatives. In certain circumstances, however, a prefabricated modular bridge may be the most viable option. The correct specification of a bridge will entail close consultation with the supplier, who should be able to provide advice on the type of bridge and the preparations required.

The Bailey bridge is the most well known prefabricated modular bridge system. It has been developed over the years by different companies under several names. Bailey bridges have been used throughout the world over the last 50 years. Older bridges within a country might be considered for use in an emergency, but this can be hazardous. Designs and materials have changed significantly. Do not use new and old panels in the same bridge, and ensure the correct manual and load tables are consulted for the specific bridge concerned. Figure 18.25 shows the main components of a typical Bailey bridge. Such bridges have two side trusses assembled from standard panels. The number of panels in the truss depends on the length, width and carrying capacity required. Trusses may be one, two or three panels high and joined side by side. A double truss single storey bridge (as shown in Fig 18.25) is known as a 'Double Single' (DS). A double truss double storey bridge is known as a 'Double Double' (DD). The trusses may be reinforced to varying degrees and the nomenclature will reflect the extent of reinforcement (e.g. DSR2).

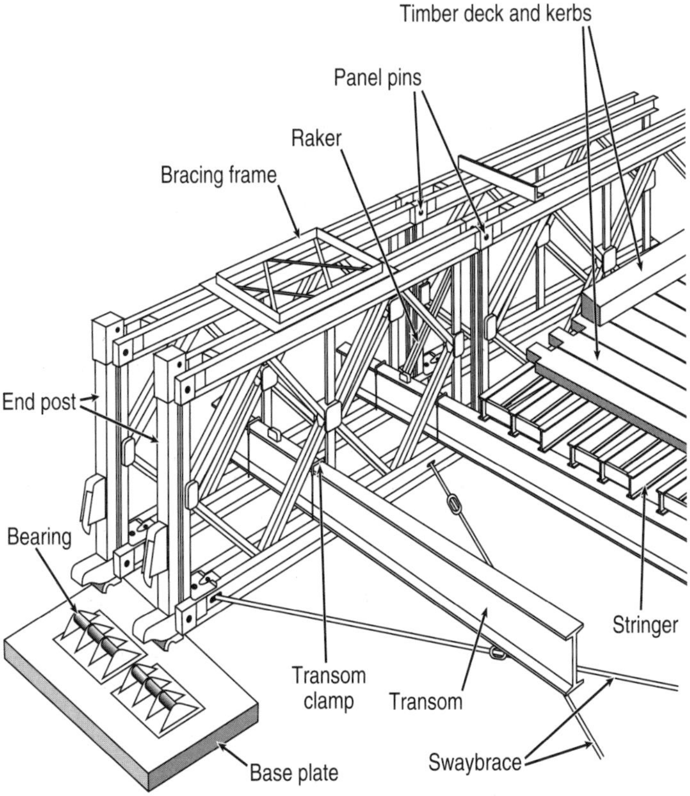

Figure 18.25 Components of a typical Bailey bridge

As much relevant information as is available should be given to a supplier as early as possible for the accurate and rapid selection of a suitable bridge. The following data should be supplied:

- Number of traffic lanes.
- Width of maximum load.
- Axle loads and spacing along the vehicle.*
- Wheel loads and spacing on the axle.*
- Tyre pressures and contact area.*
- Impact loading.*
- Number of vehicles on the bridge at one time and their spacing.*
- Pedestrian load.
- Wind velocity.
- Maximum and minimum ambient temperatures.
- Length of the gap to be bridged.
- Abutment/bank shape.
- Possibility of intermediate piers.
- Ground bearing capacity and/or description of the soils.

- Likelihood of subsidence.
- Flood level.
- Clearance required under the bridge.
- Construction area available.

(From Storey, 1983, and confirmed by Mabey & Johnson, 1995.)

In the absence of specific data on the items marked *, a widely used standard is AASHTO HS20.44 loading based on a 324 kN (32 t) vehicle with three axles and a maximum axle load of 144 kN (14.4 t).

Some pointers on method of erection

Erection of a Bailey-type bridge requires special skill and experience. The following is not intended as a guide to installation, but as a guide to understanding what is involved and hence to making the correct preparations.

In the absence of large capacity crane facilities, the common method of building a Bailey-type bridge is by cantilever launch (see Figure 18.26). The method is to launch the bridge from the home abutment on rollers and to build the bridge as it is pushed, or pulled, across the gap. To prevent the bridge from falling into the gap, the weight behind the launching rollers must always be greater than the launched section ahead. A launching nose at the front of the bridge compensates for the sag into the gap and lands on landing rollers on the far abutment.

To achieve a cantilever launch, a construction area must be available from which to launch the bridge. The area behind the launching rollers should be approximately level for a distance equal to the final span of the bridge. There should be room either side of the immediate launch area for working and stacking the bridge parts.

The end bearing positions should be above the flood level and their distance apart should be a multiple of the nominal panel lengths. It will be quicker and probably more economical to set the abutments back from the gap than to try to shorten the span, or spans, by extensive abutment construction.

18.5.6 Floating bridges and causeways

Floating bridges

Standard Bailey bridges, and other similar modular designs, can be installed on floating piers to form floating bridges. A floating installation can be used where the bridge is only temporary or the construction of conventional abutments and piers would take too long or would pose particular problems. Floating piers are based on modular construction principles, such as 'Uniflotes'. A number of floating units are assembled to form rafts of various load bearing capacities (see Figure 18.27). The load to be carried and stability required determines the number of coupled units. A bridge span, or floating bay, floats as a self-contained unit on floating piers. Each bay can be constructed separately and floated into position. The piers are maintained in position by cables anchored to the river bed and bank. Each floating unit can be supplied in a knocked-down form for ease of transport to site and to reduce freight costs.

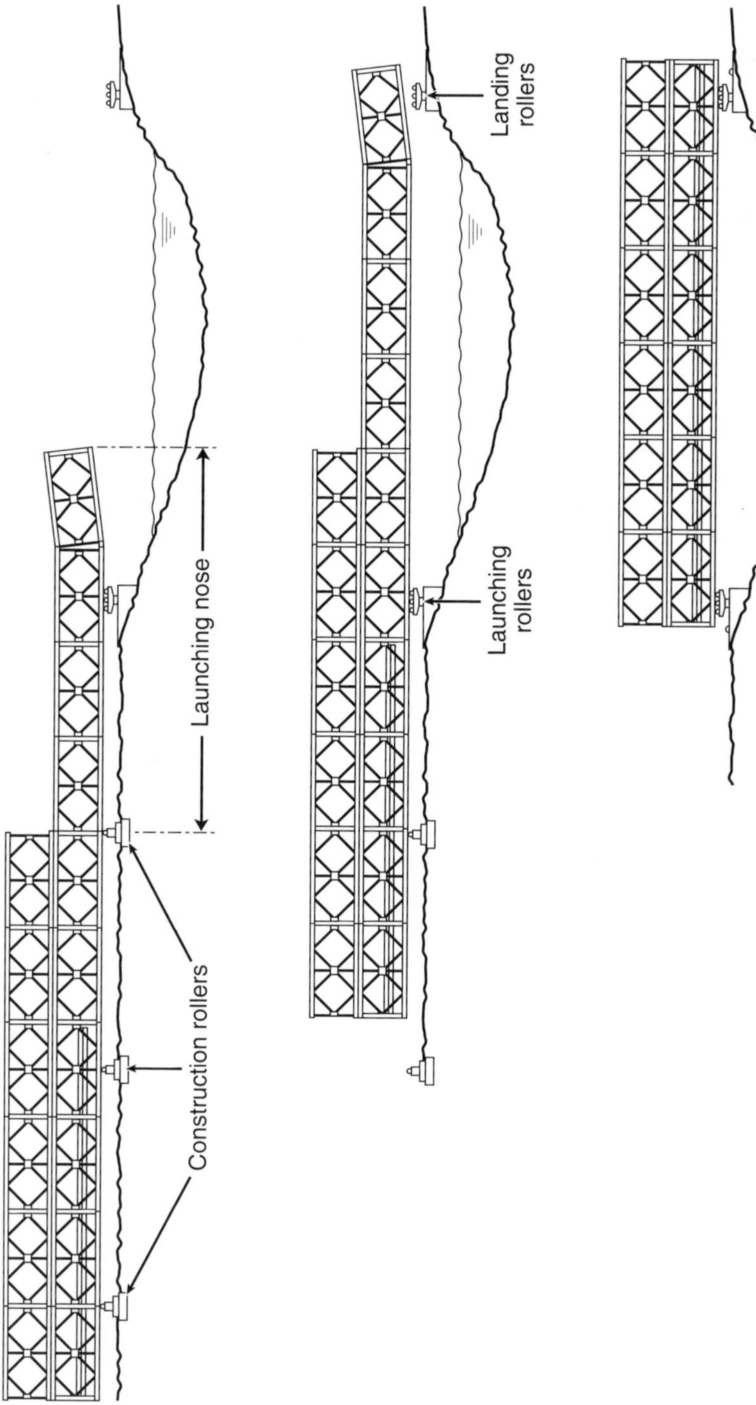

Figure 18.26 Launching a Bailey bridge
From Mabey & Johnson, 89 Compact

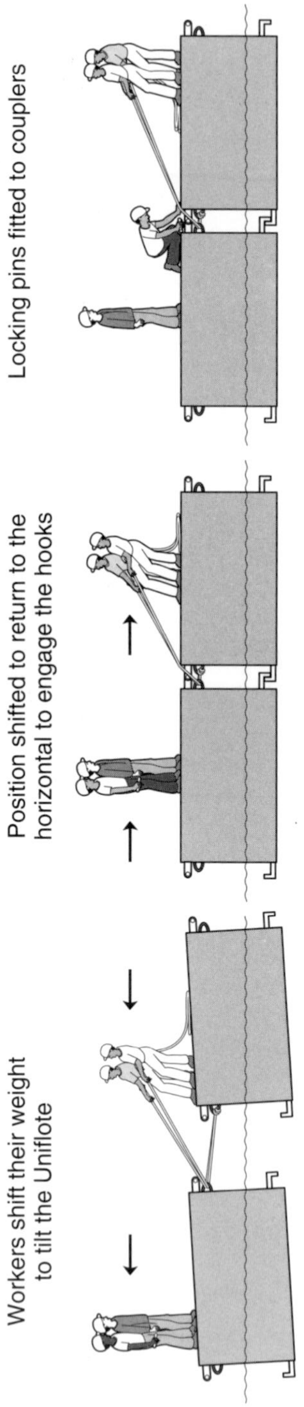

Figure 18.27 Assembling 'Uniflotes'

In addition to the information required to select a standard Bailey-type bridge (listed above), the following information for floating bridges is needed:

- High and low water levels relative to the bank height.
- River width at high and low water.
- Nature of the river bed material at anchorages up-stream and down-stream from the bridge.
- River traffic and navigation channels.
- Current and tides.

Floating bridges require regular attention and maintenance. In particular, the anchor cables require regular tensioning. After a time (sometimes within a year) corrosion can occur at the splash areas (the air/water interface) and corroded areas will need patching.

Floating causeways

A floating causeway can be constructed using the same units as those used in building floating bridge piers. Several floating units connected end-to-end with articulated connectors can form a continuous support for timber or steel decking. Articulated ramps connect with the banks. The width can be increased by connecting units side by side.

18.5.7 Aerial ropeways

The procurement and erection of a ropeway or cableway may, for example, be a solution to overcoming access problems due to flooding of a river in the wet season.

An improvised aerial ropeway

An aerial ropeway can be used to transport light relief items across a gap. However, it requires steel wire rope (SWR) and sufficient tackle of adequate strength to construct a safe crossing. The following information on aerial ropeways is from MoD (1981a).

A simple aerial ropeway for use across an approximately level gap is shown in Figure 18.28. The traveller is hauled across the gap suspended from a cable supported and anchored at both ends. The difference in level of the cable supports should not exceed 1/25th of the span.

Refer to the following appendices for construction and design guidance on the individual components:

Appendix 18 Anchorages.
Appendix 19 The construction and design details of a gyn.

Guidelines on the erection of an aerial ropeway:

- Select a site to give smooth and level landing and loading areas. Look for strong, well-rooted trees to support the cable. Determine the position of the supports and measure the gap.
- The cable used will depend on what is available. A guide to maximum loads on suspended cables is given in Table 18.11.

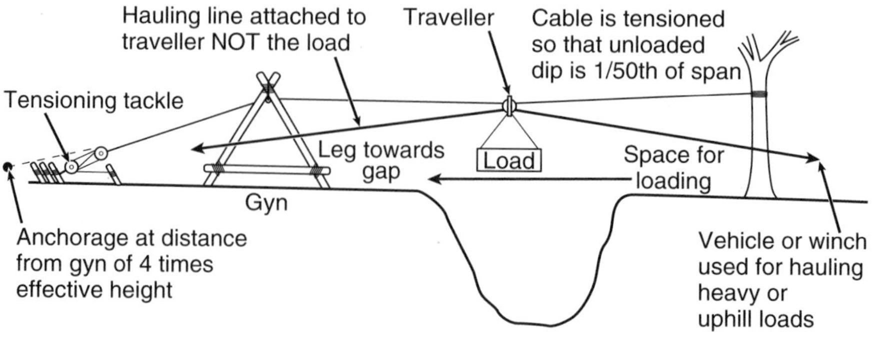

Figure 18.28 A simple aerial ropeway

Table 18.11 Maximum concentrated loads on suspended cables

Diameter of steel wire rope mm	*Tension in steel wire rope (tonnes)*	*Maximum concentrated load in kg with a safety factor of 4*					
		Span, m					
		25	*50*	*75*	*100*	*125*	*150*
8	0.5	108	104	100	96	88	86
12	1.0	212	206	200	193	187	165
16	2.8	540	518	495	476	455	417
20	4.3	863	826	794	762	725	670
24	6.5	1182	1131	1090	1042	992	910

- If natural supports cannot be found, erect a gyn from timber or steel pipe, with one leg towards the gap and slightly off the line of the cable. Include a tensioning device and anchor the cable at a distance from the support of not less than four times the effective height of the support.
- Typical travellers are shown in Figure 18.29. Lifting tackle attached to the traveller is required to lift and lower the load. Use a single snatch block for light loads. For heavier loads and for ropeways on slight slopes, use a two block traveller. Ensure the traveller is secured by the hauling rope before attaching to the cable.
- Either use two haul ropes or a single haul rope arranged to return through a snatch block so that both haulage and return can be operated from one end. Manual power or a powered winch can be used for hauling.

Prefabricated cableway

Commercially manufactured prefabricated cableways may be a solution to an access problem, where a bridge is not feasible. Erection times can be as short as two weeks although supply and transport to site may take a lot longer.

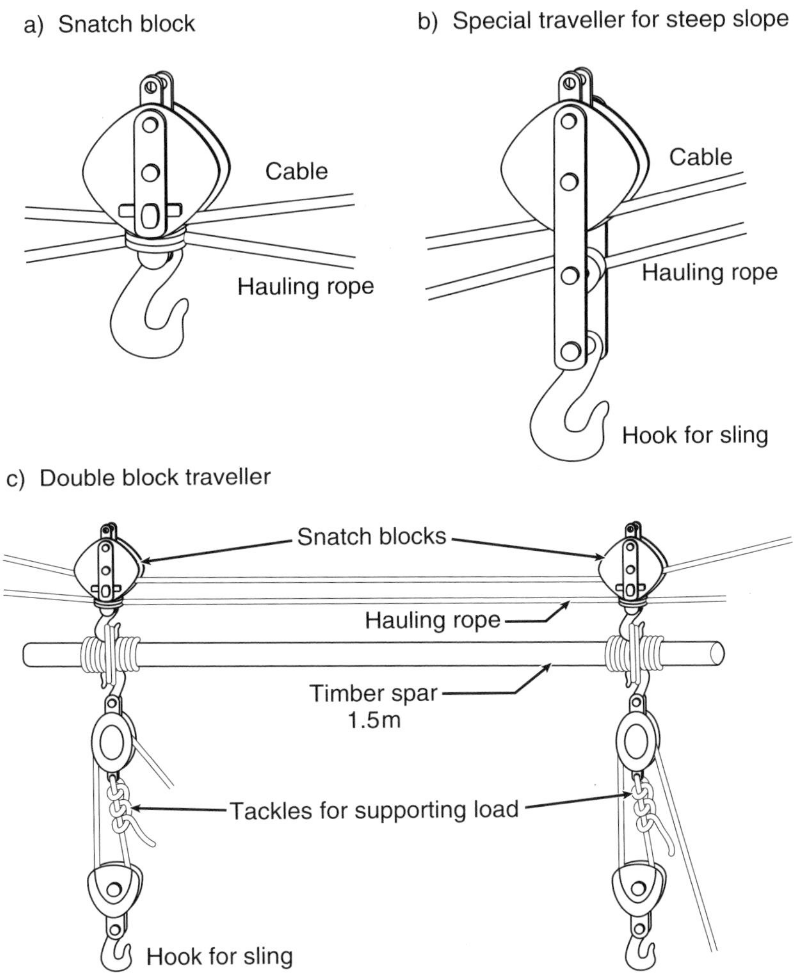

Figure 18.29 Travellers for aerial ropeways

18.6 Airstrips

18.6.1 General

Airstrips may be required in an emergency for transport or light passenger aircraft. The standard of airstrip will vary according to the aircraft type. The required airstrip parameters must be checked with the carrier, air force or pilots concerned. In many cases, the engineer in the field may be able to carry out preliminary site investigations prior to the arrival of specialists (in particular air force personnel) who will take the final decisions regarding airstrip preparation and suitability.

The preparation, improvement and maintenance of an airstrip can utilize similar labour-based approaches for those described previously for road works and it need not rely on heavy plant. The procedure for the assessment and preparation of a temporary airstrip is shown by reference to a specific example, that of an airstrip for a Hercules C130 transport aircraft. The procedures for other aircraft will need to take into account similar factors. Table 18.12 gives some of the required details for a Hercules C130 aircraft.

Table 18.12 Hercules C130 aircraft details

Plane type	*Wingspan* ft	*Length* ft	*Height* ft	*Landing* weight* lb	*Take-off* weight* lb
Mark 1	132	99	38	135 000	155 000

Note: Imperial units are commonly used in relation to aircraft and runways.
* These are maximum figures for normal operation and include total aircraft weight (self-weight, payload and fuel).

18.6.2 Temporary airstrip assessment and preparation

Survey and preparation

Dimensions The recommended dimensions of the landing strip (for a Hercules C130 transport aircraft) are:

Width 60–120 ft (18–40 m). Crosswinds increase the landing width. A wind of 35 km/h increases the width to 40 m.

Length 5000 ft (1525 m) if possible.
4000 ft (1200 m) for a 135 000 lb landing weight
3000 ft (914 m) for a 120 000 lb landing weight

The runway length is one of many factors (altitude, ambient temperature, prevailing winds and aircraft operation) which affect landing and take-off weights. Hercules C130 aircraft can land on strips down to about 2500 ft. Survey the site to ensure that it is free and clear of vertical obstructions and that no roads or tracks cross the landing strip. An additional area, termed the 'clear zone', 100 ft (30 m) wide around the ends and sides of the strip must be cleared of trees and shrubs.

Simple site test: Drive a 4×4 (Land Rover or similar) down the strip at 30 mph and if you have to hold on to your seat it is too rough!

Personnel A forward operational base for two Hercules aircraft requires many personnel (perhaps 50–100 depending on situation).

Detailed site inspection There is a plate test to simulate the aircraft wheels and this will be used by the air force or carrier involved in checking the surface strength initially and every day subsequently. Pilots and/or operators should be informed of any changes. This test is vital when weather conditions change as this may affect aircraft loads and landing possibilities.

It is not necessary for the landing strip to be perfectly level, but it is important that changes in gradient are not sudden. Longitudinal slopes should not exceed: up – 1 in 75; down – 1 in 50. There should be no gradient changes over a 150 m length of the strip. There should be sufficient cross fall to shed water to the sides.

Remove embedded rocks and sharp stones. Remove balls made of soil or clay which exceed 100 mm in diameter. Ensure that there are no ditches between the strip and the clear zone or across the strip – fill with strip material. Ruts more than 75 mm deep must be filled. Potholes more than 125 mm deep × 400 mm diameter must be filled. Remove humps more than 75 mm high × 400 mm long.

Avoid surface undulations greater than 100 mm in 50 m. Check longitudinal wavelengths against a 3 m straight edge to ensure the aircraft tyre tracks do not differ longitudinally otherwise the wings will oscillate. Use simple survey techniques to plot the strip centre line and edges to ensure they have similar wavelengths.

Vegetation in the strip overrun areas at each end should, ideally, not exceed 6 m in height for a length of 3000 ft or as instructed by the air force or carrier.

An apron for parking will be required. Allow the wing span plus 20 ft (152 ft for a Hercules) multiplied by the number of aircraft in operation. A Hercules has a turning circle of 140 ft (based on the aircraft centre line).

Operation

Site ground markers in red 'day-glo', 30 m either side of the strip centreline at the end of the landing strip and at 300 m intervals leading to the start of the landing strip. If these are not available, paint white lines instead.

Arrange an indication of wind direction at ground level – a windsock, flag or smoke.

Security – make arrangements to keep airstrip clear of people and animals. Consider the recruitment of guards. Inspect the strip regularly – at first light and last light, and 30 minutes before arrival and departure of an aircraft.

19 Shelter and built infrastructure

This chapter deals with the provision of shelter for people who have had to leave home because of a disaster; it discusses the storage required for goods and equipment, and outlines the structures and facilities needed for facilities such as health and feeding centres. Information required for assessment, procurement and installation is given. A brief outline of construction methods and materials is included. Finally, guidelines are given on the assessment of damaged buildings. Guidance on site selection and planning of temporary settlements is given in Chapter 20.

19.1 Shelter in emergencies

Shelter is an urgent basic need when displacement occurs as a result of famine or conflict or as a result of severe damage caused by earthquakes, storms or floods. Shelter should provide:

- Protection from the elements: rain, snow and wind. Warmth in cool climates and shade in hot sunny climates.
- Security against violence: people without shelter are very vulnerable. Where large numbers of people are gathered together without adequate shelter, there is great potential for conflict.
- Privacy and space for personal and communal needs.

Shelter includes basic structures and the complementary inputs of clothing, blankets, heaters and insulation.

19.1.1 Shelter options

Refer to Figure 19.1 and Table 19.1 for an overview of shelter options. The flow diagram provides guidance on assessing options for the housing of people displaced in an emergency. People may occupy empty buildings or erect basic structures from materials they find around them. It is important to understand the concerns of the whole population affected by the disaster, including the intentions of the people yet to arrive and the feelings of those already hosting migrants. Consult with local authorities, local communities, and the people who are seeking shelter to find out what is needed to meet minimum humanitarian standards and what will be allowed by the authorities. The Sphere minimum standards for shelter are listed in Appendix 3. The standards promote the need

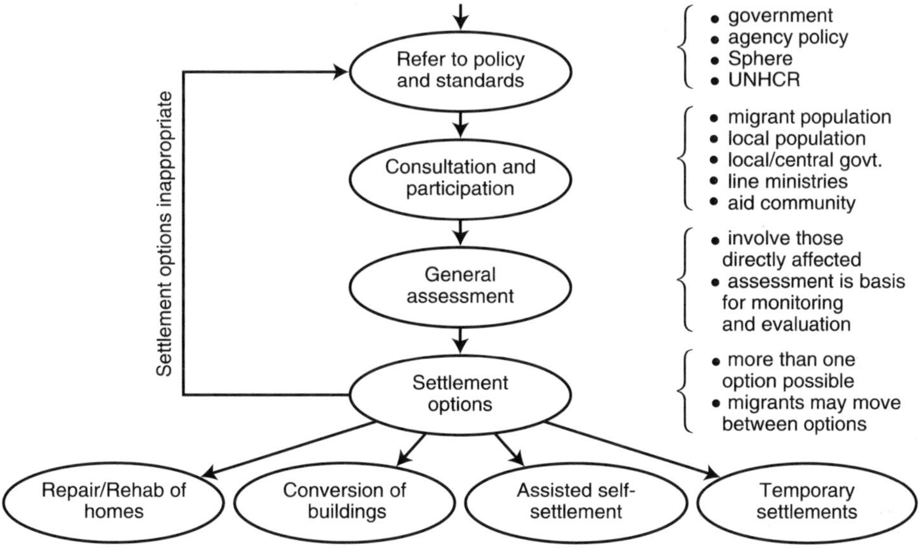

Figure 19.1 Temporary shelter options for forced migrants
Source: shelterproject.org

for a clear understanding of the emergency situation and the provision of shelter and associated needs to ensure the dignity, health and well-being of the people affected.

Meeting immediate needs often involves supplying blankets, clothing, plastic sheeting, and simple tools and materials. In some situations tents can provide the breathing space in which to reconstruct or build more permanent structures but tents are very expensive when compared to other shelter options. Tents, therefore, are used in a fraction of cases and other shelter options must be considered.

It is recommended to plan for the long term. Experience has shown that many 'temporary camps' can become permanent settlements. See Chapter 20 for further details on 'Temporary settlements', such as refugee camps.

Local solutions to the problems of shelter are generally more adaptable, responsive and culturally sensitive than imported technologies. Therefore, support local solutions and avoid imported pre-fabricated emergency shelter which can be both expensive and a long time in arriving on site.

Support early upgrading or reconstruction Following a natural disaster, people often erect temporary shelter at once and start on the reconstruction of their homes soon afterwards. Support these efforts, for example, by supplying scarce materials at subsidized prices or on credit. Only supply temporary shelter if really necessary, for example, after an earthquake, when people may be reluctant to return immediately to their homes due to the fear of further shocks. Use the opportunity to give technical support for the improvement of traditional designs to mitigate the impact of future hazards. This is, however, a

Table 19.1 Features of temporary shelter options for forced migrants

Repair/rehabilitation of homes	*Conversion of buildings*	*Assisted self-settlement*	*Temporary settlements*
Includes: • urban and rural • own or other home • increasing housing stock in region	**Includes:** • urban and rural • schools/barracks/ halls/farm buildings/ commercial structures	**Includes:** • staying with families • self-settled camps • dispersed self-settlement	**Includes:** • transit/reception • 'Supported Temporary Settlement' (or camp) • extension to an STS
Assessments • security/stability • ownership • socio-economics • demographics • likelihood of return • migrant/local cultures • climate/ environment • factors for sustained occupation • materials/skills/ tools	**Assessments** • security/stability • ownership and use • socio-economics • demographics • likelihood of return • migrant/local cultures • climate/ environment • use of outside space • materials/skills/ tools • fire/evacuation safety	**Assessments** • security/stability • socio-economics • demographics • likelihood of return • migrant/local cultures • climate/ environment • access to services • density and sustainability • fire/evacuation safety	**Assessments** • security/stability • socio-economics • demographics • likelihood of return • migrant/local cultures • climate/ environment • self-sufficiency level • integration with local community
Implementation • materials and tools • self-help and contract • support in-country materials production • communal services	**Implementation** • involve owners/ users • communal services	**Implementation** • support hosts through existing structures? • support local services	**Implementation** • involve local people/migrants/ government in site selection and physical planning • minimize environmental impact
Issues • are homes occupied? • 'ethnic cleansing': do occupiers become the owners? • how are occupiers involved? • are building materials sold on?	**Issues** • set maximum socially-sustainable stay • social/economic activities for the displaced? • long-term implications and developmental advantages? • exist strategy/ return to previous function?	**Issues** • how are local people affected? • long-term implications and developmental advantages? • How are vulnerable migrants accessed and served? • economic and environmental impact	**Issues** • are migrants and locals involved in management? • is settlement similar to migrant or local tradition? • Fire/evacuation safety • economic and environmental impact

Source: shelterproject.org

longer-term process involving close co-operation with the community. (Refer to Maskrey, 1989).

When people are displaced and gather in temporary settlements, take early action to upgrade 'emergency' shelter. Be aware that governments may not allow the construction of 'permanent' or 'semi-permanent' dwellings if they wish to discourage the long-term settlement of displaced people.

Hazards associated with shelter

Wind
Wind can kill. Shelter, service centres and storage structures must be built to withstand expected wind speeds. Free-standing, prefabricated emergency shelter can literally take off in high wind squalls if not anchored adequately. Take appropriate precautions: use guy ropes, roof bracing, the optimum orientation of structures, etc. Keep temporary water tanks at least partly full to prevent overturning and damage to dwellings and occupants (for more on wind calculations see 13.2.6).

Fire
The distance between buildings should be great enough so that a collapsed, burning building will not set fire to an adjacent building. Therefore, the distance between structures should be a minimum of twice the overall height of a structure and even greater if the materials, such as woven matting and thatch, are highly flammable. In settlements where shelter is in blocks a rule of thumb is to provide a firebreak 30 m wide between blocks or approximately every 300 m. Ensure safe methods of lighting and heating are available – avoid distributing candles for lighting. In cold climates shelters will require some form of heating and poorly utilised and maintained heaters are a potential source of fire. Train, pay and equip fire teams in settlements and collective centres. Regular fire risk inspections are advised.

Flooding
Take into account the possibility of localised flooding in the siting, design and construction of roads, buildings and shelter schemes. A raised building base or access road, for example, can act as a small dam if drainage is not provided.

Damp
Consider siting, design and construction to limit the adverse impact of damp on personal health and vulnerable commodities.

Micro-climate
In many locations there will be preferred sites to limit the severity of certain climatic conditions such as wind (locate on the lee of a hill), sun (near or under tree cover) and so on. Try to take advantage of the local environment to limit exposure to natural hazards.

19.1.2 Blankets and clothing

Supply blankets and clothing if people are exposed, or likely to be exposed in the near future, to cold or wet conditions for which they are poorly equipped. Blankets provide immediate and sometimes life-saving protection from the elements. If possible, purchase blankets, or suitable cloth material, locally. Use Box 19.1 as a guide to specifying blankets.

Box 19.1 UNHCR standard specifications for blankets

Type A woven dry raised blankets for warm climates

Composition:	Woven, minimum 30% wool. Balance of new cotton/ synthetic fibres.
Size:	150 × 200 cm, thickness 4 mm.
Weight:	1.5 kg.
T.O.G. (thermal resistance):	1.2–1.6.
Finish	10 stitches/decimetre or ribbon bordered four sides.
Packing	Water tight wrapped in pressed bales of 30 pcs. Each bale approximately 0.3 m^3 volume and weight of 48 kg.

Type B woven dry raised blankets for cool climates

Composition:	Woven, minimum 50% wool. Balance of new synthetic fibres.
Size:	150 × 200 cm, thickness 5 mm.
Weight:	1.5 kg.
T.O.G. (thermal resistance):	2.0–2.4.
Finish	10 stitches/decimetre or ribbon bordered four sides.
Packing	Water tight wrapped in pressed bales of 30 pcs. Each bale approximately 0.35 m^3 volume and weight of 50 kg.

Source UNHCR, 1999

The insulation properties of blankets and clothes decrease significantly when wet. It is better to provide good quality blankets that will keep people warm than larger numbers of cheap, poor quality blankets.

In a cold climate, priority clothing needs will be for woollen jumpers, jackets and coats, shoes and boots. The distribution of free clothing can also take work away from tailors within the local and displaced communities at a time when work creation is a priority. It may be better to supply cloth, needle and thread, and sewing machines so that people can make their own culturally appropriate clothes.

19.1.3 Family shelter

Family shelters may be constructed from traditional materials, plastic sheeting or by using tents. Basic household equipment may need to be supplied.

Local shelter materials

Local shelter materials, which may need to be supplied to enable people to build their own shelter, may include: timber, grass, corrugated steel sheets, bamboo, mud, sand, woven mats, bush poles, thatching grass, string, rope and nails (see also 19.3.1). Check with forest authorities before cutting timber – the authority may be the best supplier of timber. Woven matting, natural fibre screens and bamboo make very good ventilated walls. When necessary, rolled up plastic sheeting can be let down to make them water, draught and dust-proof.

Find out about local building techniques when determining the kind of materials to supply. Employ local techniques in the construction of camp service centres and relief staff accommodation. Box 19.2 gives an example of construction using local techniques. Traditional techniques such as these can be applied to the construction of larger, possibly rectangular, buildings for service centres and accommodation for relief personnel. Building size is limited by the length and strength of the available timber.

Box 19.2 One example of a traditional African dwelling

Walls: A common type of dwelling uses mud walls to support the roof. However, mud walls cannot be built or repaired in the rainy season as they need prolonged sunlight to dry them. In the dry season, significant quantities of water, which may not be readily available, are required to puddle the mud. An alternative roof support (shown in Figure 19.2) can be made from poles where dwellings have to be constructed at unfavourable times of the year or where the right kind of mud is not available. The roof is tied down to a circular support made of suitable fibres (stalks) which are bound together with strips of bark and bound into the Y-forks of the poles. The poles and circular support carry the roof load so the walls can, therefore, be made from a wide variety of materials. A gap left between the top of the wall and the roof provides ventilation.

Roof: An upside down cone of roof poles is formed on the ground and is bound together with fibres placed in concentric circles or in a continuous spiral. The roof is turned over and placed in position, supported at the centre on a temporary post. The roof poles are tied into position at the perimeter before the central post is removed. The roof is now ready to thatch – see Figure 19.2. The roof pitch should be at least 45° to drain the rain quickly enough to prevent soaking and rotting of the thatch.

Plastic sheeting (Adapted from Howard and Spice, 1989)

Plastic sheeting, used in combination with local materials, provides effective emergency shelter. It also has a wide range of other uses: groundsheets, feeding centre and field hospital flooring, waterproof bed covering, temporary food mound covers (sacks of flour, grain, etc.), covering stored cement bags, truck tarpaulins, waterproof knotted sacks in which individuals can carry their possessions and relief goods, and many more applications.

Always have sufficient plastic sheeting available to cover all conceivable uses and make sure people are given enough to construct weatherproof shelter. It is common to give out a cut from a standard length roll at general distributions of non-food relief items.

Plastic sheeting is available in a range of plastic materials. Polythene (LDPE) is widely available and has the advantages of low cost and low weight per unit area. Tear resistance is greatly improved by reinforcement with a square mesh of synthetic fibre welded into the sheet. Polythene is inert and it will not rot in storage or when buried; it is completely waterproof and it is unaffected by salts,

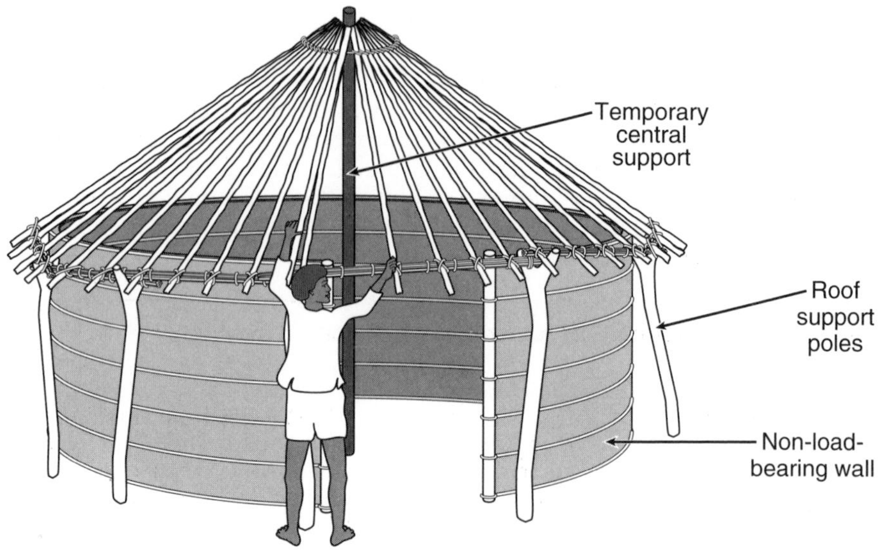

Figure 19.2 An example of a traditional African dwelling

dung, excreta and urine. However, it is susceptible to swelling by petrol and lubricating oils and to termite and rodent attack. Polythene sheet has a limited fire risk – the structure (bush poles, timber, etc.) and natural insulation materials are likely to pose a greater risk.

Polythene sheeting remains flexible well below freezing point. It begins to soften and lose strength above 80°C. Dark, especially black, plastic sheet expands significantly in direct sunlight. Allowance should be made during construction for the subsequent contraction at nightfall to prevent stretching and tearing.

The reflective surface of white plastic sheeting helps to reduce internal temperatures when used for shelter in hot climates. In colder climates, suitable material sandwiched between two sheets can greatly improve the insulation of a shelter. Suitable insulation materials include fibre glass, mineral wool, straw and hay.

Polythene sheet is made in thicknesses from 12 microns (50 gauge) to 1000 microns (4000 gauge). For emergency shelter, it is recommended that 250 or 375 microns (1000 or 1500 gauge) should be used. (For a comparison, 50 kg fertilizer sacks are usually made from 800 gauge sheeting.) The maximum available widths of single sheets are 4 m reinforced and 8 m non-reinforced. Refer to Table 19.2 for summary information on sizes and weights.

Sheeting is folded before rolling on to a 2 m wide cardboard core for ease of supply and transport. An 8 m wide sheet is folded twice and a 4 m wide sheet folded once. Plastic sheeting is available in 50 × 60 m rolls. Reinforced sheeting can be supplied with eyelets at specified intervals for tying.

Using plastic sheeting in combination with traditional materials One of the most effective uses of plastic sheeting is to weatherproof a makeshift shelter.

Table 19.2 UNHCR plastic sheeting and tarpaulin specifications

Multi-purpose plastic sheeting in rolls	
Material:	Woven high density polyethylene fibres, warp × weft: 10/12 × 10/12 per square inch, laminated on both sides with LDPE. Stabilized against ultraviolet rays and excess heat for long outdoor exposure.
Dimensions:	Rolls of 4 m × 50 m.
Material thickness:	200–230 microns (0.20–0.23 mm) (BS 2544).
Material weight:	180–200 g/m^2 (BS 2471).
Material density:	0.90–0.95 kg/dm^3.
Tensile strength:	Not less than 60 kg both directions of warp and weft (BS 2576, 25 mm grab test, or equivalent).
Tear resistance:	9 kg min. both directions (BS 4303, wing rip).
Flammability:	Flash point above 200°C.
Cold resistance:	To withstand temperatures of minimum –20°C.
Colour:	Green on both sides.
Reinforced plastic tarpaulins in sheets	
Material:	Woven high density black polyethylene fibres, warp × weft: 12/14 X 12/14 per square inch, laminated on both sides with low density polyethylene, with reinforced rims by heat sealing on all sides and nylon ropes in hem; 1000 denier minimum. Stabilised against ultraviolet rays and excess heat for long outdoor exposure. Provided with strong aluminium eyelets or equivalent on four sides of the single sheets at 100 cm centre to centre.
Dimensions:	Sheets of 4 m × 5 m.
Material thickness:	200–230 microns.
Material weight:	Minimum 200 g/m^2 (4.8 kg per tarpaulin).
Tensile strength:	Minimum 600 N both directions of warp and weft (BS 2576, 50 mm grab test, or equivalent).
Tear resistance:	Minimum 100 N both directions (BS 4303 wing tear or equivalent).
Flammability:	Flash point above 200°C.
Colour:	White with printed UNHCR logo on both sides.
Packing:	In bales of 5 sheets secured with band – gross weight per bale: approx. 23 kg – gross volume per bale: approx. 0.05 m^3.

Source: UNHCR, 2001.

Sheeting wrapped and tied over and around a framework of bush poles and grass protects the occupants from wind and rain. Grass and earth which may be used in the construction of roofs and walls provides insulation. Plastic sheet sandwiched between reed or bamboo matting is very effective.

Simple ridge tent A basic shelter using rope as a ridge is shown in Figure 19.3. Bury the polythene edges to anchor the sheet to the ground. In soft, light soils it may be necessary to weight the sheet with stones. Add guy ropes if strong winds are likely. In the absence of eyelets, tie a knot with the sheet corner and tie the guy rope around the knot.

'Oxfam hot climate shelter' The shelter design shown in Figure 19.4 was developed to utilize commonly available construction materials. Standard MDPE

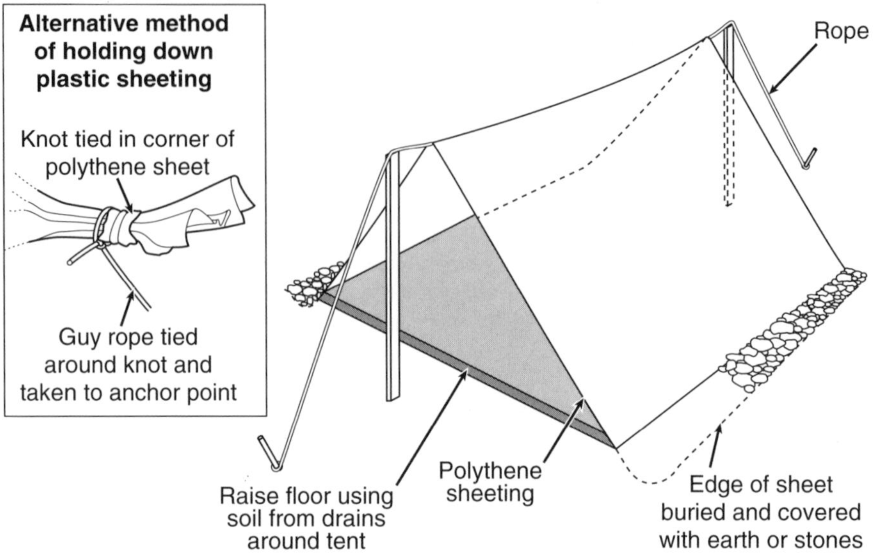

Figure 19.3 A simple plastic sheet shelter using rope as a ridge

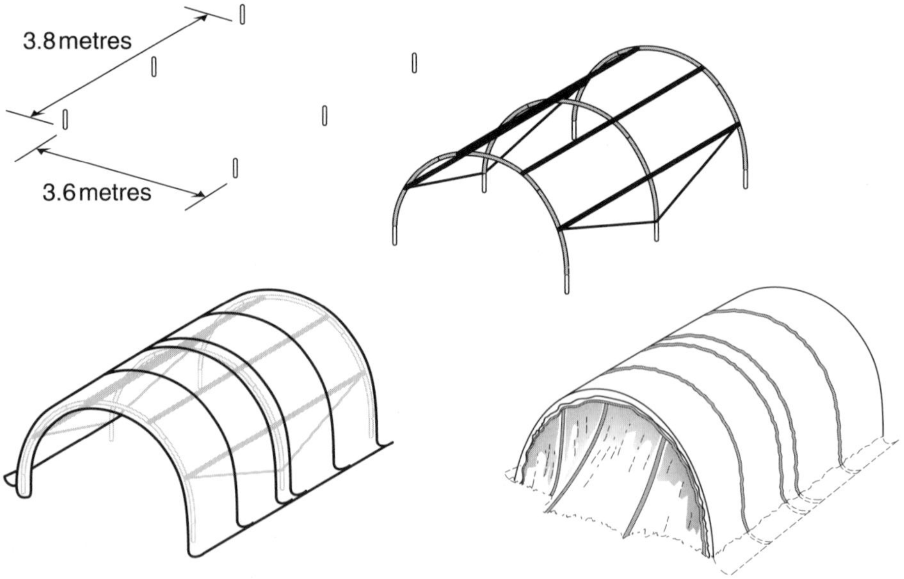

Figure 19.4 A 'shelterproject.org' shelter

pipe forms a frame which is covered with plastic sheeting for shelter or storage space. The shelter has the following advantages:

- It can be assembled from readily available, regionally purchased materials. It does not rely upon a stockpile ready to be flown into an emergency. This minimizes lead time, warehousing and logistics costs.
- The design is flexible and responsive to local conditions, easy to modify, and all the materials are useful commodities when the emergency is over.
- A kit form is available as a 'buffer stock' for immediate use.
- A winterized form is also available to widen the area of climatic appropriateness in a single or phased programme. Insulated liners for both the UNHCR tent and Oxfam shelter are under development at the Martin Centre, University of Cambridge.

Roofing and walling for health and feeding centres Use plastic sheeting and agricultural shading material over timber framework to form large buildings for use as health and feeding centres, temporary stores and workshops. Support and stretch sheeting when used as roofing, to prevent sagging when it rains. Plastic sheet roofs should have a pitch of at least 30°. Figure 19.5 shows methods of fixing to the framework to avoid tearing.

Tents

The combined purchase and transport cost of tents would, in many countries, pay for the local construction of a wooden framed structure with a metal roof. However, tents have the advantage that they can be stockpiled, and transported and erected quickly. They can also be moved easily, if necessary. Tents are, therefore, widely used. Even though tents are stockpiled, the stockpiles are limited because storage is expensive and some tent material can degrade over time.

Refer to Box 19.3 and Figure 19.6 for the UNHCR standard specification for a centre pole family tent.

Tents used in cold climates will need to be designed to take a stove and flue manifold. The amount of fuel required will depend on the thermal performance of the tent and overall shelter design. Thermal performance will depend on heat loss due to air infiltration and heat loss through the tent fabric and floor. A compromise is required between sealing the tent to prevent heat loss and allowing enough air for a comfortable and healthy living environment. More air is required if occupants smoke and when the heater/stove is being used.

Standard canvas tents provide poor insulation and significant heat is lost through the floor. Therefore, emphasis should be placed on good floor, wall and roof insulation, the control of infiltration rates and space heating. Allied to the provision of basic shelter is the fact that people who are well clothed and fed are clearly in a better position to withstand the cold.

Personal and household items

Emergency shelter may need to be complemented by the provision of items to ensure families have the basic means to survive.

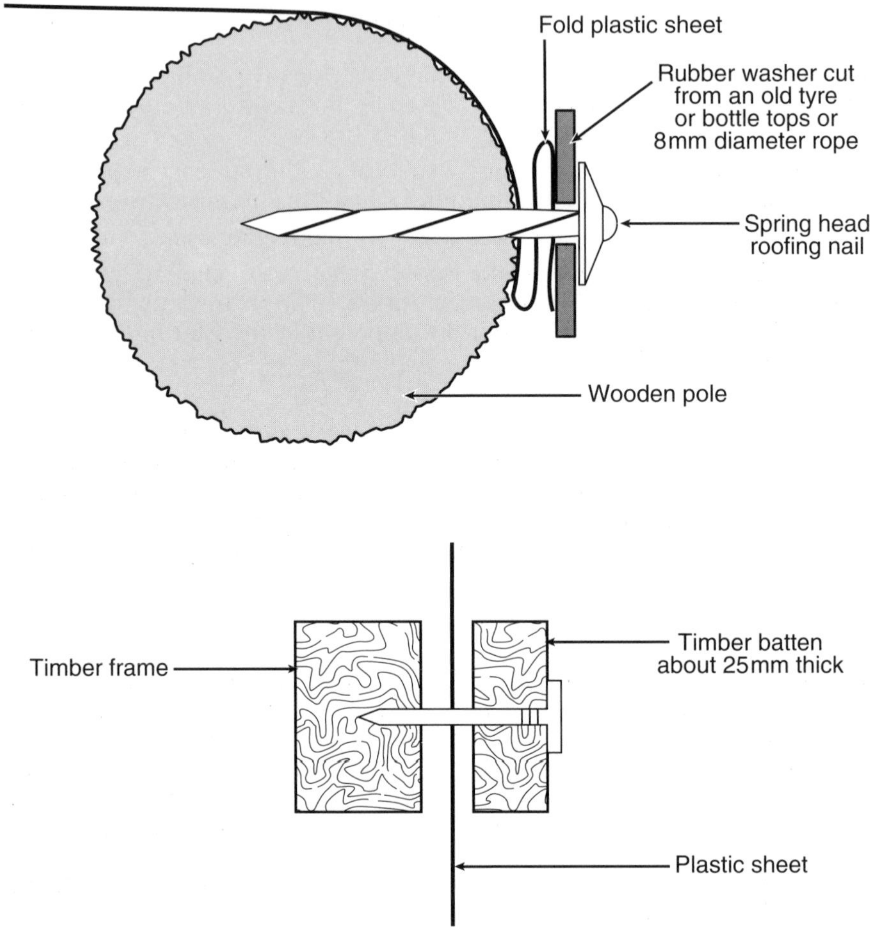

Figure 19.5 Methods of fixing plastic sheet to timber frames

Cooking fuel and utensils People who have been displaced may arrive at a camp without any cooking utensils. Provide utensils which are suited to both traditional cooking habits and to the preparation of the available relief food. Communal kitchens should only be organized as a short term measure and only when really necessary. It is better to give 'dry food rations' for people to take away and cook themselves. Supplementary feeding centres, however, will need large kitchens for daily 'wet feeding' (the provision of prepared food). See Figure 19.13 for a suitable stove design. Refer to Section 20.3.3 for details on fuel supply.

Heaters for cold climate shelters The type and size of a heater and the type and amount of fuel used will depend on the type of shelter, the climate, the availability and environmental impact of utilizing a particular fuel, cultural

Box 19.3 UNHCR standard specification for a centre pole family tent

External dimensions:	4.4 m × 4.4 m (outer fly), surface area 19.36 m^2, centre height 3 m.
Internal dimensions:	4 m × 4 m, floor area 16 m^2, centre height 2.75 m, side wall height 1.8 m (25 cm distance between outer and inner fly).
Material:	Cotton canvas 15–16 oz/m^2. Waterproofing by paraffin wax emulsion and aluminium acetate. Rot-proofing with copper napthanate.
Poles/ropes/pegs:	Four aluminium or bamboo poles for roof corners (2 m × 22 mm diameter); heavy duty sectional steel tube (or aluminium or bamboo) centre pole (3 m × 50 mm diameter). Complete with 9 mm polypropylene rope, T-bars, steel pegs, 1 kg hammer, tent repair kit, illustrated assembly instructions and contents list.
Ground sheet:	Reinforced PVC groundsheet 250 g/m^2.
Packing:	Packed in a canvas bag 2 m × 50 cm diameter. Weight 100–130 kg.

Source UNHCR, 1999

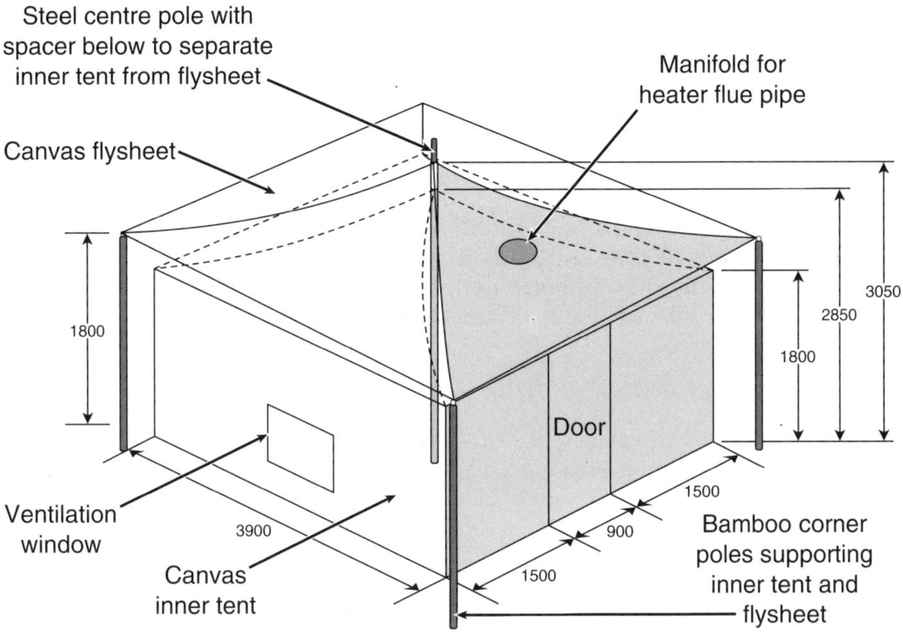

Figure 19.6 Family tent based on a UNHCR standard specification
Source: shelterproject.org

preferences, and what is available in stockpiles and in regional markets. Factors such as fuel efficiency, usable heat output, and the surface temperature of a heater and flue (for safety) will need to be taken into account in design and selection. Some heaters may also be required for cooking. In the Balkans, a locally welded steel stove with a bread oven costs approximately US$40. Heaters burning wood and/or charcoal may be undesirable in many environments and so diesel or kerosene burners are often preferred. All heaters must have flues.

Containers for water/flour/grain People will need containers for collecting and storing water and food. Recycle containers in which relief goods arrive (such as cooking oil tins). Purchase locally 10-litre plastic or galvanized steel buckets (stackable for transport) with lids. Plastic bags are also useful. Refer to 13.2.7 for details on making cement storage jars.

19.2 Built infrastructure

Built infrastructure in this context refers to a range of structures required to support a humanitarian relief operation. In particular there will be a need for warehouse facilities to store food and non-food items such as plastic sheeting, blankets, clothing, kitchen sets, hygiene kits, etc. There will also be a need for communal facilities such as health and feeding centres. The options for storage and communal centres include:

- Rent or loan of existing government or commercial buildings/warehouses.
- Repair/rehabilitation of existing buildings.
- Conversion of buildings.
- Completion of partly constructed buildings.
- Temporary shelters.
- New permanent structures.

In the assessment and design of solutions try to take into account longer-term end-use. Building with the future in mind can aid long-term development and help gain broad based acceptance and support from the local community and authorities who could ultimately benefit from the relief operation.

19.2.1 Storage requirements

There are usually two main types of store of differing capacity: large regional (axial) stores located in strategic positions; these larger stores distribute to smaller local (radial) stores (see Figure 7.1).

Food stores should:

- Protect against insect, rodent and bird pests.
- Protect against excessive moisture and warm temperatures, favourable for both insect and mould development.
- Allow adequate ventilation, yet have the facility to be made reasonably airtight for fumigation, if necessary.

- Provide for convenient loading and unloading.
- Protect against fire and theft.
- Allow for easy inspection of the stored food.
- Allow for cleaning of the storage area.
- Provide a safe, well lit working area with a firm, level floor.

Types of storage system

Storage facilities may be constructed from tarpaulins, tents, freight containers, Rubb-type shelters, and modular systems. Table 19.3 gives a guide to selecting an appropriate storage system. Modular systems and Rubb shelters are discussed in 19.2.2.

Table 19.3 A comparison of various types of store

Type of store	*Phase of emergency*	*Comments*
Tarpaulins	Initial	Easy to transport and install but very temporary, insecure and not structural
Conventional tents	Initial	Available, easy to erect, small, unstable in wind, insecure
Freight containers	Medium to long term	Durable, secure, good for offices or spare parts, heavy, small
Rubb-type	Medium to long term	Widely used, light, good clearance, insecure
Modular	Medium to long term	Secure, weatherproof, durable

Size of store

Use Table 19.4 to estimate storage requirements for different relief items.

Table 19.4 Storage volumes of common relief items

One tonne of:	*Occupies a volume of (m^3)*
Grain	2
Medical supplies	3
Compressed bales of blankets (approx 700 blankets)	4–5
Loose blankets	9
Tents (approx 25 family tents)	4–5

From UNHCR, 1999

Based on a maximum storage height of 2 m, the minimum surface area (in m^2) occupied by the goods will be half the volume (in m^3). Allow an additional surface area of 20 per cent for access and ventilation. Food will be the main and most critical item stored. Daily dry food rations weigh 500–600 g per person, of which 350–500g is a staple cereal (see Appendix 24). Ensure reserve storage is provided. Box 19.4 shows how to calculate the size of store needed.

Box 19.4 Estimating the size of stores

Estimate the size of building required to store one month's supply of food for 50 000 refugees receiving a balanced daily food ration.

Basic food ration = 600 g/day
Food for 50 000 refugees for one month = 0.6 × 50 000 × 30 kg = 900 tonnes
Allow 2 m^3 per tonne: Storage volume = 1800 m^3
If grain stored to a height of 2 m then storage surface area = 900 m^2
Allow 20% for access and ventilation 180 m^2
Total floor space required = 1080 m^2

Size of stores could be: either one store, 50 m × 22 m, OR two stores, 36 m × 15 m each

19.2.2 Types of storage facilities

Tarpaulins

Tarpaulins are a simple and quick method of protecting food mounds and other relief goods in an immediate emergency. Try to raise items off the ground on pallets, wooden boarding or, at the very least, lay plastic sheet on the ground. Tarpaulins are only a short-term solution and more secure, weatherproof storage should be arranged for the longer term.

Conventional tents

Conventional tents can be used for the storage of small quantities of quick throughput items. They are light to transport, quick to erect and easily moved. Large marquee tents should be first laid out on the ground before lifting by an organized team. The disadvantages of conventional tents is that they provide little security against theft and they are unstable in high winds. Therefore, alternatives may need to be sought.

Containers

Standard freight containers used to transport relief items can be re-used to provide storage and office and workshop space (see 17.3.1, Figure 17.7). Containers provide secure weather-proof, rodent-proof and fire-proof storage.

Raise containers off the ground slightly to give ventilation underneath and to reduce underside corrosion. Basic foundation supports may be required, depending on the soils and the loaded weight of each container. There is a considerable rise in the internal temperature of steel containers in hot, sunny climates and this may restrict the storage of some items, especially food. Shade from a simple pitched roof (perhaps using local thatch) can limit heat gain and reduce internal temperatures. Windows can be cut into the sides to give light to an office or workshop.

Several containers can be arranged in various configurations: in rows, as closed storage compounds, or stacked (assuming suitable cranage). Containers can be placed apart and the gap spanned with a fabric or plastic sheeting roof cover to give a working area or further storage. Figure 19.7 shows a possible arrangement.

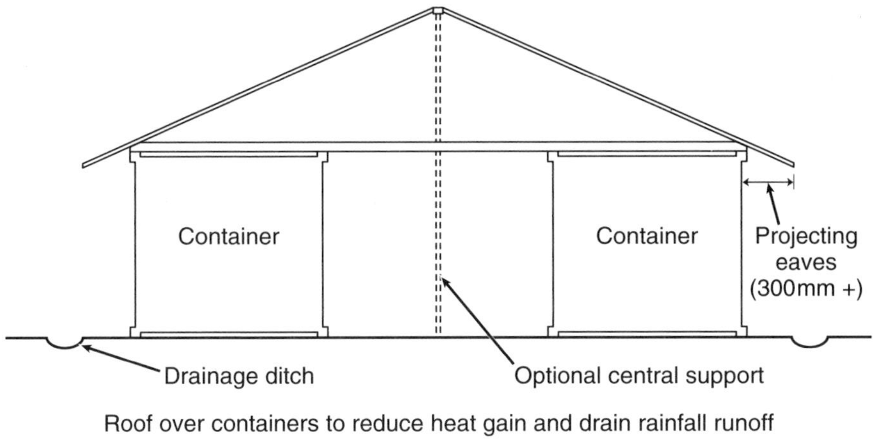

Figure 19.7 Typical container shelter arrangements

Prefabricated redeployable building systems

Modular metal framed shelters Large prefabricated metal frame shelters are commonly used for the storage of food aid. They have also been used as health and feeding centres, and for short term accommodation in transit centres. The following details are based on Rubb shelters, widely used in emergency relief.

The structure is a lattice of galvanized tubular steel frames. They can be supplied in any length, in multiples of 3 m. Tubular purlins span between each frame to provide support for the cladding (Figure 19.8). Cladding is a UV-stabilized cover of fire retardant PVC-coated polyester fabric. Extra fabric protection for hot, tropical climates can be supplied. The standard colour is a translucent white for the transmission of daylight. The sections are joined during erection by overlapping waterproof lace-up joints. End-sections are supplied ready-made. The fabric is tensioned over the frame and anchored to the foundation. Shelters can be insulated by attaching a second skin to the inside of the framework. The cavity can be filled with insulating material such as fibre glass or mineral wool.

Shelters can be erected on an uneven surface or sloping ground. Foundations vary, depending on the size of the building, the time for which the shelter will be standing and the ground conditions. Foundation alternatives include (see Figure 19.9):

- Ground anchors (steel spikes) for suitable soil conditions.
- A sand foundation.
- Ballast weights.
- Expansion bolts for fixing to concrete.
- Bolts for resin anchors.
- Steel channel.

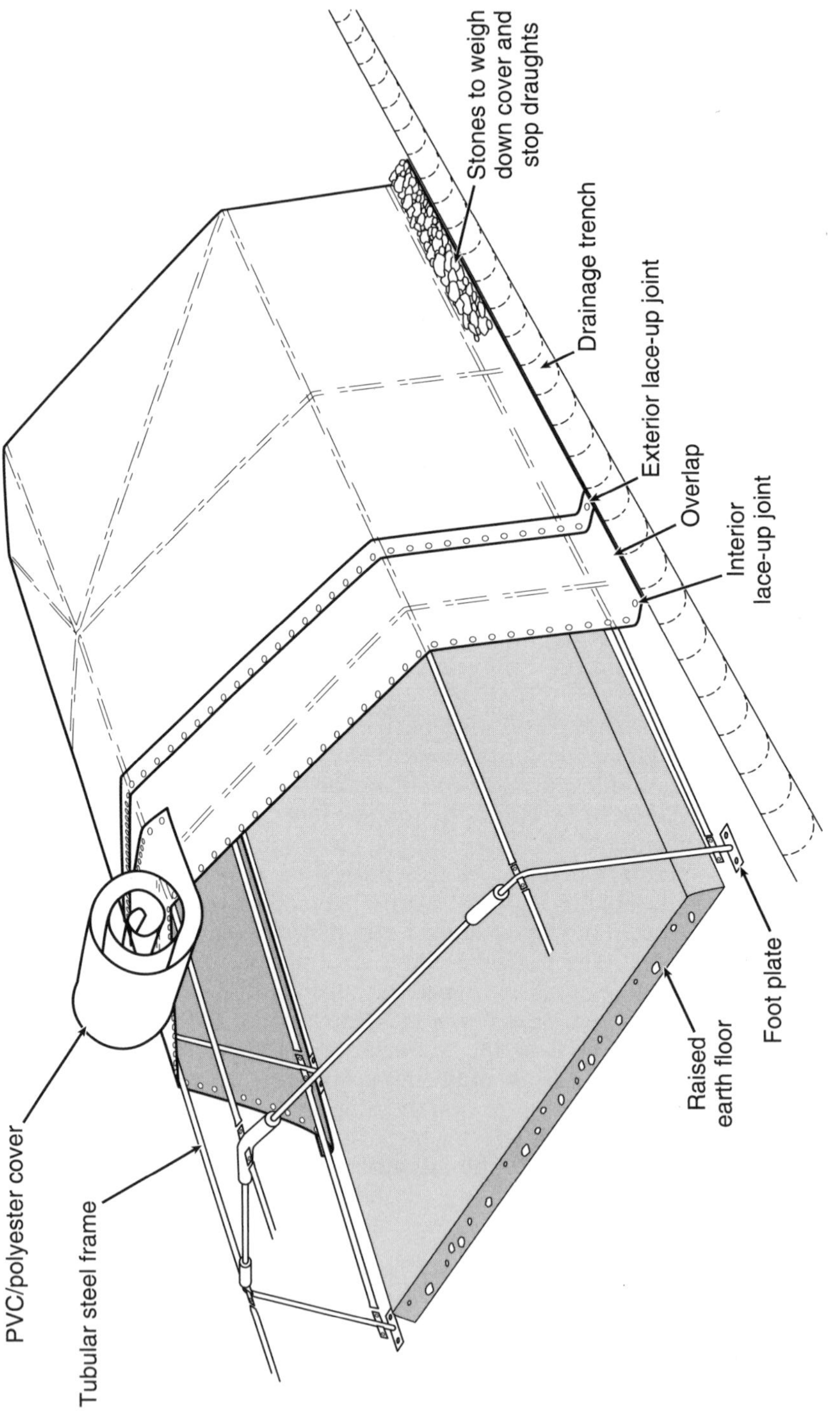

Figure 19.8 A modular metal framed shelter (based on the Rubb shelter)

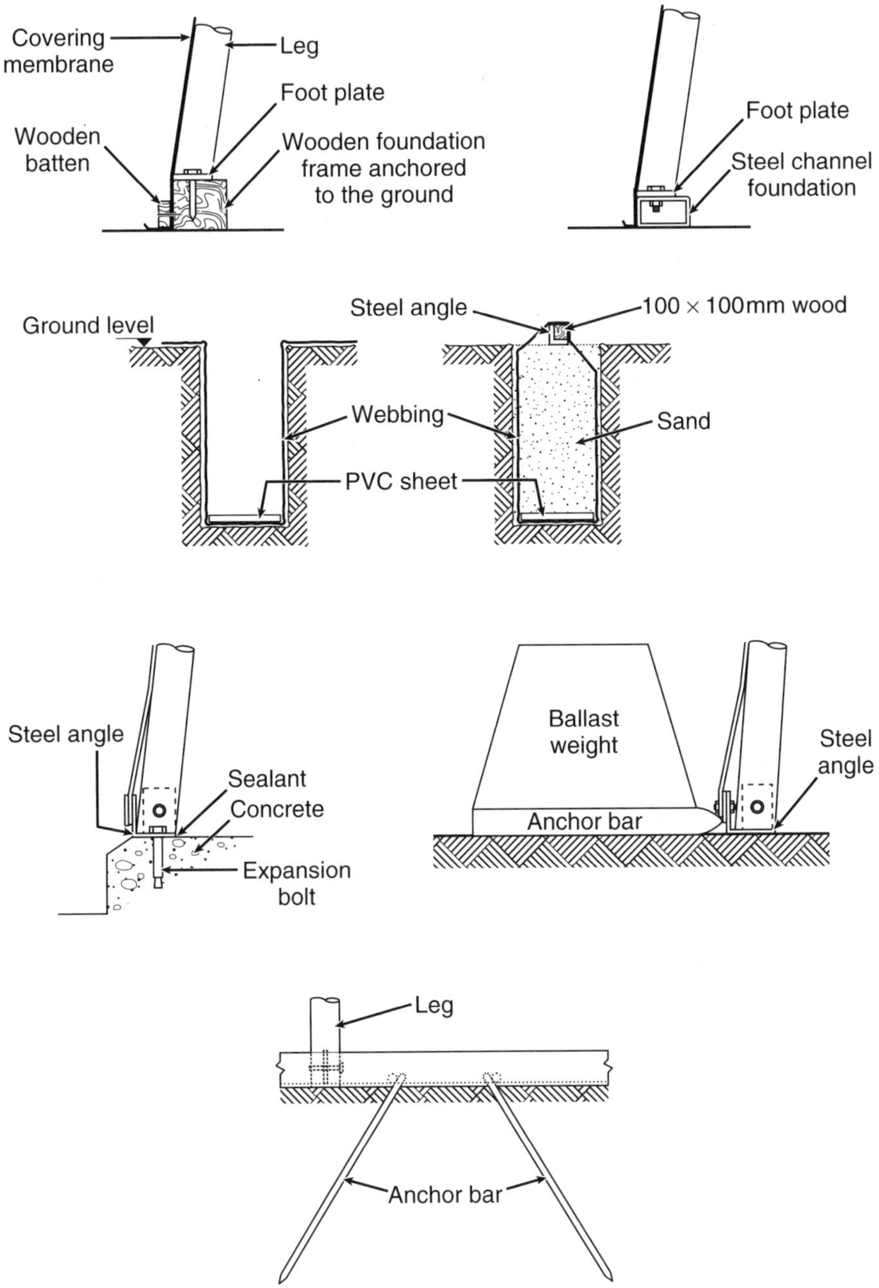

Figure 19.9 Alternative foundation arrangements for metal framed shelters

When erecting these shelters, consider security and rainfall runoff. The doors can be locked, but the shelter material can easily be cut with a knife. Therefore, if security is a concern, the shelters must be enclosed within a fenced compound. The roof has no eaves, so rainwater must be directed away from the shelter perimeter by drainage ditches. Dig the trenches before placing the fabric on the frame and use the excavated soil to form a raised floor inside. Space shelters at least 2 m apart so that runoff from one shelter does not flood an adjacent shelter.

Selected dimensions and weights of commonly used shelters are given in Table 19.5. Shelters are available with a range of sidewall heights in single and multi-spans up to 60 m by any length.

Table 19.5 Dimensions and weights of metal framed shelters

Dimensions (width × length), m	6 × 6	8 × 9	10 × 9	12 × 9
Weight, including cover, kg	1099	1652	1881	2269
Standard door opening (w × h), m	3.3 × 3.3	3.5 × 3.3	4.5 × 3.9	5.5 × 3.9
Snow loading capacity, kg/m²	109	95	45	55

From the Rubb THA range

Pre-stressed modular systems Modular systems using stressed skin sections are an alternative to large tented structures. Steel sections form an arch to give rigidity, so no framework is required. The span is determined by the width of the arch section. Sections are simply added on to extend the length. The following details are based on Conport 'Flospan' structures (see Figure 19.10).

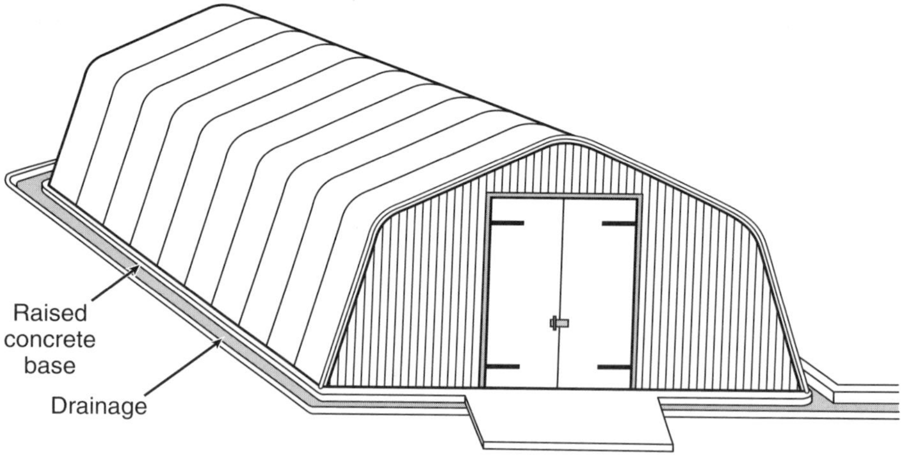

Figure 19.10 A pre-stressed modular building
From Conport, Flospan

Buildings with fully clad walls and ends are secure and weather-proof. Fully clad buildings are safe in winds up to 50 m/s (112 mph). The galvanized steel panels result in significant heat gain in hot, sunny climates. Air circulation is limited, but it can be improved by ridge and gable end vents. Specify GRP rooflights for internal daylight illumination. The steel sections nest together for transportation. Erection is relatively quick and does not require lifting gear. The panels simply bolt together. Note that an arch shape restricts the stacking of stored items, as the side wall is inclined at an angle.

19.2.3 Hospitals, health and feeding centres

In natural disasters, existing health premises may sustain damage. Carry out a rapid assessment of structural stability (see Section 19.4). Provide suitable local building materials and plastic sheeting or tarpaulins and organize repairs so that essential services can be continued. In emergencies involving displaced people, it may be possible to expand existing facilities to accept increased patient numbers, depending on local circumstances. However, health care for large numbers of displaced people often requires the establishment of new health facilities.

Hospital tents are used in the immediate emergency phase and for short-term camps. An 80 m^2 ridge or frame tent with a centre height of 3–4 m and high side walls can accommodate 10 beds or 40 patients without beds. Tents should have windows with roll-up flaps and fly/mosquito nets. Tents are an interim measure. The design of permanent and semi-permanent buildings will vary considerably and must be decided between health staff and the engineer. Figure 19.11 shows a health centre for 24-hour care built in Hartisheik refugee camp, Ethiopia. Smaller out-patient clinics with individual consulting rooms can be built using a single rectangular block design. Refer to Section 19.3 for construction details.

Feeding centres

Supplementary and therapeutic feeding centres for malnourished children may be an urgent requirement in certain emergencies (such as those arising from drought, famine or conflict). See Appendix 24 for explanations of terms used in emergency feeding programmes. The recommended maximum number of beneficiaries per supplementary feeding centre is 500.

Large tented feeding centres may not give sufficient ventilation in certain climates. Simple sun shade structures made from tree poles and thatch may be suitable in the dry season. However, in the rainy season, more substantial protection is required. Figure 19.12 shows a typical design using local timber (in this case eucalyptus poles). The roof and walling may be made from plastic sheet, corrugated steel sheets, or local materials (refer to the relevant sections on these materials).

Feeding centres need kitchens to boil water and prepare food. Figure 19.13 shows a stove made from locally available materials. Field experience suggests that this design uses up to two-thirds less fuel than drums heated on open three-stone fires on the ground.

19.3 Building construction

19.3.1 Materials

The rapid increase in demand for building materials following a disaster can result in rising prices and sometimes shortages. Supplying building materials at

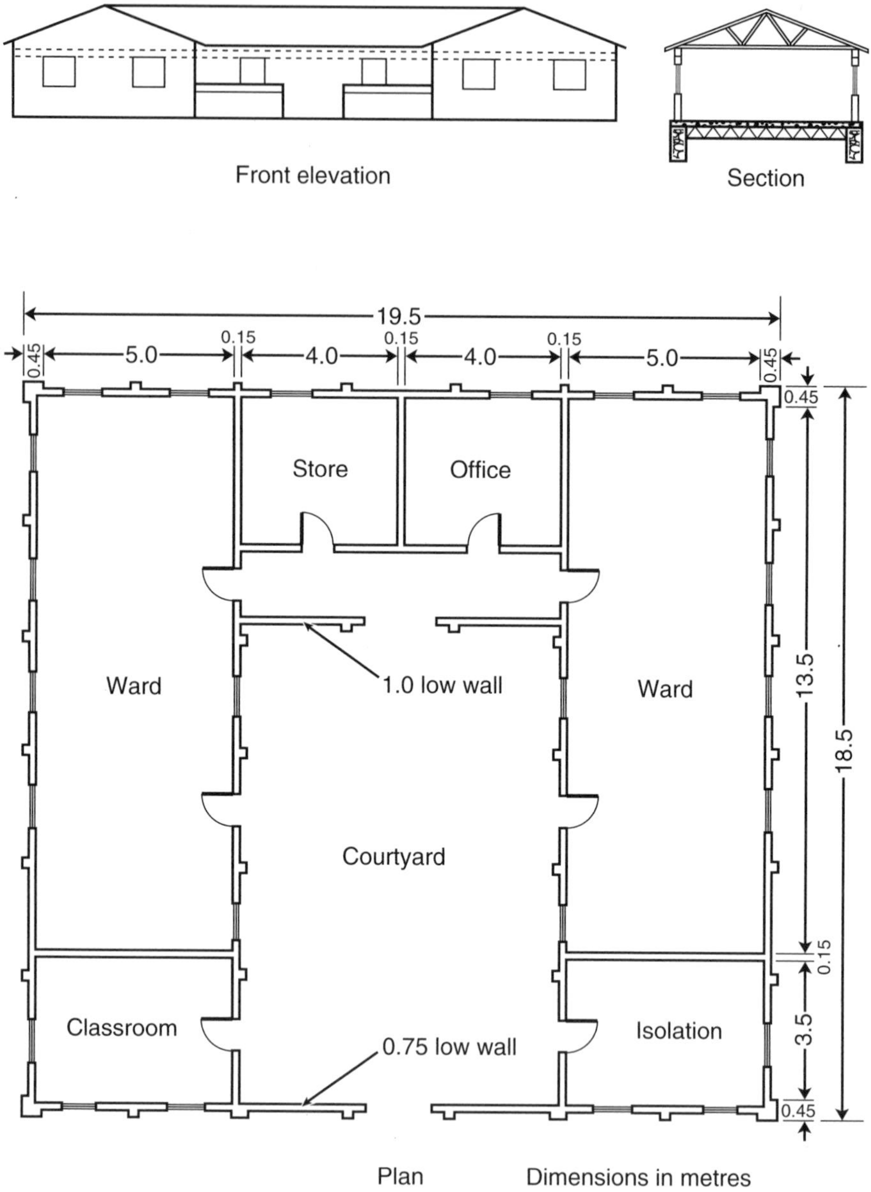

Figure 19.11 An example of a health centre for 24-hour care

subsidized prices can help people to reconstruct their own homes. Where possible, collaborate with other agencies to purchase and transport materials in bulk. This can help to limit localized price rises and the consequent adverse impact on host communities.

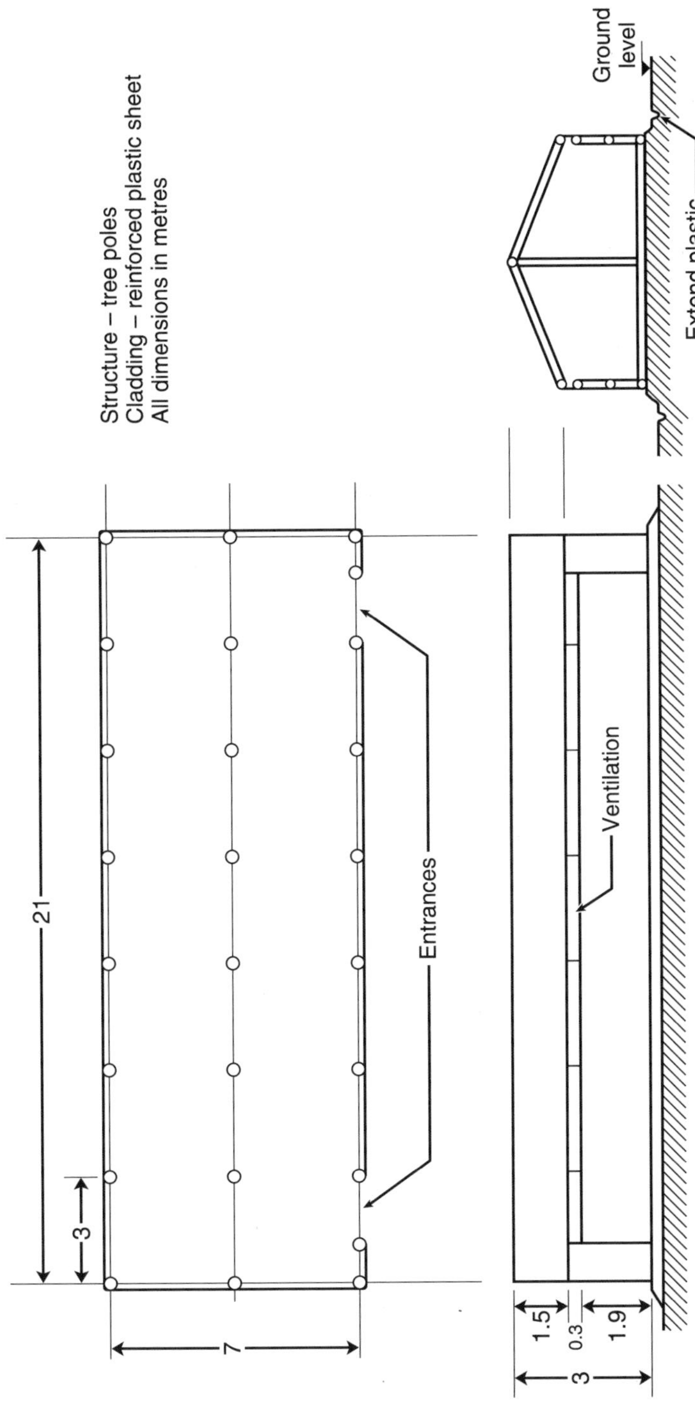

Figure 19.12 An example of a feeding centre shelter

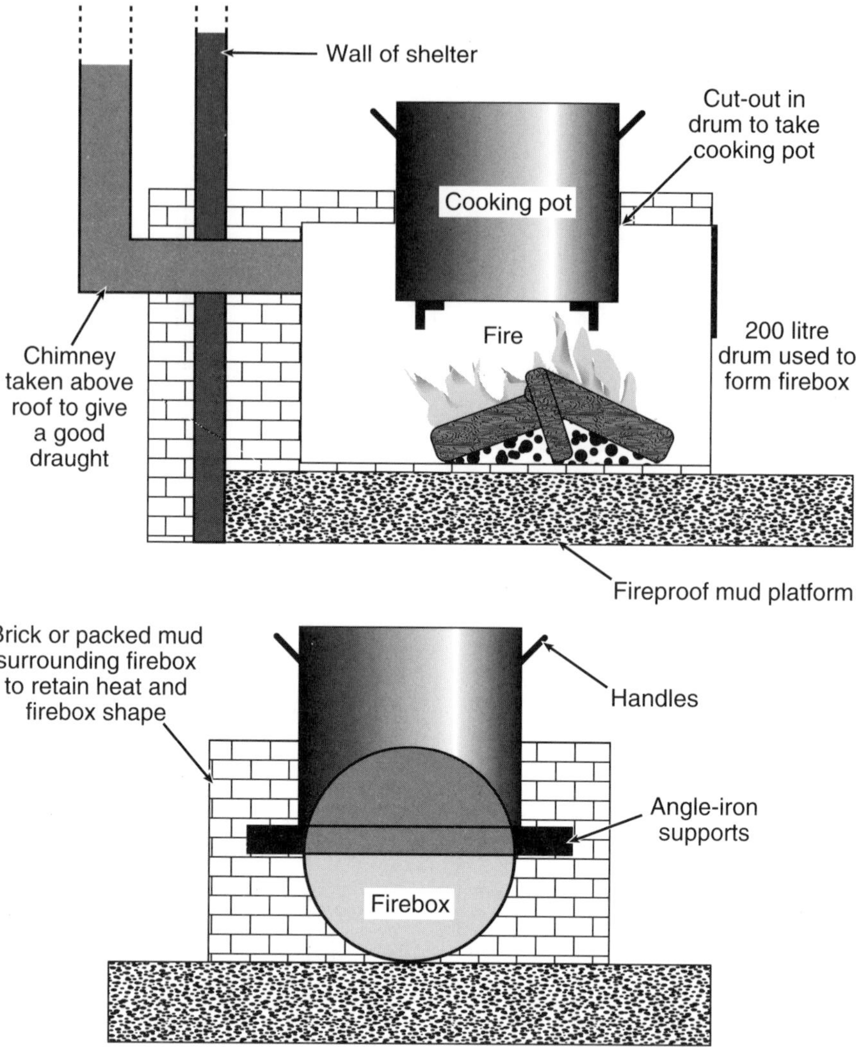

Figure 19.13 A fuel efficient stove for feeding centre kitchens

The price of cement is often controlled. Bulk supplies may have to be ordered from a government distribution corporation. Small quantities may be available quickly via alternative channels. Beware of variable cement quality.

Natural deposits of sand and stone may 'belong' to specific communities. Do not assume that sand in a dried up river can be taken free of charge. Check on local customs and legal ownership. Host communities may contract to collect, load and/or supply sand and stone.

See 19.1.3 for details of plastic sheeting and local materials.

Cement, lime and concrete

Cement Ordinary Portland cement is used for general purpose and structural concrete. Alkalis released when cement is mixed with water can be harmful to the skin. Labourers working with cement and concrete should be made aware of this risk and protective clothing supplied. Wash affected eyes with plenty of water and seek medical attention.

Cement is generally supplied in 50 kg bags. Store cement dry. If kept for long periods, the cement will absorb moisture from the atmosphere and set in lumps. Lumps too hard to be crushed in the hand should be discarded. Cement bags should not be stacked high (maximum four bags) as the compaction will encourage hardening. Raise bags off the ground during storage and keep them dry by covering with plastic sheeting. Store bags close together to reduce the circulation of damp air. Stack bags so that they can be used on a 'first in, first out' basis.

Lime and pozzolana Where periodic shortages of ordinary Portland cement occur, local supplies of lime and pozzolana may provide more than adequate substitutes and reduce the quantity of cement necessary for many construction jobs. Where such alternatives exist, local expertise may have developed in the use of these materials – use it.

The manufacture of lime varies considerably in quality and quantity between large industrial plants and small scale village kilns in developing countries. Lime is used in a variety of ways:

- To make lime mortars and lime concrete.
- To improve the workability of a sand/cement mortar.
- For lime-wash.
- To make blocks.
- To stabilize soils in road construction.

Pozzolanas contain silica or alumina in a state which is available for reaction with lime. Although not cementitious themselves, pozzolanas mixed with lime cause the mix to set and harden in the presence of water. Pozzolanas can be used in conjunction with lime in mortars, plasters and blockmaking. Pozzolanas can reduce by up to 30 per cent the quantity of Portland cement required for making mass and reinforced concrete. This also gives a stronger concrete, more resistant to sea water and chemical attack. Natural pozzolanas may be obtained from volcanic ash or tuff, pulverized fired clay (broken bricks and tiles), and ash from agricultural waste (burnt rice husks). Artificial pozzolanas are obtained from pulverized fuel ash (p.f.a.).

19.3.2 Concrete

Concrete is a controlled mixture of: cement; fine aggregate < 5mm (sand or crushed rock); coarse aggregate (gravel) 6–20 mm; and water. Water makes the concrete sufficiently workable for mixing, placement and compaction, and reacts chemically with the cement to give a hard and strong material.

A concrete mix is expressed in the proportions of each constituent it contains by volume or by weight. Mixing by volume is the only practical method in many emergency situations. The mix becomes stronger as the ratio of cement:aggregate increases. Concrete mixes by volume (cement:sand:coarse aggregate) and their common applications are shown in Table 19.6.

The amount of water in a mix is critical to the strength of concrete. For hand mixing, a water:cement ratio of about 0.55, by weight, gives a strong concrete, so a 50 kg bag of cement will need 27.5 kg (27.5 litres) of water. This ratio is for aggregates that are not absolutely dry. Where very dry aggregates are used (for instance, in hot arid climates) a little extra water is needed or the mix will be too stiff for good compaction. Compaction is important because entrapped air reduces concrete strength and durability. A poorly proportioned mix will need excess water to improve its workability (how easily it can be compacted). This excess water will dry out creating voids or capillaries, so weakening the concrete. Correct proportioning of ingredients will help to ensure that the concrete is both workable and strong.

If workability is poor with hand mixing, the usual response on site is to throw in some more water. In addition to weakening the concrete, as described above, this can wash out cement from the mix on the platform. Adjust mixes based on appearance and cohesiveness to give good workability with the minimum of water.

To avoid handling and storing partly opened bags, use mixes based on whole bags of cement (see Table 19.6). The volume of a 50kg bag of cement is about 33 litres but will vary slightly depending on the degree of compaction. The mixes described are designed to give strength with good workability, although they do not conform exactly to traditional proportions. The traditional mixes are listed for comparison.

Aggregates must be durable and clean. The grading of aggregate affects the amount of water which must be added to a mix to achieve a certain workability. Generally, a fine grading requires more water than a coarse grading. Refer to Appendix 20 for methods of identifying and testing aggregates. Fine aggregates pass through a 5 mm sieve and coarse aggregates are retained.

The size of coarse aggregate depends on the type of work. The maximum size for reinforced concrete is usually about 20 mm. A smaller size may be required for thin sections and a larger size can be used in mass concrete. All-in aggregate refers to fine and coarse aggregates mixed together. Rounded aggregate (such as river gravel) needs less water to produce good workability than sharper aggregates (such as crushed rock from a quarry). In some cases, stone breaking may be the only way of obtaining aggregate. This is an arduous task but it does provide work. In countries where there is no stone, silt and clay is fired and crushed to use as aggregate.

Obtain fine aggregates from naturally occurring deposits such as river beds. Local builders and contractors will know where to go. To obtain sand from the river bed, dig below the silt level. Bends in streams and rivers will naturally grade fine and coarse aggregate – search for the best deposits. Sand must be 'sharp sand', not soft. Damp sand can occupy as much as one-third more volume than either dry or saturated sand. Mixes referred to by volume apply to dry sand. If damp sand is used (for example, from river deposits) the mix will

Table 19.6 Concrete mixes by volume

Mixes		*Use*	*'One bag mixes'*				*Batch volumes*	
Nearest traditional mix for comparison	*Standard BS 5328 mixes*		*Aggregate volumes (litres) per 50kg bag of cement*		*Approx yield, m³*	*Number of mixes per m³*	*for 1m³ (approx.) Cement – bags Aggregate – litres*	
1:3:6 or 1:8 all-in	ST1 (C7P)	Foundations, pipe surrounds	Fine Coarse	130 180	0.24	4.2	Cement Fine Coarse	4.2 560 780
1:2.5:5 or 1:6 all-in	ST2 (C10P)	Foundations where ground conditions are poor or where it is difficult to keep excavations dry	Fine Coarse	110 160	0.21	4.8	Cement Fine Coarse	4.8 540 790
—	ST3 (C15P)	General mass concrete. Minimum for structural unreinforced concrete	Fine Coarse	90 150	0.19	5.4	Cement Fine Coarse	5.4 510 800
1:2:4	ST4 (C20P)	As for ST3 but where greater durability is required, such as solid floors, pump bases. Minimum recommended for reinforced concrete in mild conditions*	Fine Coarse	80 130	0.17	6.0	Cement Fine Coarse	6.0 490 800

* Mild conditions – completely protected against weather or aggressive conditions, except for a brief period of exposure to normal weather during construction.
Use a 1:1.5:3 mix for reinforced concrete in severe conditions. Severe conditions are defined as exposed to sea water, acidic water, driving rain, alternate wetting and drying, and to freezing while wet.
BS 5328:1981 designation: the **C** stands for compressive strength; the number indicates the characteristic crushing strength in **N/mm²** that the concrete can be expected to achieve **at an age of 28 days**; and the **P** indicates a prescribed mix.
The information in this table is based upon the use of a BS 12 cement with a standard strength class of 42.5. If cements of lower strength class are used (i.e. those containing pulverized fuel ash, ground blastfurnace slag or limestone) the proportions of aggregate should be reduced by 10 per cent. The yield will be reduced accordingly.
(Adapted from the Cement and Concrete Association construction guide).

contain less sand than required and the workability will be poor. A rough rule is to use 25 per cent more damp sand than the dry mix specification.

Water should be as clean as possible. Impurities will weaken a concrete but this can be offset to a limited extent by increasing the cement content. While sea water does not normally adversely affect the strength or durability of ordinary Portland cement concrete, it is not recommended for reinforced concrete because of the danger of corrosion of the reinforcement steel.

Mixing concrete It is preferable to use gauge boxes or a bucket levelled off with a straight edge for the uniform measurement of aggregates. A gauge box has no bottom and is filled on a mixing board. Size gauge boxes according to the mixes required. For example, 367 mm (length) × 300 mm (width) × 300 mm (depth) gives a box of volume 0.033 m^3 (the volume of a 50 kg bag of cement).

Mix concrete on a clean surface such as a large piece of packing case plywood. Cast a rough mixing slab if there is time. Materials should be well mixed while dry (turned over three times) until uniform in colour and texture. Form a crater in the pile and add some of the water. Mix, adding water as necessary, and turn over several more times until plastic and uniform in colour. The mix should be such that, when patted with a shovel, the surface is smooth but without excess cement water.

Placement and compaction Formwork (shuttering) retains the fresh concrete until it gains sufficient strength to support itself. Formwork must be adequately supported and braced to withstand the pressure of the wet concrete before it sets. Use a mould oil to stop concrete adhering to the formwork.

Concrete must be well compacted to eliminate air voids and to achieve maximum strength. Compaction needs a vigorous action with shovels and wooden or steel rammers. If available, a poker vibrator should be placed vertically to the full depth of concrete for about 15 seconds, and removed slowly to prevent the formation of voids. Repeat every 150–250 mm across the surface.

Curing Sufficient water is essential for the concrete to harden through hydration. The concrete must be kept moist or 'cured' to ensure that it does not dry out. Poorly cured concrete will not attain its full strength and may shrink and crack. Pay particular attention to curing in a hot, dry or windy climate when evaporation rates can be high. Cure concrete by:

- Covering or wrapping with plastic sheet.
- Covering or wrapping with wet hessian sacking or cement bag paper which is kept damp. A further cover made of plastic sheet will reduce evaporation, but the hessian underneath must be kept damp.
- Regular spraying or dowsing with water.

Horizontal slabs can be cured by:

- Covering with wet sand, which is kept damp.
- Flooding with water (ponding) within a low clay dam.

Start curing as soon as the concrete has set, or straight away in hot and dry weather. Ensure coverings are securely held down at the edges, to prevent air flow underneath and to stop coverings from being blown away. Hardening rates are dependent on ambient temperature. Table 19.7 shows typical curing times.

Table 19.7 Concrete curing times

Curing time, days	*Crushing strength as % of 28-day strength of concrete cured at 20 °C*	
	at 4 °C	*at 20 °C*
4	20	40
7	40	65
28	77	100

Concreting in cold weather The rate of hardening is retarded in cold weather and stops if the concrete freezes. Freezing water expands and this can prevent the concrete from ever attaining full strength. The hydration reaction generates heat, so insulation with straw and thick fabric covers will help to retain heat. A higher proportion of cement will generate more heat and gain strength earlier. Use warm water for wetting the concrete during curing. Protect from the chill effect of the wind. In low temperatures above freezing:

- Increase the curing time.
- Insulate the concrete to prevent heat loss.

In freezing temperatures, take the above measures and in addition:

- Heat the water and aggregate to not more than hand hot before mixing.
- Ensure that surfaces in contact with the fresh concrete are not frozen.
- Enclose the concrete and continue to provide heat.

Reinforced concrete Concrete is strong in compression (when being pushed together) but weak in tension (when being pulled apart). Steel bars or rods carefully placed in the concrete provide the reinforcement which enables the combined materials to resist tensile and shear stresses. Examples of lintels, simply supported floor slabs and columns are shown in Figure 19.14. Tables 19.8 and 19.9 give the dimensions of reinforcement for reinforced concrete lintels and simply supported floor slabs.

Table 19.8 Reinforcement for lintels to support a 225mm thick wall (see Figure 19.14a)

Clear span mm	*Length mm*	*Depth mm*	*Thickness mm*	*Reinforcement (2 hooked, 2 cranked)*
1800	2250	150	225	4 × 8mm bars
2400	2850	200	225	4 × 10mm bars
2750	3200	225	225	4 × 12mm bars

From Stern, 1983

a) Typical lintel reinforcement

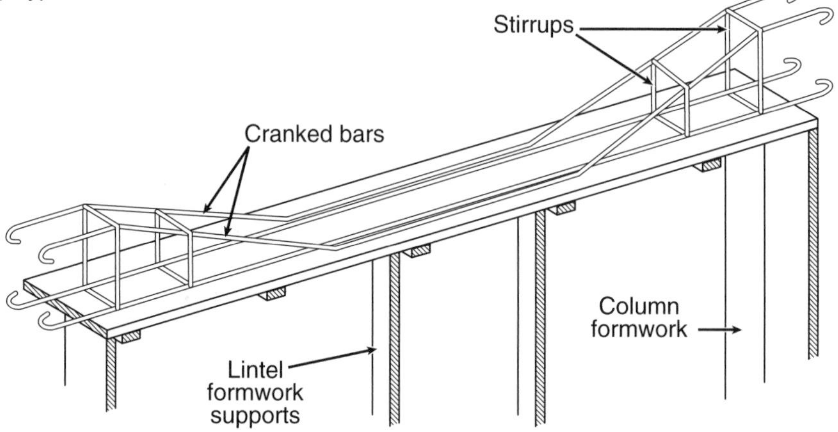

b) Simply supported reinforced concrete slab

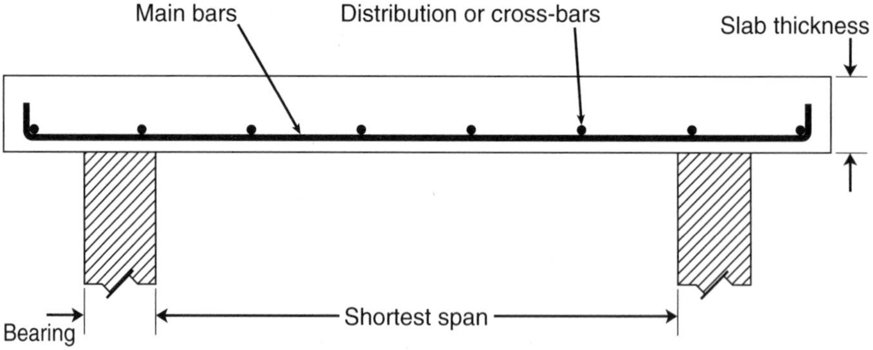

Figure 19.14 Examples of reinforced concrete construction

(Continued over)

c) Typical column reinforcement

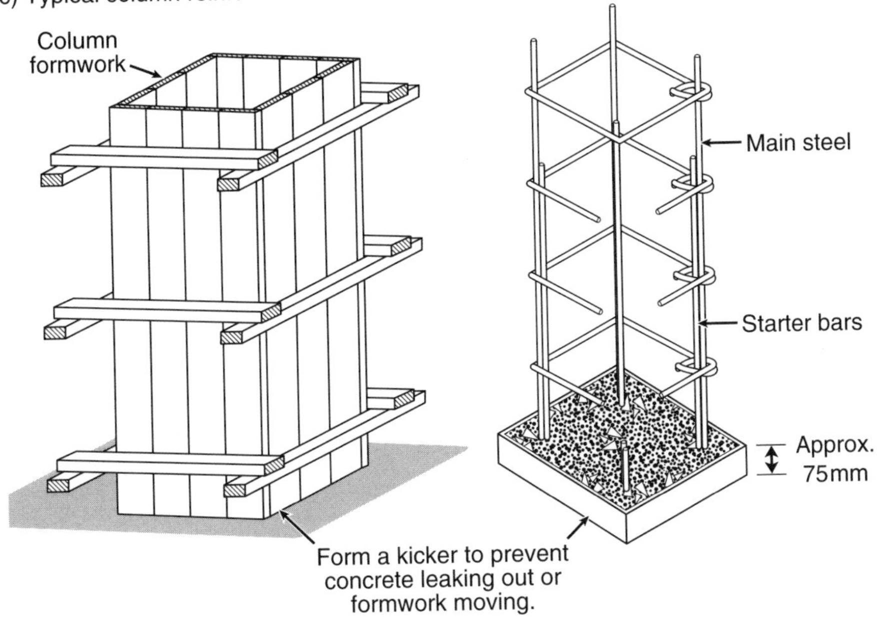

d) Typical concrete beam carrying a floor

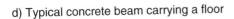

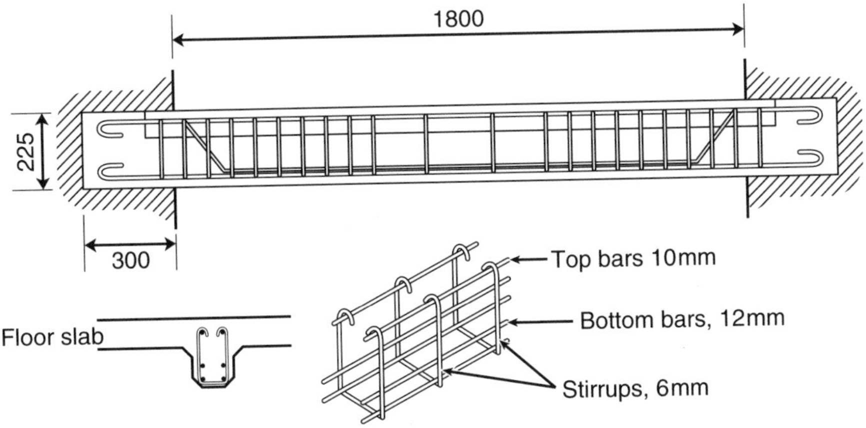

Figure 19.14 (cont.)

Table 19.9 Reinforcement for simply supported domestic floor slabs (see Figure 19.14b)

Span mm	*Thickness of slab mm*	*Bearing at ends mm*	*Main bars run in the direction of the span*		*Cross-bars No. × dia.*
			Diameter, mm²	*Centres, mm*	
900	100	75	10	250	4 × 8mm
1200	100	115	10	250	5 × 8mm
1500	100	115	10	250	6 × 8mm
1800	120	115	10	200	7 × 8mm
2100	135	150	10	200	9 × 8mm
2400	150	150	10	200	7 × 10mm

From Stern, 1983

Warning

The correct use of reinforcement is very important to prevent sudden and catastrophic failure, particularly with beams, columns or floor slabs. Do not attempt such construction unless you are professionally competent.

The most common reinforcement is plain round mild steel bar available in the following sizes: 6, 8, 10, 12, 16, 20, 25, 32 and 40 mm. Steel reinforcement should be free from dirt, oil, grease and loose rust before concrete is placed. Reinforcement should be covered by concrete to a depth of at least the diameter of the reinforcement bars, preferably more. Prefabricated reinforcement mesh of small diameter bars, or wire ('weld mesh'), can be used for floor slabs (such as workshop floors and pump platforms).

Ferrocement

Ferrocement is a combination of cement-rich mortar and wire mesh. Its main application in emergency work is in the construction of ferrocement water tanks. Construction details can be found in 13.2.5.

19.3.3 Brick, block and mud walls

Fired clay bricks

Fired bricks are made where there is suitable clay (or shale). If bricks are available, there will also be skilled bricklayers. Work with them and utilize their local techniques. Bricks fired in 'clamps' will not all be thoroughly burnt. Check samples of bricks before purchasing. A well-fired brick should give a clear ringing sound when struck. Under-fired bricks can be used for covering the next clamp of bricks for firing.

Sand-cement blocks

Sand-cement blocks are commonly made using a hand operated 'blockmaking machine'. Powered models for batch production include vibrators to compact the mix. Various sizes of solid or hollow block can be made. The size and shape can be altered by the inclusion of wooden inserts in the mould box.

The sand-cement is mixed dry with just enough water added to moisten the materials. A typical mix is in the proportions 1:6 'all-in', by volume, of cement and a well graded fine to coarse sand. Do not mix more sand and cement than can be handled in one hour or materials will be wasted. A dry mix block is removed straight after pressing for curing. Protect blocks from the sun and wind. Cover with damp sacking and/or plastic sheeting and keep the blocks regularly moistened for several days (preferably seven days) by sprinkling with water. Do not let the sacking dry out or it will draw water from the blocks, weakening them.

Mud walls

Mud walls are found in many parts of the world. Mud is a durable material in low-rainfall climates and it provides good heat insulation. Utilize local techniques, if appropriate. There are various types of mud wall:

- Combination walls – mud in combination with a supporting framework usually constructed to give a thin wall. Examples include: wattle and daub; double-layer framework with mud infill.
- Large load-bearing walls built in layers of moulded mud lumps.
- Mud brick walls (adobe) – bricks or blocks made from wet earth (and possibly straw for reinforcement), shaped in a mould, then removed and dried for wall construction.
- Rammed earth (also known as Pisé) – layers of earth compacted between wooden or metal formwork. The compaction makes the walls stronger and more water resistant than other types of mud wall. Use L-shaped formwork to produce strong corners.
- Compressed blocks are made by compacting a damp soil of high sand content with just enough clay to act as a binder. Compaction is by hand in a mould or, more usually, in a block press.

The use of a stabilizer considerably improves the strength and water resistant characteristics of mud walls (see below).

Stabilized soil blocks

Stabilized soil blocks are an alternative to sand-cement blocks where cement may be scarce, or expensive. They are also an alternative to fired bricks where fuelwood is scarce or its use may unacceptably deplete vegetation. Soil stabilization is only necessary if the strength and weather-proof characteristics of the earth construction need to be improved. The addition of a stabilizer to a soil can increase its strength, limit variations in cohesion and size due to changes in moisture content, improve resistance to erosion by wind and rain, and inhibit attack by insects.

A manual block press is used to make compacted stabilized soil blocks. Many low-cost, portable, manual block presses are based on the CINVA-Ram design (VITA, 1975); see Figure 19.15.

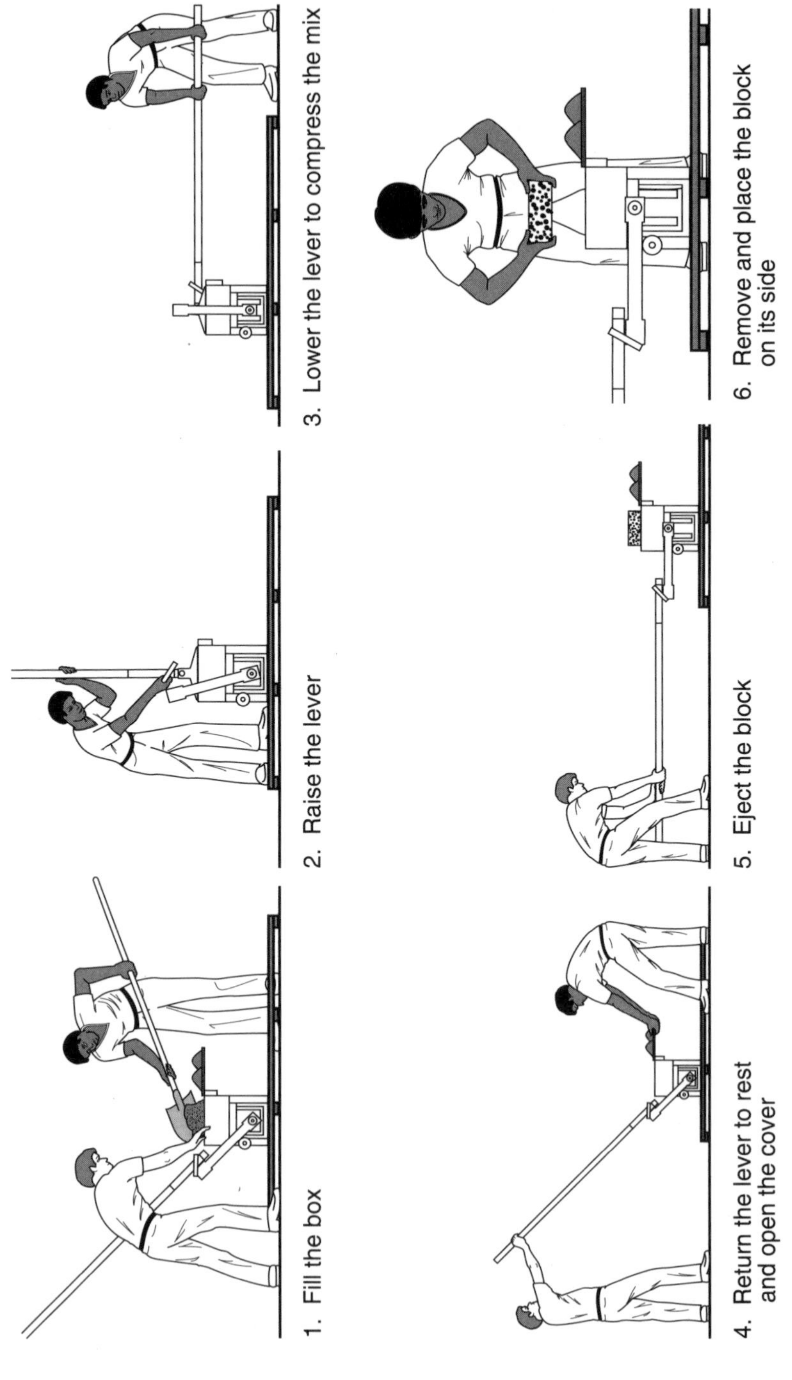
1. Fill the box
2. Raise the lever
3. Lower the lever to compress the mix
4. Return the lever to rest and open the cover
5. Eject the block
6. Remove and place the block on its side

Figure 19.15 Operation of the CINVA-Ram block press
(VITA, 1975)

Cement and building lime are common stabilizers for making blocks, and typical mix ratios are given in Table 19.10. Correct soil selection is critical to making a satisfactory block (see Appendix 20 for details). Mix ratios depend on the type of soil available and the pressure of compaction. A moist rather than a wet mix will give greatest strength. Limit soil particle size to no more than 6 mm. Refer to Appendix 20 for methods of soil identification and the shrinkage test. In the absence of a shrinkage test, try the mixes in Table 19.10. The best mix is found by testing the strength and waterproof resistance of finished blocks of different mixes after curing. Cure cement-stabilized blocks for 15 days and lime-stabilized blocks for 30 days. Keep blocks wet for at least the first five days. A team of four or five people should be able to produce 300+ blocks per day.

Table 19.10 Mixes for stabilized soil blocks

Soil content	*cement:soil*	*lime:soil*
Sandy soil (10% clay)	1:10	lime is unsuitable
Clay between 10–20%	1:7	1:15
Greater than 20% clay (more clay needs more lime)	1:12	1:6

Soil with greater than 50% clay content is unsuitable.

19.3.4 Mortar and plaster

Mud and stabilized block walls will need protection in wet climates. Providing a large roof overhang prevents direct contact with rain but splashing from the ground can wet the bottom of the walls. Rendering of the external wall (or bottom metre) with sand/cement or sand/lime/cement will give some protection.

The fine aggregate used in making concrete is usually too coarse for good block or bricklaying mortar. A finer-graded sand is required, which gives good workability and a smooth joint finish. Cement and sand alone can produce a harsh mortar which does not hold together well in use. Adding lime improves workability and gives a denser mortar. In the absence of cement, lime can be substituted, but it takes longer to gain strength. Use hydrated building lime – agricultural lime is unsuitable. Be careful when working with lime as it can be harmful to the skin and eyes. Workers should be warned. Table 19.11 gives typical mortar and plaster mixes. The mixes are based on good quality building lime and clean sand.

Table 19.11 Mortar and plaster mixes*

Cement mortar for general purpose use (but the mix can be harsh)	(cement:fine sand) 1:4
Cement lime mortar for block and bricklaying, plasters and renders	(cement:lime:sand) 1:1:6
Lime mortar for block and bricklaying	(lime:fine sand) 1:3
Mud mortar for mud bricks	(earth:sand) 1:2

*Mixes are expressed in ratios by volume

19.3.5 Timber

The quality and strength of wood varies so widely that local advice should be sought on the timber available. Newly felled timber has a high moisture content and is described as being 'green'. Timber increases in strength as it dries out during seasoning until it reaches a moisture content of about 18 per cent, which is in equilibrium with that of the air. In addition to indigenous timber, eucalyptus poles are frequently available (100–150 mm diameter) and are commonly used in construction.

Timber protection

Timber is vulnerable to termite attack in many tropical countries (termites are also called white ants because of their appearance). Subterranean termites pose the greatest risk to building timber. They live underground or in termite mounds. Wood is their main food. They tunnel through soil and on reaching the surface, they create runways of continuous tubes of soil which can reach inside buildings. Structural timber, attacked by termites, can fail within a matter of months. Therefore, use chemical or physical barriers to protect timber against termite attack. Poisoning the soil around foundations and walls forms a chemical barrier. Obtain local advice on suitable chemical treatments. There are restrictions on some insecticides used for soil poisoning.

Physical protection:

- Use metal termite shields about 300 mm above ground level angled down at about 45 degrees (Figure 19.16). By being raised off the ground, the timber support posts are also protected from rotting due to excessive moisture.
- Fill cracks in floor slabs.
- Blocks at and beneath ground level should be solid or hollow blocks filled with mortar.
- Seal gaps between pipes and service entry points.

19.3.6 Building details

It is beyond the scope of this book to give more than a brief outline of selected details of building construction. The details shown have been used successfully to construct semi-permanent and permanent buildings in relief programmes. Adapt the techniques according to the materials, tools and skills available and refer to the Bibliography for further detailed information.

Bracing structures

In emergency construction there may be neither the time nor the data to carry out conventional structural design calculations. However, there are a few basic principles which, if applied to simple structures, can greatly improve the effectiveness of building design:

- Analyse visually which members are in tension and which in compression.
- In timber or steel framed buildings keep corners square by using cross-bracing (see Figure 19.23).

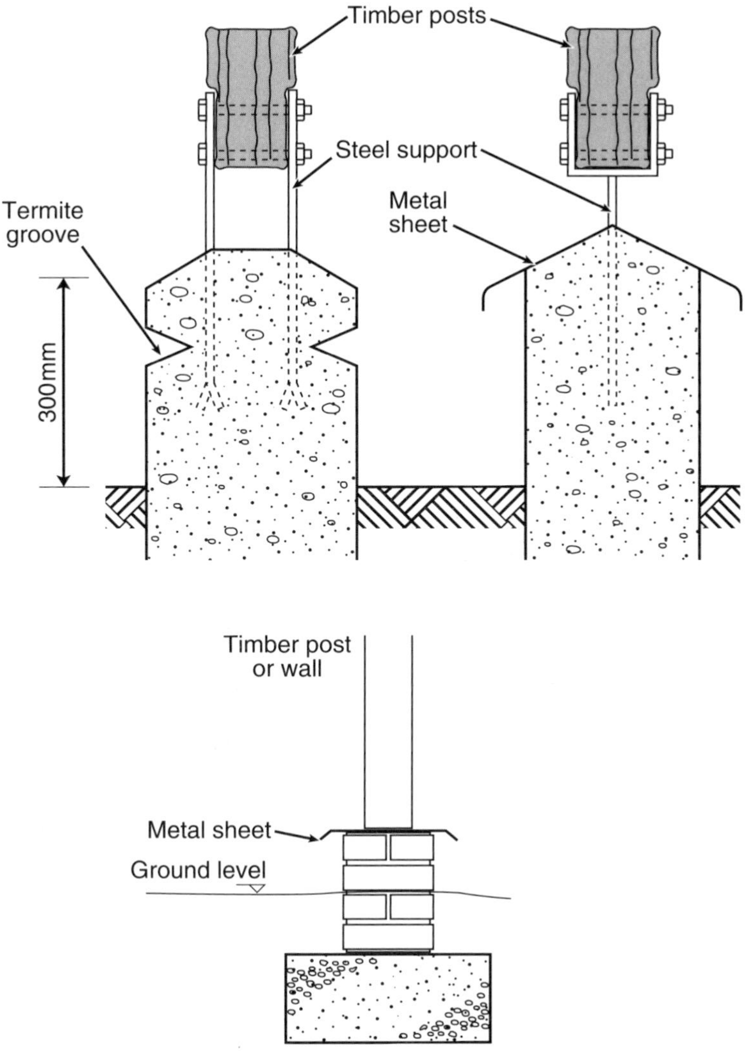

Figure 19.16 Methods of protecting against termites

- Some methods of preventing the weight of a roof pushing supporting walls out include (see Figure 19.20):
  - Support the apex of the roof with a centre pole.
  - Tie the rafters at the bottom using a tie.
  - Use a roof truss.
  - Use a circular wall as in Figure 19.2.

Refer also to Section 19.4.1.

Foundations

Figure 19.17 shows a typical foundation utilizing local stone. A concrete footing could also be used (Figure 19.16).

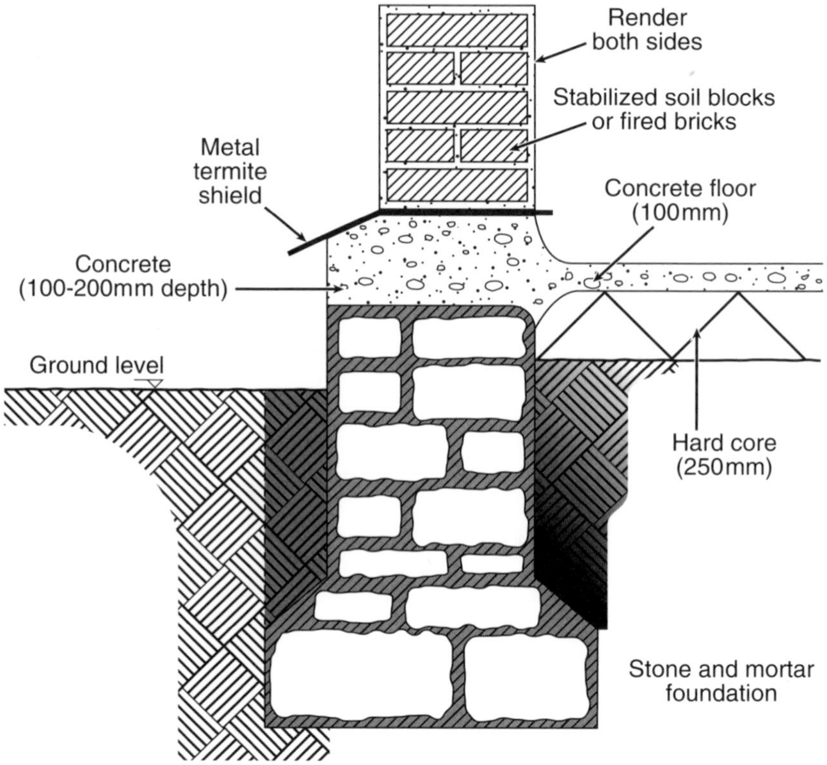

Figure 19.17 Typical foundation details

Walls

One of the main rules of brick and block-laying concerns bonding. Bricks or blocks must be lapped over each other in successive courses along the wall and across its thickness. Bonding maintains the strength of a wall, ensures loads are distributed, and gives resistance to lateral pressure. The two main methods of bonding are shown in Figure 19.18.

Roofing

Wind creates areas of high pressure and suction on external surfaces of a building, which can result in serious damage (Figure 19.19). Regular gusts can result in cyclic loadings on walls and roofs which can lead to failure. In windy areas, fix roofs securely to supports and walls. Tie rafters down at the apex of pitched roofs to prevent them being sucked upwards and blowing apart in high winds. Methods of supporting a roof are shown in Figure 19.20. See Figure 19.21 for methods of securing roofs to wall plates, walls and timber supports. If

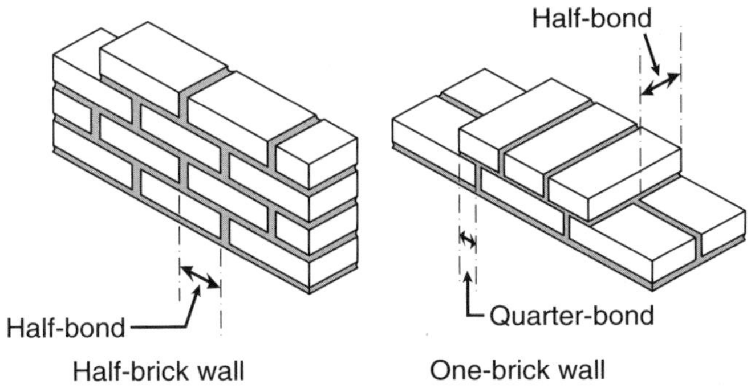

Figure 19.18 Methods of bonding a brick wall

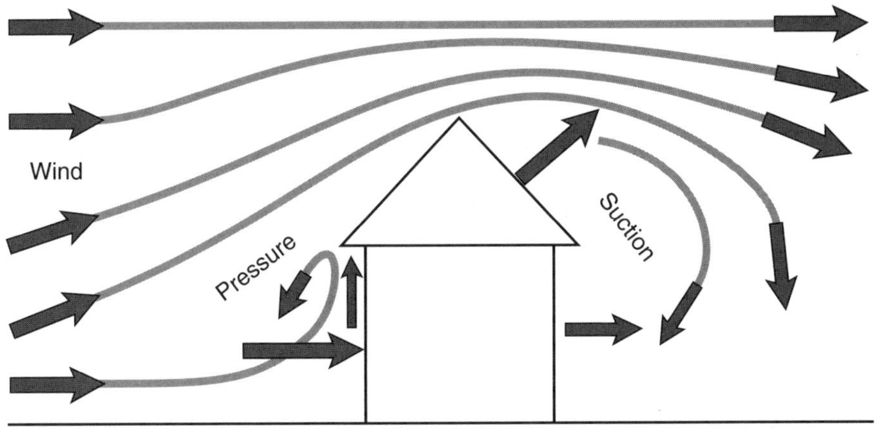

Figure 19.19 Areas of pressure and suction on a building due to wind

necessary, include extra battens and purlins around roof edges (which are particularly vulnerable) and tie them together wherever they cross.

Corrugated metal sheets

Corrugated galvanized steel sheets are widely available, and they are a better 'temporary' roofing option than imported plastic sheeting – particularly for service centres such as clinics and feeding centres. Thicker grade corrugated sheets withstand the wind and rain better than plastic sheeting and they last a lot longer. Corrugated steel sheets can also be used for walling. Details on corrugated galvanized steel sheet are given in Tables 19.12, 19.13 and 19.14 (Stern, 1983).

Table 19.12 Thickness of steel sheet in standard wire gauge (swg)

swg	16	18	20	22	24	26	30
mm	1.626	1.219	0.914	0.711	0.559	0.457	0.315

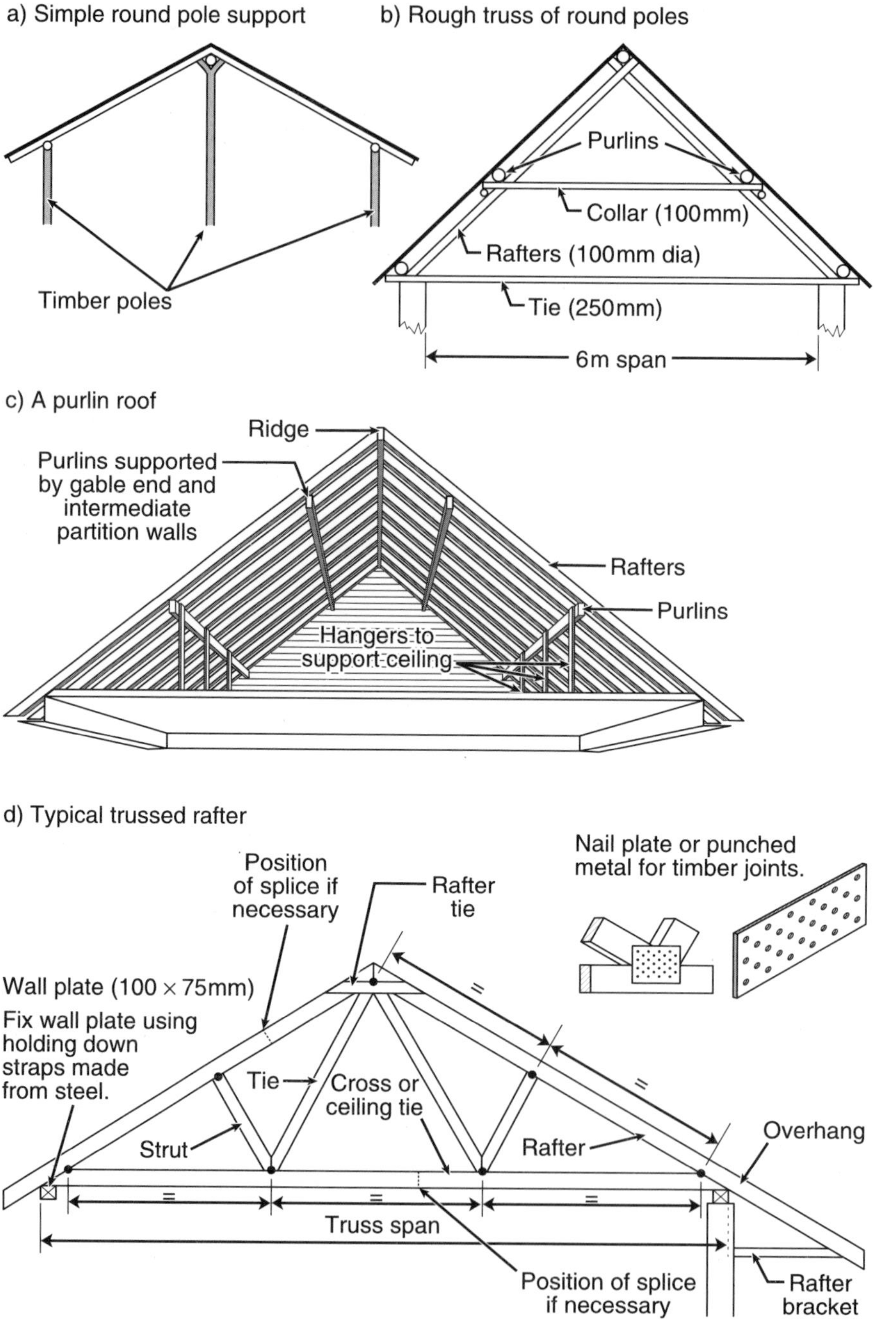
a) Simple round pole support
Timber poles
b) Rough truss of round poles
Purlins
Collar (100mm)
Rafters (100mm dia)
Tie (250mm)
6m span
c) A purlin roof
Ridge
Purlins supported by gable end and intermediate partition walls
Rafters
Purlins
Hangers to support ceiling
d) Typical trussed rafter
Position of splice if necessary
Rafter tie
Nail plate or punched metal for timber joints.
Wall plate (100 × 75mm)
Fix wall plate using holding down straps made from steel.
Tie
Cross or ceiling tie
Strut
Rafter
Overhang
=
Truss span
Position of splice if necessary
Rafter bracket

Figure 19.20 Methods of supporting a roof

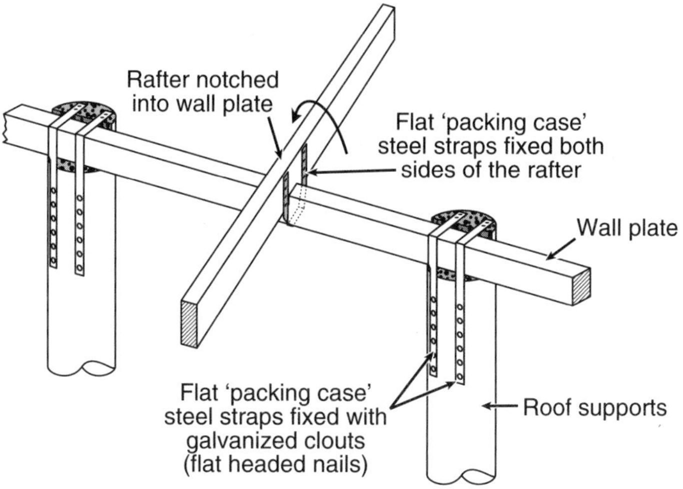

Method of strapping down rafters and wall plates to roof support timbers.

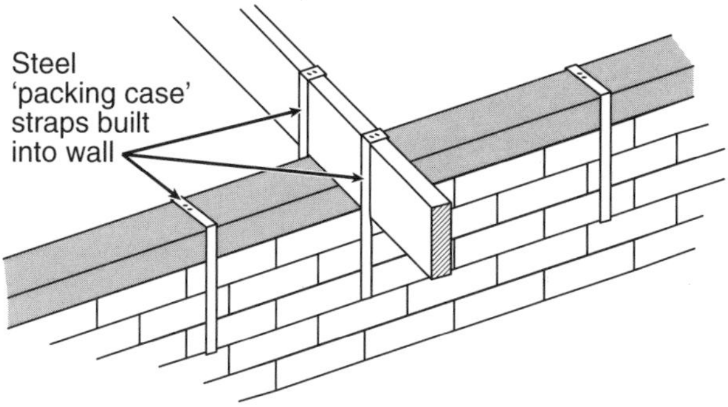

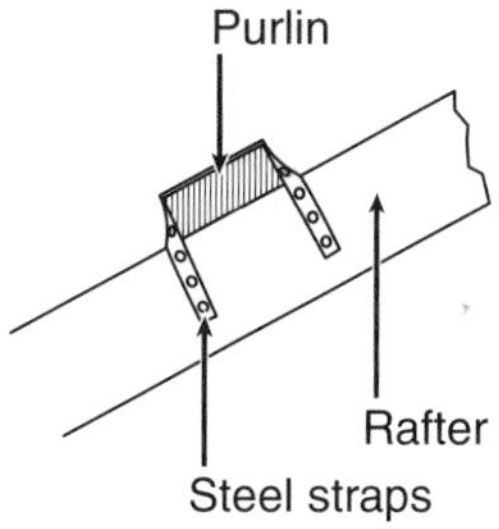

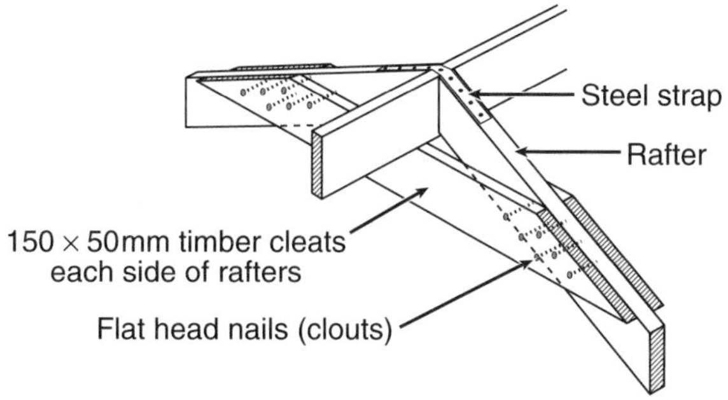

Add cleats at the roof apex to tie rafters together, to prevent them being sucked upwards and apart in high speed winds.

Figure 19.21 Methods of securing a roof

Table 19.13 Numbers of 0.65 m wide corrugated steel sheets to cover 10 m² of roof

Length of sheet (m)	*50 mm side lap 150 mm vertical lap*	*125 mm side lap 150 mm vertical lap*
1.80	9.78	11.21
2.10	8.21	9.50
2.40	7.20	8.23
2.70	6.35	7.26
3.00	5.68	6.58

For 10 m² of this roofing you need: 53 galvanized roofing nails and washers. Weight: 0.95 kg for 112 mm nails and 0.32 kg for washers.

Table 19.14 Numbers of 0.65 m and 0.8 m wide corrugated steel sheets per tonne

Length of sheets, m	*Number of sheets per tonne*			
	18 swg		*24 swg*	
	0.65m wide	*0.8m wide*	*0.65m wide*	*0.8m wide*
1.80	74	64	158	132
2.10	64	55	135	113
2.40	56	47	118	99
2.70	49	42	105	88
3.00	44	38	95	79

Corrugated sheets are fixed as shown in Figure 19.22. Use dome head nails and rubber washers to fix the sheets. Hammer nails through the ridges, not the valleys. Do not drive the nails too hard. Single or two-piece adjustable ridging covers the roof apex. Reverse ridging to make valleys which are fixed to battens and then fastened to the rafters.

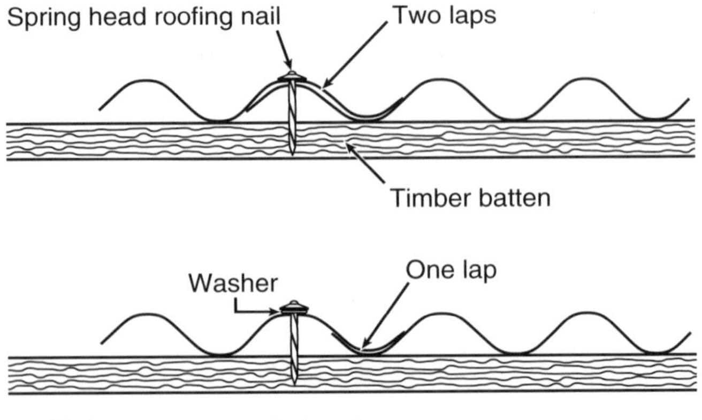

Figure 19.22 Fixing corrugated sheeting

Corrugated metal sheets can be thatched to reduce heat gain in a hot climate. Thatch can provide some insulation in a cold climate. Insulation can be placed between roofing sheets and a lining sheet, if required.

Corrugated aluminium sheets are sometimes supplied as part of prefabricated building systems because they are lighter than steel and do not rust. However, aluminium sheets are not as robust as steel and need careful handling. Sizes are similar to steel sheets.

Thatch

Compared to a corrugated steel roof, a thatched roof:

- Copes with high winds better because it is flexible and permeable.
- Is cool during the day, warm at night and quiet when it rains.
- Requires only rough cut bush poles for roof timbers.
- Requires considerable labour and skill for collection, combing and placement.
- Has a greater fire risk.

If thatch is used, take special fire precautions:

- Ensure cooking and heating fires are controlled and safe.
- In areas with severe electric storms, erect a lightning conductor pole beside the building and above the height of the thatched roof.
- Do not pass electric lighting cable across roofing poles or wrap it around them. A thatched roof 'gives' in strong winds. The relative movement between poles and cable can remove the insulation cover very quickly, resulting in a short-circuit, sparking and fire.

19.4 Damage assessment and building survey

Damage to buildings may be due to the direct consequences of a disaster (flood, hurricane, conflict) or through longer-term deterioration (such as corrosion or termite attack). An engineer may be called upon to assess the safety of a building for use during an emergency. This brief overview provides a simple, rational approach to building damage assessment for the non-structural engineer. Refer to Section 19.3 for construction details. Refer to the literature given in the Bibliography for specific information on earthquake and hurricane design, inspection and repair.

19.4.1 Damage assessment

Assessment is divided into two parts:

- The integrity of the structure as a whole.
- The safety aspects of non-structural elements, such as cladding.

Structural integrity

The most immediate concern in the short-term is gravity load carrying capacity. This can be jeopardized by:

- Loss of strength (caused by corrosion, rot, damage, etc.).
- Lateral (horizontal) instability (for instance, slender walls not supported horizontally).
- Loss of bearing (for example, when a small bearing surface, such as a floor joist, on which elements normally sit, has rotted away).

To assess structural integrity:

- Look at the foundations. Gross settlement can cause loss of load carrying capacity. Rain and flooding can weaken potentially unstable slopes and cause failure in poorly founded structures.
- Look behind the façade of the building and identify what is really holding it up. How are all the loads transmitted to the foundations?
- Establish the major load bearing elements: beams, columns, walls, etc. and how the structure resists lateral forces.

Methods of improving the rigidity of a structure are illustrated in Figure 19.23. Beams, walls and columns do not give stability on their own. Minimal lateral stability is needed for carrying vertical loads. The method of lateral stability can sometimes be difficult to establish. Lateral stability may be:

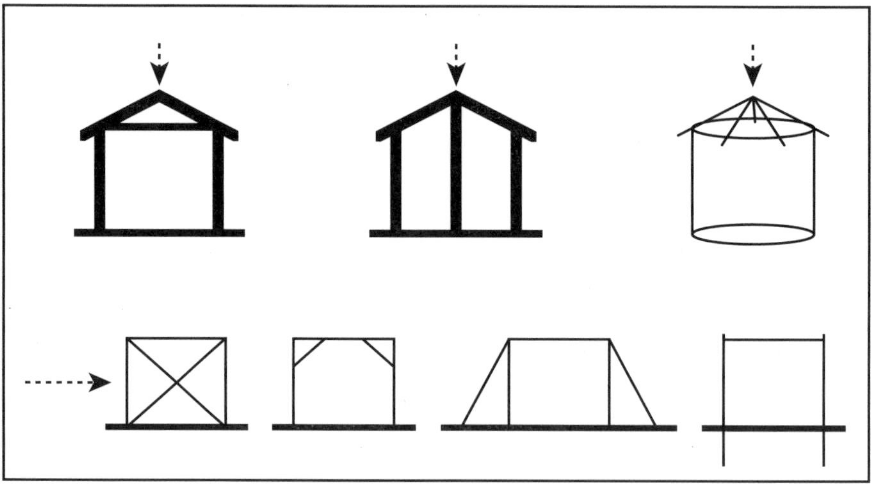

Figure 19.23 Methods of bracing structures

- Designed into the joints. Examples include bolted or welded steel joints; reinforcement bars tied into each other and the junction of concrete columns and beams cast together at the same time.
- Provided by diagonal cross-bracing.
- Incorporated in solid walls. Buttress piers and returns to a brick wall will improve its lateral stability (Figure 19.24).

Take account of any alterations and extensions that may have been made, as buildings are sometimes altered without considering structural stability. For

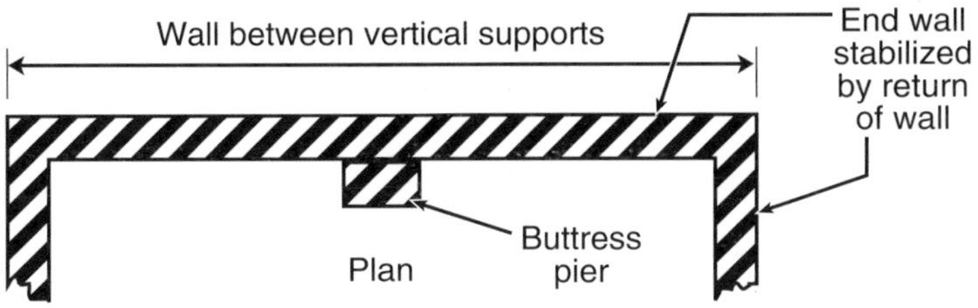

Figure 19.24 The lateral support of walls

example, the removal of walls providing lateral or vertical support, or the addition of extra storeys for which the building was not originally designed, can seriously weaken buildings.

After establishing how a building is stabilized structurally, it is important to inspect the major structural elements. Take one of the following actions if damage is found:

- If the damage is not serious as the members are more substantial than required, decide that the building is safe.
- Take remedial action by supporting or replacing structural members.
- Condemn the building as unsafe for use.

Non-structural elements

Identifying damage to non-structural elements should be more straightforward. Look for loose components which may fall and cause injury. Cladding panels, coping stones, panes of glass, etc. may have been disturbed and pose a hazard. In particular, inspect elements which normally sit on a small bearing surface, such as parapet walls to the top of buildings.

19.4.2 Notes on materials

Brickwork, blockwork and stone

Construction in brickwork, blockwork and cut stone tends to be resistant to damage. Problems arise when a wall loses its lateral restraint. A typical example of instability occurs in a gable wall at roof level. Damaged roof timbers, which would normally provide lateral restraint, may leave an unrestrained gable end wall (Figure 19.25). A chimney in the wall may provide sufficient stability.

Shell damaged brickwork may not be as dangerous as it looks. Where a hole is blown through a wall, brickwork will bridge a gap forming an approximate 45° arch. Bricks may need to be removed below the line of the arch for safety. There must be enough brickwork left to one side of the arch to take the resulting vertical and horizontal loads (Figure 19.26).

The poor tensile strength of earth buildings, coupled with sometimes poor building technique and lack of reinforcement, makes them prone to earthquake damage. Reconstruction provides an opportunity to improve traditional building techniques, and the following points should be considered when building with earth in an earthquake zone (Norton, 1986):

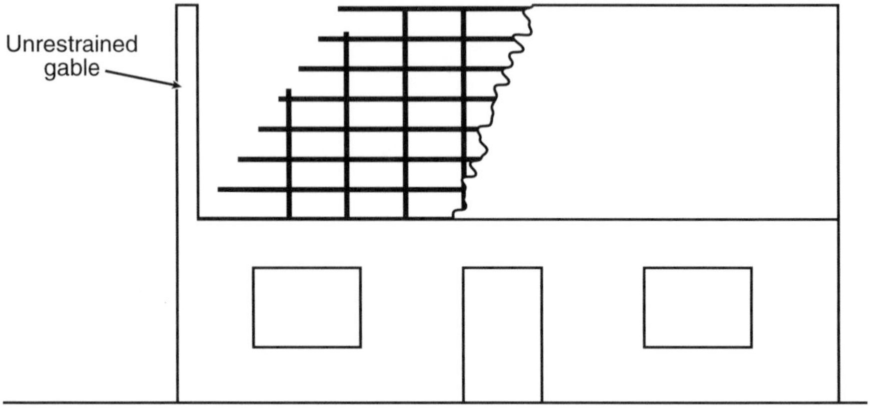

Figure 19.25 An unrestrained gable wall

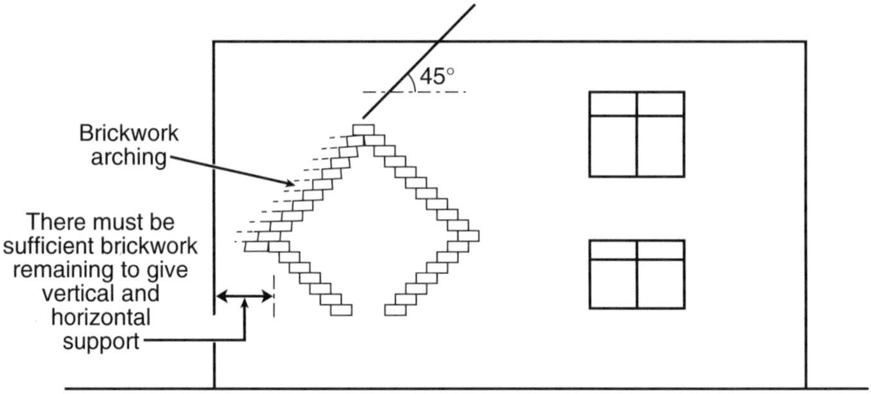

Figure 19.26 Arching in damaged brickwork

- A building can be tied together horizontally by the foundations, by a continuous ring beam at the top of the walls, and by intermediate horizontal rings such as extended lintels. Possible reinforcement includes timber in the wall and reinforced concrete made with steel bars or bamboo.
- A building can be tied together vertically with posts or reinforcing bars within the walls, particularly at corners, wall junctions and at the sides of openings. Use cross-bracing (see Figure 19.23).
- Horizontal and vertical framework and reinforcement should be tied together.
- Bricks and blocks should be well bonded.
- Openings (doorways and windows) should not be positioned close to corners and wall junctions.

- A building should be simple and symmetrical, preferably rectangular or circular. The length:width ratio should be no greater than three. Avoid buildings above a single storey.

Steelwork

The load bearing capacity of a steel member in compression will be drastically reduced if it is bent. It will need temporary propping and eventual replacement.

Corrosion can have a significant effect on steelwork. Rust expands to many times the volume of the original steel. Therefore, the rust may not be as bad as it looks if it is confined to non-joint areas. Scrape right back to the original metal before measuring the thickness of steel left. Corrosion is very bad if lamination has occurred, in which the edge of a steel plate looks as if it has split into thin layers. Corrosion in joints (bolts, rivets and welds) can be highly critical. Rust at a joint can push steel sections apart and possibly break the bolts. Check bolts for tightness.

Steel members may crack, although this is unusual. The most likely place is at welds and holes. An old crack will have a thin line of rust along it.

Reinforced concrete

Reinforced concrete members which exhibit significant cracks may have been overstressed. If the cracking is in a position likely to be in tension then consider propping. Old cracks may be the result of poor curing and shrinkage during construction. Therefore, check that the crack looks fresh. Exposed reinforcement should not necessarily be a cause for alarm. Most reinforced concrete showing exposed surface reinforcement is adequate in the short-term. It will become critical once corrosion sets in.

Timber

There is usually a fair margin of safety where timber is used in construction. The main original design criterion was probably to limit deflection. A reasonable assessment of damaged timber strength can be gauged by observing deflection under given loads. However, insect attack (such as termites or beetles) and both wet and dry rot can quickly result in failure.

Temporary methods of shoring

Temporary methods of shoring are illustrated in Figures 19.27, 19.28 and 19.29 (from Chudley and Greeno, 2001).

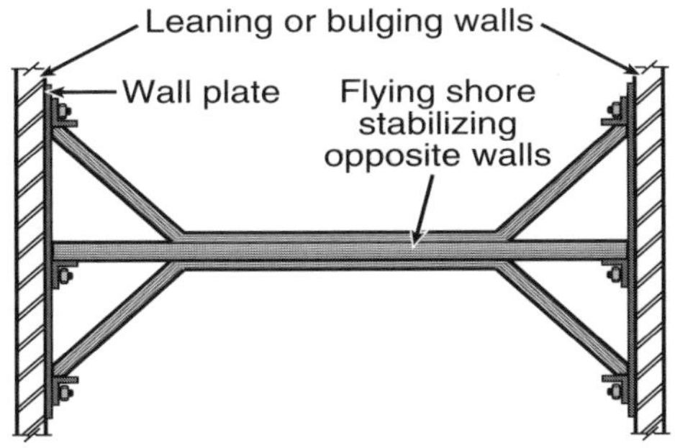

Figure 19.27 Flying shore

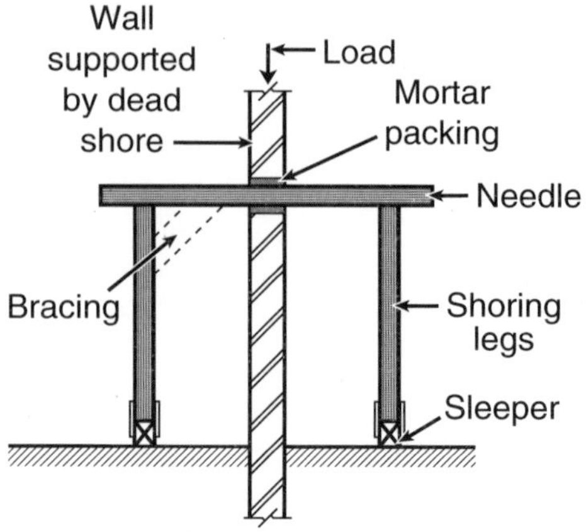

Figure 19.28 Dead shore

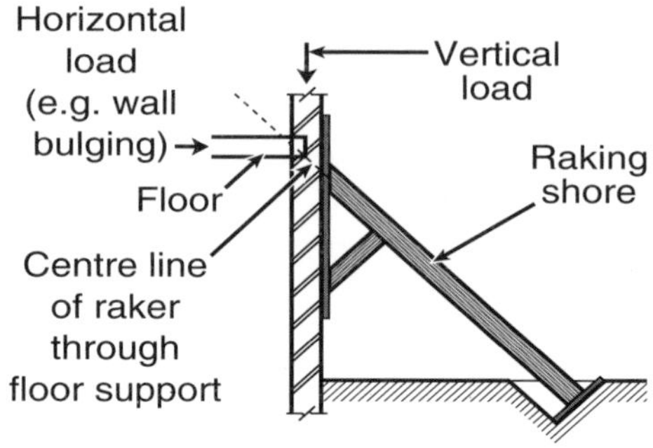

Figure 19.29 Raking shore

20 Temporary settlements

This chapter outlines some of the key factors affecting site selection and temporary settlement planning, and gives guidance figures and notes on camp administration, layout and infrastructure.

The selection of sites and planning of temporary settlements is considered because of the frequency with which relief workers are involved in supporting temporary settlements for displaced people. It is not intended as an endorsement of camps as the only solution to the problems faced by people who have been displaced, as there are clearly alternatives which are briefly described in this chapter. In the aftermath of a natural disaster, communities are keen to return home and the emphasis should be on supporting the rehabilitation of infrastructure and rebuilding permanent homes rather than sustaining temporary settlements.

20.1 Introduction

20.1.1 Preparedness planning

In many cases, the movement of large numbers of people as a consequence of war, famine or political unrest can be predicted. Where possible, it is better to take action to provide assistance to people before they have to move and then, if they still need to move, to have contingency plans in place to provide appropriate assistance on the scale required.

Figure 19.1 indicates the range of shelter options with 'supported temporary settlement' (STS) being one of several possibilities.

Whilst some migrations of displaced people occur in a matter of hours or days, in other circumstances there will be warning signals. Although it may be difficult to predict when and where the first people will arrive at the start of an emergency, the movement of subsequent migrants can sometimes be anticipated or planned. Only a short time will be available in which to prepare for their arrival. It is important that full use is made of this time for preparedness planning including site selection, ordering of equipment and materials and recruitment of staff.

The option of planning a new settlement arises when extending or transferring people from an existing settlement or where sufficient warning of arrival is given.

20.1.2 Self-settlement

Not all people who are displaced seek a camp for shelter and support. Many people, and in some cases the majority, will self-settle in dispersed communities, settle with host families (especially where there are close ethnic and cultural ties) or live in rented accommodation. Dispersal throughout a region in small settlements and local villages may have less of an impact on local food and other resources than larger settlements. However, dispersed self-settlement can result in inequitable access to services and resources, especially for the vulnerable, aggravate health problems, and impact unfairly on the host population. Support may need to be directed to host communities sheltering displaced families.

People who are displaced are often the first to select a site to settle, usually where there is water and security. If they have crossed into a different country they often do not want to move far away from the border, unless in a conflict zone. The site may well be vacant only because it is inherently unsuited to long-term habitation or that it is not currently being cultivated as it is out of season.

In the initial stages, temporary support measures should be considered whilst more fundamental questions are asked, such as:

- If the settlement can or must remain where it is, how does it function and how can it be improved?
- If the site is not suitable, can people move to a better site?

20.1.3 Moving people

People may need assistance to move from their present site for the following reasons:

- Political or security concerns.
- Poor access to water.
- Poor drainage and impermeable soils.
- Poor access for relief supplies.
- Potential for long-term environmental damage.
- Legal and social problems over the use of the land.
- Repatriation to their home communities.

It will clearly be necessary to prepare a plan with the people concerned, especially those who are particularly vulnerable. In preparing the plan, consider the following:

- Type of vehicle. Buses are best provided they can negotiate the route and are available. However, people may have to be moved by truck. It is better to travel in a truck which is moving than in a bus which is stuck. See Section 17.2.2 for guidance on convoy driving.
- Way stations. Plan for frequent stops and ensure that all concerned know where they are. Ensure water and sanitation facilities are available.
- Boarding the vehicles. Try to ensure that there is an orderly system of embarkation, which does not separate children from their families, and that the elderly and sick are given assistance.
- Travel sickness: control food at departure and way stations. People should be advised not to eat meals less than four hours before embarkation. Drivers should keep speeds down to reduce bumps and dust.
- If using trucks, reduce shocks from bumps by placing bedding (or sand) on the floor.

- Climate: In hot areas, provide covers for shade. Move at cooler times of the day. In cold areas, provide blankets and hot tea at way stations. Beware of enclosing the backs of trucks – exhaust fumes can be sucked in.
- Ensure the drivers are well looked after and do not get over-tired. Provide relief drivers.

Transit centres

Transit centres provide rest and nourishment for people travelling between sites and during repatriation. The period of stay may only be a few hours or overnight. People should not remain for extended periods. Transit centre requirements include:

- Basic services – water, food, sanitation, secure shelter for overnight stays and protection from rain, wind, the cold or the sun.
- A simple and easily understood system of passage through the centre.
- A method of monitoring arrivals and departures.
- Facilities for supervisory staff and for drivers of buses and trucks.
- Basic registration and health screening may help to identify particularly vulnerable people and assist preparations for arrival at the destination.

20.2 Site selection

20.2.1 Selection process

These guidelines are for the selection of sites for supported temporary settlements and transit centres. The starting point for these guidelines assumes that an assessment of the appropriate response to providing shelter and services has already been conducted and that a decision has been made to select sites and support temporary settlement. This preliminary assessment is critical, since supported temporary settlement camps should not be assumed to be the solution. The assessment, for instance, may provide good reasons to support alternatives to camps. See 19.1.1 Shelter options and Figure 19.1 for an overview of shelter options and the assessment process.

Great care should be taken in selecting the best available site or sites – they may be home to many thousands of people for months or even years. A poor site can add significantly to the misery of the residents and complicate the task of planning and settlement management. The best solution is for the displaced to be able to return to a safe, secure home as soon as possible. However, it should be recognized that many 'temporary camps' do become permanent or semi-permanent settlements.

A systematic process for site selection is shown in Figure 20.1 and the various steps are expanded below.

Step 1: Form a selection/assessment team.
Form a site selection team to comprise representatives from the people who have been displaced, the host population, host government, UNHCR (or lead agency) and its implementing partner agencies.

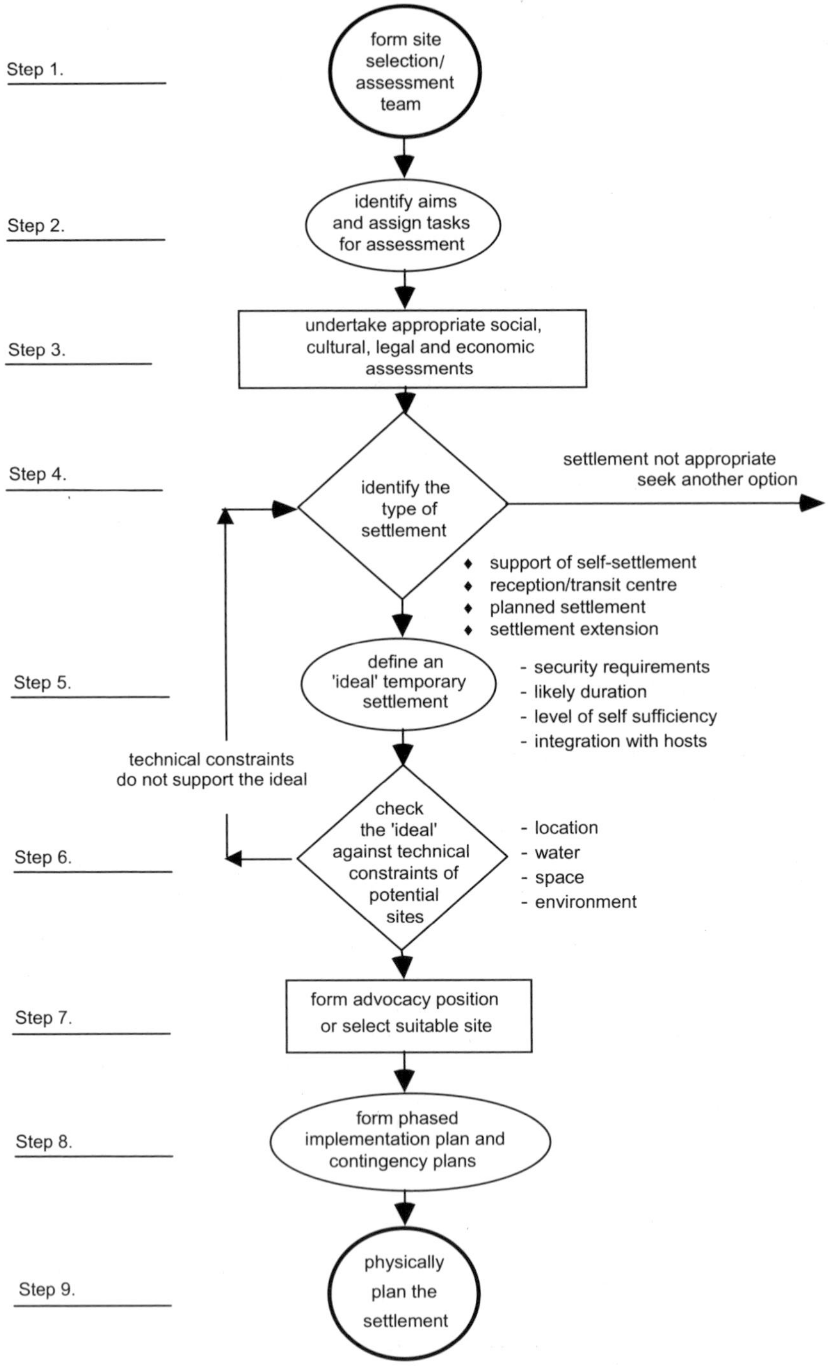
Step 1.
form site selection/ assessment team
Step 2.
identify aims and assign tasks for assessment
Step 3.
undertake appropriate social, cultural, legal and economic assessments
Step 4.
identify the type of settlement
settlement not appropriate seek another option
support of self-settlement
reception/transit centre
planned settlement
settlement extension
Step 5.
define an 'ideal' temporary settlement
- security requirements
- likely duration
- level of self sufficiency
- integration with hosts
technical constraints do not support the ideal
Step 6.
check the 'ideal' against technical constraints of potential sites
- location
- water
- space
- environment
Step 7.
form advocacy position or select suitable site
Step 8.
form phased implementation plan and contingency plans
Step 9.
physically plan the settlement

Figure 20.1 Site selection decision-making flow diagram
Source: shelterproject.org

Step 2: Identify aims and assign tasks.
Identify the assessment aims, available resources and personnel. Draw up an assessment programme integrating the needs of individual sectors (food, health, sanitation, etc). Delegate tasks to individual personnel or teams.

Step 3: Undertake appropriate social, economic and environmental assessments of the displaced people and host community. Refer to Chapter 5 for assessment guidelines and techniques.

Step 4: Identify the type of settlement.
Four types of temporary settlement are considered for support by the aid community: non-dispersed self-settlement, transit and reception centres, planned temporary settlements, and extensions to planned temporary settlements. Each typology has its associated requirements and likely impacts. Assessments (Step 3) may indicate that a temporary settlement is not appropriate, in which case another option should be sought, such as dispersed self-settlement or settlement within host communities. It should be emphasized that temporary settlements are not suitable for all situations. Technical constraints (Step 6) may also indicate that the type of settlement has to be reconsidered.

Step 5: Define an ideal temporary settlement.
Defining an ideal temporary settlement avoids being influenced by the constraints of the sites that are currently available. Determining an 'ideal' settlement (although attaining it might be unlikely) ensures that objectives remain clear and site selection is not driven by short-term technical considerations. Key issues to consider in defining the 'ideal' may include security; the likely life-span of the settlement; the level and forms of self-sufficiency that might be reached by migrants; and the optimum degree of integration between migrant and host economies and communities.

Step 6: Check 'ideal' against the constraints of sites.
Once the form that the temporary settlement would ideally take has been understood and defined it is necessary to consider whether the siting options available meet the necessary criteria. See the following section on 'Site selection criteria and weightings' for checking against specific sites.

Responses to the technical constraints of an 'ideal' site design should occur with continual reference back to the 'ideal' template, rather than incrementally creeping away from the 'ideal'. Some compromise is inevitable but when the technical constraints are so great that the principles underlying the 'ideal' are undermined a new 'ideal' settlement should be defined (Step 5).

If none of the potential sites offer the necessary attributes the team should reconsider what type of settlement is appropriate (Step 4). For example, if sufficient land is not available to support the level of agriculture, and therefore self-sufficiency, considered appropriate for the design population, then an alternative solution needs to be explored.

Step 7: Form advocacy position or select suitable site.
If the host government has proposed sites the assessment/selection team can use the systematic method to present arguments for, and against, the selection of individual sites and to advocate solutions based on rational assessment rather than political, or any other, bias. If no sites have been proposed, the

method can be used to identify suitable sites for recommendation to the government. If people have self-settled, the method can be used to assess whether or not they are on suitable sites.

Step 8: Form phased implementation plan and contingency plans.
After a site is selected, a programme of implementation needs to be formed that responds to consecutive phases of operation: the temporary settlement will need to perform different functions during the emergency and the later, care and maintenance, phases. Each phase will present different potential impacts and opportunities. Contingency plans will also be required to respond to scenarios that may develop later in the programme, such as further influxes, or an outbreak of cholera. Potential scenarios will need to be identified and evaluated, leading to a series of indicators to signal the implementation of contingency plans.

Step 9: Physically plan the settlement.
The site must be planned to allow for the appropriate location of family plots and of facilities and infrastructure, such as clinics, leisure areas, and water distribution systems. Each sector of work will require specialist attention. Refer to the planning guidelines later in this section.

20.2.2 Site selection criteria and weightings

The following criteria are suggested for consideration when assessing site suitability at Step 6 (check the 'ideal' against the constraints of potential sites) in the selection process outlined above. In any specific situation, the assessment team should add any other criteria that are considered relevant.

Non-technical criteria

Political and security issues Proximity to an international or regional border may cause political and insecurity problems. On the other hand, a government may want to limit the spread of refugees into their country by restricting them to a border area.

Social, legal and cultural issues Try to gauge the feelings of local inhabitants towards the nearby settlement of outsiders. For example, the use of land for a temporary settlement may cause friction with local farmers, herders, nomads and landowners. If nobody is using the land already it is usually for a good reason. If it isn't obvious – find out why! Be aware that some sites may have special ritual or spiritual significance to local people – in some cases specific water sources may be considered as holy places. Check on land rights and the seasonal use of land for farming and grazing at each proposed site. Previous land use must be considered. UNHCR has a policy of not offering financial compensation for land.

Technical criteria

Area of site There must be enough space for the planned population and for future growth. Refer to the recommended guideline figures given in 20.3.3, Box 20.1. Space for animals and cultivation may also need to be considered in relation to each site and the resources available to support animals and garden plots.

Access The site should be accessible to relief supplies. Where access may be interrupted for significant lengths of time, sufficient storage must be made available. Access may be easy during the dry season but impossible during the rains.

Location Access and proximity to local settlements. Consider flood hazards: avoid flat areas, depressions, swamps, river banks or lakeshore sites.

Topography Look for gentle slopes (1 per cent minimum for gravity water distribution and 5–6 per cent maximum) with natural drainage.

Soil type The soil type affects sanitation, water pipelines, road and building construction, drainage and the living environment (dust and mud). Good sanitation is critical to the proper functioning of a camp. In many circumstances pit latrines will be the first choice for toilets – if possible, choose permeable, sandy, soils. Avoid 'black cotton soil' and fine clays as they give poor percolation for latrines and make access by truck very difficult. Avoid rock as it is unsuitable for latrine construction. A high water table makes latrine construction difficult.

Water source The water source should be close enough to avoid tankering or pumping the water over long distances. Is sufficient water, which is of reasonable quality or which is amenable to treatment, available all the year? Is there sufficient quantity of water for the settlement population, the host population, livestock and agriculture? If there are no surface water sources (streams, rivers or ponds), is groundwater likely to be accessible (shallow wells, boreholes)? See Chapters 11, 12 and 13. Remember the weight of daily water requirements is at least 10 times the weight of daily dried food requirements.

Vegetation Fuel will be needed for cooking, and wood and grass for shelter. A consequence of the removal of grass and tree cover is soil erosion. If people have animals, is there any grazing available?

Fuelwood After water collection, obtaining fuel for cooking is one of the top day-to-day priorities. The availability of fuelwood is a key factor in site selection and camp management. Liaise with the local forestry department and try to site the camp in well-wooded countryside, where fuelwood, particularly dead wood, is available. Live wood can be used for shelter construction but, because of its moisture content, it is heavy and difficult to burn compared with dry dead wood. Given the choice between cutting live wood nearby and collecting dead wood from a distance, people may choose to walk considerable distances (perhaps several kilometres) for the dead wood. Avoid selecting a site near existing settlements as most of the dead wood will already have been collected and competition for the remaining fuelwood may cause friction. If fuelwood is not available, then it may have to be trucked in or alternative forms of fuel, such as kerosene or charcoal, and cooking stoves supplied (see Section 20.3.3).

Environmental impact The environmental impact of a temporary settlement is likely to be significant because of: the high population density and the ensuing high demand for fuel and vegetation; the likelihood that the settlement will be located in environmentally fragile areas; the low incentive residents will have to maintain the environment. This may result in rapid deforestation and soil erosion. Careful siting and good management can do much to mitigate these effects. Where possible, avoid siting on steep slopes where soil erosion is likely to be high, and choose sites with good vegetative cover. Do not remove vegetative cover unless it is absolutely necessary to do so. Consider the impact on the local inhabitants of severe environmental degradation and competition for scarce resources. Consider the distance to other temporary settlements – each settlement will have a 'radius of influence' – if they are too close these areas may overlap. See UNHCR (1998) for guidelines on environmental management for refugee operations.

Effective natural resource management can be assisted by carefully considered site selection together with an appropriate density and dispersal of the displaced population. For example, five dispersed settlements of 10 000 people each may be preferable to one concentrated settlement of 50 000 people.

Environmental health hazards Consider the impact of the site environment on health, for example, the potential for transmitting malaria, river blindness, bilharzia, etc. Consider the effects on local inhabitants. While not recommended, streams or rivers may be used for bathing and laundry, which may pollute streams far downstream. Water abstraction will reduce flow rates.

Weightings

Once the list of criteria is drawn up, the next step for the selection team is to decide what weight should be given to each criterion. The weightings should reflect the relative importance of each criterion. One method is to award a percentage figure, with 100 per cent reflecting a criterion with the highest relevance and zero per cent being irrelevant. Some criteria may be 'veto' criteria – for example, if the site is regularly flooded it may be so unacceptable that the camp cannot be sited there.

For the weighting system to work, the criteria must be treated as positive attributes. A negative attribute, such as the environmental fragility of a site, must be turned into a positive criterion such as environmental robustness.

20.2.3 Ranking sites

Once the criteria and weightings have been agreed, the next step is to visit each site and assess its merits against the list of criteria by, for example, awarding marks out of 100. These marks could be recorded on a chart as shown in Table 20.1 below.

In this hypothetical example, site C was vetoed as being prone to regular flooding. Site D came out with the highest ranking and would appear to be the preferred site. This method is a tool to give guidance and to be used in advocating for suitable sites. The final selection must be approved by the relevant authorities.

20.3 Temporary settlement planning

Settlement planning can be contentious and it requires a good general knowledge of the issues, strong leadership skills and an ability to reach consensus. There will be conflicting priorities and not everyone can be satisfied.

Table 20.1 Assessing sites for a temporary settlement using matrix ranking

Site selection criteria	*Weighting, %*	*Sites (see note below)*						
		A		B		C	D	
Political and security issues	85	*70*	60	*20*	17		*40*	34
Social, legal, cultural issues	45	*60*	27	*55*	21		*35*	16
Area of site	35	*50*	18	*30*	11		*10*	35
Access	21	*75*	16	*40*	8		*60*	13
Topography	55	*50*	28	*80*	44	veto	*30*	17
Soils	76	*50*	31	*20*	15		*70*	53
Water sources	85	*30*	26	*50*	43		*85*	72
Vegetation	15	*30*	5	*65*	10		*80*	12
Fuelwood availability	35	*20*	7	*70*	25		*85*	30
Robust environment	15	*40*	6	*30*	5		*60*	9
Environmental health	21	*30*	6	*45*	9		*60*	13
Totals (weighted marks)			**230**		**208**			**304**

The first number is 'marks out of 100' for that site, the second is the mark adjusted by the weighting percentage. For example Camp B scores *45* under the environmental health criterion, which is weighted at 21%. Thus the overall weighting is 21% of *45* = 9.

20.3.1 Key principles

For new settlements, planning should be carried out well before residents arrive. For existing self-settled sites, an assessment should be initiated as soon as possible before key facilities are established in poor locations. Planners and managers should be identified and given the resources to plan effectively whilst others provide ongoing services. Unstructured planning should not be left to overworked field staff.

To be effective, planning should be based on a good understanding of the social, political, cultural, environmental and economic context. Good relations need to be formed with both the local and migrant communities since the success of a settlement very much depends on the relations that can be established and maintained. Attempt to arrange for people displaced from the same villages and communities to settle in the same area of the settlement.

It has become good practice to establish 'Refugee Affected Area Programmes' to support communities in the locality of temporary camps. Projects often involve the support of local infrastructure and services. If started early, such programmes can have a positive impact in building relations. Opportunities may be lost if programmes are started too late.

Expertise is particularly important in determining the layout of a site, drawing up a sanitation and water plan, assessing the best means of access, and advising on appropriate shelter.

Key issues include:

- The desired population density on one or a series of dispersed settlements.
- Participation and self-reliance. See Chapters 1 and 5 for more details.
- Flexibility and a long-term view. Temporary settlements may become established in a matter of days but may last for weeks, months or often years.
- The promotion of effective environmental sanitation. Much illness and death can be prevented if basic sanitation measures are taken. More details can be found in Chapter 10.
- Location with respect to water sources and fuel for cooking. More details are given later in this chapter and in Chapters 11–13.
- Co-ordination and integration of all sectors. It is important that all relief agencies co-ordinate their efforts. In a refugee emergency, UNHCR usually take a co-ordination role. See Chapter 2 for more details.

Settlement size

A small number of larger settlements may be easier to serve than many small settlements. The host government may prefer larger settlements on political and, perhaps, military grounds. However, large settlements may have greater internal social problems and have proportionally a greater adverse impact on the immediate local environment and social and physical infrastructure. If there is a choice, a population of 20 000 is a reasonable compromise. Pressure to develop settlements larger than 50 000 should be strongly resisted.

20.3.2 The settlement planning process

Refer to Section 5.2 for general guidelines on the planning process. This needs to be a staged approach as the situation changes from the immediate emergency stage through to stabilization and longer-term settlement. The fundamental planning element is the population involved. This will depend on the present estimated population, the movement of people in and out of the settlement, and future population growth.

Key activities in the planning process include:

- Formation of the assessment and planning team.
- The assessment and selection of suitable sites.
- An assessment of the present and future needs.
- An assessment of the existing resources.
- The design of the settlement and services.
- The preparation of contingency plans.

Where possible the planning team should include people with relevant specialist knowledge and representatives of the displaced population, the host community, local government and aid agencies. From time to time the planning team may need to consult more widely to get detailed information on the views of all groups.

The following issues need to be addressed:

- How the planning process and implementation are to be carried out and managed, and by whom.
- Procedures between the host government, the relief agencies and the displaced population to ensure good co-ordination.
- Key aspects of settlement planning as outlined in the following section.
- Priorities, objectives and the levels of service to be achieved.
- Available time: when will people arrive? How long is there for planning and preparation?
- Livestock that may accompany the migrants.
- Land for small-scale cultivation, if allowed by the host government.
- The settlement layout.
- A sanitation and water plan.
- A plan for the supporting infrastructure and services:
  Shelter; roads; storage facilities and workshops; grain mills; feeding centres; out-patient and in-patient care; cold chain facilities for the transport and storage of medicines; markets; schools; places of worship; government and relief agency accommodation; etc.
- Needs, costs and budgets for principal items.
- Logistical needs – communication.
- A system of agreeing and monitoring targets and assigning agency responsibility for reaching each target.
- Identification of the needs which are not being addressed.
- Consideration of the longer-term developmental uses of infrastructure to the local community once the temporary settlement is no longer required and becomes vacant.
- Monitoring of the social, economic and environmental impact on the local community, the country and the settlement population.

A bar chart is useful to indicate the timing of activities and the links between them. The example in Figure 20.2 shows some of the activities which should be listed and illustrates how a bar chart can highlight bottle-necks and delays before services become available. Critical dates can be noted on the chart (such as the onset of the rains or flooding of a river) to highlight the need to accomplish tasks within a certain time. Targets (milestones) can be marked to show the date by which major activities should be completed. For example, pumps cannot be installed on a borehole until the site is selected, the layout planned and the boreholes drilled. Progress can be monitored, and the chart used as a reporting tool, by adding a column to indicate the degree of progress at any one time (for instance, roads 40 per cent complete).

Settlement reorganization

It may sometimes be necessary to reorganize an already settled camp. However, beware of reorganizing the layout just because it appears to be chaotic. There may be an underlying order, that has evolved according to the

	Task	Tasks to complete	Agency	Week 1	2	3	4	5
1	**Site** Locate site		Govt	●●				
2	Plan layout	1	Govt HCR	●●●	●●●			
3	Site drainage	1,2	MoW		●●			
7	Site ready for first arrivals					*		
8	People arrive					●●	●●●●	●●●●
12	**Shelter** Buy and distribute poles		HCR/SCF	●●●●	●●	●●●		
13	Distribute plastic sheet		SCF			●●	●●●●	
20	**Water supply** Drill boreholes	1.2	UNICEF			●●●●	●●●●	●●●●
21	Install pumps	1,2,20	Oxfam				●●●	●●●●
30	**Medical** Build health centre	1,2	MSF		●●	●●●●●	●●●	
31	Run clinics		MSF			●●	●●●●	●●●●
40	**Roads** Hire contractor	1	Govt HCR	●●				
41	Construct main access road	1,40	Contractor		●●●●	●●●●●	●●●●	
42	Construct camp roads	1,2,40	Contractor			●●●●●	●●●●	●●●●

Figure 20.2 Example of a settlement planning bar chart

needs of the settlement residents, which may not be immediately apparent to an outsider from a different culture who has only recently arrived. The best way of finding out more is to ask the residents.

Reorganization is rarely straightforward and becomes more difficult as time moves on and residents invest more and more time and effort in the existing layout. Try and reorganize as early as possible before the settlement becomes well established. An existing camp may be reorganized in the following ways:

- Reduce a high population density by moving some shelters whilst leaving others. This can also assist the regrouping of former communities and families that may have been divided during the early stages of an emergency.
- Clear a new area for relocation from an existing block. Clear the old block and relocate from a second existing block.

20.3.3 Settlement layout and services

The physical layout of a settlement can have a significant impact on security, cultural activities and social cohesion. Although shelters arranged in straight lines on a close grid pattern may appear to ease some aspects of management, such as the distribution of plots and the provision of access roads, such a pattern is not normally conducive to social cohesion nor the need for cultural space. Find out what suits the residents (see Section 5.3).

- Ascertain how people lived before the emergency and observe how they have spontaneously settled. A spontaneous layout which is apparently chaotic may have quite a strong underlying logic.
- Ask representatives of the displaced community how they would like to see the settlement laid out. Use sketches on paper, maps and air photos, to involve and inform the residents.

In planning the layout, start with the smallest social unit, which may be the family (or extended family) plot, and build up using a basic unit of family plots to form blocks and sectors as shown in Table 20.2.

Table 20.2 An example of camp building blocks

1	families			=	4 to 6	people
16	families	= 1	community	=	80	people
16	communities	= 1	block	=	1250	people
4	blocks	= 1	sector	=	5000	people
4	sectors	= 1	camp	=	20 000	people

Figure 20.3 is an example of a layout used in the large Rwandan refugee camps in Tanzania. This shows how the building block approach has been adapted.

An alternative to the rigid grid layout at community level is a community cluster layout. An example is shown below in Figure 20.4 using clusters of 16 families. Compared with the rigid grid system, the families have a smaller family plot but have access to a protected community space. Depending on the size of the cluster and the level of service provided this community space could be used for certain services, such as water points, communal latrines, laundry slabs or children's play areas. The clusters can be arranged in a block or grid system, so simplifying the planning and installation of roads and water pipelines.

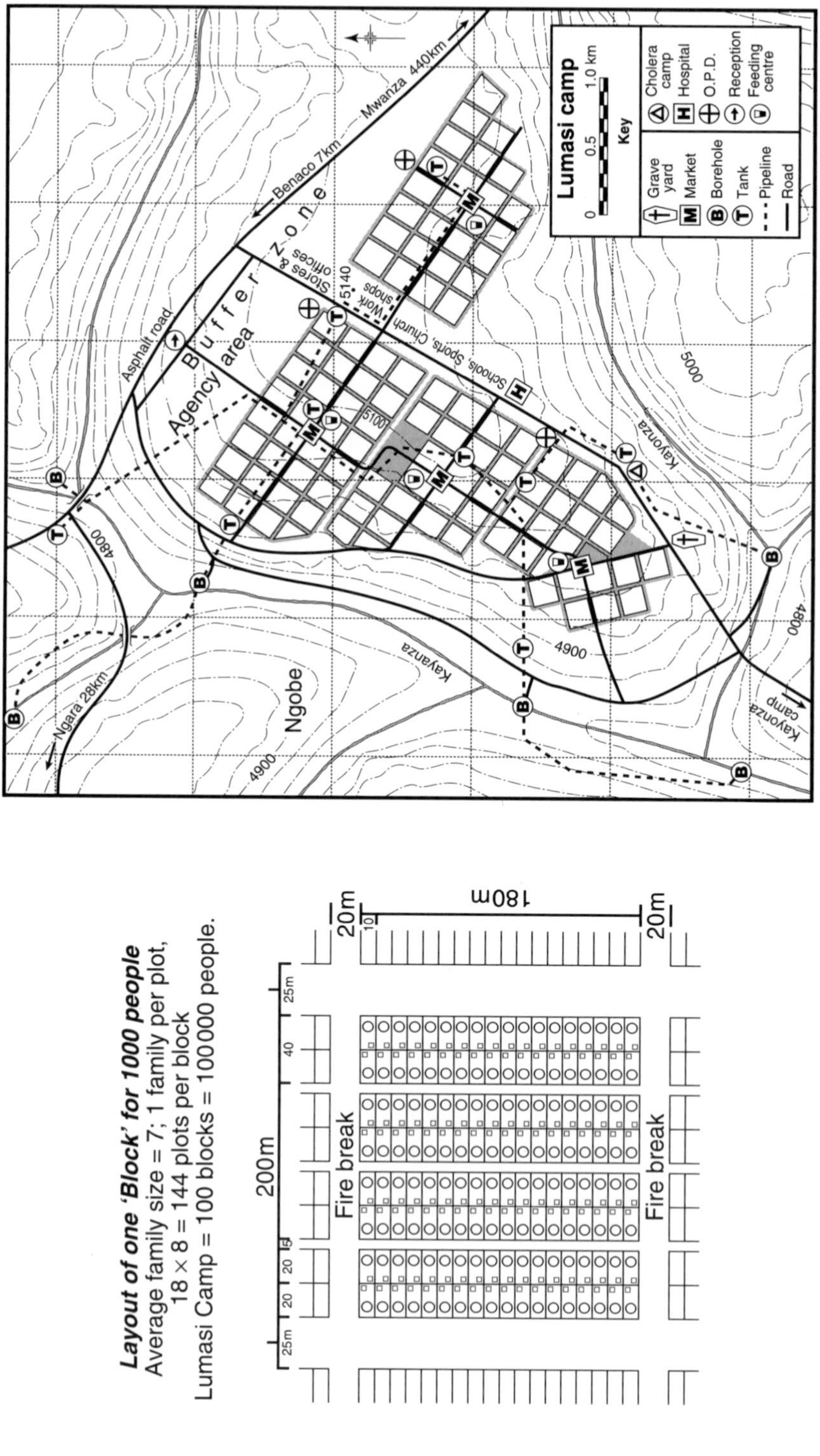

Figure 20.3 An example of the layout of a large camp – Lumasi camp in Tanzania 1994

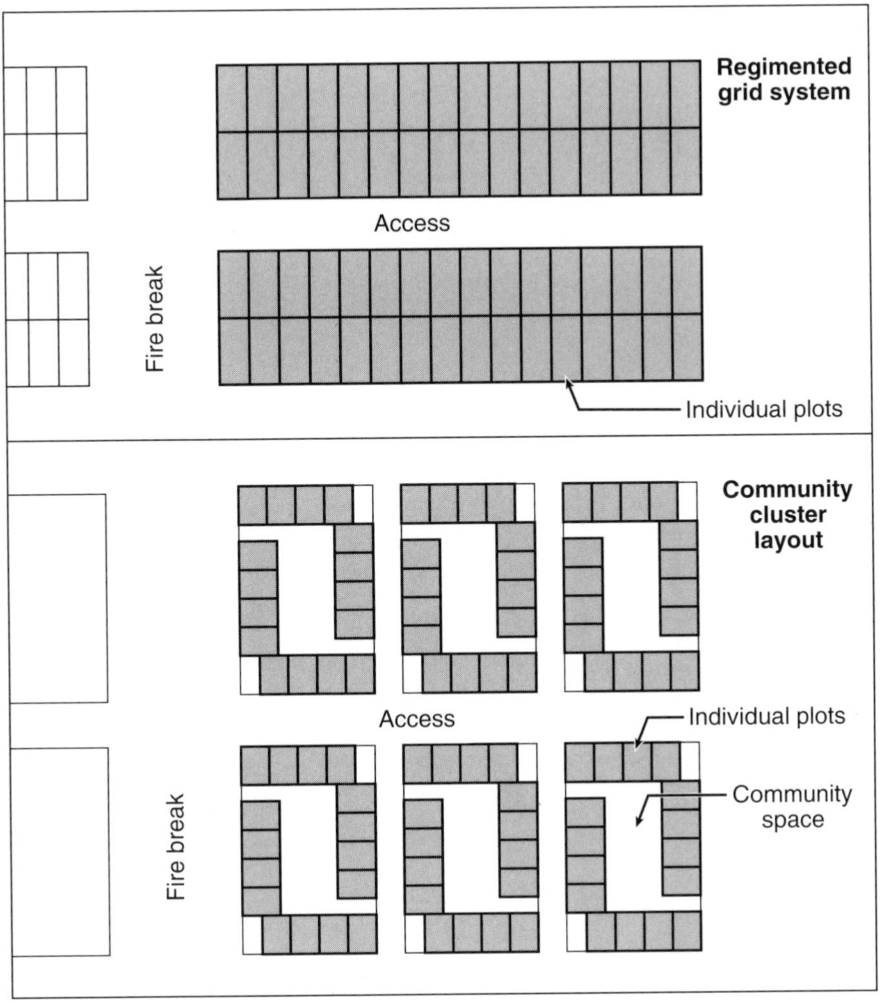

Figure 20.4 Rigid grid and community cluster layout

Settlement minimum standards

Box 20.1 gives key planning indicators for settlement layout and services. In severely overcrowded, spontaneously settled camps it may be very difficult to achieve the standards during the initial emergency phase and realistic compromises will have to be made. However, the figures do provide the basis for planning and they are standards to achieve which have been agreed within the humanitarian community.

Draw camp layout plans to a scale of 1:5000–1:25 000 for use by administrators, community representatives and relief personnel.

Box 20.1 Key planning indicators for settlement layout and services

Total surface area of settlement 45 m^2/person* (Sphere)

Includes infrastructure (e.g. roads, sanitation, schools, offices, water systems, security/fire breaks, markets, storage facilities, shelter locations), but excludes land for agriculture (crops and livestock).

Covered area available		Averages 3.5–4.5 m^2/person (Sphere)
Fire breaks		2 m between dwellings 6 m between clusters of dwellings 15 m between blocks of clusters (Sphere)
Sanitation		
	Toilet usage:	Toilets arranged by household(s) and/or segregated by sex. Maximum of 20 people per toilet (Sphere) 1 family of 6–10 persons (UNHCR)
	Distance of toilets from dwellings:	No more than 50 m from dwellings, or no more than one minute's walk (Sphere)
	Distance of latrines and soakaways from water sources:	At least 30 m from any groundwater source and the bottom of any latrine is at least 1.5 m above the water table. Distances may be increased for fissured rock and limestone, or decreased for fine soils. Drainage or spillage from toilets does not run towards surface water or groundwater sources. (Sphere)
	Public toilets:	Separate toilets for women and men for markets, distribution centres, health centres, etc. (Sphere)
	Solid waste:	No dwelling is more than 15 m from a refuse container or household refuse pit, or 100 m from a communal refuse pit. One 100 litre refuse container per 10 families, where domestic refuse is not buried on site. (Sphere) 2 refuse containers per 1 community of 80–100 people (UNHCR)
Water collection points		
	Minimum number of water points:	1 tap per 250 people (Sphere) 1 tap per community of 80–100 people (UNHCR)
	Distance between water point and shelter:	500 m maximum

Health facilities

'Agencies should aim to strengthen local health services rather than to create separate services' (Sphere)

Health centre	1 per site (20 000 people)
Feeding centre	1 per site (20 000 people)
Referral hospital	1 per 10 sites (200 000 people)

Other facilities

Distribution points:	4 per site (20 000 people)
Market:	1 per site (20 000 people)
School block:	1 per sector (5000 people)

* Plan for population growth (design for the long term) of about 3–4% per year. Also make provision for overspill due to a sudden influx of new arrivals. Plan for departures.

(Sphere) refers to the Sphere Minimum Standards in Disaster Response (Sphere, 2000)
(UNHCR) refers to the standards in the UNHCR *Handbook for Emergencies* (UNHCR, 1999)

If space allows, anticipate the natural evolution of the site. Most people will quickly adapt temporary shelter to suit their needs and plots of sufficient size are needed to allow development to take place. Allocate space for future facilities by taking a long-term view: community activities, market areas, schools, vocational training centres, and agriculture. Use the natural features of a site to break up the landscape and facilitate drainage and settlement access. Take account of the prevailing wind so that it blows first through living areas, then kitchens/feeding centres and lastly latrines.

Control surface runoff. Surface runoff during intense rain can cause sudden and massive erosion on bare soil. Runoff from a settlement is likely to have a high pathogen load and to cause pollution of downhill water sources. Control the runoff from bare areas within a settlement by using banks, laid with a very gentle slope, approximately along the contours. Allow a 30 m spacing between banks. The banks are laid to divert runoff to protected drainage lines. Such banks should be high enough to discourage vehicles passing over them, perhaps 0.5 m high and 2.0 m wide. If significant runoff is likely from areas above a settlement, construct banks to control this runoff. See Chapter 18 for more details on drainage and erosion control.

Design for security. The grouping of family plots into community units provides a defined, secure space within each unit. People know each other and strangers will stand out. The circumstances of an emergency may give rise to additional personal security risks. Women may be vulnerable to harassment and rape. Ethnic and factional divisions can provoke violent confrontations. In these circumstances the protection aspects of 'shelter' may mean keeping different groups of people apart and may also require the provision of secure compounds for particularly vulnerable people.

Reception and registration

To receive assistance, displaced people are generally required to register. Aid agencies depend on registration figures to plan the level and type of assistance. Registration is difficult and time consuming for everyone concerned, not least for those being registered. It is important that registration facilities are carefully designed.

A reception area should be set up outside the settlement to receive and register new arrivals before they become integrated within the camp. The registration site should preferably be a large, flat, open space. In hot climates, shade and a potable water supply are important. In a cold climate, shelter, clothing and heating will be required. There must be latrines or marked out defecation areas. Land may have to be allocated for accompanying animals. There may be a need for temporary first-night shelter.

A registration site comprises three main areas:

- Pre-registration: a waiting area where information can be given on the registration process.
- Registration: the actual registration process including the allocation of relief items.
- Post registration: space for dispersal.

Mark out the site with rope using natural barriers (buildings and roads), where available. The registration area must be clearly marked out as a closed area to aid the efficient management of the registration process. See Telford, 1997 for further guidance on registration procedures. Services such as immunization might also be provided and non-food items allocated: ration cards, water containers, cooking pots, shelter materials, etc.

Information useful for planning can be collected during the registration process. Data on numbers of people, nutritional status, family composition can be obtained. These data are very important for planning purposes and need to be checked carefully. Refugee numbers are frequently overestimated, perhaps by as much as 50 per cent.

Food warehousing, distribution and feeding centres

Major warehousing should be located on the outside of a settlement. This avoids heavy traffic passing through the settlement. Smaller distribution centres can be located on market squares. Make efficient use of infrastructure by alternating the use of distribution centres as market stalls. Guide figures for feeding centres and feeding programmes are given in Appendix 24.

Fuel supply

Fuel for cooking is an essential daily requirement. Options for fuel include wood, charcoal and kerosene. In many situations, wood from surrounding forests is a likely fuel. Liaise closely with the local forestry department. Factors influencing the amount of fuelwood needed include:

- The type of wood (heavy dense hardwoods, such as teak, usually have a higher calorific content than light softwoods, such as pine).
- The cooking technology (three stones, fuel efficient stoves, charcoal burners).
- The type of food and cooking methods (dried beans may need to be simmered for hours and require a lot of fuel – much fuel can be saved if the beans are pre-soaked for several hours).
- The climate (if it is cold, people will need fires for heat).

A family may require up to 10 kg of dry fuelwood per day. If fuelwood is not available locally then it will have to be brought into the settlement. A settlement of 20 000 people may consume several tens of tonnes of fuelwood per day. The more accessible the fuelwood, the more cooking will be done. This has significant logistical, administrative and environmental implications.

One possibility for controlling the use of fuelwood is to allocate plots of woodland to specific groups. A group might consist of one or more blocks of about 1000 people (see above). The group could be given sole rights to a plot and the responsibility of managing the fuelwood in that plot. Such an approach should only be attempted with the full co-operation of the local forestry department. Where the transport of large quantities of fuelwood to the settlement is difficult, consider providing transport for the wood collectors from the settlement to the fuelwood source.

Fire precautions

Take precautions against the risk of uncontrolled fires as temporary settlements are particularly vulnerable. Create an awareness of potential fire risks and draw up contingency plans to deal with a fire:

- Leave sufficient space between shelters and service centres to create fire breaks, escape routes and emergency access. See Box 20.1. Local inhabitants may burn vegetation in the dry season – provide fire breaks around the settlement to protect against these.
- Highlight the dangers of careless cooking and heating arrangements. Establish controls, if necessary (for instance, limit fires to cooking outside only).
- Do not allow rubbish to accumulate or to be burnt on site. Take it far away to burn or bury.
- Include fire breaks in settlement designs. Try to establish fire breaks in spontaneously settled camps through localized reorganization.
- Prepare contingency plans. If people know in advance what to do when a fire breaks out then they are more likely to react quickly, correctly and safely.
- Establish a fire alarm system and make it known to everyone. Consider establishing a fire fighting squad equipped with suitable implements – shovels, beaters, sand buckets, etc.

It is essential to stop a fire spreading. If a fire is out of control it is usually better to try and contain rather than fight it.

Procedure in the event of fire:

1. Raise the alarm.
2. Quickly evacuate people and animals from danger.
3. Check that all dwellings at risk or to be pulled down have no occupants, especially non-mobile infants and the elderly.
4. Contain the fire by pulling down lines of tents, huts, fences, etc. to form a fire break.

Markets

Market areas are important trading and social centres but they can pose health risks where food and drink is for sale. If acceptable, consider several small market areas rather than one big market. Provide properly supervised latrines and a system of rubbish collection. Keep water out of the immediate area but include a distribution point nearby. Market squares are good locations for distribution centres.

Slaughter areas

Provide areas for the slaughter of livestock. If possible, provide a concrete slab with good drainage to carry away blood and animal droppings. Ensure that this does not drain directly into a water course. A gantry may be desirable for hanging carcasses. Find out what cultural practices pertain. Monitor the condition of slaughter areas to ensure that they are kept in a hygienic condition.

Animals

Livestock should be kept outside a settlement, to reduce health risks, but they should be close enough to be watched and have access to a water source. Smaller dispersed settlements are more appropriate for communities with herds of animals. If people keep small numbers of goats or chickens then consider distributing chicken wire.

Schools and social service centres

Social and community services should be located within a settlement, possibly adjacent to market squares.

Roads and traffic

Drainage often decides routes. Provide sufficient cross-drainage (culverts or dips) to drain water away from shelters and services (see Chapter 18). Locate support centres, such as feeding centres, away from dusty or potentially dangerous major access roads. Limit traffic to certain routes otherwise vehicles will be driven everywhere, becoming both a nuisance and a danger to everyone. If reckless driving or dust caused by traffic is a problem, lay speed bumps. Do not allow vehicles to drive across open defecation fields.

20.4 Settlement management

In the planning of a supported temporary settlement it is important to consider who will manage the settlement and to ensure that there is as much self-management as possible. In refugee camps, high level management will normally be shared between UNHCR and the host government. Specific tasks may be managed by local or international agencies and NGOs (see Chapter 2). Settlement management has several aspects:

- Co-ordination of the activities of the various agencies.
- Representation – how are the views of the various groups within the settlement population put forward? Are there elections for leaders? How are the views of the local host community taken into account?
- Day-to-day management – who carries out food distribution, posts notices, calls meetings?

Consider the mechanisms of representation within the camp – have traditional systems survived and are they relevant to the conditions of settlement? In most cases, the maintenance of traditional structures has benefits such as: the encouragement of social bonding; the promotion of feelings of security and stability; the creation of social controls; the establishment of responsibility for shelter plots and communal facilities; the efficient management of the relief effort. However, in many camps women and children may form up to 80 per cent of the population, with many males absent. In such cases traditional structures, if male-dominated, may not be able to deal with the real needs of the camp. It may be necessary to promote stronger representation of women's and children's needs.

A highly politicized population may already be well organized. However, the representative validity of a political organization must be assessed to ensure that all groups are represented adequately.

If there are no clear forms of leadership, establish a management and representational system by recruiting from within identifiable groups of residents. This might be on a family, block, and section basis. The residents should select their own representatives. The recruitment of other staff from within the community can follow a similar pattern. Recruit against relevant criteria for the work such as literacy, numeracy, specialist knowhow or skill and for extension workers, the respect with which they are held by the community. See Section 6.2 for further details on staff recruitment and management.

In some cases it may be necessary, and advisable, to recruit staff and extension agents from the host community. This may be due to a lack of particular qualifications and skills within the displaced community, because of host government stipulations, or to establish a balanced mix of staff recruited from the displaced and local host communities.

Appendices

1 Acronyms and abbreviations

ACF	Action Contre la Faim
ACT	Action by Churches Together
ADRA	Adventist Development and Relief Agency
ALNAP	Active Learning Network for Accountability in Practice
AusAID	Australian Agency for International Development
BPRM	United States Dept of State Bureau of Population, Refugees and Migration
CAD	Children's Aid Direct
CAFOD	Catholic Fund for Overseas Development
CDC	Centers for Disease Control and Prevention
CIDA	Canadian International Development Agency
CIMIC	Civil and Military Co-operation
CRS	Catholic Relief Services
CSM	Corn-Soya Milk
CWS	Church World Service
DAC	Development Assistance Committee (OECD)
DANIDA	Danish International Development Assistance
DART	USAID/OFDA Disaster Assistance Response Team
DFID	Department for International Development
DPKO	UN Department of Peacekeeping Operations
DSM	Dried skimmed milk
ECHO	European Community Humanitarian Office
EPI	Expanded programme of immunization
ERT	Emergency Response Team
FAO	Food and Agriculture Organization of the United Nations
FFW	Food-for-work
GIS	Geographical Information Systems
GPS	Global Positioning System
HPN	Humanitarian Practice Network
IAPSO	Inter-Agency Procurement Services Office (UNDP)
IASC	UN Inter-Agency Standing Committee
IBRD	International Bank for Reconstruction and Development (The World Bank)
ICRC	International Committee of the Red Cross
ICVA	International Council of Voluntary Agencies
IDP	Internally Displaced Persons
IFRC	International Federation of Red Cross and Red Crescent Societies

ILO	International Labour Organization
INGOs	International Non-governmental Organizations
IRC	International Rescue Committee
IMC	International Medical Corps
ITDG	Intermediate Technology Development Group
LPO	Local purchase order
LWF/S	The Lutheran World Federation/Service
MCH	Mother and child health
MISP	Minimum Initial Service Package
MSF	Médecins Sans Frontières
NGO	Non-governmental organization
OAS	Organization of American States
OAU	Organization of African Unity
OCHA	UN Office for Coordination of Humanitarian Affairs
ODI	Overseas Development Institute
OECD	Organization for Economic Co-operation and Development
OFDA	Office of Foreign Disaster Assistance (USAID)
ORS	Oral rehydration salts
OSOCC	On-Site Operations Co-ordination Centre
PAHO	Pan-American Health Organisation
PEM	Protein-energy malnutrition
PTSS	Programme and Technical Support Section (UNHCR)
QUIP	Quick Impact Project
RedR	Register of Engineers for Disaster Relief
SAR	Search and Rescue
SCF	Save the Children Fund
SCHR	Steering Committee for Humanitarian Response
SDC	Swiss Agency for Development and Co-operation
SFP/C	Supplementary feeding programme/centre
Sida	Swedish International Development Co-operation Agency
SOP	Standard Operating Procedure
TFP/C	Therapeutic feeding programme/centre
UNCHS	United Nations Centre for Human Settlements (also known as 'Habitat')
UNDAC	UN Disaster Assessment and Coordination
UN-DMT	UN Disaster Management Team
UNDP	United Nations Development Programme
UNEP	United Nations Environment Programme
UNESCO	United Nations Educational, Scientific and Cultural Organization
UNFPA	United Nations Population Fund
UNHCR	United Nations High Commissioner for Refugees
UNICEF	United Nations Children's Fund
UNIPAC	UNICEF Procurement and Assembly Centre
UN OHCHR	UN Office of the High Commissioner for Human Rights
UNRWA	UN Relief and Works Agency for Palestine Refugees in the Near East
UNSECOORD	United Nations Security Co-ordinator

UNV	United Nations Volunteers
USAID	United States Agency for International Development
VOICE	Voluntary Organisations in Co-operation in Europe
WCRWC	Women's Commission for Refugee Women and Children
WFP	World Food Programme
WHO	World Health Organization
WMO	World Meteorological Organization
WSB	Wheat-soya blend

2 Web sites

Africa On Line – www.africaonline.com

Active Learning Network for Accountability and Performance in Humanitarian Assistance (ALNAP) – www.odi.org.uk/alnap/index.html

AlertNet (The Reuters Foundation) – www.alertnet.org
Press agency reports on humanitarian issues and the latest emergencies.

Amnesty International – www.amnesty.org

Asian Disaster Preparedness Centre – www.adpc.ait.ac.th

BBC News – www.bbc.co.uk/hi/english/world

Benfield Greig Hazard Research Centre, University College London – www.bghrc.com

Center for Disease Control (CDC), Atlanta, USA – www.cdc.gov

Center for Refugee and Disaster Studies, Johns Hopkins University – www.jhsph.edu/research/emergencies/

CRED (Center for Research on the Epidemiology of Disasters) – www.md.ucl.ac.be/entites/esp/epid/mission

CRID (Regional Disaster Information Centre Latin America-Caribbean) – www.disaster.into.desastres.net/crid

Crosslines Global Report, an independent journal of humanitarian reporting – www.ichr.org/xlines/default.htm

DFID, The UK Department for International Development – www.oneworld.org/dfid

Disaster Relief Organisation – www.disasterrelief.org/

US Environmental Protection Agency – www.epa.gov

Forced Migration Review – www.fmreview.org

HelpAge International – www.helpage.org

The Human Rights Watch World Report – www.hrw.org

Humanitarian Affairs Review – www.humanitarian-review.org

Humanitarian Practice Network – www.odihpn.org.uk

Humanitarian Resource Institute, Emerging Infectious Disease Network (EIDNet) – www.humanitarian.net/eidnet

Humanitarian Times – www.humanitariantimes.com

Humanitarianism and War Project – www.stg.brown.edu/projects/hw/about.html

Humanity CD-ROM Libraries – www.humanitylibraries.net/

InterAction, American Council for Voluntary International Action – www.interaction.org

International Disaster Relief Resources List – www.idealist.org

ICRC, International Committee of the Red Cross – www.icrc.ch

IFRC, International Federation of Red Cross and Red Crescent Societies – www.ifrc.org
Includes reports on humanitarian emergencies and the annual World Disaster Report

ICG (International Crisis Group) – www.crisisweb.org

ITDG, Intermediate Technology Development Group Ltd – www.itdg.org

The Journal of Humanitarian Assistance – www.jha.ac

Journal of Refugee Studies – www.oup.co.uk/refuge

Lonely Planet Online – www.lonelyplanet.com

Mango – www.mango.org.uk
Mango provides financial management services to aid agencies. Download free accounting tools.

MSF – www.msf.org

Natural hazards disasters network – www.jiscmail.ac.uk/lists/natural-hazards-disasters.html

Norwegian Refugee Council – www.nrc.no/idp.htm

OneWorld web site of over 200 'global justice' organisations – www.oneworld.org

OCHA, UN Office for the Co-ordination of Humanitarian Affairs – www.reliefweb.int

RedR – Engineers for Disaster Relief – www.redr.org
Background on RedR, how to apply to join the register, programme of short training courses, information on the technical support service, and links to other web sites.

ReliefGuide – www.reliefguide.com/supplierg/
Database of equipment and service suppliers & consultants

PAHO Pan-American Health Organization – www.paho.org/disasters/

PAHO Virtual Disaster Library – www.paho.org/English/PED/about-VDL.htm

People in Aid – www.peopleinaid.org
Includes reports on insurance for aid workers and health & safety guidelines.

Refugee Studies Programme, Oxford University – www.qeh.ox.ac.uk/rsp/

Sanitation Connection – www.sanicon.net

Sphere Project – www.sphereproject.org

United Nations – www.un.org & web site locator – www.unsystem.org

UNHCR – www.unhcr.ch

UNICEF – www.unicef.org

University of Wisconsin, Disaster Management Center – http://epdweb.engr.wisc.edu/dmc/

USAID – www.info.usaid.gov

USAID/OFDA Field Operations Guide(FOG) – www.info.usaid.gov/ofda/fog.htm

US Committee for Refugees – www.refugees.org

Working Group on Humanitarian and Emergency Assistance (WGHEA) – www.nrc.ch

WELL – www.lboro.ac.uk/well
WELL is a resource centre able to provide advice on environmental health issues.

3 Sphere minimum standards

This appendix provides a summary of the Sphere minimum standards. The Sphere Handbook (Sphere, 2000) provides much more detail covering indicators, guidance notes and contextual information, all of which are important for the interpretation and application of the standards.

Minimum standards in water supply and sanitation

1 Analysis

Analysis standard 1: initial assessment
Programme decisions are based on a demonstrated understanding of the emergency situation and on a clear analysis of the health risks and needs relating to water supply and sanitation.
Analysis standard 2: monitoring and evaluation
The performance of the water supply and sanitation programme, its effectiveness in responding to health problems related to water and sanitation, and changes in the context are monitored and evaluated.

Analysis standard 3: participation
The disaster-affected population has the opportunity to participate in the design and implementation of the assistance programme.

2 Water supply

Water supply standard 1: access and water quantity
All people have safe access to a sufficient quantity of water for drinking, cooking and personal and domestic hygiene. Public water points are sufficiently close to shelters to allow use of the minimum water requirement.
Water supply standard 2: water quality
Water at the point of collection is palatable, and of sufficient quality to be drunk and used for personal and domestic hygiene without causing significant risk to health due to water-borne diseases, or to chemical or radiological contamination from short term use.
Water supply standard 3: water use facilities and goods
People have adequate facilities and supplies to collect, store and use sufficient quantities of water for drinking, cooking and personal hygiene, and to ensure that drinking water remains sufficiently safe until it is consumed.

3 Excreta disposal

Excreta disposal standard 1: access to, and numbers of toilets
People have sufficient numbers of toilets, sufficiently close to their dwellings to allow them rapid, safe and acceptable access at all times of the day and night.
Excreta disposal standard 2: design and construction
People have access to toilets which are designed, constructed and maintained in such a way as to be comfortable, hygienic and safe to use.

4 Vector control

Vector control standard 1: individual and family protection
People have the means to protect themselves from disease vectors and nuisance pests when they are estimated to be a significant risk to health or well-being.
Vector control standard 2: physical, environmental and chemical protection measures
The number of disease-bearing vectors and nuisance animals that pose a risk to people's health and well-being are kept to an acceptable level.
Vector control standard 3: good practice in the use of chemical vector control methods
Vector control measures that make use of pesticides are carried out in accordance with agreed international norms to ensure that staff, the people affected by the disaster and the local environment are adequately protected, and to avoid creating resistance to pesticides.

5 Solid waste management

Solid waste management standard 1: solid waste collection and disposal
People have an environment that is acceptably free of solid waste contamination, including medical wastes.

Solid waste disposal management standard 2: solid waste containers/pits
People have the means to dispose of their domestic waste conveniently and effectively.

6 Drainage

Drainage standard 1: drainage works
People have an environment that is acceptably free from risk of water erosion and from standing water, including storm water, flood water, domestic wastewater and wastewater from medical facilities.
Drainage standard 2: installations and tools
People have the means (installations, tools etc) to dispose of domestic wastewater and water point wastewater conveniently and effectively, and to protect their shelters and other family or communal facilities from flooding and erosion.

7 Hygiene promotion

Hygiene promotion standard 1: hygiene behaviour and use of facilities
All sections of the affected population are aware of priority hygiene practices that create the greatest risk to health and are able to change them. They have adequate information and resources for the use of water and sanitation facilities to protect their health and dignity.
Hygiene promotion standard 2: programme implementation
All facilities and resources provided reflect the vulnerabilities, needs and preferences of all sections of the affected population. Users are involved in the management and maintenance of hygiene facilities where appropriate.

8 Human resource capacity and training

Capacity standard 1: competence
Water supply and sanitation programmes are implemented by staff who have appropriate qualifications and experience for the duties involved, and who are adequately managed and supported.

Minimum standards in nutrition

1 Analysis

Analysis standard 1: initial assessment
Before any programme decisions are made, there is a demonstrated understanding of the basic nutritional situation and conditions which may create risk of malnutrition.
Analysis standard 2: response
If a nutrition intervention is required, there is a clear description of the problem(s) and a documented strategy for the response.
Analysis standard 3: monitoring and evaluation
The performance and effectiveness of the nutrition programme and changes in the context are monitored and evaluated.
Analysis standard 4: participation
The disaster-affected population has the opportunity to participate in the design and implementation of the assistance programme.

2 General nutritional support to the population

General nutritional support standard 1: nutrient supply
The nutritional needs of the population are met.
General nutritional support standard 2: food quality and safety
Food that is distributed is of sufficient quality and is safely handled so as to be fit for human consumption.
General nutritional support standard 3: food acceptability
Foods that are provided are appropriate and acceptable to the entire population.
General nutritional support standard 4: food handling and safety
Food is stored, prepared and consumed in a safe and appropriate manner, both at household and community level.

3 Nutritional support to those suffering from malnutrition

Targeted nutritional support standard 1: moderate malnutrition
The public health risks associated with moderate malnutrition are reduced.
Targeted nutritional support standard 2: severe malnutrition
Mortality, morbidity and suffering associated with severe malnutrition are reduced.
Targeted nutritional support standard 3: micronutrient deficiencies
Micronutrient deficiencies are corrected.

4 Human resource capacity and training

Capacity standard 1: competence
Nutrition interventions are implemented by staff who have appropriate qualifications and experience for the duties involved, and who are adequately managed and supported.
Capacity standard 2: support
Members of the disaster-affected population receive support to enable them to adjust to their new environment and to make optimal use of the assistance provided to them.
Capacity standard 3: local capacity
Local capacity and skills are used and enhanced by emergency nutrition programmes.

Minimum standards in food aid

1 Analysis

Analysis standard 1: initial assessment
Before any programme decisions are made, there is a demonstrated understanding of the basic conditions that create risk of food insecurity and the need for food aid.
Analysis standard 2: monitoring and evaluation
The performance and effectiveness of the food aid programme and changes in the context are monitored and evaluated.
Analysis standard 3: participation
The disaster-affected population has the opportunity to participate in the design and implementation of the assistance programme.

2 Requirements

Requirements standard

The food basket and rations are designed to bridge the gap between the affected population's requirements and their own food sources.

3 Targeting

Targeting standard

Recipients of food aid are selected on the basis of food need and/or vulnerability to food insecurity.

4 Resource management

Resource management standard

Food aid commodities and programme funds are managed, tracked, and accounted for using a transparent and auditable system.

5 Logistics

Logistics standard

Agencies have the necessary organizational and technical capacity to manage the procurement, receipt, transport, storage and distribution of food commodities safely, efficiently and effectively.

6 Distribution

Distribution standard

The method of food distribution is equitable, and appropriate to local conditions. Recipients are informed of their ration entitlement and its rationale.

7 Human resource capacity and training

Capacity standard 1: competence

Food aid programmes are implemented by staff who have appropriate qualifications and experience for the duties involved, and who are adequately managed and supported.

Capacity standard 2: local capacity

Local capacity and skills are used and enhanced by food aid programme

Minimum standards in shelter and site planning

1 Analysis

Analysis standard 1: initial assessment

Programme decisions are based on a demonstrated understanding of the emergency situation and on a clear analysis of people's needs for shelter, clothing and household items.

Analysis standard 2: monitoring and evaluation

The performance and effectiveness of the shelter and site programme and changes in the context are monitored and evaluated.

Analysis standard 3: participation

The disaster-affected population has the opportunity to participate in the design and implementation of the assistance programme.

2 Housing (shelter)

Housing standard 1: living quarters

People have sufficient covered space to provide protection from adverse effects of the climate. They have sufficient warmth, fresh air, security and privacy to ensure their dignity, health and well-being.

3 Clothing

Clothing standard

The people affected by the disaster have sufficient blankets and clothing to provide protection from the climate and to ensure their dignity, safety and well-being.

4 Household items

Household items standard 1: items for households and livelihood support

Families have access to household utensils, soap for personal hygiene and tools for their dignity and well-being.

Household items standard 2: environmental concerns

Fuel, economic cooking implements and stoves are made available, and their use is promoted.

5 Site selection

Site standard 1: site selection

The site is suitable to host the number of people involved.

Site standard 2: site planning

Site planning ensures sufficient space for household areas and supports people's security and well-being. It provides for effective and efficient provision of services and internal access.

Site standard 3: security

Site selection and planning ensures sufficient personal liberty and security for the entire affected population.

Site standard 4: environmental concerns

The site is planned and managed in such as way as to minimize damage to the environment.

6 Human resource capacity and training

Capacity standard 1: competence

Shelter and site interventions are implemented by staff who have appropriate qualifications and experience for the duties involved, and who are adequately managed and supported.

Capacity standard 2: local capacity

Local skills and capacity are used and enhanced by shelter and site programmes.

Minimum standards in health services

1 Analysis

Analysis standard 1: initial assessment

The initial assessment determines as accurately as possible the health effects of a disaster, identifies the health needs and establishes priorities for health programming.

Analysis standard 2: health information system – data collection
The health information system regularly collects relevant data on population, diseases, injuries, environmental conditions and health services in a standardized format in order to detect major health problems.
Analysis standard 3: health information system – data review
Health information system data and changes in the disaster-affected population are regularly reviewed and analysed for decision making and appropriate response.
Analysis standard 4: health information system – monitoring and evaluation
Data collected is used to evaluate the effectiveness of interventions in controlling disease and in preserving health.
Analysis standard 5: participation
The disaster-affected population has the opportunity to participate in the design and implementation of the assistance programme.

2 Measles control

Measles control standard 1: vaccination
In disaster-affected populations, all children 6 months to 12 years old receive a dose of measles vaccine and an appropriate dose of vitamin A as soon as possible.
Measles control standard 2: vaccination of newcomers
Newcomers to displaced settlements are vaccinated systematically. All children 6 months to 12 years old receive a dose of measles vaccine and an appropriate dose of vitamin A.
Measles control standard 3: outbreak control
A systematic response is mounted for each outbreak of measles within the disaster-affected population and the host community population.
Measles control standard 4: case management
All children who contract measles receive adequate care in order to avoid serious sequellae or death.

3 Control of communicable diseases

Control of communicable diseases standard 1: monitoring
The occurrence of communicable diseases is monitored.
Control of communicable diseases standard 2: investigation and control
Diseases of epidemic potential are investigated and controlled according to internationally accepted norms and standards.

4 Health care services

Health care services standard 1: appropriate medical care
Emergency health care for disaster-affected populations is based on an initial assessment and data from an ongoing health information system, and serves to reduce excess mortality and morbidity through appropriate medical care.
Health care services standard 2: reduction of morbidity and mortality
Health care in emergencies follows primary health care (PHC) principles and targets health problems that cause excess morbidity and mortality.

5 Human resource capacity and training

Capacity standard 1: competence

Health interventions are implemented by staff who have appropriate qualifications and experience for the duties involved, and who are adequately managed and supported.

Capacity standard 2: support

Members of the disaster-affected population receive support to enable them to adjust to their new environment and to make optimal use of the assistance provided to them.

Capacity standard 3: local capacity

Local capacity and skills are used and enhanced by emergency health interventions.

4 Situation report

The following guide to a sitrep format is primarily for use by the field person responsible for reporting to the agency headquarters. It is intended to give an idea of the sort of information that the agency is interested in, and the sort of information that you should be reporting on to your manager beyond the purely technical aspects of your programme.

SITREP NO. ..... FOR PERIOD .... TO ....

MAIN DEVELOPMENTS IN EMERGENCY
Summary of main developments since last report including, where significant:

- Main changes in emergency needs, including security.
- Main developments in political situation and government activity towards agencies.
- Progress/problems in relevant operations of other agencies.

PROGRESS OF YOUR AGENCY'S RESPONSE
For each project sector being implemented:

- Progress in implementing previous plans and difficulties or developments affecting progress; main issues occupying staff time.
- How project is to change, or new projects to be added, to accommodate developments in the situation, and how problems facing the project are to be approached.
- Priorities for action – plans for near and mid-term future, and assumptions on which these are based.

Also include report on deployment, movement and morale of staff, and proposed changes in staffing.

VISITS
Report on visits to local office or programme by non-agency staff, or by agency staff to places relevant to the emergency.

PUBLIC PROFILE
Report on lobbying activity – main issues raised and with whom; priorities, aims and strategy to take these issues forward. Lobbying issues or changes of strategy that field would like HQ to take forward.

Press line – should indicate which information is confidential and what might usefully be publicized and how.

REVIEW OF OBJECTIVES

- Summary of main uncertainties in emergency situation or in overall relief effort and possible outcomes.
- What are the present priorities for your team?
- Have original programme objectives, and activities designed to achieve them, been changed, or the emphasis within aims or strategies altered?

REPORTS PRODUCED
List reports you have written (tours, meetings, projects) since last written sitrep and circulation.

5 Contract documentation

This straightforward sample document may be adapted for a variety of contracts.
(With thanks to John Tait, RedR Member).

Title page

CONTRACT
between
HELP NGO
and

....

for

....

at

....

Project no.:
Contract no.:

End of title page

Section 1 Agreement

1.1 The Parties

This Contract is established between the Parties as follows:
HELP NGO, hereinafter known as NGO, of

....

and

....hereafter known as the Contractor, of
....
for the provision of..
as defined below.

1.2 Documents making up the Contract.

Only the documents listed below are contractual. All other documentation or prior verbal agreements have no contractual validity.
Notice that the Contractor's Tender is not included.

1.0 Agreement
2.0 The Scope of Work
3.0 Technical Specification
4.0 Drawings
5.0 Bill of Quantities
6.0 Services provided by the NGO to the Contractor
7.0 Programme
8.0 Terms of Payment
9.0 Guarantees

Appendices e.g. Power of Attorney (authority to sign Contract)
Invoice Form
Change Order Form
Other (e.g. special requirements of funding agencies)

1.3 Agreement

The Parties therefore agree as follows:

The Contractor agrees to perform the work and the NGO agrees to pay the Contractor in accordance with the provisions of the Contract documentation listed in Article 1.2 above.

For the NGO:
Name:
Title:
Signature:
Date:

For the Contractor:
Name:
Title:
Signature:
Date:

Section 2 Scope of Work

2.1 *Describe in clear and simple terms what the Contractor is expected to do.*

If it is for a complete job include wording such as: 'Provide all necessary labour, material, tools, equipment and services, except those furnished by the NGO as noted in Section 6 below, to build (how many units) of ... ... at (location).'

Refer to the Technical Specification and Drawings as appropriate.

Section 3 Technical Specification

3.1 *If a Technical Specification is required it should be included here. Note the title, reference number, revision number and date of issue.*

Section 4 Drawings

4.1 *If there are drawings or sketches include them here. List titles, numbers, revision numbers and date of issue. Even if they are hand drawn sketches give them a number and date so they can be recognized.*

Section 5 Bills of Quantities (Bill of Materials)

5.1 *If these form part of the contract list titles, descriptions, numbers and dates of issue.*

Describe how they are to be used in the final measurement of the works and for payment. Refer to Section 8 as required.

Section 6 Services to be provided to the Contractor by the NGO

6.1 Only those items of material or services listed specifically in this section will be provided to the Contractor for use by the Contractor in executing the Contract.

List here anything appropriate: fuel, special materials, camp facilities, etc. Identify quantities, how delivered and checked, whether paid for or free issue.

Section 7 Programme

7.1 *Make up a simple bar chart (see Section 5.2.3). Where there are specific target dates, intermediate or end dates these should be stated clearly in this section.*
e.g. 'the first 20 latrines must be completed no later than ... ... and the entire job no later than ... ...'.

Do not sign open-ended contracts or contracts of indefinite duration. It is easier to write a Change Order (see at the end of this sample contract) to extend a contract than sort out problems arising from ongoing commitments. This applies particularly to the hire of vehicles and equipment. It is best to make such contracts from month to month.

Section 8 Terms of Payment

8.1 Method of Measurement

This depends on how the Contract is to work. It is best to relate payment to clearly identifiable units. For example:

Number of finished latrines, huts, houses built.
Number of truck trips signed for.
Number of days' use of vehicles.
Payment of labour against approved timesheets.
Lengths of wood cut.
How Bills of Quantities are used to describe how the estimated quantities will be re-measured at the end of the job for adjustments to payments.

8.2 Method of Payment

Against an invoice within .... days of submission and with all the required support documents.

A standard procedure avoids receiving many scraps of illegible paper and makes it easier in accounting. If necessary, give the Contractor a model invoice to use with the Contractor's letterhead.

8.3 Cash Flow and Retention

Small contractors often need a down-payment to get their first material. If possible, they should provide a bank bond for the amount advanced.

It is always wise to keep a retention (5–10%) for say, a month (actual period depends on the job), after completion to cover for any hidden faults that need correcting after takeover.

A typical cash flow might look like this:

Down-payment	10% Contract price	With Contract	400
Progress payment 1	Per amount completed	End month 1	est 1000
Progress payment 2	Per amount completed	End month 2	est 1000
Progress payment 3	All work completed	End month 3	est 1000
Retention release	10% Contract price	End month 4	400
	Total Contract price	Monetary unit	3800

8.4 Contract not to exceed

Payments under this contract cannot exceed the amount of – *include the above total contract price* – without prior authorization of the NGO and issue of the appropriate Change Order in the form attached as an appendix to this document.

Any commitments made by the Contractor in excess of the above authorized maximum are made under the Contractor's entire responsibility and will not be reimbursed by the NGO.

Section 9 Guarantees

If any longer-term guarantees are required they should be specified in this section.

Appendices

A Power of Attorney (authorization to sign contracts)

This is a document signed by a Director or Chairman of the Contractor and notarized which certifies that the person signing the contract is duly authorized to do so. Where payment is to be made to an individual the same kind of authorization is needed.

B Invoice

A standard invoice can save time and ensures you receive a document with the necessary information that you and your accountants need for payment and audit. Discuss the format with the agency accountants.

C Change Order

This is the standard way to modify the Terms and Conditions of the Contract. See the sample that follows.

Sample Change Order

HELP NGO

Project: **Project No.:**

Project location:

CHANGE ORDER

Contractor:	**Contract No.:**	**Contract date:**
	Change Order No.:	**Change Order date:**

The Terms and Conditions of the above Contract are hereby amended as indicated below. All other Terms and Conditions remain in force in accordance with the original agreement.

Include amendments here

Previous Contract price:
Addition/Deduction by this Change Order: __________
Revised Contract price: __________

The changes as set out above are hereby agreed between the parties.

For the NGO:	For the Contractor:
Name:	Name:
Title:	Title:
Signature:	Signature:
Date:	Date:

6 Water well construction contract guidelines

The following format for a water well (borehole) construction contract is an edited version of guidelines drawn up by UNHCR and intended for use by its implementing partners (usually NGOs) in executing a borehole drilling programme employing a contractor. The contract should be adapted to individual circumstances. The contract and its supervision must take into account the feasibility of adhering to the accuracy of specifications and balance their relevance against the urgency with which water needs to be pumped out of the ground.

Key: A: Number of wells to be drilled
B: Location of drilling sites
C: UNHCR's implementing partner for the project.

General clauses

1.1 SUBJECT OF THE CONTRACT

The subject of the contract comprises the construction of (A) water wells for potable water supplies for refugee settlements in (B).

The contractor will carry out the drilling work and provide the proper tools, machinery, implements, materials and labour for due construction of the wells, their development and pump testing. The contractor will provide the casing and screen materials to the quality specifications given hereunder.

1.2 INFORMATION SUPPLIED BY (C)

(C) will supply to the contractor all the information available to (C) about the hydrogeological conditions in the area to be drilled. It should be clear that this information does not hold (C) responsible for the locally different conditions at each specific drilling site or for particular problems the contractor may encounter.

1.3 DRILLING SITES

(C) will indicate the drilling sites and provide the required permits for the use of the land where the contract is to be carried out.

The contractor will be responsible for all the damages occurring outside the allocated land.

The contractor will clear all debris of any kind, and leave the land, as far as it is possible, in its original condition after the well has been constructed, developed and pump tested.

1.4 ABANDONED WELL

If the contractor is not able to finish the drilling or has to abandon the well due to loss of tools or any other accident or contingency, the contractor will remove the casing or drive pipes already placed in the hole and refill it with clay or concrete, at the contractor's expense. All material extracted from such holes will be considered the property of the contractor.

In the case of an abandoned well, (C) will not pay for any of the work carried out and will give advanced authorization for the drilling of a new borehole near the abandoned well.

Technical specifications

2.1 BOREHOLES

2.1.1 Information concerning each borehole

The contractor will supply a detailed borehole log of: drilling rates; the appearance of the water; soil sampling details and the types of rock found; type and size of well casing; position, type and size of screen and other relevant well construction details.

2.1.2 Casing and diameters

The drilling of each borehole will be carried out according to the characteristics specified in the 'Table of Tentative Specifications' (at the end of this document) using the correct drilling tools, drive pipes, casing pipes, gravel packs and sanitary protection (see Specification 2.5), based on the actual characteristics of the aquifer formations. The casing pipe and sanitary protection (seals) should isolate each aquifer from other formations which are considered unsuitable for the exploitation of wholesome water.

The well design is to be authorized by (C) before the casing pipes and screens are introduced into the well.

2.1.3 Pipes and screen filters

The contractor will supply all pipes, screen filters and fittings for the proper casing of the wells at the agreed price.

2.1.4 Drilling equipment and depth of drilling

The contractor will use drilling equipment capable of drilling to a depth 25 per cent deeper than indicated in the 'Table of Tentative Specifications'. The use of cable tool, rotary or down-the-hole hammer (air percussion) rigs is acceptable.

The depths indicated in the 'Table of Tentative Specifications' should only be regarded as a guide.

If the actual characteristics of the wells being drilled justify any change in these specifications, the contractor will request the authorization of (C) for such changes to be made.

These communications will be made verbally and shall be properly recorded by (C).

In every case, if the actual characteristics of the well differ from those indicated in the 'Table of Tentative Specifications', and once these changes have been authorized by (C), a proper price adjustment will be made according to the final depth of the well and the unit price rendered by the contractor in the original proposal.

2.2 WELL PLUMBNESS AND ALIGNMENT

2.2.1 Tests

The well will be tested for plumbness and alignment by means of a straight, 12 metre long, steel pipe that will be passed down the whole depth of the well. The maximum external diameter of the pipe will be 13 mm less than the internal diameter of the well casing. The pipe will be supplied by the contractor.

2.2.2 Minimum requirements

The test pipe described in 2.2.1 should easily pass down the whole depth of the well. The deviation from plumbness of the well's axis should never be more than two-thirds the inside diameter of the smallest casing. If these minimum requirements are not met, the contractor will, if possible, correct the defects. If not, (C) will reject the well and no payments will be made for its drilling and completion. This test should normally be made before pump testing the well.

2.3 WELL COMPLETION AND TEST PUMPING

2.3.1 Pumping tests

The contractor will have a pumping unit capable of discharging 50 per cent more water, at the well's pumping water level, than the maximum yield indicated for each well in the 'Table of Tentative Specifications'.

Once the well construction is finished, the well will be developed by hydraulic surging (by means of a packer piston or compressed air). Immediately after this operation is completed, the well will be cleaned and the pumping unit introduced into the well. The contractor will communicate (3 days in advance) the date the pumping test is to be carried out. The test pumping of the well will be performed as follows.

Pumping test
The test will consist of continuously pumping the well at the maximum yield specified in the 'Table of Tentative Specifications' for the respective well or at any other rate previously defined between the contractor and (C), according to the outcome of the drilling. The duration of the test will be 48 hours. The measuring of the dynamic water levels will be performed according to the logarithmic timescale schedule normally used for test pumping water wells.

Other specifications
The contractor will convey the pumped water at least 200 m away from the well such that no pumped water will be left standing within a radius of 200 m of the well. The contractor will provide all the necessary equipment for this to be achieved.

The contractor will provide all the necessary equipment (weirs, pipes, gauges, etc.) for the proper measurement of discharge rates and water levels.

2.3.2 Well yield

After the pumping tests have been carried out, (C) will decide the recommended yield for each well, according to the test results, appropriate hydrogeological techniques and the actual needs.

2.4 PROTECTION OF THE WATER QUALITY, DISINFECTION AND SAMPLING

2.4.1 Well pollution

The contractor will take maximum care to avoid the physical, chemical or bacteriological contamination of the well water during construction. If water is polluted due to the contractor's neglect, the contractor will be obliged to carry out all the necessary operations, at the contractor's cost, to remove such pollutants from the well.

2.4.2 Well sterilization

Once the well has been completed and tested, the contractor will sterilize the well with a chlorine solution yielding at least 50 mg/l of active chlorine in all parts of the well.

The chlorine solution may be prepared from calcium hypochlorite, sodium hypochlorite or gaseous chlorine. The chlorine solution should stay in the well for at least four hours at the specified concentration.

2.4.3 Rock samples

The contractor will keep rock samples taken during the drilling operations in properly packed and identified sample bags and will make them available to (C) upon request.

The contractor will take at least one sample every three metres of drilling and at every change in rock formation. Each sample should weigh a minimum of 500 grammes.

For each sample not taken, the contractor will be fined an amount equal to 1 per cent of the total value of the well contract. This amount will be deducted from the final payment. If the total number of samples not taken is more than

15 per cent of the specified number, the well should be started again and (C) will not make any payments for the work already done.

2.4.4 Water samples

The contractor will take two water samples for laboratory analysis after completion of the long duration pumping test. One sample will be used for physical and chemical analysis. It should be put in a clean and properly sealed plastic or glass container. Its volume should not be less than 5 litres.

The other sample will be used in a bacteriological analysis. The sample should be divided and placed into three separate sterilized and properly sealed containers. The volume of each container should not be less than 100 ml. The samples will be handed to (C) as soon as the samples are taken.

2.4.5 Sand particle content in pumped water

The water drawn out of the well will be acceptable if it has a sand particle content of less than 5 g/m^3. If this maximum limit is not met, the contractor will make all necessary adjustments to the well structure, at the contractor's expense, to meet this specification.

2.5 FINISHING WORKS

2.5.1 Temporary lid

The contractor will take precautions against the entrance of pollutants into the well, including surface water, both during drilling and after completion of the well. For this purpose, the contractor will provide a lid to be placed over the mouth of the well at any time the drilling rig is not in operation. The lid will be placed on top of the well on completion of well construction.

2.5.2 Artificial filter packs

If necessary, an artificial properly graded gravel pack will be placed in the annular space between the hole wall and the outer face of the casing according to the 'Table of Tentative Specifications'. Proper techniques will be used for the accurate placing of this pack. The gravel to be used should be clean, well-rounded and the grains should be hard, of alluvial origin and in size between 0.5 to 2.5 cm diameter. The gravel shall be approved by (C).

2.5.3 Sanitary protection seal

All the wells that have been successfully tested shall have a proper protective sanitary seal cast in concrete by the contractor. The protective seal shall be placed from 3.5 metres below ground level to 0.25 metres above ground and will occupy an annular space between the hole wall and the outer face of the casing.

Table A6.1 Table of Tentative Specifications (to be completed by C's consultant)

Well site location	Drilling diameter mm	Diameter of casing mm	Max drilling depth mm	Length of casing m	Length of screen m	Min exp yield l/s	Max exp yield l/s	Remarks

Min = Minimum; Max = Maximum; exp = expected
l/s: litres per second m: metre mm: millimetre

7 Employment contract and job description

(To be adapted to suit particular circumstances)

Sample employment contract

1. OFFER OF EMPLOYMENT
On behalf of [name of agency] I am offering you the position of Sanitation Engineer.

2. TERMS AND CONDITIONS
Your terms and conditions of employment are set out in this appointment letter. This document will constitute your contract of employment with [name of agency].

3. SALARY AND ALLOWANCES
Your initial basic salary will be .... You will be entitled to claim subsistence expenses when you are asked by your manager to travel for work purposes outside your normal place of work. These expenses will be limited to ..../day. You will be paid monthly on the last Friday of the month.

4. PERIOD OF APPOINTMENT
Your appointment will be effective from 01/02/02 for a period of 1 year and will end on 31/01/03. There will be a review of this term in 9 months' time, when this expiry date will be confirmed with you or renewed for a further term with your consent.

5. PROBATIONARY AND NOTICE PERIODS
The first 3 months of your employment will be regarded as probationary. During this period 2 weeks' notice is required to be given in writing by either party. Once the probationary period is complete and your appointment has been confirmed, you are entitled to receive and required to give 6 weeks' notice of termination, which must be given in writing.

6. DUTIES AND RESPONSIBILITIES
Your duties and responsibilities are as detailed in the job description. In this position you will report to the senior environmental health engineer and your operating base will be [insert area where work is to be undertaken]. You may be asked to work in other areas away from this centre as the need arises. You must be willing to undertake such assignments unless good reason can be shown to the contrary.

7. DISCIPLINARY PROCEDURES
You will be subject to the standard agency disciplinary procedures as set out in the relevant notice which is available for inspection at the local office. It is your responsibility to ensure that you have read, understood and are familiar with these procedures.

8. HOURS OF WORK
Your hours of work will be 48 hours per week from Monday to Saturday starting at 7.30a.m. and finishing at 4.30p.m. including an hour for lunch. The agency requires a flexible approach to these work hours and if longer hours of work are required during peak work periods a flexible approach is expected of you. The agency does not pay overtime but will make every attempt to compensate for extra hours worked in the form of time off in lieu during quiet work periods. You are entitled to 4 weeks' holiday per year plus national public holidays.

9. SICKNESS ABSENCE AND MEDICAL BENEFITS
You will be entitled to reclaim medical expenses related to yourself and your immediate family. Your immediate family is made up of your spouse(s) and legal children. All medical expense claims must be substantiated by official receipts from your doctor. You are not entitled to reclaim dental or optical expenses unless incurred as a result of an accident at work. You must provide a doctor's certificate to verify days absent from work due to sickness after three days of absence. Periods of less than three days do not require a certificate but your manager must be informed of the reason of your absence during the first day.

10. ACCEPTANCE
Please would you confirm your acceptance of this offer by signing and dating the attached copy of this letter and returning it to this office within one week of receipt.

I accept the appointment referred to in the above contract on the terms and conditions set out in the letter and attached appendices.

Signed .... Date ....

Sample job description

SANITATION ENGINEER

RESPONSIBLE TO: Senior Environmental Health Engineer

STAFF REPORTING: Sanitation Construction Teams, Foremen, Drivers, Storemen.

PURPOSE: To improve and maintain environmental health status in the temporary settlements where [name of agency] is working.

TASKS:

1. Assist in the design of an appropriate sanitation programme for the temporary settlements in which [name of agency] is working. The programme is to include the provision of latrines, bathing areas, clothes washing facilities, and

services which facilitate household waste disposal, drainage and vector control. This will involve consultation and discussion with the camp planners to ensure an appropriate camp layout.

2. Consult with displaced population on what constitutes an appropriate design for the sanitation programme.

3. Liaise closely with the hygiene education team in order to co-ordinate activities for the overall improvement in environmental health of the camp populations.

4. Supervise the construction of all structures associated with the sanitation component of the environmental health programme. Wherever possible and feasible encourage the involvement of the camp population in the sanitation programme.

5. Be responsible for ordering all construction materials and chemicals for the sanitation programme. These materials must be ordered in sufficient time to ensure that agreed stock levels at camp and regional level are maintained at all times.

6. Help the hygiene education team to monitor the effect of the sanitation programme by assisting with regular monitoring of fly populations, litter surveys, observation of the hygiene standards of latrines, wash areas and so on.

7. Provide regular weekly summaries and monthly reports to the senior environmental health engineer, commenting on progress according to agreed targets, working relationships with, and progress of, contractors, and cash expenditure.

8. Collaborate closely with the water engineer and water construction team to ensure optimum location of sanitation facilities in relation to water points.

9. Assist the senior environmental health engineer to draw up a maintenance schedule for all sanitation facilities. Compile a maintenance manual for the programme for the benefit of new staff members and to provide continuity.

10. Be willing to undertake any reasonable task asked of him/her by the senior environmental health engineer or country director.

8 Sanitary survey checklists

Sanitary surveys are described in Section 9.1.2.

Figure A8.1 and the accompanying checklist indicate the kind of visual reminder and questions to include on a sanitary survey form for use by field workers. Questions for other water source checklists are also suggested, but they must be adapted and further appropriate questions added according to the situation.

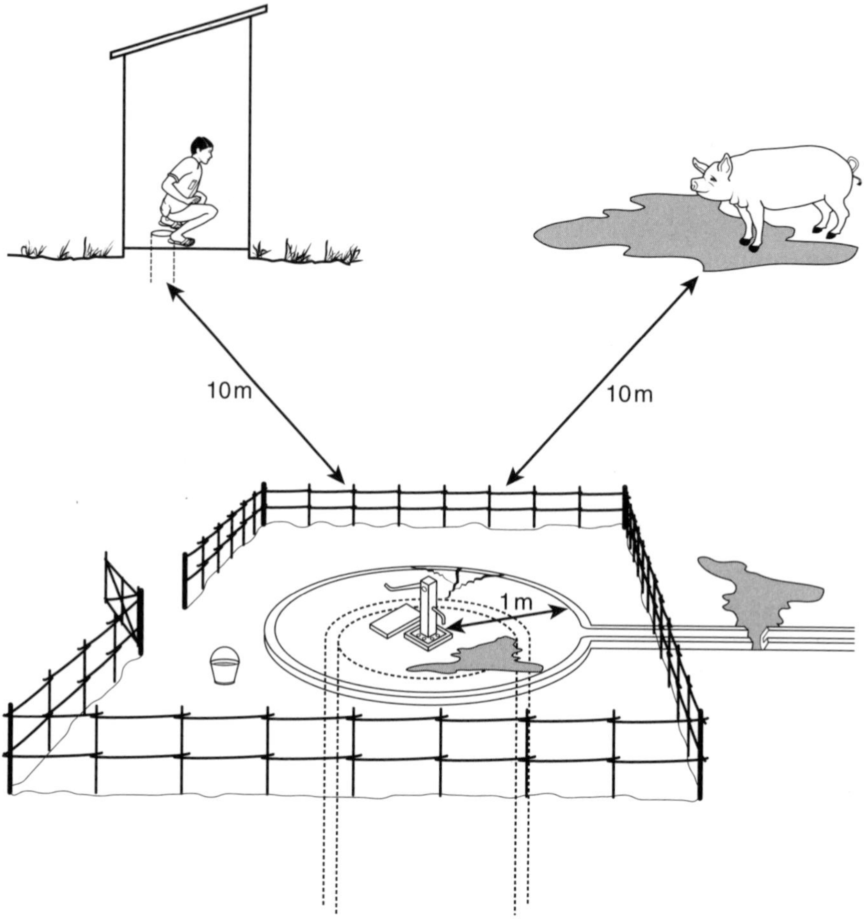

Figure A8.1 Sanitary survey of a dug well fitted with a handpump

1. Dug well (or borehole) fitted with a handpump

	Yes	No
Is there a latrine within 10 m of the well?		
Is the latrine on higher ground than the well?		
Is there any other source of pollution within 10 m?		
Is there inadequate fencing around the well?		
Is the apron less than 1 m radius around the handpump?		
Is there ponding of water around the well?		
Is the drainage channel broken or is it dirty?		

	Yes	No
Is there any ponding of water around the handpump?		
Are there any cracks in the well apron?		
Is the handpump loose at the point of attachment?		
Is the cover of the well insanitary?		
Is the well poorly sealed for 3 m below ground level?		
Is the handpump broken?		

Risk score (the number of '**Yes**' answers): ☐

2. Open dug well

Similar to list 1 but replacing questions about the handpump with questions about the alternative method of lifting. For example:

	Yes	No
Do people use their own rope and bucket to collect water?		
Are ropes and buckets contaminated in use?		
Is there a poor well wall which will allow spilt and surface water into the well?		
Is the well left open when not in use?		

3. Borehole fitted with a powered pump

List adapted to account for the greater drawdown of a powered pump and to refer to the sanitary state of the pump house floor. For example:

	Yes	No
Is there a latrine within 50 m of the well?		
Is there any other source of pollution within 50 m?		
Is there inadequate fencing around the pump house?		
Is the pump house floor cracked?		
Is there ponding of water on the floor?		
Is the pump loose at the point of attachment to the floor?		

4. Protected spring

	Yes	No
Is the spring source open to surface water contamination?		
Is the spring wall or box cracked?		
If there is an inspection cover, is it cracked or not in position?		
Is the overflow pipe screen missing or insanitary?		
Is there inadequate fencing around the spring source?		

	Yes	No
Is the cut-off ditch above the spring blocked or non-existent?		
Is there a latrine uphill of the spring?		
Is there any other source of pollution uphill of the spring?		
Is there ponding of water at the collection point?		
Is the drainage away from the spring blocked?		

5. Chlorinated and piped supply

	Yes	No
Are there any pipe leaks?		
Are there any leaks from valves?		
Is there ponding of water in the valve boxes?		
Are break pressure tank covers missing or cracked?		
Do pipes pass closer than 10 m to latrines, sewers or drains?		
Are there cracks in the water storage tank wall or roof?		
Is the storage tank inspection cover missing or cracked?		
Is there less than 0.2 mg/l free residual chlorine at every tap?		

(Lloyd and Helmer, 1991)

9 Discharge measurements and estimates

Bucket and stop-watch

Do not make flow measurement more complicated than it needs to be for the degree of accuracy required. A reasonably accurate and easy method of measuring low flows from a pipe, borehole or spring is to use a bucket and stop-watch.

The measurement of discharge over V-notch and rectangular-notch weirs

A weir is suitable for measuring the flow from large springs or small streams. A pre-fabricated weir box can measure the discharge from pipes, boreholes, etc. To place a weir in a stream it will be necessary to divert or dam the flow temporarily with sand bags. Ensure weirs are:

- Sharp-crested – made of thin steel plate not more than 2 mm thick; thicker plywood can be chamfered to give a sharp 2 mm thick crest.
- Sealed to prevent leakage – dig the weir plate into the bed and banks and seal with clay.

- Vertical and perpendicular to the channel with the crest horizontal – use a spirit level.
- Fully contracted – the bed and sides of the approach channel should be sufficiently far from the weir crest to have no significant effect on the flow.
- Free-flowing – the downstream water level should be below the crest.

The approach velocity should be less than 0.15 m/s. Place stones below the overflow to prevent erosion around the bottom of the plate.

To avoid the effect of drawdown at the crest, the depth above the weir, h, should be measured at a distance of more than 4 h upstream. Accurately position the measuring staff to ensure that the zero mark is level with the vertex of the V-notch or at the level of the rectangular weir crest. This can be done using a spirit level and string, or a plastic tube water-level.

Up to about 70 l/s the V-notch weir gives better overall accuracy than a rectangular weir.

V-notch weir

For a V-notch weir of dimensions shown in Figure A9.1:

$$Q = 0.533 \sqrt{(2g)}\ C \tan(\theta/2)\ h^{2.5}$$

where: Q (m^3/s) is the discharge rate
θ is the angle of the notch
h (m) is the depth of water above the vertex of the notch
C is the coefficient of discharge which varies according to the dimensions of the weir and channel.

Within the accuracy of field measurements it is practical to simplify the calculations by taking an approximate constant value of C = 0.59 for discharge over 60° and 90° V-notch weirs within the limits of the weir dimensions shown in Figure A9.1.

For a 60° V-notch: $Q = 0.80h^{2.5}$
For a 90° V-notch: $Q = 1.39h^{2.5}$

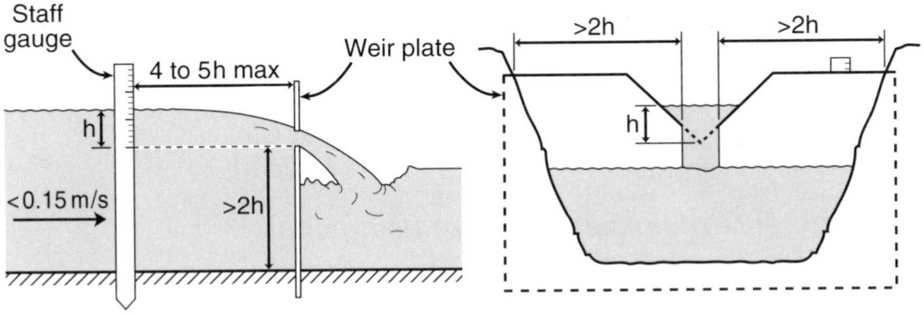

Figure A9.1 Fully-contracted flow over a V-notch weir

Table A9.1 Flow over V-notch weirs

h, mm	*Q, l/s 90° V-notch*	*Q, l/s 60° V-notch*
40	0.4	0.3
50	0.8	0.5
60	1.2	0.7
70	1.8	1.0
80	2.5	1.5
90	3.4	1.9
100	4.4	2.5
110	5.5	3.2
120	7.0	4.0
130	8.5	4.9
140	10	5.9
150	12	7.0
175	18	10
200	25	14

Rectangular weir

For a rectangular weir of dimensions shown in Figure A9.2:

$$Q = 0.667 \sqrt{(2g)}\ C\ b\ h^{1.5}$$

where: Q (m^3/s) is the discharge rate
h (m) is the depth of water over the crest
b (m) is the width of the weir notch
C is the coefficient of discharge.

The value of C varies according to:

- The ratio of the width of the notch, b, to the width of the approach channel, B.
- The ratio of the depth of water over the crest, h, to the height of the crest relative to the channel floor, p.

Within the accuracy of field measurements it is practical to simplify the calculations by taking an approximate constant value of C = 0.6 for discharge over rectangular-notch weirs within the limits of the dimensions shown in Figure A9.2. Then,

$$Q = 1.77\ b\ h^{1.5}$$

Measurements of flow in a stream using floats

Where a water course is too wide or is unsuitable for a temporary weir, a rough estimate of the flow can be obtained from the measurement of the velocity of a float. From the average flow velocity (V) and the average cross-sectional area

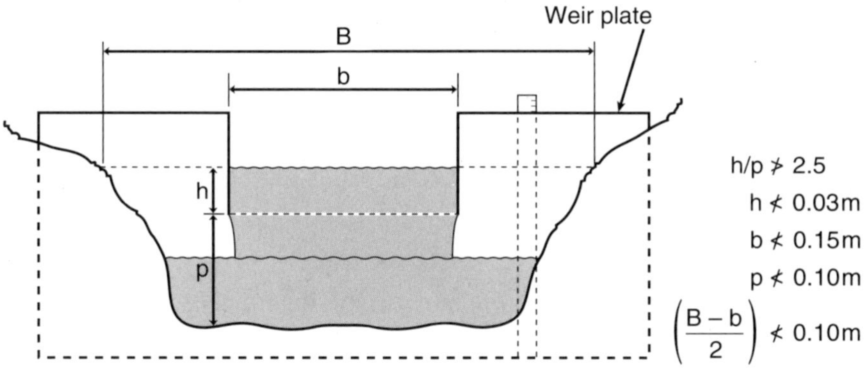

Figure A9.2 Fully-contracted flow over a rectangular weir

Example: Flow over a rectangular weir of notch width, b = 0.6 m

h, mm	Q, l/s	h, mm	Q, l/s
50	12	160	68
60	16	170	74
70	20	180	81
80	24	190	88
90	29	200	95
100	34	210	102
110	39	220	110
120	44	230	117
130	50	240	125
140	56	250	133
150	62	260	141

(A) of a uniform straight section of channel, the rate of flow (Q) is given by:

$$Q = V A$$

where: Q is the rate of flow (m^3/s)
V is the average velocity of flow (m/s)
A is the average cross-sectional area of the stream (m^2).

Floats give an approximate mid-stream surface velocity. The surface velocity is multiplied by a coefficient to give the average velocity. The depth of the channel will determine the coefficient. This varies from 0.66 for channels less than 300 mm deep to 0.85 for depths over 6 m. A figure of 0.8 is often used for small streams.

A fruit makes a good float as it is less affected by wind than a stick. Weighted floats can also be used to give an estimate of the average velocity.

Choose a relatively straight section of stream of reasonably uniform cross-section. Record the time taken for a float to travel a measured distance between two points – at least 10 times the channel depth: the longer the better. Take an average of several readings to give the float velocity.

Surface floats such as blocks of wood, tins, bottles, or oranges Surface floats will give the surface velocity (V_s) which must be adjusted to give the average velocity, $V_a = 0.8\ V_s$
Surface floats are affected by wind.

Sub-surface floats A floating buoy and weighted container set at 0.6 of the depth, measured from the surface, will give an estimate of the average velocity. Sub-surface floats are less affected by wind.

Rod floats A weighted rod that will float vertically with its lower end just above the channel bed can give a good approximation of the average velocity. The rod length is critical.

Measure the cross-sectional area of the channel with a depth pole and measuring tape at several points in the timed section. Estimate the flow rate from the measured average velocity and the cross-sectional area.

Estimating flows in streams at critical periods

Stream gauging gives an estimate of flow at a particular time. Flow data for other times may be needed such as:

- The dry season minimum flow, to ensure that the supply will be adequate and that the intake will not run dry.
- The wet season maximum flow, so that pumps can be protected from peak flood flows.

Sources of information for estimating flows:

- Records from similar streams.
- Local knowledge.
- Observation and survey – signs of flood levels in the channel banks.
- Records of rainfall and catchment size.

Records from similar streams

For the recorded basin, measure the catchment area A1 which drains to the measuring station. For the unrecorded basin, measure the catchment area A2 which drains to the point where the flow is to be estimated. Obtain the flow Q1 for the recorded basin at the time of the year required (such as dry season). Estimate the flow Q2 for the unrecorded basin at the same time of year using: $Q2 = Q1 \times A2/A1$.

Note that this method is accurate only when the streams have similar characteristics (slopes, soils, vegetation, size) and rainfall.

Local knowledge

Obtain records of the depth of flow at a particular time of year (such as high flood in the rainy season) together with a survey of the cross-section and slope of the stream. Estimate using Manning's formula:

$$Q = \frac{A \times R^{0.67} s^{0.5}}{n}$$

Where Q = discharge (m^3/s)
A = wetted area (m^2)
R = A/P where P = wetted perimeter (m)
s = slope (m/m)
n = Manning's roughness coefficient ($s/m^{0.33}$)

Suitable values of n are:

straight river with earth bed	0.02–0.025
straight river with stony bed	0.03–0.04
winding river with earth bed	0.03–0.05
winding river with stony bed	0.04–0.08

Measurement of constant discharges from pipes

A weir box

Use a V- or rectangular-notch weir placed in a rectangular box. Fit baffles to still the incoming flow. Measure the head between 100 mm and 720 mm upstream of the weir. Do not measure the head near the inlet or in a downstream corner of the box.

For a weir box of dimensions:
Length 1.50 m, Width 0.92 m, Height 0.45 m

use the following expressions to calculate the flow.

For a 90° V-notch weir box,

Q = flow rate (m^3/s); h = head (m) above the vertex of the V-notch; C = 0.6 (approx); $Q = 1.42\ h^{2.5}$, giving the following:

h, mm	Q, l/s	h, mm	Q, l/s
40	0.4	120	7.1
60	1.3	140	10.4
80	2.6	160	14.6
100	4.5	180	19.5

For a rectangular-notch weir box,

Q = flow rate (m^3/s); h = head (m) above the vertex of the weir sill; b = width of a rectangular weir; C = 0.6 (approx); $Q = 1.77\ b\ h^{1.5}$

Measurement of flow from a horizontal pipe

Flow can be gauged by measuring the co-ordinates of the water trajectory from a horizontal pipe as indicated in Figure A9.3.

The discharge, Q m^3/s, is given by:

$$Q = CAx \sqrt{(g/2y)}$$

where: C is a coefficient (1.0 – 1.1)
A is the cross-sectional area of the pipe (m^2)
x and y are as shown in Figure A9.3 (mm)
where x > 20 mm and y > 20 mm

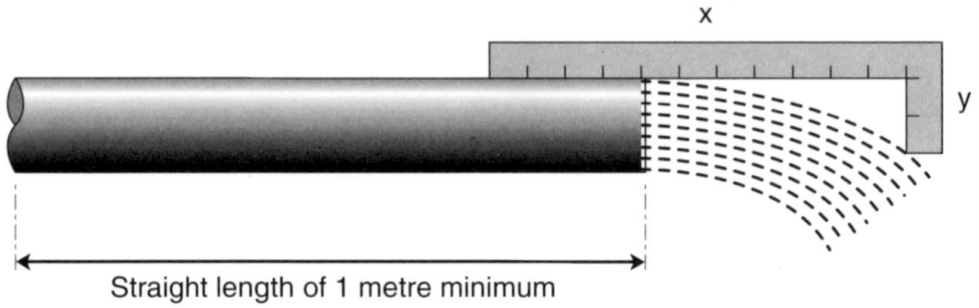

Figure A9.3 Measurement of flow from a horizontal pipe

10 Aquifer properties and well hydraulics

Hydraulic conductivity, k, is a measure of permeability and is a constant relating to an aquifer's capacity to allow water to flow through it. For an aquifer whose properties are equal in all directions (isotropic) and homogenous, Darcy's law states:

$$Q = k\,A\,I$$

where:

Q is the flow rate through the aquifer (m^3/day)
A is the cross-sectional area of the aquifer (m^2)
I is the hydraulic gradient (m/m)
k has the units of m/day.

Table A10.1 shows the order of magnitude of k for different materials. Useful aquifers have k values of over 0.5 m/day.

Transmissivity (transmissibility), T, is the rate of groundwater flow under unit hydraulic gradient through an aquifer cross-section of unit width and is expressed as:

$$T = k\,b$$

Table A10.1 Approximate hydraulic conductivities for different materials

Material	*Hydraulic conductivity, k (m/day)*
Clay	10^{-5} to 10^{-7}
Silt	10^{-1}
Fine sand	10^{-1} to 10
Coarse sand	10 to 2×10^{2}
Gravel	10 to 10^{3} plus

Source: Kruseman and De Ridder, 1979

where:

k is the average hydraulic conductivity (m/day)
b is the thickness of the saturated part of the aquifer (m)
T is the transmissivity (m^2/day).

The cone of depression in a clayey aquifer of low transmissivity is deep, steep sided, and of small radius. A gravel aquifer of high transmissivity has a flat cone of large radius. Therefore, the distance between wells to prevent well interference, and between wells and latrines to prevent contamination, is more critical in sand/gravel aquifers than in aquifers of lower transmissivity.

Aquifer storage

Specific yield, S_y, refers to storage in an unconfined aquifer.

Specific yield is the volume of water which will drain from a unit volume of unconfined aquifer by gravity and is given by:

$$S_y = \frac{V_w}{V_b}$$

where:

V_w is the volume of water that will drain by gravity from rock or soil
V_b is the volume of water in an initially saturated rock or soil

Specific yield is dimensionless and is often expressed as a percentage. Illustrative specific yields of different soils and rock are given in Table A10.2.

Table A10.2 The specific yield of different materials

Material	*Specific yield %*
Clay	1–10
Sand	10–30
Gravel	15–30
Sandstone	5–15
Shale	0.5–5
Limestone	0.5–5

Storage coefficient, S, refers to storage in a confined aquifer.

The storage coefficient can be defined as the volume of water released from storage per unit change of head per unit surface area of confined aquifer. It takes into account the elasticity of the aquifer and the compressibility of water. S is dimensionless and, for a confined aquifer, ranges from 10^{-5} to 10^{-3}. For an unconfined aquifer, S is the same as the specific yield, S_y.

Specific capacity and drawdown of a well The specific capacity is the ratio of the discharge, Q, to the drawdown, s, of a well (Q/s).

The specific drawdown is the reciprocal of specific capacity: s/Q.

11 Hand augers

Box A11.1 lists the components of a hand auger set. Lightweight sets can be used for soil surveys and heavier sets for drilling wells.

Table A11.1 Equipment and materials for augering wells of different diameters

Equipment and materials	*Set 1 mm*	*Set 2 mm*	*Set 3 mm*
Diameter of the first auger	100	150	180
Outer diameter of temporary casing	90	125	160
Inner diameter of temporary casing	76	108	146
Diameter of the second auger for drilling inside temporary casing	70	100	140
Outer diameter of permanent casing	63	75	110
Inner diameter of permanent casing	58	69	101
Gravel pack thickness	13	25	25
Recommended max. diameter of pump cylinder	55	66	96

Source: Van Reekum Materials b.v.

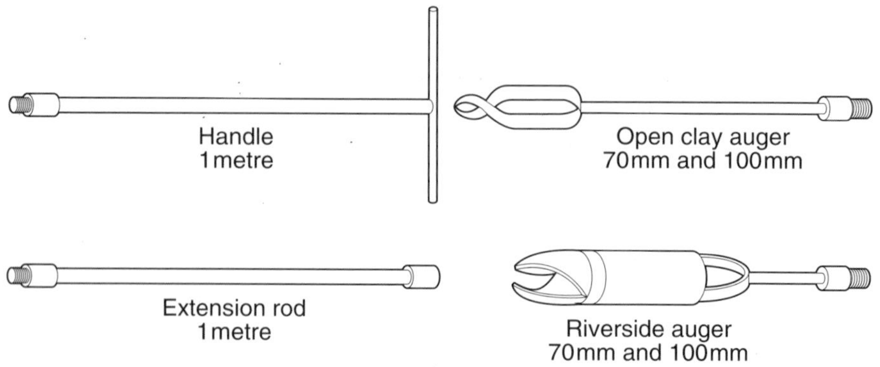

Box A11.1 The components of hand auger sets

Hand auger set for surveys to a depth of 15 m. Rods and augers with conical screw thread connections

No.	Description	Outside diameter mm
1	'T' handle, length 0.5 m	
1	'T' handle, length 1.0 m	
15	Extension shafts, length 1.0 m	
22	Male thread protectors	
22	Female thread protectors	
1	Clay auger	(70)
1	Clay auger	(100)
1	Riverside auger	(70)
1	Riverside auger	(100)
1	Bailer with flap valve	(63)
Tool kit:		
2	Extension rod catchers	
2	Pipe wrenches	
1	Screwdriver, length 30 cm	
1	Thread cleaning brush	
Optional casing set (depending on soils):		
20	ABS casings, length 1.0 m	(90)
3	ABS slotted casings, length 1.0 m	(90)
23	Male thread protectors	(90)
23	Female thread protectors	(90)
1	Steel casing shoe	
1	Steel casing head	
2	Casing clamps	
1	Casing retriever	

Hand auger set for the construction of a 150 mm hand drilled borehole to a depth of 15 m. Finished internal diameter of final casing: 70 mm

No.	Description	Outside diameter mm
1	Cross-piece and handles	
1	Tool guide	
15	Extension rods, length 1.0 m	
5	Spare rod connectors	
1	Clay auger	(100)
1	Clay auger	(150)
1	Riverside auger	(100)
1	Riverside auger	(150)
1	Spare riverside auger blade	(100)
1	Spare riverside auger blade	(150)
1	Flight auger	(150)
1	Stone auger	(100)
1	Stone auger	(150)
1	Stone catcher	(100)
1	Chisel	(100)
15	Drilling casings, length 1.0 m	(125/108)
1	Casing shoe	(125/108)
1	Casing head	(125/108)
2	Casing clamps	(125)
1	Bailer with flap valve	(90)
Tool kit:		
2	Rod catchers/lifters	
1	Hammer	
1	Screwdriver	
1	Adjustable spanner	
1	Mechanical sounding device	

Each gravel packed installation will require a recommended final casing of 75/69 mm PVC casing suitable for a 50 mm diameter pump cylinder.

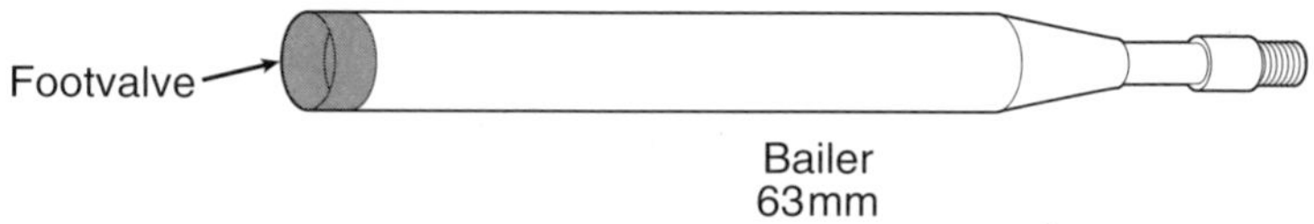

12 Compressed air tool package for open well construction

Quantity	*Item*
1	Trailer mounted air compressor (35 l/s free air delivered at 7 bar). Service kits (500/1000 hour) for compressor, depending on run time.
1	Lightweight (24 kg) pneumatic breaker. A number of tools to fit breaker according to the type of rock and amount of work: – moil point chisel tools for breaking soft rock – narrow chisel tools for splitting rock.
1	Lightweight hand-held rotary rock drill for drill diameters of 19–35 mm and drilling depths up to 3 m. Also a number of drill steels to fit rock drill, according to the type and amount of work. A typical series of drill steels with chisel bits is:

Length, mm	*Diameter, mm*
800	33
1200	32
1600	31
2000	30

2	Extension hoses compatible with tools (typical length 15 m).
2	Short length hoses compatible with tools (length 3 m).
1	In-line mineral oil lubricator. Lubricant compatible with the above.
1	Water separator (optional).
Assorted	Claw couplings: hose nipples, external thread and internal thread couplings.
10	Spare packing for couplings.
8	Covers for coupling connections on tools and hoses when not in use.

13 Pipe and hose specifications

The metric and inch systems of pipe designation are not the same:

- The inch system relates to the nominal pipe bore or internal diameter.
- The metric system relates to the outside diameter.

Note on pressures (see Appendix 25):
1 bar = 10 m H_2O (approx) = 1 atmosphere = 14.22 lbf/in^2 (p.s.i.)

Polyethylene pressure pipes

Polyethylenes are manufactured by a variety of processes in different parts of the world. Quality will vary and the data given in this appendix relates to pipe manufactured to internationally accepted standards. In addition, the polyethylene materials may not always be compatible for fusion jointing. Check trial joints before fusion jointing PE pipes of unknown specification or dissimilar PE materials.

PE pipes are referred to by the Standard Dimension Ratio (SDR):

$$SDR = \frac{\text{Mean outside diameter}}{\text{Minimum wall thickness}}$$

Blue MDPE

OD mm	Approx. bore mm	SDR	Maximum working pressure @ 20°C bar	Approx. weight kg/m
20	15	9	12	0.128
25	20	11	12	0.165
32	26	11	12	0.274
50	41	11	12	0.658
63	51	11	12	1.040
90	73	11	10	2.103
125	101	11	10	4.043
180	146	11	10	8.392
250	203	11	10	16.094

The maximum recommended working pressure is reduced with increase in temperature. To obtain the revised maximum recommended working pressure above 20°C, multiply the recommended maximum working pressure at 20°C by the reduction factors listed below.

Temperature	*Reduction factor*
25°C	0.80
30°C	0.63

MDPE retains ductility well below freezing and the recommended maximum operating temperatures at 20°C continue to apply.

MDPE pipe is available in coils or in straight lengths as follows:

- 90 mm OD and above in straight lengths of 6 and 12 m
- 20 mm to 180 mm OD in coils of varying length from 25 m to 250 m depending on the diameter.

Coiled pipe is particularly advantageous in an emergency because it reduces the number of joints to be made and it can be uncoiled and laid very quickly.

However, care must be taken when handling and laying coiled pipe due to the high amount of energy stored. Coils are supplied securely strapped and they must be uncoiled very carefully.

Black polyethylene pressure pipe

Black pigmented PE pipe is suitable for use above ground.

Nominal maximum working pressures:
SDR 11 10 bar (12 bar for sizes 90–180 mm) blue markings
SDR 17.6 6 bar (7.5 bar for sizes 90 – 180 mm) red markings

HDPE

Specifications based on HDPE pipe used in Nepal (Jordan, 1984)

OD mm	Class	Approx. bore mm	Approx. weight kg/m
32	III	27	0.22
	IV	24	0.33
50	III	42	0.47
	IV	38	0.80
63	III	53	0.74
	IV	48	1.26
90	III	76	1.68
	IV	70	2.32

Class III 6 bar; Class IV 10 bar

PVC pressure pipe

PVC-u inch sizes based on BS 3505:1986

Nominal size inches	Class	Nominal bore mm	Approx. weight kg/m
3	C	80	1.61
	D	80	1.95
	E	80	2.35
4	C	100	2.48
	D	100	3.23
	E	100	3.87
6	C	150	5.38
	D	150	7.04
	E	150	8.49
8	C	200	8.39
	D	200	10.86
	E	200	13.04

Standard length of pipe: 6 m.

Pressure ratings at 20°C: Class C 9 bar; Class D 12 bar; Class E 15 bar.

PVC-u metric size based on UK Water Industry Specification 4-31-06

Outside diameter mm	Pressure rating at 20°C	Mean bore mm	Approx. weight kg/m
90	8 bar	84	1.2
	12.5 bar	81	1.8
110	8 bar	103	1.8
	12.5 bar	99	2.8
160	8 bar	150	3.8
	12.5 bar	144	5.9
200	8 bar	187	6.0
	12.5 bar	180	9.2

The maximum recommended working pressure is reduced with increase in temperature. To obtain the revised maximum recommended working pressure, reduce the rating by 2% per degree C above 20°C.

PVC-u pipes are susceptible to failure through fatigue when subjected to pulsating pressures. Therefore, where surge pressures are likely to be encountered, the total of the working pressure and surge pressure must not exceed the maximum rated pressure of the pipe.

Galvanized steel (GI pipe)

A standard joint for galvanized steel pipe for water supplies is the taper/parallel screwed and socketed joint in which the tubes have a taper thread and the joint

Table A13.1 Maximum design pressures for galvanized steel tubes to BS 1387 with taper/taper screwed and socketed joints for carrying cold water

Nominal size	**Thread**	**Medium**			**Heavy**		
mm	Inches	Pressure bar	Thickness mm	Weight m/tonne	Pressure bar	Thickness mm	Weight m/tonne
15	½	35	2.6	787	42	3.2	667
20	¾	35	2.6	610	42	3.2	516
25	1	35	3.2	398	42	4.0	329
32	1¼	28	3.2	309	35	4.0	254
40	1½	28	3.2	268	35	4.0	220
50	2	24	3.6	190	31	4.5	156
65	2½	24	3.6	148	31	4.5	121
80	3	21	4.0	114	28	5.0	93
100	4	17	4.5	78	21	5.4	66
125	5	17	5.0	57	21	5.4	53
150	6	14	5.0	48	17	5.4	45

Source: British Steel plc, Tubes & Pipes

sockets have parallel threads. However, it is not considered practical to give precise limits for working pressures as the effectiveness of the joint is a key factor. The screwed joint is very dependent on size, local service conditions, pipe supports and jointing techniques.

Steel tubes are categorized as Light, Medium and Heavy. It is only practical to use Medium and Heavy for threaded joints. As an approximate guide, pressures not exceeding those shown in the following table can be considered for tubes manufactured to BS 1387 and used with taper/taper screwed joints. But beware, tubes available internationally may not comply with this standard.

Tubes are colour coded with 50 mm wide bands:

Light – Brown   Medium – Blue   Heavy – Red

Galvanized pipe is galvanized internally and externally. Note that the galvanized finish is removed when cutting new threads which can result in corrosion at the joints.

PVC reinforced suction hose

Commonly available in coils of 30 m

Nominal ID inches	Nominal ID mm	Working pressure at 20°C bar	Approx. weight kg/m
2	50	5	1.0
3	75	4	1.6
4	100	3	2.7

NOTE: The characteristics of flexible PVC hose vary widely between types of hose and manufacturer. The above working pressures are only a guide and are significantly reduced at higher temperatures.

14 Pipe and hose fittings

The following brief guide is to aid in the correct identification of fittings so that errors in ordering and purchasing due to the use of incorrect terms can be avoided. Sketches of selected fittings are shown alongside the names of fittings of a similar type which are commonly available.

Standard method of specifying fittings:

- For fittings with two outlets, specify the larger first.
- For fittings with more than two outlets (such as Tees), first specify the straight line outlets, followed by the branch outlet size.
- The size of two outlets of the same size on the same straight line is specified only once.

Compression fittings for plastic pipe

(*Names in English, French and Spanish*, courtesy Astore SpA)

Coupling
Manchon
Manguito

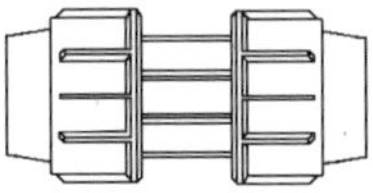

Reducing coupling
Manchon réduit
Manguito reducido

Male adaptor
Raccord male
Emplame macho

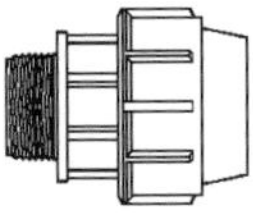

Female adaptor
Raccord femelle
Emplame hembra

90° Elbow
Coude à 90°
Codo a 90°

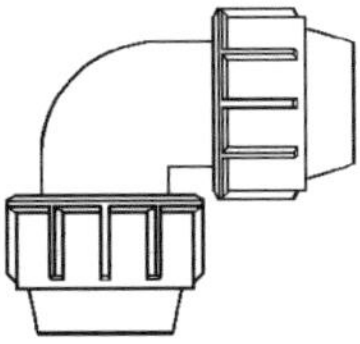

90° Tee or 'T'
Té à 90°
T a 90°
OR
with threaded female offtake
avec derivation taraudée femelle
con derivaciòn fileteada hembra
OR
male/filetée/macho

Flanged joint
Joint à bride
Empalme con arandela

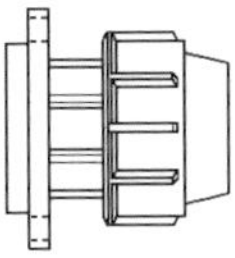

Clamp saddle
Collier de prise
Colarin de toma

Plug
Bouchon femelle
Tapon

Fittings for PE pipes

PE pipe and fittings may be joined using compression fittings described previously or by welding. The two methods of welding are 'electrofusion' and 'butt fusion'.

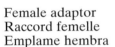

Electrofusion joints require purpose made couplers, reducers and fittings with the appropriate terminals for electrofusion.

Butt fusion joints can be made between plain ended pipe – special couplers are not needed. Fittings for butt fusion must be 'pupped' to give sufficient length of straight pipe leading from the fitting for the jointing process (see 13.4.1).

Fittings for PVC-u pipes

Fittings are produced for a range of joints: 'O' ring push-fit, spigot and socket, solvent cement, stub collar and backing flange, and other combinations of joints. When ordering, specify the type of joints required.

Common fittings available:

Bends: 90°, 45°, 22½°, 11¼°

Coupler (socket × socket)
(Can be used for pipe repairs and to take up expansion and contraction)

'O' ring coupler, with or without central register
(Can be used for pipe repairs and to take up expansion and contraction)

Straight coupling (plain socket × plain socket)

Reducing socket (socket × socket)

Straight connector (socket × tapered pipe thread)

Adaptor nipple (spigot × taper thread)

Union (socket × socket with nut) – to provide a means of future disconnection

90° Elbow (socket × socket)

Equal tee (socket × socket × socket)

End cap (socket)

Socket flange (socket × PVC flange)

Socket stub flange (socket × metal backing ring)

Reducing flange adaptor (flange to parallel spigot)

Hose fittings

Lug fittings, male and female –
parallel thread hosetails in brass, malleable iron and polypropylene

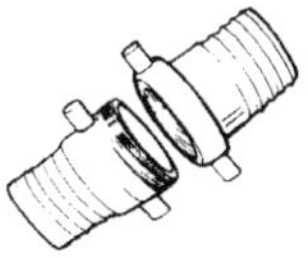

Flange hosetails in steel –
stipulate correct flange specification

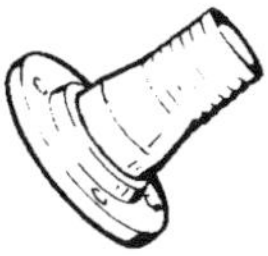

Bauer couplings –
galvanized steel quick fit male and female couplings

Instant fire hose couplings – in gunmetal or aluminium alloy

Foot valve and strainer – with a male or female pipe thread, or hosetail for connection to suction pipe

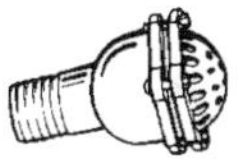

Malleable iron threaded fittings

Malleable iron fittings may be supplied 'Black', with an oil finish for protection against rust prior to fitting, or 'Galvanized', for long term corrosion protection. When ordering, stipulate whether 'Black' or 'Galvanized' finish is required.

Hexagon nipple

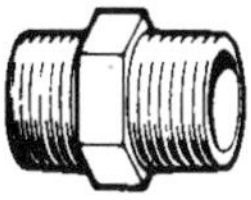

Hexagon nipple, reducing

Hexagon bush

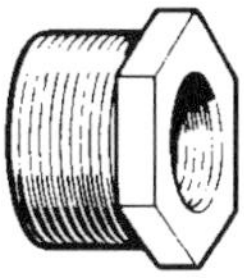

Socket (parallel thread and taper thread)

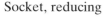

Socket, reducing

Plug

Cap

Tees:
equal; reducing on branch; reducing on run; reducing on run and branch; increasing on branch

Pitcher tee

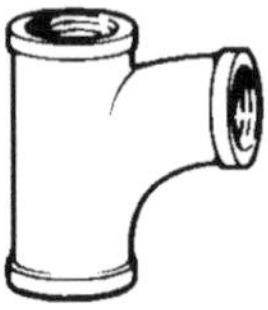

Cross

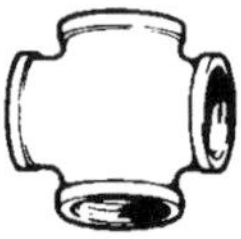

Elbows: equal; reducing; male and female; 45°

Twin elbow

Bend

Bend, male

Bend, male and female

Return bend (180°)

Union, flat seat + gasket

Union, spherical seat

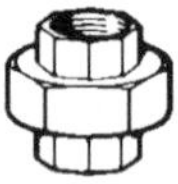

Round flange, drilled or undrilled

Ferrule straps

Self-tapping with integral cutter for underpressure tappings into PE and PVC pipe (F. W. Talbot & Co. Ltd).

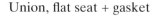

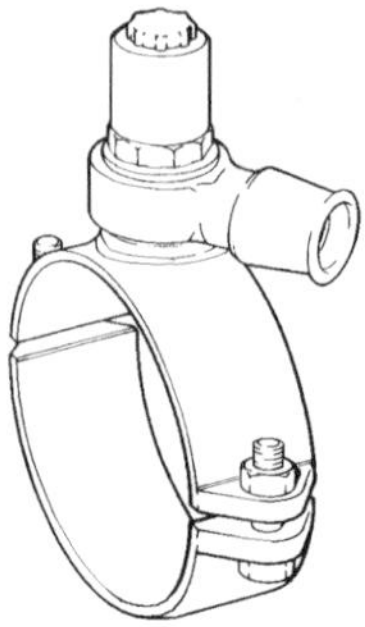

15 Valves

This appendix gives details of gate, globe, butterfly, non-return, float-operated and air valves.

Gate valve (also called sluice valve)

A gate valve is used to isolate flow. It is not designed to regulate or throttle flow for long periods, although for short periods and in an emergency it is used in this way. Only the last 10–15 per cent travel of the gate towards closure has any substantial effect on the flow rate.

Valves should not be closed suddenly as this will cause an immediate increase in pressure (water hammer) which could damage pipe and fittings. Gate valves avoid sudden closure problems because they can only be screwed down relatively slowly. Overtightening gate valves can damage the mating faces and valve threads.

Gate valves should be inspected for leaking valve stems. The stem seal may be a compression packing or an 'O' ring. Packing must be tightened only enough to prevent leakage and no further. Packed glands can be temporarily repaired with natural string or other material which expands when wet.

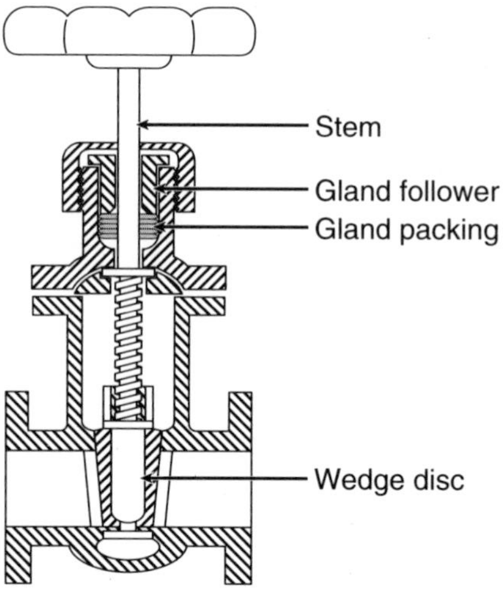

Figure A15.1 Gate valve

Globe valve (screw-down stop valve)

Globe valves are used on small diameter pipe (up to 50 mm) for the control of flow in service pipes, such as to tapstands. It is important to install the valve the correct way round in a pipe, as flow is only possible in one direction. An arrow on the valve body indicates the direction of flow. Pressure drop across the valve is high when open. Check and repair leaking glands as for the gate valve.

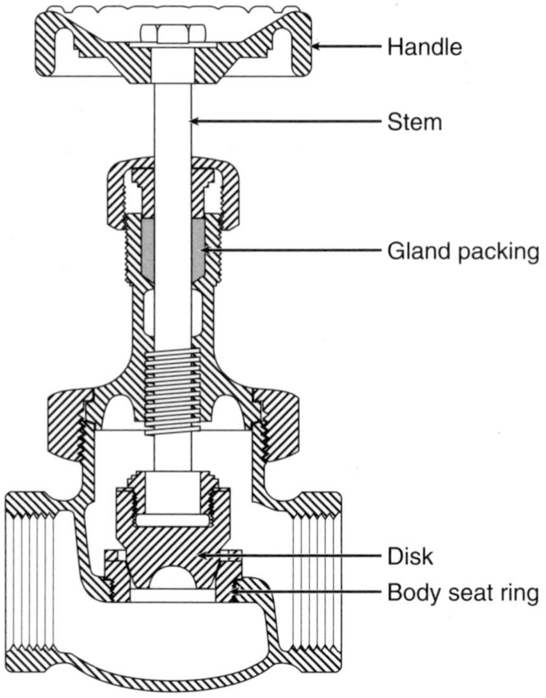

Figure A15.2 Globe valve

Butterfly valve

A butterfly valve is easy to open and close. As the valve is closed, the rate at which the flow is cut off diminishes, making it suitable for flow regulation. Valves should not be closed suddenly, as this would cause an immediate increase in pressure (water hammer) which could damage pipe and fittings. Pressure drop across the valve is small when fully open.

Non-return valve (reflux or check valve)

Non-return valves allow the flow of water in only one direction. An arrow on the valve body indicates the direction of flow. Most non-return valves are of either the 'swing' or the 'lift' type.

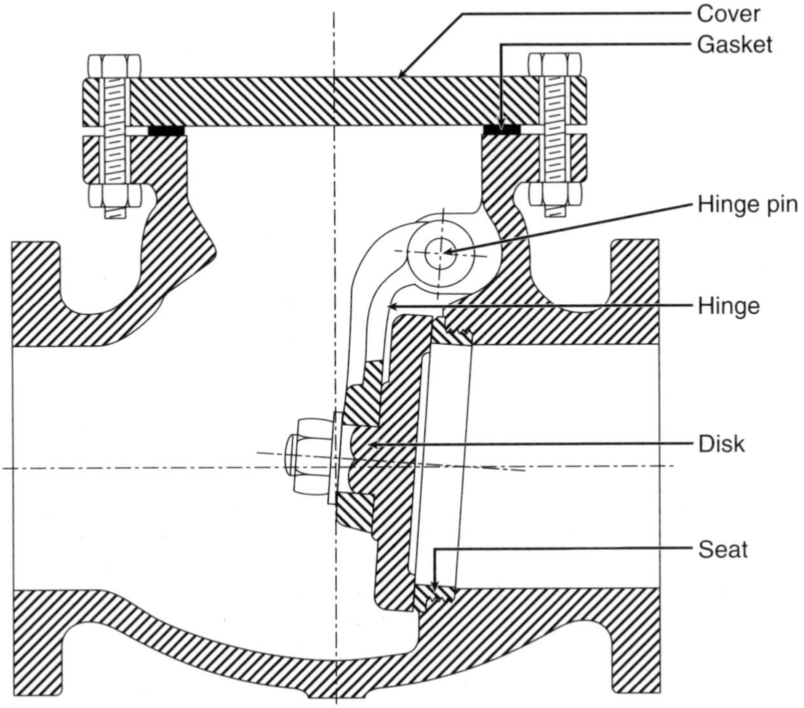

Figure A15.3 Swing non-return valve

A swing check valve has a hinged disk which seals on a tilted plate. During flow, the disk swings clear to allow full bore flow with little head loss. A common problem is breakage of the disk hinge if the valve is not correctly rated for the working pressure, or if the system experiences excessive water hammer.

A lift check valve operates in a similar manner to the globe valve. A disk sits on a horizontal seat until it is lifted by flow under pressure. It falls back when flow ceases. This type of non-return valve must be installed horizontally and is often used as a pump suction foot-valve.

Air valve

An air valve automatically releases accumulated air in a pressurized pipe or allows air to escape when the pipe is filling or allows air to enter when a pipe is emptying.

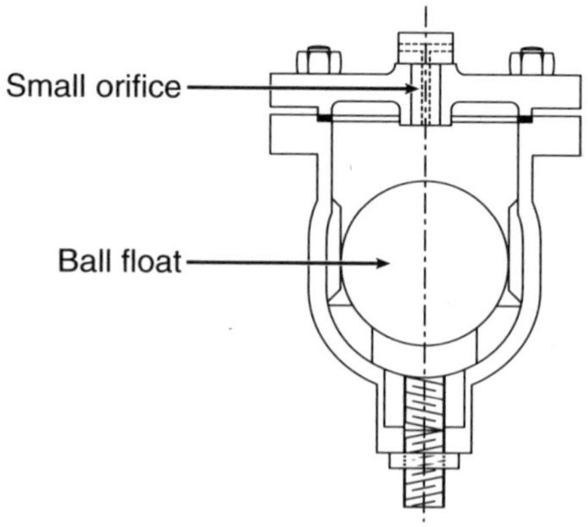

Figure A15.4 Air valve

An air release valve consists of a floating ball which rises and falls in a small chamber. When air enters the chamber of an air-release valve, the ball will fall as the water surface drops. This action opens a small orifice for the air to escape. As the air escapes the ball floats back up and closes the orifice.

An air valve which allows large quantities of air into or out of a pipeline during emptying or filling has a large orifice. A double orifice air valve has two float chambers, one with a small orifice and the other with a large orifice, to cater for all situations.

All air valves must be installed upright to function correctly. An isolation valve is normally included to isolate the air valve for maintenance and repair.

A substitute for an air valve, if one is not available, is a manually operated gate valve on a 'T-branch'. Alternatively, a regularly used tapstand, or single tap, sited at a high point will release air.

In relatively low pressure plastic pipe, a hole can be made in the pipe with a hot nail and plugged with a screw, to act as a manual air release. The hole can be left open if slight water loss is acceptable.

Float-operated valve

Float-operated valves automatically maintain the level of water in a tank to prevent overflowing.

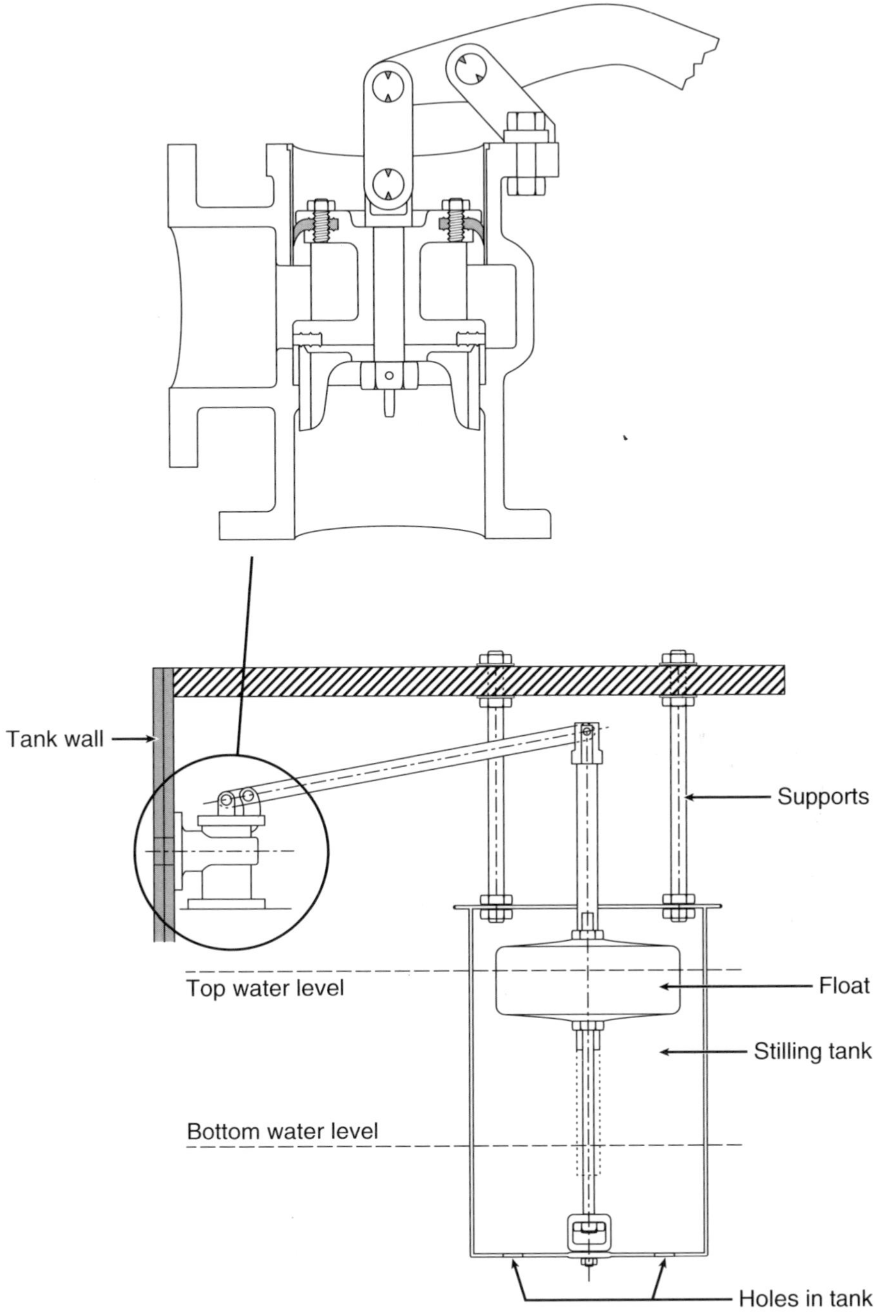

Figure A15.5 Float-operated valve

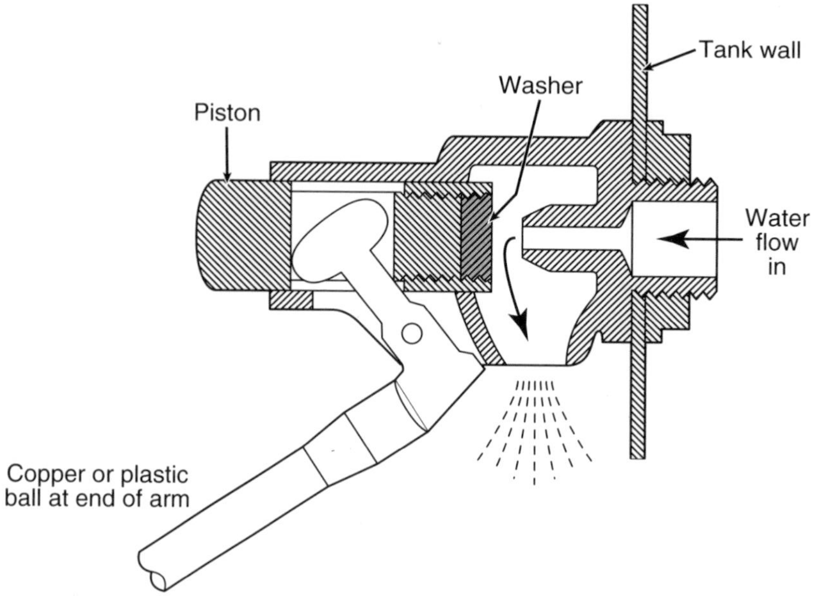

Figure A15.6 Ball float valve

16 Water flow in pipes – head loss data

Table A16.1 Hydraulic tables for small diameter plastic pipes

Based on the Colebrook-White formula
Roughness, k = 0.06 mm; Temperature = 15°C

For intermediate values draw a graph for the relevant size.

MDPE OD mm	Internal diameter mm	Flow Q l/s	Flow Q m^3/d	Hydraulic gradient 1 in n	Velocity V m/s	Head loss H m/100 m	$V^2/2g$ m
20	15.25	0.06	5.2	65	0.33	1.55	0.01
20	15.25	0.12	10.4	19	0.66	5.38	0.02
20	15.25	0.18	15.6	9	0.99	11.32	0.05
20	15.25	0.24	20.7	5	1.31	19.35	0.09
20	15.25	0.30	25.9	3	1.64	29.43	0.14
20	15.25	0.36	31.1	2	1.97	41.57	0.20
25	20.25	0.08	6.9	153	0.25	0.65	0.00
25	20.25	0.16	13.8	45	0.50	2.24	0.01
25	20.25	0.24	20.7	21	0.75	4.68	0.03
25	20.25	0.32	27.6	13	0.99	7.96	0.05
25	20.25	0.40	34.6	8	1.24	12.07	0.08
25	20.25	0.48	41.5	6	1.49	16.99	0.11

(cont.)

MDPE OD mm	Internal diameter mm	Flow Q l/s	Flow Q m^3/d	Hydraulic gradient 1 in n	Velocity V m/s	Head loss H m/100 m	$V^2/2g$ m
32	25.75	0.12	10.4	240	0.23	0.42	0.00
32	25.75	0.24	20.7	70	0.46	1.43	0.01
32	25.75	0.36	31.1	33	0.69	3.00	0.02
32	25.75	0.48	41.5	20	0.92	5.09	0.04
32	25.75	0.60	51.8	13	1.15	7.71	0.07
32	25.75	0.72	62.2	9	1.38	10.85	0.10
50	40.40	0.20	17.3	852	0.16	0.12	0.00
50	40.40	0.70	60.5	91	0.55	1.10	0.02
50	40.40	1.20	103.7	34	0.94	2.95	0.04
50	40.40	1.70	146.9	18	1.33	5.66	0.09
50	40.40	2.20	190.1	11	1.72	9.22	0.15
50	40.40	2.70	233.3	7	2.11	13.61	0.23
63	50.90	0.40	34.6	765	0.20	0.13	0.00
63	50.90	1.50	129.6	70	0.74	1.42	0.03
63	50.90	2.60	224.6	25	1.28	3.95	0.08
63	50.90	3.70	319.7	13	1.82	7.70	0.17
63	50.90	4.80	414.7	8	2.36	12.65	0.28
63	50.90	5.90	509.8	5	2.90	18.80	0.43
75	60.55	0.80	69.1	516	0.28	0.19	0.00
75	60.55	2.60	224.6	60	0.90	1.66	0.04
75	60.55	4.40	380.2	22	1.53	4.46	0.12
75	60.55	6.20	535.7	12	2.15	8.55	0.24
75	60.55	8.00	691.2	7	2.78	13.95	0.39
75	60.55	9.80	846.7	5	3.40	20.63	0.59
90	72.90	1.00	86.4	851	0.24	0.12	0.00
90	72.90	3.50	302.4	87	0.84	1.15	0.04
90	72.90	6.00	518.4	32	1.44	3.15	0.11
90	72.90	8.50	734.4	16	2.04	6.10	0.21
90	72.90	11.00	950.4	10	2.64	10.00	0.35
90	72.90	13.50	1166.4	7	3.23	14.85	0.53
110	89.10	1.40	121.0	1231	0.22	0.08	0.00
110	89.10	5.00	432.0	121	0.80	0.82	0.03
110	89.10	8.60	743.0	44	1.38	2.27	0.10
110	89.10	12.20	1054.1	23	1.96	4.41	0.20
110	89.10	15.80	1365.1	14	2.53	7.24	0.33
110	89.10	19.40	1676.2	9	3.11	10.75	0.49
125	101.20	2.00	172.8	1203	0.25	0.08	0.00
125	101.20	7.00	604.8	122	0.87	0.82	0.04
125	101.20	12.00	1036.8	44	1.49	2.25	0.11
125	101.20	17.00	1468.8	23	2.11	4.37	0.23
125	101.20	22.00	1900.8	14	2.74	7.17	0.38
125	101.20	27.00	2332.8	9	3.36	10.64	0.57

PVC-u DN"/ OD mm	Internal diameter mm	Flow Q l/s	Flow Q m^3/d	Hydraulic gradient 1 in n	Velocity V m/s	Head loss H m/100 m	$V^2/2g$ m
2"/60	54.00	0.50	43.2	685	0.22	0.15	0.00
2"/60	54.00	1.50	129.6	94	0.65	1.06	0.02
2"/60	54.00	2.50	216.0	37	1.09	2.73	0.06
2"/60	54.00	3.50	302.4	19	1.53	5.14	0.12

(cont.)

PVC-u DN"/ OD mm	Internal diameter mm	Flow Q l/s	Flow Q m^3/d	Hydraulic gradient 1 in n	Velocity V m/s	Head loss H m/100 m	$V^2/2g$ m
2"/60	54.00	4.50	388.8	12	1.96	8.28	0.20
2"/60	54.00	5.50	475.2	8	2.40	12.16	0.29
3"/90	81.00	1.20	103.7	1022	0.23	0.10	0.00
3"/90	81.00	4.20	362.9	105	0.82	0.96	0.03
3"/90	81.00	7.20	622.1	38	1.40	2.62	0.10
3"/90	81.00	10.20	881.3	20	1.98	5.07	0.20
3"/90	81.00	13.20	1140.5	12	2.56	8.31	0.33
3"/90	81.00	16.20	1399.7	8	3.14	12.34	0.50
4"/114	104.00	2.20	190.1	1158	0.26	0.09	0.00
4"/114	104.00	7.50	648.0	123	0.88	0.81	0.04
4"/114	104.00	12.80	1105.9	45	1.51	2.22	0.12
4"/114	104.00	18.10	1563.8	23	2.13	4.29	0.23
4"/114	104.00	23.40	2021.8	14	2.75	7.02	0.39
4"/114	104.00	28.70	2479.7	10	3.38	10.42	0.58
6"/168	153.00	6.00	518.4	1233	0.33	0.08	0.01
6"/168	153.00	22.00	1900.8	112	1.20	0.89	0.07
6"/168	153.00	38.00	3283.2	40	2.07	2.52	0.22
6"/168	153.00	54.00	4665.6	20	2.94	4.95	0.44
6"/168	153.00	70.00	6048.0	12	3.81	8.19	0.74
6"/168	153.00	86.00	7430.4	8	4.68	12.22	1.12

Value of the coefficient, k, in the expression $kV^2/2g$ due to losses in bends and fittings:

Entrances		**Bends**	**90 deg**	**45 deg**	**90 deg tee**	
Bellmouth	0.1	Medium	0.4	0.2	In line flow	0.4
Sharp	0.5	Elbow	1.0	0.4	Branch to line	1.5
Plain suction	0.9					
Re-entrant	1.0	**Valves**				
Sharp exit	1.0	Open gate valve	0.1	Open globe valve	7.5	

Equivalent pipe lengths (length:diameter ratios) of various fittings

	length:diameter ratio
Pipe bend (of radius 3 to 5 diameters)	5
Pipe bend (of radius 2 to 3 diameters)	10
Elbow	33
Tee (flow in the main line)	27
Tee (flow from main to the branch)	68
Gate valve (fully open)	7
Non-return valve (flap type)	50
Foot valve and strainer	70

17 Gabions and mattresses

(The following is based on information provided by Maccaferri Ltd)

Gabions and mattresses (also called Reno mattresses) are boxes formed from hexagonal woven steel mesh. They are placed in position on site and

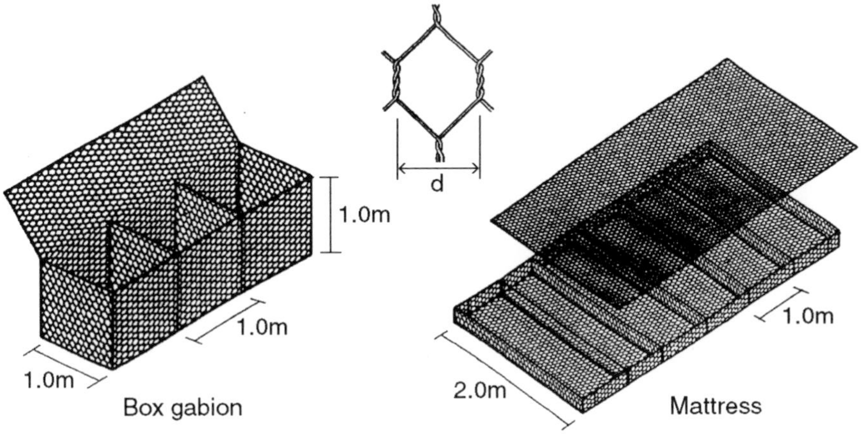

Figure A17.1 A box gabion and mattress

filled with stone. Adjacent units are tied together with wire lacing to give a stable but flexible wall or base structure. Typical examples are shown in Figure A17.1.

The advantages of using gabions are:

- Flexibility: a gabion structure can tolerate movement due to settlement, flood waters and shifting stream beds.
- Foundation preparation: ground only requires to be levelled.
- Placement by hand: a machine for the placement of stone and boxes is not essential, although it may be useful. Construction with gabions is suited to an unskilled labour-intensive workforce.
- Convenient to transport: gabions are supplied folded flat in compressed bundles and opened up on site.
- Use of local materials: gabions are filled with stone which can be obtained locally in many cases.

A gabion structure is also permeable although, if required, it can be sealed with a mix of suitable clays and plastic sheeting to form a low dam or impermeable wall.

Installation

Foundations

The basic requirement for a foundation is that it is reasonably flat. Stone can be placed if this makes working easier.

Assembly

Unfold, stretch out and flatten each gabion on a hard flat surface. Fold the sides to make a box. Boxes and mattresses may have internal diaphragm walls which are also folded vertically. The edges are strengthened with thicker selvedge

Table A17.1 Typical gabion and mattress sizes

Box gabions		*Mattresses*	
Unit size (m)	*No. of partitions*	*Unit size (m)*	*No. of partitions*
1 × 1 × 1	0	3 × 2 × 0.5	2
1.5 × 1 × 1	0	6 × 2 ×0.5	5
2 × 1 × 0.5	1	3 × 2 × 0.3	2
2 × 1 × 1	1	6 × 2 × 0.3	5
3 × 1 × 0.5	2	3 × 2 × 0.17	2
3 × 1 × 1	2	6 × 2 × 0.17	5

wire which protrudes from each side. Use the selvedge wire to tie the corners. Tie galvanized binding wire at the top corners and, with a continuous piece of wire, lace the panels with alternating single and double loops about every 100 mm. A pair of 8-inch (20 mm) long nose pliers are recommended for binding.

Place empty gabions in position and lace them all together. Before filling with stone it is important to stretch empty gabions in line. This can be achieved by filling one central or end gabion to provide an anchor against which to pull the rest. Use pieces of strong timber or steel rods to spread the load across the end gabion when stretching, using a 'Tirfor' type of winch or a team of labourers.

Multi-layered gabion structures should be wired to adjacent layers above and below.

Filling with stone

Stone used for filling should be hard and durable. Woven mesh is sized according to the width of opening, d, shown in Figure A17.1. Standard mesh sizes are 80 mm and 60 mm. Stone should be graded between 100 mm to 150 mm. If this size is difficult to obtain then the core can be filled with smaller sized material, provided that the facing material can retain it.

Bracing wires must be fixed to exposed faces to prevent bulging. Fill 1 m high gabions one-third full and then place bracing wires between the sides. Continue filling and place another row of bracing wire when two-thirds full. Half-metre high gabions can be braced at the mid-point, if required. Overfill each gabion by 30 mm to allow for settlement. Fold the lid down and lever into position for lacing to the front, sides and diaphragm walls.

The installation procedure is similar for mattresses. On slopes, mattresses may need to be pegged into position during filling.

Standard sizes

Gabions and mattresses come in a variety of unit sizes, mesh sizes, wire diameter and numbers of partitions (diaphragm walls). The following are typical.

Mesh sizes: 60 and 80 mm Wire diameter: 2.5, 2.7, 3.0 mm

Note: Wire can be coated in PVC to provide improved resistance to corrosion.

Typical applications

Gabions:
- Dry land retaining wall
- River training
- Soil conservation/gulley erosion control
- Bridge and culvert abutments and protective walls
- Improving fords (see 18.5.3, Figure 18.18)
- Low dams and weirs.

Mattresses:
- Stabilization of drainage channels
- Bridge and culvert protective aprons
- Protection of pipes at wadi crossings.

18 Anchorages

Anchorages are needed in a variety of situations – for example, bridging, lifting, vehicle recovery, and stabilizing sheer legs and structures. The following is a guide to anchorages which can be improvised in the field.

Natural or structural anchorages

A tree can be strengthened as an anchorage by tying it back to another tree or to a picket holdfast. Two trees close together can be used with a stout timber log between them to spread the load. Always try to spread loads taken on stone masonry and brickwork. The pull should be taken as close to the ground as possible.

Picket holdfasts

A picket is a stout pole up to about 1.5 m long. One end is pointed for driving into the ground. Pickets are used singly or in groups lashed together. Various combinations are shown in Figure A18.1.

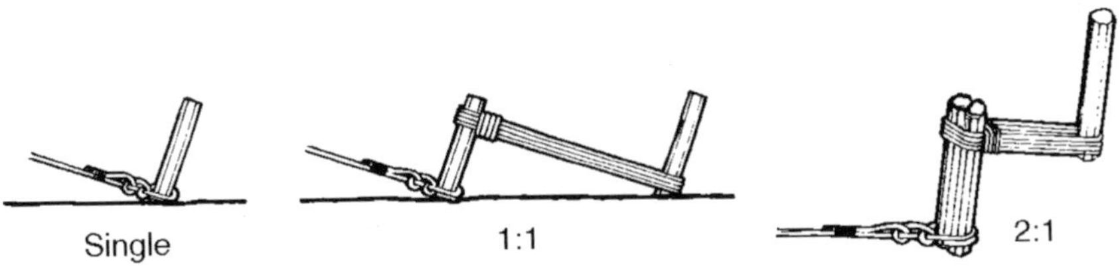

Figure A18.1 Combinations of picket holdfasts

Key points when using picket holdfasts in normal ground:

- Pickets should be driven at least a metre into the ground at right-angles to the line of pull.
- The lashings connecting the pickets should be at right-angles to the pickets.
- Lashings should come from the head of the picket in front to the bottom of the back-up picket.
- There should be no slack in the lashings.

Holdfasts can be used in rock by chiselling holes with a 'jumper bar' and jamming steel crowbars or angle iron into the holes. Wire ties can be used for back-up lashings.

Withdraw pickets in the same line as they were driven in or they may break.

Baulk anchorage

This anchorage uses a log or stout timber (a baulk), held by a series of picket holdfasts (Figure A18.2). Use for loads of 2 to 10 tonnes.

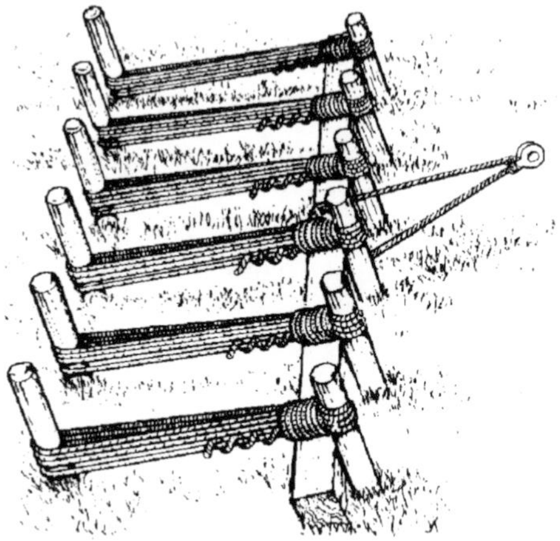

Figure A18.2 A baulk anchorage

Key points when using a baulk anchorage:

- There should be the same number of holdfasts either side of the pull.
- Holdfasts should not be less than 0.5 metres apart.
- The log must bear evenly on all the pickets.
- The log should rest on the ground and soil removed for the rope to pass around the log.
- Square section timber must be bedded into the ground so that a flat face bears evenly on all pickets.

Buried log anchorage

A buried log anchorage is used for pulls above about 10 tonnes. A log, or several logs, are buried horizontally in a trench (Figure A18.3).

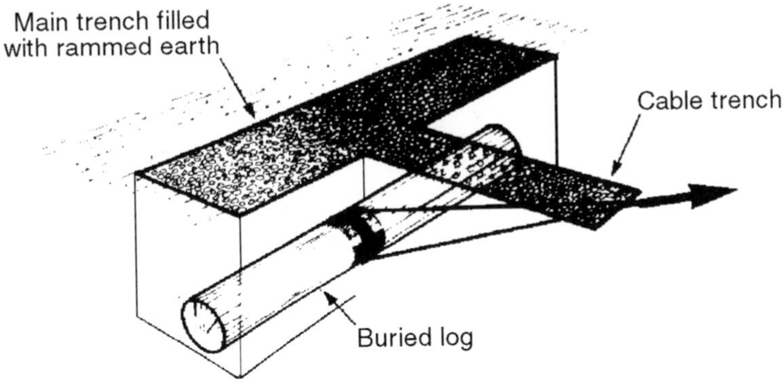

Figure A18.3 A buried log anchorage

Key points when using a buried log anchorage:

- The log, timber or steel pipe must be chosen to resist failure due to shear or bending.
- The trench is dug with a vertical face at right-angles, in the horizontal plane, to the direction of pull.
- The optimum burial depth is half the length of the log.
- The trench for the cable is dug as narrow as possible.
- The main trench is filled and rammed with earth; the cable trench is left open for the inspection and adjustment of cable and fastenings.

(Adapted from MoD, 1981a)

19 Sheers and gyns

Sheers

A sheer is a hoisting apparatus of two poles or spars tied together at the top and with the feet separated. To assemble the sheer, the spars are laid on the ground and the bark stripped away at the point of the lashing. Lash the spars together while they are side-by-side so that when they are opened out the lashing will be tight. If the spars are large they may need to be opened some distance before lashing. A typical arrangement is shown in Figure A19.1. Note that the guy ropes are arranged so that they draw the spars together when loaded. The load sling is passed over the fork formed by the spars.

Sheers can be used to move a load in a straight line swung between the legs until the sheers lean at a limiting slope of 3:1. In this case the base of the spars must be well anchored.

General rules for loads:

- Sheer legs made of 4in spars are suitable for lifting up to 4 tonnes.
- Sheer legs made of 6in spars are suitable for lifting up to 10 tonnes.

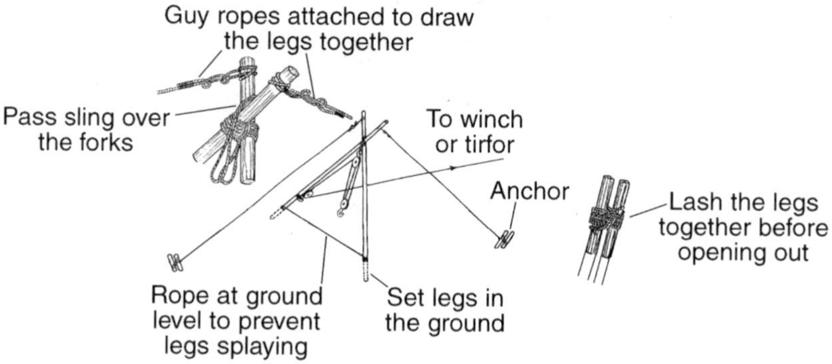

Figure A19.1 Sheers

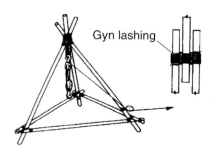

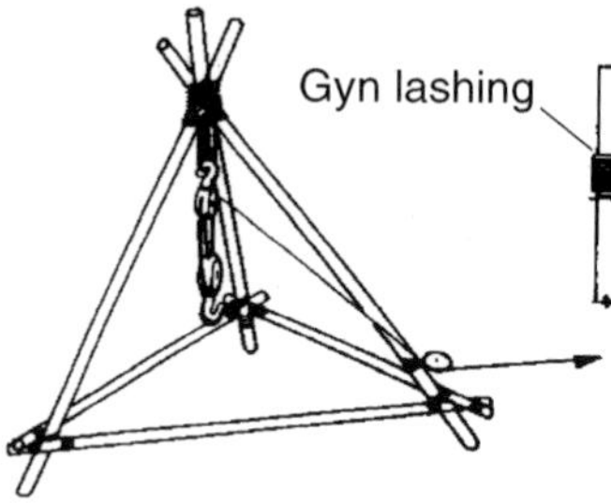

Figure A19.2 Gyn

Gyns

A gyn is shown in Figure A19.2. Gyns can only be used to lift vertically or to support a vertical load. A gyn occupies little space and no guys are required. To erect the gyn, lay two spars in one direction and the middle spar in the other direction as shown in Figure A19.2. Lash the three spars together before crossing the two outer spars until the feet of the spars are a distance apart of about half the length of the spars. Lash poles between the feet of the spars to fix their distance apart. Place the load sling across the top lashing and lift the spars. Push the middle spar into the triangle formed by the other two spars and the bottom pole until an equilateral triangle is formed on the ground by the feet of the spars. The top lashing can be prevented from slipping during lifting by a nail driven into the middle spar just below the lashing. Anchor the feet of each spar to prevent movement when loaded. The head of the gyn should be placed above the load to be lifted. Guy ropes should be fixed if there is a chance of a load moving sideways.

(Adapted from MoD, 1981a)

20 Soil classification, identification and testing

Table A20.1 Soil classification by size

Classification		*Upper size limits, mm*
Gravel	Coarse	60
	Medium	20
	Fine	6
Sand	Coarse	2
	Medium	0.6
	Fine	0.2
Silt	Coarse	0.06
	Medium	0.02
	Fine	0.006
Clay		0.002

Note: Precise classifications vary according to application. For example, aggregates for concrete mixes are defined as: sand < 5 mm; gravel > 5 mm.

Soil analysis

Simple field tests

- Smell – if a soil smells at all it contains decaying organic material.
- Look and feel – if the soil stains your hands it contains silt and/or clay. Sand does not stick between finger print ridges like silt and clay.

Grading a soil

There are several fields of engineering where it may be necessary to estimate the different sizes of particles in a soil sample: aggregates for concrete, water well construction, filter sands, dam embankments and filters, road gravels. Choose the type of soil grading test according to the accuracy required. Note: a poorly graded soil is either uniformly graded (particles nearly all the same size) or a size is missing.

Vibration test Place a handful of dry soil on a flat board, lift one end slightly and tap gently to separate the particles. This will give a very rough visual indication of grading.

Settling test A settling test separates different sizes of particles in water to give a rough indication of grading. Put a handful of soil in a clear glass jar and fill two-thirds full with water. Close the jar and shake vigorously to break up the soil. Place the jar on a flat surface and start timing.

After 25 seconds	Mark the depth of settlement. This roughly indicates the stone and sand portion of the soil.
After 60 seconds	Mark the depth of settlement. Most of the silt should have settled.
After 24 hours	Clay will have settled but some colloidal clay may still remain in suspension.

The volumes settled out can be converted to a percentage of the total sample.

Sieve analysis An accurate indication of the particle size distribution of a soil can be obtained by a sieve analysis.

Shake a weighed sample of dry soil through a series of sieves of decreasing mesh size. Gently break up lumps of clayey soil to grade the whole sample. Weigh the samples retained on each sieve and convert into a percentage of the total weight of the sample. Small hand shaken nests of sieves (about 75 mm in diameter) and mechanical balances are available for field analysis. An alternative to weighing samples is to assume the material has the same density and estimate relative volumes.

Plot the weight passing (or relative volumes) as a percentage against the sieve mesh size on arithmetic or semi-logarithmic paper. This gives a grading curve (also called a grain-size distribution curve). The use of a logarithmic scale for the mesh size stretches the finer section and compresses the coarser section of the curve. Note that in some applications the cumulative weight retained (not passing) is plotted against mesh size.

The slope and shape of a grading curve describes a soil according to particle size.

The classification of silts, sands, gravels and so on according to grain size varies depending on the application. Table A20.1 is widely used.

Grain sizes are commonly referred to as the percentage passing. For example, the D60 size of a sample is the mesh size through which 60 per cent of the sample will pass.

Effective Size (ES) is the D10 size (or the mesh size which will retain 90 per cent of a sample).

The slope of a grading curve can be described by the Sorting Coefficient.
The Sorting Coefficient (SC) is the D60 size divided by the D10 size.

Well sorted	$SC < 2.5$
Poorly sorted	$SC > 5$

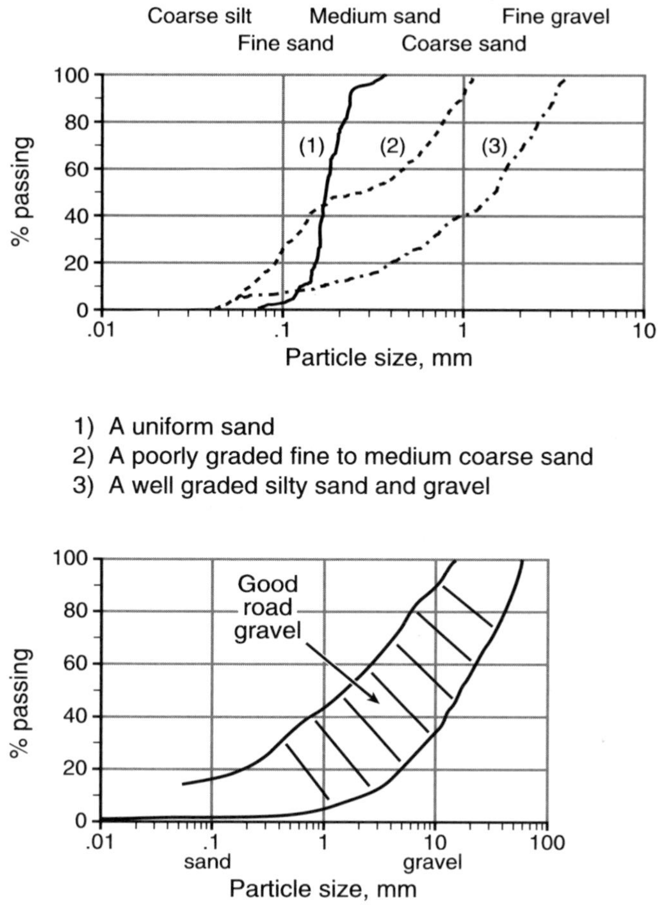

Figure A20.1 Typical grading curves

Note that the Sorting Coefficient is also referred to as the Uniformity Coefficient.

Soils have characteristic curve shapes as shown in Figure A20.1. Granular materials deposited by flowing water usually have an S-shape. S-shaped curves usually have a higher porosity than curves with a 'tail'.

The 'Filter Rule' for graded media

Successive layers of graded media are used in a range of situations to prevent the migration of fine material into a coarse material: water filters, drains, infiltration galleries, etc. The following rule for the optimum sizing of media has been found to hold in practice.

The rule for preventing the migration of finer material into a coarser material is based on the D15 size (i.e. the mesh size which passes 15 per cent of the material). Each successive layer of material should comprise particles such that the D15 size of one layer is 9 times the D15 size of the adjacent layer. If the ratio is more than 9 then migration is likely to occur. This applies to material at least 50 per cent compacted.

For practical purposes, each layer should be thick enough to ensure that any movement during or after construction does not break up the continuity of each layer.

Table A20.2 Example of soil grading

Layer	*Layer thickness*	*15% size*
Silt	'Thick'	0.01 mm
Fine sand	0.3 m	0.1 mm
Coarse sand	0.3 m	0.9 mm
Gravel	0.45 m	8.1 mm

An alternative to successive layers of graded media is to use a geotextile for the separation of media. Refer to 'Geotextiles' below for more details.

Shrinkage test

The shrinkage test is used to estimate the amount of lime or cement needed as a stabilizer for stabilized cement blocks.

Make a mould for a shrinkage test from plywood or metal sheet.

Dimensions: 600 mm × 40 mm × 40 mm.

- Make a wet paste with the soil sample and fill the mould. Tamp to fill the corners and smooth the surface.
- Dry in the sun for about 3–5 days, or longer in the shade.
- Push the dried sample to one end and measure the shrinkage.

Note: the soil is unsuitable if it has many cracks.

Table A20.3 Using the shrinkage test to determine cement requirements

Shrinkage	*Cement:soil ratio required*
Less than 15 mm	Too much sand and the soil is unsuitable for stabilized soil blocks
15mm–30 mm	1:16
30mm–45 mm	1:14
45mm–60 mm	1:12
Greater than 60 mm	Too much clay for blockmaking

If lime is used as a stabilizer instead of cement, the quantity of lime used is double the amount of cement indicated in Table A20.3.

Table A20.4 Approximate load-bearing capability of soils for foundations

Material	*kg/cm²*
'Rock'	5
Hard clay, gravel and coarse sand	4
Loose medium sand and medium clay	2
Loose fine sand	1
Soft clay	0–1

Infiltration rates – a field test

Force a steel cylinder of about 300 mm diameter into the soil so that it stands upright. Place an upright ruler or gauge stick marked in millimetres within the cylinder. Fill the cylinder with water and measure the fall in water level at convenient intervals (5, 10, 20, 30 minutes) as water infiltrates into the soil. This gives an approximate infiltration rate.

If water is to percolate through a trench, then dig a trial section of trench and carry out a similar test to the above omitting the cylinder. This takes into account infiltration through the trench sides.

Guideline infiltration rates according to soil type Use Figure A20.2 to identify soil types. The infiltration rates of sewage and sullage will decrease over time due to the build-up of organic material in soil pores. Therefore, approximate guideline infiltration rates for both clean water and wastewater are given.

Table A20.5 Approximate clean water and wastewater infiltration rates according to soil type

Soil type	*Infiltration rate litres/m²/day (mm/day)*	
	Clean water	*Wastewater*
Sand	720–2400	33–50
Sandy loam	480–720	24
Silt loam	240–480	18
Clay loam	120–240	8
Clay	24–120	Unsuitable for soak pits or trenches

(From Stern, 1979, and Reed and Dean, 1994)

Geotextiles

Geotextiles are used for many applications including separation, filtration/drainage, erosion control and soil reinforcement.

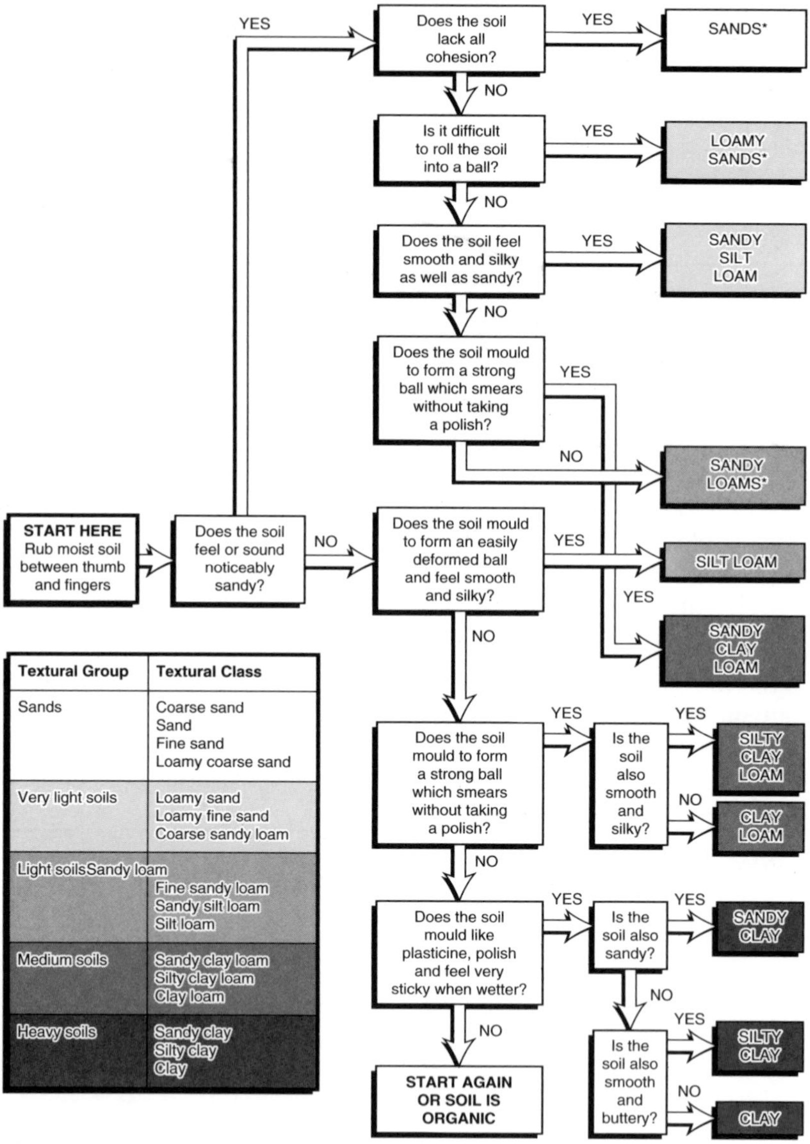

Textural Group	Textural Class
Sands	Coarse sand Sand Fine sand Loamy coarse sand
Very light soils	Loamy sand Loamy fine sand Coarse sandy loam
Light soils	Sandy loam Fine sandy loam Sandy silt loam Silt loam
Medium soils	Sandy clay loam Silty clay loam Clay loam
Heavy soils	Sandy clay Silty clay Clay

*Coarse, medium and fine categories of sands, loamy sands and sandy loams may be determined by the size of sand particles which can be detected by feel:

Coarse: particles approximately the size of granulated sugar.
Medium: particles feel like grains of table salt.
Fine: particles smaller than table salt grains but can be felt
If in doubt, grittiness can be heard if the moist soil is rubbed close to the ear.

Published by kind permission of CIBA-Agriculture (UK)

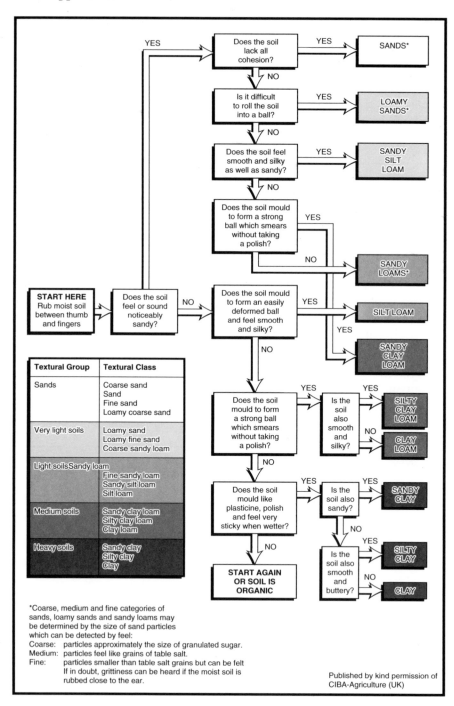

Figure A20.2 Guide to soil identification

Terram®, and similar geotextiles, are supplied in 4.5 m wide rolls. When placed in position, adjacent rolls should be overlapped by 0.3 m–1.0 m. Selection of Terram grade is based on strength versus filtration characteristics, if cost is not a major factor.

Terram is available in the following grades:
500, 700, 900, 1000, 1500, 2000, 3000, 4000.

For normal road separation use Terram 1000. For very soft soils (for example, in road soft spot improvements) use Terram 1500 or 2000.

21 Temporary support of excavations

Excavations can pose a hazard to people working within and around them, and precautions must be taken to keep them stable and safe. In addition, adequate measures should be taken to ensure that any excavation, however shallow, does not pose a hazard to people generally.

Stability of excavations

The angle at which the sides of an excavation can be dug and remain stable depends on a number of factors:

- Type and condition of soil.
- The presence of groundwater.
- The presence of surface water and rainfall runoff.
- Loadings imposed by spoil heaps, local buildings and traffic.
- Depth of excavation.
- Time for which excavation is left open.
- The weather.

Protect excavations from rainfall runoff by digging uphill catchwater drains.

Gauge the safe angle of excavated slopes by looking at the natural angle of repose of locally exposed soils. Natural angles of repose and temporary slopes will depend on whether the site is predominantly wet or dry. Stable dry slopes can easily collapse with, for example, the onset of the rains at the end of the dry season.

A guide to safe temporary slopes is given in Table A21.1.

Table A21.1 Temporary slopes in different ground conditions

Ground	*Temporary slope (degrees from the horizontal)*	
	'Dry'	*'Wet'*
Boulders	35–45	30–40
Gravel/sand	30–40	10–30
Silt	20–40	5–20
Clay	30–45	10–20

(Refer to Appendix 20 for the identification of soils)

Temporary trench support

Temporary support to trenches may be needed in unstable ground and where trenches are to be left exposed for some length of time (for example, deep trench latrines). Timber boards, bamboo, matted cane and bush poles can be used to support the vertical sides of trenches temporarily. Struts and waling will be necessary to prop between the walls as shown in Figure A21.1. Struts should be placed at least every 1.8 metres but may need to be positioned closer, depending on trench use. For example, in trench latrines, struts should be placed in line with each partition to prevent fouling. A second level of struts will be required if the depth of the trench exceeds 2 metres.

To prevent people, soil or items falling into a trench, a barrier can be formed by extending the height of the trench support above ground level. Fence off or cover an open trench when it is not being worked in or used.

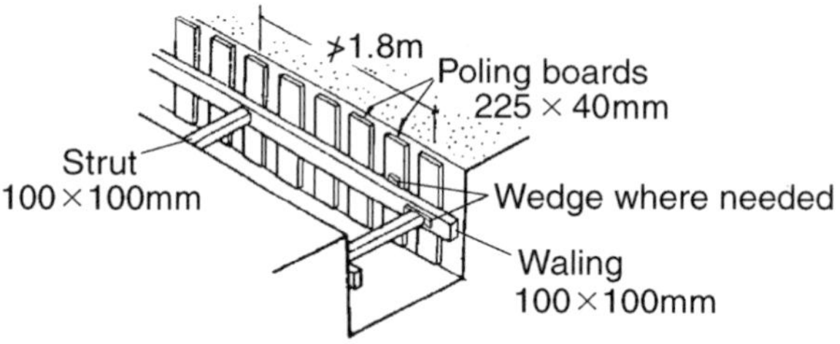

Poling boards may be open (as shown) or continuous close boarding

Figure A21.1 Typical temporary trench support

22 Beam calculations

Figure A22.1 gives maximum bending moments, shear forces and deflections for simply supported and built-in beams. For a beam with several loads, the bending moment, shear force and deflection can be found by adding the values due to each load acting separately.

Where: W = point load; w = load per unit length;
E = Young's modulus; I = second moment of area

Values of Young's modulus, E:

Steel 202 000 N/mm^2
Timber 3–12 000 N/mm^2

$$\text{Maximum stress in a beam} = \frac{\text{Maximum bending moment (M)}}{\text{Section modulus (Z)}}$$

The second moment of area, I, and section modulus, Z, for selected sections are shown in Figure A22.2.

Point loads

	Maximum bending moment	*Maximum shear force*	*Maximum deflection*
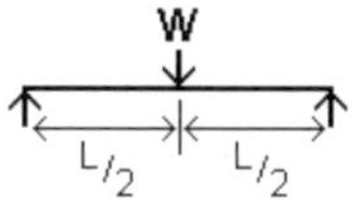	$\frac{WL}{4}$	$\frac{W}{2}$	$\frac{1}{48}\frac{WL^3}{EI}$
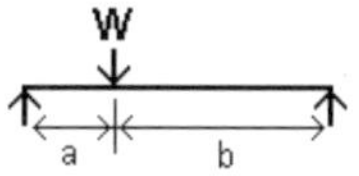	$\frac{Wab}{L}$	$\frac{Wb}{L}$	$\frac{1}{48}\frac{WL^3}{EI}\left[\frac{3a}{L} - 4\left(\frac{a}{L}\right)^3\right]$
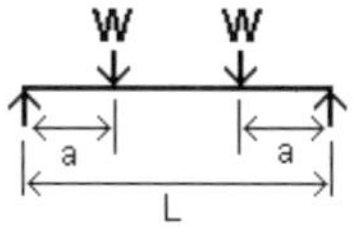	Wa	W	$\frac{1}{6}\frac{WL^3}{EI}\left[\frac{3a}{4L} - \left(\frac{a}{L}\right)^3\right]$
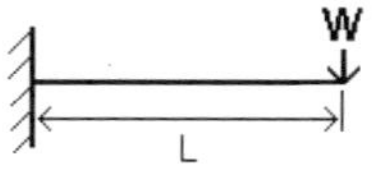	WL	W	$\frac{1}{3}\frac{WL^3}{EI}$
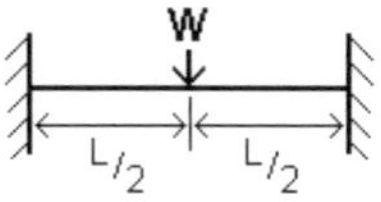	$\frac{WL}{8}$ at ends and at mid-span	$\frac{W}{2}$	$\frac{1}{192}\frac{WL^3}{EI}$

Uniformly distributed loads

	Maximum bending moment	*Maximum shear force*	*Maximum deflection*
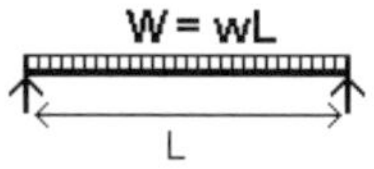	$\frac{WL}{8}$	$\frac{W}{2}$	$\frac{5}{384}\frac{WL^3}{EI}$
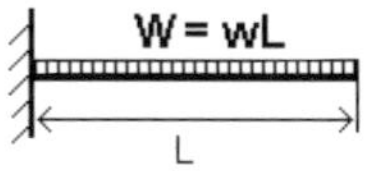	$\frac{WL}{2}$	W	$\frac{1}{8}\frac{WL^3}{EI}$
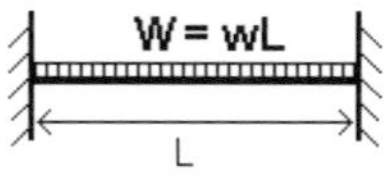	$\frac{WL}{12}$ at ends	W	$\frac{1}{384}\frac{WL^3}{EI}$

Figure A22.1 Beam bending moments, shear forces and deflections

In beam design it is generally recommended that the deflection of timber and steel beams is limited to 0.003 of the span.

Strengths and moduli of elasticity for ‘dry’ Canadian spruce, pine and fir are given in Table A22.1 for comparative purposes.

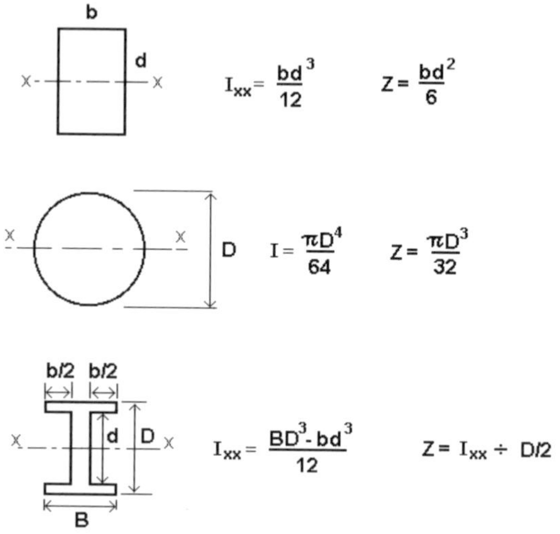

Figure A22.2 Second moment of area and section modulus for selected beam sections

Table A22.1 Comparative values for 'dry' softwood timbers

Stress parallel to the grain N/mm²				*Young's modulus N/mm²*	
Bending	*Tension*	*Compression*	*Shear*	*Mean*	*Minimum*
4.8	3.3	4.8	0.79	8000	4300

23 Basic engineering surveying and setting out

Engineering surveying

A small hand-held satellite-based GPS (Global Positioning System) can be useful and quick to locate positions, store them in various grid formats and display or download to a computer to print out. A combination hand-held GPS with altimeter can provide co-ordinates and elevations although a second altimeter at a base station will be required to adjust altitude readings for variations in atmospheric pressure. The following notes outline basic methods for more accurate surveying, setting out and mapping than can normally be achieved with a simple GPS.

Engineering surveying involves measuring the location of points in vertical and horizontal planes in order to produce a map. Locating points in a vertical plane is called levelling.

When carrying out a survey it is important to start drawing the map as soon as possible. It is recommended that you map the data every day, especially in the initial stages of your fieldwork. Do not wait until you have collected all the survey information, as you may be making errors and have to go back and collect it all again. A list of basic surveying equipment is given in Box A23.1. Even if you have no equipment, some useful spatial data may be obtained by pacing and visual observation.

Levelling

The relative level of two points may be obtained by measuring the vertical distance of each point above or below a level line (see Figure A23.1). This usually involves sighting along a level line and noting where the level line cuts a ruler or staff held vertically.

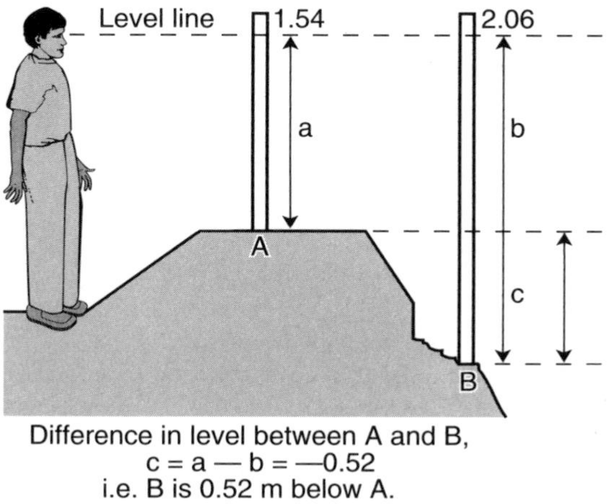

Figure A23.1 Measuring differences in level

Using a surveyor's level A surveyor's level is designed principally to measure differences in level. However it can also be used to measure distances and horizontal angles. The instrument consists of a telescope which can be mounted on a tripod and rotated through a level plane. Before taking any readings, the instrument should be carefully levelled – this can be done crudely using the tripod legs, and then accurately using the adjustment screws on the instrument. Self levelling levels need only crude adjustment.

To take levels, the staff is placed on the point of interest and held carefully in a vertical position. The level is pointed at the staff and focused. A typical view through the telescope is shown in Figure A23.2. When the telescope is level the centre stadia hair shows where the level line from the telescope intersects the staff. If the staff is tilted slightly around the vertical, then the lowest reading on the staff is correct. In this case the reading is 2.553, which means that the ground on which the staff is standing is 2.553 m below the level of the telescope. Significant errors may occur if readings are taken at distances greater than 50 m, especially in hot and hazy conditions.

Box A23.1 Equipment for basic surveying

Measuring equipment:

- A dumpy level or equivalent with a levelling staff.
- An engineer's 50 m or 30 m steel or plastic tape.
- A 3 m pocket tape.
- Half a dozen ranging rods and some stout wooden or steel pegs.

A field compass should be used to take bearings. A pocket-size abney level allows you to take levels with a reasonable degree of accuracy and is highly recommended as part of your field kit. A levelling staff may be fabricated from timber. The markings on the staff should be clearly visible through a telescope – see Figure A23.2 below for a typical pattern of markings on a staff.

Booking equipment:

- Survey book or shorthand notebook.
- Clipboard with protective sheet of plastic, and clips to prevent pages lifting in the wind.
- Pencils, pens, ruler, calculator.

Mapping equipment:

- Pencils and rubbers, pens, scale rulers, good (large) protractor.
- Paper: A1 or A2 cartridge paper, squared if possible, and tracing paper.
- Calculator.
- Compass; a long beam compass is desirable.

Before starting a levelling survey, the accuracy of the instrument should be checked (see below).

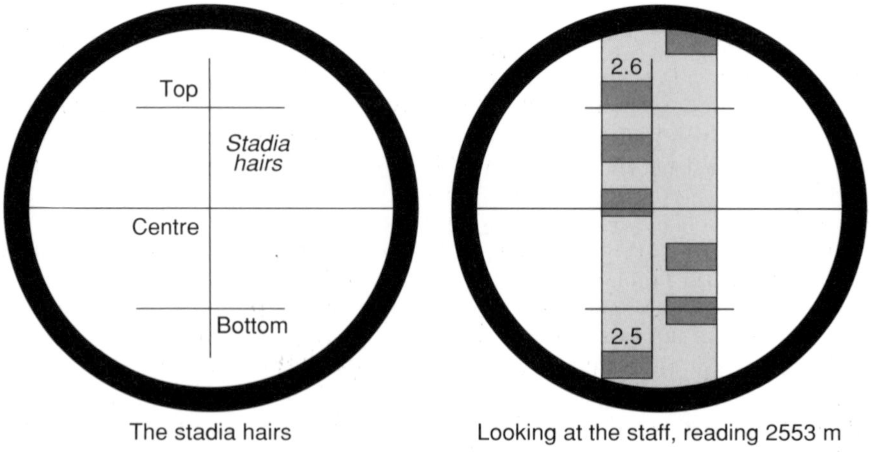

Figure A23.2 View through a level's telescope

Carrying out the survey To carry out a levelling survey, one must first start from a known, permanent and fixed starting point. This should be a clearly identifiable mark such as on a bridge, a large durable building, an immovable rock, or a permanent well. Figure A23.3 below shows how a typical levelling survey might progress.

In location L1, the first sighting through the level to the known point is known as the backsight (BS1). As the level of this point is known, the height of the level line (or height of collimation) may be determined by adding the value of staff reading (4.075 m) to the value of the known level (if not known, then it may be assigned an arbitrary level of 100 000 m), giving $HoC_{L1} = 104.075$. The levels (termed reduced levels) of all other points around location 1 may then be obtained by keeping the level at point L1 and moving the staff to the other points, noting the staff reading and subtracting that reading from the height of collimation.

To continue the survey, the staff should remain at the last point of measurement before moving the level to the next location, L2. The last reading taken from location L1 is termed the fore-sight (here FS1). When the level is set up at location L2, a reading, termed a backsight (here BS2) is taken back to the staff (which has not been moved). As the level at the staff is known, the height of collimation of the level at location L2 is the reduced level at the staff plus BS2. All other points around location L2 can be levelled and booked as in Table A23.1.

Before carrying out a levelling survey it is important to agree a system of hand signals with the staff operator. Shouting instructions up to a distance of 50 m is very tiring.

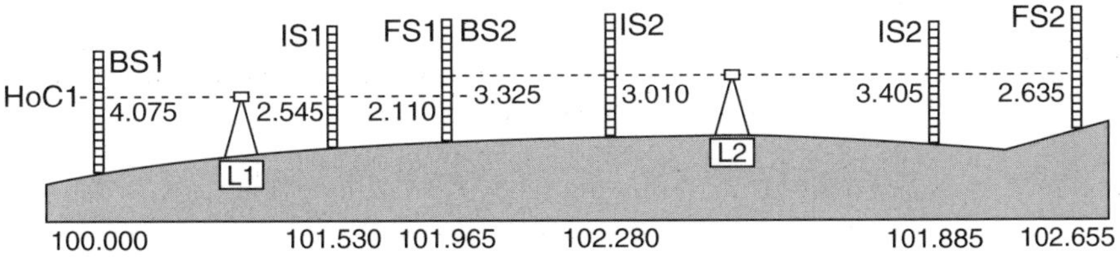

Figure A23.3 Conducting a levelling survey

Errors Errors are inevitable, arising from inaccuracies in the instrument, a staff not held vertically, reading errors or booking errors. To ascertain the degree of error it is important to close the day's survey at a point of known level. It is common practice to plan the survey in a loop so that you finish at the point where you started. The level you calculate for this point at the end of your survey will not be the same as the value you started with, as errors occur. The permissible error in mm is $20\sqrt{n}$, where n is the number of stations of the level. Thus, for seven stations, the permissible error is $20\sqrt{7} = 53$ mm.

When using the height of collimation method of booking, the arithmetic can be checked by subtracting the sum of the backsights from the sum of the

Table A23.1 Level booking form

Station	*Back-sight*	*Inter-mediate sight*	*Fore-sight*	*Ht of collimat.*	*Reduced level*	*Remarks*
L1	4 075			104 075	100 000	Assumed ht of start pt, bridge foot
		2 545			101 530	junction of roads
			2 110		101 965	gatepost
L2	3 325			105 290	101 965	gatepost
		3 010			102 280	well plinth
		3 405			101 885	south streambank
			2 635		102 655	north streambank

foresights. The difference should be equal to the difference between the reduced level of the first and last point.

Checking the accuracy of the level In a correctly set instrument, the line of sight of the telescope is level. Over time the line of sight may depart from level, causing an error. The magnitude of this error may be checked as follows (see Figure A23.4).

Set the instrument up on gently sloping ground, over a point marked Y. Set staffs 1 and 2 equidistant from Y, perhaps 20 m. In this example the instrument is shown reading below level.

As XY = YZ, then CA = DB, and the actual difference in height between X and Z, $h_{xz} = CX - DZ = AX - BZ$

Move the instrument to W, close to staff 2. Now the measured difference in height, $H_{xz} = EX\text{-}FZ$. The error in elevation measured from W is

$$h_{xz} - H_{xz} = (AX - BZ) - (EX - FZ) = EG$$

The actual error in the reading from W to staff 1 is EL.
Now $EL/LW_1 = EG/GF$, giving

$$EL = LW_1 \times (EG/GF)$$

with LW_1 and GF measured and EG calculated above.

If the magnitude of the error is more than 20 mm for 30 m distance, the cross-hairs of the instrument need to be adjusted – a job for a specialist.

Mapping

A key principle in map-making is 'from outside to inside'. Where possible, start with fixed and known points and locate the area that you are mapping in detail on a small-scale map (1:250 000 or 1:1 000 000).

Due North should be measured as accurately as possible and indicated on your map.

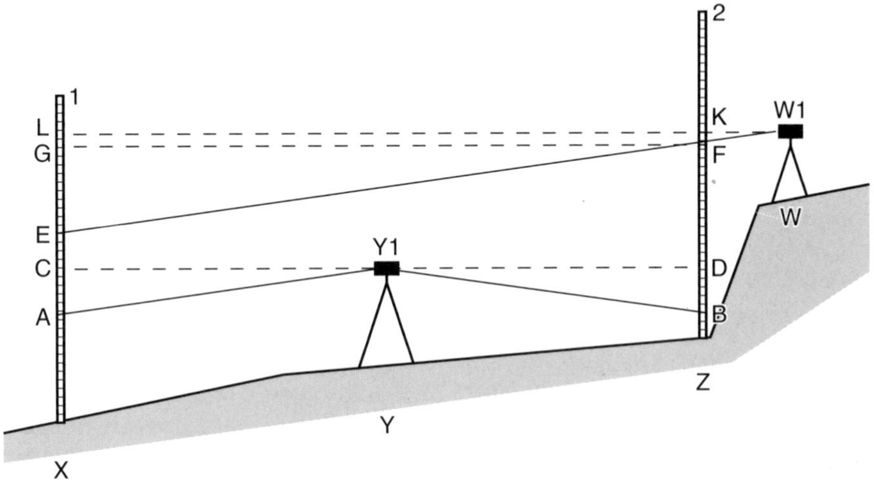

Figure A23.4 Checking the accuracy of a level

The relative location of points of interest can be determined by triangulation, where:

- Each of three sides of a triangle can be measured.
- The length of two sides and the angle between them are known.
- The length of one side and the internal angles at each end can be measured.

It is important to be able to measure distances accurately and, if possible, angles.

Distances may be measured by:

- Pacing: check the length of your average pace by measuring the actual length of 50 paces with a tape. A quick but imprecise method.
- Driving: using the odometer on the vehicle.
- Chaining or taping: specialized surveying chains or tapes may be used. This method is accurate but time consuming.
- Tacheometry: theodolites and many levels have a facility for measuring distance using tacheometry. This involves taking readings from a staff held vertically over the point to be measured against the stadia hairs seen in the intrument's telescope. Referring to Figure A23.2, the reading for the top stadia (T) is 2 590 and the bottom (B) 2 518. There is a direct relationship between these stadia readings and the distance to the staff. Each instrument has its own precise relationship but in general it is close to: distance, d = 100 (T-B), in this case 7.2 m. This relationship should be checked before beginning any survey by measuring a known distance, which has been accurately measured by tape. Tacheometry is quick and sufficiently accurate for most engineering reconaissance surveys.

Angles may be measured by:

- Protractor, or instrument such as a level.
- Taking compass bearings.

With a field compass or surveyor's level, angles may generally be read only to an accuracy of about 30 minutes. Over a distance of 100 m this gives a distance error of 0.87 m. This level of accuracy is acceptable for rapid reconaissance mapping, but not where great precision is required.

Procedure for collecting mapping data using tacheometry Prepare data booking forms (see Tables A23.1 and A23.2) to allow you to record accurately all the relevant data for each point to be measured. When using a surveyor's level, a form may be designed to collect tacheometric and levelling data at the same time.

Make a rough field sketch of the area to be mapped, including approximate locations of the stations for the instrument. The stations should form a loop, so that you finish at the starting point. This ensures that you can check the magnitude of errors. Take the compass bearing of at least one measured line.

Table A23.2 Tacheometry booking form

Station	*Levelling data (see Table A23.1) reduced levels*	*Stadia readings Top*	*Bottom*	*Distance (m)*	*Angle reading*	*Remarks*
L1						Instrument location L1
L1–1	100 000	2 064	1 336	72 8	0 0°	SE cnr of compound
L1–2	101 175	0 879	0 172	70 7	18 5°	NE cnr of compound
L1–5	101 015	1 383	0 648	73 5	160 5°	Foresight to L1–5
L1–6	99 608	2 423	1 761	66 2	222 5°	Foresight to L1–6
L2						Instrument location L2
L1–6	99 608	2 934	2 276	65 8	0°	Backsight to L1–6
L1–5	101 015	1 845	1 209	63 6	60 3°	Backsight to L1–5

Note: Distance is calculated from stadia readings and included angles from angle readings. Levels given are reduced levels calculated as in Table A23.1.

Referring to Figure A23.5, set up the instrument at a point L1 close to your base station. Measure and record the distance from L1 to L1–1. Take a compass bearing along this line. Measure and record the angle between L1–1 and L1–2 and the distance L1 to L1–2. Repeat the procedure for all points around L1.

Before changing the instrument location to L2, leave clear markers at two of the points located from L1, for example L1–5 and L1–6. This is necessary to locate L2 on the map. Readings are taken at L2 as they were at L1. The process is continued until the area to be mapped is covered.

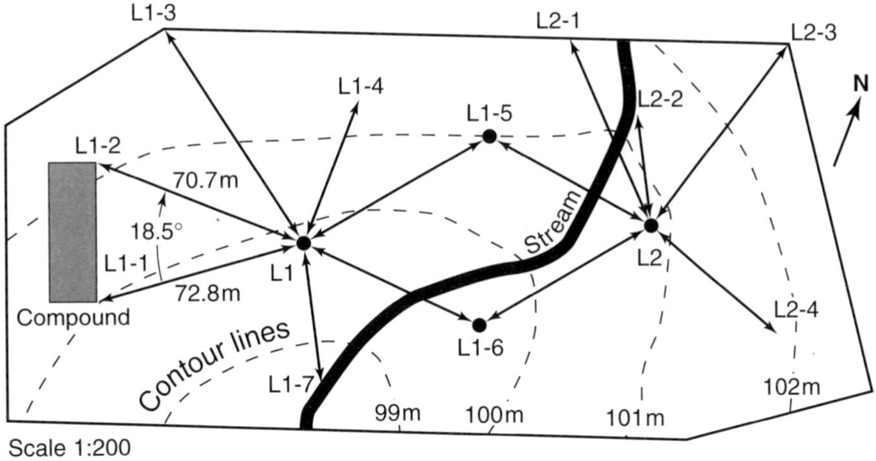

Figure A23.5 Collection of mapping data

During the course of the survey add as much detail to your field sketch as possible.

Transferring the data to a map

While collecting the data it is necessary to understand how the information will be placed on a blank sheet of paper to draw up a map.

Using distance measurement only Looking at Figure A23.5, L1, L1–1 and L1–2 can be accurately located by measuring the distance L1–1 to L1–2, L1 to L–1 and L1 to L1–2. These points can be located on a scale drawing using a compass and scale rule.

Using angle and distance If angle and distance can be measured then L1–2 can be located by measuring the distance from L1 to L1–1 and L1 to L1–2 and the angle at L1 between L1–1 and L1–2. With these measurements, the three points can be plotted on paper using a scale rule and accurate protractor. If your protractor is not accurate, then use the following formula to calculate the distance between L1–1 and L1–2.

$$A^2 = B^2 + C^2 - 2\,BC \cos \alpha$$

where: A = distance between L1–1 and L1–2
B = distance between L1 and L1–1
C = distance between L1 and L1–2
α = angle at L1 (18.5°)

The points may now be plotted with a scale rule and compass. Location L2 is fixed on your sheet of paper using the distances you have measured from two of the points located from L1 (L1–5 and L1–6).

The levels of the points of interest should be noted. Contour lines may be drawn.

Setting out

Setting out is the marking out on the ground of the plan of a building, the route of a pipeline, or road, or the location and arrangement of a site (tents, water treatment works etc.). Choose a method suited to the accuracy required and avoid over-complex time consuming procedures.

Use wooden pegs or short lengths of reinforcing bar to mark out the ends of trenches or corners of buildings.

Linear measurements

Approximate horizontal distances and plan area can be rapidly estimated by pacing. Gauge and check the length of your own pace over a known measured distance to assess accuracy. Use a 30 m steel or fibre-glass measuring tape for more accurate measurements.

Angles

Set out a right-angle using a 3-4-5 triangle. This can be done in several ways:

- In the form of a builder's square – make a 'builder's square' from accurately cut and fixed pieces of planed wood (Figure A23.6a) or simply cut from a sheet of plywood.
- Peg out both ends of one side (3 m) of the triangle. Attach a string (of 4 m length) to one peg and another string (of 5 m length) to the other peg. Stretch out the strings to meet each other and a right angle will be formed at the corner (Figure A23.6b).
- An alternative to string is to wrap the measuring tape itself around the pegs and position to the correct lengths.

An equilateral triangle will give an angle of 60° and, when used together with a builder's square, an angle of 30°, and multiples thereof (Figure A23.6a).

Squareness

Check the squareness of a rectangle by measuring the length of the diagonals. They should be equal.

Profile boards

Profile boards enable the width, direction and, possibly, depth of a trench to be monitored during excavation. A typical arrangement is shown in Figure A23.7. The centre line and width of the trench can be marked on the profile board with nails or saw cuts. Further dimensions, such as wall width, or road drain profile, can be set out in the same way.

Establish the line of a trench with tight string and then mark out on the ground with lines of sand or piles of soil. For excavation by hand, mark out

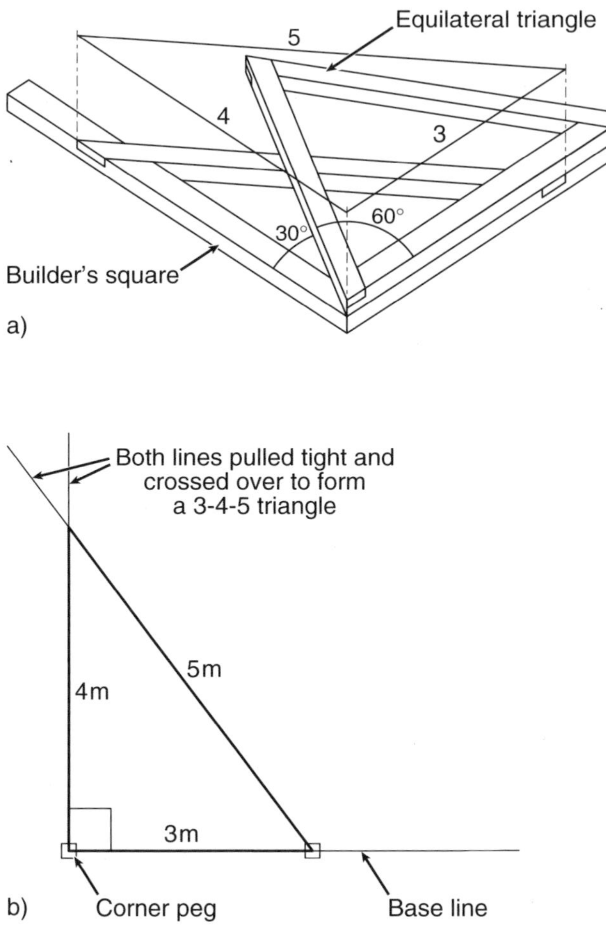

Figure A23.6 Setting out angles

the trench width. For excavation by mechanical digger, mark the trench centre line.

Levelling

If profile boards are to be used to control the depth of the excavation, they must be set level relative to a site datum. (A profile board set at a certain height above a required level is also called a sight rail.) Use a traveller (also called a boning rod) to control the depth of a trench as shown in Figure A23.7. A similar approach can be used to level an area of ground where this may be critical, for example, when erecting an emergency water treatment works.

A set of two sight rails and a boning rod is used to control the gradient of a pipeline or drain as shown in Figure A23.8.

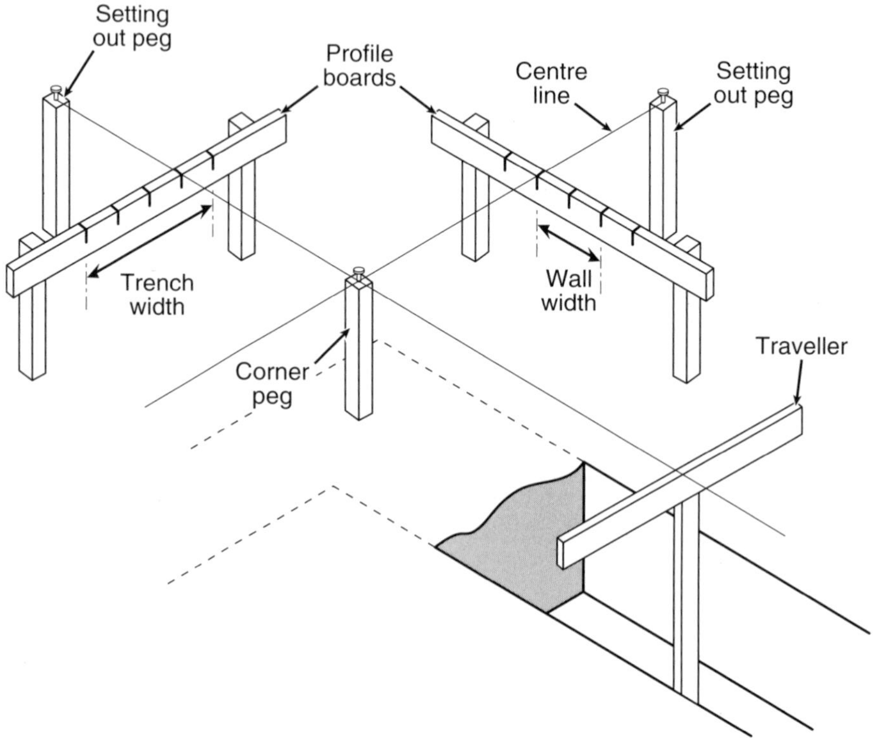

Figure A23.7 A typical layout of profile boards and traveller

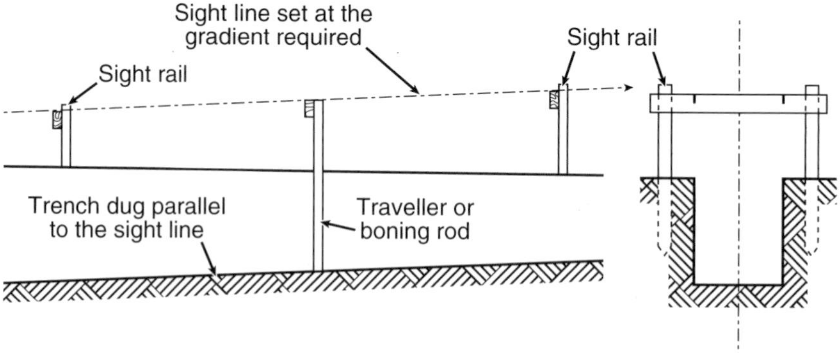

Figure A23.8 Controlling the gradient of a trench

Further simple methods of levelling over short distances:

- Straight edge and a spirit level: to extend the range of a spirit level, lay it along the edge of a timber board about 3 m long with two straight and parallel edges. To check the spirit level is accurate, reverse the level on the straight edge. Check the accuracy of the board by reversing it after levelling.

To cancel out any possible inaccuracy, reverse the board at each successive position.

- Line and line-level: a line-level is a small spirit level with two hooks for hanging on a taut string. The method is only accurate if the spirit level is positioned at the mid-point of the string and the string is pulled tight.
- Water level: the water level is useful for quickly transferring levels, especially around corners, within an accuracy of about ± 5 mm. A water level can be made from a length of clear plastic tubing with an internal diameter of about 10 mm. The tubing need only be clear at each end and other tubing can be used in between. Tape each end to matching graduated rules. Almost fill the tube with water, ensuring that no bubbles are trapped. Hold the ends side by side and, when the levels are the same, mark this level on the rules. Place a stopper in each end when moving them about to prevent the loss of water. Precautions to take: check the levels side-by-side before use; avoid temperature differences between each end (for instance, if one end is left in direct sunlight); ensure air bubbles are not trapped in the tube.

24 Food and nutrition

Data on food and nutrition may be useful to the engineer in determining food transport and storage requirements, when constructing feeding centres and when discussing requirements with health and nutrition workers.

Average food rations

Average food rations must provide the following:

Initial survival	1500 kcal/person/day of energy
Long-term standard	1900 kcal/person/day of energy plus 50 g of protein

Typical daily standard ration (food basket) per person:

- A staple food to provide the bulk energy and protein requirement, e.g. 350–500g of cereal.
- An energy-rich food, for instance 20–40g of oil.
- A protein-rich food, such as 50–100g of pulses.

Total weight of daily food ration: about 500–600 g per person (useful for estimating logistics requirements).

Blended food supplements are for use by small children, the sick and the malnourished:

CSM (Corn-soya milk) WSB (Wheat-soya blend)

Cooking fuel

Approximate guide: a medium sized family requires about 8 kg of fuelwood for cooking each day.

Supplementary feeding

Supplementary feeding is for those who are moderately malnourished; it is given in addition to normal feeding. The WHO standard definition of moderate malnourishment is anyone between 70 and 80 per cent normal weight-for-height. A feeding programme is necessary when the malnutrition rate is more than 15 per cent of the refugee population who are less than 80 per cent weight-for-height (infants are determined by weight-for-length, WFL).

Table A24.1 Typical additional daily ration required for a supplementary feeding programme

Item	*Amount (g)*
Cereal	60
Oil	10
Dried skimmed milk (DSM)	25
Sugar	5
Total additional daily ration	100

Recommended maximum number of beneficiaries per supplementary feeding centre: 500.

Therapeutic feeding

Therapeutic feeding is for severely malnourished children and adults. Criteria for therapeutic feeding: children less than 70 per cent weight-for-height and children with kwashiorkor; malnourished adults; pregnant women with anaemia.

Food: high energy milk or semi-liquid porridge. A minimum per day per kilogram body weight of 150 kcal of energy and 3–4 g protein.

Recommended maximum number of beneficiaries per therapeutic feeding centre: 50.

(Adapted from Mears and Chowdhury, 1994)

25 Unit conversion tables

Length

	m	ft	in	km	miles
1 m	1	3.281	39.37	1×10^{-3}	6.214×10^{-4}
1 ft	0.3048	1	12.00	3.048×10^{-4}	1.894×10^{-4}
1 in	0.0254	0.0833	1	2.54×10^{-5}	1.578×10^{-5}
1 km	1000	3281	3.937×10^{4}	1	0.6214
1 mile	1609	5280	6.336×10^{4}	1.609	1

1 nautical mile (UK) = 1.853 km   1 degree of latitude is about 111 km

Area

	m^2	ft^2	acre	hectare
1 m^2	1	10.76	2.471×10^{-4}	1.0×10^{-4}
1 ft^2	9.29×10^{-2}	1	2.29×10^{-5}	9.29×10^{-6}
1 acre	4.047×10^{3}	4.356×10^{4}	1	4.047×10^{-1}
1 hectare	1.0×10^{4}	1.076×10^{5}	2.471	1

Volume

	m^3	l	UK gal	US gal	ft^3
1 m^3	1	1.0×10^{3}	2.200×10^{2}	2.642×10^{2}	35.32
1 l	1.0×10^{-3}	1	0.220	0.2642	3.532×10^{-2}
1 UK gal	4.546×10^{-3}	4.546	1	1.200	0.1605
1 US gal	3.785×10^{-3}	3.785	0.8326	1	0.1337
1 ft^3	2.832×10^{-2}	28.32	6.229	7.480	1

Discharge (Volume rate of flow)

	l/s	m^3/s	m^3/d	UK gal/day	ft^3/s
1 l/s	1	1.0×10^{-3}	86.40	1.901×10^{4}	3.531×10^{-2}
1 m^3/s	1.0×10^{3}	1	8.640×10^{4}	1.901×10^{7}	35.313
1 m^3/d	1.157×10^{-2}	1.157×10^{-5}	1	2.200×10^{2}	4.087×10^{-4}
1 UK gal/day	5.262×10^{-5}	5.262×10^{-8}	4.546×10^{-3}	1	1.858×10^{-6}
1 ft^3/s	28.32	2.832×10^{-2}	2.447×10^{3}	5.382×10^{5}	1

Note: the cubic metre per second (m^3/s) is also known as the 'cumec'
the cubic foot per second (ft^3/s) is also known as the 'cusec'

Velocity

	m/s	km/h	mile/h	ft/s
1 m/s	1	3.6	2.237	3.281
1 km/h	0.2778	1	0.6214	0.9113
1 mile/hour	0.447	1.609	1	1.467
1 feet/second	0.3048	1.097	0.6818	1

Mass

	kg	lb	t	UK ton
1 kg	1	2.205	1×10^{-3}	9.842×10^{-4}
1 lb	0.454	1	4.536×10^{-4}	4.464×10^{-4}
1 metric tonne (t)	1000	2205	1	0.984
1 UK ton	1016	2240	1.016	1

1 US ton = 2000 lb

Density

	g/cm^3	kg/m^3	lb/in^3	lb/ft^3
1 g/cm^3	1	1000	0.0361	62.43
1 kg/m^3	1×10^{-3}	1	3.61×10^{-5}	0.0624
1 lb/in^3	27.68	27.68×10^3	1	1728
1 lb/ft^3	0.016	16.02	5.787×10^{-4}	1

Pressure

	kgf/cm^2	bar	kN/m^2	lbf/in^2 (psi)
1 kgf/cm^2	1	0.981	98.1	14.223
1 bar	1.02	1	100	14.504
1 kN/m^2	0.01	0.0098	1	0.145
1 lbf/in^2 (psi)	0.07	0.0689	6.89	1

1 Pa (pascal) = 1 N/m^2
1 N/mm^2 = 1MN/m^2 = 1 MPa
101 325 Pa = 1 standard atmosphere (atm) = 1.01325 bar
100 kPa = 1 bar
10.33 m head of water = 1 atm
2989 Pa = 1 ft head of water = 22.42 mm of mercury (mmHg)
1 mmHg = 0.0394 inch of mercury (inHg)
1 MPa = 145 lbf/in^2 (psi)

Force

	N	kgf	lbf	pdl
1 N	1	0.1019	0.2248	7.2330
1 kgf	9.8066	1	2.2046	70.9316
1 lbf	4.4482	0.4536	1	32.1740
1 poundal (pdl)	0.1382	0.0141	0.0311	1

1 N = 1 kg m/s^2
1 pdl = 1 lb ft/s^2

Torque (Moment of force)

	Nm	kgf m	lbf ft	lbf in
1 Newton metre (Nm)	1	0.1020	0.7376	8.8507
1 kilogram-force metre (kgf m)	9.8066	1	7.2330	86.7962
1 pound-force foot (lbf ft)	1.3558	0.1382	1	12.0000
1 pound-force inch (lbf in)	0.1130	0.0115	0.0833	1

Power

	kW	CV	bhp
1 kilowatt (kW)	1	1.3596	1.3410
1 metric horsepower (CV)	0.7355	1	0.9863
1 brake horsepower (bhp)	0.7457	1.0139	1

The metric horsepower, Cheval Vapeur, is variously denoted as CV, ch and PS.

Fuel consumption (volume/distance)

	l/km	UKgal/mile	USgal/mile
1 litre/kilometre (l/km)	1	0.354	0.425
1 UK gallon/mile (UKgal/mile)	2.825	1	1.201

Fuel consumption (distance/volume)

	km/l	mile/UKgal	mile/USgal
1 kilometre/litre (km/l)	1	2.825	2.352
1 mile/UK gallon (mile/UKgal)	0.354	1	0.833

Specific fuel consumption

1 gram/kilowatt hour (g/kWh) = 1.644×10^{-3} pounds/horsepower hour (lb/hp h)

Energy

1 Joule (J) = 0.2388 calorie (cal) = 9.4781×10^{-4} British thermal unit (Btu)

Temperature

F° = 9/5 C° + 32°

C° = 5/9 (F° – 32°)

Concentration

1 mg/l = 1 part per million

1 kg/m^3 = 1 g/dm^3 = 1 g/l

Metric prefixes

Prefix	Symbol	Factor by which the unit is multiplied
giga	G	1 000 000 000
mega	M	1 000 000
kilo	k	1 000
hecto	h	100
deca	da	10
deci	d	0.1
centi	c	0.01
milli	m	0.001
micro	μ	0.000 001

Bibliography

The chapters and appendices in which a reference is cited are given in brackets at the end of the reference, e.g. [17,9,A2].

Adams, J. (1999) *Managing water supply and sanitation in emergencies*, Oxford: Oxfam [6, 9, 10, 11, 12, 13].

Alvan Blanch Development Co. Ltd., Chelworth, Malmesbury, Wiltshire SN16 9SG [15].

American Water Works Association (AWWA) (1971) *Water quality and treatment*, 3rd edition, New York: McGraw-Hill (Figure adapted from Packham R.F. (1963), *Proc. Soc. Water Treat. Exam.*, 12:15) [13].

Anderson, M. (1999) *Do no harm: how aid can support peace – or war*, Lynn Reinner

Anderson, M. and Woodrow, P. (1998) *Rising from the ashes: development strategies in times of disaster*, London: ITDG Publishing.

Anderson, M. (1994) *People-oriented planning at work, using POP to improve UNHCR programming. A practical planning tool for refugee workers.* Geneva: UNHCR. [5].

Antoniou, J., Guthrie, P., De Veen, J. (1990) *Building roads by hand, An introduction to labour-based road construction*, London: Longman on behalf of the ILO, Geneva (copyright 1990 International Labour Organization) [18].

Atalanta PumpSets Ltd., UK (PumpSets@aol.com) [14].

Aysan, Y., Clayton, A., Cory, A., Davis, I. and Sanderson, D. (1995) *Developing Building for Safety Programmes: guidelines for organizing safe building programmes in disaster-prone areas*, London: ITDG Publishing.

Ball, P. (2001) *Drilled wells*, St. Gallen, Switzerland: SKAT.

Bartram, J. and Howard, G. (1994) *The prevention and control of cholera*, in 'Waterlines', Vol.12, No.4, April 1994, London: ITDG Publishing. [9].

Baumann, E. (2000) *Water lifting*, St. Gallen, Switzerland: SKAT.

Beenhakker, H.L. with Carapetis, S., Crowther, L., Hertel, S. (1987) *Rural transport services, a guide to their planning and implementation*, London:ITDG Publishing [18].

Benenson, A.S. (editor) (1995) *Control of communicable diseases in man*, 16th edition, A report of the American Public Health Association, Washington: APHA [10].

Birley, M.H. (1989) *Guidelines for forecasting the vector-borne disease implications of water resources development*, PEEM Guidelines Series 2, VBC/89.6, WHO/FAO/UNEP [12].

Blaikie, P., Cannon, T. Davis, I. and Wisner, B. (1994) *At Risk: natural hazards, people's vulnerability and disasters*, London & New York: Routledge.

Boot, M.T. and Cairncross, S. (Editors) (1993) *Actions speak, the study of hygiene behaviour in water supply and sanitation projects*, The Hague: IRC and the London School of Hygiene and Tropical Medicine. [9].

Brandberg, B. (1997) *Latrine Building: A handbook for implementing the SanPlat system*, London: ITDG Publishing [10].

Brassington, R. (1988) *Field Hydrogeology*, Open University Press and Halsted Press (John Wiley & Sons).

Buttle, M. and Smith, M. (1999) *Out in the cold: emergency water and sanitation for cold regions*, Loughborough University: WEDC.

Busvine, J.R. (1982) *Control of domestic flies*, Ross Institute Bulletin No.5, 7th edition, London: Ross Institute [10].

Cairncross, S. and Feachem, R. (1993) *Environmental Health Engineering in the Tropics: An Introductory Text*, 2nd Edition, Chichester: John Wiley & Sons.

CARE (1997) *Land Mine Safety Handbook*, Atlanta: CARE.

Chalinder, A. (1998) *Temporary human settlement planning for displaced populations in emergencies*, HPN Good Practice Review No.6, London: ODI.

Chudley, R. and Greeno, R. (2001) *Building construction handbook*, 4th edition, Oxford: Butterworth-Heinemann Ltd. [19].

Clark, L. (1988) *The Field Guide to Water Wells and Boreholes*, Open University Press and Halsted Press (John Wiley & Sons).

Clayton, A. and Davis, I. (1994) *Building for Safety Compendium – an annotated bibliography and information directory for safe building*, London: ITDG Publishing.

Coburn, A., Hughes, R., Spence, R. and Pomonis, A. (1995) *Technical principles of building for safety*, London: ITDG Publishing [19].

Conport Structures, 27A Sloane Square, London, SW1W 8AB [19].

Corsellis, T. (2000) *RedR Construction in Emergencies course handouts*, Tom Corsellis, Martin Centre, University of Cambridge, England [19, 20].

Crabtree (1994) Catalogue of commercial and industrial circuit protection and control equipment, Walsall:Crabtree Electrical Industries Ltd. [16].

Cutts. M and Dingle, A. (1998) *Safety First, Protecting NGO Employees Who Work in Areas of Conflict*, 2nd edition, London: SCF [4].

Darcy, J. (1997) *Human rights and international legal standards: what do relief workers need to know?*, London: HPN, ODI [1, 4].

Davis, I. (1982) *Shelter after Disaster: Guidelines for Assistance*, http://www.reliefweb.int/library/documents/2003/undro-shelter-jul82.htm

Davis, M. (1994) *How to make low-cost building blocks: stabilized soil block technology*, London: ITDG Publishing [19].

De Montfort University (2000) Low cost medical waste incinerator – manufacturing, operation and maintenance instructions. The Innovative Technology Centre, De Montfort University, Leicester.

DoD (1993) 'Practical ways to prevent the spread of cholera', in *Dialogue on Diarrhoea* (DoD) Spring 1993, London: AHRTAG. [9].

Driscoll, F.G. (1986) *Groundwater and wells*, 2nd edition, Minnesota: Johnson Division [13].

Drouart, E. and Vouillamoz, J-M. (1999) *Alimentation en eau des populations menacées*, Paris: Hermann.

Environmental Protection Agency (EPA) (1980) *Design Manual: On-site wastewater treatment and disposal systems*, Report EPA-600/2–78-173, Cincinnati: EPA [10].

Euroconsult (1989) *Agricultural compendium for rural development in the tropics and sub-tropics*, Amsterdam: Elsevier.

Feachem, R.G. (1993) personal correspondence with RedR [13].

Ferron, S., Morgan, J. and O'Reilly, M. (2000) *Hygiene promotion, a practical manual for relief and development*, London: ITDG Publishing/CARE International [9].

Fischer R. and Ury, W. (1992) *Getting to YES*, London: Century-Hutchinson [6].

Franceys, R., Pickford, J. and Reed, R. (1992) *A guide to the development of on-site sanitation*, Geneva: WHO [10].

Gawlinski, J. and Graessle, L. (1988) *Planning together*, London: Bedford Square [6].

Gosling, L. and Edwards, M. (1995) *Toolkits, a practical guide to assessment, monitoring, review and evaluation*, London: Save the Children.

Grundfos Pumps Ltd., Grovebury Road, Leighton Buzzard, Bedfordshire LU7 8TL [14, 16].

Hamill, L. and Bell, F.G. (1986) *Groundwater resource development*, London: Butterworths [12].

Harrell-Bond, B. (1986) *Imposing aid,* Oxford: Oxford University Press [1].

Hausman, B. (1994) *Guidelines for epidemics: cholera*, Amsterdam:MSF [9].

Help Age International (2000) *Older people in disasters and humanitarian crises: guidelines for best practice*, London: HelpAge International [1].

Hindson, J., revised by Howe, J. and Hathaway, G. (1983) *Earth roads: their construction and maintenance*, London: ITDG Publishing [18].

House, S. & Reed, R. (1997) *Emergency water sources: guidelines for selection and treatment*, Loughborough: WEDC.

Howard, J. & Spice, R. (1989) *Plastic sheeting: Its use for emergency shelter and other purposes, an Oxfam technical guide*, 3rd revision, Oxford:Oxfam [19].

The Humanitarian Practice Network (HPN) – formerly known as the Relief and Rehabilitation Network (RRN) – publications come in three formats: Good Practice Reviews, Network Papers and a newsletter called *Humanitarian Exchange*.

Hulscher, W. and Fraenkel, P. (1994) *The Power Guide: an international catalogue of small-scale energy equipment*, 2nd edition, London: ITDG Publishing [14].

IFRC annual publication. *World Disasters Report*, Geneva: International Federation of Red Cross and Red Crescent Societies.

ICRC, undated. *Coping with Stress*, Geneva: ICRC Publications [3].

IRC (1983) edited by Hofkes, E.H., *Small community water supplies. Technology of small water supply systems in developing countries*, TP18 (enlarged edition), The Hague: IRC [13].

IRC (1990) compiled by Smet, J.E.M. and Visscher, J.T. *Pre-treatment methods for community water supply. An overview of techniques and present experience*, The Hague: IRC [13].

Jahn, S.A.A. (1981) *Traditional water purification in tropical developing countries*, Eschborn: GTZ [13].

Jordan, T.D. (1984) *A handbook of gravity-flow water systems*, London: ITDG Publishing [13].

Key, D. (Editor) (1995) *Structures to withstand disaster*, London: Thomas Telford.

Kruseman, G.P. and De Ridder, N.A. (1979) 'The analysis of pumping test data', *ILRI Bulletin 11*, Wageningen, The Netherlands: ILRI [A10].

Lacarin, C. and Reed, R. (1999) *Emergency vector control using chemicals: a handbook for relief workers*, Loughborough: WEDC [10].

Land Rover (1989) *Working in the wild: Land Rover's manual for Africa*, Solihull: Land Rover [17].

Lewis W.J. *et al.* (1980) 'The pollution hazard to village water supplies in eastern Botswana', *Proceedings of the Institution of Civil Engineers*, 69: 281–293. [10].

Lines, J. and Kolsky, P. (undated), *Relative importance of vector breeding places and a prioritised list of possible engineering interventions*, unpublished course notes, London School of Hygiene and Tropical Medicine [10].
Lister-Petter (undated), *Diesel engine theory*, Edition Four, Publication 027–08649, Dursley: Lister-Petter Ltd. [15].
Lloyd, B. and Helmer, R. (1991) *Surveillance of drinking water quality in rural areas*, UK: Longman [11].

Mabey & Johnson Ltd., Floral Mile, Twyford, Reading, Berks RG10 9SQ, UK [18].
Maccaferri Ltd., 4B The Quorum, Oxford Business Park, Garsington Road, Oxford OX4 2JY, UK [A17].
Manfield, P. and Corsellis, T. (1999) *Cold climate emergency shelter systems, a research project for humanitarian organisations*, The Martin Centre for Architectural & Urban Studies, University of Cambridge.
Maskrey, A. (1989) *Disaster mitigation: a community based approach*, Development guidelines No.3, Oxford:Oxfam [19].
Mears, C. and Chowdhury, S. (1994) *Health care for refugees and displaced people*, Oxfam practical health guide no. 9, Oxford:Oxfam [9, A24].
MoD (Ministry of Defence) (1981a) *Military engineering Vol II, Field engineering, Pamphlet No 1, Basic field engineering*, London: HMSO [18, A18, A19].
MoD (Ministry of Defence) (1981b) *Military engineering Volume II, Field engineering Pamphlet No. 9, Water Supply*, London: HMSO [13].
MoD (Ministry of Defence) (1994) *Military engineering Vol II, Field engineering, Pamphlet No 7A, Classification of bridges*, London: HMSO [18].
Monarflex, Lyon Way, St. Albans, Hertfordshire, AL4 0LB [19].
Mono Pumps Ltd., H_2O Waste-Tec, Horsfield Way, Bredbury Park, Stockport, SK6 2SU, UK [14].
Morgan, J. (1993) Internal Oxfam Report, October 1993 [9].
MSF (1988) *Organisation d'un camp de refugies*, Modules 1, 2, 3, 4 Paris: MSF [9].
MSF (1992) *Technicien sanitaire, en situation précaire*, premiere édition, Paris: MSF [10].
Mulemba, F. and Nabeth, P. (1994) 'Environmental sanitation for the control of cholera in Lisungwi refugee camp, Malawi', *Waterlines*, Vol.12, No.4, April 1994, London: ITDG Publishing. [9].
Murlis, J. and Stephenson, R. (1981) 'Insect pest control in refugee camps', *Disasters*, Vol.5, No.3 [10].

Nelson, K.D. (1985) *Design and construction of small earth dams*, Melbourne: Inkata Press [12].
Nilsson, A. (1988) *Groundwater dams for small-scale water supply*, London: ITDG Publishing [12].
Nissen-Peterson E. (1992) *How to build cylindrical water tanks with domes, volumes* $23m^3$ *and* $46m^3$, ASAL Consultants Ltd., PO Box 867, Kitui, Kenya.
Norton, J. (1986) *Building with earth, A handbook*, London: ITDG Publishing [19].

OCHA (2000) *Guiding principles on internal displacement*, OCHA [1].
Ockwell, R. (1986) *Assisting in emergencies: a resource handbook for UNICEF field staff*, New York: UNICEF.
ODI Quarterly. *The Journal of Disaster Studies, Policy and Management*, London: Overseas Development Institute/Blackwell Publishers.
O'Keefe, P. and Middleton, N. (1998) *Disaster and Development – politics of humanitarian aid*, London: Pluto Press.

Oxfam (1988) OXFAM/Delagua water testing kit, Oxford: Oxfam [11].
Oxfam (2000) Personal communication with Richard Luff, Oxfam [13].

Paul, D. (1999) *Protection in practice: field level strategies for protecting civilians from deliberate harm*, RRN Network Paper 30 [1, 4].

Payne, L. (1998) *Rebuilding Communities in a Refugee Settlement – a casebook from Uganda*, Oxford: Oxfam.

People in Aid (1998) *The People in Aid Code of best practice in the management and support of aid personnel*, London: Overseas Development Institute.

Petbow (undated), Installation manual for generating sets, Sandwich, Kent:Petbow Generators UK [16].

PIARC (1994) *Road maintenance handbook Volume 1.* UK: Transport Research Laboratory [18].

Pickford, J. (1991) *The worth of water*, London: ITDG Publishing [13].

Reed, R. due to be published in 2002. *Emergency sanitation*, Loughborough: WEDC.

Reed, R. and Dean, P.T. (1994) 'Recommended methods for the disposal of sanitary wastes from temporary field medical facilities', *Disasters*, Vol.18, No.4 [10, A20].

Reed, R. (1994) *Sanitation for refugees and similar emergency situations*, unpublished technical guide prepared for Oxfam.

Roberts, D.L. (1999) *Staying Alive, safety and security guidelines for humanitarian volunteers in conflict areas*, Geneva: ICRC [4].

Rottier, E. and Ince, M. (2001) *Controlling and preventing disease, the role of water and sanitation interventions*, Loughborough: WEDC.

RRN (1994) *The 1994 Code of Conduct for the International Red Cross and Red Crescent Movement and NGOs in disaster relief*, Network Paper 7, London: ODI.

Rubb Buildings Ltd, Dukesway, Team Valley Trading Estate, Gateshead, Tyne and Wear NE11 0QE [19].

Rubb Inc., P.O. Box 711, Sanford, ME 04073, USA [19].

SCF(UK)/UNHCR/Ethiopian Ministry of Health and Administration for Refugee Affairs (1989) Quoted by Toole, M.J. & Bhatia, R. in *Journal of Refugee Studies*, Vol., No.3/4, 1992, Oxford: OUP [9].

Schulz, C. and Okun, D.A. (1992) *Surface water treatment for communities in developing countries*, London: ITDG Publishing Ltd [13].

Sphere (2000) *The Sphere Project: Humanitarian Charter and Minimum Standards in Disaster Relief.* Published on behalf of the Sphere Project by Oxfam, Oxford.

Stephens, T. (1991) *Handbook on small earth dams and weirs*, Bedford: Cranfield Press [12].

Stephenson, R.S. (1983) 'Vehicle workshop operations', *Disasters*, March 1983 [17].

Stern, P.H. (1979) *Small scale irrigation, a manual of low-cost water technology*, London: ITDG Publishing/International Irrigation Information Center [A20].

Stern, P. (editor) *et al.* (1983) from an original work by F. Longland, *Field Engineering: a guide to construction and development work in rural areas*, London: ITDG Publishing [19].

Storey, T. (Engineers) Ltd. (1983) *Acrow panel bridge technical handbook*, 3rd edition, Weybridge: Thos. Storey (Engineers) Ltd. [18].

SWS Filtration Ltd., Hartburn, Morpeth, Northumberland NE61 4JB [12].

Talbot, F.W. & Company Ltd., Winnall Valley Road, Winchester, Hampshire, SO23 8LL, UK [13, A14].

Tampere Convention on the Provision of Telecommunications Resources for Disaster Mitigation and Relief Operations. www.reliefweb.int/telecoms/tampere [10]

Telford, J. (1997) *Counting and identification of beneficiary populations in emergency operations: registration and its alternatives*, HPN Good Practice Review No5, London: ODI [20].

Terram®, Mamhilad Park, Pontypool, Gwent NP4 0YR, UK [A20].

Theis, J. and Grady, H.M. (1991) *Participatory rapid appraisal for community development*, London: IIED/Save the Children Federation [5].

Thomson, M.C. (1990) *Controlling insects and disease in displaced populations*, Refugee Programme Newsletter (RPN), No.8, May 1990, Oxford:RSP [10].

Thomson, M.C. (1995) *Disease prevention through vector control: guidelines for relief organizations*, Oxfam practical health guide No.10, Oxford: Oxfam [10].

TRRL (1985) *Maintenance techniques for District Engineers, Overseas Road Note 2*, 2nd Edition, Crowthorne: Transport and Road Research Laboratory [18].

TRRL (1988) *Bridge inspector's handbook, Overseas Road Note 7*, Vol 2, Crowthorne: Transport and Road Research Laboratory [18].

TRRL (1992) *A design manual for small bridges, Overseas Road Note 9*, Crowthorne: Transport and Road Research Laboratory [18].

UN Guidelines on the Protection of Refugee Women – available on-line at: www.theirc.org/wcrwc/wc_guidelineswomen.html [1].

UNHCR (1989) *Supplies and Food Aid Handbook*, Geneva: UNHCR [7, 17].

UNHCR (1992) *Water manual for refugee situations*. Geneva: UNHCR PTSS.

UNHCR (1993) *Dealing with the media*, Geneva: UNHCR [3].

UNHCR (1998) Environmental guidelines:

Refugee Operations and Environmental Management: Key Principles for Decision-Making. [Also available in French.]

Refugee Operations and the Environmental Management: Selected Lessons Learned. [Also available in French.]

Environmental Guidelines: Domestic Energy in Refugee Situations.

Environmental Guidelines: Forestry in Refugee Situations.

Environmental Guidelines: Livestock in Refugee Situations.

UNHCR (1999) *Handbook for emergencies*, Second edition, Geneva: UNHCR.

UNHCR (2000) *The state of the world's refugees: A humanitarian agenda*. Geneva: UNHCR [1].

UNHCR (2001) Personal communication with the Supply and Transport Section of UNHCR [19].

UNICEF (undated), *Standing ferrocement water tank construction manual*, Nairobi: UNICEF Technology Support Section, Nairobi, Kenya [13].

USAID/OFDA (1998) *Field Operations Guide for Disaster Assessment and Response*, Version 3, Washington: Bureau of Humanitarian Response/Office of Foreign Disaster Assistance. Available on-line at: www.info.usaid.gov/ofda/.

US Committee for Refugees, *Annual World Refugee Survey*, US Committee for Refugees.

Van Brabant, K. (2000) *Operational Security Management in Violent Environments, A Field Manual for Aid Agencies*, Good Practice Review 8, Humanitarian Practice Network (HPN), London: Overseas Development Institute [4].

Van Reekum Materials b.v., Kanaal Noord 115, P.O. Box 98, NL7300 AB Apeldoorn, The Netherlands [12].

VITA (1975) *Making building blocks with the CINVA-Ram block press*, Arlington: VITA (Volunteers In Technical Assistance) [19].

Watt, S.B. (1978) *Ferrocement water tanks and their construction*, London: ITDG Publishing [13].

Webber, N.B. (1971) *Fluid mechanics for civil engineers*, London: Chapman & Hall.

Wegelin, M. (1986) *Horizontal-flow roughing filtration (HRF): a design, construction and operation manual*, IRCWD Report No. 06/86, Duebendorf: International Reference Centre for Waste Disposal [13]

Wegelin, M. (1994) Personal communication [13].

WHO (1972) *Vector control in International Health*, WHO Non-serial Publication, Geneva: WHO [10].

WHO (1982) *Manual on environmental management for mosquito control: with special emphasis on malaria vectors*, WHO Offset Publication No.66, Geneva: WHO [10].

WHO (1984a) *Guidelines for drinking-water quality, vol.2: health criteria and other supporting information*, Geneva: WHO [11].

WHO (1984b) *Chemical methods for the control of arthropod vectors and pests of public health importance*, Geneva: WHO [10].

WHO (1985a) *Guidelines for drinking-water quality, vol.3: drinking-water quality control in small-community supplies*, Geneva: WHO [11].

WHO (1989) *Disinfection of rural and small-community water supplies: a manual for design and operation*, Medmenham: WRc [13].

WHO (1990) *Equipment for vector control*, 3rd edition, Geneva: WHO [10].

WHO (1993) *Guidelines for cholera control*, Geneva: WHO [9].

WHO/UNEP (1991) *Manual on water and sanitation for health in refugee camps*, Jordan: WHO/UNEP [10].

WIG Engineering Ltd., Mill Road, Kirtlington, Oxfordshire OX5 3JE [12].

Wilson, K. and Harrell-Bond, B. (1990) *Dealing with dying*, Refugee Programme Newsletter (RPN), No.9, August 1990, Oxford: RSP [10].

World Vision (1998) *A Shield About Me, safety awareness for world vision staff*, WVI.

Index

PRACTICAL ACTION
Publishing

developmentbookshop.com

developmentbookshop.com offers over 1000 publications for practitioners on aspects of international relief and development work.

Buy on-line now and receive a 10% discount!

- Improved layout, secure on-line shopping, automated shipping cost calculator and advanced search facility.
- The on-line catalogue includes all of the publications advertised in our full annual printed catalogues, as well as books from other publishers distributed by Practical Action Publishing. The site is kept up-to-date with all of our latest publications and includes featured products and special offers.
- We offer a full delivery service worldwide; each year, we despatch over 20,000 books to more than 100 countries.
- An affiliate marketing option provides an incentive for individuals and organisations to provide links to developmentbookshop.com
- Whether you are a development practitioner, a policy-maker, a volunteer working in the field, or a development studies student, you are sure to find the book you need at developmentbookshop.com.

Visit www.developmentbookshop.com to start browsing our collection now.

Practical Action Publishing (formerly *ITDG Publishing*) is the new trading name for Intermediate Technology Publications Ltd.

publishinginfo@practicalaction.org.uk
T: +44 (0) 1926 634501 F: +44 (0) 1926 634502
Practical Action Publishing, The Schumacher Centre for Technology and Development, Bourton on Dunsmore, Rugby, Warwickshire, CV23 9QZ, UK.

RedR Mission

RedR – Engineers for Disaster Relief – relieves suffering in disasters by selecting, training and providing competent and effective personnel to humanitarian relief agencies world-wide.

As an international, non-profit NGO with offices in London, Canberra, Auckland, Ottawa and Geneva, RedR aims:

- To provide competent and effective relief personnel at short notice
- To improve the competence of relief personnel
- To work with other agencies to improve the availability and effectiveness of relief personnel.

Recruitment

RedR recruits to its register people with the competence and aptitude to be effective in humanitarian relief. RedR members are offered high quality training and then, if available, they undertake short-term assignments with front-line humanitarian relief agencies. After their assignment, many RedR members return to their usual employment or become available for another posting.

Training

If you are involved in humanitarian relief, or considering relief work for the first time, RedR Training can help you to adapt existing skills, discover more about relief work, prepare for assignments and boost your confidence. The emphasis of RedR Training is on active learning through participatory group exercises, case studies, role play, focused discussion, simulations and practice with equipment used in the field. Training is planned and delivered in collaboration with relief agencies and specialist organisations.

Technical Support

The RedR website supports its members in the field by providing a Technical Support Service through which technical queries are answered by RedR members with expertise in several specialist areas. Access the service through the website which also provides a comprehensive range of resources, information and links to other sites.

Visit the RedR website, **www.redr.org** for more information about RedR and for contact details of RedR offices worldwide.

UK contact details:
RedR – Engineers for Disaster Relief
1 Great George Street, London, SW1P 3AA
Tel: 00 44 (0) 207 233 3116
Fax: 00 44 (0) 207 222 0564
Email: info@redr.demon.co.uk

Registered Charity No.1079752. Registered in England and Wales as Company No. 3929653 limited by guarantee.